# Colombia

## a Lonely Planet travel survival kit

### Krzysztof Dydyński

**Colombia**

**2nd edition**

**Published by**
   **Lonely Planet Publications**
   Head Office:   PO Box 617, Hawthorn, Vic 3122, Australia
   Branches:      155 Filbert St, Suite 251, Oakland, CA 94607, USA
                  10 Barley Mow Passage, Chiswick, London W4 4PH, UK
                  71 bis rue du Cardinal Lemoine, 75005 Paris, France

**Printed by**
   SNP Printing Pte Ltd, Singapore

**Photographs by**
   Krzysztof Dydyński

   Front cover: Old Balconied Houses of Cartegena, Krzysztof Dydyński
   Back cover: Chiva, Krzysztof Dydyński

**First Published**
   1988

**This Edition**
   August 1995

**Although the authors and publisher have tried to make the information as accurate as possible, they accept no responsibility for any loss, injury or inconvenience sustained by any person using this book.**

National Library of Australia Cataloguing in Publication Data

Dydyński, Krzysztof
   Colombia – a travel survival kit.

   2nd ed.
   Includes index.
   ISBN 0 86442 234 2.

   1. Colombia – Guidebooks.
   I. Title (Series: Lonely Planet travel survival kit).

918.6104632

text & maps © Lonely Planet 1995
photos © photographers as indicated 1995
climate charts compiled from information supplied by Patrick J Tyson, © Patrick J Tyson, 1995

## Krzysztof Dydyński

Krzysztof Dydyński was born and raised in Warsaw, Poland. Though he graduated in electronic engineering and became an assistant professor in the subject, he soon realised that there's more to life than microchips. In the mid-1970s he took off to Afghanistan and India and has been back to Asia several times since. In the 1980s a newly discovered passion for Latin America took him to Colombia, where he lived for over four years and travelled throughout the continent. In search of a new incarnation, he has made Australia his home and worked for Lonely Planet as an artist and designer. Apart from this guide he is the author of travel survival kits to *Poland* and *Venezuela* and has contributed to other Lonely Planet books.

## From the Author

Many friends, colleagues and travellers – both Colombians and foreigners – have kindly contributed to this book and deserve the highest praise. I would like to thank all those people for their advice, information, hospitality and much else.

My sincere gratitude to Marc Chernick (USA) who contributed to the sections on modern politics, guerrillas and mafias, and to Jim Ross (UK) without whose help this guide could never have been completed.

Warmest thanks to Mauricio Afanador (Col), Tulia Camacho (Col), Jaime De Greiff (Col), Gerhard Dilger (D), Lina Espinosa (Col), Mary Galvis de Melendro (Col), Stephan Havel (D), Luis Enrique La Rotta (Col), Marion Lokhorst (C), Didier Martin (F), Juana Méndez (Col), Gonzalo Ospina (Col), Jorge 'El Rumbero' Parra (Col), Juan Pablo Ruiz (Col), Cristóbal 'Quapp' von Rothkirch (Col), Margarita Rubiano (Col) and Gerhild Schiller (D).

Special appreciation goes to Angela Melendro who not only was a great companion on the road, but also provided invaluable advice, assistance and help throughout the project.

I've received an amazing number of letters from travellers in response to the first edition of this book. Thanks to all of you, and please keep them coming. Following is the list of the travellers (apologies if I've misspelt your name) who took the time to write to Lonely Planet, providing information, comments and suggestions for this edition. Parts of some of these letters were extracted for use in the text in this book.

Claudine Amiel-Tison (F), Arjen Arnold (NL), Bryan Bakker (USA), Ori Bar On (Isr), Ulrike Bär (D), Juliane Baron, Andrew Bartram (UK), Thomas Bauer (D), Hannah Beardon, Nathalie Benzing (C), Priscilla Berry (USA), David Biagioni (AUS), Gian Bifulco (J), Lesley Blackie (UK), Erik Bloom (USA), Jérome Bonnard (F), Michel Bresson (F), Kathy Connelly (USA), Xavier Cortal Escarra (Sp), Richard Craven (UK), Tony Cucuzzella, Anne D'Heygere (B), Cathy Davidson (UK), Barry Didato (USA), Vincent van Es (NL), I R Farnell (UK), Arnold Fieldman (USA), Ed Frijters (B), Steven Fruhwirth, Guy Gagné (C), Ian Gates (UK), Kenrick Ghosh (UK), Stephen Greig (AUS), Daniel Guerrero (Chi), Anne Hägler (CH), Bob Hancox (UK), Christine & Luc Hegetschweiler-Rotzler (CH), Martin Hendriks (NL), Andreas Hofer (A), Lawrence J Hribar (USA), Adam

Jones (C), Felipe Kay (USA), Freddy Koekoek (NL), Astrid Könneke (D), Mark Laptin (UK), Mabel Macdonald (USA), Andrew Magratten (USA), Ezio Manzione (I), Nathalie Matha (F), Tony McKenzie (UK), Mark Metelmann (UK), Guillermo Moreno (AUS), P Narendran (UK), Marco Nowinski (D), Kirk Nyland (USA), Joop Nijboer (NL), Toot Oostueen (NL), Richard Patience (N), Fiorenzo Peloso (CH), Robert Pichler (A), Samantha Pickering (AUS), Oliver Plath (D), Didier Presutto (F), Stefan Rammelt (D), Genevieve Raymond, Sophie & George Redman (UK), Charlotte Roberts (UK), Konni Rojewski (D), Peter Roth (UK), Gavin Schmidt (C), Karsten Schönborn (D), Thilo Schultze (D), Gerd Schurbohm (D), Daniel Sevier (USA), Aylá S Sevin (Tur), Martin Spencer (AUS), Manfred Stamm (D), Judy Stoft (USA), Cristina Strauss (CH), Mark Terlien (NL), Paul Terlien (NL), Alan Thompson (UK), Kate Trollope (UK), Ellen Uytendaal (NL), Dorine Vanleke (B), Moira Wakefield (UK), Christian Widor (A), Pat Yale (UK), Emmanuel Ypsilanti (Gr) and Wolfgang Zilm (D).

A – Austria, AUS – Australia, B – Belgium, C – Canada, CH – Switzerland, Chi – Chile, Col – Colombia, D – Germany, F – France, Gr – Greece, I – Italy, Isr – Israel, J – Japan, N – Norway, NL – Netherlands, Sp – Spain, Tur – Turkey, UK – United Kingdom, USA – United States of America

## From the Publisher

This book was edited at Lonely Planet's Melbourne office by Rowan McKinnon, Nick Tapp, David Collins, Janet Austin, Rob van Driesum, Adrienne Costanzo and anyone else standing nearby. Sally Steward helped with the language section, Steve Womersley and Janet Austin did the proofing and Sharon Wertheim produced the index. The maps were drawn by Glenn Beanland, Marcel Gaston and Sandra Smythe with help from Maliza Kruh, Rachel Black and Jacqui Saunders. The book was designed by Marcel Gaston with help from Tamsin Wilson. Tamsin and Trudi Canavan did the illustrations, and Vallerie Tellini designed the cover. Special thanks to Adrienne Costanzo and Tamsin Wilson for their help and advice.

## Warning & Request

Things change – prices go up, schedules change, good places go bad and bad places go bankrupt – nothing stays the same. So if you find things better or worse, recently opened or long since closed, please write and tell us and help make the next edition better.

Your letters will be used to help update future editions and, where possible, important changes will also be included in a Stop Press section in reprints.

We greatly appreciate all information that is sent to us by travellers. Back at Lonely Planet we employ a hard-working reader's team to sort through the many letters we receive. The best ones will be rewarded with a free copy of the next edition or another Lonely Planet guide if you prefer. We give away lots of books, but unfortunately, not every letter/postcard receives one.

# Contents

**INTRODUCTION**..................................................................................................9

**FACTS ABOUT THE COUNTRY**......................................................................10

History .......................................10　　Flora & Fauna.......................... 32　　Arts & Culture ..........................39
Government ..............................28　　Economy ..................................36　　Society & Conduct....................45
Geography ................................28　　Population & People.................. 37　　Religion....................................47
Climate .....................................30　　Education ..................................39　　Language...................................47

**FACTS FOR THE VISITOR**.............................................................................**56**

Visas & Embassies ................... 56　　Cultural Events ..........................64　　Film & Photography .................72
Documents...............................57　　Post & Telecommunications.... 65　　Health.......................................74
Customs ....................................58　　Time..........................................67　　Women Travellers.....................88
Money.......................................58　　Electricity.................................67　　Dangers & Annoyances ............88
When to Go ...............................61　　Laundry....................................67　　Activities..................................95
What to Bring ...........................61　　Weights & Measures................ 67　　Accommodation.......................96
Tourist Offices .........................63　　Books .......................................67　　Food & Drink...........................98
Useful Organisations ...............63　　Maps ........................................71　　Entertainment.........................106
Business Hours & Holidays ..... 64　　Media .......................................72　　Things to Buy.........................106

**GETTING THERE & AWAY**...........................................................................**109**

Air...........................................109　　Tours ......................................127　　Warning...................................128
Land ........................................119　　Arriving in
Sea ..........................................127　　& Leaving Colombia.............. 128

**GETTING AROUND**......................................................................................**130**

Air...........................................130　　Train.......................................135　　Boat.........................................139
Bus..........................................132　　Car & Motorcycle...................135　　Tours.......................................139
Chiva.......................................134　　Bicycle ...................................138　　Local Transport ......................140
Colectivo .................................135　　Hitching ..................................139

**BOGOTÁ**.....................................................................................................**142**

History ....................................142　　Getting There & Away............179　　Salto de Tequendama .............190
Climate ....................................143　　Getting Around .......................181　　Zoológico Santa Cruz .............190
Orientation...............................144　　**Around Bogotá ................ 183**　　Fusagasugá.............................191
Information...............................144　　Zipaquirá.................................183　　Zabriskie.................................191
Things to See ...........................153　　Nemocón..................................185　　Parque de Chicaque ................191
Festivals & Events...................164　　Tausa.......................................185　　Bojacá.....................................192
Places to Stay..........................165　　Guatavita.................................185　　Facatativá................................192
Places to Eat ...........................170　　Laguna de Guatavita................186　　Guaduas...................................192
Entertainment .........................176　　Suesca.....................................186　　Salto de Versalles ...................193
Things to Buy .........................178　　Parque Nacional Chingaza ..... 188

**BOYACÁ, SANTANDER & NORTE DE SANTANDER**.....................................194

**Boyacá............................194**　　La Candelaria..........................211　　Laguna de Tota.......................221
Tenza.......................................194　　Chiquinquirá ...........................212　　**Sierra Nevada del Cocuy 221**
Around Tenza .........................196　　Muzo.......................................214　　Güicán.....................................221
Tunja.......................................197　　Paipa.......................................215　　El Cocuy.................................223
Puente de Boyacá ...................204　　Pantano de Vargas ..................215　　Güicán-El Cocuy Trek ............223
Villa de Leyva ........................205　　Duitama...................................215　　**Santander........................ 227**
Around Villa de Leyva ...........209　　Sogamoso................................217　　Socorro....................................227
Santuario de Iguaque...............210　　Monguí ...................................220　　San Gil ...................................230
Ráquira ....................................211　　Tópaga ....................................220　　Barichara.................................232

| | | |
|---|---|---|
| Guane.....235 | Bucaramanga.....236 | Cúcuta.....244 |
| Cueva del Yeso.....235 | Girón.....240 | Villa del Rosario.....249 |
| Aratoca.....235 | **Norte de Santander.....241** | Ocaña.....249 |
| Cañón del Chicamocha.....235 | Pamplona.....241 | Los Estoraques.....252 |

## CARIBBEAN COAST.....253

| | | |
|---|---|---|
| **Cesar.....255** | Santa Marta.....281 | Mompós.....318 |
| Valledupar.....255 | El Rodadero.....285 | **Sucre & Córdoba.....322** |
| **La Guajira.....258** | Taganga.....285 | Sincelejo.....322 |
| Maicao.....260 | Parque Nacional Tayrona.....286 | Tolú & Coveñas.....324 |
| Uribia.....262 | Isla de Salamanca.....288 | Islas de San Bernardo.....325 |
| Manaure.....263 | Ciénaga Grande de Santa | Montería.....325 |
| Cabo de la Vela.....263 | Marta.....289 | Arboletes.....326 |
| Parque Nacional Macuira.....264 | **Atlántico.....290** | **Urabá.....327** |
| Riohacha.....264 | Barranquilla.....290 | Turbo.....327 |
| Santuario Los Flamencos.....268 | Around Barranquilla.....297 | Necoclí.....331 |
| **Sierra Nevada Ciudad** | Volcán de Lodo El Totumo.....298 | Capurganá, Sapzurro & |
| **Perdida.....272** | **Bolívar.....299** | Acandí.....331 |
| Nabusímake.....275 | Cartagena.....299 | Parque Nacional Los Katíos.....333 |
| Nabusímake-Pico Colón Trek 276 | Around Cartagena.....316 | |
| **Magdalena.....281** | San Jacinto.....318 | |

## SAN ANDRÉS & PROVIDENCIA.....336

| | |
|---|---|
| **San Andrés.....337** | **Providencia.....344** |

## THE NORTH-WEST.....347

| | | |
|---|---|---|
| **Chocó.....347** | Hacienda Fizebad.....375 | Cartago.....398 |
| Quibdó.....349 | Sonsón.....376 | Roldanillo.....401 |
| Istmina.....352 | Abejorral.....376 | Armenia.....401 |
| Bahía Solano & El Valle.....352 | Jericó.....376 | Calarcá.....405 |
| Parque Nacional Ensenada de | Andes.....377 | Circasia.....405 |
| Utría.....354 | Jardín.....377 | Filandia.....407 |
| **Antioquia.....355** | Río Claro Area.....379 | Salento.....407 |
| Medellín.....355 | Caverna Del Nus.....382 | Cocora.....407 |
| Santa Fe de Antioquia.....368 | **Zona Cafetera.....383** | Reserva Natural Acaime.....408 |
| Puente de Occidente.....370 | Manizales.....383 | Parque Nacional Los Nevados 409 |
| Circuito de Oriente.....371 | Salamina.....390 | **Tolima.....412** |
| Marinilla.....371 | Riosucio.....390 | Ibagué.....412 |
| El Peñón.....372 | Marmato.....391 | Girardot.....415 |
| Rionegro.....373 | Pereira.....391 | Cueva del Cunday.....416 |
| Carmen de Viboral.....374 | Marsella.....396 | Ambalema.....417 |
| La Ceja.....374 | Termales de Santa Rosa.....396 | Armero.....418 |
| Salto de Tequendamita.....375 | Belén de Umbría.....397 | Mariquita.....418 |
| Retiro.....375 | Parque Ucumarí.....398 | Honda.....419 |

## THE SOUTH-WEST.....422

| | | |
|---|---|---|
| **Valle del Cauca.....422** | Around Juanchaco.....445 | Villavieja.....469 |
| Cali.....422 | Isla Gorgona.....445 | Desierto de la Tatacoa.....470 |
| Parque Nacional Farallones de | **Cauca & Huila.....449** | Aipe.....470 |
| Cali.....436 | Popayán.....449 | Piedra Pintada.....471 |
| Haciendas El Paraíso & | Silvia.....453 | **Nariño.....471** |
| Piedechinche.....437 | Coconuco.....454 | Pasto.....471 |
| Buga.....438 | Parque Nacional Puracé.....454 | Volcán Galeras.....476 |
| Embalse Calima.....439 | San Agustín.....456 | Laguna de la Cocha.....477 |
| Darién.....440 | Cueva de los Guácharos.....461 | Sibundoy.....478 |
| Buenaventura.....441 | La Plata.....463 | Ipiales.....479 |
| La Bocana.....444 | Tierradentro.....464 | Santuario de las Lajas.....481 |
| Juanchaco & Ladrilleros.....444 | Neiva.....466 | Volcán Cumbal.....482 |

Volcán Azufral ..........................483　Reserva Natural La Planada ... 484　Tumaco.....................................485

## THE AMAZON BASIN .................................................................................................487

Florencia...................................491　Mocoa ......................................493　Leticia ......................................497
San Antonio de Getucha..........492　Puerto Asís ..............................494　Around Leticia .........................503
Curillo......................................493　Puerto Inírida .........................496
Puerto Guzmán ......................493　Mitú.........................................496

## LOS LLANOS ...........................................................................................................507

Villavicencio............................510　Parque Nacional Serranía de　Puerto Carreño .......................516
　　　　　　　　　　　　　　　la Macarena.............................515　Parque Nacional El Tuparro ...518

## GLOSSARY .............................................................................................................519

## INDEX .....................................................................................................................527

Maps .........................................527　Text ..........................................527

# Map Legend

## BOUNDARIES

International Boundary
Internal Boundary
Regional Boundary
National Park Boundary

## ROUTES

Freeway
Highway
Major Road
Unsealed Road or Track
City Road
City Street
Railway
Underground Railway
Walking Track
Walking Tour
Ferry Route

## AREA FEATURES

Park, Gardens
National Park
Built-Up Area
Pedestrian Mall
Market
Cemetery
Reef
Beach or Desert

## HYDROGRAPHIC FEATURES

Coastline
River, Creek
Intermittent River or Creek
Lake, Intermittent Lake
River Flow
Canal
Swamp

## SYMBOLS

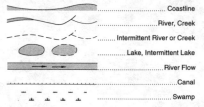

CAPITAL ............ National Capital
Capital ............ Departmental Capital
CITY ............ Major City
City ............ City
Town ............ Town
Village ............ Village
■ ............ Place to Stay
▼ ............ Place to Eat
▼ ............ Pub, Bar
Post Office, Telephone
Tourist Information, Bank
Transport, Parking
Museum, Youth Hostel
Caravan Park, Camping Ground
Church, Cathedral
Mosque, Synagogue
Hospital, Police Station

Airport, Airfield
Swimming Pool, Gardens
Shopping Centre, Zoo
Winery or Vineyard, Picnic Site
One Way Street, Route Number
Archaeological Site or Ruins
Stately Home, Monument
Castle, Tomb
Cave, Hut or Chalet
Mountain or Hill, Lookout
Lighthouse, Shipwreck
Pass, Spring
Underground Station
Ancient or City Wall
Rapids, Waterfalls
Cliff or Escarpment, Tunnel
Railway Station

Note: not all symbols displayed above appear in this book

# Introduction

For most travellers, Colombia is unknown territory – a land of myths, of cocaine, emeralds and the mysterious El Dorado. It is the land of Gabriel García Márquez and his famous *One Hundred Years of Solitude* – a tale as magical as the country itself. And it is the land which bears the name of Columbus, discoverer of the Americas, but where people have changed the order of the letters to make Locombia, the mad country.

Colombia certainly doesn't have a good international reputation. The news which repeatedly hits the media worldwide may give the impression that it's a lawless domain of drug lords and guerrillas, pushed to the brink of civil war. From closer up, however, the picture is quite different. It has a stable economy, with people pursuing orderly lives, surprisingly relaxed and easy-going – albeit perhaps more temperamental and intense than those in neighbouring nations.

Due to its bad press, Colombia has been the forgotten part of the popular Latin American 'gringo trail' that wends from Mexico down through Ecuador, Peru and Bolivia. It is looked upon as a country to get through quickly rather than as a place to visit. As a result, there are only a handful of popular tourist sites while the rest of Colombia hardly ever sees a foreign traveller. There are almost no beaten trails, gringo hotels or 'thrilling tours' businesses, and this makes Colombia a wonderful country for independent travel.

Colombia's geography is one of the most diverse in South America, as are its flora and fauna. The inhabitants, too, form a palette of ethnic blends uncommon elsewhere on the continent, and include a few dozen Indian groups, some of which still live traditional lifestyles. In its people, climate, topography, culture, crafts and architecture, Colombia is representative of most other Latin American countries. In effect, it's several countries rolled into one.

Through its stormy and turbulent history, Colombia has been soaked with blood in innumerable civil wars. The country has endured the largest and longest guerrilla insurgency on the continent. It is also the world's major producer of cocaine. With such a background, it's no wonder that violent acts may occur here more frequently than elsewhere, meaning Colombia is not as safe as neighbouring countries.

These comments might make you hesitate to visit Colombia, but don't be put off. If you take the necessary precautions, Colombia is worth the challenge. It is one of the most exotic, sensual, wild, complex and fascinating of countries. And it's hard to find such open, hospitable, spirited and stimulating people as in Colombia.

# Facts about the Country

## HISTORY
### The Pre-Columbian Period

Colombia lies at the gateway to South America, which means the continent's first inhabitants, Indians who migrated from North and Central America, passed through here on their way south. Most of the migrating tribes continued further south, where they developed well-known cultures such as the Nazca, Tiahuanaco and Inca, but some hunting and fishing communities settled in what is now Colombia. Several of these groups formed permanent settlements, which ultimately reached a remarkably high level of development.

In contrast to the Aztecs or Incas who dominated vast territories, a dozen independent Colombian cultures occupied relatively small areas in the Andean region and along the Pacific and Caribbean coasts. Despite trading and cultural contacts, the tribes essentially developed independently.

Little is known about these pre-Colombian cultures, partly because few of them left spectacular, enduring monuments. There are only three important archaeological sites in the country: San Agustín, Tierradentro and Ciudad Perdida. Most cultures left behind only artefacts, mainly in gold and pottery. There has been little investigation of these cultures, but their art reveals a high degree of craftsmanship, and their goldwork is the best in the continent.

Among the most outstanding cultures were the Tayrona, Sinú, Muisca, Quimbaya, Tolima, Calima, Tierradentro, San Agustín, Nariño and Tumaco. Evidence of the most ancient culture was discovered in Puerto Hormiga near Cartagena – pottery excavated there dates from about 3000 BC, making it the oldest on the continent. The Tierradentro and San Agustín cultures flourished long before the Spanish conquest, but the others were believed to be at the height of their cultural and social development when the Spaniards arrived.

San Agustín is one of the most extraordinary ceremonial centres in South America, noted for the hundreds of monolithic statues and tombs scattered over a wide area. The culture developed between the 6th and the 14th centuries AD. By the time the Spaniards arrived, it had died out and many of the remains had been covered by vegetation. It was not until the middle of the 18th century that the site was discovered. Since then, the mysterious statues have attracted many archaeologists, making San Agustín the most studied pre-Columbian civilisation in Colombia. Nevertheless, many facets of the culture remain enigmatic.

Another culture with developed funeral rites flourished in Tierradentro. The Indians living there kept the ashes of tribal elders in underground burial vaults scooped out of soft rock. The walls and ceilings of these chambers were decorated with paintings. Tierradentro's stone sculpture and pottery had certain affinities with that of San Agustín, but Tierradentro's funeral vaults are unique in South America. Archaeologists are still not sure when they were constructed, and know little about the builders or their culture.

The Muisca culture became widely known for the part it played in the Spanish myth of El Dorado. The Muiscas (often confusedly called the Chibchas because they formed the most important group of the Chibcha linguistic family) had a thriving, wealthy civilisation which occupied what are now the departments (administrative divisions) of Cundinamarca and Boyacá. They were Colombia's largest indigenous group at the time of the Spanish conquest, with a population estimated by some chroniclers to have been as high as 500,000.

Around the 3rd century BC, the Muiscas took advantage of fertile soils and rich salt and emerald mines, and created extensive trading links with other cultures. They had a complex, pyramidal social and political

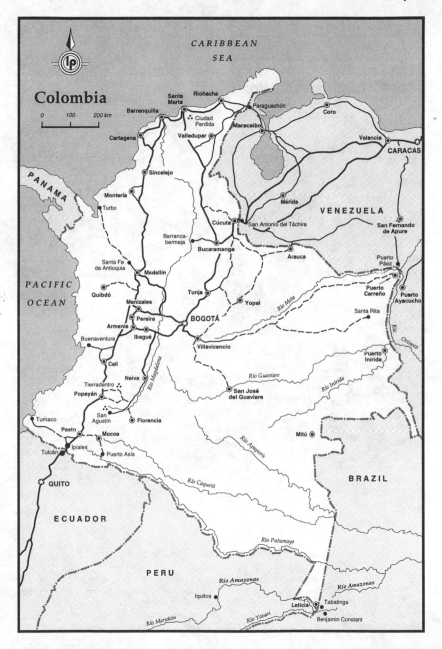

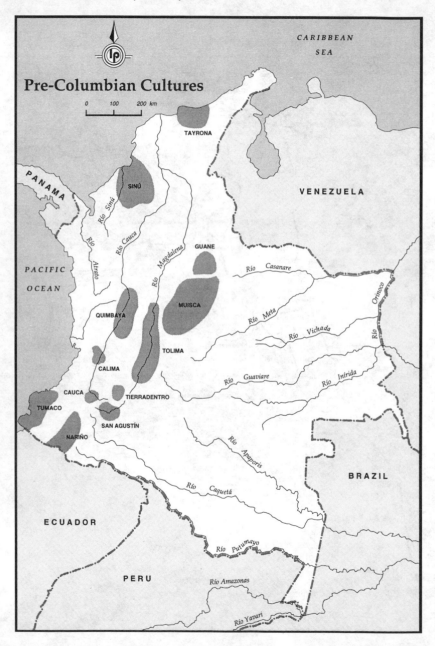

## Pre-Columbian Cultures

structure and a developed religious culture. They were skilled artisans, renowned for the technical quality of their pottery, the variety of motifs in their goldwork and their cotton fabrics. They also made many rock paintings, drawings and carvings, though their meaning remains a mystery. The Spaniards destroyed most of the Muisca ceremonial centres, and only a few sites exist today.

The Tayrona (or Tairona) developed from about the 5th century AD in the Sierra Nevada de Santa Marta. They were considered to be one of the most advanced of the early Indian civilisations, but it was only after the discovery of the Ciudad Perdida, the Lost City, in 1975 that their greatness as builders and urban planners was confirmed. The Ciudad Perdida, thought to be their capital, is one of the largest ancient cities ever found in the Americas. Spectacularly set on steep slopes in the heart of a lush rainforest, it consists of several hundred stone terraces linked by a network of stairs.

Tayrona artwork is renowned both for its detail and the simplicity of its lines. Unlike most other cultures, Tayronas rarely used pure gold in their jewellery, opting instead for a mixture of gold and copper. Quartz, rock crystal, cornelian and other semiprecious stones were used to make ceremonial and decorative objects. The Spaniards quickly became aware of the riches of the Tayronas and plundered the region in their obsessive pursuit of El Dorado. The Indians resisted strongly but were wiped out over the course of almost 100 years of struggle.

Other pre-Columbian cultures left few important architectural remains or ceremonial sites, yet they developed a remarkable degree of artistry, especially in pottery and goldwork.

One of the most advanced cultures was the Quimbaya, which occupied the region of the present-day departments of Caldas, Risaralda and Quindío. They were a peaceful, farming tribe, particularly noted for the perfection of their goldwork. Their favourite motifs were human figures, distinguished by their realism, delicate lines and peculiar beauty.

The Calimas lived further to the south, in the Dagua and Calima valleys. Evidence of their culture was discovered only 50 years ago and has still not been widely researched. What is known is that the Calima valley was a crossroads for several pre-Columbian groups, all of whom left their mark on the region. The Calima emerged from this convergence of cultures and later influenced others, especially the Tumaco.

The Tolima inhabited the area of the present-day department of Tolima and the northern part of Huila. The dominant groups of the culture were the Panches to the north and the Pijaos to the south. Both were formidable warrior tribes and practised cannibalism. They were also first-rate goldsmiths and developed a style not found elsewhere.

The Sinú (or Zenú), whose origin dates from the 1st century AD, inhabited the Caribbean lowlands between the Sinú and the San Jorge rivers. The Sinú and the Tayrona were the first Indian tribes to attract the attention of the gold-hungry conquerors.

The Nariño lived in the south-western region of Colombia. They were influenced by cultures further south, particularly the Incas. They produced remarkable pottery, often richly decorated and painted.

The Tumaco culture on the Pacific coast is one of the oldest in Colombia, dating from about the 10th century BC. It is noted for the erotic art associated with its fertility cult. The Tumaco were influenced by the coastal cultures of Ecuador, Costa Rica, Guatemala and Mexico. This is evident in the similarities of many of their art forms, especially their ceramic human heads and figures.

For more information about the art of these cultures, see the Arts section later in this chapter.

## The Spanish Conquest

Colombia is named after Christopher Columbus, although he never set foot on Colombian soil. It was Alonso de Ojeda, one of his companions on his second voyage, who landed at the Cabo de la Vela on the Guajira Peninsula in 1499. He briefly explored the Sierra Nevada de Santa Marta

Christopher Columbus

and was astonished by the wealth of the local Indians. Their gold and their stories about fabulous treasures inland gave birth to the myth of El Dorado, a mysterious kingdom abundant in gold. In its most extreme interpretation, it was believed to be a land of gold mountains littered with emeralds.

The legend of El Dorado became linked to the Muiscas and their famous Laguna de Guatavita. There, the expectations of the Spaniards were to some degree confirmed by the rituals of the Indians, who threw gold offerings into the sacred waters (though little has been found despite numerous efforts). There were, however, plenty of regional El Dorados. Wherever the Spaniards encountered Indians using or wearing gold objects (which was quite natural to the natives), they proclaimed a new El Dorado.

These El Dorados included the legendary golden range in the Sierra Nevada de Santa Marta which, in fact, never existed; Danaybe, the golden city in the department of Antioquia, which gave rise to feverish but fruitless expeditions; the tombs of the Sinú Indians in the valley of the Sinú River, which were thought to be full of gold; and even the vast regions of the Llanos and the Amazon where many conquerors found only their death.

From the moment the Spaniards arrived in South America, their obsession with El Dorado became the principal force driving them into the interior. They did not find El Dorado, but their search resulted in the rapid colonisation of the highlands.

Attracted by the riches, Alonso de Ojeda decided to explore other coastal regions and sailed as far as the Golfo de Urabá, where he founded San Sebastián de Urabá, the first Spanish settlement. Alonso de Ojeda was wounded in fights with the Indians and retreated to Santo Domingo, where he died soon after. The Indians destroyed San Sebastián de Urabá.

Despite the setback, news of the riches continued to spread and the shores of present-day Colombia became the target of numerous coastal expeditions. Francisco Pizarro, (in)famous for his conquest of the Incas, first sought his fortune in Colombia. Several ephemeral towns were founded in this early period, such as Anades, Santa Cruz and, the best-known, Santa María La Antigua, from where Vasco Núñez de Balboa set off to discover the Pacific. None of them exist today; they were all soon razed by the Indians.

It was not until 1525 that Rodrigo de Bastidas founded Santa Marta, the earliest surviving town. Bastidas had accompanied Alonso de Ojeda on his voyage and taken part in Juan de la Cosa's expedition of 1501. He had learned about the treasures of the Tayronas, and Santa Marta was founded to establish a gateway to the Sierra Nevada de Santa Marta.

The Indians were at first tolerant and even cordial to the conquerors but rebelled when the Spaniards tried to take their land and enslave them. In 1532, the Indians stopped sending food supplies to Santa Marta and the town's population began to starve; many were forced to return to Spain.

Pedro de Heredia laid the first stones of Cartagena, the second settlement along Colombia's Caribbean coast, in 1533. Cartagena soon became the main centre of trade, surpassing the half-abandoned Santa Marta.

In 1536, three independent parties began to advance into Colombia's interior from different directions. The parties were under the command of Gonzalo Jiménez de Quesada, Sebastián de Belalcázar and Nikolaus Federmann. Although all three were drawn by the Indian treasures, none intended to reach Muisca territory, where they finally met.

Jiménez de Quesada left Santa Marta, probably because of food shortages, and pushed up the Magdalena Valley with the intention of reaching Peru. He would probably have continued further south if not for the Indians who told him of the rich salt mines. He changed his route, climbed the Cordillera Oriental and arrived in Muisca territory early in 1537.

At the time, the Muiscas were divided into two clans – the southern one ruled by the Zipa from Bacatá (present-day Bogotá) and the northern empire under the Zaque in Hunza (present-day Tunja). The two caciques quarrelled over territory and this rivalry considerably helped Jiménez de Quesada conquer the Muiscas without undue difficulty. In August 1538, he founded Santa Fe de Bogotá on the site of Bacatá. In spite of spectacular Indian ceremonies at the Laguna de Guatavita, he found little gold, and even thought about leaving the nascent town and continuing on to Peru.

Sebastián de Belalcázar advanced from the south. He had deserted from Francisco Pizarro's army during the conquest of Peru and escaped towards the north in hope of reaching the Caribbean coast. He founded Quito, Popayán and Cali and originally intended to continue northward along the Cauca Valley, but the Indians' stories of the Guatavita rituals changed his mind. He crossed the Cordillera Central, followed the Magdalena Valley, climbed the Cordillera Oriental and reached Bogotá soon after it was founded.

The third expedition, led by German Nikolaus Federmann, set off from the Venezuelan coast. After successfully crossing Los Llanos, the expedition climbed the Cordillera Oriental and arrived in Bogotá shortly after Belalcázar.

Thus, in a short period of time, a large part of the colony was conquered and a number of towns were founded. Other important towns settled in the early years of Spanish colonisation include Mompós (1537), Tunja (1539) and Santa Fe de Antioquia (1541).

## The Colonial Period

When the three *conquistadores* found themselves face to face in Bogotá, rivalry soon developed. It was not until 1550 that King Charles V (Carlos V) of Spain, in an effort to establish law and order, created the Real Audiencia del Nuevo Reino de Granada, a tribunal based in Bogotá. It was principally a court of justice but its duties went beyond normal legal and penal affairs. Administratively, the new colony was subject to the Viceroyalty of Peru (Virreynato del Perú) which ruled from Lima.

In 1564, the Crown established a new system, the Presidencia del Nuevo Reino de Granada, which had dual military and civil power and greater autonomy. Authority was in the hands of the governor, appointed by the King of Spain. The Nuevo Reino at that time comprised present-day Panama and all of Colombia except what is today Nariño, Cauca and Valle, which were under the jurisdiction of the Presidencia de Quito.

The population of the colony, initially consisting of indigenous communities and the Spanish invaders, diversified with the arrival of blacks, brought from Africa to serve as the workforce. Cartagena was granted the privilege of being the exclusive slave-trading port, in which blacks were sold as slaves and distributed throughout the colony. Most of them were set to work in mines and plantations, mainly on the Caribbean and Pacific coasts. During the 16th and 17th centuries the Spaniards shipped in so many blacks that they eventually surpassed the indigenous population in number.

The demographic picture became still more complex when the three racial groups

## Simón Bolívar

'There have been three great fools in history: Jesus, Don Quixote and I' – this is how Simón Bolívar summed up his life shortly before he died. The man who brought independence from Spanish rule to the entire north-west of South America – today's Venezuela, Colombia, Panama, Ecuador, Peru and Bolivia – died abandoned, rejected and poor.

The Bolívar family had come to the New World from Spain in 1557. They first settled in Santo Domingo, but in 1589 moved to Venezuela, where they were granted a hacienda in San Mateo, near Caracas. Members of Venezuela's colonial elite, they were well off and steadily extended their possessions. One of their descendants, Juan Vicente Bolívar, acquired a town house in Caracas. He was 47 years old when, in 1773, he married 15-year-old María de la Concepción Palacios y Blanco. They had four children; the second, born on 24 July 1783, was named Simón.

Juan Vicente died in 1786 (Simón was then three years old) and María six years later. The boy was brought up by his uncle and was given a tutor, Simón Rodríguez, an open-minded mentor who had a strong formative influence on his pupil.

In 1799 the young Bolívar was sent to Spain and France to continue his education. After having mastered French, he turned his attention to that country's literature. Voltaire and Rousseau became his favourite authors. Their works introduced him to new, progressive ideas of liberalism and – as it turned out – were to determine the course of his career.

In 1802, Bolívar married his Spanish bride, María Teresa Rodríguez del Toro, and a short time later the young couple sailed to Caracas. Their married life lasted only eight months; María Teresa died of yellow fever. Bolívar never married again, although he had many lovers. The most devoted of these was Manuela Sáenz, whom he met in Quito in 1822 and who accompanied him almost until his final days.

The death of María Teresa marked a drastic shift in Bolívar's destiny. He returned to France, where he met with the leaders after the French Revolution, and then travelled to the USA to take a close look at the new order after the War of American Independence. By the time he returned to Caracas in 1807, he was full of revolutionary theories and experiences taken from these two successful examples. It didn't take him long to join clandestine, pro-independence circles.

At the time, disillusionment with Spanish rule was close to the point of breaking out into open revolt. On 19 April 1810 the Junta Suprema was installed in Caracas and on 5 July 1811 the Congress declared independence. This turned out to be only the beginning; the declaration triggered a long, bitter war, most of which was to be orchestrated by Bolívar.

Bolívar's military career began under Francisco de Miranda, the first Venezuelan leader of the independence movement. After Miranda was captured by the Spaniards in 1812, Bolívar took over command. Over the following decade, he hardly had a moment's rest; battle followed battle with astonishing frequency until 1824. Of those battles personally directed by Bolívar, the forces of independence won 35. Of these, the key strategic achievements were the Battle of Boyacá (7 August 1819), which secured the independence of Colombia; the Battle of Carabobo (24 June 1821), which brought freedom to Venezuela; and the Battle of Pichincha (24 May 1822), which led to the liberation of Ecuador.

Bolívar's long-awaited dream materialised: Gran Colombia, the unified state comprising Venezuela, Colombia and Ecuador, became reality. However, the task of setting the newborn country on its feet proved to be even more difficult than that of winning battles. 'I fear peace more than war', Bolívar wrote in one of his letters, aware of the difficulties ahead.

The main problem was the question of the political organisation of Gran Colombia. Bolívar, then the president, favoured a strong central rule, but the central regime was increasingly incapable of governing such an immense country with its great racial and regional divisions and differences. Gran Colombia began to collapse from the moment of its birth.

Bolívar insisted on holding the weak union together, but matters began to slip out of his hands. His impassioned and vehement speeches – for which he was widely known – no longer swayed the growing opposition. His glory and charisma faded.

As separatist tendencies escalated dangerously, Bolívar removed Vice-president Santander from office by decree and, in August 1828, assumed dictatorship. This step brought more harm than good. His popularity waned further, as did his circle of personal friends and supporters. A short time later, he miraculously escaped an assassination attempt in Bogotá. Disillusioned and in bad health, he resigned the presidency in early 1830 and decided to travel to Europe. The formal disintegration of Gran Colombia was just months away.

Venezuela separated from Gran Colombia, and the Venezuelan Congress approved a new constitution and banned Bolívar from his homeland. A month later, Antonio José de Sucre (remembered for inflicting final defeat on Spain in the Battle of Ayacucho on 9 December 1824), the closest of Bolívar's friends, was assassinated in southern Colombia. These two pieces of news reached Bolívar shortly before he was to have boarded a ship bound for France. Depressed and ill, he accepted the invitation of a Spaniard, Joaquín de Mier, to stay at his house, Quinta de San Pedro Alejandrino, in Santa Marta. A bitter remark written in Bolívar's diary at this time reads: 'America is ungovernable. Those who serve the revolution plough the sea.'

Bolívar died on 17 December 1830 of pulmonary tuberculosis. A priest, a doctor and a few officers were by his bed, but none of his close friends. Joaquín de Mier donated one of his shirts to dress the dead body, as there had been none among Bolívar's humble belongings. So died perhaps the most important figure in the history of the South American continent.

It took the Venezuelan nation 12 years to acknowledge its debt to the man to whom it owed its freedom. In 1842, Bolívar's remains were brought from Santa Marta to Venezuela and deposited in the cathedral in the capital, Caracas. In 1876, they were solemnly transferred to the National Pantheon in Caracas, where they now rest.

Today Bolívar is once again a hero – his reputation polished and inflated to almost superhuman dimensions. His cult is particularly strong in Venezuela but he is also widely venerated in all the other nations he freed. His statue graces almost every central city square, and at least one street in every town bears his name. If one could gather together all the portraits of Bolívar produced over the past two centuries, perhaps none of the world's largest museums would be big enough to accommodate the collection.

El Libertador – as he was named at the beginning of the liberation campaign and is still commonly called today – was without doubt a man of extraordinary gifts and talents. An idealist with a poetic mind and visionary ideas, his goal was not only to topple Spanish rule but to create a unified America. This, of course, was an impossible ideal, yet the military conquest of some five million sq km remains a phenomenal accomplishment. This inspired amateur without any formal training in the strategy of war won battles in a manner which still confounds experts today. The campaign over the Andean Cordillera in the rainy season was described 100 years later as 'the most magnificent episode in the history of war'.

Voices critical of Bolívar's faults and short-comings are now almost never heard, yet he was frequently accused of despotism and dictatorship when he ruled Gran Colombia. It was Bolívar himself who once said: 'Our America can only be ruled through a well-managed, shrewd despotism.'

The complexity of Bolívar's character allows almost anyone – be they conservative or liberal, leftist or rightist, dictator or guerrilla – to identify with his words and works and adopt them as their own. One of the final, prophetic remarks in Bolívar's diary reads: 'My name now belongs to history, it will do me justice.' And history has duly done so. ∎

Simón Bolívar

began to mix together, producing various fusions, including *mestizos* (people of European-Indian blood), *mulatos* (of European-African ancestry) and *zambos* (African-Indian). Yet, throughout the whole of the colonial period, the power was almost exclusively in the hands of the Spaniards.

Prompted by the growth of the Spanish Empire in the New World, Philip V (Felipe V) decided, in 1717, to divide the vast Virreynato del Perú into smaller territorial and administrative units. The Presidencia del Nuevo Reino de Granada became an autonomous viceroyalty, independent of the Virreynato del Perú. It was abolished in 1723 but re-established in 1739 and lasted until Colombian independence. The Virreynato de la Nueva Granada comprised the territories of what are today Colombia, Panama, Venezuela and Ecuador. Santa Fe de Bogotá became the viceroyalty's capital.

As Spanish domination of the continent increased, so did the discontent of the inhabitants. Slavery, and the monopoly of commerce, taxes and duties – amongst other factors – slowly gave rise to protests, particularly towards the end of the 18th century. The first open rebellion against the colonial authorities was the revolt of the Comuneros in Socorro in 1781. It was principally a local protest against tax increases levied by Spain to finance its wars against England, but it soon spread throughout the region and took on pro-independence overtones. The revolt was brutally crushed and its leaders executed, but this only led to further discontent.

Disillusionment was not only felt by the lower classes; it also appeared in the higher Creole class. The *criollos*, Colombian-born whites, were generally excluded from senior administrative posts and reproached the Crown for treating them as second-class citizens. Of the 170 viceroys who governed the New World, only four were Creoles.

It was during this period that a national consciousness evolved which helped pave the way to independence. The pioneering Botanical Expedition led by José Celestino Mutis gathered a number of scientists together and gave impetus to studies in the natural riches of the country. Intellectual circles and literary salons, which explored South American and not just Spanish issues, also began to emerge.

In 1794, Antonio Nariño translated Thomas Paine's *Rights of Man* into Spanish. The pamphlet was a touchpaper of revolt in a country where slavery was widespread. Nariño was condemned to prison in Africa but managed to escape and return clandestinely to the country.

Ultimately it was a series of external events, such as the North American and the French revolutions and, most importantly, the invasion of Spain by Napoleon Bonaparte, that precipitated independence. When, in 1808, Napoleon replaced the Spanish king Ferdinand VII (Fernando VII) with his own brother Joseph, the colonies refused to recognise the new monarch. One by one, towns began to declare their independence from Spain. The first to do so were Mompós and Cartagena. In Bogotá, the Corte Suprema de la Nueva Granada (Supreme Court) was established, the first central state body whose members were to be elected from the different provinces.

Many of the provinces, however, refused to send their representatives and became fierce advocates of regional autonomy. Thus, in spite of a united front against Spain, internal rivalries between centralists and federalists ensued. This continued to be the central political division of post-independence Colombia and gave rise to numerous conflicts and civil wars.

In 1812, Simón Bolívar, who was to become the hero of the independence struggle, appeared on the scene. El Libertador, as he came to be known, eventually liberated Venezuela, Colombia, Panama, Ecuador, Peru and Bolivia – the so-called *países bolivarianos* – from Spanish rule.

Bolívar left Caracas, his place of birth, and launched his brilliant campaign to seize Venezuela from Cartagena in 1813. He won six battles against the Spanish Army but was unable to hold Caracas and withdrew to Cartagena.

By then, the situation in Europe had

changed. When Napoleon was defeated at Waterloo, Spain recovered its throne and set about reconquering its colonies. Troops were sent under Pablo Morillo and, in 1815, after a four-month siege, Cartagena was retaken. The 'pacifying' Spanish troops then reconquered the interior and colonial rule was re-established by 1817.

Bolívar retreated to Jamaica after the defeat of Cartagena, and took up arms again. He landed on the Venezuelan coast, assembled an army of horsemen from Los Llanos and, strengthened by a British legion, set out on his decisive campaign. Before freeing Venezuela, he marched over the Cordillera Oriental into Colombia and claimed victory after victory. The last and most decisive battle took place at Boyacá on 7 August 1819. Three days later he arrived triumphantly in Bogotá. Independence was won.

## The Post-Independence Period

The revolutionary congress met in Angostura (modern-day Ciudad Bolívar, in Venezuela) in December 1819. Still euphoric with victory, the delegates proclaimed the Gran Colombia, a new state uniting Venezuela, Colombia and Ecuador (though Venezuela and Ecuador were still under Spanish rule; the former was eventually liberated in 1821, the latter in 1822). The Angostura Congress was followed by another congress held in Villa del Rosario near Cúcuta in 1821. It was there that the two opposing tendencies, centralist and federalist, came to the fore. Bolívar supported a centralised republic, while Francisco de Paula Santander favoured a federal republic of sovereign states.

Bolívar succeeded in imposing his will and the Gran Colombia came into being. Bolívar was elected president and Santander became vice-president.

The Gran Colombia began to disintegrate from the moment of its inception. Bolívar was occupied fighting for the independence of Peru, and left real power in Santander's hands. It soon became apparent that a central regime was incapable of governing such a vast territory, and the Gran Colombia split in

1830. Bolívar's dream of a sacred union of the nations he had freed came to an end. Disillusioned and ill, he died soon after, in December 1830, in Santa Marta.

The two political currents born in the struggle for independence were formalised in 1849 when two political parties were established: the Conservatives with centralist tendencies, and the Liberals with federalist leanings. The country became the scene of fierce rivalries between the two forces, resulting in a sequence of insurrections, chaos and civil wars. In the course of the 19th century, the country experienced no less than eight civil wars, and between 1863 and 1885 there were more than 50 insurrections.

In 1899, a Liberal revolt turned into a full-scale civil war, the so-called War of a Thousand Days. The carnage left 100,000 dead and resulted in a Conservative victory. In 1903, the United States took advantage of the country's internal strife and fomented a secessionist movement in Panama, then a Colombian province. By creating a new and independent republic, the USA was able to build an inter-ocean canal across the Central American isthmus under its control. Colombia did not recognise the sovereignty of Panama or settle its dispute with the USA until 1921.

It's worth remembering that the independence movement and the subsequent governments were almost entirely in the hands of Creoles. They paid little attention to Indians and blacks, and not much more to mestizos or mulatos, who continued to be exploited under conditions similar to or worse than those prevailing under Spanish rule. Although slavery was officially abolished in 1849, in many regions it continued well into the 20th century. For instance, during the rubber boom in the Amazon, some Indian tribes were brought to the brink of extermination by enslavement.

## The 20th Century

After a period of relative peace, the struggle between Liberals and Conservatives broke out again in 1948 with La Violencia, the most cruel and destructive of Colombia's many civil wars. With a death toll of some 300,000,

La Violencia was one of the bloodiest conflicts in the western hemisphere, comparable only to the Mexican Revolution and the American Civil War.

The first urban riots broke out in Bogotá on 9 April 1948 following the assassination of Jorge Eliécer Gaitán, a charismatic and populist Liberal leader. Liberals soon took up arms throughout the country. In Barrancabermeja (in the department of Santander), labour leaders, Liberals and Communists declared a revolutionary junta, while the captain of the municipal police force headed to the mountains with his men and formed the first band of guerrillas.

In Los Llanos, Liberals created an army of over 20,000 peasants which ransacked the symbols and strongholds of Conservatism. This included the burning of churches and the assassination of priests, as well as some armed confrontations with the Conservative-dominated military and the destruction of towns and villages inhabited by members of the opposing party.

To comprehend the brutality of this period, one must understand that Colombians were traditionally born either a Liberal or a Conservative and reared with a mistrust of the members of the other party. In the 1940s and 1950s, these 'hereditary hatreds' prevailed over any rational difference of ideology or politics, and were the cause of countless atrocities, rapes and murders, particularly in rural areas. Hundreds of thousands of people took to the hills and shot each other for nothing more than the name of their party.

After 1948, the fighting transferred from the urban areas to the countryside. The political leaders of both parties, safely entrenched in the cities, supported the actions of their followers, providing ideological justification, arms and supplies. By 1953, however, some of the peasant *comandantes* of the Liberal guerrillas had begun to demonstrate a dangerous degree of independence. They introduced revolutionary language into their communiqués and in some cases made alliances with the small bands of communist guerrillas which operated in some areas during this period.

As it became evident that the partisan conflict was taking on revolutionary overtones, the leaders of both the Liberal and Conservative parties made the decision to support a military coup as the best means to retain power and pacify the countryside. The 1953 coup of General Gustavo Rojas Pinilla is the only military intervention Colombia has experienced this century.

One of the first actions of the newly installed military government was to offer an amnesty to the Liberal guerrillas. Shortly thereafter, over 6000 peasant fighters, mostly from Los Llanos, handed over their arms to government authorities. Those that did not were pursued and punished. This model of amnesty and repression was to be applied several times over the next 30 years.

## Changing Names

Colombia changed names several times. Before independence, it formed a part of the Virreynato de la Nueva Granada. After independence, it was part of the Gran Colombia. When the Gran Colombia came to an end in 1830, the country took the name of the República de Nueva Granada. This lasted until 1857, when it became the Confederación Granadina. In 1861, the name was changed again to Estados Unidos de Nueva Granada, then in 1863 to Estados Unidos de Colombia (United States of Colombia), and finally, in 1886 to the República de Colombia, which is the name it bears today.

Each of these changes corresponded to a new constitution. Those of 1857 and 1863 were federalist and the constitution of 1863 gave almost complete sovereignty to the provinces, only deferring the authority to conduct foreign affairs to the central government. The constitution of 1886 was centralist and principally the work of Rafael Núñez – president, poet, journalist and philosopher. A modified version of this constitution was in force for over a century, until 1991. ■

The dictatorship of General Rojas was not to last. In 1957, the political leaders of the two factions signed a pact that guaranteed an arrangement to share power for the next 16 years. The agreement, later approved by a plebiscite (in which women were, for the first time, allowed to vote), became known as the Frente Nacional (National Front). During the life of the accord, the two parties agreed to alternate the presidency every four years and evenly divide all posts within government ministries, state agencies, the national Congress and the judiciary. Thus, in spite of the loss of some 300,000 lives during the years of La Violencia, the same men returned to power. Moreover, they no longer needed to contest it.

The National Front eliminated political competition – a central feature of democracy – and repressed (often forcefully) all political activity that remained outside the scope of the two parties. To its credit, the National Front also brought peace to the country, a degree of political stability and moderate but steady economic growth during a crucial transition from a semi-feudal, agrarian society to a capitalist, industrial economy.

The National Front formally came to an end in 1974, when Liberal President Alfonso López Michelsen was elected. However, after 16 years of coalition government, both the Liberal and Conservative parties were unwilling to abandon their joint monopoly on state power. The parties still preferred to divide the benefits of an expanding bureaucracy between them, rather than to compete for access to limited institutional resources. A modified version of the National Front was to last another 17 years.

Colombian presidents are constitutionally limited to one four-year term. López was succeeded by another Liberal, Julio César Turbay Ayala (1978-1982). The Conservatives regained the presidency in 1982 with the election of Belisario Betancur. However, don't let the party labels confuse you. Turbay was one of the most conservative presidents in recent Colombian history, launching a major military campaign against the country's Marxist guerrillas and repressing labour strikes

and demonstrations. In contrast, Conservative president Betancur presented himself as a populist and opened direct negotiations with the guerrillas in a bid to reincorporate the armed opposition into the nation's political life and restore peace to the country.

The 1980s proved to be a dramatic and traumatic period in Colombia's political life. The first negotiations with the guerrillas ended in renewed hostilities and a new round of blood-letting (see the Guerrillas section). The rupture was poignantly symbolised by the takeover of Bogotá's Palace of Justice by the M-19 guerrillas in November 1985. The military surrounded the building and, after 28 hours of fighting, left it in flames. When the fighting was over, more than 100 people lay dead, including an estimated 35 guerrillas and 11 Supreme Court justices. Of those who survived, many disappeared. According to human rights organisations, the 'disappearances' were the work of the military, hunting for accomplices of M-19.

Following the massacre at the Palace of Justice, Colombia entered a period which came to be known as the 'dirty war'. Unknown paramilitary forces killed or 'disappeared' thousands of left-wing political activists, amnestied guerrillas, labour leaders and human rights workers. Amnesty International declared Colombia a 'human rights emergency' in 1988. It was soon learnt that the paramilitary squads were backed by members of the Armed Forces, allied to newly rich drug traffickers, local politicians and landowners.

## Recent Developments

Colombia's political crisis and escalating violence came to a head between 1989-1991. By the late eighties, the drug traffickers (see the Drug Cartels section) began to direct their guns at members of the ruling political class in a naked play for power. The upsurge in drug-related violence provoked a strong response from the government of President Virgilio Barco (1986-90). After drug lords gunned down the leading Liberal presidential candidate, Luis Carlos Galán, President

Barco declared an all-out war against drug traffickers. Colombia was now engaged in two internal wars, one against guerrillas, and another against drug cartels.

At the outset of the 1990s, the country reached the brink of chaos. Ordinary citizens began to lose faith in governmental institutions, and students took to the streets to call for change. In a 1990 plebiscite, the Colombian people voted overwhelmingly for a Constitutional Assembly to reform the constitution and address the crisis. Special elections were held in which former guerrillas, indigenous leaders, Protestants, popular leaders, as well as members of the two traditional political parties were elected.

The Constitutional Assembly met from January to July 1991 and extensively reformed the institutional structure of Colombian politics, replacing the bipartisan power-sharing arrangement of the National Front. In its place, the constitution affirmed a more pluralist conception of politics, which incorporated former guerrilla groups, Indian communities, blacks, non-Catholics and others who had previously felt excluded from the political process.

The constitution of 1991 is pioneering in its conceptions of human rights, ethnic pluralism and ecological preservation. The challenge for Colombia in the 1990s is to fully implement the new constitution, and to convert it into 'a peace treaty for all Colombians', as President César Gaviria (1990-94) proposed on 4 July 1991 when the new political charter took effect.

The first part of President Gaviria's term brought some hope for the 'peace treaty': Colombia's most notorious drug trafficker, Pablo Escobar, surrendered and the Coordinadora Guerrillera Simón Bolívar (the unified guerrilla front) declared a truce to negotiate with the government. However, Escobar escaped from his palace-like prison (commonly known as La Catedral) and, after peace talks bogged down, the guerrillas returned to the hills.

Predictably, drug trafficking and guerrillas occupied the agenda for most of Gaviria's remaining time in office, keeping the president busy resolving emergencies rather than constitutional issues. It seems likely that this nightmare will continue during the term of the current president.

The 1994 election campaign was probably the most apathetic in the country's recent history. Differences between the candidates for the traditional parties, the Liberal Ernesto Samper and the Conservative Andrés Pastrana, were barely distinguishable and neither candidate captured the attention of the electorate. In a typically Colombian manner, the bored voters forged the name of the would-be winner: Pastramper. Not far from truth, as it was to turn out.

Only a third of the electorate bothered to vote: Samper won 45% of the vote and Pastrana collected a marginal 0.3% less. Antonio Navarro Wolff of ADM-19 came third with a humiliating 4% of the vote. The elections proved that despite the new constitution and the hopes for a more pluralist system, bipartisan dominance was still very much intact.

As none of the candidates won half of the votes, a second, deciding round was held three weeks later between the two major contenders. Election Day coincided with Colombia's appearance in the soccer World Cup and voters predictably preferred to drink booze in preparation for the TV transmission rather than turn up at the ballot-box. With a low turnout, Samper eventually won, capturing just over 50% of the vote.

## Guerrillas

Guerrillas play an important part in Colombian political life. Their roots extend back to the period of La Violencia in the 1940s and 1950s, making them the oldest insurgent forces in Latin America. During the 1960s, the Sino-Soviet split and the influence of the Cuban revolution spawned several new guerrilla movements, each representing a different programme for Marxist revolution. In the 1970s, several nationalistic groups took up arms, seeking to overthrow what they referred to as a closed and unrepresentative political system dominated by the traditional oligarchy.

By the late 1970s, Colombia had perhaps a dozen different guerrilla groups, each with its own ideology and its own political and military strategies. The movements which have had the biggest impact on local politics (and left the largest number of dead) include the FARC (Fuerzas Armadas Revolucionarias de Colombia, see FARC), the ELN (Ejército de Liberación Nacional), the M-19 (Movimiento 19 de Abril) and the EPL (Ejército Popular de Liberación).

Over the years, four guerrilla groups have laid down their arms and joined the electoral process. Most other groups have stopped armed action. However, the two major guerrilla groups, FARC and ELN, and a dissident faction of the third group, EPL, continue to engage in armed struggle.

Colombia's peculiar geography facilitated much of the country's endemic political violence. Over 50% of the country comprises vast lowlands to the east of the Andes – the Llanos to the north and the Amazon to the south – which are sparsely populated and relatively inaccessible. Guerrilla groups prospered in these regions, often controlling large areas and providing public services which the state was unable or reluctant to supply.

In the late 1970s and early 1980s, when the traditional parties were in crisis and divorced from Colombia's social and economic realities, the nation's insurgency movements emerged as key protagonists in Colombian politics. Yet their participation was limited to military operations, including the takeover of small villages and towns, and dramatic propaganda exercises, such as the seizure of the Dominican Republic's embassy in Bogotá by the M-19, during which 15 ambassadors were held hostage for two months.

During the reign of the National Front, the government implemented counter-insurgency programmes which emphasised sporadic warfare and military participation in rural development. However, in 1982, in the face of mounting guerrilla actions and declining support for the traditional parties, the newly elected president, Belisario Betancur, dramatically changed the direction of government policy. Betancur officially recognised that poverty, unemployment, inadequate state services and undemocratic institutional structures contributed to the spread of Colombia's armed movements. Belisario – as he was popularly known – called for a 'democratic opening' of Colombia's political institutions.

Upon taking office, Belisario offered an unconditional amnesty and released over 400 political prisoners from the nation's jails, including dozens of top guerrilla leaders. Two years later, in 1984, the government signed ceasefire agreements with four of the principal groups and promised to promote basic structural changes to the system, particularly agrarian reform and guarantees for opposition movements and parties.

However, the ceasefire agreements ended in failure. By 1986, all the major groups had reverted to armed struggle, and the country entered a bloody phase of conflict, the 'dirty war', during which many amnestied guerrillas, some elected to congress and mayorships, were assassinated.

In 1989, as the violence was reaching its zenith and becoming complicated by the war against drug trafficking, President Virgilio Barco re-initiated negotiations with several guerrilla movements. The first to enter into agreements was the M-19. The M-19 was a nationalist group, militarily weak, but through its spectacular actions and Robin Hood imagery, it had developed a degree of popular approval, though not direct support. In 1990, the M-19 formally surrendered its arms to an international delegation and requested that the weapons be melted down and converted into a statue of peace.

A month after laying down his arms, M-19 leader and presidential candidate, Carlos Pizarro, was assassinated on a commercial airliner on his way to a campaign stop. Pizarro's funeral attracted tens of thousands of mourners who marched through the streets of Bogotá. It was a moment of national catharsis and led to a greater outpouring of support for the M-19. The M-19, now known as the Alianza Democrática M-

19, refused to be intimidated by the violence and fielded its new leader, Antonio Navarro Wolff, as its presidential candidate. Navarro Wolff received an unprecedented 12% of the vote in the presidential election and established the ADM-19 as a significant challenger to the Liberal and Conservative parties.

Several months later, in special elections for the Constitutional Assembly, the ADM-19's vote increased to 27%, and Navarro Wolff emerged as a co-president of the constitutional convention. By this time, the government had successfully negotiated peace treaties with two other guerrilla movements, the EPL and the Quintín Lame, a group that fought for the rights of the indigenous people in the department of Cauca. Both groups were guaranteed participation in the writing of the new constitution. The EPL soon changed its name to Esperanza, Paz y Libertad (Hope, Peace and Liberty) and allied itself with the ADM-19. The Quintín Lame allied itself with other indigenous groups in the Constitutional Assembly, and made headway in securing indigenous rights. A third group, the PRT (Partido Revolucionario de los Trabajadores), a small movement operating in the Caribbean coastal region, negotiated an end to its armed struggle shortly after the conclusion of the Constitutional Assembly, and also allied itself with the ADM-19.

Despite these successes, the government failed to reach agreement with the two largest, and militarily strongest guerrilla groups, the FARC and the ELN. The FARC was historically linked to the Communist Party of Colombia and was pro-Soviet. The ELN, originally pro-Castro, later became a hardline Christian Marxist group headed by Spanish former priests. By the early 1990s, these two groups, together with a dissident faction of the EPL which had refused to surrender its arms, were united in a guerrilla coalition called the Coordinadora Guerrillera Simón Bolívar.

The government continued to negotiate with the Coordinadora Guerrillera in the aftermath of the Constitutional Assembly, but did not reach agreement; negotiations have since been suspended indefinitely.

Despite the new constitution and a different domestic and international political environment, the breakdown of talks has resulted in continued violence and confrontation. The main change is that the guerrillas have now lost much of their popular support and international support from Moscow and Havana. They now rely on extortion, robbery and kidnapping to finance their struggle. They are also increasingly involved in the drug business.

The guerrilla presence continues to be significant in Los Llanos, parts of the Amazon and in isolated areas of the eastern and central cordilleras. Yet most analysts believe that the guerrillas have little future. Their options are to negotiate with the government – as the other guerrilla movements did – and convert their armed struggle into a legal, political movement, or to continue to fight without popular support and risk degenerating further into criminality and banditry.

Colombian history demonstrates that it is difficult to achieve victory over guerrilla armies which maintain a strong base of popular support, but possible to defeat bandits, or *bandoleros*, which have lost support and are unable to sustain their armed actions. So, theoretically at least, the guerrillas' future seems uncertain.

It should be noted that the Colombian guerrillas have still not employed the type of terrorist actions known in Europe and the Middle East. They do not place bombs in theatres and supermarkets, and the fighting is mostly limited to remote, isolated areas. They do not have a history of targeting tourists, but travellers should not venture too far into regions known to be guerrilla strongholds and should check local newspapers to avoid areas where there have been recent skirmishes. The problems travellers encounter in these zones will probably not be caused by the guerrillas but by the security forces patrolling the area.

**Drug Cartels**
Colombia is the biggest producer of

cocaine, controlling some 80% of the world market. It is also the third largest grower of marijuana. Since the late 1980s, the country has begun growing opium poppies, and producing high-grade heroin. The vast majority of these drugs are produced for export, primarily to the USA, but also to Europe.

The production and trafficking of these drugs, which is, of course, illegal, is controlled by regional mafias, referred to as cartels. The Medellín Cartel has been on the front pages of the world's newspapers for the past decade. It was the strongest cartel during the 1980s and dominated a significant portion of the cocaine business, but it has since been overshadowed by the Cali Cartel. Apart from these major cartels, there are regional groupings in Bogotá, Santa Marta, Bucaramanga and other cities.

The cartels started in a small way in the early 1970s using primitive smuggling methods. The cocaine was packed into shoe heels or sewn into the linings of suitcases or coats, and smuggled overseas by *mulas* (payed persons carrying drugs) on regular commercial flights. The cartels bought the cocaine paste in Bolivia and Peru, refined it in clandestine laboratories hidden in the Colombian jungles and distributed the pure product to the USA, mainly through Florida.

The boom years began in the early 1980s, and the Medellín Cartel became the principal mafia. Its leaders – Pablo Escobar, Jorge Luis Ochoa, Gonzalo Rodríguez Gacha and Carlos Lehder – lived quietly in freedom and luxury. Lehder founded a newspaper and a political party, Movimiento Nacional Latino. Escobar also founded a newspaper and, in 1982, was elected to the Congress! By 1983, Escobar's personal wealth was estimated to be US$2 billion, making him the richest criminal in the world. He financed the construction of a barrio for 200 poor families in Medellín, and for this and several other benevolent actions, he was called the Robin Hood Paisa.

In mid-1983, Tranquilandia, the largest cocaine laboratory in history, went into production on the banks of the Río Yarí in Los Llanos.

It had 14 independent, fully equipped laboratories, a water and electricity supply, roads, dormitories and its own airstrip. It produced 3500 kg of pure cocaine every month.

The climate in which such laboratories could operate changed in August 1983 when Belisario Betancur appointed Rodrigo Lara Bonilla Minister of Justice. Bonilla launched a campaign against the drug trade, which led *El Espectador*, one of Bogotá's leading daily papers, to publicise some of Escobar's former crimes. The war between the cartel and the government began.

In March 1984, police raided Tranquilandia and arrested everyone working there. The police confiscated seven aeroplanes, a number of weapons and vehicles, and all the chemicals on the premises. Fourteen tonnes of cocaine were reportedly seized and thrown into the river!

The cartel bosses disappeared from public life. All of them except Lehder left for Panama, from where, in May 1984, they proposed an unusual peace treaty to President Betancur. For immunity from prosecution and extradition, they offered to invest their capital in national development programmes. More tantalising still, they proposed to pay Colombia's entire foreign debt, some US$13 billion! After much consideration, their proposals were turned down by the government.

The Medellín Cartel continued to operate throughout the 1980s and began to invest its profits in land, and later in industry. As the drug traffickers became major landowners, they began to create private armies to protect their investments. The most notorious of these was the MAS (Muerte a Secuestradores, or Death to Kidnappers), a group created after Ochoa's sister was kidnapped.

In 1984, the Medellín Cartel assassinated its major adversary, Justice Minister Rodrigo Lara Bonilla. The government responded by implementing an extradition treaty that had been signed years earlier with the US but never enforced. Four minor drug traffickers were swiftly sent to the US to stand trial. The Medellín Cartel immediately began a campaign against the extradition. Calling themselves the 'extraditables', they declared, 'better a grave in Colombia than a jail in the US'. The campaign won a degree of nationalist support against the treaty.

The government refused to soften its stand, so the cartel bosses began to target the treaty's prominent supporters, such as Guillermo Cano, the publisher of *El Espectador*, who was assassinated in late 1986. Eventually, even the Attorney-General was gunned down in the escalating conflict over the treaty.

Colombia's security forces retaliated. In February 1987, the anti-narcotics police, with the cooperation of the US Drug Enforcement Agency (DEA), captured and extradited to the US one of the top cartel leaders, Carlos Lehder.

Until 1989, the drug war had consisted of strong declarations from both sides, and a few showpiece acts of violence and revenge. This changed when the cartel assassinated the leading presidential candidate, Luis Carlos Galán, in August 1989. For the next six months, all hell broke loose. Galán's murder led to a declaration of all out war by the government, and the US immediately offered US\$65 million in emergency aid and logistical support.

In the opening salvo of this new war, President Barco confiscated 989 buildings and ranches, 367 aeroplanes, 73 boats, 710 vehicles, 4.7 tonnes of cocaine, 1279 guns and 25,000 rounds of ammunition. The traffickers responded with a hair-raising campaign of terror, burning the farms of regional politicians in Antioquia and detonating bombs in banks, newspapers offices, political party headquarters, and private homes in Bogotá, Cali, Medellín and Barranquilla.

In September 1989, an explosion destroyed the headquarters of *El Espectador*. In November, a mid-air bombing killed all 101 passengers and six crew members aboard an Avianca flight from Bogotá to Cali. In December, a huge truck bomb ripped into the bottom floors of the national police agency (DAS) in Bogotá; the blast was so powerful it damaged buildings twenty blocks away.

The war culminated in a massive manhunt that led to the killing of another cartel leader, Gonzalo Rodríguez Gacha, known as 'El Mexicano', who was suspected of masterminding the terror. After his death, the remaining cartel leaders urged the government to negotiate. Lengthy negotiations led to the surrender of the three Ochoa brothers, Pablo Escobar and their aids.

The deal they struck required the drug traffickers to surrender and plead guilty to just one crime in exchange for guarantees that they would not be extradited and would serve a reduced sentence in a specially-built prison in Envigado, the home town of Pablo Escobar, on the outskirts of Medellín. At the same time, the Constitutional Assembly formally rejected the extradition treaty for Colombian nationals, removing the issue from both Colombian politics and the drug war.

With the surrender or death of all the top leaders of the Medellín Cartel, the narco-terrorism subsided, though the drug trade continued unaffected. An estimated two to three tonnes of top quality cocaine continued to enter the USA every week in large cargoes smuggled by sea or air. Although Escobar and his associates ran their business from behind bars, they were unable to maintain domination of the market.

Narco-terrorism resumed in July 1992 when Pablo Escobar escaped from his La Catedral jail following the government's bumbling attempts to move him to a more secure prison. Over the next year and a half, the elite 1500-man Search Block sought Escobar, tracking down and killing most of his close aids and collaborators. Finally, in December 1993, after 499 days of searching, the special unit located Escobar and shot him dead. The government trumpeted its victory.

Yet the final victory is a long way ahead. Drug trafficking hasn't diminished as the government hoped it would – in fact it's steadily growing. While Colombia's elite force concentrated its resources, hunting one man and persecuting one cartel, the other cartels were quick to take advantage of the opportune circumstances.

The Cali Cartel, which developed during the 1980s, swiftly moved into the shattered Medellín Cartel's markets, and became

Colombia's largest drug trafficker. The Cali organisation, led by the Rodríguez Orejuela brothers, rules the industry in a quieter, more business-like manner. It's probably no less ruthless than its Medellín rival, but certainly more discreet and sophisticated, avoiding open violence and terrorism if it is not 'necessary'. The cartel's lawyers are negotiating a surrender of the cartel leaders with the government, and some of the minor bosses have already turned themselves in.

By 1994, the Cali Cartel was thought to control over 80% of New York's cocaine market and had dominant shares in other US and European markets. There are rumours that the surviving Medellín bosses may join the Cali network to create a supercartel, a mafia more powerful than anything Colombia has seen. The Cali bosses have also diversified into opium poppies and heroin, reflecting the change in consumer habits in the USA. So, although the worst days of narco-terrorism seem to have passed, the drug trade continues to flourish. And until the USA rethinks its drug strategy, including the legalisation of drugs, there's little hope that the cartels will simply walk away from a US$5-billion-a-year business.

## GOVERNMENT

The president (presidente) is elected for a four-year term and cannot be re-elected. If no candidate obtains an absolute majority (half of all votes) in the first round, a second and deciding round between the two leading contenders is held three weeks later. The president is the head of the state, of the government and of the armed forces, as well as the supreme administrative authority. The president is empowered to nominate ministers.

The Congress (Congreso) consists of two houses, the 102-seat Senate (Senado) and the 163-seat Chamber of Representatives (Cámara de Representantes). The members of the Congress are elected for a four-year term.

The Supreme Court (Corte Suprema de Justicia), the highest judicial body, is entitled to review legislation and to judge the president and the members of the Congress. The death penalty was abolished in 1910.

Administratively, the country is divided into 32 departments (departamentos) ruled by governors (gobernadores), and Bogota's Special District (Distrito Especial) ruled by the city's mayor (alcalde mayor). The governors and the mayor are elected by the people.

The Colombian flag has three horizontal belts: the upper half is yellow and the lower one is half blue and half red.

## GEOGRAPHY

Colombia covers 1,141,748 sq km, an area roughly equal in size to that of France, Spain and Portugal combined. It is the fourth largest country in South America, after Brazil, Argentina and Peru. It occupies the north-western part of the continent and is the only country in South America with coasts on both the Pacific (1350 km long) and the Caribbean (over 1600 km).

Colombia is bordered by Panama in the north-west (266 km shared border), Venezuela in the north-east (2219 km), Brazil in the south-east (1645 km), Peru in the south (1626 km) and Ecuador in the south-west (586 km).

The western part of Colombia (about 45% of the country) is mostly mountainous. The 8000-km Cordillera de los Andes runs the length of South America and, on reaching Colombia (in Nariño), splits into three ranges: the Cordillera Occidental, Cordillera Central and Cordillera Oriental. The three chains fan out northwards across the country and descend to the Caribbean.

The Cordillera Occidental is the lowest of these ranges; it runs parallel to the Pacific coast for about 1100 km before petering out in northern Antioquia. The Cordillera Central, which is considered an extension of the main Andean range, is the highest and most volcanic. It contains many snow-capped peaks, including Nevado del Huila (5750 metres), and Los Nevados, a chain of volcanoes dominated by the Nevado del Ruiz (5325 metres). The Cordillera Oriental is the longest and widest massif. It spreads across the middle of the country, bordered by the vast plains of Los Llanos to the east. The range culminates in the snowy summits of the Sierra Nevada del Cocuy, topped by Ritacuba

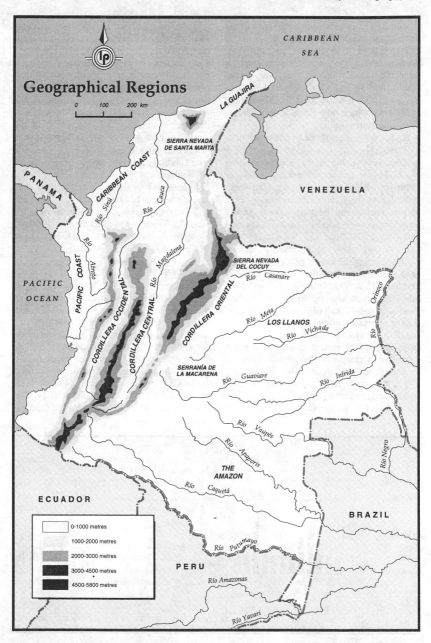

## Geographical Regions

0    100    200 km

CARIBBEAN
SEA

LA GUAJIRA

SIERRA NEVADA
DE SANTA MARTA

PANAMA

CARIBBEAN COAST

Río Sinú

Río Cauca

VENEZUELA

PACIFIC COAST

Río Atrato

PACIFIC
OCEAN

Río Magdalena

CORDILLERA OCCIDENTAL

CORDILLERA CENTRAL

SIERRA NEVADA
DEL COCUY

CORDILLERA ORIENTAL

Río Casanare

Río Meta    LOS LLANOS

Río Vichada

Río

Orinoco

SERRANÍA DE
LA MACARENA

Río Guaviare

Río Inírida

Río Vaupés

Río Apaporis

THE
AMAZON

Río Caquetá

Río Negro

ECUADOR

BRAZIL

0-1000 metres

1000-2000 metres

2000-3000 metres

3000-4500 metres

4500-5800 metres

Río Putumayo

PERU

Río Amazonas

Río Yavari

Blanco (5330 metres), after which it heads north-eastwards into Venezuela.

Two valleys, the Valle del Cauca and Valle del Magdalena, are sandwiched between the three cordilleras. Their rivers flow northwards, more or less parallel, until the Cauca River (1350 km long) joins the Magdalena (1538 km), which then flows into the Caribbean near Barranquilla.

Apart from the three Andean chains, Colombia boasts one other exceptional mountain range, the Sierra Nevada de Santa Marta. This is an independent and relatively small formation rising from the Caribbean coast. It is the highest coastal mountain range in the world, and its permanently snow-capped peaks – Simón Bolívar (5775 metres) and Cristóbal Colón (5775 metres) – are Colombia's highest mountains.

Over 50% of the territory east of the Andes is a vast lowland which can be broadly divided into two regions: Los Llanos to the north and the Amazon to the south. Los Llanos, roughly 250,000 sq km in area, is a huge open savannah lying in the basin of the Río Orinoco. It descends gradually from about 500 metres at the foot of the Cordillera Oriental in the west to some 50 metres at the Venezuelan border in the east.

The Amazon, stretching over some 400,000 sq km, occupies all of Colombia's south-east. Most of this land is covered by a thick rainforest crisscrossed by rivers. It is mostly unexplored and uninhabited. The major rivers of the Colombian Amazon are the Caquetá and Putumayo, both tributaries of the Amazon River.

Colombia is a country of geographical contrasts and extremes. Among some its curiosities are a desert on La Guajira, in the north-eastern tip of the country; the jungle of the Pacific coast, which holds one of the world's rainfall records; and the Serranía de la Macarena, an isolated mountain formation rising abruptly from the eastern plains to some 1000 metres.

Colombia has several small islands. The major ones are the archipelago of San Andrés and Providencia in the Caribbean Sea, the Islas del Rosario and Islas de San Bernardo along the Caribbean coast, and Gorgona and Malpelo in the Pacific Ocean.

## CLIMATE

Colombia is close to the equator, so the average temperature varies little throughout the year. Temperatures vary with altitude, however, creating climatic zones, which range from hot lowlands to permanent snow. As a general rule, the temperature falls about 6°C with every 1000-metre increase in altitude. If the average temperature at sea level is 30°C, it will be around 24°C at 1000 metres, 18°C at 2000 metres and 12°C at 3000 metres. Because of the varied topogra-

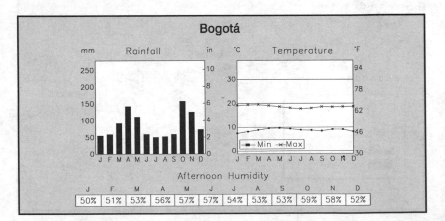

| Afternoon Humidity | | | | | | | | | | | |
|---|---|---|---|---|---|---|---|---|---|---|---|
| J | F | M | A | M | J | J | A | S | O | N | D |
| 50% | 51% | 53% | 56% | 57% | 57% | 54% | 53% | 53% | 59% | 58% | 52% |

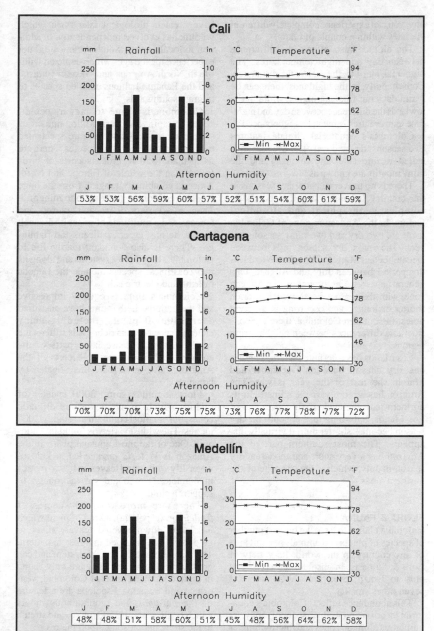

## Cali

| | mm Rainfall in | °C Temperature °F |
|---|---|---|

**Afternoon Humidity**

| J | F | M | A | M | J | J | A | S | O | N | D |
|---|---|---|---|---|---|---|---|---|---|---|---|
| 53% | 53% | 56% | 59% | 60% | 57% | 52% | 51% | 54% | 60% | 61% | 59% |

## Cartagena

| | mm Rainfall in | °C Temperature °F |
|---|---|---|

**Afternoon Humidity**

| J | F | M | A | M | J | J | A | S | O | N | D |
|---|---|---|---|---|---|---|---|---|---|---|---|
| 70% | 70% | 70% | 73% | 75% | 75% | 73% | 76% | 77% | 78% | 77% | 72% |

## Medellín

| | mm Rainfall in | °C Temperature °F |
|---|---|---|

**Afternoon Humidity**

| J | F | M | A | M | J | J | A | S | O | N | D |
|---|---|---|---|---|---|---|---|---|---|---|---|
| 48% | 48% | 51% | 58% | 60% | 51% | 45% | 48% | 56% | 64% | 62% | 58% |

phy, you can experience completely different climates within a couple of hours.

The altitude also affects the difference between day and night temperatures. The higher the altitude, the greater the difference. Consequently, in the highlands, there can be warm days but freezing nights, while in the lowlands the difference between day and night-time temperatures is much less pronounced.

Colombia's equatorial climate features two seasons, dry and wet. The dry season is called *verano* (literally, summer) and the rainy months are known as *invierno* (winter).

There is no universal pattern of seasons in the country because rainfall depends on complex geographical and altitudinal factors. In the Andean regions of Colombia there are two dry and two rainy seasons per year. The main dry season falls between December and March, with a shorter and less dry period between July and August. This general pattern varies throughout the Andean zone, with the seasons being wetter or drier, shorter or longer, and occurring at different times. In southern Colombia, there are considerable differences between neighbouring regions.

Los Llanos has a definite pattern. There is one dry season between December and March; the rest of the year is wet. The Amazon has a more variable climate. In its northern part, the cycle is similar to that of Los Llanos, but going further south the dry season becomes shorter until it virtually disappears. The most southern part of the Amazon has a very short and moderate dry season in July, which is the opposite of the northern areas.

## FLORA & FAUNA

Colombia claims to have the highest number of species of plants and animals per unit area of any country in the world. Its variety of flora & fauna is, in absolute terms, second only to Brazil, even though Colombia is seven times smaller.

This abundance reflects Colombia's equatorial location and its diverse topography. Its numerous climatic zones and micro-climates have created biological islands in which wildlife has evolved independently. In addition to local factors, South America did not experience the ice ages which depleted wildlife in North America and western Eurasia, and the Panama Isthmus enabled species to migrate southwards.

Colombia is home to jaguar, ocelot, peccary, tapir, deer, armadillo, numerous species of monkey and the rare spectacled bear, to mention just a few species. There are more than 1550 recorded species of birds (more than the whole of Europe and North America combined), ranging from the huge Andean condor to the tiny hummingbird. There is a variety of macaws, parrots and toucans and a multitude of water birds, such as ibis, herons, egrets, pelicans and flamingos. There is also abundant marine life in Colombia's major river systems and along its two coastlines; species include the famous piranha and electric eel.

Colombia's flora is equally impressive and the national herbariums have classified over 130,000 plants, including many endemic species. This richness is still not the whole picture, because large parts of the country, such as inaccessible parts of the Amazon, have never been investigated by botanists.

Flora includes some 3000 species of orchid, which grow in various climatic zones, but are most common at roughly 2000 metres. The widest variety is found in Antioquia. One of the most unusual plants in the Amazon is *Victoria amazonica*, a kind of water-lily with round leaves up to two metres in diameter, which are strong enough to support a child.

There are more than 70 species of *frailejones* (espeletia), a kind of plant which has large, down-covered leaves, silver to gold in colour, arranged in a rosette pattern. The mature plants have a thick stem and can grow up to 10 metres. They are only found in limited highland areas of Colombia, Venezuela and Ecuador. Espeletia are a feature of the *páramos*, the mountainous moors which begin at about 3500 metres and stretch to the snow line at some 4600 metres.

Faces of Colombia

Chivas – Old-style buses still popular today

Jaguar

## National Parks

Preservation of Colombia's ecosystem began in 1960 when the first nature reserve, the Cueva de los Guácharos, was created. Today, the network of reserves includes 33 national parks, six relatively small areas called *santuarios de fauna y flora*, two *reservas nacionales* and one *area natural única*. Their combined area constitutes 7.9% of the country's territory. The national park system continues to grow and several new parks are to be opened shortly.

The system has been run by Inderena (Instituto Nacional de los Recursos Naturales Renovables y del Ambiente), a branch of the Ministry of Agriculture. Inderena has its headquarters in Bogotá and branch offices in most departmental capitals and towns and cities close to parks. However, this is currently being changed.

The Ministry of the Environment (Ministerio del Medio Ambiente), created in 1994, is taking over the issues of the national parks through one of its own departments, the Unidad Administrativa Especial del Sistema de Parques Nacionales, in conjunction with regional organisations.

In this book you will still find Inderena listed as the body managing individual parks. In practice, the change will not affect the information given, since the new Unidad Administrativa is taking over Inderena's offices. The addresses and telephone numbers given in the book are likely to remain the same; only the name of the organisation occupying them will change.

Unfortunately, there have never been sufficient funds or personnel to guard the parks properly. In many areas, simply decreeing a region a national park has not eliminated deforestation, contamination, hunting or fishing.

Only a handful of the parks provide

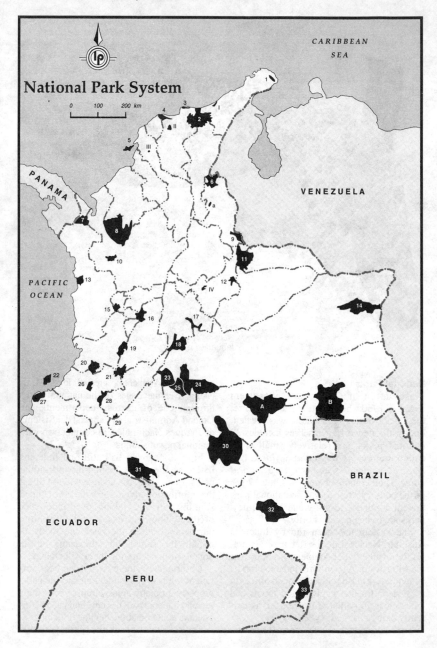

| Parque Nacional | | Location (Department) | Area (sq km) |
|---|---|---|---|
| 1 | Macuira | Guajira | 250 |
| 2 | Sierra Nevada de Santa Marta | Magdalena/Cesar/Guajira | 3830 |
| 3 | Tayrona | Magdalena | 150 |
| 4 | Isla de Salamanca | Magdalena | 210 |
| 5 | Corales del Rosario | Bolívar | 195 |
| 6 | Catatumbo Bari | Norte de Santander | 1581 |
| 7 | Los Katíos | Antioquia/Chocó | 720 |
| 8 | Paramillo | Antioquia/Córdoba | 4600 |
| 9 | Tama | Norte de Santander | 480 |
| 10 | Las Orquídeas | Antioquia | 320 |
| 11 | El Cocuy | Boyacá/Arauca | 3060 |
| 12 | Pisba | Boyacá/Casanare | 450 |
| 13 | Ensenada de Utría | Chocó | 540 |
| 14 | El Tuparro | Vichada | 5480 |
| 15 | Tatamá | Chocó/Risaralda | 543 |
| 16 | Los Nevados | Caldas/Quindío/Risaralda/Tolima | 583 |
| 17 | Chingaza | Cundinamarca/Meta | 503 |
| 18 | Sumapaz | Cundinamarca/Meta/Huila | 1540 |
| 19 | Las Hermosas | Tolima/Valle | 1250 |
| 20 | Farallones de Cali | Valle | 1500 |
| 21 | Nevado del Huila | Cauca/Huila/Tolima | 1580 |
| 22 | Isla Gorgona | Cauca (Pacific Ocean) | 492 |
| 23 | Cordillera de los Picachos | Caquetá/Meta | 4390 |
| 24 | Serranía de la Macarena | Meta | 6300 |
| 25 | Tinigua | Meta | 2018 |
| 26 | Munchique | Cauca | 440 |
| 27 | Sanquianga | Nariño | 800 |
| 28 | Puracé | Cauca/Huila | 830 |
| 29 | Cueva de los Guácharos | Huila | 90 |
| 30 | Chiribiquete | Caquetá/Guaviare | 12,800 |
| 31 | La Paya | Putumayo | 4220 |
| 32 | Cahuinari | Amazonas | 5750 |
| 33 | Amacayacu | Amazonas | 2930 |

**Santuario de Fauna y Flora**

| | | | |
|---|---|---|---|
| I | Los Flamencos | Guajira | 70 |
| II | Ciénaga Grande de Santa Marta | Magdalena | 230 |
| III | Los Colorados | Bolívar | 10 |
| IV | Iguaque | Boyacá | 67 |
| V | Galeras | Nariño | 76 |
| VI | Isla de la Corota | Nariño | 0.08 |

**Reserva Nacional Natural**

| | | | |
|---|---|---|---|
| A | Nukak | Guaviare | 8550 |
| B | Puinawai | Guainía | 10,925 |

**Area Natural Única**

| | | | |
|---|---|---|---|
| a | Los Estoraques | Norte de Santander | 6.40 |

accommodation and food facilities; several more offer only camping possibilities. The remaining parks have no tourist amenities and some, especially those in the Amazon, are virtually inaccessible.

Theoretically, you need a permit from Inderena (or the new Unidad Administrativa) to visit the parks, though you will only be asked for the permit in a few parks. Permits can be obtained in Inderena's (the Unidad's) Bogotá office and in some of the regional branch offices. Refer to the Inderena section in the Bogotá chapter for more information.

## ECONOMY

It may come as a surprise, but Colombia has had one of the highest rates of economic growth of any Latin American country over the past 20 years. During this period, the country's GDP has more than doubled – growing faster than the much-publicised economies of both Chile and Mexico, and only a little slower than that of Brazil.

Colombia's exports have not only expanded almost tenfold over the last 20 years, they have also changed radically in composition: primary products (except for fuels) have shrunk, and the share of manufactured goods has tripled to account for one-third of the total.

Colombia today has a diversified economy and produces an array of domestically manufactured products to meet local demand. The country exports coffee, oil, coal, nickel, flowers, bananas, sugar, cotton, textiles, pharmaceuticals and a host of other competitive manufactured goods. Colombia was one of the few Latin American countries to avoid the debt crisis of the 1980s and the bouts of hyper-inflation which plagued many of its larger neighbours. Today, the

---

**Underground Economy**

The unknown element in any portrait of the Colombian economy is the impact of the underground economy and of Colombia's illegal exports which, by all estimates, account for a significant portion of GNP. The biggest illegal export, without doubt, is cocaine, which earns an estimated US$5 billion annually, US$3 billion of which is thought to be re-invested in Colombia.

The country is also the world's third leading producer of marijuana. In the 1980s, the US DEA (Drug Enforcement Agency) sprayed most of Colombia's marijuana fields with herbicide, practically eliminating all production. At this time, production was concentrated mostly in the Sierra Nevada de Santa Marta and La Guajira. Today the crop is back, and is grown in many regions of the country; it has become a major revenue earner.

The new, illegal Colombian export is heroin. The industry is nascent but is quickly making inroads into northern markets, taking advantage of the transport networks established for the cocaine trade. Colombian heroin is evidently of high quality and competes with the best available from Afghanistan or the Golden Triangle.

Illegal exports are not confined to drugs. Colombia has been commercially producing emeralds for over a century, but the state has been unable to control the trade. Though difficult to assess, the value of the emerald trade is considerable because Colombia produces half of the world's emeralds and the Colombian stones are generally regarded as the finest. Emeralds are among the most expensive precious stones, and a good one can be worth more than a diamond of the same weight. The biggest emerald in the world, the 632-carat *Patricia*, was found at the beginning of the century in Peñas Blancas in Boyacá ; you can see it in the Museum of Natural History in New York.

It is hardly surprising that Colombia has become an illegal exporter of animals, mostly birds, given the amazing variety of exotic wildlife. The birds are caught in Colombian forests and re-appear in US or European pet shops; macaws sell for anywhere between US$1000 and US$10,000, depending on the particular specimen.

Colombia is also thought to be one of the leading producers of counterfeit US dollars. According to rough estimates, about a quarter of all fake US dollars circulating worldwide are printed in Colombia, mainly in Cali. Like the other illegal products, they are of excellent quality, and are virtually indistinguishable from the genuine article. ■

country has a relatively large middle class, and an economy robust enough to support sustained economic growth.

Colombia's traditional export is coffee, and until the late 1970s the crop was responsible for about half of the country's legal foreign exchange earnings. Coffee was brought from Abyssinia, present-day Ethiopia, and introduced to Colombia in the 18th century. The first commercial plantations began operating at the beginning of the 19th century, and today the country is the world's second largest coffee producer, after Brazil. Coffee is cultivated in most departments, but the majority comes from Caldas, Risaralda and Quindío, the so-called *zona cafetera*.

The other main agricultural products include sugar (with production concentrated in the Cali region), cotton and bananas. Thanks to the diversity of the climatic zones, crops such as rice, maize, potatoes, tobacco, barley, beans and cocoa are also grown, making Colombia agriculturally the most self-sufficient of Latin American countries. It is also an important producer and exporter of flowers, particularly carnations. Local sources claim that the country supplies half of the world's carnations.

Another agricultural success is beef production, which has developed rapidly over the last two decades. The hides are used to make some of the world's best leather goods for export.

Approximately 70% of Colombia's electricity needs are supplied by hydroelectric schemes.

Since the late 1980s, Colombia has become an important exporter of oil and coal. The country possesses the largest deposits of coal in Latin America, which is mined in La Guajira by a joint venture between Exxon and the Colombian government. Colombia began exporting oil from the Arauca oilfields in 1986, but discovered what is believed to be the biggest new field found in the world in the last ten years in Casanare in the early 1990s. Oil from the Casanare fields will begin to flow sometime in 1995, generating billions of additional dollars for the economy, and converting petroleum into Colombia's principal legal export.

Amongst other subsoil riches, Colombia has gold, silver, platinum, nickel, copper and iron, to list just a few. Although in plentiful supply, the sources have not been thoroughly explored or exploited.

Industry has grown notably during the last two decades, mainly in the fields of petrochemistry, metallurgy, car assembly (Renault, Chevrolet, Mazda), textiles, domestic electrical appliances, and food and agriculture.

The downside of economic success is that much wealth has become concentrated in the hands of a few. Income distribution is among the worst in Latin America, and about a quarter of the population lives in absolute poverty, unable to adequately satisfy their basic needs.

## POPULATION & PEOPLE

The 1993 national census revealed that Colombia's population had reached 35,886,280, making it the most populous country in South America, after Brazil. Population growth is about 2.2%, which is among the highest figures in Latin America. Average life expectancy is about 66 years.

The census also showed that the urban population (considered as those living in settlements of over 1500 inhabitants) rose to around 73% in 1993 from 65% in 1985.

Population density varies a great deal, with over 90% of people living in the western half of the country – in the Andean region and on the coasts. This is largely the result of historical and geographical forces. Whereas in other parts of South America the Spaniards mainly colonised only coastal areas, in Colombia they quickly ventured into the interior in search of El Dorado. The Andean zone was the first interior region to be colonised, and the colonial towns that were founded soon attracted new settlers.

Colombia's rough topography limited contact between regions, forcing them to be self-sufficient and develop independently. The result is still noticeable today. In contrast

to other countries in South America, which tend to be dominated by a single metropolis, Colombia has four distinct regional centres, each centred around a city with more than a million inhabitants. Bogotá, the capital, has over six million people and is the nucleus of central Colombia; Medellín, the second largest urban centre, has nearly two million inhabitants, and dominates the north-west; Cali, the centre of the south-west, is about the same size as Medellín; and Barranquilla, the smallest of the four, is the centre of the Caribbean coast. There are also some 30 cities with a population of more than 100,000 scattered throughout the Andean region.

Colombia is a nation of mixed races. Unlike Argentina or Uruguay, where whites predominate, or Peru or Bolivia, which have high percentages of Indians, Colombia has significant racial integration. About 75% of the population is of mixed blood, composed of 50% to 55% mestizos and 15% to 20% mulatos. There are also about 3% zambos.

The rest of the population, roughly a fourth of the nation, are pure whites, blacks or Indians. Whites, mainly descendants of the Spaniards, constitute about 20% of the population. Antioquia and the coffee region (Caldas, Risaralda and Quindío) are 'white' departments due to the traditional reluctance of the European settlers to mix either with blacks or Indians.

Blacks represent about 4% of the total population and are most numerous on the Caribbean coast (formerly the centre of the slave trade), the Pacific coast and in the Cali region. The department of Chocó has the largest black population.

Indians number between 300,000 and 400,000, representing roughly 1% of the total population. This seemingly insignificant number comprises over 50 Indian groups belonging to several linguistic families. They live in communities scattered throughout the country, usually occupying quite small areas. Some groups live in relative isolation, while others maintain contact with the outside world. In spite of these contacts, several groups have managed to preserve their culture and traditions. It is estimated that about 200 indigenous dialects are still used in the country.

## EDUCATION

According to the 1991 Constitution, education is compulsory for children between five and 15 years of age. This basic education is provided by the state and is free, but facilities are limited, especially in poor city suburbs and rural areas. Private schools fill the gap but charge high fees.

Tertiary education is mostly private, although there are some state-run universities. Bogotá has more than 15 institutions of higher education. Most cities have at least one university.

Literacy stands at 88%, though it's much lower (about 60% on average) among blacks and Indian groups.

## ARTS & CULTURE

Colombia is an ethnic mosaic and its culture, folklore, arts and crafts reflect this. The different roots and traditions of the Indians, Spaniards and Africans have combined with external influences to produce interesting fusions.

### Pre-Columbian Art

The pre-Columbian cultures of what is now Colombia left behind a number of artefacts, mostly stone sculpture, pottery and goldwork, which show a high degree of development.

The greatest masters of stone sculpture were the Agustinians of San Agustín, who left several hundred monumental stone statues. Some statues feature anthropomorphic figures, presumably depicting ancestors and gods, while others have zoomorphic forms, representing the animals of the complex religious cult of the group. The statues reveal a remarkable level of technical skills.

Pottery developed as people became sedentary farmers, although the objects they made were not always utilitarian. Funeral jars, anthropomorphic and, less frequently, zoomorphic figures have also been found,

Quimbaya ceramic female figure with child

along with ritual dishes and vases. Decorative motifs, in colour or in relief, were sometimes applied.

Pre-Columbian pottery can be seen today in most Colombian museums. There are an infinite number of forms and styles, which makes classification very difficult. One of the most characteristic forms of the Muiscas is the *múcura*, a sort of big jar, usually round in shape, with a slim neck, sometimes decorated with anthropomorphic designs. It was made for both daily needs and religious purposes. Similar múcuras are still manufactured and used in rural areas of Boyacá today.

Colombia's pre-conquest goldwork is commonly considered the best on the continent. Several cultures using similar techniques developed individual styles and forms. Gold was used in jewellery (nose rings, breastplates, headwear and bracelets) and ritual artefacts (mainly stylised human and animal figures). The best-known piece of pre-Columbian goldwork is the famous golden Balsa Muisca (Muisca Raft), which depicts the ceremonial raft holding the cacique, his dignitaries and oarsmen. The Muiscas are also widely known for their *tunjos* – flat, gold figurines depicting human figures, often warriors.

The goldwork of the Tolima and Quimbaya are also particularly distinguished. The Tolima are well known for their flat pectorals, depicting simplified human figures. The Quimbaya were masters at making *poporos*, finely proportioned lime containers embellished with realistic bas-relief human images. Other cultures noted for outstanding goldwork include the Tayrona, the Sinú and the Calima. The largest collection of pre-Columbian goldwork is held and displayed in the Museo del Oro (Gold Museum) in Bogotá.

## Crafts

Colombia's craft tradition goes back to the pre-Columbian period. After the conquest, the Indians incorporated Spanish inventions and techniques into their work, but maintained their ancient motifs and patterns. The great variety of plants and materials available contributed considerably to the diversity of crafts developed, which include basketry, weaving and pottery.

Baskets come in all sizes, shapes, colours and vegetable fibres. Fique, the agave fibre, widespread in Colombia, is popular but plenty of other materials, such as bamboo, palm leaf, reed, and even horse hair, are employed.

Weaving was well developed in pre-Columbian times but sheep, and thus wool, were introduced by the Spaniards. Although the techniques have changed, rudimentary hand looms are still used by artisans in many regions.

Pottery manufacture has adapted to present-day needs, and mainly utilitarian or decorative items are produced. Though some pottery is still made using traditional methods, the pottery wheel, introduced by the Spaniards, is the norm. The shape and decoration of modern pottery reveals many similarities with the pottery made a millennium ago.

Folk art differs widely between the regions, and is best represented in the areas where Indian groups still live today, such as on the Pacific coast, in the Amazon and La Guajira. Boyacá department is the biggest producer of handicrafts. Although there are no pure, indigenous descendants living there, the mixed mestizo population have maintained and developed the ancient craft of the Muiscas and enriched it with new forms.

## Music

Music formed an integral part of the religious ceremonies, festivities and battles in pre-Columbian times. The indigenous people used only wind and percussion instruments (there were no string instruments on the continent before the Spanish conquest), but little is known of their musical forms and only a handful of instruments have survived.

The musical world became much more complex and diversified with the arrival of the Spaniards and the blacks, both of whom came with their own musical traditions and instruments. The imported musical rhythms gradually fused with one another and with traditional Indian music, to produce new forms and rhythms. Different forms evolved in different regions, giving Colombia a heterogeneous musical identity.

Colombia's unique geographical location has made it a melting pot for two distinct and flourishing musical cultures: the African-originated rhythms of the Caribbean basin, and the Andean Indian music of the highlands of Bolivia and Peru. Both have influenced local rhythms, though the Caribbean contribution is far more noticeable.

In very broad terms, the country can be divided into four musical zones: the two coasts, the Andean region and Los Llanos. All the rhythms listed below have corresponding dance forms.

The Caribbean coast vibrates with hot African-related rhythms, such as the *cumbia*, *mapalé* and *porro*, which have many similarities with other Caribbean musical forms.

The music of the Pacific coast, such as the *currulao*, is more purely African, with strong use of drums, but tinged with Spanish influences.

Colombian Andean music has been strongly influenced by Spanish rhythms and instruments, and differs noticeably from the Indian music of Peru or Bolivia. Among the typical forms are the *bambuco*, *pasillo* and *torbellino*; all instrumental and using predominantly string instruments.

The music of Los Llanos, *música llanera*, is sung and usually accompanied by a harp, *cuatro* (a sort of four-string guitar) and maracas. It has much in common with the music of the Venezuelan Llanos.

Apart from these traditional forms, two newer musical styles have conquered large parts of the country. They are the *salsa*, which spread throughout the Caribbean in the 1960s; and the *vallenato*, which emanated from La Guajira and Cesar. The latter is based on the European accordion.

Foreign musical trends are quickly assimilated. For example, the *nueva trova cubana* (new Cuban song) is quite fashionable, as is the Mexican *ranchera*. Tango is probably more widely heard in Antioquia than in Argentina. On the San Andrés Island, locals have developed their own distinctive sound, which is similar to reggae.

## Architecture

No pre-Columbian dwellings have survived because they were generally built from perishable materials. Stone was used only by the most developed groups, and on a limited scale, mostly for foundations and cult centres. The most outstanding example of pre-Columbian urban planning is the Ciudad Perdida, the city of the Tayrona Indians in the Sierra Nevada de Santa Marta. Although the dwellings have all disappeared, the stone structures, including a complex network of terraces, paths and stairways, are still in place.

Indian dwellings were usually built of wood or vegetable fibres and thatched with palm leaves or other locally available products. This tradition is still followed today by descendants of the Indians, so the present-day homes of the Kogis in the Sierra Nevada de Santa Marta are probably much the same as those of the Tayrona some 700 years ago.

After the arrival of the Spaniards, bricks and tiles became the main construction materials. The colonial towns the Spaniards founded in the early days of the conquest followed rigid standards laid down by the Spanish Crown. The towns were constructed on a grid pattern, focussed on the Plaza Mayor (main square), which was always lined by the church and government house. This pattern was applied both during and after the colonial period, and is the dominant feature of Colombia's cities, towns and villages.

The houses were built in the popular Andalusian style. They were mostly whitewashed, one or two-storey structures with patios and, usually, balconies.

Spain's strong Catholic tradition led to the construction of numerous churches and convents in the colony – the central areas of Cartagena, Tunja, Bogotá, Popayán and Pasto are good examples. The churches built in the early days of the conquest were generally small and modest, but in the later period they tended to reach monumental dimensions. Despite austere exteriors, their interiors are usually rich in decoration, and apart from the well-preserved colonial towns, they represent the best, if not the only, vestiges of colonial splendour.

In the 19th century, despite independence, the architecture continued to be predominantly Spanish in style. Very little French, English or Italian influence was felt and new houses hardly differed from the colonial constructions of three centuries earlier. There were obviously some regional variations, notably Antioquia, which developed a decorative, intricate style of ornamental carving for doors and windows.

Modern architectural trends only began to appear in Colombia after WW II. This process accelerated during the 1960s as skyscrapers appeared on urban horizons. The most interesting examples are to be found in Bogotá and Medellín.

## Visual Arts

The colonial period was dominated by Spanish religious art, and although the paintings and sculptures of this era were generally executed by local artists, they reflected the Spanish trends of the day. Much of their work consisted of paintings of saints, carved wooden statues, gilded retables and elaborate altarpieces, some of which can still be seen in old churches and museums.

Two interesting variations – both originating from Spain – left a strong mark on Colombia's colonial art. One is the Islamic-influenced Mudéjar art *(arte mudéjar)* which developed in Spain between the 12th and 16th centuries and is at its best in the internal decoration of the churches in Tunja and Bogotá. The other is the style known as the Quito School *(escuela quiteña)* which flourished in Quito after the conquest and influenced religious woodcarving in southern Colombia.

Gregorio Vásquez de Arce y Ceballos (1638-1711) was the most remarkable painter of the colonial era. He lived and worked in Bogotá, and left behind a collection of more than 500 works, now distributed among the city's churches and museums. Gaspar de Figueroa was another artist noted for his achievements.

With the arrival of independence, visual arts departed from strictly religious themes, but it was not until the revolution in European painting in the early 20th century that Colombian artists began to experiment and produce original art.

Many painters and sculptors who started their careers in the 1930s and 1940s developed interesting individual styles. Among the most distinguished are Pedro Nel Gómez, known mainly for his murals but also for his watercolours, oils and sculptures; Luis Alberto Acuña, a painter and sculptor who used motifs from pre-Columbian art; Guillermo Wiedemann, a German who spent most of his creative period in Colombia and drew inspiration from local themes, though he later moved into abstract art; Enrique Grau, inclined mostly to figurative art; Alejandro Obregón, one of the most popular figures in Colombian painting, tending to abstract forms; Omar Rayo, known for his abstract and figurative prints; Edgar Negret, an abstract sculptor; Eduardo Ramírez Villamizar, who expressed himself mostly in geometric forms; and Rodrigo Arenas Betancur, Colombia's most famous monument-maker.

These masters were followed by a slightly younger generation, born mainly in the 1930s, such as Armando Villegas, a Peruvian living in Colombia, whose influences ranged from pre-Columbian motifs to surrealism; Leonel Góngora, noted for his erotic drawings; and the most internationally-renowned Colombian artist, Fernando Botero, whose somewhat ironic painting and sculpture is easily recognisable by the characteristic fatness of the figures.

The recent period has been characterised by a proliferation of schools, trends and techniques. The artists to watch out for include Bernardo Salcedo (conceptual sculpture and photography), Miguel Ángel Rojas (painting and installations), Lorenzo Jaramillo (expressionist painting), Gabriel Silva (painting), María de la Paz Jaramillo (painting), Doris Salcedo (sculpture and installations), Antonio Caro (conceptual art), Alicia Barney (art influenced by ecological issues), María Fernanda Cardozo (installations), Rodrigo Facundo (mixed techniques exploring violence and death) and Catalina Mejía (abstract painting).

Colombia today is considered one of Latin America's leading representatives in visual arts. Plenty of exhibitions featuring contemporary art are put on by museums and private commercial art galleries. Several magazines are devoted to art, including *Arte en Colombia* and *Número*. Bogotá, with its hundred or so galleries, plus university art faculties, has the most active cultural life, making it the main centre for contemporary art. In Bogotá you have the best chances of seeing fresh, forward-looking and creative works by both renowned and emerging artists.

## Literature

It is generally assumed that Colombian literature, like all national literatures in South America, began during the Spanish conquest when the journals and chronicles of expeditions were published. They narrated early impressions and recorded the discovery of the New World. The oldest, written by Martín Fernández de Enciso in 1519, was titled *Suma de Geografía (Essential Geography)*.

Yet it is a mistake to place the origins of Colombian literature strictly in this period. Many of the important cultural motifs of the new colony were taken from the oral histories of the indigenous communities. The Spanish myth of El Dorado, which became one of the nation's most enduring legends, was derived from the rituals of the Muiscas, the Indian tribe that inhabited the savannah of Bogotá.

Almost all literature during the colonial period was written by the Spaniards; this imposed not only the Spanish language, but a whole Spanish cultural perspective. A more independent approach emerged only at the end of the 18th century, with the birth and crystallisation of revolutionary trends, which led to the publication of political literature expressing the ideals and ambitions of the nation. This period also witnessed the birth of scientific literature, the first important account being the study published after the Botanical Expedition led by José Celestino Mutis in 1783.

Following independence, Colombian literature became intoxicated with the imagery of freedom and the Romanticism then dominant in the European schools. Rafael Pombo (1833-1912) is generally acclaimed as the father and most outstanding representative of Colombian romantic poetry. He is also noted for his children's literature and fairy tales, such as *El Renacuajo Paseador*. Jorge Isaacs (1837-95), another notable author of the period, is particularly remembered for his romantic novel *María*, which is still popular.

Several literary schools emerged in the late 19th and early 20th centuries, but most of them followed the European trends of the day. One such school was *modernismo*, the literature dominated by principles of form and aesthetics. The Colombian poet José Asunción Silva (1865-96), best known for his *Los Nocturnos*, is considered the precursor of modernism in America. He planted the seeds that were later developed by the well-known Nicaraguan poet, Rubén Darío.

Another literary school that found fertile soil in Colombia was the *nueva sensibilidad*, which introduced the ideas of irrationalism, free expression and the language of the avant-garde. The leading exponent of this school was Porfirio Barba Jacob (1883-1942), 'the poet of death', who was strongly influenced by Baudelaire.

Other men of letters during this period include José Eustasio Rivera (1889-1928), best known for his novel *La Vorágine*; and one of Colombia's greatest satirists León De Greiff (1895-1976), who combined humour, poetry and criticism in works such as *Tergiversaciones de Leo le Gris* and *Libro de los Signos*.

After WW II, Latin America experienced a literary boom that thrust at least a dozen great authors into the international sphere. These writers succeeded in transforming the pathos of life, with its frustrations, fantasies, and feudal institutions into a new and innovative form of literature. One of the foremost writers of this generation was the Colombian novelist Gabriel García Márquez (born 1928).

García Márquez began writing as a journalist in the 1950s, but gained fame through his novels. His *One Hundred Years of Solitude*, which appeared in 1967, immediately became an international bestseller. It mixed myths, dreams and reality, and amazed readers with a new form of expression which critics called *realismo mágico* (magic realism). In 1982, García Márquez won the Nobel Prize for literature.

García Márquez continues to publish a new book every couple of years. Among his recent works are *El General en su Laberinto*, published in 1989 and translated into English in 1990 as *The General in his Labyrinth*. It's a historical novel which recounts the tragic final months of Simón Bolívar's life. *Doce Cuentos Peregrinos* appeared in 1992 and was translated into English as *Strange Pilgrims* in 1993. It's a collection of 12 stories written by the author over the previous 18 years. His latest book, *Del Amor y otros Demonios*, was published in 1994. It's the story of a young girl, raised by her parents' black slaves, who becomes a victim of Cartagena's Inquisition after being bitten by a rabid dog.

Gabo, as he is affectionately known, is the principal figure of Colombian literature. His phenomenal success has, to a great extent, overshadowed both the accomplishments of his contemporaries and the emerging group of younger authors. Several talented writers are belatedly beginning to receive the recognition they deserve, and probably the most notable of these is the poet and novelist (and painter) Héctor Rojas Herazo (born 1921) who has brought a profound, post-modern sensibility to the novel, particularly in his monumental *Celia se Pudre* (1986).

Among other remarkable writers of García Márquez's generation are his close friend Alvaro Mutis (born 1923), whose recent novels include *Un Bel Morir* (1989) and *Abdul Bashur, Soñador de Navíos* (1991); and Manuel Mejía Vallejo (born 1923), the Antioquian writer and author of the much acclaimed *La Casa de las Dos Palmas* (1989).

Of the younger generation, seek out *La Tejedora de Coronas* by Germán Espinosa (born 1938); *Juego de Damas* and *Finale Capriccoso con Madonna* by Rafael Humberto Moreno Durán (born 1946); and *En Diciembre llegaban las Brisas* by Marvel Moreno. These are among the most ambitious and innovative novels written in Colombia in recent years.

## Theatre & Cinema

Both these artistic forms arrived relatively recently in Colombia and lack a local pedigree.

Although theatre first developed in the middle of the 19th century, it mainly followed foreign trends and remained insignificant. A genuine national theatre emerged a few decades ago in Bogotá and Cali. Since then, perhaps a 100 theatre groups have been founded, most of them small, amateur troupes.

Theatre activity is almost exclusively confined to the largest urban centres. Only Bogotá, Medellín and Cali have several groups working permanently in their own theatres. Teatro de la Candelaria in Bogotá, the TEC in Cali, and El Águila Descalza in Medellín are probably the most interesting and innovative. Several theatre schools are now contributing to the development of a national theatre, and foreign and local performers gather at the two annual international theatre festivals, held in Bogotá and Manizales.

Colombian cinema is still immature and inexperienced, far behind that of, say, Mexico or Brazil. Films of better technical quality and artistic content began to appear during the 1980s. Local production is small and few domestically produced films reach the screens because distributors prefer foreign movies, which are more likely to realise a profit.

If you're a film buff, try to see the following films which are among the highlights of Colombian cinematography: *Cóndores No Entierran Todos los Días* (1984) by Francisco Norden, *Tiempo de Morir* (1985) by Jorge Alí Triana, *Visa USA* (1986) by Lisandro Duque, *La Mansión de Araucaima* (1986) by Carlos Mayolo, *Técnicas de Duelo* (1988) by Sergio Cabrera, *María Cano La Iluminada* (1989) by Camila Loboguerrero, *Confesión a Laura* (1992) by Jaime Osorio and *La Estrategia del Caracol* (1992) by Sergio Cabrera.

Plenty of foreign films can be seen in Colombia, most of them are mainstream US movies, but there are several *cinematecas* (art cinemas) that show art movies; most of them are confined to Bogotá.

In contrast to the dearth of cinematic productions, the production of films for TV has been burgeoning. Colombians, like most Latin Americans, are fans of *telenovelas* (soap operas) and producers and directors are doing everything they can to meet the demand.

## SOCIETY & CONDUCT

The following general observations cover some typical Colombian customs and manners which might seem strange or irritating if you haven't been to South America before.

### Getting to Know Colombians

You don't have to worry about this – making contact with Colombians is very easy. On the whole, Colombians are open, willing to talk and are not shy about striking up a conversation with a stranger. They're good at picking out foreigners and will take the initiative by asking a question or making an innocent joke behind your back, inviting you to respond. If you do respond, they will often invite you to have a coffee or a beer at the nearest corner.

This gregariousness may vary from region to region: the Bogotanos (inhabitants of Bogotá) are cooler than, say, the Caleños (people of Cali) – like the climate in their respective cities – and the people of the Pacific coast are more reserved than those of the Caribbean. But wherever you are, you are unlikely to be alone or feel isolated, especially if you can speak a little Spanish.

Latin America is not like Asia, where the distinct religious, philosophical and social systems often combine with the language barrier to hinder contact between locals and Westerners, reducing the pleasure of travel to observation of an intriguing and exotic but not entirely accessible culture. The latinos have much in common with Westerners which helps enormously.

Although Colombians are generally friendly and straightforward, there are a few distinctive traits to keep in mind.

You will probably meet many extremely friendly people, ready to do everything for you, promising you the earth. Take it easy because that effusiveness often has a very short life. Just like anywhere else in the world, some people just expect to profit from you and soon lose interest when nothing can be gained. There is, however, a more general Latin American characteristic, which is related to the concept of *aquí y ahora* (here and now). Little importance is given to the future or past. The passionate 'friend' of one day might hardly recognise you the next. Don't worry, there will be plenty of new faces and new promises coming your way.

*Rumbas* are a Colombian speciality. They are parties where friends gather to talk, drink and dance. They can be great fun, but if you go to such a party, don't leave your valuables unattended – better still, don't take anything of value with you.

## Noise

Noise is a constant companion in Colombia and Colombians seem to be undisturbed by noise levels 50 decibels above anything a European could stand.

Music blasts out of restaurants, is pumped into buses, and climaxes at night in discos, *tabernas* (taverns) and private rumbas. A rumba seldom ends before 3 am and a good one is supposed to last at least until dawn, with music at full volume the whole time.

TV noise can be a nightmare in budget hotels, where the insulation between the rooms and corridors is often very flimsy. Colombians enjoy TV, so many hotels provide a set in the reception area for their clients and it is usually kept on until late at night. The volume ranges from high to ultra high depending on the programme. If you are unfortunate enough to be trying to sleep during a sports transmission, particularly soccer or cycling, a good set of earplugs will be your only salvation. When you book into a hotel, look around to see where the noise-making box stands and take a room as far from it as possible. Check also that there isn't a bar or taberna downstairs or next door, especially on a Friday or Saturday night.

The noise produced by traffic is another Colombian charm. Some vehicles are, to put it modestly, not very new (by US standards they would be museum pieces) and are as noisy as tanks. To add to the cacophony, horns are used extensively, even in traffic jams, which are virtually guaranteed in Bogotá during rush hour.

## Traffic

When vehicles are not stuck in traffic jams, they run at the highest speed their engines can manage. Buses flying at breakneck speed along twisting mountain roads are a common sight.

There are lots of traffic lights in the cities, although Colombian drivers seem to consider them decorative rather than a form of traffic regulation. Their colours are the same as everywhere else, it's just that Colombians decipher their meaning more flexibly, stopping only when they have to.

Pedestrians can feel free to cross the street on both green and red lights, although it's not quite clear which is safer. Always keep a close eye out for traffic to the left and to the right (even on one-way streets) before you decide to scamper across.

## Time

Since the invention of the clock, the world has slowly turned into a more organised place. Colombia, however, has only loosely taken to the notion, and the Western concept of time is a very low priority. Terms for time do exist but their interpretation is not necessarily what Westerners might expect. *Mañana* (literally 'tomorrow', but better understood as 'in an indefinite future') is one of the most commonly used words.

Let's say that you visit somebody in their office, but the person is out. The secretary has a set answer: *ahorita viene* (or in a more charming form: *ahoritica viene*), which literally means that the person will arrive in a moment. That 'moment' is both flexible and unpredictable; it may mean five minutes but it could easily turn into five hours.

A Colombian invited to lunch on a Tuesday may arrive on Wednesday, and by his or her understanding of time, regard themselves as only a little late. You should not adopt local habits to this extent, but arriving a bit late is normal. If you are invited to a Colombian rumba at, say, 8 pm and you turn up at 9 pm, you will probably be the first guest at the party.

The same applies to meetings in the street.

Arriving half an hour later than arranged will still give you time to smoke a couple of cigarettes or read a newspaper before your friend arrives (if ever). If you become versed in this local custom, it can be a good idea to fix two or even three meetings with different people at the same time and place. Finally, somebody is likely to turn up!

Offices and institutions also have a flexible grasp of their stated working hours. The rule seems to be that if money is directly involved, the hours are more likely to be adhered to. Banks, for instance, run like Swiss watches. Shops and other commercial establishments are generally OK in this respect. Elsewhere it can differ a great deal.

The moral is to have a relaxing travel schedule to avoid irritation and take it easy if things go slower than you planned.

## Litter

Like noise, litter is an integral part of Colombian life, so be prepared to get used to it. Colombians are accustomed to throwing things away wherever they happen to be – in the streets, on the floors of restaurants, hotel rooms, buses, cinemas, in the countryside and on the beach.

You will probably feel a bit uncomfortable about this for the first few days, but with time, you will get used to the local rules and probably (because of the absence of litter bins) adopt them – you can only walk around for so long with a banana peel in your hand.

In budget hotels and restaurants you will rarely find an ashtray and asking for one may embarrass the management because they often simply don't have them. It's normal to throw cigarette butts on the floor and nobody pays the slightest attention.

## RELIGION

Roman Catholicism has been the principal religion in Colombia since the arrival of the Spaniards, and the Catholic clergy has played an important role in Colombia. The Inquisition was established in 1610, with its first court in Cartagena.

Many Indian groups were converted to the Catholic faith – only a few isolated tribes escaped the new gospel and preserved their native beliefs. The blacks were also converted to Christianity, almost entirely losing their ancestral religions.

After independence, Colombia remained a deeply Catholic nation, and enshrined this in the country's constitution. Although other creeds were officially permitted, their followers were minimal – San Andrés and Providencia islands, which were colonised by the English, were one of the few settled areas to avoid the influence of Catholicism; they remain largely Protestant to this day.

The 1991 constitution marked possibly the most important religious revolution in Colombia's history. References to the 'Sacred Heart of Jesus' were replaced by a universal 'God', eliminating the concept of a Catholic nation as it had been defined in the previous constitution.

Catholicism remains the dominant religion today, although the situation has begun to change. Over the past five years the Catholic Church has lost some three million of its followers (about 10% of Colombia's population) to rapidly growing alternative creeds. According to a recent episcopal document, there are a dozen well-known congregations, such as Anglicans, Lutherans, Calvinists, Mormons, Jehovah's Witnesses etc, and 43 minor religious groups, some of them regarded as sects.

The reasons for this transformation are complex, but are common to other Latin American countries as well. It appears Colombians have started to tire of the unreformed, conservative standpoint of the Catholic Church, which has distanced itself from contemporary life, and other churches have been quick to fill the vacuum.

## LANGUAGE

Spanish is Colombia's official language and, except for some remote Indian tribes, all Colombians speak it. There are also about 200 Indian dialects still used in the country.

In the major cities, you will find people who speak English (particularly among the upper class), but it is not a commonly understood or spoken language. The education system includes English in its curriculum but Colombians' disdainful attitude towards gringos doesn't help spread the language. As soon as you leave urban areas, Spanish is virtually the only medium of communication.

Spanish is not a complicated language so it's well worth making the effort to learn at least the essentials. Take a Spanish course or buy or borrow some books. Practise your Spanish during your trip. Colombians will encourage you, so there is no need to feel self-conscious about vocabulary, grammar or pronunciation.

A Spanish-English/English-Spanish dictionary and a phrasebook are worthwhile additions to your backpack. See the Book section in the Facts for the Visitor chapter for suggestions.

## Colombian Spanish

The Spanish spoken in Colombia is generally clear and easy to understand. There are regional variations, but these will not be noticeable to visitors, apart from perhaps the *costeños*, from the Caribbean coast who speak fast and may be difficult to understand.

The use of the forms *tu* (you, casual) and *usted* (you, formal) is flexible in Colombia. In Spain, the *tu* form is generally more familiar and used among friends, but this is not the case in Colombia. Strangers can often use *tu*, while a husband and a wife may use *usted*

Our Lady of Amparo de Chinavita

when speaking to each other and to their children. Basically, either form is OK, although the best advice is to answer in the same form that you are addressed – and always use *usted* when talking to the police.

Note that Colombians, like all Latin Americans, do not use *vosotros* (the plural of *tu*); *ustedes* is commonly used.

For some unfathomable reason, greetings in Colombia have turned into an elaborate ritual. The short Spanish *hola* has given way to an incalculable number of expressions, all of them meaning something in between 'hello' and 'how do you do'. Here are some examples:

*¿Cómo está?*
*¿Cómo ha estado?*
*¿Qué ha hecho?*
*¿Cómo le va?*
*¿Cómo me lo han tratado?*
*¿Qué tal?*
*¿Q'hubo?* or *¿Quiubo?*
*¿Qué me cuenta?*
*¿Cómo le acabó de ir?*
*?Qué más (de nuevo, de su vida)?*
*¿Qué hay (de cosas, de bueno)?*

This list could be continued for several more pages. When people meet or phone each other, they always begin the conversation with a long exchange of these and similar expressions.

It is funny, surprising, irritating, ridiculous, tiring, fascinating – but whatever you say about it, it is typically Colombian and you should learn some of these expressions to keep to the local style.

### Vocabulary

Latin American Spanish vocabulary has lots of regional variations and differs noticeably from European Spanish. Colombian Spanish has altered the meaning of some words or taken their secondary meaning as the main one. Colombians have also created plenty of *colombianismos*, words or phrases used either nationally or regionally, but almost unknown outside Colombia. You will find some colombianismos in the Glossary section at the end of the book.

Colombians and other South Americans normally refer to the Spanish language as *castellano* rather than *español*.

Note that 'll' is a separate letter and comes after 'l' in the alphabet. 'Ch' and 'ñ' are also separate letters; in the alphabet, they come after 'c' and 'n' respectively.

### Pronunciation

Spanish pronunciation is, in general, consistently phonetic, and once you are aware of the basic rules, it should cause little difficulty. Colombian Spanish, however, differs in pronunciation from Spanish spoken in Spain. The most significant pronunciation differences are: 'll' is pronounced in Colombia as 'y' (in Spain 'ly'); 'z', and 'c' before 'e' and 'i', are pronounced as 's' (not 'th' as in Spain).

**Vowels** Spanish vowels are always pronounced the same way and they all have easy English equivalents:

| | |
|---|---|
| a | is like 'a' in 'father' |
| e | is like the 'e' in 'met' |
| i | is like 'ee' in 'feet' |
| o | is like 'o' in 'for' |
| u | is like 'oo' in 'boot' |
| y | is a consonant except when it stands alone or appears at the end of a word, in which case its pronunciation is identical to Spanish 'i'. |

**Consonants** Spanish consonants generally resemble their English equivalents: pronunciation of the letters 'f', 'k', 'l', 'n', 'p', 'q', 's' and 't' is virtually identical to English, as is 'y' when used as a consonant. However, there are some major exceptions:

| | |
|---|---|
| b | resembles its English equivalent, and is undistinguished from 'v'; for clarification, refer to the former as 'b larga', and the latter as 'b corta' (the word for the letter itself is pronounced like English 'bay') |
| c | is like 's' in 'see' before 'e' and 'i', otherwise it's pronounced like the English 'k' |

**ch** is like 'ch' in 'chair'

**d** in an initial position and after 'l' and 'n', is like 'd' in 'dog'; elsewhere it's pronounced as 'th' in 'though'

**g** before 'e' and 'i', is similar to 'h' in 'hell', otherwise it's pronounced like 'g' in 'go'

**h** is never pronounced

**j** is similar to 'h' in 'hell' (the same as Spanish 'g' before 'e' and 'i')

**ll** is similar to 'y' in 'yellow'

**ñ** is similar to 'ni' in 'onion'

**q** is like 'k' in 'key'; 'q' is always followed by a silent 'u' and is only combined with 'e' as in *que* and 'i' as in *qui*

**r** is strongly rolled at the beginning of the word, or after 'n', 'l' and 's'; in other positions, it is pronounced with one trill

**rr** is always strongly rolled

**v** see 'b', above

**x** is like 'x' in 'taxi'

**z** is like 's' in 'sun'

**Diphthongs** Diphthongs are combinations of two vowels which form a single syllable. In Spanish, the formation of a diphthong depends on combinations of 'weak' vowels ('i 'and 'u') and strong ones ('a', 'e', and 'o'). Two weak vowels or a strong and a weak vowel make a diphthong, but two strong ones are separate syllables.

A good example of two weak vowels forming a diphthong is the word *diurno* (during the day). The final syllable of *obligatorio* (obligatory) is a combination of weak and strong vowels.

**Stress** There are two general rules regarding stress. Words ending in a vowel, or the letters 'n' or 's', are stressed on the second-to-last syllable. For example: *amigo* (friend) is stressed on 'mi'. For words ending in a consonant other than 'n' or 's', the stress is on the last syllable. For example: *amor* (love) is stressed on 'mor'.

Any deviation from these rules is indicated by a visible accent. Thus, *sótano* (basement), *América* and *porción* (portion)

all have the stress on the syllable with the accented vowel. Accents over capital letters are often not shown, but they still affect the pronunciation.

**Basic Grammar**

Nouns in Spanish are masculine or feminine. The definite article ('the' in English) agrees with the noun in gender and number; for example, the Spanish word for 'train' is masculine, so 'the train' is *el tren*, and the plural is *los trenes*. The word for 'house' is feminine, so 'the house' is *la casa*, and the plural is *las casas*.

The indefinite articles (a, an, some) work in the same way: *un libro* (a book) is masculine singular, while *una carta* (a letter) is feminine singular. Their plurals are respectively: *unos libros* (some books), *unas cartas* (some letters).

Most nouns ending in 'o' are masculine and those ending in 'a' are generally feminine. Normally, nouns ending in a vowel add 's' to form the plural, while those ending in a consonant add 'es'.

Adjectives usually come after the noun they describe, and agree with its gender and number. Possessive adjectives *mi* (my), *tu* (your), *su* (his/her) etc come before the noun and agree in number with the thing (or things) possessed, not with the possessor. For example, 'his suitcase' is *su maleta*, while 'his suitcases' is *sus maletas*. A simple way to indicate possession is to use the preposition *de* (of). 'Juan's room', for instance, would be *la habitación de Juan* (literally, 'the room of Juan').

Personal pronouns are usually not used with verbs. There are three main categories of verbs: those whose infinitive ends in 'ar', such as *hablar* (to speak); those which end in 'er', such as *comer* (to eat); and those which end in 'ir', such as *reír* (to laugh). There are also many irregular verbs, such as *ir* (to go) and *venir* (to come).

A characteristic feature of American Spanish is an extremely common use of diminutives. They either describe the smallness of something or, more often, express affection. They are formed by adding suffixes

-*ito/a*, -*cito/a*, -*illo/a* and -*cillo/a* to nouns and adjectives. For example, *cafecito* is the diminutive form of *café* (coffee), means 'small coffee', and *amorcito* is a tender version of *amor* (love) used as a form of address.

## Greetings & Civilities

| Good morning. | *Buenos días.* |
| Good afternoon. | *Buenas tardes.* |
| Good evening. | *Buenas noches.* |
| Good night. | *Buenas noches.* |
| Goodbye. | *Adiós/Chao.* |
| Please. | *Por favor.* |
| Thank you. | *Gracias.* |
| Excuse me. | *Disculpe/Excuse/Perdone.* |
| I'm sorry. | *Disculpe/Lo siento.* |

## Essentials

| Yes. | *Sí.* |
| No. | *No.* |
| with | *con* |
| without | *sin* |
| here | *aquí* |
| there | *allí, allá* |
| Where? | *¿Dónde?* |
| Where is ...? | *¿Dónde está/queda ...?* |
| When? | *¿Cuándo?* |
| How? | *¿Cómo?* |
| I would like ... | *Me gustaría ...* |
| How much? | *¿Cuánto?* |
| How many? | *¿Cuántos?* |

## People

| Madam/Mrs | *Señora* |
| Sir/Mr | *Señor* |
| Miss | *Señorita* |
| man | *hombre* |
| woman | *mujer* |
| husband | *marido, esposo* |
| wife | *mujer, esposa* |
| boy | *chico, muchacho* |
| girl | *chica, muchacha* |
| child | *niño/a* |
| father | *padre, papá* |
| mother | *madre, mamá* |
| son | *hijo* |
| daughter | *hija* |
| brother | *hermano* |
| sister | *hermana* |
| grandfather | *abuelo* |
| grandmother | *abuela* |
| family | *familia* |
| friend | *amigo/a* |

| I | *yo* |
| you (singular) | *tú* (informal), *usted* (formal) |
| he | *él* |
| she | *ella* |
| we | *nosotros/as* |
| you (plural) | *ustedes* |
| they | *ellos/ellas* |

## Language Difficulties

Do you speak English?
  *¿Habla inglés?*
Does anyone here speak English?
  *¿Alguien habla inglés aquí?*
I don't speak Spanish.
  *No hablo castellano.*
I understand.
  *Entiendo.*
I don't understand.
  *No entiendo.*
Please speak more slowly.
  *Por favor hable más despacio.*
Could you repeat that please?
  *¿Puede repetirlo, por favor?*
What does it mean?
  *¿Qué significa? ¿Qué quiere decir?*
Please write that down.
  *Por favor escríbalo.*

## Getting Around

| plane | *avión* |
| train | *tren* |
| bus | *bus* |
| small bus | *buseta* |
| ship | *barco, buque* |
| boat | *lancha, bote* |
| car | *carro* |
| taxi | *taxi* |
| truck | *camión* |
| pick-up truck | *camioneta* |
| bicycle | *bicicleta* |
| motorcycle | *motocicleta* |
| to hitchhike | *echar dedo* |
| | |
| airport | *aeropuerto* |
| train station | *estación del tren* |

| | |
|---|---|
| bus terminal | *terminal de buses* |
| bus stop | *paradero, parada* |
| port | *puerto* |
| wharf, pier | *muelle* |
| | |
| city | *ciudad* |
| town | *pueblo* |
| village | *pueblito, caserío* |
| road | *carretera* |
| freeway | *autopista* |
| tourist office | *oficina de turismo* |
| petrol station | *bomba de gasolina* |
| police station | *estación de policía* |
| embassy | *embajada* |
| consulate | *consulado* |
| bank | *banco* |
| public toilet | *baño público* |
| | |
| entrance | *entrada* |
| exit | *salida* |
| open | *abierto/a* |
| closed | *cerrado/a* |
| | |
| ticket | *boleto, pasaje* |
| ticket office | *taquilla* |
| first/last/next | *primero/último/próximo* |
| 1st/2nd class | *primera/segunda clase* |
| one-way/return | *ida/ida y vuelta* |
| left luggage | *guardaequipaje* |

Where is...?
   *¿Dónde queda/está...?*
How can I get to ...?
   *¿Cómo puedo llegar a ...?*
I would like a ticket to ...
   *Quiero un boleto/pasaje a ...*
What's the fare to ...?
   *¿Cuánto cuesta a ...?*
When does the next bus leave for ...?
   *¿Cuándo sale el próximo bus para ....?*

## Geographical Terms

| | |
|---|---|
| bay | *bahía* |
| beach | *playa* |
| cave | *cueva* |
| channel | *caño* |
| hill | *cerro* |
| mount | *pico* |
| mountain | *montaña* |

| | |
|---|---|
| mountain range | *cordillera, sierra, serranía* |
| pass | *paso* |
| rapids | *raudales* |
| ravine | *quebrada* |
| river | *río* |
| sea | *mar* |
| valley | *valle* |
| waterfall | *cascada, salto* |

## Accommodation

| | |
|---|---|
| hotel | *hotel, residencias, hospedaje* |
| room | *habitación* |
| single room | *habitación sencilla* |
| double room | *habitación doble* |
| toilet, bath | *baño* |
| shared bath | *baño compartido* |
| private bath | *baño privado* |
| shower | *ducha* |
| towel | *toalla* |
| soap | *jabón* |
| toilet paper | *papel higiénico* |
| bed | *cama* |
| double bed | *cama matrimonial* |
| bed sheets | *sábanas* |
| pillow | *almohada* |
| blanket | *manta, cobija* |
| fan | *ventilador* |
| air conditioning | *aire acondicionado* |
| key | *llave* |
| padlock | *candado* |
| | |
| cheap | *barato/a* |
| expensive | *caro/a* |
| clean | *limpio/a* |
| dirty | *sucio/a* |
| good | *bueno/a* |
| poor | *malo/a* |
| noisy | *ruidoso/a* |
| quiet | *tranquilo/a* |
| hot | *caliente* |
| cold | *frío/a* |

Do you have rooms available?
   *¿Hay habitaciones?*
May I see the room?
   *¿Puedo ver la habitación?*

What does it cost?
*¿Cuánto cuesta?*
Does it include breakfast?
*¿Incluye el desayuno?*

## Food

Only a few basic words are given here. See the Food & Drink section in the Facts for the Visitor chapter for more terms.

| | |
|---|---|
| the bill | *la cuenta* |
| cup | *taza* |
| dish | *plato* |
| fork | *tenedor* |
| glass | *vaso* |
| knife | *cuchillo* |
| menu | *menú, carta* |
| plate | *plato* |
| spoon | *cuchara* |
| teaspoon | *cucharita* |

| | |
|---|---|
| bread | *pan* |
| butter | *mantequilla* |
| egg | *huevo* |
| fish | *pescado* |
| fruit | *fruta* |
| ham | *jamón* |
| meat | *carne* |
| milk | *leche* |
| pepper | *pimienta* |
| potatoes | *papas* |
| rice | *arroz* |
| salad | *ensalada* |
| salt | *sal* |
| sugar | *azúcar* |
| vegetables | *verduras* |
| water | *agua* |

## Toilets

The most common word for 'toilet' is *baño*, but *servicios sanitarios*, or just *servicios* (services) is a frequent alternative. Men's toilets will usually be labelled by a descriptive term such as *hombres* or *caballeros*. Women's toilets will be labelled with *señoras* or *damas*.

## Shopping

| | |
|---|---|
| shop | *almacén, tienda* |
| shopping centre | *centro comercial* |

| | |
|---|---|
| price | *precio* |
| change | *vueltas* |
| money | *dinero, plata* |
| coin | *moneda* |
| banknote | *billete* |
| cash | *efectivo* |
| cheque | *cheque* |
| credit card | *tarjeta de crédito* |

| | |
|---|---|
| expensive | *caro* |
| cheap | *barato* |
| big | *grande* |
| small | *pequeño* |

How much is it?
*¿Cuánto cuesta/vale?*
I (don't) like it.
*(No) me gusta.*
Do you have...?/Are there....?
*¿Hay...?*

## Post & Telecommunications

| | |
|---|---|
| post office | *oficina de correo* |
| letter | *carta* |
| parcel | *paquete* |
| postcard | *tarjeta postal* |
| airmail | *correo aéreo* |
| registered mail | *correo certificado* |
| stamps | *estampillas* |
| letter box | *buzón* |

| | |
|---|---|
| public telephone | *teléfono público* |
| telephone card | *tarjeta telefónica* |
| long-distance call | *llamada de larga distancia* |
| international call | *llamada internacional* |
| person to person | *persona a persona* |
| collect call | *llamada de pago revertido* |

## Times & Dates

Eight o'clock (8.00) is *las ocho*, while 8.30 is *las ocho y treinta* (literally, 'eight and thirty') or *las ocho y media* (eight and a half). Quarter to eight (7.45) can be *las ocho menos quince* (literally, 'eight minus fifteen'), *las ocho menos cuarto* (eight minus one quarter), *un cuarto para las ocho* (one quarter to eight) or *quince para las ocho* (fifteen to eight).

A 24-hour clock is often used for transport schedules. In everyday conversations, however, people commonly use the 2 x 12 hour system and, if necessary, add *de la mañana* (in the morning), *de la tarde* (in the afternoon) or *de la noche* (at night).

What time is it?
  *¿Qué horas son? ¿Qué hora es?*
It's 1pm.
  *Es la una de la tarde.*
It's 7 am.
  *Son las siete de la mañana.*
It's 7.15.
  *Son las siete y cuarto.*
It's late.
  *Es tarde.*
It's early.
  *Es temprano.*

| | |
|---|---|
| time | *hora, tiempo* |
| today | *hoy* |
| tonight | *esta noche* |
| this week | *esta semana* |
| now | *ahora* |
| yesterday | *ayer* |
| day before yesterday | *anteayer, antes de ayer, antier* |
| last week | *la semana pasada* |
| tomorrow | *mañana* |
| day after tomorrow | *pasado mañana* |
| next week | *la semana entrante* |

| | |
|---|---|
| second | *segundo* |
| minute | *minuto* |
| hour | *hora* |
| day | *día* |
| week | *semana* |
| month | *mes* |
| year | *año* |
| century | *siglo* |

| | |
|---|---|
| early | *temprano* |
| late | *tarde* |
| soon | *pronto* |
| already | *ya* |
| right away | *en seguida* |

| | |
|---|---|
| Monday | *lunes* |
| Tuesday | *martes* |
| Wednesday | *miércoles* |
| Thursday | *jueves* |
| Friday | *viernes* |
| Saturday | *sábado* |
| Sunday | *domingo* |

| | |
|---|---|
| January | *enero* |
| February | *febrero* |
| March | *marzo* |
| April | *abril* |
| May | *mayo* |
| June | *junio* |
| July | *julio* |
| August | *agosto* |
| September | *septiembre* |
| October | *octubre* |
| November | *noviembre* |
| December | *diciembre* |

| | |
|---|---|
| rainy season | *invierno* |
| dry season | *verano* |

| | |
|---|---|
| spring | *primavera* |
| summer | *verano* |
| autumn | *otoño* |
| winter | *invierno* |

## Numbers

| | |
|---|---|
| 0 | *cero* |
| 1 | *uno* |
| 2 | *dos* |
| 3 | *tres* |
| 4 | *cuatro* |
| 5 | *cinco* |
| 6 | *seis* |
| 7 | *siete* |
| 8 | *ocho* |
| 9 | *nueve* |
| 10 | *diez* |
| 11 | *once* |
| 12 | *doce* |
| 13 | *trece* |
| 14 | *catorce* |
| 15 | *quince* |
| 16 | *dieciseis* |
| 17 | *diecisiete* |
| 18 | *dieciocho* |
| 19 | *diecinueve* |

| 20 | veinte |
|---|---|
| 21 | veintiuno |
| 30 | treinta |
| 40 | cuarenta |
| 50 | cincuenta |
| 60 | sesenta |
| 70 | setenta |
| 80 | ochenta |
| 90 | noventa |
| 100 | cien |
| 101 | ciento uno |
| 200 | doscientos |
| 500 | quinientos |
| 1000 | mil |
| 100,000 | cien mil |
| 1,000,000 | un millón |
| 2,000,000 | dos millones |

| 1st | primero/a |
|---|---|
| 2nd | segundo/a |
| 3rd | tercero/a |
| 4th | cuarto/a |
| 5th | quinto/a |
| 6th | sexto/a |
| 7th | séptimo/a |
| 8th | octavo/a |
| 9th | noveno/a |
| 10th | décimo/a |
| 11th | undécimo/a |
| 12th | duodécimo/a |
| 20th | vigésimo |

**Emergencies**

See the Health section in the Facts for the Visitor chapter for more useful terms.

| accident | accidente |
|---|---|
| ambulance | ambulancia |
| clinic | clínica |
| dentist | dentista, odontólogo |
| doctor | doctor, médico |
| help | auxilio, ayuda |
| hospital | hospital |
| medicine | medicina, remedio |
| pharmacy | droguería |
| police | policía |

I feel bad.
  *Me siento mal.*
I have a fever.
  *Tengo fiebre/temperatura.*
Please call a doctor/the police.
  *Por favor llame a un doctor/la policía.*
Where is the nearest hospital?
  *¿Dónde queda el hospital más cercano?*
Could you help me, please?
  *¿Me podría ayudar, por favor?*
Could I use your telephone?
  *¿Podría usar su teléfono?*
I want to call my embassy.
  *Quiero llamar a mi embajada.*

# Facts for the Visitor

## VISAS & EMBASSIES

According to visa regulations introduced in November 1992, only Chinese nationals need a visa to enter Colombia. Citizens of any other country will simply get an entry stamp in their passport from the DAS immigration post when they arrive at any Colombian international airport or land border crossing. Immigration will note in your passport the period you can stay in the country – usually 90 days, the maximum allowed.

Officially, an onward ticket is required, but you will probably never be asked to show one when you enter the country. This requirement is, however, often enforced by airlines and travel agents, who may refuse to sell you a one-way ticket to Colombia unless you have an onward ticket. Remember the golden rule at border crossings: the smarter your appearance, the less hassle you are likely to get.

You are entitled to one 30-day extension of your stay, which can be obtained from DAS in the major cities; it costs US$18. If you want to stay in Colombia longer, go to any of the surrounding countries and come back.

If you intend to visit other countries in the region, think about the visas you will need before you arrive in South America. Many travellers simply get their visas successively as they journey through the continent, but this strategy may not always work well.

Venezuela, in particular, may prove a hard nut to crack. All nationals entering the country overland require visas, and these are very difficult to get in Colombia and Venezuela's other neighbouring countries. In Colombia, for example, only the Venezuelan consulate in Cúcuta will issue a tourist visa, so if you intend to travel overland, you are strongly advised to get this visa in your country of residence (where it's much easier to obtain). There's no problem if you fly into Venezuela because the airline will automatically supply you with a so-called Tourist Card, which entitles you to a 60-day stay.

Colombia's other neighbours are easier to enter. Most nationals do not need visas for Ecuador or Peru, but those who do can easily obtain them in the respective consulates. Visas to Panama and Brazil are easily obtainable as long as you present an onward ticket. It's always best to check the visa regulations before you travel and, if possible, get the visas you need at home.

### Colombian Embassies & Consulates

Although you no longer need to get a visa, you may want to contact Colombian embassies or consulates for information. It's a good idea to call them to ask for current visa requirements because these regulations tend to change frequently.

Australia
   101 Northbourne Ave, Turner, ACT 2601 (☎ (06) 257 2027)
   5th floor, 220 Pacific Hwy, Crows Nest, NSW 2065 (☎ (02) 955 0311, 922 5597)
Canada
   1010 Sherbrooke West, Suite 420, Montreal, Quebec H3A 2R7 (☎ (514) 849 4852, 849 2929)
   1 Dundas St West, Suite 2108, Toronto, Ontario M5G 1Z3 (☎ (416) 977 0098)
France
   11 Rue Christophe Colomb, Paris 8 (☎ (1) 47 23 36 05, 47 23 30 72)
Germany
   Friedrich-Wilhelm Strasse 35, Bonn (☎ (0228) 234 565)
   Clara Zetkin Strasse 89, 1080 Berlin (☎ (030) 229 2669, 229 1994)
   Rudolfstrasse 13-17, 6000 Frankfurt am Main (☎ (069) 251 650)
UK
   Suite 10, 140 Park Lane, London W1Y 3DF (☎ (0171) 495 4233)
USA
   2118 Leroy Place, Washington DC (☎ (202) 387 8338)
   122 South Michigan Ave, Suite 1441, Chicago, Illinios 60603 (☎ (312) 341 0658)
   2990 Richmond Ave, Suite 544, Houston, Texas 77098 (☎ (713) 527 8919, 527 9093)
   280 Aragon Ave, Coral Gables, Miami, Florida 33134 (☎ (305) 448 5558, 441 0437)
   10 East 46th St, New York, New York 10017

(☎ (212) 949 9898)
595 Market St, Suite 2130, San Francisco, California 94105 (☎ (415) 362 0080)

## Foreign Embassies in Colombia

Almost all countries which maintain diplomatic relations with Colombia have their embassies in Bogotá (refer to that chapter for addresses).

## DOCUMENTS
### Passport

A valid passport is the most essential document. Once in Colombia, you must carry it with you at all times. There are numerous police/military checkpoints on the roads, particularly in guerrilla areas, and identity checks are normal procedure. At each checkpoint, you will probably be asked to show your passport. In cities and towns, document checks on the street are not uncommon, and if you don't have your papers with you, you will be taken straight to the police station.

Some guidebooks and local sources say that you can photocopy your passport, authenticate the copy at a notary and use it as your identity document. However, according to the (DAS) Departamento Administrativo de Seguridad – the security police who are also responsible for immigration – this is not true.

### International Health Certificate

Visitors to Colombia are not required to have any vaccinations, although those arriving from an area infected with yellow fever or cholera may be asked for an International Health Certificate proving that they have been inoculated against these diseases.

The fact that they please border officials, of course, is not the main reason for recommending vaccinations against endemic diseases, and you should seriously think about getting some for your own protection.

A yellow fever vaccination is highly recommended for every visitor to Colombia. If you're continuing on to Brazil, Brazilian authorities may not grant entrance without it.

Other commonly recommended vaccinations for travel in South America are those for typhoid, tetanus and polio, as well as gamma globulin or Havrix as protection against hepatitis. Smallpox has been wiped out worldwide, so immunisation against this disease is no longer necessary. Refer to the Health section in this chapter for more details on predeparture preparations.

### Other Documents

A student card is of very limited use in Colombia. You may save a few pesos on museum entry costs but that's about it. There are no student discounts on domestic flights or buses. A hostelling card is more useful because there are some youth hostels in Colombia. See the Useful Organisations section in the Bogotá chapter for further information.

If you bring your own vehicle or plan to hire a car, make sure you have your domestic driving licence and an International Driver's Permit.

Don't forget to get insurance for both your luggage and health. Even if you don't need to use it, it will help you sleep more peacefully.

For security reasons, it's worth having photocopies of your passport, airline tickets and travellers' cheque numbers. Needless to say, keep them separate from the originals. It's also worth bringing several passport-sized photographs for any visas or documents you might need to get in Colombia.

### Letter of Introduction

A letter of introduction may be useful if you plan to explore remote areas, especially those noted for guerrilla activity (guerrillas operate in many regions and are very mobile, so it's easy to step into such a zone unintentionally).

The letter is not for the guerrillas but for the military or police forces patrolling the area. They may be suspicious about tourists travelling in such areas, and will be inclined to suspect them of being involved or collaborating with the guerrillas. It could be hard to make the authorities understand that you are innocently wandering around in a place that no Colombian would dare visit.

An official letter of introduction usually helps to convince the authorities of your legitimate purposes. Furthermore, such a letter means that somebody stands behind you, no matter whether it's the Red Cross, a mountaineering club or an ornithological society. Without the backing of an official organisation, you are merely a private citizen – that is, someone who is easy to rip off.

The letter of introduction must be in Spanish. Keep it simple and don't invent anything too elaborate; just say that you are travelling to study architecture, observing the flora or learning about handicrafts. Don't mention anything to do with journalism, interviews or political interests because these are viewed with suspicion. State clearly in the letter that photography is part of your programme because taking pictures arouses police suspicion. The more stamps and signatures on the document, the stronger your protection is considered to be. Get the letter from your university, friendship society, mountaineering club etc. If you come without one and head for remote areas, try to get a letter from the tourist office.

## CUSTOMS

You are allowed to bring in personal belongings and presents that you intend to give to Colombian residents. You can bring in cameras (still, cine and video), a personal computer, a typewriter, a portable radio/cassette recorder, camping equipment, sporting accessories and the like, but the quantity, kind and value of these items should not arouse suspicions that they may have been imported with a commercial purpose in mind. Basically, only bring in one of each item, and if it's not a present, make sure it comes replete 'with evident traces of use'.

Customs procedures on arrival and departure are little more than a formality, and your luggage is likely to pass through with only a cursory glance. However, thorough checks occasionally happen (more often at airports than at land borders) and when they do, they can be exhaustive – including a body search. These searches are not conducted to find your extra Walkman; they are looking for

drugs. Smuggling drugs across the border will provide you with the best opportunity to have an extended look at the inside of a Colombian jail.

You may be asked on departure for receipts for emeralds, antiques, and articles of gold and platinum purchased in Colombia.

## MONEY

There is no black market in Colombia, and you will probably not get a better exchange rate than that offered by a bank. Under these circumstances, it's advisable to carry most of your money in travellers' cheques and credit cards and only keep an emergency reserve in cash. US dollars are by far the most widely used and accepted foreign currency, so stick with greenbacks. Some US dollars in small notes may be useful if you get stuck without pesos in a remote area. American Express is the most popular travellers' cheque in Colombia. Don't take obscure travellers' cheques from small banks because you may find them impossible to cash. Visa and MasterCard are the most useful credit cards.

There is a limit on the amount of foreign currency a tourist can spend in Colombia. This is meant to make it harder to launder drug money as 'travel expenses'. The maximum a tourist can exchange during any one visit to the country is US$25,000. When you enter Colombia, customs officials now stamp a seal in your passport, where every foreign exchange transaction has to be recorded. If you don't get this stamp on the border, it will probably be issued by the first bank you use for a foreign exchange transaction.

### Currency

The official Colombian currency is the *peso*, comprising 100 *centavos*. There are five, 10, 20, 50, 100, 200 and 500-peso coins, and paper notes of 100, 200, 500, 1000, 2000, 5000 and 10,000 pesos. A 20,000 peso note was planned and may be in circulation by the time you arrive. Forged notes do exist, so pay attention to exactly what you get – they are generally of poor quality and easy to recognise. Counterfeit notes can frequently be seen on display in shops and restaurants which have been duped.

## Changing Cash & Travellers' Cheques

The best place to go to change money is a bank. Banks change cash and travellers' cheques, and pay peso advances to credit card holders. However, banking practices change constantly from bank to bank, city to city, day to day, and can be complicated by countless local factors – the bank may reach its daily limit of foreign exchange, it may run out of money, or the cashier may simply be out of the office. So don't expect all banks to handle foreign exchange transactions – some don't handle any – and don't assume that the bank you went to one day will necessarily accommodate you the next.

All banks in Colombia (except for those in Bogotá) have the same opening hours: Monday to Thursday from 8 to 11.30 am and 2 to 4 pm, and on Friday from 8 to 11.30 am and 2 to 4.30 pm. Banks in Bogotá do not have a lunch break, but they open one hour later and close one hour earlier. However, opening hours do not mean much because banks usually offer foreign exchange services for limited hours, which may mean only one or two hours daily; each branch of every bank seems to have its own schedule (your best chances are in the morning).

Keep in mind that if the bank states that it changes money until say 11 am, it means just that: they will simply stop at 11 am no matter how many people are still in the queue. To make matters more complex, some banks may have their own upper and/or lower limits on exchange transactions. A bank might tell you that they can only change up to US$100, while another may refuse to change your money unless it's US$1000 or more.

You need your passport to conduct any banking operation. Some banks will also request a photocopy of your passport (two pages are required, the one with your photograph and personal details, and the one with the entry stamp). Make sure you always have the photocopy with you when visiting a bank; some banks will want to photocopy your passport. Others won't change your travellers' cheques until they've seen your purchase receipt (the form titled 'purchase record customer's copy' issued when you buy the cheques). The banks are often crowded and there's so much paperwork involved in foreign exchange transactions that you should set aside an hour to change money; it will occasionally take even longer.

The banks which are most likely to exchange your cash and/or travellers' cheques are Banco Anglo Colombiano, Banco Unión Colombiano, Banco Popular, Banco Industrial Colombiano and Banco Sudameris Colombia.

The Colombian representative of American Express is Tierra Mar Aire (TMA) travel agency. It has offices in most major cities, including Bogotá, Barranquilla, Cali, Cartagena, Manizales, Medellín and Santa Marta (refer to the respective sections for addresses). You can report the loss or theft of American Express traveller's cheques at any of these offices, but probably only the Bogotá office will be able to refund them. None of the TMA offices exchanges traveller's cheques.

You can change cash (but not travellers' cheques) in *casas de cambio* (authorised money exchange offices) which are found in most major cities and border towns. They are open until 5 or 6 pm on weekdays, and usually until noon on Saturday. They deal mainly with US dollars and offer rates about 2% lower than the banks.

You can also change cash dollars on the street, but it's not recommended. The only street money markets worth considering are those at the borders, where there may be simply no other place to change money. There are moneychangers at every land border crossing. They change pesos into the currency of the neighbouring country and vice versa. Cúcuta, Ipiales and Maicao (and their respective border points) are the busiest centres for money dealers. The rate they offer is usually fixed, so don't waste time looking for a special deal; just ask a few first to check, and then change your money. If one moneychanger offers a significantly better rate, be cautious because it may be a scam. Change all the money from the country you are leaving (unless you plan to return soon) because the further you get from the frontier, the more difficult the currency will be to change.

### Credit Cards

Credit cards are very useful in Colombia. They are not as universal as they are in Western countries, but they have become quite popular over the past decade. A number of banks will accept credit cards and pay a peso advance.

On the whole, it's easier to get local currency with a credit card than to exchange travellers' cheques. This is particularly true in smaller cities where there may be no bank eager to change either cash or cheques, but there is usually one which will accept your card. Furthermore, you get more money with a card than you do for travellers' cheques (see the following section).

Visa and MasterCard are by far the most popular credit cards in Colombia. The banks which are most likely to give advance payments on Visa are Banco de Bogotá, Banco de Colombia, Banco del Estado and Banco Colombo Americano, while MasterCard is accepted by Banco Industrial Colombiano and Banco de Occidente.

Of the two cards, Visa is the more universal and is honoured by a larger number of banks. Other credit cards, such as American Express or Diners Club, may also be useful but fewer banks will cash them. Credit cards are generally accepted in top-class hotels and restaurants, and when buying air tickets; elsewhere, their use is limited.

### Exchange Rates

The exchange rate for travellers' cheques will always be some 2% to 5% higher than that for cash. Some banks charge a commission when they change cheques, so the difference can be less; always ask whether commission is charged before signing your cheques. Exchange rates for both cash and travellers' cheques vary from bank to bank, and the difference can be significant (up to

2%); this probably justifies shopping around before deciding which bank to use.

The banks (but not casas de cambio) offer Colombians lower cash exchange rates than they offer foreigners, so you may be approached by locals (who usually hang around the bank door) asking you to change their dollars for them. They often want to change as much as US$20,000. Although you are officially allowed to change up to US$25,000, and might get a US$100 reward for the favour, be aware that you are probably money laundering. Not many backpackers turn up at a bank to change US$20,000 cash in one go, so you will not be discreet; don't take the risk.

The exchange rate for credit cards is about 4% to 7% higher than the rate for travellers' cheques – a bonus for plastic money holders – but there is a degree of uncertainty about obtaining money this way. Banks pay you advances in pesos and will inform you of the conversion rate, but the whole transaction is done 'behind your back'. You can only find out how much they actually charged your card when you get the statement from your bank at home. This may not always be the figure quoted by the Colombian bank. There have been complaints received from travellers who discovered on returning home that their peso advances were calculated on an inexplicably low rate. In most cases, however, credit cards work fine and will provide you with more pesos per dollar than either cash or travellers' cheques.

As this book went to press, the approximate exchange rates for the Colombian peso were:

| | | |
|------|---|-------------|
| A$1 | = | 634 pesos |
| C$1 | = | 622 pesos |
| DM1 | = | 633 pesos |
| FF1 | = | 179 pesos |
| UK£1 | = | 1407 pesos |
| US$1 | = | 874 pesos |
| ¥1 | = | 10 pesos |

The depreciation of the peso against hard currencies has been fairly constant over the two past decades, usually about 25% per year. This is quite an achievement on a continent where almost all countries experienced a period of hyper-inflation in the 1980s.

### Costs

Compared to other South American countries, Colombia is in the middle-price bracket; it's more expensive than Ecuador and Peru, but cheaper than Venezuela and Brazil.

How much you spend in Colombia largely depends on what degree of comfort you require, what kind of food you eat, where you go, how fast you travel and the means of transport you use. If, for instance, you are used to rental cars and plush hotels, you can easily spend just as much as you would in the West. If you're a budget traveller, prepared for basic conditions and willing to endure some discomfort on the road, a daily average of around US$20 should be sufficient. This would cover accommodation in budget hotels, food in low to middle-range restaurants and getting around at a reasonable pace by bus. If you want to leave a comfortable margin for beers, taxis, movies and other extras, add US$5 per day. These averages don't include air travel, rental cars and tours.

If you seriously economise, it's possible to cut the average daily cost down to US$15, but this will limit your experience of the country and can turn your trip into more of an endurance test than a holiday.

Accommodation, food and transport are the three major items of expenditure. If you are prepared for basic conditions, you shouldn't have to spend more than US$4 a night (on average) for a budget hotel. The cost will be lower (or the standard better) if you travel in a group or, better still, as a couple.

Food costs vary greatly, though if budget dining is what you're used to, it shouldn't come to more than US$8 a day. Because of the climate, you'll drink a lot of soft drinks, mineral water etc, but they are fortunately cheap.

The amount you spend on transport can vary widely depending on how far and how fast you travel. Obviously, if you plan to stay on a beach or wander leisurely through one particular region, it will be far cheaper than if you rush like a rocket from one end of the country to the other.

Buses are the main mode of transport and are relatively cheap; city buses cost next to nothing. Taxis aren't expensive (especially if you're in a group) and they are definitely worth considering for trips to or from bus terminals and airports, when you're carrying all your gear with you. Flights are fairly costly – roughly triple the cost of bus rides. River transport is almost as expensive as flying. If you plan on exploring the outlying regions, such as the Amazon, Chocó or La Guajira, you will spend considerably more on transport.

Museum admission fees are low – in most cases, well under US$1 – and entertainment and cultural events (cinema, theatre, music) are also fairly inexpensive. On the other hand, visits to nightclubs can deplete your funds quickly, especially if you adapt to the Colombian way of drinking.

### WHEN TO GO

The most pleasant time to visit is in the dry season, between December and March or in July and August. This is particularly true if you intend to do any trekking because rain may spoil the fun of walking. The dry season also gives visitors a better chance to savour local cultural events because many festivals and fiestas take place during this period.

Keep in mind, however, that most Colombians take their holidays between late December and mid-January so transport is more crowded, hotels tend to fill up faster and prices may rise slightly during this period. If you travel at this time, you will have to plan your trip a little ahead and do more legwork to find a place to stay, but you'll also enjoy more contact with travelling Colombians, who will be in a relaxed, holiday spirit.

### WHAT TO BRING

The best advice is to take as little as possible – a large, heavy backpack will soon become a nightmare. You can buy almost anything you might need in Colombia (clothes, footwear, toiletries, stationery and most medicines) so don't bring hundreds of envelopes to send letters home, or a huge bottle of shampoo or a giant tube of toothpaste to last the whole trip. Pay attention to the most important items such as a good backpack, comfortable shoes, a basic set of clothes and photographic gear. If you plan on trekking, however, you need to be more prepared.

### Carrying Bags
For most travellers, there is nothing better than a strong backpack – make sure it's well constructed because overland travel destroys packs rapidly. A small day pack is recommended for city walks, short side trips and for carrying your essential items and valuables with you on buses.

### Clothes
The Colombian climate varies with altitude, so you need to be prepared for both hot and cold weather. A warm shirt with long sleeves is essential but also pack a T-shirt for the lowlands, and a jacket and sweater for the highlands. Take a light, waterproof jacket because the weather changes constantly; even the dry season can be fickle in some regions. A hat and sunglasses are useful. Flip-flops (thongs) are recommended to protect feet against fungal infections easily picked up in shabby hotel bathrooms. Take a set of smart clothes for dining out in fancy restaurants and special occasions.

The rest is up to you. Some people always wear jeans while others prefer light, loose trousers; most travellers wear sneakers, but others alternate between sandals and hiking boots. Whatever you pack, don't bring any khaki coloured clothing or any army surplus uniforms. You will look like a soldier or a guerrilla and shooting is the only form of communication between the two.

### Useful Items
A sleeping bag is only necessary if you intend to go trekking; even the cheapest hotels provide sheets and blankets. A torch (flashlight) is essential for visiting caves, the Tierradentro tombs, and for occasional blackouts. A travel alarm clock or alarm wristwatch is necessary for catching early buses (some leave at 3 or 4 am and you can't rely on the management of a budget hotel to wake you). A small combination lock or a padlock is useful in budget hotels. Plastic bags of different sizes will protect your gear from rain and dust. An umbrella can be an alternative to a rainproof jacket. Earplugs may be necessary if you are not a heavy sleeper. The usual travel accessories, such as penknife, string and a sewing kit are always useful.

All of the items listed above are readily available in Colombia, particularly in the larger urban centres, so you do not have to bring them all with you. In Bogotá, for instance, any time it begins to rain, the streets immediately fill up with hundreds of enterprising umbrella sellers.

A small English/Spanish, Spanish/English dictionary and a phrasebook are worthwhile additions. You might also want to bring some paperbacks because the choice of foreign-language books offered by local bookshops is limited.

Consider bringing some simple gifts with you, because it's nice to give something to people for their hospitality or help. Foreign coins, stamps, postcards, small handicrafts from your country are merely a few suggestions.

### Medicines
Make sure you bring any prescription medicines you normally use. If you wear glasses or contact lenses, bring a spare pair with you. If you plan on visiting remote areas, a small medical kit is recommended – refer to the Health section for details.

### Trekking Equipment
If you plan to go trekking in the mountains or visiting the jungle, you should bring a tent, sleeping bag, warm clothes etc. Trekking equipment is expensive in Colombia, not easy to find and almost impossible to hire. Two of Colombia's best mountain treks are

in the Sierra Nevada del Cocuy and the Sierra Nevada de Santa Marta – see these sections for more details on trekking gear.

## TOURIST OFFICES

The Corporación Nacional de Turismo (CNT) is the national tourist information board. Until recently, it had a score of offices throughout the country and plenty of free publications but, unfortunately, it is gradually disintegrating. At the time of writing, CNT still had offices in half a dozen cities, including Bogotá. Regional tourist information bureaux are attempting to fill the vacuum, with varying degrees of success. Addresses and phone numbers are given in the relevant sections throughout this book. The best and most helpful tourist office is in San Agustín. Colombia's national parks are administered by Inderena which has offices throughout the country, and these may be a useful source of information.

There are Colombian tourist offices in New York, 140E 57th St, NY 10022, and in Caracas, PB 5, Av Urdaneta, Ibarras a Pelota. Colombian consulates and embassies may provide limited tourist information, and overseas offices of the main national airline, Avianca, may occasionally have brochures.

## USEFUL ORGANISATIONS

Only international organisations are listed in this section. For information about useful organisations within Colombia, see the Bogotá chapter.

### South American Explorers Club

One of the most useful sources of information and help for visitors to South America is the South American Explorers Club (☎ (607) 277 0488), 126 Indian Creek Rd, Ithaca, NY 14850, USA. The club provides services, information and support to travellers, scientific researchers, mountaineers and explorers. It sells a wide range of books, guides and maps of South America, and publishes a quarterly journal and a mail order catalogue. If you're travelling in South America, note that the club maintains clubhouses in Quito (Ecuador) and Lima (Peru).

Membership costs US$30 a year per individual; US$40 per couple.

### Information for Disabled Travellers

Disabled travellers from the USA can contact the Society for the Advancement of Travel for the Handicapped (☎ (718) 858 5483), 26 Court St, Brooklyn, New York, NY 11242 for information. In the UK, a useful contact is the Royal Association for Disability & Rehabilitation (☎ (0171) 242 3882), 25 Mortimer St, London W1N 8AB.

### Environmental Organisations

Many international organisations are promoting preservation of the rainforest and other endangered environments. For more details, contact any of the following groups:

Australia
> Friends of the Earth, 312 Smith St, Collingwood, Vic 3066 (☎ (03) 419 8700)
> Greenpeace Australia Ltd, PO Box 800, Surry Hills, NSW 2010 (☎ (02) 211 4066)

UK
> Friends of the Earth, 26/28 Urderwood St, London N17JU (☎ (0171) 490 155)
> Survival International, 310 Edgeware Rd, London W2 1DY (☎ (0171) 723 5535)
> Greenpeace, Canonbury Villas, London N1 2PN, UK (☎ (0171) 354 5100)

USA
> The Rainforest Action Network (RAN), 301 Broadway, Suite A, San Francisco, CA 94133 (☎ (415) 398 4404)
> Conservation International, 1015 18th St, NW, Suite 1000, Washington, DC 20036 (☎ (202) 429 5660)
> Cultural Survival, 215 First St, Cambridge, MA 02142 (☎ (617) 621 3818)
> The Nature Conservancy, 1815 N Lynn St, Arlington, VA 22209 (☎ (703) 841 5300)
> Survival International USA, 2121 Decatur Place, NW, Washington, DC 20008 (☎ (202) 265 1077)
> Friends of the Earth, 218 D St, SE, Washington, DC 20003 (☎ (202) 544 2600)
> Greenpeace, 1436 U St, NW, Washington, DC 20009 (☎ (202) 462 8817)
> Earthwatch, 680 Mt Auburn St, Box 403, Watertown, MA 02272 (☎ (617) 926 8200)
> The Chico Mendes Fund, Environmental Defence Fund, 257 Park Ave South, New York, NY 10010 (☎ (212) 505 2100)
> Rainforest Alliance, 270 Lafayette St, Suite 512, New York, NY 10012 (☎ (212) 941 1900)

The Rainforest Foundation Inc, 1776 Broadway, 14th floor, New York, NY 10019 (☎ (212) 431 9098)

## BUSINESS HOURS & HOLIDAYS
### Business Hours

The office working day is theoretically eight hours long, from 8 am to noon and 2 to 6 pm, Monday to Friday. In practice, offices tend to open later and close earlier. Bogotá is slowly adopting the so-called *jornada continua*, a working day without a lunch break, which finishes two hours earlier. However, if you try to arrange something between noon and 2 pm at any office which has adopted this practice, you will find that most of the staff have gone to lunch – old habits die hard.

Banks have the most reliable business hours, and all have identical opening hours (see the Money section), except for Bogotá where banks work the jornada continua.

As a rough guide, shopping hours are from about 9 am to 12.30 pm and 2.30 to 6.30 pm, Monday to Saturday. Some stores don't close at lunchtime, others don't open Saturday afternoon, others are open on Sunday.

Museums and tourist sites have variable opening hours. Stated opening times are supplied in the main text, but be careful because actual opening hours may differ. Churches are an even bigger puzzle, seeming to base their opening times on individual direction from Heaven. Some are open all day, others for only certain hours, and the rest are locked except during mass, which may be only once a week. Cinemas usually have three shows daily, at 3, 6 and 9 pm, but there is no hard and fast rule concerning the actual starting time of the film; a half-hour delay isn't unusual. The last movie is the one most likely to begin on schedule (or even before) because the operators want to go home as soon as possible.

### Public Holidays

The following days are observed as public holidays in Colombia:

1 January
  *La Circuncisión* (Circumcision)

6 January*
  *Los Reyes Magos* (Epiphany)
19 March*
  *San José* (St Joseph)
March/April (Easter, dates vary)
  *Jueves Santo* (Maundy Thursday)
  *Viernes Santo* (Good Friday)
1 May
  *Día del Trabajo* (Labour Day)
May (date varies)*
  *La Ascensión del Señor* (Ascension)
May/June (date varies)*
  *Corpus Cristi* (Corpus Christi)
June (date varies)*
  *Sagrado Corazón de Jesús* (Sacred Heart)
29 June*
  *San Pedro y San Pablo* (St Peter & St Paul)
20 July
  *Día de la Independencia* (Independence Day)
7 August
  *Batalla de Boyacá* (Battle of Boyacá)
15 August*
  *La Asunción de Nuestra Señora* (Assumption)
12 October*
  *Día de la Raza* (Discovery of America)
1 November*
  *Todos los Santos* (All Saints' Day)
11 November*
  *Independencia de Cartagena* (Independence of Cartagena)
8 December
  *Inmaculada Concepción* (Immaculate Conception)
25 December
  *Navidad* (Christmas Day)

When the dates marked with an asterisk (*) do not fall on a Monday, the holiday is moved to the following Monday, to make a three-day long weekend, referred to as the *puente*.

## CULTURAL EVENTS

The Colombian calendar is full of festivals, carnivals, fairs and beauty pageants. Colombians love fiestas and they organise them whenever they can or whenever they feel like it. A tourist guide of events listed some 200 celebrations, ranging from small, one-day, local affairs to international festivals lasting several days. This means that almost every day there is a fiesta going on somewhere in Colombia.

A number of the feasts and celebrations follow the Church calendar: Christmas, Easter and Corpus Christi are often solemnly

Buses and busetas in central Bogotá

Left:    Central Bogotá
Right:    Bullring and planetarium in central Bogotá
Bottom:    Sunset over Bogotá

Friday; the most prominent celebrations are in Popayán and Mompós; March or April

*Festival Iberoamericano de Teatro* – Bogotá; biennially in April

*Festival de la Leyenda Vallenata* – Valledupar; April

*Festival Internacional de Cine* – Cartagena; June

*Festival Folclórico y Reinado del Bambuco* – Neiva; June

*Feria de las Flores* – Medellín; August

*Festival Latinoamericano de Teatro* – Manizales; September

*Reinado Nacional de Belleza* – Cartagena; November

*Reinado del Coco* – San Andrés; November

*Festival Folclórico y Turístico del Llano* – San Martín (Meta); November

*Feria de Cali* – Cali; December

## POST & TELECOMMUNICATIONS
### Post

The Colombian postal service is operated by two companies, Avianca and Adpostal. Both cover national and international post, but Avianca only deals with airmail, so if you want to ship a parcel overseas, you need Adpostal. Both operators seem to be efficient and reliable. International airmail letters take somewhere between a week and two weeks to reach their destination.

The post offices controlled by Avianca are in every city which Avianca flies to, and in some other places where they have an office only. The post and airline offices are usually in the same building or next door to one another. Adpostal has offices in the large cities, and also covers smaller towns where Avianca doesn't provide services.

**Postal Rates** Both operators have similar airmail rates for letters, postcards and packages. The domestic rates are reasonably cheap but international airmail is fairly expensive. A postcard to anywhere in the Americas costs US$0.60; a 20-gram letter costs US$1.20, and a 100-gram letter costs about US$4. A 500-gram package costs around US$6.50, a one-kg package US$12, and a two-kg package US$24. The rates for postcards, letters and packages sent to anywhere outside the Americas are about 15% higher. Registered mail costs US$1.20 on top of the ordinary rate.

The Adpostal surface-mail rates are far

celebrated, particularly in more traditional rural communities. The religious calendar is dotted with saints' days, and every village and town has its own patron saints – you can take it for granted that the locals will be holding a celebratory feast on those days. In many cases, religious ceremonies have become more generic celebrations and have turned into popular feasts.

The following list is a brief selection of the biggest events. More information on these and other fiestas can be found in the appropriate sections.

*Carnaval de Blancos y Negros* – Pasto; January

*Carnaval del Diablo* – Riosucio (Caldas); biennially in January

*Feria de Manizales* – Manizales; January

*Carnaval de Barranquilla* – Barranquilla; February or March

*Festival Internacional de Música del Caribe* – Cartagena; March

*Semana Santa* (Holy Week) – climaxes on Good

cheaper. Shipping a package to the USA will cost about US$2.50 per kg, and US$3.50 per kg to anywhere else in the world. The maximum allowed weight of the package is 20 kg. It will take up to two months for the package to reach its destination. The service appears to be fairly reliable.

**Poste Restante** The *poste restante* system is operated by Avianca and functions reasonably well. They hold mail for one month, sometimes longer, after which they return uncollected letters to the sender. The service costs US$0.25 per letter, and you need to present your passport or another identity document to collect mail. The letters are sorted in alphabetical order but sometimes they don't distinguish between the given name and the surname, so check under both. If you want to have letters sent to you, they should be addressed to your name only (don't use any Mr, Ms etc because it might cause confusion), c/o Poste Restante, Lista de Correo Aéreo, Avianca – Oficina Principal, city, department, Colombia. Theoretically, you can receive poste restante letters in any city where Avianca has a post office, but not all provincial offices do a good job. The most reliable office is in Bogotá.

## Telephone

The telephone system is controlled by Telecom (Empresa Nacional de Telecomunicaciones), which has offices almost everywhere, even in the most remote villages. In major cities, offices are open late; in rural areas, they tend to close earlier. The system is largely automated for both domestic and international calls.

Public telephones dot the streets of the larger cities, but many are out of order. If you can't find a public telephone in working order, try the nearest Telecom office, which should have at least one that is working. Public telephones use coins, although newly-installed telephones accept phone cards *(tarjeta telefónica)*. Phone cards can be used for international, inter-city and local calls, so it's worth buying one if you think you might be using public telephones

frequently. The cards can be bought at Telecom offices.

**International Calls** The international telephone service is expensive. When dialling direct, either from a public or private telephone, the call will be charged according to the length of time you talk. If you place the call through the international operator, either at a Telecom office or from a private telephone, the minimum charge is the same as a three-minute call. This will cost about US$7 if you're calling to the USA and US$9 to anywhere outside the Americas. Each extra minute costs a third more. For a person-to-person call *(persona a persona)*, add an extra minute's charge. Waiting time for a connection doesn't usually exceed 15 minutes, but sometimes it can take an hour or more to get through.

Collect calls *(llamadas de pago revertido)* are possible to a number of countries, including the USA, Canada, the UK, France, Italy and New Zealand, but not to Australia, Germany or Denmark. The list seems to change from year to year, so check with the Telecom office. If the called party refuses to accept payment for the call, you'll be charged US$1 by Telecom.

The country code for Colombia is 57. To call a telephone number in Colombia from abroad, dial the international access code of the country you're calling from, the country code (57), the area code (they are given below, but drop the initial '9') and the local telephone number.

**National Calls** You can call direct to just about anywhere in Colombia. A three-minute local call within a city costs about US$0.10. The cost of intercity calls rises with distance, and reaches about US$0.30 a minute for connections between the most distant localities.

Area codes for the departmental capital cities are listed below. The codes of the places detailed in this book have been included in the relevant sections. They are always given under the name of the city or town.

| | |
|---|---|
| Arauca (Arauca) | 9818 |
| Armenia (Quindío) | 967 |
| Barranquilla (Atlántico) | 958 |
| Bogotá (Cundinamarca) | 91 |
| Bucaramanga (Santander) | 976 |
| Cali (Valle) | 923 |
| Cartagena (Bolívar) | 953 |
| Cúcuta (Norte de Santander) | 975 |
| Florencia (Caquetá) | 988 |
| Ibagué (Tolima) | 982 |
| Leticia (Amazonas) | 9819 |
| Manizales (Caldas) | 968 |
| Medellín (Antioquia) | 94 |
| Mitú (Vaupés) | 9816 |
| Mocoa (Putumayo) | 988 |
| Montería (Córdoba) | 947 |
| Neiva (Huila) | 988 |
| Pasto (Nariño) | 927 |
| Pereira (Risaralda) | 963 |
| Popayán (Cauca) | 928 |
| Puerto Carreño (Vichada) | 9816 |
| Puerto Inírida (Guainía) | 9816 |
| Quibdó (Chocó) | 949 |
| Riohacha (Guajira) | 954 |
| San Andrés (San Andrés) | 9811 |
| San José del Guaviare (Guaviare) | 986 |
| Santa Marta (Magdalena) | 954 |
| Sincelejo (Sucre) | 952 |
| Tunja (Boyacá) | 987 |
| Valledupar (Cesar) | 955 |
| Villavicencio (Meta) | 9866 |

## Fax

Faxes can be sent from the major branches of Telecom offices. There's also a growing number of private companies in the larger cities offering fax services. The best hotels will also send and receive faxes for you, but will charge heavily for this already expensive service.

## TIME

Colombia is five hours behind GMT (UTC). There is no daylight-saving time. When it is noon in Bogotá, the time in other cities around the world is:

| | |
|---|---|
| Auckland | 5 am next day |
| Berlin | 6 pm |
| Buenos Aires | 2 pm |
| Caracas | 1 pm |
| Frankfurt | 6 pm |
| Hong Kong | 1 am next day |
| Lima | noon |
| London | 5 pm |
| Los Angeles | 9 am |

| | |
|---|---|
| Melbourne | 3 am next day |
| Mexico | 11 am |
| Montreal | noon |
| New York | noon |
| Paris | 6 pm |
| Quito | noon |
| Río de Janeiro | 2 pm |
| San Francisco | 9 am |
| Sydney | 3 am next day |
| Tokyo | 2 am next day |
| Toronto | noon |
| Vancouver | 9 am |

## ELECTRICITY

Electricity is 110V, 60 cycles AC, throughout the country, except for small areas in Bogotá where the old, 150V system still exists. Plugs are the two-pin American flat type, so take conversion plugs if you need them.

## LAUNDRY

There are dry cleaners in the larger cities; they usually take one to two days to clean clothes. Top-class hotels offer faster laundry facilities. Self-service laundrettes don't exist, but there are some laundries which offer service washes.

## WEIGHTS & MEASURES

The metric system is commonly used, except for petrol which is measured in US gallons. Food is often sold in *libras* (pounds) which is roughly equivalent to half a kg. There is a conversion table at the back of this book.

## BOOKS

You will get far more out of your visit if you read about the country before you arrive. There is quite a choice of English-language books about Colombia, some of which are recommended below; check specialist encyclopaedias for more information.

If you can read Spanish, you'll find plenty of invaluable sources of information in Colombia itself. The country produces lots of books and publications, few of which have been translated into foreign languages.

### History, Politics & Economics

A very readable overview of Spanish colonisation is provided by John Hemming's *The Search for El Dorado*. The book is a fascinating insight into the conquest of Venezuela and Colombia. Equally captivating is *The Explorers of South America* by Edward J Goodman (Collier–MacMillan, London, 1972, reprinted by University of Oklahoma Press, Norman and London, 1992), which recounts some of the more incredible expeditions to the continent, some of which refer to Colombia.

*Colombia* by Françoise de Tailly (Delachaux & Niestlé, Neuchâtel, Switzerland, 1981) is a general book, richly illustrated, which covers pre-Columbian cultures, history, economics, people and folklore. The book has two dual language editions: Spanish/English and French/ German.

The well-balanced *Colombia: Portrait of Unity and Diversity* by Harvey F Kline (Westview Press, Boulder, USA, 1983) is an overview of Colombian history.

There's a good selection of titles covering Colombia's modern history. *The Politics of Colombia* by Robert H Dix (Praeger, New York and London, 1987) is a concise analysis of recent politics. Other recommended titles which may help to explain Colombia's complicated political scene include: *Colombia: Inside the Labyrinth* by Jenny Pearce (Latin American Bureau, London, 1990), *The Politics of Coalition Rule in Colombia* by Jonathan Hartlyn (Cambridge University Press, Cambridge, 1988) and *The Making of Modern Colombia: A Nation in Spite of Itself* by David Bushnell (University of California Press, Berkeley, 1993).

For a detailed insight into Colombia's drug cartels, read *The White Labyrinth: Cocaine and Political Power* by Rensselaer W. Lee III (Transaction Publishers, New Brunswick, USA and London, 1991) and *Kings of Cocaine* by Guy Gugliotta & Jeff Leen (Simon & Schuster, 1990). The latter book, written by *Miami Herald* journalists, reads like a thriller. Other books on the subject include *Coca and Cocaine: An Andean Perspective* (Greenwood Press, Westport, USA, 1993) and *Drug Policy in the Americas* (Westview Press, Boulder, USA and Oxford, 1992).

*The Colombian Economy* (Westview Press, Boulder, USA, 1992) is a detailed survey of the country's economy over the past couple of decades.

If you want to keep a close eye on Colombia's current politics and economics, there's probably nothing better than the newspaper *Latin American Regional Reports*, published weekly by Latin American Newsletters (☎ (0171) 251 0012, fax 253 8193), 61 Old St, London EC1V 9HX. Telephone or write for current subscription rates (which are high).

## Geography & Wildlife

The famous German geographer and botanist, Alexander von Humboldt, explored regions of Colombia, Venezuela, Ecuador and Peru, describing it in amazing detail in his three-volume *Personal Narrative of Travels to the Equinoctial Regions of America, 1799-1801*. It's a fascinating, historical read.

Travellers with a serious interest in South American wildlife can choose between a number of general books and practical guides. *World of Wildlife – Animals of South America* by F R de la Fuente (Orbis Publishing, 1975) is a good, basic reference work. *Neotropical Rainforest Mammals – A Field Guide* by Louise H Emmons (University of Chicago Press, Chicago 1990) is a practical guide containing descriptions and illustrations of several hundred species, many of which can be found in Colombia.

If you're interested in birds, start with *A Guide to the Birds of South America* (Academy of Natural Science, Philadelphia). Alternatively, try the comprehensive reference work, *The Birds of South America* by R S Ridgley & G Tudor (University of Texas Press, 1989). It comes in several volumes; amateurs will find it extremely detailed and technical. Get a copy of *A Guide to the Birds of Colombia* by Stephen L Hilty & William L Brown (Princeton University Press, New Jersey, 1986) to take with you on your trip. Colour plates in the guide help to identify particular species. *South American Birds – A Photographic Aid to Identification* by John S Dunning (1987) is another practical guide you could stuff in your backpack.

A recommended rainforest guide is *Rainforests – A Guide to Research and Tourist Facilities at Selected Tropical Forest Sites in Central and South America* by James L Castner (Feline Press, Florida, 1990). It has useful background information and descriptions of about 40 rainforests in half a dozen countries.

*Colombia – Parques Nacionales* (Inderena, Bogotá, 1986, 2nd edition), is the most comprehensive book about the Colombian national parks and their wildlife; it has excellent text and photographs. However, the book is in Spanish only, and is virtually unobtainable outside Colombia. *Nuevos Parques Nacionales* (Inderena, Bogotá, 1992) is the equally admirable sequel, which features new parks.

*Orquídeas Nativas de Colombia* (Editorial Colina, Medellín, 1991) is a marvellous four-volume edition about Colombian orchids. The set contains about 600 descriptions of native species (of some 3000 to be found in the country), each illustrated with a splendid photograph – a treat for orchid lovers.

### Society, Culture & Arts

There are not many English-language publications about the pre-Hispanic communities of Colombia, even though they were among the most developed cultures on the continent. A good introduction to aboriginal civilisations is provided by *Colombia* (published in the series *Ancient Peoples and Places)* by Gerardo Reichel-Dolmatoff (Thames & Hudson, London, 1965). The book outlines Colombia's cultural development from its beginnings to the Spanish conquest.

Reichel-Dolmatoff is perhaps the most prominent authority on Colombian indigenous cultures; one of his outstanding achievements is *Los Kogi – una Tribu de la Sierra Nevada de Santa Marta* (Procultura, Bogotá, 1985), a very comprehensive, two-volume study of the Indians of the Sierra Nevada, unfortunately available only in Spanish.

*Colombia before Columbus: The People, Culture, and Ceramic Art of Prehispanic Colombia* by Armand J Labbé is a wonderful, glossy introduction to the impressive pottery of the country's indigenous inhabitants.

*Historia del Arte Colombiano* (Salvat Editores, Barcelona) is an illustrated, multi-volume, 1680-page, comprehensive guide to Colombian arts from pre-Columbian times to the present. It is in a class of its own and is highly recommended, though it only has a Spanish-language version.

### Travelogues & Personal Narratives

*The Fruit Palace* by Charles Nicholl (Picador, London, 1985) is an excellent and fascinating introduction to Colombia's crazy reality. It's a journalist's account of what was intended to be an investigation of cocaine trafficking in Colombia. The author did not get to the heart of the cartels, but he provides a vivid picture of the country, from Indian mountain villages to shabby bars.

*A Traveller's Guide to El Dorado and the Inca Empire* by Lynn Meisch (Penguin Books, 3rd edition, 1984) provides interesting information about food, folk art, fiestas and music in Colombia, Ecuador, Peru and Bolivia.

*The Heart of the World* by Alan Ereira (Jonathan Cape, London, 1990) is a story about the Kogi Indians. Written by a filmmaker who made a documentary on the Indians for the BBC, the book gives an insight into a culture which has rarely been penetrated by outsiders, let alone foreigners.

### Travel Guides

You won't find many English-language guidebooks about Colombia. Its lawless image has discouraged travel writers from exploring more than a handful of cities and a few tourist attractions. There doesn't appear to be any other comprehensive guidebook focused solely on Colombia, although the country is included in several general guides either covering the Andean region or the entire South American continent.

Lonely Planet's *South America on a Shoestring* (5th edition, 1994) is recommended for budget travellers who want a single book covering the continent.

Another option in this category is the *South American Handbook* (Trade & Travel Publications, Bath, UK). It caters for a wide range of travellers, from penurious backpackers to business travellers, so there's a lot of extraneous information for most readers.

*Travellers Survival Kit: South America* by Emily Hatchwell & Simon Calder (Vacation Work, Oxford, 1992) also covers the entire continent but is much more general than the other two.

*Ecuador, the Galápagos & Colombia* by John Paul Rathbone (Cadogan Books, London, and Globe Pequot Press, Connecticut, 1991) has colourful, general descriptions of cities and places of interest. However, its coverage is not very extensive and it is not strong on practical information. *Michael's Guide to Ecuador, Colombia and Venezuela* by Michael Shichor (Inbal Travel Information, Tel Aviv, 1988) is sketchy and out of date.

*Guía Turística: Colombia* by Raúl Jaramillo Panesso (Grupo Editorial Norma, Bogotá, 1992) is the best locally published general guidebook to the country. The guide contains lots of photographs and regional maps, but little practical information. The sections referring to the most popular tourist destinations have English translations.

### Useful Local Publications

Colombia does not produce many travel publications, but it does publish a lot of beautiful coffee-table books about Colombian nature, architecture and art which are tempting souvenirs. They may also give you an idea of where you would like to go and what you would like to see. Just skim through the titles you are interested in at any of the good bookshops, then go to a library to have a closer look and take notes.

*Colombia* by Patrick Rouillard (Editorial Colina, Medellín, 1985) is one of the best photographic records of Colombia. Spanish, English, French and German versions are available. Rouillard has produced several other photographic books, including *Antioquia*, *Cartagena de Indias*, *San Agustín* and *Boyacá*, all of which boast splendid photographs.

### Colombian Literature

Colombia's most famous contemporary writer is Gabriel García Márquez, winner of the 1982 Nobel Prize for literature. You shouldn't set off for Colombia before reading at least his most famous novel, *One Hundred Years of Solitude*. It's a very good aid to understanding Colombian culture, mentality and philosophy. Although considered by critics and readers to be a highly imaginative work, the book is actually solidly based on acute observation – its vividness reflects Colombian reality as much as it reveals García Márquez's vibrant imagination.

For more information about Colombian literature, refer to the Arts & Culture section (Literature) in the Facts about the Country chapter.

### Phrasebooks & Dictionaries

Lonely Planet's *Latin American Spanish Phrasebook* is a worthwhile addition to your backpack. A good alternative is the *Latin-American Spanish for Travellers* published by Berlitz. The latter is available with a cassette to help you improve your pronunciation.

Spanish is one of the world's major languages, so there are loads of Spanish-English dictionaries available. One of the best examples is the *University of Chicago Spanish-English, English-Spanish Dictionary*, whose small size, lightness and thoroughness makes it useful for overseas travellers.

For something more comprehensive, look for the *Pequeño Larousse Español-Inglés, English-Spanish*, which is one of the most helpful compact dictionaries available. It's published as either a single volume or two separate volumes, but contains the same amount of information in each edition.

## MAPS

If you require anything other than a general map of the country, you will have difficulty finding it outside of Colombia, or even outside of Bogotá. Check with good travel bookshops and specialised map shops to see what's available. In the USA, Maplink (☎ (805) 965 4402), 25 E Mason St, Dept G, Santa Barbara, CA 93101, has an excellent supply of maps. A similarly extensive selection of maps is available in the UK from Stanfords (☎ (0171) 836 1321), 12-14 Long Acre, London WC2E 9LP.

For general maps of South America with excellent topographical detail, it's hard to beat the sectional maps published by International Travel Maps (ITM), 345 West Broadway, Vancouver, BC V5Y 1P8, Canada. Coverage of Colombia is provided in *South America – North West* (1993, 2nd edition). This and other ITM maps are sold by a number of distributors in Europe and North America. Availability in Australia is still patchy – Melbourne Map Centre (☎ (03) 569 5472) or Bowyang's (☎ (03) 670 4383) in Melbourne have the best supply.

Within Colombia, folded national road maps are produced by several publishers and distributed through bookshops. *Mapa vial de Colombia* (scale 1:2,000,000), published by Rodríguez in Bogotá, is probably the best. It can be bought in better bookshops.

The widest selection of maps of Colombia is produced and sold by the Instituto Geográfico Agustín Codazzi (IGAC). This is the government mapping body, and it has its head office in Bogotá. It produces general maps of Colombia (political, physical,

### Orientation

Colombian cities, towns and villages have traditionally been laid out on a rigid grid pattern. The streets running north-south are called Carreras, often abbreviated on maps to Cra, Cr or K; those running east-west are called Calles, labelled on maps as Cll, Cl or C. This simple pattern is complicated in larger towns and cities by diagonal streets, called either Diagonales (more east-west and thus like Calles), or Transversales (more like Carreras).

All streets are numbered and the numerical system of addresses is used. Each address consists of a series of numbers, eg Calle 23 No 5-43 (which means that it is the house on Calle 23, 43 metres from the corner of Carrera 5 towards Carrera 6), or Carrera 17 No 31-05 (the house on Carrera 17, five metres from the corner of Calle 31 towards Calle 32). Refer to the Orientation map for examples. The system is very practical and you will soon become familiar with it. It is usually easy to find an address.

In the larger cities the main streets are called Avenidas or Autopistas. They have their own names and numbers, but are commonly known just by their names.

Cartagena's old town is probably the only Colombian city where centuries-old street names have withstood the modern numbering system.

The Colombian system of designating floors is the same as that used in the USA; there is no 'ground floor' – it is the *primer piso* (1st floor). Thus, the European 1st floor will be the *segundo piso* (2nd floor) in Colombia. ■

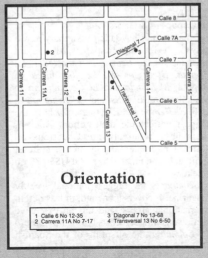

## Orientation

| | |
|---|---|
| 1 Calle 6 No 12-35 | 3 Diagonal 7 No 13-68 |
| 2 Carrera 11A No 7-17 | 4 Transversal 13 No 6-50 |

road/tourist etc) and regional maps for each department.

Other useful IGAC maps include the 1:100,000 scale *planchas* (sheets), broken down into more detailed 1:25,000 scale maps. The latter are the best maps for trekking; the topography is usually correct but they are not very up-to-date and ignore local variations in the naming of villages, creeks and rivers etc.

The maps are based on aerial photos and have some white patches in spots which were under cloud when the photos were taken. Maps of the frontier areas are not available, nor of the areas where there are military bases or strategic installations.

The IGAC also publishes many city maps and specialist maps (soils, geology etc). If the colour printed maps are out of stock, they will make a copy from the originals. The price is about US$1 to US$2 per sheet, depending on the kind of map and its format.

Some leaflets issued by tourist offices contain regional and city maps but they are of variable quality and value, and cover only the most touristy areas.

## MEDIA
### Newspapers & Magazines

All major cities have their own daily newspapers. The leading newspapers in the largest cities include: *El Tiempo, El Espectador, La Prensa, El Siglo* and *La República* in Bogotá; *El Mundo* and *El Colombiano* in Medellín; and *El País* and *El Occidente* in Cali. *El Tiempo* and *El Espectador* have the biggest nationwide distribution. Both of them have relatively good sections on national and international news, culture, sport and economics. They cost US$0.30 on weekdays, US$0.40 on weekends.

*Semana* is the biggest national weekly magazine. It covers local and, in less detail, international affairs, and has an extensive section on culture. It costs US$1.50. *Cambio 16 Colombia*, the offspring of the Spanish *Cambio 16*, began in June 1993, and is becoming an increasingly popular weekly magazine. It also provides a coverage of

local and international politics, but gives less space to culture.

*The Colombian Post* is the only local paper published in English. This young 16-page weekly has, so far, patchy distribution and is difficult to find; major newsstands in Bogotá are the best places to look for it. It costs US$1.

International daily papers and periodicals, such as the *International Herald Tribune, The Times, Der Spiegel* and *Le Monde*, can be found at a few selected newsstands and bookshops, mainly in Bogotá. *Time* and *Newsweek* have the widest distribution of the foreign news publications.

### Radio & TV

There are over 500 FM and AM radio stations in Colombia. They are all commercial and consist mainly of music programmes (Western pop, salsa and merengue and other local rhythms). Even middle-size towns have their own local radio stations.

Colombian TV dates from 1954 and since 1981 all programmes have been broadcast in colour. There are three nationwide television channels, all broadcast by the state monopoly Inravisión. In the late 1980s, three regional channels, Telepacífico, Teleantioquia and Telecaribe, began broadcasting.

Satellite TV has boomed in Bogotá and, to a lesser extent, in other major cities. The *parabólica* (satellite dish) has become the ultimate status-symbol, and a new feature of the city skyline.

Major newspapers list the programmes of all TV channels which can be picked up locally.

### FILM & PHOTOGRAPHY

Colombia's spectacular geography, diverse wildlife, colonial architecture and pot pourri of races means there's plenty to capture on film or video. Unfortunately, the country is not particularly safe, so you have to be very careful with your equipment and shoot photographs discreetly to avoid attention – this is particularly true in the large cities. In rural areas, taking photographs is not as stressful, but use common sense and keep your camera out of sight when you are not using it.

Except for the usual restrictions on photographing military installations and other strategic facilities, you can take pictures of just about anything. Taking photographs is permitted in virtually every church and in many museums (though some don't allow the use of flashes).

## Photographic Equipment

Bring all necessary equipment from home. Cameras and accessories can be bought in Colombia, but the choice is limited and unpredictable, and the prices are hardly welcoming. It's difficult to get cameras repaired in Colombia, so make sure your gear is reliable.

The first thing to consider before you leave home is which camera and accessories you will need. Some travellers are happy with a small, aim-and-shoot automatic camera, while others travel with their backpacks almost brimming over with photographic gear.

An automatic 35-mm reflex with a zoom lens is the most universal choice for general photographic purposes, including landscapes, portraits and architecture. The choice between a zoom and a set of straight lenses is a matter of individual preference. Zooms are definitely more convenient because you can frame your shot easily and work out the optimum composition. The problem is that they absorb a lot of light and require higher speed film for photographs taken in anything other than bright daylight.

A fixed focal length lens will yield better results and greater clarity, but you have to carry several different lenses and change them according to the particular shot.

For serious wildlife photography you will need a long telephoto lens. A reasonable length would be somewhere between 200 and 300 mm. A 500-mm lens will bring the action even closer, but is much heavier, and requires faster film or a tripod. Long lenses are also useful for taking photographs of people, but do it discreetly and be sensitive. If necessary, ask for permission to photograph and don't insist or take a picture if permission is denied.

In certain touristy areas, some locals may expect payment for being photographed. Avoid this by getting to know the people beforehand and promising to send them a copy of the photograph (make sure you do!), or simply don't take a picture if the person insists on payment. Remember, the disease spreads quickly: any payment will immediately encourage other locals to do the same. It will be dreadful to see the whole village population coming out to pose for tourists' cameras and shouting 'one photo one dollar', as is the custom in some regions of the world.

A wide-angle lens can be useful, sometimes indispensable, for photographing architecture or tight interiors. The macro, which comes as a standard feature in most zooms, comes in handy for taking photos of small insects and tiny flowers. A UV filter is essential when photographing at high altitudes to minimise the effect of ultraviolet rays.

A tripod is an important but heavy and bulky piece of equipment. It is particularly useful in dim interiors (for example in churches) and may also be necessary when using long lenses. If you decide to take one, don't forget to also take a cable release.

A flash is, thankfully, a lighter accessory. Other useful items include a spare set of batteries for your camera, a lens cleaning kit and plenty of silica-gel packs and plastic bags to protect your gear from the humidity, dust, sand and water.

Whatever combination of lenses and accessories you decide to bring, make sure they are carried in a sturdy bag which will protect them from the elements and the rugged treatment they're sure to receive. It's much better if the bag is scruffy because it's less likely to attract the attention of thieves. Needless to say, make sure your equipment is insured.

## Film

The price of film in Colombia is roughly comparable to that in the USA. There's a decent choice of films in Bogotá and a few other big cities, but elsewhere it may be difficult to get the type and speed you need.

Kodak, Fuji and, to a lesser extent, Agfa are the most popular brands.

Negative films are found almost everywhere but slide films, especially high-speed or professional ones, are harder to get. Prints can usually be processed within an hour or two at photographic laboratories, and the quality is usually OK; E6 slide processing is not as common and the quality is not always good. See the Bogotá chapter for where to buy slide films cheaply and where to process them.

If you plan on taking slides and don't visit Bogotá, it's best to bring films with you and have them processed back home.

Bring a variety of film stock: rainforests are surprisingly dark and may require very fast films – ISO (ASA) 400 and upwards – and often even a tripod, but snowy peaks and sunny, white beaches don't require anything faster than ISO (ASA) 50.

Heat and humidity can ruin films, so remember to keep them in the coolest, driest place available, both before and after exposure. Films should be processed soon after exposure, but don't panic about it: you'll often get a better result by waiting to have them developed in a reliable laboratory at home rather than processing them immediately in an unknown, local outlet.

Use a lead film bag to protect films from airport X-ray machines. This is important for the sensitive high-speed films; films with speeds of ISO (ASA) 100 or lower come through unharmed.

### Video

Betamax is Colombia's standard video format for recording from TV and viewing rented movies at home. VHS does exist, but is less popular. Most amateurs shooting their own videos opt for a Video 8 mm system. The equipment, cassettes and accessories for all systems are available, but the variety is both limited and expensive.

If you decide to bring a video camera, don't forget to bring a conversion plug to fit electric sockets (American flat two-pin type) if you have a different system at home.

Remember that Colombia's electricity is 110V, 60 cycles.

## HEALTH

Colombia is not the most disease-ridden part of the world, but certain precautions should be taken. The medical standards and the variety of diseases make health more of a problem than in the West. Fortunately, the local pharmacy network is quite developed and extensive: there are *droguerías* (pharmacies) even in small towns, and those in the cities are usually well stocked. Water is safe to drink from the tap in Bogotá and several other large cities, but if you prefer to avoid it, there's always a choice of bottled waters and other drinks readily available in shops. No vaccinations are required for entry to Colombia, unless you come from an infected area.

Travel health depends on your predeparture preparations, your day-to-day health care while travelling and how you handle medical problems or emergencies that develop. The list of potential dangers included in this section may seem quite frightening, but don't panic: with some basic precautions and adequate information, few travellers experience more than minor stomach upsets.

This section includes preventative measures, descriptions of symptoms and suggestions about what to do if there is a problem. It isn't meant to replace professional diagnosis or prescription, and visitors to Colombia should discuss with their physician the most up-to-date methods used to prevent and treat the threats to health which may be encountered.

If a serious medical problem arises during the trip, seek qualified help wherever possible because self-diagnosis and treatment can be risky. Your embassy or consulate can usually recommend a good place to go for medical help. Five-star hotels can also recommend doctors, though usually ones with five-star prices – this is when the medical insurance really comes in useful.

### Predeparture Preparations
**Health Insurance** It's a good idea to get a

travel insurance policy to cover medical problems, regardless of how fit and healthy you are – anyone can be involved in an accident.

There are a wide variety of policies and your travel agent will have recommendations: The international student travel policies handled by STA and other student travel organisations are usually good value. When buying a policy, it's important to check the small print:

- Some policies specifically exclude 'dangerous activities' which can include scuba diving, motorcycling or even trekking. If these activities are on your agenda, such a policy is of limited value.
- You may prefer a policy which pays doctors or hospitals directly, so you don't have to pay them on the spot and claim the money back later. If you have to claim later, make sure you keep all documentation. Some policies ask you to make a reverse charge call to a centre in your home country so an immediate assessment of your problem can be made.
- Check if the policy covers ambulances or an emergency flight home. If you have to stretch out across a few airline seats, someone has to pay for them.

**Travel Health Information** In the USA, you can contact the Overseas Citizens Emergency Center and request a health and safety information bulletin on Colombia by writing to the Bureau of Consular Affairs Office, State Department, Washington, DC 20520. This office also has a special telephone number for emergencies while abroad: ☎ (202) 632 5525.

The International Association for Medical Assistance to Travellers (IAMAT), 417 Center St, Lewiston, New York, NY 14092 can provide travellers with a list of English-speaking physicians in Colombia.

In the UK, contact Medical Advisory Services for Travellers Abroad (MASTA) (☎ (0171) 631 4408), Keppel St, London WC1E 7HT. MASTA provides a variety of services, including a choice of concise or comprehensive 'Health Briefs' and a range of medical supplies. Another source of medical information and supplies is the

British Airways Travel Clinic (☎ (0171) 831 5333).

In Australia, make an appointment with the Traveller's Medical & Vaccination Centre in Sydney (☎ (02) 221 7133) or Melbourne (☎ (03) 602 5788) for general health information pertaining to Colombia and requisite vaccinations for travel in South America.

There are a number of books on travel health. *Staying Healthy in Asia, Africa & Latin America* (Volunteers in Asia) is probably the best all-round guide to carry because it's compact, very detailed and well organised. *Travellers' Health* by Richard Dawood (Oxford University Press) is comprehensive, easy to read and authoritative, but it's rather large to lug around.

The Center for Disease Control's (CDC) *Health Information for International Travel* (a supplement of *Morbidity & Mortality Weekly Report)* and the World Health Organisation's (WHO) *Vaccination Certificate Requirements for International Travel & Health Advice to Travellers* are useful references.

**Medical Kit** Give some thought to a medical kit for your trip. The size and contents of your first-aid kit will depend on your knowledge of first-aid procedures, where and how far off the beaten track you are going, how long you will need the kit for, and how many people will be sharing it.

It's not necessary to take every remedy for every illness you might contract during your trip. Colombian pharmacies stock all kinds of drugs and medication is cheaper than in the West. There are few restricted drugs; almost everything (including antibiotics, contraceptive pills and syringes) is sold over the counter. Many drugs are manufactured locally under foreign licence; be sure to check expiry dates.

Travellers should be aware of any drug allergies they may have, and avoid using such drugs or their derivatives. Since common names of prescription medicines in Colombia may be different from the ones you're used to, ask a pharmacist before taking anything you're not sure about.

A possible kit may include:

- Any prescription medicine you normally take
- Aspirin or Panadol – for pain or fever
- Antihistamine (such as Benadryl) – useful as a decongestant for colds and allergies, to ease the itching from insect bites, or to help prevent motion sickness
- Antibiotics – useful if you're travelling well off the beaten track; unlike in the West, many antibiotics are available in Colombia without a prescription
- Kaolin and pectin preparation, such as Pepto-Bismol, for stomach upsets, and Imodium or Lomotil to temporarily relieve diarrhoea in case of emergencies or during long-distance travel
- Rehydration mixture – for treatment of severe diarrhoea; this is particularly important if travelling with children
- Antiseptic liquid or cream and antibiotic powder – for cuts and grazes
- Calamine lotion – to ease irritation from bites or stings
- Ear and eye drops
- Foot and groin (antifungal) powder
- Bandages and band-aids
- Scissors, tweezers and a thermometer (note that mercury thermometers are prohibited by airlines)
- Insect repellent, sunscreen, suntan lotion, chapstick, and water purification tablets
- Sterile syringes (be sure you have at least one large enough for a blood test – those normally used for injections are too small)
- Plastic container with a sealable lid, to pack your medical kit in

Ideally, antibiotics should be administered only under medical supervision and should never be taken indiscriminately. Overuse of antibiotics can weaken your body's ability to deal with infections naturally, and can reduce the drug's efficacy in future. Take only the recommended dose at the prescribed intervals and continue using the antibiotic for the prescribed period, even if the illness seems to have been cured. Antibiotics are quite specific to the infections they treat, so if there are any serious unexpected reactions, discontinue use immediately. If you are not sure whether you have the correct antibiotic, don't use it at all.

**Health Preparations** Make sure you're healthy before you start travelling. Have your teeth checked and make sure they are OK.

If you wear glasses or contact lenses, bring a spare pair and your optical prescription. Losing your glasses can be a real problem, although in many Colombian cities you can get new spectacles made up quickly, cheaply and competently.

At least one pair of high-quality sunglasses is essential because there is strong glare, and dust and sand can get into the corners of your eyes. A hat, sunscreen lotion and lip protection are also important.

If you require a particular medication, take an adequate supply with you because it may not be available locally. Take the prescription specifying the generic rather than the brand name (which may not be stocked); it will make getting replacements easier. It's also a good idea to have the prescription with you to prove you're using the medication legally. Customs and immigration officers may get excited at the sight of syringes or mysterious powdery preparations. The organisations listed under Travel Health Information can provide medical supplies and multilingual customs documentation.

**Immunisations** No immunisations are necessary for Colombia, unless you are coming from an infected area. However, the further off the beaten track you go, the more necessary it is to take precautions. All vaccinations should be recorded on an International Health Certificate, which is available from your physician or government health department.

Plan your vaccinations ahead of time: some require an initial shot followed by a booster, while others cannot be administered at the same time as other vaccinations. Most travellers from Western countries will have been immunised against various diseases during childhood, but your doctor may still recommend booster shots. The period of protection offered by vaccinations differs widely. Note that some are not advisable for pregnant women.

The list of possible vaccinations includes:

*Cholera* Colombian authorities may require that you have a cholera vaccination if you are coming from an infected area. Protection is not very effective, lasts only for a maximum of six months and is not suitable for pregnant women.

*Hepatitis* Protection can be provided in two ways – either with the antibody gamma globulin or with a new vaccine called Havrix. The latter provides long-term immunity (possibly more than 10 years) after an initial course of two injections and a booster one year later. Havrix may be more expensive than gamma globulin but it certainly has advantages, including length of protection and ease of administration. It takes three weeks before the vaccine provides satisfactory protection – hence the need for careful planning prior to travel. Gamma globulin is not a vaccination but a ready-made antibody which has proven successful in reducing the chances of contracting infectious hepatitis (hepatitis A). Because it may interfere with the development of other immunities, it should not be given until at least 10 days after administration of the last vaccine. It should be administered as close to departure as possible because of its relatively short protection period – normally about six months.

*Polio* This has been wiped out in Colombia, but is endemic in Brazil, where recent outbreaks have been reported in the southern states. Westerners will usually have had an oral polio vaccine while at school, but you should undertake a booster course if more than 10 years have elapsed since your last vaccination.

*Tetanus* Most people in developed countries have been vaccinated against this disease at school age. Boosters are necessary every 10 years and are recommended as a matter of course.

*Typhoid* Protection lasts for three years and is useful if you are travelling for longer periods in rural tropical areas. The vaccination consists of two injections, taken four weeks apart, so you have to think well ahead, especially if you plan on having a gamma globulin shot as well (see above). You may get some side effects, such as pain at the injection site, fever, headache and a general feeling of being unwell.

*Yellow Fever* Protection lasts 10 years and is recommended for all travel in South America. You usually have to go to a special yellow fever vaccination centre. Vaccination isn't recommended during pregnancy, but if you must travel to a high-risk area, it is probably better to take the vaccine.

## Basic Rules

Paying attention to what you eat and drink is the most important health rule. Stomach upsets are the most common travel health problem, but most of these upsets will be relatively minor. Don't be paranoid about trying local food – it's part of the travel experience and you wouldn't want to miss it.

**Water & Drinks** The tap water in Bogotá and several other large cities is safe to drink, although bottled water and soft drinks are easily available. Outside the big cities, tap water isn't always drinkable. If you don't know for certain whether or not the water is safe, don't drink it. This goes for ice as well.

In rural areas, take care with fruit juice, particularly if water may have been added. Milk should be treated with suspicion because it is often unpasteurised. Boiled milk is fine if it is kept hygienically, and yoghurt is always good. Hot tea or coffee should also be OK, since the water will probably have been boiled. Even in the most remote villages bottled drinks are almost always available.

The problems begin when you venture into wilderness areas, where there are no Coca Cola stands. One solution is to bring drinkable water with you; the other is to purify the local water. The simplest way of purifying water is to boil it thoroughly; technically this means boiling it for 10 minutes. Remember that at higher altitudes, water boils at lower temperatures, so germs are less likely to be killed.

Simple filtering will not remove all dangerous organisms, so if you cannot boil suspect water, it should be treated chemically. Chlorine tablets (Puritabs, Steritabs or other brand names) will kill many but not all pathogens. Iodine is an effective water purifier and is available in tablet form (such as Potable Aqua), but follow the directions carefully and remember that too much iodine is harmful. If you can't find tablets, tincture of iodine (2%) or iodine crystals can be used.

**Food** Salads and fruit should, theoretically at least, be washed with purified water, or peeled whenever possible. Ice cream is usually OK, but beware of street vendors selling ice cream that has melted and been refrozen. Thoroughly cooked food is safe but not if it has been left to cool or if it has been reheated. Take great care with shellfish or fish, and avoid undercooked meat. If a place looks clean and well run and if the vendor also looks clean and healthy, then the food is probably all right. In general, places that are packed with locals will be fine, while empty restaurants are questionable.

**Nutrition** If your diet is poor or you're travelling hard and fast and missing meals, you can soon start to lose weight and place your health at risk.

Make sure your diet is well balanced. Eggs, beans, lentils and nuts are all safe sources of protein. Fruit you can peel (bananas, oranges or mandarins, for example) is always safe and a good source of vitamins. Eat sufficient rice and bread. Remember that although food is generally safer if it is cooked well, overcooked food loses much of its nutritional value. If your diet isn't well balanced or if your food intake is insufficient, it's a good idea to take vitamin and iron pills.

Many of Colombia's regions are hot, so make sure you drink enough – don't rely on thirst alone to tell you when to drink. Not needing to urinate or dark-yellow urine are signs of dehydration. Always carry a water bottle with you on trips off the beaten path. On the other hand, excessive drinking can cause excessive sweating. This can lead to a loss of salt resulting in muscle cramps. If you find that your sweat is not salty, add more salt than usual to your food.

**Everyday Health** Normal body temperature is 37°C (98.6°F); more than 2°C higher is a 'high' fever. A normal adult pulse rate is 60 to 80 beats per minute (children 80 to 100, babies 100 to 140). You should know how to take a temperature and a pulse rate. As a general rule, the pulse increases about 20 beats per minute for each °C rise in fever.

Respiration rate can also be an indicator of health or illness. Count the number of breaths per minute: between 12 and 20 is normal for adults and older children (up to 30 for younger children, 40 for babies). People with a high fever or serious respira-

tory illness (like pneumonia) breathe more quickly than normal. More than 40 shallow breaths a minute usually means pneumonia.

Many health problems can be avoided by taking care of yourself. Wash your hands frequently – it's quite easy to contaminate your own food. Clean your teeth with purified water rather than water which has come straight from the river. Avoid extremes of temperature: keep out of the sun when it's hot, dress warmly when it's cold.

Colombia's topography means travel in the country is almost always up or down, from steamy lowlands to cold, windy highlands, or vice versa. If you travel by bus, the climate can change considerably within a couple of hours, so have appropriate clothes handy to avoid getting frozen solid and catching colds, coughs etc.

Some diseases can be avoided by dressing sensibly. Worm infections can be caught by walking barefoot, and dangerous coral cuts are likely if you walk over coral without shoes. Avoid insect bites by covering bare skin and using insect repellents or a mosquito net at night. Seek local advice: if you're told water is unsafe due to crocodiles or piranhas, obviously don't go in.

### Diseases of Insanitation

**Diarrhoea** Sooner or later, usually at the most inconvenient moment, diarrhoea makes its appearance on every trip. It's probably the most common illness among travellers. In general, it is not a serious problem, simply a reaction to a change of diet and lack of resistance to local strains of bacteria. A few rush toilet trips with no other symptoms is not indicative of dysentery, so don't panic and start stuffing yourself with pills.

Moderate diarrhoea, involving half a dozen loose movements in a day, is more of a nuisance, but still no reason to load up on antibiotics because they can do more harm than good. If the bacteria in your body build up immunity to the antibiotics, the drugs may not work when you really need them.

Dehydration is the main danger with diarrhoea, particularly for children, so fluid replenishment is the number one treatment. Weak black tea with a little sugar, soda water, or soft drinks allowed to go flat and diluted 50% with water are all good. The *aromáticas*, herbal teas which are widely available in Colombia, are probably the best.

If possible, don't eat, rest and avoid travelling. If you can't stand starving, keep to a light diet of dry toast, biscuits and plain rice, but stay away from sweets, fruit and dairy products.

Lomotil or Imodium can relieve the symptoms, although they do not actually cure the problem. Use these drugs only if absolutely necessary – for example, if you must travel – but don't take them if you have a high fever or are severely dehydrated.

If recovery doesn't come after a few days, and the symptoms persist or become more serious, it's probably time for antibiotics. These can be very useful in treating severe diarrhoea, especially if it is accompanied by nausea, vomiting, stomach cramps or mild fever. Ampicillin, a broad spectrum penicillin, is usually recommended. However, before you start using it, go to see a doctor to be tested, because the diarrhoea may be the symptom of other problems such as dysentery, giardia, cholera and so on.

**Dysentery** This serious illness is caused by contaminated food or water and usually shows up as severe diarrhoea, often with blood or mucus in the stool, and painful gut cramps. There are two kinds of dysentery: bacillary and amoebic.

Bacillary dysentery is characterised by rapid development; its typical symptoms are a high fever, acute diarrhoea, headache, vomiting and stomach pains. It is highly contagious. Since it is caused by bacteria, it responds well to antibiotics and it generally doesn't last more than a few days. Even if it's not treated by antibiotics, it will disappear pretty fast without further complications.

Amoebic dysentery is, as its name suggests, caused by amoebas (a parasite, not a bacteria). It takes longer to develop, usually has no fever or vomiting, but is a more serious illness. It is not a self-limiting disease: if left

untreated, it will persist and can recur and cause long-term damage.

A stool test is necessary to determine which kind of dysentery you have, so you should seek medical help. In case of an emergency, note that Tetracycline is the prescribed treatment for bacillary dysentery, whereas Metronidazole (Flagyl) is normally used for amoebic dysentery.

**Giardiasis** Caused by giardia, an intestinal parasite which is present in contaminated water, the symptoms of this disease include stomach cramps, nausea, a bloated stomach, headache, foul-smelling diarrhoea and frequent gas. Giardiasis can appear weeks after you have been exposed to the parasite. The symptoms may disappear for a few days and then return; this can go on for several weeks. Metronidazole is the recommended drug, but it should only be taken under medical supervision. Antibiotics are of no use.

**Hepatitis** There are seven strains of hepatitis, named after the first seven letters of the alphabet, and they are all caused by a virus which attacks the liver. Hepatitis A is the most common form of the disease and is spread by contaminated food or water. The symptoms appear between two and six weeks after contraction and include fever, chills, headache, fatigue, feelings of weakness, lack of appetite, and aches and pains. The most tell-tale bad signs are dark urine (no matter how much liquid you drink), light-coloured faeces, and conspicuously yellowish eyes. An infected person will also experience tenderness in the right side of the abdomen, where the liver is located.

You may seek medical advice but, in general, there is not much you can do apart from rest and low-fat diet. Stop smoking and drinking alcohol immediately. As soon as you discover the disease, you should be extremely careful not to give it to travelling companions or other people. Maintain strict personal hygiene and don't share any eating or drinking utensils.

The severity of the disease varies; sometimes it may last two or three weeks and give you only a few bad days, but it may last for several months with a few really bad weeks. The more rest and the better diet you have, the faster the disease will clear up.

If you contract hepatitis A during a short trip to South America, there's probably nothing better to do than to make arrangements to return home. If you can afford the time, however, the best cure is to stay in bed and only get up to go to the toilet. Arrange for somebody to bring you food and drinks if you're not travelling with a reliable companion. Keep to a diet rich in proteins and vitamins.

After two or three weeks, you should feel like living again; this is the time to start thinking about continuing your trip. Take it easy at first, and keep to your diet until your health returns to normal, which should take another two or three weeks. Forget alcohol and cigarettes for the next six months; your liver needs this long to completely recover.

How to guard against hepatitis? Theoretically, by avoiding contaminated food and water. Some cautious guidebooks give wise advice about not eating salads, drinking only boiled water, using your own eating utensils etc. It's easy to say but harder to do. Use common sense and don't get paranoid about it.

The best preventative measures against hepatitis A are the new Havrix vaccine or a jab of immune serum globulin (commonly called gamma globulin). Havrix provides long-term immunity (up to 10 years) but is more expensive than gamma globulin. The latter is not 100% effective but may at least mitigate the severity of an infection. Gamma globulin should be taken just before departure and, if your trip is a long one, booster shots are recommended every three or four months while you're away (beware of unsanitary needles). A gamma globulin jab is also recommended if you come in contact with an infected person; and if you come down with hepatitis, anyone who has been in recent contact with you should have the shot too.

Hepatitis B, which used to be called serum hepatitis, is spread through contact with infected bodily fluids, which may be transmitted through sexual contact, unsterilised needles or blood transfusions. Avoid having your ears pierced, tattoos done or getting injections in establishments where you have reasons to doubt their sanitary conditions. The incubation period of hepatitis B is between four and 24 weeks, which means that you may already be at home for several months before the symptoms appear. They are much the same as those of hepatitis A, except that they are more severe and may lead to irreparable liver damage or liver cancer.

Although there is no treatment for hepatitis B, an effective (but expensive) vaccine is available in most countries. The immunisation schedule requires two injections at least a month apart, followed by a third dose five months after the second. Gamma globulin is not effective against hepatitis B.

Hepatitis C is similar to B but less common. Hepatitis D is also similar to B and always occurs in conjunction with it; its occurrence is currently limited to drug users. Hepatitis E is similar to A and is spread in the same manner, by contaminated water or food. Late in 1994 a new hepatitis virus was detected and called hepatitis F, and only a couple of months later US scientists discovered hepatitis G. Tests are available for the A, B, C and D strains but they are expensive. Travellers shouldn't be too paranoid about the proliferation of hepatitis strains; they are fairly rare (so far), and following the precautions for strains A and B should be all that's necessary to avoid them.

**Cholera** This disease is transmitted orally by the ingestion of contaminated food or water. The symptoms, which appear one to three days after infection, consist of a sudden onset of acute diarrhoea with 'rice water' stools, vomiting, muscular cramps, and extreme weakness. You need medical attention but your first concern should be rehydration. Drink as much water as you can – if it refuses to stay down, keep drinking anyway. If there is likely to be a considerable delay in getting medical treatment, begin a course of Tetracycline, but it should not be administered to children or pregnant women.

The cholera vaccination is not very effective, to say the least: protection is estimated (depending on the authority) at between 20% and 80% efficiency. It only lasts for a maximum of six months and can produce some side effects. It's probably worth getting vaccinated anyway because there have been outbreaks of cholera over the last three years in various South American countries, including Colombia, Peru, Venezuela, and Brazil. Fortunately, they haven't reached epidemic proportions.

**Typhoid** This is another gut infection which travels via contaminated water and food. Vaccination against typhoid is not 100% effective and, since it is one of the most dangerous infections, medical attention is necessary if you are infected. Early symptoms are similar to those of many other travellers' illnesses – you may feel as though you have a bad cold or the flu combined with a headache, a sore throat and a fever. The fever rises a little each day until it exceeds 40°C, while the pulse rate slows – unlike a normal fever where the pulse increases. These symptoms may be accompanied by vomiting, diarrhoea or constipation.

In the second week, the high fever and slow pulse continue and a few pink spots may appear on the body. Trembling, delirium, weakness, weight loss and dehydration set in. If there are no further complications, the fever and other symptoms will slowly fade during the third week. Medical attention is essential, however, since typhoid is extremely infectious and possible complications include pneumonia or peritonitis (burst appendix).

When feverish, the patient should be kept cool. Watch for dehydration. The recommended antibiotic is Chloramphenicol, but Ampicillin causes fewer side effects.

**Viral Gastroenteritis** As the name implies, this disease is caused by a virus, not by a bacteria. It is characterised by stomach cramps, diarrhoea, and sometimes by vomiting and a slight fever. All you can do is rest and drink lots of fluids.

## Insect-Borne Diseases

**Malaria** The disease is caused by a blood parasite which is transmitted by mosquitoes. Only the females spread the disease, but you can contract it through a single bite from an insect carrying the parasite. Malaria sporozites enter the bloodstream and travel to the liver where they mature, multiply and infect the red blood cells. This process takes between one and five weeks. Only when the infected cells re-enter the bloodstream and burst do the dramatic symptoms begin. They include (in this order) gradual loss of appetite, malaise, weakness, alternating shivers and hot flushes, diarrhoea, periodic high fever, severe headache, vomiting and hallucinations. Diagnosis is confirmed by a blood test and the treatment has to begin immediately; otherwise the disease can be fatal.

A vaccine against malaria has recently been invented by a Colombian scientist, Manuel Elkin Patarroyo. It's still in the experimental stage and, so far, hasn't been introduced on the market, but commercialisation is expected soon. Check with the World Health Organisation (WHO) because Patarroyo granted them the exclusive rights for the production and distribution of the vaccine.

The value of protection provided by a range of prophylactics is a subject of debate. They are not always effective because new drug-resistant strains of malaria are constantly being discovered. They may also cause side effects, sometimes dangerous ones and occasionally even fatal. Lastly, they may obscure diagnosis when the disease eventually develops, thus leading to improper treatment. Some doctors openly state that antimalarial drugs do not actually prevent the disease but only suppress its symptoms.

The problem in recent years has been the emergence of increasing resistance to commonly used antimalarials like chloroquine, maloprim and proguanil. Newer drugs such as mefloquine (Lariam) and doxycycline (Vibramycin, Doryx) are often recommended for chloroquine and multidrug-resistant areas. Expert advice should be sought because there are many factors to consider when deciding on the type of antimalarial medication, including the region to be visited, the risk of exposure to malaria-carrying mosquitoes, your current medical condition, and your age and pregnancy status. It is also important to discuss the side-effects of the medication, so you can work out the risk to benefit ratio. Be sure of the correct dosage of the medication prescribed to you. Some people inadvertently have taken weekly medication (chloroquine) on a daily basis, with disastrous effects. While discussing dosages for prevention of malaria, it is often advisable to include the dosages required for treatment, especially if your trip is through a high-risk area that is isolated from medical care.

Antimalarial prophylactics are normally begun two weeks before reaching the malarial area. They should be continued during the course of travel and for several weeks after. You can get antimalarial tablets in virtually every pharmacy in Colombia.

Primary prevention should always be to avoid mosquitoes. The mosquitoes that transmit malaria bite from dusk to dawn and during this period travellers are advised to:

- Wear light coloured clothing
- Wear long trousers and long-sleeved shirts
- Use mosquito repellents containing the compound DEET on exposed areas
- Avoid highly scented perfumes or aftershaves
- Use a mosquito net – it may be worth bringing your own.

Mosquitoes are prevalent throughout Colombia and can live up to about 3000 metres. However, the anopheles, ie those which can transmit the disease, are mostly confined to lowland areas. For example, you will see mosquitoes in Bogotá but the chances of catching malaria there are next to nil. The risk of infection is highest in steamy rainforest regions such as Chocó and the Amazon. Some parts of the Caribbean coast and Los Llanos are also risky areas, particularly so during the rainy season.

Of the four main existing types of malaria, two (vivax and falciparum) can be contracted in Colombia, the latter being the most dangerous one; it attacks the brain and is responsible for the very serious cerebral malaria.

The symptoms of malaria only appear several weeks after contraction, which may lead to confusion in diagnosis. By the time symptoms appear, you may be home and local doctors will not be looking for such an exotic disease. Make sure you give your doctor details of your trip.

**Yellow Fever** This is found in most of South America, except for the Andean highlands and the southern part of the continent. This viral disease, which is transmitted by mosquitoes, first manifests itself as fever, headaches, abdominal pain and vomiting. There may appear to be a brief recovery before it progresses into its more severe stages, including possible liver failure. There is no treatment apart from keeping the fever as low as possible and avoiding dehydration. The yellow fever vaccination gives good protection for 10 years, and is highly recommended for every person travelling on the continent.

**Typhus** This is spread by ticks, mites and lice. It begins as a severe cold followed by a fever, chills, headaches, muscle pains and a body rash. There is often a large and painful sore at the site of the bite, and nearby lymph nodes become swollen and painful.

Trekkers may be at risk from cattle or wild game ticks. Seek local advice about whether or not ticks are present in the area and check yourself carefully after walking in suspect areas. A strong insect repellent can help; serious walkers should consider treating their boots and trousers with repellent.

### Diseases Spread by People & Animals
**Tetanus** This potentially fatal disease is difficult to treat but is easily prevented by immunisation. Tetanus occurs when a wound becomes infected by a germ which lives in human and animal faeces. Clean all cuts, punctures and animal bites. Tetanus is also

known as lockjaw because the first symptom may be a stiffening of the jaw and neck or difficulty swallowing; this can be followed by painful convulsions of the jaw and body.

**Rabies** Rabies is present in most of South America. It is caused by a bite or scratch by an infected animal. Bats and dogs are the most notorious carriers. Any bite, scratch or lick from a mammal should be cleaned immediately and thoroughly. Scrub the site with soap and running water and then clean it with an alcohol solution. If there is any possibility that the animal is infected, medical help should be sought. Even if the animal is not rabid, all bites should be treated carefully because they can become infected or result in tetanus. Avoid any animal that appears to be foaming at the mouth or acting strangely.

If you are bitten, try to capture the offending animal so that it can be tested. If that's impossible, you must assume the animal is rabid. Rabies is almost always fatal if untreated, so don't take the risk. The rabies virus incubates slowly in its victim, so while medical attention isn't urgent, it shouldn't be delayed.

The treatment consists of a series of injections (usually seven) around the navel over consecutive days. A rabies vaccination is now available and should be considered if you intend to spend a lot of time around animals.

**Worms** These parasites are common in most humid, tropical areas. They can be present on unwashed vegetables or in undercooked meat, or you can pick them up through your skin by walking barefoot. Infestations may not show up for some time and although they are generally not serious, they can cause further health problems if left untreated. A stool test on your return home is not a bad idea if you think you may have contracted them. Once the test pinpoints the problem, medication is usually available over the counter and the treatment is easy and short.

The most common form you're likely to contract are hookworms. They are usually caught by walking barefoot on infected soil. The worms bore through the skin, attach themselves to the inner wall of the intestine and proceed to suck your blood, resulting in abdominal pain and sometimes anaemia.

**Fungal Infections** Hot-weather fungal infections are most likely to occur between the toes or fingers or around the groin. The infection is spread by infected animals or humans; you may contract it by walking barefoot in damp areas, for example.

To prevent fungal infections wear loose, comfortable clothes, avoid artificial fibres, wash frequently and dry thoroughly. Use thongs (flip-flops) while taking a shower in bathrooms of cheap hotels.

If you become infected, wash the infected area daily with a disinfectant or medicated soap, and rinse and dry well. Apply an antifungal powder like the widely available Tinaderm. Try to expose the infected area to air or sunlight as much as possible, and wash all towels and underwear in hot water and change them often.

**Syphilis & Gonorrhoea** Sexual contact with an infected partner can result in you contracting a number of diseases. While abstinence is 100% effective, the use of a condom lessens the risk of infection considerably.

The most common sexually transmitted diseases are gonorrhoea and syphilis, which in men first appear as sores, blisters or rashes around the genitals and discharge or pain when urinating. Symptoms may be less marked or not present at all in women. Syphilis' symptoms eventually disappear but the disease continues and may cause severe problems in later years. Gonorrhoea and syphilis are treatable with antibiotics.

**HIV & AIDS** Like almost everywhere else, these diseases have become a concern in Colombia. Although there are no credible statistics, it's estimated that at least 100,000 Colombians are HIV-positive. HIV (Human

Immunodeficiency Virus), is likely to develop into AIDS (Acquired Immune Deficiency Syndrome). It is impossible to detect the HIV-positive status of an otherwise healthy-looking person without a blood test. Although in the West the disease is most commonly spread through intravenous drug use and male homosexual activity, in South America it is transmitted primarily through sexual contact between heterosexuals.

HIV/AIDS can also be contracted through infected blood transfusions; and you should be aware that most developing countries cannot afford to screen blood for transfusions. The virus may also be picked up through injection with an unsterilised needle. Acupuncture, tattooing and ear or nose piercing are other potential dangers.

There is currently no cure for AIDS.

### Climate & Altitude-Related Illnesses

**Sunburn** The sun's rays in tropical zones are more direct and concentrated than in temperate zones. In highland areas, such as the Andean regions, you will be additionally exposed to hazardous UV rays and can become sunburnt surprisingly quickly, even through cloud. Use a sunscreen and take extra care to cover areas which are not normally exposed to sunlight – for example, your feet. A hat provides added protection, and sunglasses will prevent eye irritation (especially if you wear contact lenses). Fair-skinned people should be particularly careful about sunburn.

**Prickly Heat** This is an itchy rash caused by excessive perspiration trapped under the skin. It usually strikes people who have just arrived in a hot climate and whose pores have not yet opened sufficiently to cope with the increased sweating. Frequent baths and application of talcum powder will help relieve the itchiness.

**Heat Exhaustion** Serious dehydration or salt deficiency can lead to heat exhaustion. Salt deficiency, which can be brought on by diarrhoea or vomiting, is characterised by fatigue, lethargy, headaches, giddiness and muscle cramps. Salt tablets may help. The best way to avoid heat exhaustion is by drinking lots of liquids and eating salty foods.

Anhydrotic heat exhaustion, caused by an inability to sweat, is quite rare. Unlike the other forms of heat exhaustion, it is likely to strike people who have been in a hot climate for some time, rather than newcomers.

**Heatstroke** This serious, sometimes fatal, condition can occur if the body's heat-regulating mechanism breaks down and the body temperature rises to dangerous levels. Long, continuous periods of exposure to high temperatures can leave you vulnerable to heatstroke. Alcohol intake and strenuous activity can increase chances of heatstroke, especially among new arrivals to a hot climate.

Symptoms include minimal sweating, a high body temperature (39°C to 40°C), and a general feeling of being unwell. The skin may become flushed and red. Severe throbbing headaches, decreased coordination, and aggressive or confused behaviour may be signs of heatstroke. Eventually, the victim may become delirious and go into convulsions. Get the victim out of the sun, if possible, remove clothing, cover with a wet towel and fan continually. Seek medical help as soon as possible.

**Cold** Too much cold is just as dangerous as too much heat, and may lead to hypothermia. Many of Colombia's regions are highlands, where hypothermia is a potential threat.

Hypothermia occurs when the body loses heat faster than it can produce it. It is caused by exhaustion and exposure to cold, wet or windy weather. It is surprisingly easy to progress from being very cold to dangerously cold due to a combination of wind, wet clothing, fatigue and hunger, even if the air temperature is well above freezing.

It is best to dress in layers; silk, wool and some of the new artificial fibres are all good insulating materials. A hat is important because a lot of heat is lost through the head. A strong, waterproof outer layer is essential, and keeping dry is vital. Carry food containing simple sugars to generate heat quickly, and lots of fluid to drink.

Symptoms of hypothermia include exhaustion, numb skin (particularly toes and fingers), shivering, slurred speech, irrational or violent behaviour, lethargy, stumbling, dizzy spells, muscle cramps and violent bursts of energy.

To treat hypothermia, get the sufferer out of the wind or rain, remove their clothing if it's wet and replace it with dry, warm garments. Give them hot liquids – not alcohol – and easily digestible food. This should be enough for the early stages of hypothermia, but if it has gone further, it may be necessary to place sufferers in a sleeping bag and get in with them in order to provide as much warmth as possible. If no improvement is noticed within a few minutes, seek help, but don't leave the victim alone while doing so. The body heat of another person is more important in the short term than medical attention.

**Altitude Sickness** Known locally as *soroche,* Altitude Sickness, and its more serious form, Acute Mountain Sickness (AMS), occur at high altitudes and in extreme cases can be fatal. They are caused by ascending to high altitudes so quickly that the body does not have time to adapt to the lower oxygen concentration in the atmosphere. Light symptoms can appear at altitudes as low as 2500 metres, and they become increasingly severe the higher up you go. Most people are affected to some extent at altitudes between 3500 and 4500 metres.

Colombia has a very rough topography. Some roads cross the cordilleras at well over 3000 metres, and villages at these altitudes are not unusual. If you plan on trekking in the mountains, you will probably go much higher. Some people suffer mild symptoms flying to Bogotá (2600 metres) from low-lying areas, but these usually pass quickly.

The best way to minimise the risk of altitude sickness is to ascend slowly, to increase liquid intake and to eat meals containing energy-rich carbohydrates.

Even after acclimatisation, you may still have trouble if you visit high-altitude areas. Headaches, nausea, dizziness, a dry cough, breathlessness and loss of appetite are the most frequent symptoms. As long as they remain mild, there's no reason to panic, but the ascent should be halted and the sufferer watched closely and given plenty of fluids and rest. If the symptoms become more pronounced or there is no improvement after a few hours, descend to a lower altitude.

Often a descent of a few hundred metres is enough to provide considerable relief. Descend further and rest for a day or two. Don't take risks with altitude sickness; many people have died because they have ignored the early symptoms and pressed on to higher altitudes.

Altitude sickness is completely unpredictable – youth, fitness or experience at high altitudes are no protection. Even people who have had no problems at high altitudes before may suddenly suffer altitude sickness at relatively low altitudes.

### Cuts, Bites & Stings

**Cuts & Scratches** In warm, moist, tropical lowlands, skin punctures can easily become infected and may have difficulty healing. Even a small cut or scratch can become infected and this can lead to serious problems.

The best treatment for cuts is to cleanse the affected area frequently with soap and water and to apply Mercurochrome or an antiseptic cream. Whenever possible, avoid using bandages, which keep wounds moist and encourage the growth of bacteria. If the wound becomes tender and inflamed, use a mild, broad-spectrum antibiotic. Remember that bacterial immunity to certain antibiotics may build up, so it's not wise to take these medicines indiscriminately or as a preventative measure.

Coral cuts are notoriously slow to heal because coral injects a weak venom into the wound. Avoid coral cuts by wearing shoes when walking on reefs.

**Bites & Stings** The plethora of ants, gnats, mosquitoes, bees, spiders, flies and other exotic creatures living in Colombia means that you may experience a variety of bites and stings. Some are more dangerous or annoying than others, but it's best to protect yourself from bites altogether. Cover your skin, especially from dusk to dawn when many insects, including malaria-transmitting mosquitoes, feed. The problem is more serious in rural areas than in cities, and dense rainforests are probably the worst.

Wear long-sleeved shirts and long trousers, instead of T-shirts and shorts, and wear shoes instead of sandals or thongs. Use insect repellent on exposed skin and, if necessary, spray it over your clothes. Sleep under a mosquito net if you are outdoors or if your hotel room does not have a sufficiently strong fan. Burning incense also lowers the risk. Good repellents, mosquito nets and incense are available in Colombia.

If you are bitten, avoid scratching because this easily opens bites and may cause them to become infected. Use creams and lotions which alleviate itching and deal with infections. They are sold in local pharmacies.

Bee and wasp stings are usually more painful than dangerous. Calamine lotion will give some relief and ice packs will reduce the pain and swelling.

Body lice and scabies mites are common, but shampoos and creams are available to eliminate them. In addition to hair and skin, clothing and bedding should be washed thoroughly to prevent further infestation.

Bedbugs love to live in the dirty mattresses and bedding of seedy hotels. If you see spots of blood on bedclothes or on the wall around the bed, look for another hotel. Bedbugs leave itchy bites; calamine lotion may help alleviate them.

Leeches may be present in damp rainforests. They attach themselves to your skin and suck your blood. Trekkers may get them on their legs or in their boots. Salt or a lighted cigarette end will make them fall off.

Do not pull them off because the bite is more likely to become infected and the head of the leech can remain in your body. An insect repellent may keep them away.

Vaseline, alcohol or oil will persuade a tick to let go. You should always check your body if you have been walking through a tick-infested area because ticks can spread typhus. They like the warmest parts of the body and often go to the gentital area or the armpits, so be sure to inspect all of these areas.

It's rather unlikely that you'll get stung by a scorpion or a spider, but if you do, it may be severely painful (though rarely more than that). They tend to shelter in shoes and clothing, so check them before putting them on. Also, check your bedding or sleeping bag before going to sleep.

**Snakebite** There's only a small chance of being bitten by a snake in Colombia, but you should take precautions.

To minimise the chances of being bitten, wear boots, socks and long trousers when walking through undergrowth. A good pair of canvas gaiters will further protect your legs. Don't put your hands into holes and crevices, and be careful when collecting firewood. Check shoes, clothing and sleeping bags before use.

Snakebites do not cause instantaneous death and antivenenes are available. If someone is bitten, it's vital that you identify the snake, or at the very least, be able to describe it.

Keep the victim calm and still, wrap the bitten limb tightly, as you would a sprain, then attach a splint to immobilise it. Seek medical help immediately and, if possible, bring the dead snake along for identification. Don't attempt to catch the snake if there is a chance of being bitten again. Tourniquets and sucking out the poison are now comprehensively discredited.

If you plan on seriously trekking in the wilderness, antivenenes for some local snakes (but not all) can be bought in Bogotá. Antivenenes must be kept at a low temperature, otherwise their efficiency quickly decreases. It's a good idea to carry a field guide with photographs and detailed descriptions of possible perpetrators.

## Motion Sickness

If you are prone to motion sickness, try to choose a place that minimises disturbance – near the wing on an aircraft, midship on a boat or between the front and the middle of a bus. Eating lightly before and during a trip will reduce the chances of motion sickness. Fresh air almost always helps, but reading or cigarette smoking makes matters worse.

Commercial motion-sickness preparations, which can cause drowsiness, have to be taken before the trip; if you're already feeling sick, it's too late. Dramamine tablets, one of the most popular medications, should be taken three hours before departure. Ginger can be used as a natural preventative and is available in capsule form.

## Women's Health

**Gynaecological Problems** Poor diet, lowered resistance due to antibiotic use or even contraceptive pills, can lead to vaginal infections when travelling in hot climates. Keep the genital area clean, and wear skirts or loose-fitting trousers and cotton underwear to help prevent infections.

Yeast infections, characterised by an itchy rash and discharge, can be treated with a vinegar or lemon-juice douche or with yoghurt. Nystatin suppositories are the usual medical prescription. Trichomonas is a more serious infection; symptoms include a discharge and a burning sensation when urinating. Male sexual partners must also be treated, and if a vinegar-water douche is not effective, medical attention should be sought. Flagyl is the most frequently prescribed drug.

**Pregnancy** Most miscarriages occur during the first three months of pregnancy, so this is the most risky time to travel. The last three months should also be spent within reasonable reach of good medical care because serious problems can develop at this stage. Pregnant women should avoid all unnecessary medication, but vaccinations should still be taken when possible. Additional care should be taken to prevent illness and particular attention should be paid to diet and nutrition.

## Back Home

Be aware of illnesses after you return home; take note of odd or persistent symptoms of any kind, get a check-up and remember to give your physician a complete travel history. Most doctors in temperate climates will not be looking for unusual tropical diseases. If you have been travelling in malarial areas, have yourself tested for the disease.

## Health Glossary

This basic glossary of illnesses and other health-related terms may be useful. See the Language section in the Facts about the Country chapter for emergency terms and phrases.

AIDS – *SIDA (síndrome de inmunodeficiencia adquirida)*
allergy – *alergia*
antibiotic – *antibiótico*
bite – *picadura* (insect, snake) *mordedura* (dog)
blood – *sangre*
blood test – *examen de sangre*
cold or flu – *gripa, resfriado*
cholera – *cólera*
condom – *condón, preservativo*
cough – *tos*
cramp (menstrual) – *cólico*
cramp (muscular) – *calambre*
cut – *cortadura, cortada*
diarrhoea – *diarrea*
disease – *enfermedad*
dizziness – *mareo*
dysentery – *disentería*
earache – *otitis, dolor de oído*
fatigue – *fatiga, cansancio*
fever – *fiebre*
headache – *dolor de cabeza*
heart attack – *ataque cardíaco, infarto*
hepatitis – *hepatitis*
health – *salud*
heatstroke – *insolación*
HIV – *VIH (virus de inmunodeficiencia humana)*
injection – *inyección*
insurance – *seguro*
itching – *ardor*
malaria – *malaria*
medication – *droga, medicamento, remedio*

miscarriage – *aborto*
nausea –*náusea*
pain – *dolor*
penicillin – *penicilina*
contraceptive pills – *pastillas anticonceptivas*
pneumomia – *pulmonía*
polio – *polio*
pregnancy – *embarazo*
prescription – *receta, fórmula*
rabies – *rabia*
rash – *escozor, rasquiña*
stomach – *estómago*
symptom – *síntoma*
syringe – *jeringa*
sore throat – *dolor de garganta*
sunburn – *quemadura de sol*
tablets – *pastillas*
tetanum – *tétano*
toothache – *dolor de muelas*
typhoid – *fiebre tifoidea*
vaccination – *vacuna*
vomiting – *vómito*
weakness – *debilidad*
wound – *herida*
yellow fever – *fiebre amarilla*

## WOMEN TRAVELLERS

Colombia is very much a 'man's country'. Machismo and sexism are palpable throughout society: from the level of the family, right up to the top government ranks. The dominant Catholic church with its conservative attitude towards women doesn't help matters. In this context, it's not difficult to imagine how a gringa travelling by herself is regarded.

Women travellers will attract more curiosity, attention and advances from local men than they would from men in the West. Many Colombian men will stare at women, use endearing terms, make comments on their physical appearance and, in some cases, try to make physical contact. It is the Colombian way of life, and Colombian men would not understand if someone told them that their behaviour constituted sexual harassment. On the contrary, they would argue that they are just paying the woman a flattering compliment.

Gringas are often seen as exotic and challenging conquests. Local males will immediately pick them out in a crowd and use a combination of body language and flirtatiousness to capture their attention. These advances may often be light-hearted, but can sometimes be more direct and rude. In either form, women may find them annoying. Men in large cities, especially when they are in male-only groups, will generally display more bravado and be more insistent than those in small villages.

The best way to deal with unwanted attention is usually to ignore it. Maintain your self-confidence and assertiveness and don't let macho behaviour disrupt your holiday. Dressing modestly may lessen the chances of you being the object of macho interest, or at least make you less conspicuous to the local peacocks.

Travelling with a man solves much of the problem because local men will see your male companion as a protector and a deterrent. Travelling with another woman will make things easier; the harassment is likely to continue, but you will at least have the emotional support of your companion.

Harassment aside, women travelling alone face more risks than men on their own. Women are often prime targets for bagsnatchers and assault. Rape is a potential danger in all countries, but female travellers need not walk around Colombia in a constant state of fear. Just be conscious of your surroundings and aware of situations that could be potentially dangerous. Shabby barrios, solitary streets and beaches, and all places considered male territory, such as bars, sports matches, mines and galleras should be considered risky. Do not hitchhike alone.

There isn't a wide network of women's support services in Colombia, but in Bogotá you can get some information on what's available from Centro de Información y Recursos para la Mujer Pro Mujer (☎ 245 1678, 245 0563), Avenida 39 (Calle 41) No 19-23, or the Casa de la Mujer (☎ 248 2469), Carrera 18 No 59-60.

## DANGERS & ANNOYANCES

Colombia is not the safest of countries. Don't expect to be fleeced by thieves or attacked by robbers the moment you enter the country but you should be on your guard and know something about how they operate.

This section covers a variety of potential dangers and may look alarming, but don't panic; the intention is not to frighten you by listing how many bad things can happen to you, but to demonstrate how you can prevent mishap.

While travelling, keep an eye on the current guerrilla movements, so you don't get caught in the crossfire. The local press is a good source of information. Unfortunately, certain regions of Colombia (parts of the Amazon basin, Los Llanos, Urabá, Magdalena Medio and the Sierra Nevada de Santa Marta) are becoming off limits for secure travel.

## Predeparture Precautions

The most important rule when packing is to take only those items which you are prepared to lose. Try to take only used or cheap items. Take as little as possible, because the less you carry with you, the less you have to lose. Don't bring jewellery, chains, expensive watches or anything flashy – this will only increase the chances of robbery. Don't bring anything of such sentimental value that its loss would cause significant grief. If you insist on taking an expensive item (such as a camera), try to make sure it's a standard model which is easy to replace.

The only guarantee of replacement is to have travel insurance. A good policy is essential for two reasons: it gives you psychological comfort while travelling (because you know that a loss won't ruin you or the trip); and it gives you the actual security of replacement if something is lost (touch wood). Loss through violence or petty theft is always a stressful experience, but if you have insurance and follow the advice above, you'll get through it with less trauma.

If you are careful about choosing what you take, you'll find there is only a handful of items which you really wouldn't like to lose, including money, documents, your passport and air-tickets. Keep these items as secure as possible (see the Accessories section which follows).

Take photocopies of your passport (the pages which show passport number, name, photograph, location where issued, expiration date and visas) and your airline tickets; write down the details and numbers of travellers' cheques, credit cards, contact addresses etc. Keep one copy with you, one with your belongings and another with your travelling companion.

Don't take your original address/phone book (especially if it is the only copy); instead make copies of the phone numbers and addresses you are likely to use during the trip. Take notes of the serial numbers of your camera, lenses, camcorder and any other pieces of high-tech gear you'll be taking with you, and carry the copy with you.

Take most of your money in travellers' cheques and credit cards, leaving only an emergency amount in cash (preferably US dollars). Keep a record of the date when, and the place where, you purchased your cheques – this information may be necessary if you need to report their loss or theft. Make sure you know the number to call if you lose your credit card, and be quick to cancel it if it's lost or stolen.

Cabling money is time-consuming, difficult and expensive. You must know the name and address of both the bank sending (record this and keep this with your documents) and the bank receiving the money.

Travelling with a friend or two is theoretically always safer than travelling on one's own. An extra pair of eyes makes a lot of difference.

## Accessories

It's best if your backpack is fitted with double zippers, which can be secured with small combination locks. Padlocks are also good, but are easier to pick. A thick backpack cover or modified canvas sack improves protection against pilfering, the planting of drugs, and general wear and tear. Double zippers on your day pack can be secured with safety pins which will make it harder for petty thieves to get at your belongings. Some cautious travellers deter razor-thieves by lining the inside of their day pack (and even their backpack) with lightweight wire mesh. A spare combination lock or padlock is useful for replacing the padlocks on your hotel door.

A swanky camera bag is not a good idea; take something less conspicuous. Many travellers carry their photographic equipment in day packs. If you have a choice, bring a plain, sober day pack rather than one which is fluorescent orange or purple.

Various types of money belt are available. These can be worn around the waist, neck or shoulder. Those made of leather or cotton are more comfortable than the synthetic variety. Money belts are only useful if worn under clothing – pouches worn outside clothing attract attention and are easy prey. Determined thieves are wise to conventional money belts. Some travellers also sew cloth pouches into their trousers or other items of clothing. Other methods include belts with a concealed zipper compartment and bandages or pouches worn around the leg.

If you wear glasses, secure them with an elastic strap to prevent them falling off and breaking, and to deter petty theft.

## Precautions in Colombia

Theft and robbery are the most common travellers' dangers. Generally speaking, the problem is more serious in the largest cities; Bogotá, Medellín and Cali are the worst. The more rural the area, the quieter and safer it is. The favourite setting for *ladrones* (thieves) are crowded places such as markets, festivals and fiestas, bus terminals and buses (both long-distance and urban). The *atracadores* (robbers or muggers) prefer empty streets, especially at night.

The most common methods of theft are snatching your day pack, camera or watch, pickpocketing, or taking advantage of a moment's inattention to pick up your gear and run away – nothing particularly new, it just happens more frequently than in other countries. Some thieves are more innovative and will set up an opportune situation to separate you from your belongings. They may begin by making 'friends' with you, or pretend to be the police and demand to check

your belongings. The imagination of Colombians is infinite in this respect, so keep your wits about you.

The best way to prevent losing everything in one fell swoop is to distribute your valuables about your person and luggage. It's a good idea to carry a small emergency packet containing the important records of your passport, cheques, credit cards, tickets etc plus a US$100 bill. Keep the packet separately in a safe place. Some travellers sew it inside their trousers or skirt, but keep in mind that good-looking, expensive clothes are also appreciated by robbers.

Try not to attract the attention of thieves and muggers. Your dress is an important piece of information for them. One rule that works quite well in risky areas is 'the shabbier you look, the better', but use common sense and wear more decent clothes in less dangerous places. Your dress should be casual and inexpensive; it's best to follow local fashion.

If you carry a day pack, it's safer to wear it strapped to your front rather than on the back, so you can keep a constant eye on it. Many local youths now carry their packs that way, so you won't stand out of the crowd.

If you're in a bus terminal, restaurant, shop or any other public place and have to put your day pack down, put your foot through the strap. If you have a camera, don't wander around with it dangling over your shoulder or around your neck – keep it out of sight as much as possible. Your camera bag – if you've opted to bring one and carry it with you – will certainly fuel the appetite of thieves and robbers. In genuinely risky areas, you shouldn't carry your camera at all. If you have to, for whatever reason, camouflage it the best you can – an ordinary plastic bag from a local supermarket is one possible way to disguise it.

Get used to keeping small amounts of money, approximately equivalent to your expected daily expenditure, in a pocket or another easily accessible place. You can then pay your expenses without extracting a bundle of notes and attracting attention. This money is also useful in case you are assailed:

muggers can become very annoyed if you don't have anything for them, and they may then react unpredictably. The rest of your money should be well hidden, in a body pouch, money belt etc. Leave your wallet at home because it's an easy target for pickpockets.

Remember that a hotel (even a budget hospedaje) is almost always safer than the street of a large city. If you can, leave your money and valuables somewhere safe before walking around the city streets, particularly at night.

Behave confidently when you're on the street; don't look lost or stand with a blank expression in the middle of the street or in front of the bus terminal. Helpless-looking tourists are the favourite victims of thieves and robbers.

Before arriving in a new place, make sure you have a map or at least a rough idea about orientation. Try to plan your schedule so you don't arrive at night, and use a taxi if this seems the appropriate way to avoid walking through high-risk areas. Be vigilant and learn to move like a street-smart local.

Thieves often work in pairs or groups: one or more will distract you, while an accomplice does the deed. There are hundreds, if not thousands, of possible ways to distract you, and new scams are dreamt up every day. To name a few 'standards': someone 'accidentally' bumps into you (sometimes throwing you off balance); a group of strangers appear in front of you and greet you jovially as if you were lifelong friends; a woman drops her shopping bag right at your feet; a character spills something on your clothes or your day pack; several kids start a fight around you. Try not to get distracted – of course, it's easier said than done.

Keep your eyes open while you're leaving your hotel, bank, casa de cambio etc. Look around to see whether there is anyone watching you, and if you notice you're being followed or closely observed, let them understand that you are aware and alert.

If you happen to be in a crowded place (urban bus, market, bus terminal, busy street etc) keep a close eye on your pockets and day pack. Even if you have a cheap watch, it's better to keep it in your pocket rather than on your wrist – it attracts attention.

On intercity bus journeys, put your backpack in the luggage compartment, where it will be relatively safe. Don't put your day pack or handbag on the floor or on the luggage rack – keep it under your arm next to you or, if you are with a companion, wedge it between the two of you. On long night bus rides, it is better if one of your party is awake.

Robbery is far more dangerous than theft. Armed hold-ups become more common every year and the large cities are particularly noted for them. The usual weapon is a knife, but guns are not unheard of. The assault usually goes something like this: you are stopped on the street by a man or, more often, a group of men; they show you a knife to be better understood and either ask for your money and valuables, or set about searching for themselves. Even if they don't show you a knife, you can take it for granted that they have one. It is best to give them what they are after. Don't try to escape or struggle – your chances are slim. The favourite places for robberies are slum areas, especially at night when there's nobody around. Unfortunately, hold-ups are now becoming more and more common in central districts during daylight hours.

Don't count on any help from other passengers or passers-by. A thief or robber can quietly walk away with your gear and nobody will stop them. This indifference is simply due to fear – both of robbers and of having to make a statement to the police. Sadly, this apathy is also shared by a large part of the police force, who rarely react if they see a thief running through the streets.

If you do get your passport and other valuables stolen, go to the police station to make a *denuncia*, a report. They will give you a copy which serves as a temporary identity document, and if you have insurance, you will need to present it in order to make a claim. See whether the copy they hand you is legible. The reports are produced on typing machines using several carbon copies. If you get the last one, it may be undecipherable, which could cause problems.

Don't expect your things to be found, because the police are unlikely to even try to do anything about it. They are seldom able to find stolen cars or aeroplanes (yes, it became popular to steal light planes for drug trafficking), so how can you expect something as small as your camera to be found.

I've heard of only one case of recovery in more than four years of living in Colombia. A friend was robbed of his cameras; he went looking for the robbers and finally found them. He then made heroic efforts to get the police to arrest the thieves, and when they finally did, and recovered his gear, it took over a month of wrestling with the police to get it back.

In the first edition of this guidebook, I included a couple of theft and robbery stories. One of them was:

Once, I met a foreigner travelling whose entire luggage was a small cardboard box. This is perhaps typical of Colombians, but not foreign tourists, so I asked the fellow about his peculiar 'backpack'. He said the bus he was on was hijacked and all the passengers lost their stuff. They were going by night bus from Cúcuta to Bogotá and, in the middle of nowhere, two gentlemen got up from their seats, approached the driver with revolvers and asked him kindly to turn off onto a rough road they pointed to. They drove a few km until they reached a truck where some accomplices were waiting. The robbers transferred all the luggage, not forgetting the passengers' money and valuables, slashed the tyres of the bus and disappeared into the night. I've heard of several more similar cases, all happening at night, usually on pullmans.

Unfortunately, bus robbery has been on the increase over the past few years. The robbers often don't bother to ride on the bus; they just set up a 'checkpoint' on the road and stop passing vehicles of their choice. It's not uncommon for them to wear army clothes. They also seem to have become more 'efficient', concentrating essentially on money, jewellery and other easy-to-pinpoint valuables, ignoring the main luggage because it is too time-consuming to inspect and too heavy to carry away.

The attacks on buses have been mostly confined to certain areas and particular routes, including the notorious Pasto-Popayán road, but they are spreading to other regions. So far, the robbers have mainly targeted night buses. It's wise to travel during the day.

Another story in the previous edition went like this:

A couple took a taxi from the bus terminal in Bogotá to the centre. When they stopped at one of the traffic lights, the engine died. The driver tried to start it again but without success. He then asked the passengers to push the taxi, which they kindly did. The engine started and the taxi vanished with their backpacks on board. The tourists managed to note down the registration number and reported it to the police but there was no such number in the register book.

The taxi transport at Bogotá's bus terminal is now well organised and is safe, but I've heard similar stories occurring elsewhere. Never put yourself in a situation where you are separated from your luggage, even during the loading and unloading of the taxi. Don't get in a taxi if the driver has a companion. This is becoming popular nowadays because taxi drivers prefer to have the company of a friend or a family member (particularly at night) for their own security. However, this may also mean insecurity for you.

In the heart of Bogotá, usually on the Carrera Séptima, the following is a common scenario:

A man approaches you asking for directions or something else to make contact; he says that he is from some other Latin American country. Soon, a well-dressed fellow appears, he guesses immediately that both of you are foreigners, shows his 'police' document (a very good fake) and tells a story about a drugs check or something, asking you to show your documents, money etc. Your *amigo latino* turns out his pockets without any hesitation and hands everything over to 'the policeman', who checks it and gives it back. Now it's your turn...

This example also comes from the previous edition and doesn't need any update: apparently the same men and their pupils perform the same old trick.

## Police

Colombian police have a mixed reputation. Corruption, abuse of power, use of undue authority – among other things – are frequently reported by the media. The high crime rate, violence, drug trafficking and the guerrilla insurgency doesn't make the police's job easy, and consequently it doesn't turn officers into angels. With this in mind, it's best to stay a safe distance from them – although Colombian police are everywhere, so it's not that easy.

While travelling, you'll experience plenty of stops at *retenes*, police checkpoints. They stop and control the traffic passing through, mostly trucks and public buses. They check the identity documents of passengers and, sometimes, search their luggage. There are not many retenes on the main 'safe' routes, and the occasional searches are often superficial. However, on roads crossing contraband and guerrilla areas, checkpoints are more numerous and the searches more scrupulous. It can take half an hour to inspect the bus and all passengers are usually ordered off.

These routine road checks are boring and annoying but rarely more than that. The problem begins when you are travelling on your own into a remote area which hardly ever sees tourists. Moreover, if you take pictures, you never know what might result. The police in such areas may be extremely suspicious and unfriendly, and your unexpected arrival may be automatically attributed to guerrillas, drug trafficking or spying. This is where a letter of introduction comes in handy to establish the reason for your presence (see the Documents & Paperwork section at the beginning of this chapter).

If you happen to get involved with the police, keep calm and be polite, but not overly friendly. Don't get angry or hostile – it only works against you. Keep a sharp eye out when they check your gear because things sometimes 'disappear'.

Police ID checks in cities are not common but they do occur, so always have your passport with you. If you don't, you may end up at the police station. By law, you must carry your passport with you at all times. A certified photocopy of the passport is not a legal identity document, although some police officers may be satisfied with it.

Be wary of criminals masquerading as plain-clothes police. They generally operate in large cities and frontier areas. The most common scenario is that you are stopped on the street by a plain-clothes 'police officer' (or 'officers') who will identify himself with a fake ID, then request to inspect your passport, money and belongings. The reason given for the inspection could be suspicion of drug possession, searching for false dollars etc. If you hesitate, the 'officer' may try to persuade you to go with him to the police station in his vehicle or in a taxi (which are, of course, as genuine as the officer himself). Under no circumstances should you agree to the search or a lift. Call a uniformed police officer, if there happens to be one around. If not, insist on phoning a bona fide police station or going on foot; and preferably have a travelling companion or a witness accompany you.

On a more positive note, there's an increasing number of so-called tourist police. They are uniformed and easily recognisable by the *policía de turismo* labels printed on their arm bands. These forces have been formed and trained to attend to tourist needs and, accordingly, operate mainly in the popular tourist destinations such as Bogotá, Medellín, Cali, Cartagena and Popayán. They are usually friendlier and more helpful than ordinary police.

## Drugs

Colombia is the capital of cocaine. The industry is well developed and although laboratories are hidden out of sight, the white powder is available throughout the country. *Basuco*, the base from which cocaine is refined, is even more easily available than cocaine. It's a dirt powder or sugar-like crystal substance which is smoked in ciga-

Arhuaco Indian withdrawing lime from a gourd.
The coca leaves are carried in his mochila

rettes like marijuana. It is harmful and may cause painful side effects.

After a boom in the early 1980s, basuco lost some of its popularity to crack, another coca-derived substance. Crack, which is a mixture of cocaine, sodium bicarbonate and ammonia, is stronger than basuco and cheaper than cocaine. It has become popular in Western countries among those who either cannot afford cocaine or don't like it. Crack exists in Colombia, but has already gone out of fashion. Colombia also produces marijuana; some consider it to be the best in South America.

In May 1994, Colombia's constitutional court legalised the possession of drugs for personal use. The ruling makes it legal to possess small amounts of drugs (including hard drugs such as cocaine, crack and heroin), although the production, trafficking and sale of drugs remains illegal. The legal quantities are 20 grams of cannabis and one gram of cocaine.

Despite this ruling, it's best to keep well away from drugs; do not carry even the smallest quantity. The Colombian authorities are continuing their severe campaign against drugs and the police follow that line. Police searches can be thorough, and if they find drugs, even for your personal use, they may take advantage of it to threaten you with arrest, looking for a payoff. There have been reports of drugs being planted on travellers, so be careful and keep your eyes open. Watch carefully while police officers search your luggage.

You may be coaxed to buy dope on the street, especially in the big cities, but don't accept this offer. The vendors may well be setting you up for the police; or their accomplices will stop you two blocks away, show you false police documents and threaten you with jail unless you pay them off.

Always refuse if a stranger at an airport asks you to take their luggage on board as part of your luggage allowance. Smuggling dope across borders, particularly at airports, is a dangerous and crazy idea.

**Burundanga**
Burundanga is a drug used by thieves and robbers to eliminate the victim's ability to respond. It is obtained by quite a simple process from a species of tree, commonly called *borrachero* or *cacao sabanero*, which is widespread in Colombia. The drug is then put into food or drink and given to the chosen victim. It can be added to virtually any substance – sweets, cigarettes, chewing gum, spirits, beer – and it has no noticeable taste or smell.

The main effect after a 'normal' dose is the loss of will, even though you remain conscious. The thief can then ask you to hand over your valuables and you will obey without resistance. Cases of rape under the effect of burundanga are known. Other effects are loss of memory and sleepiness, which can last from a few hours to several days. An overdose can be fatal.

Burundanga is not only used to trick foreign tourists – many Colombians have been on the receiving end as well, losing their cars, contents of their homes, and sometimes their life. Unfortunately, use of the drug has been spreading, even into neighbouring countries, so think twice before accepting a cigarette from a stranger or a drink from a new 'friend'.

It is ironic that the *borrachero* which is the source of this drug is a beautiful tree with exquisite bell-shaped flowers.

## Irritations

Road traffic in Colombia is fast and chaotic; this becomes a problem in the large cities where traffic is heavy and peak hour results in total disorder. Drivers don't obey traffic rules: they run red lights, drive like maniacs and crawl against the flow up one-way streets. This can make crossing the street a tricky experience; take it for granted that no driver will stop to give you right of way.

Air pollution is largely a by-product of the busy traffic and the poor mechanical condition of most vehicles, many of which belch clouds of smoke like steam locomotives. The pollution may be appalling to visitors from 'clean' countries.

There are no self-contained public toilets in Colombia. If you are unexpectedly caught in need, use a toilet in a restaurant. Choose better-looking establishments because basic eateries either don't have toilets or, if they do, you're better off not witnessing them. If you feel uncomfortable about sneaking in just to use the toilet, order a soft drink, a beer or a coffee. Museums and large shopping centres usually have toilets.

You will rarely find toilet paper in these toilets, so make sure you carry some with you at all times. In bus terminals and some airports, you have to pay a small fee to use the toilet, but in return you usually receive a short piece of single-ply toilet paper which will almost certainly be too small to be of any practical use.

Toilet plumbing in budget hotels might not be up to the standard you are accustomed to. The tubes are narrow and the water pressure is weak, so toilets usually can't cope with toilet paper. A wastebasket is normally provided; but if there is no receptacle, or if it's already full, toss the used toilet paper on the floor and someone will eventually get around to removing it.

If you ask for information or directions, don't always expect a correct answer, especially in rural areas. The *campesinos* (peasants) have different notions of time and space. Even if they have no idea they will often tell you anything just to appear helpful and knowledgeable. Ask several people the same question and if one answer seems to pop up more frequently than the others, it may be the correct one. Avoid questions which can be answered by 'yes' or 'no'; instead of 'is this the way to...?' ask 'which is the way to ...?'.

## ACTIVITIES

Colombia has more than 30 national parks, offering walks ranging from easy, well-signposted trails to jungle paths where you may need a machete. If you arrive in Bogotá, contact Sal Si Puedes, who organises weekend walks in the area and longer treks in other regions (see Information in the Bogotá chapter).

Sierra Nevada de Cocuy and Sierra Nevada de Santa Marta provide Colombia's best high-mountain trekking, mountaineering and rock climbing; guides and equipment are available in Bogotá. If you want to try some rock climbing closer to Bogotá, Suesca is the most popular place.

Beach lovers can indulge themselves on Colombia's 3000 km of coastline. Parque Tayrona has perhaps the most amazing beaches, but many other seaside areas, such as Cabo de la Vela and Sapzurro are also magnificent. There is good snorkelling and scuba diving off the Archipiélago de San Andrés and Providencia, and around the Islas del Rosario.

Fishing enthusiasts are spoilt for choice: Colombia has two coasts and no shortage of rivers. Angling is not popular in Colombia so buy an *atarraya* (a fishing net) and follow the local style.

Speleologists can explore Colombia's caves; one of the most spectacular is the Cueva de los Guácharos in Huila, but there are also some excellent caves in eastern Antioquia and western Santander.

## ACCOMMODATION

Accommodation which is listed in this book is ordered according to price, beginning with the cheapest. Budget travellers should read these sections from the beginning; more affluent visitors would be wise to leapfrog to the closing paragraphs.

Where the hotels are broken down into price categories, bottom-end accommodation includes anything costing less than US$12 for a double, mid-range hotels run from approximately US$12 to US$25 per double, and anything over US$25 for a double is considered top end.

### Camping

Camping is not popular in Colombia, and there are only a handful of genuine camp sites in the country. Unofficial camping is theoretically possible almost anywhere outside the urban centres, but given the country's dangers, you should be very careful. If you intend to camp, get permission to pitch your tent next to a peasant's house or in the grounds of a holiday centre so that you have some protection. Camping rough is never safe, but is much safer far away from human settlements, such as in the mountains. Even there, you shouldn't leave your tent or gear unattended.

If you camp in wilderness or other fragile areas, try to minimise your impact on the environment. Biodegradable items can be buried but food residue, cigarette butts and other rubbish should be carried out. Even if you bury it animals can dig it up and scatter it about. If there are no toilet facilities, select a site at least 50 metres from water sources, and bury waste. If possible, burn used toilet paper or bury it well. Use biodegradable soap products. Wash dishes and brush your teeth well away from watercourses. Make sure you have a sufficient stock of sturdy bags to take your garbage out of the area.

### Hostels

Colombia recently became a member of the International Youth Hostel Federation. There are not many hostels at the moment but their number is expected to increase in future. The Colombian Youth Hostel Association (Alcom) has its main office in Bogotá. See the Useful Organisations section in the Bogotá chapter for details.

### Hotels

There are so many places to stay in Colombia that the problem is not finding a hotel but choosing which one to stay in. There are, however, almost no gringo hotels. Except for in a handful of places which have gained popularity among travellers, you are unlikely to meet other foreigners.

Places to stay appear under a variety of names including *hotel, residencias, hospedaje, pensión, hostería, hospedería, estadero, apartamentos, amoblados, posada* etc. For the budget places, residencias and hospedaje are the most popular names. 'Hotel' generally means a place of a higher standard, or at least a higher price, but not always.

Standards vary a great deal and there doesn't appear to be a simple correlation between quality and price. Some cheap hotels charge fairly reasonable rates for a good, clean room while others demand twice as much for a scruffy, dingy cell. If a place is touristy, it doesn't necessarily mean that accommodation is more expensive. Isolated regions are usually dearer – the Amazon, Los Llanos, San Andrés and Providencia are the most noticeable examples.

Budget accommodation is usually clustered around the bus company offices, the bus terminal, or the market. On the whole, residencias and hospedajes are unremarkable places without any style or atmosphere. This is particularly true in the cities, where they are generally poor or overpriced, or both. At their most primitive, you get a spartan room, a bed with a bumpy mattress and sometimes a chair and/or a table. Hardboard partitions instead of walls are not unusual, which makes noise and security a problem.

Some budget hotel rooms have a toilet and shower attached (in this book simply called

A Bullfight in the Plaza de Santa Maria in Bogotá
B Street corner in La Candelaria, Bogotá
C Car park in Central Bogotá
D Public telephone in Bogotá
E Is Bogotá unsafe?

Left: Iglesia de Santa Clara La Real, Tunja
Right: Iglesia de Santo Domingo, Tunja
Bottom: Casa del Fundador, Tunja

bath). The bathroom is usually separated (at least partially) from the room but not always. A real bath (ie a large, enamel container you can fill with water) is virtually unknown in the cheapies, though they are usually available in top-class hotels. Note that cheap hotel plumbing can't cope with toilet paper, so throw it in the box or basket which is usually provided.

In hot places (ie lowland areas), a ceiling fan or a table fan is often provided. The latter is almost always a better solution because you can adjust it to the desired speed or move it nearer or further away according to your needs. Ceiling fans usually only have on/off switches, and 'on' may be worse than 'off'. If the fan is very efficient and right above the bed, you may freeze at night. Fans are often in a dilapidated state and can be very noisy.

In general, even the cheapest budget hotels provide a sheet and some sort of cover (another sheet or blankets depending on the climatic zone). Most of them will also give you a towel, a small piece of soap and a roll of toilet paper.

Always have a look at the room before booking or paying. When inspecting the room, make sure the toilet flushes and the shower works. Check that the fan works and that the lock on the door is sufficiently secure. In the hotels in the highlands, pay attention to how many blankets you are given and check the hot water if the hotel claims to have it. If you're not satisfied with the room you're shown, ask to see another.

Mid-range hotels are usually found in the centre of towns, close to the main square. They are often undistinguished places, not much better than budget hospedajes. Their advantage is their location, and you can also often expect your own bathroom. Some have air-con instead of a fan. Generally, these hotels are more modern than the cheapies, which are usually located in old houses. It's still a good idea to have a look at the room before paying.

At the upper end of the price scale you have a choice of decent hotels, topped by international chains such as Hilton and Intercontinental. If money is no barrier, you can have a swimming pool, sauna, colour TV, air conditioning etc. Most cities have at least one such hotel, with a substantially wider choice in Bogotá, Cartagena and San Andrés.

**Hotel Pricing** Budget hotels have different systems of charging. Some charge per person, so each person pays the same regardless of whether they stay in a single, double or larger room. This usually works out cheaper if you are travelling on your own, but not if you are in a bigger party. Other cheapies charge per bed, no matter how many people squeeze into it!

The majority, however, charge per room, with doubles usually costing about 50% more than a single. The prices of the cheapies start around US$2 to US$3 for a single room, and US$3 to US$5 for a double.

Many cheap hotels have *matrimonios*, rooms with one double bed intended for married couples. Some, however, are not interested in the sex of the people who want to share the bed. A matrimonio is cheaper than a double room, and can be only slightly more expensive than a single (or even the same price). Travelling as a couple considerably reduces the cost of accommodation.

In the middle and top-end hotels, a double room usually costs only about 20% to 30% more than a single.

Room prices in Colombian hotels are the same for locals and foreigners. In virtually every middle and top-range hotel, a 14% IVA (VAT) tax will automatically be added to the price they display. Many cheapies will also charge this tax, but not all. The tax has been included in the prices given in this book.

**Hotel Security** By and large, hotels are safe places, though certain precautions are always advisable. Most budget places lock their doors at night; some even keep them locked during the day, opening them only for guests. The biggest danger of being ripped-off is from other guests. The thief's 'work' is made easier by the partial hardboard partitions between the rooms and the flimsy catches and easily-picked padlocks on the doors. Hotels provide padlocks, but it's recommended that you use your own combination lock (or padlock) instead. A hotel padlock obviously increases the number of people with access to your room. As a rule, the bigger hotels are less safe because the atmosphere is more impersonal; a thief won't stand out in a crowd.

Most budget hotels offer a deposit facility, which usually means that the management will put your gear in their room. This reduces the risk, but doesn't eliminate it completely. In most cheapies, the staff won't want to give you a receipt for your valuables, and if you insist on one, they may simply refuse to guard them. Decide for yourself if it's safe.

Better hotels usually have the reception desk open around the clock, with proper facilities to safeguard guests' valuables.

Remember that a hotel (no matter which sort of hotel it is) is almost always safer than the street of a big city at night.

### Other Accommodation

Brothels are not uncommon in Colombia. In the cities they tend to concentrate in 'red-light' streets, but sometimes they simply merge into streets with normal hotels. They are easily recognisable by the hordes of *putas* (prostitutes) waiting at the entrance. The brothels are usually located in the cheapest hospedajes in town, and the surroundings are far from pleasant.

Love hotels are more common than brothels. These places are designed for couples with an urgent need to be together for a while. They have rooms with a double bed and a private bath, and are rented by the hour. The standards of these hotels varies but, by and large, they are not bad and usually don't admit prostitutes.

Many budget hotels double as love hotels. Sometimes you can identify them by the management's first question, which is likely to be: '¿Para un rato o p'amanecer?' (for a while or for the whole night?). However, it's often impossible to recognise them and to avoid staying in one from time to time.

It's probably not worth keeping away from love hotels at any cost because they can be as good and safe as normal budget hotels (the guests have more interesting things on their minds than stealing your belongings). The staff also usually keep the 'sex' section separate from the other hotel rooms, so excited couples won't disturb you sleeping at night.

### FOOD & DRINK

**Food** It's hard to starve in Colombia. There's a huge number of places to eat, ranging from street stalls to excellent, well-appointed restaurants. Even the smallest village will have a place to eat – a restaurant, the market or, at the very least, a private house which serves meals.

Colombian cuisine varies regionally, but this variety unfortunately doesn't apply to the cheapest meals, which are, with some local additions, the same the length and breadth of the country. The basic meal is the *comida corriente*. At lunchtime (roughly from noon to 2 pm) it is called *almuerzo* (lunch), sometimes with additional descriptions such as *ejecutivo* or *casero*. At dinner time (usually after 6 pm) it changes to *comida* (dinner), but remains identical to the lunch.

It's a set two-course meal consisting of *sopa* (soup) and *bandeja* or *seco* (main course), and usually it includes a *sobremesa* (a dessert or a drink). The main course contains a small piece of meat, chicken or fish (look closely, it can be very small!) served with rice, pasta, red beans, lentils or vegetables, sometimes with fried plantains and a small salad. In cheap restaurants, the sobremesa is likely to be just a drink: usually a *gaseosa* (bottled fizzy drink) or, less often, a sort of watered down fruit juice or *agua de panela*. The drink may or may not be included in the meal price.

The comida corriente is the principal diet of the vast majority of Colombians and some budget restaurants not only offer nothing else, but serve the same meal for months without changing the combinations. The meal may also appear on the menus of higher-class establishments, where they are usually more diversified and tastier, and you can expect a genuine dessert rather than a drink only.

Some restaurants serve set meals non-stop from noon until they close at night, but most serve them only at lunchtime and, less often, only in the evening. The comida corriente is the cheapest way to fill yourself up, costing roughly half the price of any à la carte dish (which doesn't include either soup or a drink). The comida costs somewhere between US$1 and US$2, but can be more expensive in remote regions.

Budget restaurants supplement the comida with a short list of popular dishes, which almost always includes *carne asada* (roasted or grilled beef) and *arroz con pollo* (rice with chicken).

If you're on a tight budget, be prepared to stick to the comida corriente in seedy restaurants. The way to diversify and enrich your diet is to eat at the street stalls and the market. Food stalls are a common part of the urban landscape and are likely to be found in the city centre, around the bus terminals (new bus terminals often contain cafés and restaurants inside) and in the market. Every town has a market with stalls serving food which is usually fresh, tasty and cooked in front of you.

Roasted or barbecued chicken restaurants are another interesting alternative to the comida. There are plenty of them; the most popular chains are *Kokoriko*, *La Brasa Roja*, *Frisby*, *Cali Mío* and *Cali Vea*. Just look for any 'Pollo Asado' sign. Chicken is served with potatoes or, less often, with chips; salad is extra. Half a chicken with potatoes will cost between US$3 and US$4.

Most Colombians are carnivores. They don't consider a dish a serious meal if it is served without meat. Only over the last decade has there been a noticeable trend towards vegetarian food. There are still not many vegetarian restaurants, but they are appearing in increasing numbers. They are usually simple venues serving a limited menu of dishes, and are generally cheap or very cheap. If you can't find one, order a comida corriente in any restaurant and ask them to replace the meat with fried eggs or an additional portion of vegetables.

There is a great variety of regional food. Some local specialities have spread through-

out the country, but others remain characteristic only to their region of origin. Some restaurants specialise in the food of certain regions (such as *La Fonda Antioqueña* – a chain serving Antioquian specialities), while others offer popular dishes from different regions. Depending on the class of the restaurant, you will pay somewhere between US$3 and US$10 for a typical main course.

Western food is readily available, either in the well-known fast-food chains (Wimpy, Burger King and the like), expensive restaurants or top-class hotels.

Chinese cuisine is also quite popular. Colombia's large cities have sizeable Chinese communities, and many Chinese run their own restaurants. The cheapest ones have mixed Colombian/Chinese dishes and are not particularly good. At the other end of the scale, there are fine, authentic Chinese restaurants, which are not overly expensive. You shouldn't pay more than US$10 for a really good meal.

**Colombian Cuisine** The following list includes some of the most common dishes and snacks (see the Food & Drink Glossary for more snacks and descriptions of accompaniments):

*Ajiaco* – a soup with chicken, potatoes of three different varieties, corn on the cob and a herb called guasca; served with capers and cream, and accompanied by avocado; a Bogotano speciality

*Arepa* – a toasted or fried maize pancake, which is plain by itself and is included as an accompaniment to some dishes; it also has more interesting forms such as *arepa con queso* (with cheese) or *arepa de huevo* (a maize dough fried with an egg inside); the latter is typical of the Caribbean coast

*Arroz con chipichipi* – rice with small shellfish; typical of the Caribbean coast

*Arroz con coco* – rice cooked in coconut milk; a speciality of the Pacific and Caribbean coasts

*Arroz con pollo* – rice with chicken and vegetables, found on the menu of almost all restaurants

*Bandeja paisa* – (also called *plato montañero*), a typical Antioquian dish consisting of *frijoles* (red beans), minced beef, *chorizo* (sausage), rice, *patacón* (fried plantain), a fried egg, *chicharrón* (fried pork rind), *arepa* and avocado; it is found almost everywhere

*Cabrito* – grilled goat, usually served with yucca and *arepa*; a speciality of Santander

*Carne asada* – roast or grilled beef, served with rice, chips, yucca etc, depending on the region; a must on every menu

*Cazuela de mariscos* – a stew of shellfish, fish, squid and vegetables; a speciality of the coast but also available in better restaurants in the interior

*Cuchuco* – a heavy soup made of ground corn, wheat or maize with a piece of pork, potatoes and other vegetables; originally from Boyacá

*Cuy* or *cui* – guinea pig grilled on a spit; typical of Nariño

*Chocolate santafereño* – traditionally, a cup of hot chocolate, cheese (which is put into the chocolate and then spread on a piece of bread), a small *tamal*, scrambled eggs with onion and tomato, *almojábanas* and biscuits; the common version includes just hot chocolate, cheese and bread; a Bogotano speciality

*Churrasco* – a large steak, typical of Argentina but widespread in Colombia

*Empanada* – a fried pasty stuffed with rice, vegetables and meat; there are numerous regional variations which can include fish, seafood, chicken, cheese etc. The *empanada de pipián*, typical of Popayán, is stuffed with potato and peanut and comes with a hot peanut sauce.

*Fritanga* – a popular dish, often sold in markets, street stalls, and in roadside restaurants. It may include any of these: *chicharrón* (deep fried pork rind), *morcilla* (pork tripe stuffed with rice and peas), *chorizo* and *longaniza* (two types of sausages), *bofe* (beef lung), *corazón* (beef heart), *hígado* (beef liver), *papa criolla* (a small, yellow potato), *papa salada* (a skinned potato boiled and sprinkled with salt), *plátano maduro* (ripe plantain), *mazorca* (corn on the cob).

*Hormiga culona* – large fried ants; probably the most exotic Colombian speciality, unique to Santander and available only in season (March to May); it's not a dish you order in a restaurant, but a snack you buy by weight in shops

*Lechona* – a pig carcass, stuffed with its own meat, rice and/or dried peas and then baked; traditionally it is baked for several hours in a wood-fired *horno de barro*, a dome-shaped oven made of mud and brick; a speciality of Tolima

*Mazamorra* – boiled maize in milk; typical to Antioquia, but there are regional variations (eg *peto* in Cartagena)

*Mazamorra chiquita* – a hearty soup with meat, tripe, different types of potatoes and other vegetables; a speciality of Boyacá

*Mondongo* – a seasoned tripe cooked in bouillon with maize, potatoes, carrots and other vegetables; popular in many regions

*Mute* – a soup typical to Santander, prepared from pork, beef and tripe with potatoes, maize and other vegetables

*Puchero* – a broth with chicken, pork, beef, potato, yucca, cabbage, corn and plantain; accompanied by rice and avocado; a Bogotá speciality

*Rondón* – the most typical dish of San Andrés, made with coconut milk, yucca, plantain, fish and sea snails

*Sancocho* – a very common dish found everywhere, a kind of vegetable soup with fish, meat or chicken; it has many regional varieties, the most popular of which is *sancocho de gallina*, chicken soup with potatoes, plantain, yucca and corn on the cob; *sancocho de pescado* is a speciality of the Caribbean coast

*Sobrebarriga* – stewed, baked or fried brisket or flank of beef served with rice, potatoes and vegetables

*Tamales* – chopped meat with vegetables and other ingredients (varying widely depending on the region) folded in a maize dough, wrapped in banana leaves and steamed; it's always served in the leaf (don't eat it!); the most famous tamales come from Tolima, but there are plenty of regional varieties

*Viudo de pescado* – river fish soup (mainly *bocachico*) cooked with potatoes, yucca and plantains; typical of Tolima and Huila

If you are interested in Colombian cuisine and cooking, *Gran Libro de la Cocina Colombiana* (Círculo de Lectores, Bogotá, 1984) is a good cookbook featuring regional Colombian dishes.

**Fruit** Fruit really deserves a whole chapter because there's an amazing variety. Apart from widely known fruits such as bananas, pineapples, oranges, mangos, papayas etc, Colombia has many fruits found only in tropical South America or even, in some cases, only in particular regions of Colombia. You shouldn't leave Colombia without trying *guayaba* (guava), *maracuyá* (passion fruit), *guanábana*, *lulo*, *curuba*, *zapote*, *mamoncillo*, *uchuva*, *fraijoa*, *granadilla*, *tomate de árbol*, *borojó* and *mamey*, to name just a few. Refer to the Food & Drink Glossary for descriptions.

Check out *Frutas en Colombia* by Eduardo Sarmiento Gómez (Ediciones Cultural, Bogotá, 1986) which has photographs and descriptions of over 120 fruits found in the country.

## Drinks

**Non-Alcoholic Drinks** Coffee is not only the most popular drink in Colombia, it's almost a ritual. *Tinto* (a small cup of black coffee) is served everywhere. Its quality, however, varies from place to place; in some cafés it's hard to believe how such muck can be made from excellent Colombian beans.

Other coffee drinks are *perico* or *pintado* (a small, milk coffee) and *café con leche* (which is larger and uses more milk). Milk in cafés is not always available but you can easily buy it in shops and supermarkets.

Tea is poor in quality and not very popular. In contrast, *aromáticas* – herbal teas made with various plants like *cidrón* (citrus leaves), *yerbabuena* (mint) and *manzanilla* (camomile) – are very cheap and good. *Agua de panela* (unrefined sugar melted in hot water) is another tasty drink; in hot climates it's usually served cold with lemon juice; in the highlands it comes hot and often includes a piece of cheese.

Fizzy soft drinks (*gaseosas*) are cheap (US$0.15 to US$0.25 per bottle) and available everywhere. Colombia is the world's third largest consumer of soft drinks, and has the highest per capita consumption. Apart from locally produced well-known Western drinks, such as Coca-Cola, Pepsi, Sprite etc, there are a variety of Colombian drinks such as Colombiana, Uva (grape) and Manzana (apple) – the local concoctions leave a lot to be desired.

**Alcoholic Drinks** Beer is very popular and generally quite good. There are several local brands; Águila, Poker, Bavaria and Club-Colombia are the most popular. A bottle of beer (a third of a litre) costs about US$0.25 in the shops, US$0.30 and upwards in restaurants. The *refajo*, an equal mixture of beer and a fizzy drink, is a popular accompaniment to meals. It is produced commercially under the brand name Cola & Pola.

Colombian wine is poor, not popular and best avoided. There are some imported Chilean and Argentine wines, which are of acceptable quality. European wines are very expensive.

Cerveza Aguila, a popular Colombian beer

*Aguardiente* is the most popular spirit and is consumed mostly by the male half of the population. It's a local alcohol flavoured with anise, and is produced by several companies under their own brand names: Aguardientes Cristal and Néctar are the most popular in the Bogotá region, but Aguardiente Medellín is considered to be the best. A more refined, 'lady-like' version of aguardiente is the *mistela*, a home-made sweet liquor, produced by preserving fruit or herbs in syrup aguardiente.

*Ron* (rum) is another popular spirit, mainly on the coast and in Antioquia and Caldas. Some brands are pretty good. Recommended dark rums are Ron Viejo de Caldas and Ron Medellín; the best white rums are Ron Tres Esquinas and Ron Blanco.

You'll find *guarapo* and *chicha* in some regions, usually in rural areas. They are home-made alcoholic beverages obtained by the fermentation of fruit or maize in sugar or panela water. Most are low in alcohol, but some varieties can lay you out pretty quickly.

## Food & Drink Glossary

The following is a glossary of food and drink terms you are likely to come across in Colombia:

*aceite* – oil
*aceituna* – olive
*agria* – popular name for beer

*agua* – water
*agua aromática* – herbal tea
*agua de panela* – drink made of *panela* melted in hot water
*aguacate* – avocado
*aguardiente* – sugarcane spirit flavoured with anise
*ají* – red chilli pepper
*ajo* – garlic
*alcaparra* – caper
*aliño* – combination of spices
*almeja* – clam
*almendra* – almond
*almojábana* – a sort of small bread made from corn-flour and cottage cheese
*almuerzo* – lunch
*almuerzo corriente* – set lunch
*amarga* – popular name for beer
*apio* – celery
*arepa* – toasted or fried maize pancake
*arequipe* – milk pudding made of milk and sugar (sometimes *panela*) boiled until thick; similar to fudge but a bit runnier
*aromática* or *agua aromática* – herbal tea
*arroz* – rice
*arveja* – green peas
*atún* – tuna (fish)
*auyama* – pumpkin
*avena* – cold drink made from oats and milk, with cinnamon and cloves
*azúcar* – sugar

*bagre* – catfish
*banano* – banana
*bandeja* – main course
*bebida* – drink, beverage
*berenjena* – eggplant
*bizcocho* – cake
*bocachico* – a river fish; very tasty but with plenty of bones
*bocadillo* – a sweet made of guava paste and wrapped in banana leaf; often eaten with a piece of cheese (*bocadillo con queso*)
*bofe* – beef lungs
*borojó* – grapefruit-sized round fruit with dirt-brown peel, endemic on the Pacific coast; used for juices which are alleged to be aphrodisiacs
*breva* – fig
*brevas con arequipe* – figs stuffed with a type of fudge, served in syrup
*brócoli* – broccoli
*buñuelo* – a small ball of deep fried maize dough and cheese
*butifarras* – small, smoked meat balls, sprinkled with a few drops of lemon juice; typical of the Caribbean coast

*cachama* – tasty river fish
*calabacín* – zucchini, courgette

*calabaza* – squash
*calamar* – squid
*calao* – toasted bread
*caldo* – broth
*caldo de menudencias* – broth with chicken giblets
*caldo de papa* – broth with pieces of meat, potatoes and coriander; an energy-boosting Colombian breakfast
*camarón* – small shrimp
*canela* – cinnamon
*canelazo* – hot drink made of *aguardiente*, *agua de panela* and cinnamon
*cangrejo* – crab
*caracol* – snail
*carajillo* – black coffee with liquor
*carne* – meat
*carne a la llanera* – beef grilled on a spit
*carne de cerdo* – pork
*carne de res* – beef
*carne guisada* – stewed beef
*carne molida* – mince meat
*carne oreada* – sun dried, grilled beef
*casabe* – a very large, dry, flat, round bread made from *yuca brava* (a kind of yucca), common in Los Llanos
*cebolla* – onion
*cebollín* – scallion, spring onion
*cerdo* – pork
*cerveza* – beer
*ceviche* – raw fish or prawn marinated in lemon juice
*cigarrería* – a sort of delicatessen
*cilantro* – coriander
*ciruela* – plum
*cocada* – a sweet made from coconut
*coco* – coconut
*coctel* – cocktail
*colaciones* – butter biscuits; a speciality of Cundinamarca
*colí* – a kind of plantain used in soup
*colicero* or *sopa de colí* – a soup made of *colí* and other vegetables
*coliflor* – cauliflower
*comida* – dinner
*comida corriente* – set meal
*cordero* – lamb
*corvina* – blue fish
*costilla* – rib

*crema de leche* – cream

*criadillas* – bull's testicles

*cuajada* – unsalted, white, fresh cheese wrapped in banana leaf

*cuajada con melao* – a typical desert, consisting of a piece of *cuajada* in *panela* syrup

*cubio* – a white and purple tuber, mainly found in Boyacá

*curuba* – oval-shaped fruit, with soft, yellow peel and orange-coloured meat, growing only in Cundinamarca and Boyacá; the *sorbete de curuba* is second to none – don't miss it

*champiñón* – mushroom

*champús* – a cold drink made from rice and *lulo* fruit; typical of Valle del Cauca

*changua* – a light breakfast soup made of milk, containing an egg, a *calao* and coriander; in some regions potatoes are added

*chicha* – a thick, alcoholic beverage made from corn

*chicharrón* – deep fried piece of salted pork rind, added to the *bandeja paisa* and some other dishes

*chipichipi* – a tiny shell fish

*chirimoya* – custard apple

*chivo* – goat

*choclo* – sweet corn

*chocolate* – chocolate

*chontaduro* – the fruit of a palm, cooked and eaten with salt; very popular in Valle del Cauca

*chorizo* – seasoned sausage

*chuleta* – chop, rib steak

*chunchullo* – beef tripe, boiled and then fried

*dedos de queso* – white cheese strips wrapped in pastry and deep fried

*desayuno* – breakfast

*durazno* – peach

*ensalada* – salad

*espárrago* – asparagus

*espinaca* – spinach

*fraijoa* or *feijoa* – aromatic fruit with green peel and white meat similar in texture to the guava; the peel can be eaten

*fresa* – strawberry

*frijoles* or *fríjoles* – red beans

*fritanguería* – street stand serving *fritanga*

*fuente de soda* – budget cafeteria serving snacks, ice creams, fruit salads etc

*galleta* – biscuit, cracker

*gallina* – hen

*gamitana* – river fish typical to the Amazon; one of the most delicious fish

*garbanzo* – chickpea

*gaseosa* – bottled soft drink

*golosinas* – snacks, sweets

*granadilla* – a round, orange-sized fruit with a hard yellow peel dotted with brown freckles; inside, it has grey, sweet flesh; comes from the same family as the passion fruit

*grasa* – fat

*guama* – a fruit with a hard, thick skin which looks like a huge string bean; the edible part is the inside cotton-like flesh covering the seeds

*guanábana* – soursop

*guarapo* – fermented drink made from fruit and sugarcane juice

*guasca* – a herb typical of the Colombian highlands, used in soups; a must in the *ajiaco*

*guayaba* – guava

*haba* – large lima bean common in the Andes

*habichuela* – string bean

*helado* – ice cream

*hielo* – ice

*hígado* – liver

*huevo* – egg

*huevos fritos* – fried eggs

*huevos pericos* or *huevos revueltos* – scrambled eggs

*jaiba* – a species of crab

*jamón* – ham

*jugo* – juice

*langosta* – lobster

*langostino* – large shrimp, large prawn

*lapingacho* – fried pancake made from mashed potato and cheese; Ecuadorian dish popular in Nariño

*leche* – milk

*lechuga* – lettuce

*lenteja* – lentil

*limón* – lemon

*limonada* – lemonade

*lomito* – sirloin

*lomo* – loin

*longaniza* – a type of sausage

*lulo* – golf ball-sized, ideally round fruit with prickly yellow skin (don't handle it) and very soft flesh; makes a delicious juice

*maíz* – corn, maize

*maíz pira* – popcorn

*mamey* – a grapefruit-sized fruit with brown skin and bright yellow flesh

*mamoncillo* – grape-sized fruit, with green skin and reddish edible flesh which you suck until you get to the core

*mandarina* – mandarin, tangerine

*mango* – mango

*maní* – peanuts

*manjarblanco* – a kind of fudge made of milk, rice and sugar, sometimes with figs

*mantecada* – cake made of cornflour, butter, eggs and vanilla

*mantequilla* – butter
*manzana* – apple
*maracuyá* – passion fruit
*margarina* – margerine
*marisco* – shellfish
*mariscos* – seafood
*masa* – dough
*masato* – low-alcohol home-made beverage made of rice, wheat or corn, flavoured with cinnamon and cloves
*mazorca* – sweet corn on the cob
*mejillones* – mussels
*melao* – sugarcane syrup
*melocotón* – peach
*melón* – cantaloupe, rockmelon
*menudencias* – chicken giblets
*mero* – grouper or sea bass
*milanesa* – thin steak
*mistela* – home-made alcoholic drink made with *aguardiente* sweetened with herbs or fruits for several weeks
*mogolla chicharrona* – a bread with small pieces of fried pork rind
*mora* – blackberry
*morcilla* – tripe stuffed with rice, peas and herbs, boiled and then fried
*mostaza* – mustard
*muchacho* – roast beef

*naco* – mashed potatoes
*naranja* – orange
*nata* – milk skin
*nicuro* – a river fish
*níspero* – a perfectly round, billiard ball-sized, brown fruit with soft, fleshy meat; delicious in juices
*nuez* – nut, walnut

*ñame* – a type of yam, edible tuber

*oblea* – two thin, crisp pancakes with *arequipe* in the middle
*ostra* – oyster
*ostrería* – street stand serving seafood cocktails

*paella* – Spanish dish of rice, pork, chicken and seafood
*pan* – bread
*pan de bono* – a small bun made of maize flour, yucca starch and white cheese
*pan de yuca* – a half-moon bread made of yucca starch and cheese
*panela* – unrefined and uncrystalised raw sugar obtained from sugarcane syrup and sold in brown-coloured blocks
*papa* – potato
*papa criolla* – literally 'creole potato', a species of small, yellow potato endemic to Colombian highlands, mainly Cundinamarca and Boyacá
*papas fritas* – chips
*papayuela* – a small and very aromatic papaya from the Andean region, with a different taste from the common lowland papaya
*pargo* – red snapper
*pastel* – pastry
*pastelería* – cake shop
*patacón* – piece of plantain, squashed and then fried
*patilla* – watermelon
*pato* – duck
*pavo* – turkey
*pechuga* – breast (poultry)
*pepino* – cucumber
*pera* – pear
*perejil* – parsley
*pernil* – leg of pork or poultry

*perro caliente* – hot dog
*pescado* – fish that has been caught and is considered to be food
*peto* – boiled maize in hot milk, sweetened with panela
*pez* – a live fish
*pimentón* – capsicum
*pimienta* – pepper
*piña* – pineapple
*piqueteadero* – budget, short-order restaurant or roadside stand serving basic food
*pitaya* – tuna; prickly pear cacti fruit (don't handle it) that has yellow to red peel with a delicate soft, sweet meat and very small black seeds
*plátano* – plantain (green banana)
*pola* – popular name for beer
*pollo* – chicken
*ponqué* – cake
*postre* – dessert
*postre de natas* – a dessert made from milk skin; speciality of Cundinamarca and Boyacá
*principio* – accompaniment (of main dish)
*pulpo* – octopus

*quesillo* – fresh, white cheese wrapped in banana leaf; a speciality of Espinal in Tolima but also found elsewhere
*queso* – cheese

*raspao* – ice ball made by scraping a block of ice and adding artificial flavours; sold only on the street
*refajo* – a drink made of beer and soft drink (usually the 'Colombiana', the most popular Colombian fizzy drink)
*rellena* – tripe stuffed with rice, peas and herbs
*remolacha* – beetroot
*repollo* – cabbage
*riñones* – kidneys
*róbalo* – snook, bass
*ron* – rum
*roscón* – sweet bread with guava paste inside
*ruya* – a small edible tubercule, typical of Boyacá and Cundinamarca

*sabajón* – a thick beverage made of *aguardiente*, egg and milk
*sal* – salt
*salchicha* – sausage
*salmón* – salmon
*salpicón* – small pieces of different fruits in a fruit juice or fizzy drink
*salsa* – sauce
*salsa de tomate* – tomato sauce, ketchup
*sardina* – sardine
*seco* – main course
*sierra* – king mackerel, sawfish
*sopa* – soup
*sorbete* – milk shake; fruit juice with milk

*tamarindo* – tamarind
*té* – tea
*ternera* – veal
*tienda* – grocery
*tisana* – herbal tea
*tocineta* – bacon
*tomate* – tomato
*tomate de árbol* – tree tomato, tamarillo
*toronja* – grapefruit
*torta* – tart, cake
*tortilla* – omelette
*trago* – alcoholic drink
*trigo* – wheat
*trucha* – trout

*uchuva* – a cherry tomato-sized, orange-coloured fruit; its flesh looks like that of a tomato, but it has a unique taste
*uva* – grape
*uva pasa* – raisin

*vinagre* – vinegar
*vinagreta* – salad dressing
*vino* – wine
*vino blanco* – white wine
*vino espumoso* – sparkling wine
*vino rosado* – rosé
*vino tinto* – red wine

*yuca* – yucca, cassava (edible root)

*zanahoria* – carrot
*zapote* – a brown eggplant-shaped fruit with orange fleshy fibred meat around several seeds; there is another variety found on the coast, *zapote costeño*, which is like an ostrich egg and has softer meat around a single stone

The following words will help you judge how food has been prepared:

*ahumado/a* – smoked
*a la parrilla* – broiled, grilled
*al horno* – baked
*asado/a* – roasted
*cocido/a* – boiled
*estofado/a* – braised, stewed
*frito/a* – fried
*guisado/a* – stewed
*oreado/a* – sun-dried

*bien cocido/a* – well-done
*poco cocido/a* – rare
*término medio* – medium
*tres cuartos* – medium well

## ENTERTAINMENT
### Cinema
Cinema is popular in Colombia; virtually every town has a cinema, and Bogotá has more than 50. Most movies are regular Hollywood fare, which arrive in Colombia a few months after their US release. If you need something more mentally stimulating, try the cinematecas (art cinemas) in Bogotá.

Most movies are screened in their original language with Spanish subtitles. A cinema ticket costs between US$1 and US$2. Cinemas in the lowlands are air-conditioned, so they can be pretty cold sometimes; come prepared.

### Theatre & Classical Music
Most of Colombia's theatre is confined to the three largest cities, Bogotá, Medellín and Cali. Other cities have theatres but the choice, and usually the quality of the productions, is not impressive. Much the same can be said about other areas of artistic expression, such as ballet, opera and classical music.

### Nightlife
Many Colombian discos play salsa and other Caribbean rhythms. They are called salsotecas. The music is usually recorded but can sometimes be live. Salsotecas are in plentiful supply in Bogotá and Cali, and also exist in Cartagena, Barranquilla, San Andrés and many other cities.

Colombians also like Western pop, so if you can't live without it, you'll find a choice of night venues. Remember to leave valuables, cameras, day packs etc in your hotel or in another reliable place before setting off for the night. Take only the money you expect to spend that night and enough for a taxi back to your hotel.

### Spectator Sports
Soccer and cycling are the most popular imported spectator sports. Colombia regularly takes part in international events in these two fields, such as the World Cup and the Tour de France, and has recorded some successes. The national soccer league has matches most of the year.

Colombians are passionate about corrida (bullfighting), which was introduced by the Spaniards. Most cities and towns have plaza de toros (bullrings). The bullfighting season usually peaks in January (when the top-ranking matadors are invited from Spain); minor bullfights take place irregularly throughout the rest of the year.

Cockfighting is another cruel, thrilling 'sport'. It's popular in Colombia and much of South America. Galleras (cockfight rings) can be found in most cities.

The coleo, a sort of rodeo popular in Los Llanos, is an equally exciting but thankfully bloodless spectacle. The aim of the coleo, also known as las coleadas, is to knock over a bull by grabbing its tail from a galloping horse.

The tejo is yet another popular local sport, or rather a form of leisure activity. Its origins reputedly date back to pre-Columbian times, when it was known in Chibcha language as turmequé. It's still referred to as turmequé in some regions, especially in Boyacá. The players throw metal disks (known as tejos) towards a wooden structure – located, traditionally, 18 metres away – which is filled with soft earth, sand or clay. A metal bowl (bocín) is put in the middle of this 'cushion' and a small envelope of gunpowder (mecha) is placed in the bocín. The aim is to throw the tejo in such a way that it hits the mecha and makes it explode. A tejo session is invariably accompanied by huge amounts of beer.

## THINGS TO BUY
Colombia is the world's largest producer of emeralds and the local stones are most sought after for their quality. If you have extra pesos to spend, the best place to buy them is Bogotá because it has the best selection and the most reasonable prices. Good stones are obviously not cheap, but they are half the price they are in, say, the USA. However, if you aren't knowledgeable about emeralds you are unlikely to strike a good deal, so leave well alone.

Bogotá is also the best centre for original antiques, particularly pre-Columbian pottery. Prices are high, so don't expect to

Cockfight

find a bargain. You may occasionally be approached by locals offering pottery for sale in archaeologically-rich zones, but it's usually of mediocre quality and may not be genuine.

The best filigree gold and silver jewellery is found in Mompós. Santa Fe de Antioquia also has good goldwork.

Colombian handicrafts vary region by region. Some areas and towns are famous for particular local crafts. Boyacá is probably the largest handicraft manufacturer; it produces excellent handwoven items, basketry and pottery. The basketwork of the Pacific coast is also interesting; the best selection is in Cali. Pasto is noted for decorative items

covered with the *barniz de Pasto*, a kind of vegetable resin.

Pitalito has become famous for its ceramic miniatures of *chivas*. A chiva is a sort of Disneyland bus which was, until the 1960s, the main mode of rural public transport. Chivas are still common on country roads. Today, miniatures of chivas are produced in many regions.

Hammocks are another tempting buy and come in plenty of regional variations, from the simple, practical hammocks made in Los Llanos (especially good to buy in Villavicencio) to the more decorative ones made in San Jacinto, and the still more elaborate *chinchorros* of the Guajiro Indians. Another well-known Indian craft is the *mola* (rectangular cloth with coloured designs) made by the Cuna Indians, probably best bought in Capurganá.

*Ruanas*, the Colombian woollen ponchos, are found in the colder parts of the Andean zone, where the climate justifies it. In many villages, they are still made by hand with simple patterns and natural colours. The best selection is probably in Bogotá.

The best and most fashionable *mochilas* (a kind of woven hand bag) are those of the Arhuaco Indians from the Sierra Nevada de Santa Marta. They are not cheap, but if you buy them in Sierra Nevada de Santa Marta, they will be half the price they are in Bogotá.

Colombian leather goods are relatively cheap and are among the best in South America.

There are leather bags and suitcases of every shape, size and style. Bogotá has the widest choice, but you can find a good selection in other cities. In Medellín you can buy a *carriel*, a typical Antioquian leather hand bag for men. Leather boots are another attractive purchase.

Colombia publishes an assortment of well-edited and illustrated coffee-table books about the country's nature, art and architecture. The best choice is in the bookshops of the large cities. If you're interested in local music, there are lots of records and cassettes (costing roughly US$4). Although the technical quality may not be impressive, many of them can't be found elsewhere. An increasing variety of local music is recorded on CDs (US$10 to US$14). Bogotá has the widest selection.

# Getting There & Away

## AIR

Colombia's location at the northern edge of South America means it has good and relatively cheap air links with both Europe and North America. Most visitors fly to Colombia's major international airport in Bogotá, but some travellers use Colombia's other international airports, particularly Cartagena and San Andrés.

If you plan on flying within Colombia, note that Avianca, the major national carrier, offers a domestic air pass, but it has to be bought overseas. See the Air section in the Getting Around chapter for details.

### Buying the Ticket

Your plane ticket will probably be the single most expensive item in your budget, and buying it can be an intimidating business. It's worth remembering that round-trip fares are almost always cheaper than two one-way tickets. Similarly, a single air ticket which includes a number of stopovers will be cheaper than a number of separate tickets for the same route. Note also, that the straight return ticket may not necessarily be the cheapest option for flying to Colombia. Other types of discount airfares, such as RTW, circle or open jaw tickets (see Air Travel Glossary) may work out cheaper. They can also be more attractive because they allow you to visit other countries, rather than just Colombia.

Air tickets bought from travel agents are generally cheaper than those bought directly from an airline, even if they cover the same route and have similar conditions or restrictions. How much you save largely depends on where you buy. In some countries or cities there is a big trade in budget tickets; in others, the discount-ticket market is limited, and the prices not very attractive.

There is likely to be a multitude of airlines and travel agents hoping to separate you from your money, and it is always worth putting aside a few hours to research the current state of the market. Start early: some of the cheapest tickets have to be bought months in advance, and some popular flights sell out early. Talk to other recent travellers – they may be able to stop you making some of the same old mistakes. Look at the ads in newspapers and magazines (including the Latin American press published in your country), consult reference books and watch for special offers. Read the Air Travel Glossary in this chapter to get familiar with the basic terms. Then phone round travel agents for bargains. Find out the fare, the route, the duration of the journey and any restrictions on the ticket, and sit back and decide which is best for you.

Airlines can supply information on their routes, timetables and full fares; except at times of airline price wars, they do not supply the cheapest tickets. It's worth calling them anyway because they occasionally have specials; if not, you will at least know the full fare to see what you're saving when you buy from an agent.

Agents may tell you that those impossibly cheap flights they've advertised are 'fully booked, but we have another one that costs a bit more...' Or you may discover that the flight is on an airline notorious for its poor safety standards and requires a 24-hour stopover in the world's worst airport. Or they may claim they only have two seats left, which they will hold for you for a maximum of two hours. Don't panic – keep ringing around.

Use the fares quoted in this book as a guide only. They are approximate and based on the rates advertised by travel agents at the time of going to press. Quoted airfares do not necessarily constitute a recommendation for the carrier.

If you are travelling from the UK or the USA, you will probably find that the cheapest flights are being advertised by obscure bucket shops (known as consolidators in the USA) whose names haven't yet reached the telephone directory. Many such firms are honest and solvent, but there are a few rogues who will take your money, disappear, and reopen somewhere else a month or two later under a new name. If you feel suspicious about a firm, don't give them all the money at once – leave a small deposit and pay the balance when you get the ticket. Before leaving a deposit, fix all details of the ticket, including conditions, restrictions and the total fare. Otherwise you may find that when you pick up your ticket, there are some unmentioned extras on top of the previously agreed price which makes the ticket substantially more expensive; if you don't want it, your deposit is lost. If they insist on full cash in advance, go somewhere else. And once you have the ticket, ring the airline to confirm that you are actually booked onto the flight.

You may decide to pay more than the rock-bottom fare by opting for the safety of a better-known travel agent. Firms such as STA Travel, who have offices worldwide, Council Travel in the USA or Travel CUTS in Canada offer good prices to most destinations and are not going to disappear overnight, leaving you clutching a receipt for a non-existent ticket.

Once you have your ticket, write its number down, together with the flight number and other details (or make a photocopy of it), and keep the copy separate from the original. This will help you get a replacement if the ticket is lost or stolen.

It's sensible to buy travel insurance as early as possible. If you buy it the week before you fly, you may find, for example, that you're not covered for delays to your flight caused by industrial action.

## Onward Ticket Requirements

Colombia still, technically, has an onward ticket requirement; formally you are not allowed to enter the country unless you already have an onward ticket to another destination. This can be a return ticket or a ticket to another country.

This requirement is practically never enforced by Colombian immigration offi-

cials, either at the international airports or at land border crossings. However, this rule is quite strictly enforced by airlines and travel agents. If you intend to fly into Colombia but don't have an onward ticket, the airline probably won't sell you a one-way ticket and will insist that you buy a return. Even if you manage to buy a one-way ticket, you can still face problems at the airport: the airline may refuse to allow you to board the plane. These are simply carriers' preventive measures: if you arrive in a country and are refused entry, the airline is responsible for flying you back out again, so they make sure you have the necessary papers and tickets before you board.

Colombia is not a good place to buy international air tickets. Airfares to Europe and Australia are high and there are virtually no discounted tickets available. Flights to the USA are cheaper because it's closer, but discounted airfares are still few and far between. Moreover, when you buy an international ticket in Colombia, you have to pay 19% tax (9.5% on a return ticket) on top of the fare.

The onward ticket requirement and the price of air tickets in Colombia make it better to have your whole route covered by the ticket you buy at home. This will also avoid you being caught without a return ticket just when you wish to go home.

## Air Travellers with Special Needs

If you have special needs of any sort – you've broken a leg, you're vegetarian, travelling in a wheelchair, taking a baby or terrified of flying – you should let the airline know as soon as possible so that they can make appropriate arrangements. You should remind them of your needs when you reconfirm your booking (at least 72 hours before departure) and again when you check in at the airport. It may be worth ringing around the airlines before you make your booking to find out how they can handle your particular requirements.

Airports and airlines can be surprisingly helpful, but they do need advance warning. Most international airports will provide escorts from the check-in desk to the plane when needed, and there should be ramps, lifts, and accessible toilets and phones. Aircraft toilets, on the other hand, are likely to present a problem; travellers should discuss this with the airline at an early stage and, if necessary, with their doctor.

Guide dogs for the blind will often have to travel separately from their owners in a specially pressurised baggage compartment with other animals, though smaller guide dogs may be admitted to the cabin. All guide dogs are subject to the same quarantine laws (six months in isolation etc) as other animals when entering or returning to countries currently free of rabies, such as the UK or Australia.

Deaf travellers can ask for airport and in-flight announcements to be written down for them.

Children under two years of age travel for 10% of the standard fare (or free on some airlines), as long as they don't occupy a seat. They don't get a baggage allowance either. 'Skycots' should be provided by the airline if requested in advance; these are capable of carrying a child weighing up to about 10 kg. Children between two and 12 years of age can usually occupy a seat for half to two-thirds of the full fare, and do get a baggage allowance. Pushchairs (pushers) can often be taken aboard as hand luggage.

## From the USA

North America is a relative newcomer to the bucket-shop traditions of Europe and Asia, so bargain tickets cannot be bought on every corner and are usually not such a bargain. Due to aggressive competition between carriers and a lot of government red tape in determining fare structures, flights originating in the USA are subject to numerous restrictions and regulations. This is especially true of bargain tickets; anything cheaper than the standard tourist economy fare must be purchased at least 14 days, and sometimes as many as 30 days, prior to departure.

In addition, you'll often have to book departure and return dates in advance and

these tickets will be subject to minimum and maximum stay requirements: usually seven days and six months, respectively. Open tickets, which allow an open return date within a 12-month period, are generally not available in the USA, and penalties of up to 50% are imposed if you make changes to the return booking.

The easiest way to get a cheap airfare from the USA is through a travel agency selling discounted fares. The Sunday travel sections of major newspapers have advertisements from many such agencies; *The Los Angeles Times*, *The San Francisco Examiner* and *The New York Times* are all good newspapers to check.

Two of the most reputable discount travel agencies in the USA are STA Travel and Council Travel Services. Although they both specialise in student travel, they also offer discount tickets to nonstudents of all ages. You can contact their national head offices to ask about prices, find an office near you or purchase tickets by mail.

STA Travel
    5900 Wiltshire Boulevard, Los Angeles, CA 90036 (☎ (800) 777 0112, (213) 937 8722; fax (213) 937 2739)
Council Travel Services
    205 East 42nd St, New York, NY 10017 (☎ (800) 223 7402, (212) 661 1414; fax (212) 972 3231)

STA Travel has offices in Los Angeles, San Diego, San Francisco, Berkeley, Boston, Cambridge and New York. Council Travel has offices in all these cities and in 20 others around the country.

A recommended publication is the monthly newsletter *Travel Unlimited* (PO Box 1058, Allston, MA 02134) which gives details of cheap airfares and courier possibilities for destinations all over the world from the USA. Send US$5 for their latest edition, or buy a one-year subscription for US$25.

Courier flights are a relatively new concept which businesses use to ensure the arrival of urgent freight without excessive customs hassles. The system is operated by courier companies which hire couriers who commit themselves to delivering packages to

## Air Travel Glossary

**Apex Tickets** Apex stands for Advance Purchase Excursion fare. These tickets are usually between 30 and 40% cheaper than the full economy fare, but there are restrictions. You must purchase the ticket at least 21 days in advance (sometimes more) and must be away for a minimum period (normally 14 days) and return within a maximum period (90 or 180 days). Stopovers are not allowed, and if you have to change your dates of travel or destination, there will be extra charges to pay. These tickets are not fully refundable – if you have to cancel your trip, the refund is often considerably less than what you paid for the ticket. Take out travel insurance to cover yourself in case you have to cancel your trip unexpectedly – for example, due to illness.

**Baggage Allowance** This will be written on your ticket; you are usually allowed one 20-kg item to go in the hold, plus one item of hand luggage. Some airlines which fly transpacific and transatlantic routes allow for two pieces of luggage (there are limits on their dimensions and weight).

**Bucket Shops** At certain times of the year and/or on certain routes, many airlines fly with empty seats. This isn't profitable and it's more cost-effective for them to fly full, even if that means having to sell a certain number of drastically discounted tickets. They do this by off-loading them onto bucket shops (UK) or consolidators (USA), travel agents who specialise in discounted fares. The agents, in turn, sell them to the public at reduced prices. These tickets are often the cheapest you'll find, but you can't purchase them directly from the airlines. Availability varies widely, so you'll not only have to be flexible in your travel plans, you'll also have to be quick off the mark as soon as an ad appears in the press.

Bucket-shop agents advertise in newspapers and magazines and there's a lot of competition, so it's a good idea to telephone first to ascertain availability before rushing from shop to shop. Naturally, they'll advertise the cheapest available tickets, but by the time you get there, these may be sold out and you may be looking at something slightly more expensive.

**Bumped** Just because you have a confirmed seat doesn't mean you're going to get on the plane – see Overbooking.

**Cancellation Penalties** If you have to cancel or change an Apex or other discount ticket, there may be heavy penalties involved; insurance can sometimes be taken out against these penalties. Some airlines impose penalties on regular tickets as well, particularly against 'no show' passengers.

**Check In** Airlines ask you to check in a certain time ahead of the flight departure (usually two hours on international flights). If you fail to check in on time and the flight is overbooked, the airline can cancel your booking and give your seat to somebody else.

**Confirmation** Having a ticket written out with the flight and date on it doesn't mean you have a seat until the agent has confirmed with the airline that your status is 'OK'. Prior to this confirmation, your status is 'on request'.

**Courier Fares** Businesses often need to send their urgent documents or freight securely and quickly. They do it through courier companies. These companies hire people to accompany the package through customs and, in return, offer a discount ticket which is sometimes a phenomenal bargain. In effect, what the courier companies do is ship their freight as your luggage on the regular commercial flights. This is a legitimate operation – all freight is completely legal. There are two shortcomings, however: the short turnaround time of the ticket, usually not longer than a month; and the limitation on your luggage allowance. You may be required to surrender all your baggage allowance for the use of the courier company, and be only allowed to take carry-on luggage.

**Discounted Tickets** There are two types of discounted fares – officially discounted (such as Apex – see Promotional Fares) and unofficially discounted (see Bucket Shops). The latter can save you more than money – you may be able to pay Apex prices without the associated Apex advance booking and other requirements. The lowest prices often impose drawbacks, such as flying with unpopular airlines, inconvenient schedules, or unpleasant routes and connections.

**Economy-Class Tickets** Economy-class tickets are usually not the cheapest way to go, though they do give you maximum flexibility and they are valid for 12 months. If you don't use them, most are fully refundable, as are unused sectors of a multiple ticket.

**Full Fares** Airlines traditionally offer first-class (coded F), business-class (coded J) and economy-class (coded Y) tickets. These days there are so many promotional and discounted fares available that few passengers pay full fare.

**Lost Tickets** If you lose your airline ticket, an airline will usually treat it like a travellers' cheque and, after inquiries, issue you with a replacement. Legally, however, an airline is entitled to treat it like cash, so if you lose a ticket, it could be forever. Take good care of your tickets.

**MCO** An MCO (Miscellaneous Charges Order) is a voucher for a value of a given amount, which resembles an airline ticket and can be used to pay for a specific flight with any IATA (International Air Transport Association) airline. MCOs, which are more flexible than a regular ticket, may satisfy the irritating onward ticket requirement, but some countries are now reluctant to accept them. MCOs are fully refundable if unused.

**No Shows** No shows are passengers who fail to show up for their flight for whatever reason. Full-fare no shows are sometimes entitled to travel on a later flight. The rest of us are penalised (see Cancellation Penalties).

**Open Jaw Tickets** These are return tickets which allow you to fly to one place but return from another, and travel between the two 'jaws' by any means of transport at your own expense. If available, this can save you backtracking to your arrival point.

**Overbooking** Airlines hate to fly with empty seats, and since every flight has some passengers who fail to show up (see No Shows), they often book more passengers than they have seats available. Usually the excess passengers balance those who fail to show up, but occasionally somebody gets bumped. If this happens, guess who it is most likely to be? The passengers who check in late.

**Promotional Fares** These are officially discounted fares, such as Apex fares, which are available from travel agents or direct from the airline.

**Reconfirmation** You must contact the airline at least 72 hours prior to departure to 'reconfirm' that you intend to be on the flight. If you don't do this, the airline can delete your name from the passenger list and you could lose your seat.

**Restrictions** Discounted tickets often have various restrictions on them, such as necessity of advance purchase, limitations on the minimum and maximum period you must be away, restrictions on breaking the journey or changing the booking or route etc.

**Round-the-World Tickets** These tickets have become very popular in the last few years; basically, there are two types – airline tickets and agent tickets. An airline RTW ticket is issued by two or more airlines that have joined together to market a ticket which takes you around the world on their combined routes. It permits you to fly pretty well anywhere you choose using their combined routes as long as you don't backtrack, ie keep moving in approximately the same direction east or west. Other restrictions are that you (usually) must book the first sector in advance and cancellation penalties then apply. There may be restrictions on how many stopovers you are permitted. The RTW tickets are usually valid for 90 days up to a year. The other type of RTW ticket, the agent ticket, is a combination of cheap fares strung together by an enterprising travel agent. These may be cheaper than airline RTW tickets, but the choice of routes will be limited.

**Standby** This is a discounted ticket where you only fly if there is a seat free at the last moment. Standby fares are usually only available directly at the airport, but sometimes may also be handled by an airline's city office. To give yourself the best possible chance of getting on the flight you want, get there early and have your name placed on the waiting list. It's first come, first served.

**Student Discounts** Some airlines offer student-card holders 15% to 25% discounts on their tickets. The same often applies to anyone under the age of 26. These discounts are generally only available on ordinary economy-class fares. You wouldn't get one, for instance, on an Apex or an RTW ticket, since these are already discounted.

**Tickets Out** An entry requirement for many countries is that you have an onward or return ticket, in other words, a ticket out of the country. If you're not sure what you intend to do next, the easiest solution is to buy the cheapest onward ticket to a neighbouring country or a ticket from a reliable airline which can later be refunded if you do not use it.

**Transferred Tickets** Airline tickets cannot be transferred from one person to another. Travellers sometimes try to sell the return half of their ticket, but officials can ask you to prove that you are the person named on the ticket. This may not be checked on domestic flights, but on international flights, tickets are usually compared with passports.

**Travel Periods** Some officially discounted fares, Apex fares in particular, vary with the time of year. There is often a low (off-peak) season and a high (peak) season. Sometimes there's an intermediate or shoulder season as well. At peak times, when everyone wants to fly, both officially and unofficially discounted fares will be higher, or there may simply be no discounted tickets available. Usually the fare depends on your outward flight – if you depart in the high season and return in the low season, you pay the high-season fare. ■

any of the companies' destinations (see Air Travel Glossary for more information).

New York and Miami are the only places to look for courier flights to South America. For the widest selection of destinations, try Now Voyager (☎ (212) 431 1616), Air Facility (☎ (718) 712 0630) or Travel Courier (☎ (718) 738 9000) in New York, and Linehaul Services (☎ (305) 477 0651) or Discount Travel International (☎ (305) 538 1616) in Miami. As an example only, a two-week courier fare on the Miami-Bogotá-Miami flight will cost around US$300.

There are basically three routes from the USA to Colombia: via Central America, via Venezuela and directly. Your choice will mainly depend on your plans, time and money.

The first route, via Central America, is part of the great Latin American gringo trail, and has traditionally been popular with travellers. If you're interested in visiting Mexico and some of the Central American countries on the way to Colombia then this is the route to choose. It can be done all the way overland, providing you are prepared to cross the most difficult barrier – the Darién. Travellers usually go overland as far as Guatemala from where they take a flight to Colombia via San Andrés (a Colombian island). Some more adventurous backpackers wend their way as far south as Costa Rica or even to Panama, and then fly to Colombia. See the From Central America section for details on how to get from there to Colombia.

The route through Venezuela is an obvious choice if you intend to visit this country before reaching Colombia. However, it's also worth considering this way as a transportation bridge only. Some flights from the USA to Colombia via Venezuela may be cheaper than the direct US-Colombia connections.

The major US gateway for Venezuela is Miami. Plenty of airlines fly from there to Caracas and a few other Venezuelan cities. They include several major international carriers and various minor South and Central American airlines. Three Venezuelan carriers alone fly this route.

At the time of writing, the Zuliana de Aviación, a little-known Venezuelan carrier based at Maracaibo, was offering what were probably the cheapest fares to both Venezuela and Colombia. Their routes and prices (in US$) from Miami were:

| To | One-way | Return |
|---|---|---|
| Caracas | 196 | 367* |
| Maracaibo | 155 | 285* |
| Medellín | 205 | 385 |
| Bogotá | 205 | 385 |

* The return airfares marked with an asterisk are maximum 60-day fares; the others are valid for one year.

There are no advance purchase restrictions. The flights run daily on Boeing 727s. For details, contact Zuliana de Aviación's Miami office (☎ (305) 579 8780 or toll-free (800) 223 8780), Suite 200, 7001 NW 25th St, Miami, Florida 33122.

Check with the other airlines which fly from Florida to Colombia via Venezuela. For example, the major Venezuelan airline, Viasa (☎ (800) 468 4272), has Miami-Bogotá flights via Caracas (see the From Venezuela section for further information).

Direct routes from the USA to Colombia are serviced by Avianca, Aces (both Colombian airlines) and American Airlines. Ordinary full fares are costly but Apex and other discount return tickets are available. Avianca offers some promotional fares from time to time. At the time of writing, their cheapest fares were: Miami-Cartagena-Miami (US$419) and Miami-Bogotá-Miami (US$449). A maximum stay of two months was allowed for both.

You may also consider flights via San Andrés island. Sahsa (☎ (800) 327 1225) flies to San Andrés from Miami (US$260 one way), New Orleans (US$270) and Houston (US$310). You can then continue to the mainland on a domestic flight (see the From Central America section for further information).

Direct flights from the US west coast to Colombia are expensive. Avianca flies the

Los Angeles-Bogotá route, but a return ticket will cost nearly US$1000.

In the northern winter season, there are sometimes charter vacation packages to Cartagena. They go on sale for somewhere between US$500 and US$800 for airfare and a week's accommodation. Check with major travel agents for details.

Some agents advertise themselves as specialists in 'last minute' bargains. These tickets are reduced during the week prior to the flight, sometimes considerably, and can be as low as US$350. At this rock-bottom price, you can fly to Cartagena, stay the week at a top-class hotel, throw away the return portion and travel around Colombia. Make sure, however, to buy another ticket in the USA to get back home.

### From Canada

There are no direct, scheduled flights from Canada to Colombia. Anyone flying from Canada will have to fly via the usual US transit points such as Los Angeles or Miami. Another possibility is to fly to Guatemala or Honduras and continue on via San Andrés. However, flights to Central America are only slightly less expensive than flights to Colombia, so it will not be any cheaper going this way.

The cheapest flights from Canada to Colombia are from Toronto or Montreal via Miami. The prices vary according to the length of your stay. For example, the return ticket from Toronto costs about C$1000 if you stay less than 60 days and C$1300 if you want to stay longer. From the Canadian west coast, eg Vancouver, it is usually cheaper to fly to Toronto or Montreal, and then go on via Miami, rather than flying via Los Angeles.

During the winter months, there may be charter flights from Toronto and Montreal to Cartagena. If you wait until the last minute, assuming your schedule is flexible, the prices go down to around C$400 for the return flight and one week's accommodation. Phone travel agents in Toronto or Montreal for the latest specials.

The Last Minute Club and Marlin Travel are two of the agencies specialising in last-minute package discounting. They advertise on Saturdays in the travel sections of *The Toronto Star* and *The Montreal Gazette*. Even if you don't use the return section, the price is very attractive.

It's worth checking out fares at Travel Cuts, Canada's national student travel agency (you don't have to be a student to use its services). Its head office is in Toronto (☎ (416) 977 3703, 979 2406; fax (416) 977 4796), 171 College St, Toronto, Ontario M5T 1P7, and it has branch offices in Edmonton, Halifax, Montreal, Ottawa, Saskatoon, Vancouver and Victoria.

It's also worth contacting Andes Travel, one of the travel agents specialising in flights to South America. Call its office in Toronto on ☎ (416) 537 3447, or in Montreal on ☎ (514) 274 5565. Adventure Centre, which has offices in Calgary, Edmonton, Toronto and Vancouver, can also be useful.

### From Europe

A number of airlines, including British Airways, Air France, Lufthansa, Iberia, Viasa and Avianca, link Bogotá with European cities.

London is the cheapest starting point for flights to Colombia, thanks to its numerous bucket shops. Other cities with long-standing traditions in ticket discounting include Amsterdam, Brussels, Frankfurt and Paris. Elsewhere, special deals come and go, but there are usually less to choose from and the airfares are generally higher. This is particularly true in Scandinavia where budget tickets are difficult to find.

For this reason, many European budget travellers buy their tickets from London's bucket shops. In any case, it's worthwhile checking the London market before buying an expensive ticket from a local agent. Some London travel agents will make arrangements over the phone, so you don't actually have to go to London to shop around. However, you may be obliged to go to London to pick up your ticket in person because not many British agencies will want to send the ticket outside the UK.

Colombia is one of the cheapest South American destinations to reach and many travel agents list flights from Europe to Bogotá.

**From the UK** In London, you'll find discounted fares to Bogotá and all the other major destinations in South America. Several magazines advertise bucket shops, but don't take the advertised fares as gospel truth. To comply with advertising laws in the UK, companies must be able to offer some tickets at their cheapest quoted price, but they may have only one or two of them per week. If you're not one of the lucky ones, you'll be looking at higher priced tickets. The best thing to do is begin looking for deals well in advance of your intended departure, so you can get a fair idea of what's available.

One of the best sources of information about cheap fares around the world is the monthly *Business Traveller*, available at newsstands in many countries, or direct from 60/61 Fleet St, London EC4. See also the London weekly entertainment guide *Time Out*, available from newsstands in London, and *LAM*, a free London weekly magazine for entertainment, travel and jobs, available at underground stations. Another free weekly with ads for cheap airfares, *News & Travel Magazine*, is also worth checking out.

The Globetrotters Club (BCM Roving, London WC1N 3XX) publishes a newsletter called *Globe* which covers obscure destinations and can help in finding travelling companions.

When it's time to start calling agents, contact Journey Latin America (JLA) (☎ (0181) 747 3108; fax (0181) 742 1312), 14-16 Devonshire Rd, Chiswick, London W4 2HD, which specialises in flights to Latin America and will make arrangements over the phone. Ask for their useful, free magazine *Papagaio*. The company is well informed about South American destinations, have a good range of South American air passes, and can issue tickets from South America to London and deliver them to any of the main South American cities, which is

cheaper than buying the same ticket in South America. They may have interesting open jaw routes that include Bogotá.

Another reputable agency is Trailfinders (☎ 0171) 938 3939), 194 Kensington St, London W8 7RG. Their useful travel newspaper, *Trailfinder*, is free. They offer cheap flights to a wide variety of destinations; ask about RTW tickets. They have regional branches in Bristol, Glasgow and Manchester. South American Experience (☎ (0171) 379 0344) is also worth checking out. In Manchester, contact Travel Bug (☎ (0161) 721 4000).

STA Travel and Council Travel are both excellent organisations specialising in student and nonstudent budget travel. STA Travel has offices in London, Bristol, Cambridge, Leeds, Oxford and Manchester. Campus Travel also offers competitive deals. The London offices of the three agencies are:

STA Travel
    74 Old Brompton Rd, London, SW7 3LQ (☎ (0171) 937 9962)
    117 Euston Rd, London NW1 2SX (☎ (0171) 465 0484)
Council Travel
    28a Poland St, London W1 (☎ (0171) 437 7767)
Campus Travel
    52 Grosvenor Gardens, London SW13 0AG (☎ (0171) 730 8111)

Prices for discounted flights from London to Bogotá start at around UK£230 one way and UK£400 return. Bargain hunters should have little trouble finding even lower prices, but make sure you use a travel agent which is 'bonded' by the ABTA (Association of British Travel Agents). If you have bought your ticket from an ABTA-registered agent who then goes out of business, ABTA will guarantee a refund or an alternative. Unregistered bucket shops are sometimes cheaper, but can be riskier.

**From France** The Paris-Bogotá route is serviced directly by Air France and Avianca, but travel agents often use indirect routes (usually via Amsterdam or London) operated by other carriers, and they can work out to be cheaper.

Following is the list of recommended agencies in Paris. Many of them have branch offices in other major French cities.

Access Voyages
  6 Rue Pierre Lescot, 75001 Paris (☎ 40 13 02 02, 42 21 46 94)
Council Travel
  22 Rue des Pyramides, 75001 Paris (☎ 44 55 55 44, 40 75 95 10)
  31 Rue St Augustin, 75002 Paris (☎ 42 66 20 87)
Forum Voyages
  67 Ave Raymond Poincaré, 75016 Paris (☎ 47 27 89 89)
  140 Rue du Faubourg Saint Honoré, 75008 Paris (☎ 42 89 07 07)
Fuaj (Fédération Unie des Auberges de Jeunesse)
  27 Rue Pajol, 75018 Paris (☎ 44 89 87 27)
  9 Rue Brantôme, 75003 Paris (☎ 48 04 70 40)
Jumbo
  38 Ave de l'Opéra, 75002 Paris (☎ 47 42 06 92)
  62 Rue Monsieur le Prince, 75006 Paris (☎ 46 34 19 79)
Nouveau Monde
  8 Rue Mabillon, 75006 Paris (☎ 43 29 40 40)
Nouvelles Frontières
  87 Blvd de Grenelle, 75015 Paris (☎ 41 41 58 58)
OTU (Office de Tourisme Universitaire)
  39 Ave Georges Bernanos, 75005 Paris (☎ 44 41 38 50, 43 29 90 78)
STA Travel
  c/o Voyages Découvertes, 21 Rue Cambon, 75001 Paris (☎ 42 61 00 01)
Uniclam
  11 Rue du 4 Septembre, 75002 Paris (☎ 40 15 07 07)
  46 Ruc Monge, 75005 Paris (☎ 43 25 21 18)
  63 Rue Monsieur le Prince, 75006 Paris (☎ 43 29 12 36)

The cheapest Paris-Bogotá return tickets can be bought for about FF5000. Many of the listed agencies specialise in student travel and may offer even cheaper fares for students. Most discounted return tickets have a maximum stay period of two or three months, but student fares usually allow for a stay of up to six months.

## From Australia & New Zealand

Travel between Australasia and Colombia is far from convenient: the flight is arduously long, the tickets are expensive, there are a number of alternative routes with little to distinguish between them and the local travel agents have little South American experience. Colombia is certainly not a popular destination and there are few budget tickets.

In theory, there are four air routes to South America. The most popular is probably the route through Los Angeles, but getting to Colombia from there can work out to be quite expensive (see From the USA). Arrange the ticket for the whole route at home. Expect to pay between A$2200 and A$3000 for a return ticket, depending on the season, length of stay etc.

The route through Europe is the longest, but it's not as absurd as it may sound. Given the discount airfares to London, and relatively cheap fares from London to Bogotá, the total fare may be comparable or even sometimes lower than travelling through Los Angeles. It's best to arrange the ticket for the whole route in Australia or have the London-Bogotá leg prepared for you by a London agent and ready to pick up.

The shortest route to South America goes over the South Pole. Aerolíneas Argentinas, the only Latin American carrier landing in Australia, flies once weekly from Sydney to Buenos Aires with a stopover in Auckland. It's an interesting proposition if you plan on a long overland trip across the continent and decide to begin your journey from the Southern Cone, but be aware that Colombia is at the opposite end of the continent. The Sydney-Buenos Aires return excursion fare depends on the length of stay: around A$2200 with a maximum stay of 21 days; A$2350 for 45 days; and about A$2500 for six months. Up to six stopovers are permitted. New Zealanders can join the flight in Auckland, but the fares from there are only marginally lower.

Finally, you can fly right across the southern Pacific to Santiago de Chile. Lan Chile flies from Papeete (Tahiti) via Easter Island to Santiago. Associated carriers take passengers to and from Australia and New Zealand. The Sydney-Santiago return fares are roughly comparable to those for the Sydney-

Buenos Aires route. Like the previous route, you still end up quite a long way from Colombia, even if Lan Chile can bring you closer by providing you with an onward ticket to Lima at little or no extra cost.

Unless you are particularly interested in any of the four above-mentioned routes, it's worth investigating RTW tickets. RTW tickets with various stopovers can still be found for as little as A$2100, but these tend to include only northern hemisphere stopovers; RTW tickets which include Latin America or the South Pacific will automatically cost about A$1000 more. Of these, one of the most interesting options may be a one-year RTW ticket with Aerolíneas Argentinas and KLM on the route: Sydney-Auckland-Buenos Aires-Bogotá (overland to Caracas at your own expense) and then Caracas-Amsterdam-Singapore-Sydney. It's possible to include a couple of other South American destinations, such as Santiago or Lima.

Alternatively, look for a cheap northern hemisphere RTW which includes Miami, from where you can make a side trip to Colombia for a few hundred US dollars (see From the USA).

The Saturday editions of the major newspapers, *The Sydney Morning Herald* and *The Age*, carry travel sections which have discount airfare ads, but very few of them include South American destinations. It's worth getting a copy of *El Español* or the *Extra Informativo*, Spanish-language newspapers published in Australia, which list travel agents specialising in South America.

STA Travel has Australian offices in Adelaide, Brisbane, Cairns, Canberra, Darwin, Melbourne, Perth, Sydney and Townsville. In New Zealand, it has offices in Auckland, Christchurch, Dunedin and Wellington. Flight Centres International, which has offices in most major cities in Australia and New Zealand, may also have good deals.

## From Central America

Colombia has regular flight connections with all Central American capitals. Most of these flights go via the Colombian island of San Andrés, and are serviced by the Colombian airline, Sam, and/or the Honduran airline, Sahsa. Following are the airfares (in US$) to San Andrés (figures in brackets are discount 30-day return fares):

| From | Airline | Fare |
|------|---------|------|
| Managua | Sahsa | 168 (260) |
| San Salvador | Sahsa | 150 (240) |
| Guatemala City | Sam/Sahsa | 125 (215) |
| Tegucigalpa | Sahsa | 117 (200) |
| Panama City | Sahsa | 115 |
| San José | Sam | 85 |

From San Andrés, you can continue to the Colombian mainland on a domestic flight operated by several national airlines, including Sam (Sahsa flies only as far as San Andrés). See the San Andrés & Providencia chapter for further details.

If you plan on flying to San Andrés from Central America, you'll probably be obliged by the agent or airline to buy a return ticket to fulfil Colombia's onward ticket requirement. In this case, it's better to fly with Sahsa than with Sam because the Sahsa office in San Andrés may be able to refund you the difference between the return and the one-way ticket. If not, try again at the Sahsa office in Bogotá.

Make sure you only buy a ticket as far as San Andrés, and shop around for a ticket for the Colombian domestic portion after you arrive on the island. A ticket covering the whole route bought at the point of your departure will cost you more.

Considering distance and price, flights from Guatemala City and Tegucigalpa to San Andrés are the best value for money and, predictably, they have become the most popular among travellers.

Panama City is the only Central American capital from which it's cheaper to fly directly to the Colombian mainland rather than via San Andrés. One-way flight options (in US$) from Panama City to Colombia include:

| To | Airline | Fare |
|------|---------|------|
| Medellín | Copa, Sam | 115 |
| Cartagena | Copa | 118 |
| Barranquilla | Copa | 118 |
| Bogotá | Sam, Avianca | 146 |
| Cali | Avianca | 158 |

Copa (a Panamanian carrier) is not an IATA member, so its tickets are not transferable to other airlines. Copa offices in Cartagena, Barranquilla and Medellín should refund unused return halves of tickets, but check in advance. If possible, apply in Barranquilla, since applications in Cartagena are referred to Barranquilla anyway. Refunds, in Colombian currency only, take up to four days.

If you don't want to fly directly from Panama to Colombia, and would like to go at least part of the way through the Darién Gap, Ansa and Aerotaxi have internal flights to Puerto Obaldía (near the Colombian border). These flights depart from Panama City's domestic airport, at La Paitilla.

From Puerto Obaldía, it's a four-hour walk to Capurganá in Colombia, from where you can take a domestic flight to Medellín. See the From Panama section under Land for information.

### From Venezuela

There are plenty of flights between Caracas and Bogotá operated by several carriers including Avianca, Avensa and Viasa. The regular one-way fare offered by the airlines is US$194; the one-year discount return ticket costs US$250. Zuliana de Aviación, however, will fly you from Caracas to Bogotá (via Maracaibo and Medellín) for only US$116 (US$232 one-year return).

Other possible ways from Venezuela to Colombia (in decreasing order of price) include: Caracas-Cartagena with Viasa (US$172, US$199 one-year return); Caracas-Barranquilla with Lacsa (US$161, US$193 30-day return); Valencia-Bogotá with Valenciana de Aviación (US$120, US$200 60-day return); Maracaibo-Bogotá or Medellín with Zuliana de Aviación (US$75, US$150 one-year return); and Santo Domingo (near San Cristóbal)-Bogotá with Avensa (US$50, US$100 one-year return).

### From Ecuador

There are over a dozen regular flights a week between Quito and Bogotá, operated by Avianca, Ecuatoriana, Viasa and Servivensa

(US$153 one way, US$246 return, minimum stay five days, maximum two months).

Other routes between the two countries include Esmeraldas-Cali and Tulcán-Cali, both serviced by Intercontinental de Aviación and Tame and both costing US$60 one way. One other back-door route is Lago Agrio-Puerto Asís, operated by Aires (US$16 one way).

### From Brazil

Routes between Brazil and Colombia are serviced by several airlines, including Viasa and Avianca, but they are expensive. For example, the flight from Sao Paulo or Rio de Janeiro to Bogotá costs about US$800 (US$850 return).

The cheapest direct Brazil-Colombia flight is between Manaus and Bogotá; it costs about US$350. It's possible to cut this price down to around US$300 by taking a Brazilian domestic flight from Manaus to Tabatinga, crossing the border overland and then taking a Colombian internal flight from Leticia to Bogotá (refer to the Leticia section for details).

### LAND

Colombia borders Panama, Venezuela, Brazil, Peru and Ecuador, but has road connections with Venezuela and Ecuador only. These are the easiest and the most popular border crossings.

### From Panama

The Pan-American Highway does not go all the way from Panama into Colombia. It terminates in the town of Yaviza, in Panama's vast wilderness region called the Darién, and reappears some 150 km further on, far beyond the Colombian border. This break in the highway between Central and South America is known to travellers as the Darién Gap.

Notwithstanding the repetitive announcements by Panamanian and Colombian governments, it seems extremely unlikely that the missing bit of the highway will be built before the turn of the millennium. In addition to the purely technical difficulties (thick rainforest, extensive swamp areas, hundreds of streams to bridge, high rainfall etc), there are increasing ecological concerns about the destruction of the local habitat. There are also fears of spreading foot-and-mouth disease, which is presently limited to South America. Furthermore, a road link would facilitate the northbound migration of people and drugs, a nightmare for the US government.

Darién is a region of pristine tropical rainforest which UNESCO has declared a World Heritage Site. It is also designated a Biosphere Reserve. Scientists have described this region as one of the most naturally diverse in tropical America, with a large variety of flora and fauna. Cuna, Chocó, Emberá and Waunana indigenous groups inhabit different parts of the region.

Panama has established a national park, the Parque Nacional del Darién, to protect both the natural and human resources of the region. This park covers 90% of the borderland between Panama and Colombia, and at 5750 sq km, it is the largest national park in Central America. On the Colombian side, the Colombian government has established the Parque Nacional Los Katíos.

There are basically two ways through the Darién Gap. The first skirts the Caribbean coast via the San Blas archipelago, Puerto Obaldía and Capurganá, making use of boat services and involving a minimum of walking. The second goes through the jungle from Yaviza to the Río Atrato in Los Katíos national park, and you have to walk most of the way. Either of these routes can be done in as little as a week, but you should allow twice this time, especially for the jungle trip.

Remember that Panama demands onward tickets, visas and 'sufficient funds' (US$400 or more), so make sure you meet all three requirements before you leave Colombia. Many travellers have been turned back by Panamanian border officials for failing to comply with these conditions. Things are far easier going in the opposite direction: you will probably be able to get into Colombia at Turbo by just showing your passport.

If you plan on taking the jungle route, you are theoretically required by Panama's environmental agency, Inrenare, to obtain written permission before entering the Darién park. It is unlikely that anyone will ask you for this permit once you are in the park, but it's better to have one, just in case. Write to Inrenare, Departamento de Parques Nacionales y de Vida Silvestre, Box 2016, Paraíso, Ancón, Republic of Panama, or you can visit its offices in Panama City (☎ 324325; fax 324083) or El Real. Inrenare can arrange guides and boats.

## From Panama along the Caribbean Coast

This route starts at Colón (Panama) and goes via the San Blas archipelago to Puerto Obaldía, then to Capurganá (Colombia) and on to Turbo.

For the first leg of the journey, you need to find a cargo boat going to Puerto Obaldía. Merchant boats carrying passengers and supplies sail regularly from Colón to the San Blas archipelago, but there are not so many boats going all the way to Puerto Obaldía. You may decide to wait for a direct boat, or go to El Porvenir, the principal town of San Blas, and look around there. The boats usually depart around midnight from Coco Solo pier in Colón, and arrive at El Porvenir the following morning.

A boat from Colón to Puerto Obaldía will cost around US$30, meals included. It takes anywhere between four days and a week depending on how many stops the boat makes. It may stop at two dozen islands along the way – staying for a couple of hours at each one or even overnight – so you'll get a chance to visit many small islands. Make your own sleeping arrangements on deck – a hammock is very useful.

It is also possible to fly from Panama City to Puerto Obaldía; Ansa Airline (☎ 267891, 266898 in Panama City) and Aerotaxi (☎ 648644) operate daily flights on this route. The one-way fare is about US$45 with either carrier; Aerotaxi has a luggage excess charge of US$0.25 for every pound (0.45kg) the luggage weighs above the free 25-lb (11.25kg) threshold.

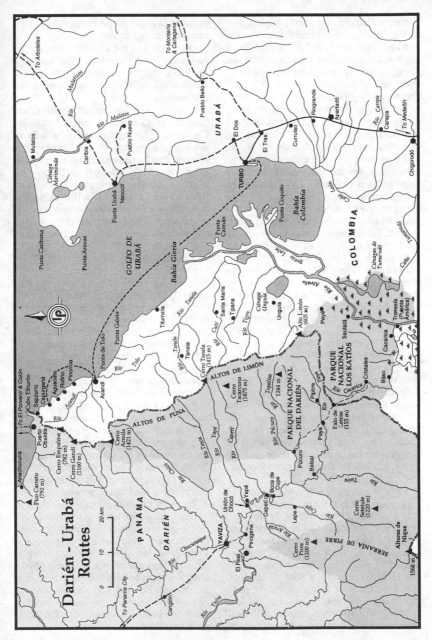

Darién – Urabá
Routes

Puerto Obaldía is a small, tropical port living off trade between Colombia and Panama. The town is nothing special, but it has beaches, palm trees and a clear, blue sea. There's a basic hotel near the airstrip (everybody will direct you there), which costs about US$5 per bed.

You need to visit the immigration inspector in Puerto Obaldía for an exit or entry stamp. If you're heading to Colombia, the formalities are usually smooth and quick, and your passport will be stamped with an exit stamp. On the other hand, if you're heading from Colombia into Panama, the immigration officer is likely to ask for your Panamanian visa, onward ticket and sufficient funds. Make sure you have all necessary papers in order. The inspector may also send you to a local doctor to have your blood tested for malaria.

Once you have your exit stamp, you can continue on to Colombia. There are two options: boat or walk. Boats depart irregularly, when they collect enough passengers, to Sapzurro (US$4, 45 minutes) and Capurganá (US$6, one hour). The boatmen will probably try to make foreign travellers pay more – by claiming it's an 'international route' or saying that your backpack is heavy etc. Alternatively, you can negotiate a boat for your party to La Miel, the last Panamanian village before the Colombian frontier. There are always fishermen around eager to get a little extra money, so the fare will never be high. Count on around US$10 per person if there are two people, less if there are more in your group. A contracted boat to Sapzurro shouldn't cost much more.

The other alternative is to walk. There's a path (often muddy in the rainy season) all the way to Acandí. The first part of the trail goes from Puerto Obaldía to La Miel, a two-hour walk. The locals in both Puerto Obaldía and La Miel say this track is unsafe for walking, although Lonely Planet has not received any confirmed reports about robberies. However, there are many misleading paths branching off inland, so you may get lost. Unless you find a local companion (who will serve as both a guide and as protection), it's probably better to do the Puerto Obaldía-La Miel portion by boat.

Once you reach La Miel, there are no problems. From the village, you ascend a small hill, pass the border marker on the top and descend to Sapzurro – which takes just half an hour.

From Sapzurro, the footpath climbs again, then drops to the next coastal village, Capurganá. This leg can easily be done in two hours. Capurganá has a choice of budget hotels and restaurants and is a pleasant place to hang around for a day or two. If you want to get out quickly, there are two flights a day from Capurganá to Medellín (US$77). Before doing so, however, present yourself at the local police post and get a written record from them explaining that you're going to do this. The note will prevent hassles at DAS in Medellín, where you'll get an entry stamp in your passport.

From Capurganá, you can take a boat to Turbo (US$12, around three hours). If there's no direct boat to Turbo on the day you wish to leave, go by boat to Acandí (US$4, one hour) and continue on another boat to Turbo (US$9, around two hours). If you are not in a hurry, it's worthwhile continuing from Capurganá to Acandí on foot. It's a lovely walk; allow yourself the best part of a day.

Whether you're heading from Panama to Colombia or vice versa, you need to call at the DAS office in Turbo to obtain an exit or entry stamp. It's very informal and quick, as long as your papers are in order. Travellers have been fined for entering Colombia via Turbo without getting an entry stamp here – so don't think you can wait until you reach Cartagena or Medellín to get one.

There is no Panamanian consulate in Turbo, so if you're heading to Panama, it's best to get your visa beforehand if you need one. You still have a chance to get one in Capurganá, but if the consulate there is closed for any reason, you will have to go a long way back to Medellín or Barranquilla to get one. Be sure you already have an onward ticket to enable you to enter Panama; many travellers have been forced to backtrack to get one.

The whole journey between Colón and Turbo can be done in a week, but you could easily take double that, especially if you have to wait for boats between Colón and Puerto Obaldía, or if you stay somewhere on the way. The San Blas archipelago, Sapzurro and Capurganá are the most pleasant places to break the journey.

See the sections on Turbo, Acandí, Capurganá and Sapzurro for further details about the Colombian portion of this route.

**From Panama through the Jungle** This trip begins in either Yaviza or El Real and goes via Boca de Cupe and Paya to Los Katíos national park. It's longer, more difficult and more dangerous than the coastal route, but it's also more spectacular and memorable.

*Warning* In addition to natural hazards, such as high rivers and mud slides (the Darién is a seismic activity zone), the human dangers to travellers in the area must not be underestimated. Although the Darién is still a wilderness, it is not unpopulated. Apart from the usual permanent inhabitants, there are always a number of people traversing the region or staying temporarily.

There's a mine in the Darién to which miners walk from both the Panamanian and Colombian sides. Many freelance miners are undocumented immigrants. There are also a lot of Latin Americans heading north to the USA, as well as smugglers of drugs and other contraband. There are also bandits who prey on jungle travellers. As a result, the route is getting more dangerous each year.

In addition, the Darién has become an area of activity for Colombian guerrillas operating from the Colombian side of the frontier. In January 1993, three US Protestant missionaries who had been working among the Cuna were kidnapped from the town of Púcuro by Colombian guerrillas. In the most recent disturbing incident, a young Canadian hiker, who attempted to cross the Darién alone, disappeared. His body was found after a search; he had been shot, apparently by guerrillas.

The guerrillas are said to have a camp in the Altos de Limón mountain area on the Panama-Colombian border, east of Púcuro, overlooking the trail from Boca de Cupe to Palo de Letras.

Several people who have made the journey recently highly recommend that foreign travellers hire a guide, not just to find the right trail (though this is part of it) but also for safety. Inrenare will arrange for a guide, as noted above. Eco-Tours (☎ 363076, 363575, 364494; fax 263550, Apartado 465) in Panama City is worth a preliminary visit and can help prospective travellers get oriented to the region.

Local Indian guides should be available as far south as Paya. They are usually willing to conduct travellers up to Cristales, but may insist on being hired in pairs. This is partly because of fear of guerrillas and partly because the business works better that way – you have to pay twice as much.

Having said all that, many people complete this route without major problems; those who have done so describe it as a unique and rewarding experience.

*When to Go & What to Bring* This trip should only be undertaken in the dry season, from mid-December to March (or possibly in July and August if little rain has fallen). The rest of the time, the trails are impossibly waterlogged and the rivers are torrents, full of broken trees and debris. On the other hand, towards the end of the dry season, the river levels drop and it's often difficult to find boats. Accordingly, it's best to go in the middle of the dry season: mid-January to mid-February is possibly the ideal period.

The trip should never been undertaken without careful preparation. One of your party should speak at least basic Spanish in order to communicate with the locals, whose help is essential in this isolated area. A letter of introduction (refer to the Documents & Paperwork section in the Facts for the Visitor chapter) may prove useful when dealing with immigration officials and the military. Don't forget to bring some small gifts for children and adults.

Ideally, you need camping gear and decent hiking boots, but otherwise keep your baggage to an absolute minimum. A compass and a machete are a must if you do not hire a guide. Remember to bring a good insect repellent.

Take an emergency package of dry food with you, and eat locally prepared meals wherever possible. You'll be able to find somebody to cook a hot meal for you in almost every village on the way. Expect to pay roughly US$5 for a meal. You'll need to carry drinking water, and be equipped to purify more as required. Be sure you drink plenty of water to avoid dehydration. Soft drinks are available in the villages on the way up to Púcuro and then from Bijao onward, but they are expensive.

A tent isn't necessary; instead, bring along a light hammock with a well-fitted mosquito net, plus two long pieces of rope to sling it. Some travellers have done the whole route without a tent or a hammock, relying entirely on the informal accommodation in the villages on the way. This is possible if you use guides, who will direct you to a village for the night and find a bed or a mattress for you. If you plan on trekking without a guide, don't set off without a hammock – there's always a risk of being lost in the middle of nowhere. In this case, you'll also need more food than just an emergency package.

You might make the whole route in eight days, but it's best to plan for a longer trip. The total cost won't be any less than flying from Panama to Colombia by the time you add up the cost of buses, boats, accommodation, food and guides, but the experience will be incomparable. Be prepared to spend about US$200 for the Panama City-Turbo route. Boats and guides will be the major items of expenditure.

From Panama City, there are two ways to start the trek: via Yaviza (far more popular) or via El Real.

**To Boca de Cupe via Yaviza** The town of Yaviza sits at the end of the Pan-American Highway, 284 km south-east of Panama City. It's reached by a daily bus (US$12), after a punishing 10-hour ride over mostly unpaved, bumpy road. The length of time it takes to complete the journey varies depending on the road conditions. The trip can usually only be accomplished in the dry season; the rest of the year, the last stretch of road often becomes impassable. If this is the case, the bus goes only as far as Canglón, 26 km before Yaviza. At times in the rainy season, the bus cannot make it further than Cañazas, leaving you stuck 106 km from Yaviza.

Alternatively, you can fly with Parsa (☎ 263883, 263803 in Panama City) from Panama City to Yaviza (Tuesday, Thursday, and Saturday; US$40 one way).

Yaviza is the last town of any size you'll see until the end of the route at Turbo. There's one hotel in town, *Las Tres Américas*, which costs US$10 per person. The restaurant close to the hotel serves basic meals.

The first leg of the route from Yaviza is a hike to Boca de Cupe, which you may be able to complete in one day if you start early. Cross the Río Chucunaque at Yaviza by canoe (US$1) and walk south for one to 1½ hours until you get to Río Tuira. Keep walking upstream along the river for another 1½ to two hours until you see the village of Pinogana on the opposite side. Wade across the river or, if the water is too high, call to someone in the village to take you across in a dugout (US$1).

From Pinogana, walk eastward for three to four hours to Aruza, passing a series of banana plantations. Chocó Indians live in the area, and you'll encounter quite a few along the way. Wade across the river at Aruza and then walk for about 45 minutes to Unión de Chocó.

If it's getting late, you can stay overnight in the village, but if the sun is still high, you may want to continue to Boca de Cupe. To do this, cross the Río Yapé to the village of Yapé and head south along the Río Tuira (keeping the river in sight) to Capetí. Finally, cross the river to Boca de Cupe. It's a pleasant walk which will take you about four to five hours from Unión de Chocó.

Wading across rivers is only possible (but

not always) in the dry season; at other times, you will require a canoe or boat, which adds to the cost and duration of the journey.

Sometimes, you may be able to find a boat going from Yaviza to Boca de Cupe. It never hurts to ask around.

**To Boca de Cupe via El Real** You can get to El Real from Panama City by banana boat. Boats depart from the Muelle Fiscal and take between 12 and 36 hours. They cost about US$25 per person, including the simple meals which are provided on board. There's no fixed schedule for these boats. If possible, try to get passage on a large boat, which is usually more comfortable.

The port of El Real is some distance from the town, so you have to go about five km upstream to the Mercadero to pick up a boat to Boca de Cupe. The best place to inquire about boats is the general store; most provisions arrive by boat, so the owner is generally clued up about what's going on. Prices for the two to four-hour boat trip to Boca de Cupe are negotiable, as are all the boat trips on this route. The fare can cost anywhere between US$10 and US$20 per person. You can camp either at the port or at the Mercadero.

**Boca de Cupe to Púcuro** Boca de Cupe is a Chocó Indian village on the Río Tuira. You get your Panama exit stamp here from a shop alongside the river. Ask for Antonio, the shop owner, and you will be directed there. According to recent reports, the immigration formalities have moved to Púcuro, but you still have to present yourself at the shop to have your passport details recorded.

You can stay overnight in Boca de Cupe with a local family, or ask for the *casa comunal*, a small community house with four double rooms (US$5 per person). Locals will soon approach you to ask if you want meals cooked for you.

In Boca de Cupe, you need to find a boat going to Púcuro. You may have to wait two or three days for a boat, and then negotiate the fare. It can cost anywhere between US$15 and US$30 for the three to five-hour

trip. You may be able to arrange a motorised dugout through the local schoolteacher, which can be cheaper.

Púcuro is the first Cuna Indian village you'll encounter; it's an interesting place, but it's also the site of recent guerrilla activity.

When the river is high, boats land right at Púcuro, but otherwise they put you down about a half-hour walk downstream from the village. Ask someone where you can stay for the night; the village chief may let you sleep in the meeting hall for a fee (the whole village will take an interest in you), but there are other possibilities.

**Púcuro to Paya** The 18-km walk to Paya, the next village, can be done in six to eight hours. It involves four river crossings, but all the rivers are fordable. You need to look hard for the trail after the third crossing, but otherwise the path is easy to follow and no guide is necessary. There is a good camping site just before the third crossing. Should you prefer to go with a guide, you can hire one in Púcuro. They charge about US$30 for this portion of the trail; don't pay in advance.

When you get to Paya, you must go to the military barracks, about two km away, for a passport (and most probably luggage) inspection. This involves wading across the river; the locals will show you the path to take to the crossing point. The soldiers will probably offer to let you stay the night in the barracks, but no food is available.

The village of Paya is a far more enjoyable place to stay. Ask the village chief where you can stay; he is likely to let you sleep in his home and his family will cook for you. Pay a reasonable fee for these services, even though he probably won't bring up the subject of payment. Make the lodging arrangements with the chief before you go to the barracks.

Paya was once the site of the Cuna 'university' to which Cunas came to study the traditional arts of magic, medicine and history. It fell on hard times about a century ago as European technology and European diseases gradually penetrated the area, but it's still an interesting place. Be discreet with your camera, and ask permission before you take photographs.

There's a foot-and-mouth disease control station in the barracks. If you're coming from Colombia, your baggage will be inspected and anything made of leather, or even vaguely resembling leather, will be dipped in a mild antiseptic to kill any pathogens.

**Paya to Cristales** From Paya, the trail goes to Cristales via Palo de Letras (the border marker between Panama and Colombia). This is the most difficult stage, and it's the part where you're most likely to get lost, so a guide is highly recommended. If you were going to hire a guide for only a part of the hike, this would be the right time to do it. In 1992, a party of six were lost here for nine days, according to rangers.

Guides can be found in Paya – ask the chief. A pair of guides (they won't like to go on their own) for the route to Cristales will cost about US$70. The trek with a guide takes eight to 10 hours. If you want to challenge this bit of jungle on your own, it will probably take you two days, if not longer.

The first part of the trail to Palo de Letras is uphill, and this is perhaps the most difficult portion. A British Army expedition came through here in 1972 and cut the trail, but it is long gone. You should reach Palo de Letras in about three hours (with guides).

At Palo de Letras, you leave behind Panama's Parque Nacional del Darién and enter Colombia's Parque Nacional Los Katíos. From the border marker, the trail goes downhill for about 20 km to Cristales; it takes about five to six hours to do this bit.

You tramp through a thick forest down to the Río Tulé and cross the river eight times (2½ to three hours from the border to the last crossing). One hour after the last crossing, you reach the Río Cacarica. Follow the river downstream for about 1½ hours until you reach Cristales.

Along most of this portion, the trail is faint and may be overgrown and confusing, particularly at the beginning of the dry season.

It virtually disappears in the course of the rainy season.

Cristales is one of the national park's ranger stations. The rangers are friendly and helpful, and will probably let you sleep in the station free of charge.

**Cristales to Turbo** The last part of the trip, from Cristales to Turbo, is by boat. If the park workers are going to Turbo for supplies, then it can all be done in one haul. If not, you'll first have to find a boat to Bijao, and then, possibly, another to Travesía (also known as Puente América), on the Río Atrato. A hired boat from Cristales to Bijao can cost up to US$40. You can walk this leg of the trip in five hours, but you are highly likely to get lost unless you hire someone to guide you.

Bijao is just a collection of poor huts inhabited mostly by blacks. The best person to ask about boats is the store owner. You may have to wait a couple of days before a boat turns up. Hiring a motorised dugout from Bijao to Travesía may cost another US$40 (three hours). There is a shop in Travesía with expensive food, soft drinks and beer. There's also a dirty, tick-infested hotel, where a bed will cost US$3. A couple of ramshackle, basic eateries serve the usual fish-and-rice meals.

Once at Travesía, you'll have no difficulty finding transport to Turbo. There are fast passenger motorboats coming from Riosucio every morning heading for Turbo (US$10, two hours). There may be another boat passing through Travesía in the afternoon. If you decide to take one of the cargo boats which ply the Río Atrato, allow a whole day for the journey; your boat may stop en route several times to load, unload, fix the engine, fish, rest, fix the engine, visit the family, fix the engine, or for a hundred other unexpected reasons. Once you get to Turbo, have your passport stamped in the DAS office. Refer to the Turbo section for details.

Instead of going straight to Turbo, it's well worth stopping in Sautatá, the visitors centre of Los Katíos park, to rest for a couple of days after the trek. See the Parque Nacional Los Katíos section for more information.

## From Venezuela

There are four border crossings between Colombia and Venezuela. By far the most popular with travellers is the route via San Antonio del Táchira (Venezuela) and Cúcuta (Colombia), on the main Caracas-Bogotá road. See the Cúcuta section for details.

Another entry point to Colombia is Paraguachón, on the Maracaibo (Venezuela) to Maicao (Colombia) road. This may be your route if you plan on heading directly to the Colombian Caribbean coast. There are buses and shared taxis between Maracaibo and Maicao. You'll find further details in the Maicao section.

The third possible route to Colombia leads through Los Llanos, from either Puerto Páez or Puerto Ayacucho (both in Venezuela) to Puerto Carreño (Colombia). See the Puerto Carreño section for details.

Finally, you can cross the border from El Amparo de Apure (Venezuela) to Arauca (Colombia), but this route is neither convenient nor safe and is rarely used by travellers. Note that Arauca department has guerrilla problems.

## From Ecuador

Almost all travellers use the Pan-American Highway border crossing at the Rumichaca Bridge between Tulcán (Ecuador) and Ipiales (Colombia). All passport formalities are done on the border. See the Ipiales section for more information.

A more adventurous entry point into Colombia is on the fringe of the Amazon, from Lago Agrio (Ecuador) to San Miguel (Colombia) and on to Puerto Asís. The region around Puerto Asís is partly controlled by the guerrillas and is unsafe. Details about this border crossing are given in the Puerto Asís section.

You can also get into Colombia by boat along the Pacific coast, from San Lorenzo (Ecuador) to Tumaco (Colombia). Read the Tumaco section for further information.

## From Brazil & Peru

The only viable border crossing from these two countries into Colombia is via Leticia in the far south-eastern corner of the Colombian Amazon. Leticia is reached from Iquitos (Peru) and Manaus (Brazil). See the Leticia section for details.

## SEA

Colombia has ports on both Pacific and Caribbean coasts, so it's possible to arrive or leave the country by sea. Sea traffic is busier on the Caribbean side: boats are frequently coming and going between the USA, Mexico, Central America, the Caribbean islands and the coasts of Colombia and Venezuela. Colombian ports on the Caribbean include Barranquilla, Cartagena, Santa Marta and Turbo.

There's less sea traffic along the Pacific coast but some boats from Ecuador, Mexico and Central America call at Buenaventura, Colombia's major Pacific port.

There are no regular passenger liners operating to either coast, so all you can do is try to get onto a cargo ship, fishing boat or yacht. These informal arrangements require time and luck, so the trip is impossible to plan in advance. Probably the best strategy is simply to ask around the docks at the port you plan to sail from. If you come up with nothing, try the next port you come to. Also try yacht marinas: boat owners may have a space for a willing helper.

Note that some boats are involved in smuggling, including drug trafficking, so think twice before boarding a boat you suspect of carrying illegal cargo. This is very difficult to determine, of course, so there's always some risk.

## TOURS
### Overland Companies

Overland trips to South America are becoming popular, especially with UK and Australasian travellers. However, there are very few tours which include Colombia in their itinerary. Contact one of the following South America overland operators, all of which are based in the UK (Exodus and

Encounter also have offices in Australia, New Zealand, the USA and Canada):

Dragoman
    Camp Green, Kenton Rd, Debenham, Suffolk IP14 6LA (☎ (01728) 861133; fax (01728) 861127)
Encounter Overland
    267 Old Brompton Rd, London SW5 9JA (☎ (0171) 370 6845)
Exodus Expeditions
    9 Weir Rd, London SW12 0LT (☎ (0181) 673 0859; fax (0181) 673 0779)
Geodyssey
    29 Harberton Rd, London N19 3JS (☎ (0171) 281 7788; fax (0171) 281 7878)
Guerba Expeditions
    101 Eden Vale Rd, Westbury, Wiltshire BA13 3QX (☎ (01373) 826611; fax (01373) 838351)
Hann Overland
    201/203 Vauxhall Bridge Rd, London SW1V 1ER (☎ (0171) 834 7337; fax (0171) 828 7745)
Top Deck
    Top Deck House, 131/135 Earls Court Rd, London SW5 9RH (☎ (0171) 244 8641; fax (0171) 373 6201)

### Environmental Tours

**UK** For information on ecotours, contact the Centre for the Advancement of Responsible Travel (☎ (01732) 352757), Tourism Concern (☎ (0181) 878 9053) and Green Flag International (☎ (01223) 893587).

**USA** Information about ecological and other types of tours can be obtained from the following organisations: North American Coordinating Center for Responsible Tourism, 2 Kensington Rd, San Anselmo, CA 94960; One World Family Travel Network, PO Box 4317, Berkeley, CA 94703; and Travel Links, Co-op America, 2100 M St NW, Suite 310, Washington DC 20036.

Earthwatch organises trips for volunteers to work overseas on scientific and cultural projects with a strong emphasis on protection and preservation of ecology and environment. Other organisations which provide tours with a similar emphasis include Conservation International and The Nature Conservancy. For the addresses of these and other environmental organisations,

see the Useful Organisations section in the Facts for the Visitor chapter.

## ARRIVING IN & LEAVING COLOMBIA

Although you no longer need a visa to enter Colombia (unless you're a Chinese citizen), you must get an entry and exit stamp in your passport from the DAS authorities when you arrive and depart from the country.

If you fly into Colombia, this will be done at the airport – Bogotá, Medellín, Cali, Pereira, Bucaramanga, Barranquilla, Cartagena and San Andrés have airports which handle international flights. At the land/sea border crossings, DAS have posts in Cúcuta, Maicao, Santa Marta, Turbo, Buenaventura, Tumaco, Ipiales, Mocoa, Leticia, Puerto Carreño and Arauca.

This means that if you arrive in Colombia by a somewhat unusual route, you won't have your passport stamped until the nearest DAS office. For example, arriving from Panama overland by the Darién Gap, you get the stamp in Turbo. The same applies when leaving Colombia overland for Panama: get the exit stamp in Turbo, although you will still be travelling for some time in Colombia before actually crossing the border.

The airport tax on international flights out of Colombia is US$17 if you have stayed in the country up to 60 days, and US$30 if you have stayed longer. The tax is payable either in US dollars or pesos at the exchange rate of the day. Other foreign currencies may be occasionally accepted, but not travellers' cheques.

## WARNING

The information in this chapter is particularly vulnerable to change: prices for international travel are volatile, routes are introduced and cancelled, schedules change, special deals come and go, and rules and visa requirements are amended. Airlines and governments seem to take a perverse pleasure in making price structures and regulations as complicated as possible. You should check directly with the airline or a travel agent to

Sierra Nevada del Cocuy

Top: The parish church in Villa de Leyva
Bottom: Handicraft shop on the central square of Villa de Leyva

make sure you understand how a fare (and ticket you may buy) works.

The travel industry is highly competitive, so you should get opinions, quotes and advice from as many airlines and travel agents as possible before you part with your hard-earned cash. The details given in this chapter should be regarded as pointers and are not a substitute for your own careful, up-to-date research.

# Getting Around

## AIR

Colombia was the first country in South America to have an airline. In 1919 the Colombian-German company SCADTA (Sociedad Colombo Alemana de Transporte Aéreo) was founded, to later become Avianca. Today the country has a well-developed airline system and one of the densest networks of domestic flights in Latin America.

## Airlines

Colombia has half a dozen main airlines and perhaps a score of other smaller carriers. Major passenger airlines include:

Avianca (Aerovías Nacionales de Colombia) – Colombia's main international airline, it flies to the USA, Europe and most Latin American capitals; at home it services about 15 major cities, all of which are departmental capitals (see the map)

Sam (Sociedad Aeronáutica de Medellín) – the Medellín-based carrier, it has international flights to Central America; within Colombia it doubles most of the major Avianca routes

Aces (Aerolíneas Centrales de Colombia) – it focuses on north-western Colombia providing access from the major cities to about 25 towns of the region; it also has daily flights to Miami

Aires – links the Andean regions with the fringes of the Amazon and Los Llanos over the Cordillera Oriental; it has flights between Bogotá, Cali, Florencia, Girardot, Ibagué, Medellín, Neiva, Pitalito, Puerto Asís, Puerto Leguízamo, San Vicente, Tame, Villavicencio and Yopal; its only international flight is between Puerto Asís and Lago Agrio (Ecuador)

Intercontinental de Aviación – despite its proud name, it has no intercontinental flights and its only international routes are Cali-Esmeraldas and Cali-Tulcán (both in Ecuador); on the domestic front, it flies between most major cities, including Arauca, Barranquilla, Bogotá, Bucaramanga, Cali, Cartagena, Cúcuta, Medellín, Pasto, Pereira, Popayán, Riohacha, San Andrés, Tumaco and Valledupar

Satena (Servicio Aéreo a Territorios Nacionales) – the commercial arm of the FAC (Colombian Air Force), it specialises in flights to the Territorios Nacionales, the vast areas of the Amazon, Los Llanos and the Pacific coast; it lands at some 50 small towns and villages which would be otherwise virtually inaccessible

Since the economic opening in 1991, reflected in the airline business by the so-called *cielos abiertos* (open skies) policy, several new carriers emerged, including AeroRepública and Isleña de Aviación, and further ones are likely to appear in the near future.

Colombian airlines operate an enormous variety of aircraft, ranging from light turbo few-seaters to jumbo jets. The planes of the major companies are relatively new and, on the whole, they are in acceptable condition, but some minor carriers (particularly cargo airlines) may fly anything that manages to take off.

The on-board service of the major carriers is OK. As the flight time is usually not longer than an hour, don't expect any gastronomic treats; on most flights you get no more than a snack. Smoking is banned on domestic flights.

## Airfares

Colombian airfares are high compared to those of, say, Venezuela or Ecuador. The prices are adjusted periodically to account for the depreciation of the peso against hard currencies.

When the open skies policy began in 1991, the airfare war between the carriers broke out. As a result, the airfares differ between the airlines and the difference over the same route may be up to 40%, or even more. Avianca and Sam keep their fares the same, and they are the most expensive carriers to fly with. Aces tends to follow the two big brothers. Before booking with them, check who else is flying the route you're interested in. For example, Intercontinental, which covers most of the major routes, may often have significantly lower airfares. The newly established airlines usually offer promotional fares, sometimes phenomenal bargains.

See the Avianca flights map, which also

130

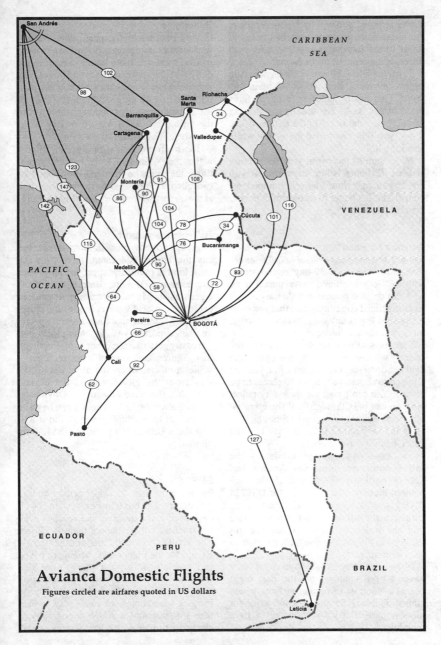

# Avianca Domestic Flights

Figures circled are airfares quoted in US dollars

shows airfares. You will find more details in the appropriate sections later in the book. Refer to the Bogotá chapter for fares with different carriers out of the capital.

There's a US$3.50 airport tax on domestic flights departing from about 30 main airports. This tax is included in the airfares listed in this book. You usually pay this tax when buying the ticket in the airline office. If not, you'll be charged at the airport while checking in.

Make sure to reconfirm your reservation at least 72 hours before departure. If you don't, you may find yourself bumped off your flight. It's better to reconfirm in person than by phone.

## Avianca Air Pass

Known as *Conozca a Colombia* or *Descubre Colombia*, this is a 30-day round ticket within Colombia offered by Avianca. The air pass can only be bought outside the country and the official conditions state that you have to fly into the country by Avianca, though this is not strictly enforced.

The pass allows for travel around the country with Avianca and Sam between any of their domestic destinations, but you are allowed to choose only up to 10 places to be visited. You can't visit the same city twice, but you can pass through it, if there are no other connections. You must submit an itinerary before beginning the journey but you don't actually have to book.

Two kinds of air pass are available – the full version including San Andrés and Leticia, costing US$325; and another one without these two destinations, for US$224 (flying with Avianca from Europe you are entitled to the full version at this price). Note that the domestic airport taxes are not included in the pass, so you must pay one on each departure.

If the prices stay as they have so far (they haven't been changed for the past eight years, in contrast to regular airfares which almost doubled), the pass is good value for money, particularly for those on a tight schedule.

## Schedules

Flights between the largest cities are frequent; for example, from Bogotá to Medellín or Cali there are more than a dozen flights daily with various carriers. Small towns may witness only a few flights a week. If you plan on travelling by air in some obscure areas, it's a good idea to get flight schedules from the airline offices. Stock up in Bogotá as elsewhere it's difficult to get them.

The main problem with domestic flights is that they often tend to be late and sometimes they can be changed, postponed or cancelled. Be prepared to spend some time at the airport waiting for your flight.

## To/From the Airport

Regardless of how close or how far from the city the airport is located, there's always some kind of public transport. In many cities (for example, Bogotá, Barranquilla, Cartagena, Santa Marta, Bucaramanga) you can get to the airport by urban bus. Some cities, such as Medellín and Cali, have a special minibus airport service. In some places you can easily get to the airport on foot (Popayán, San Andrés and several smaller towns), while in others, where the airport is a long way from the city (Pasto is the classic example), there are colectivos. Obviously, you can always take a taxi but it can be quite expensive; for example, in Medellín it will cost about US$15 compared to US$1.50 by minibus.

## BUS

Buses are the main means of getting around the country. The bus transport system is well developed and extensive, and reaches even the smallest villages where there is a road. The roads, however, are another story. Except for the main roads, which are paved and generally in a good shape, most side roads are unsurfaced and their condition often leaves a lot to be desired. In order to imagine what some back roads may be like, take into account a rough topography, a changing climate with a heavy rainy season and a lack of funds and enthusiasm when it comes to repairing the roads.

## Types of Buses

There are three principal kinds of buses: ordinary (called *corriente*, *sencillo* or *ordinario*), 1st class (which goes by a variety of names, such as *pullman*, *metropolitano*, *de lujo* or *directo*) and the air-con buses (known as *climatizado* or, more proudly, as *thermoking*).

The corriente buses range from geriatric crates to fairly good modern models; the antiques usually ply the rough minor roads, while the newer versions run on the main routes. The corrientes stop for people along the road. Some drivers seem to hunt for passengers and pick up everybody, which sometimes results in the bus being packed far beyond its capacity. The corrientes on the side roads prefer travelling by day and some start very early, with departures at 3 or 4 am.

The pullman buses are pretty good, reliable and comfortable, with plenty of leg room, reclining seats and large luggage compartments. They are predominantly long-distance buses covering the main routes, and many travel at night.

The pullmans are usually fast as they stop less often on the road to pick up passengers. Breakdowns are rare and a flat tyre is the most frequent unforeseen stop on the road. As a rule, but with many exceptions, the pullmans take only as many passengers as they have seats.

The climatizados are the best. These are the most modern buses, usually equipped with a toilet, and sometimes even with seat belts. They have expanded over the past few years, pushing most corrientes (and even some pullmans) out of the main routes. They now account for a good deal of transport between the major cities. They are the fastest and most comfortable way of travelling. They depart and arrive on schedule, stop only in a few main towns en route and won't pick up passengers elsewhere. They almost never take more passengers than they have seats.

Smoking in buses is not allowed, although in the corrientes plying back roads people smoke and nobody seems to pay attention to it. The long-distance buses stop for meals but not necessarily at mealtimes; it seems to depend on when the driver is hungry or when the bus gets to a restaurant which has an arrangement with the bus company. Don't leave any hand luggage in the bus when you get off for your meal.

The traditional bus entertainment is music – anything from vallenato via ranchera to salsa – according to the driver's taste. The volume is also at a whim of the driver, and you may sometimes experience a whole night of blasting music – not necessarily the greatest fun.

There is, however, a more disturbing entertainment – video movies. Most buses, including corrientes, are now equipped with video equipment, and this can be a nightmare when travelling by night. Bloody US action movies interlaced with sweet Mexican love stories – two Colombian favourites – played most of the night and often at full volume can be real torture. The technical quality is hardly acceptable; the videos don't track properly and the jumpy image is often unwatchable.

## Bus Companies

There are plenty of companies. The biggest ones usually have all three kinds of buses, though some don't operate the corrientes. They service large parts of the county, mostly the main interregional routes between large cities. The major companies, that supposedly have a better reputation, include Expreso Bolivariano, Expreso

Brasilia, Berlinas del Fonce, Rápido Ochoa and Copetrán.

Small companies usually provide the service within the regions and their buses mostly include corrientes and pullmans.

## Bus Terminals

Almost every large city has its *terminal de buses*, a central bus terminal. A few cities which still haven't got terminals are in the process of building them. In smaller cities and towns, where there are no central terminals, buses depart from the bus company offices which usually tend to gather along one or two adjacent streets.

The standard of the bus terminals varies widely from place to place. Bogotá, Medellín, Cali, Cartegena and Bucaramanga all have modern, well-organised, purpose-built terminals. Regardless of how far or how close to the city centre the terminal is, it's always serviced by city buses or busetas.

## Tickets & Fares

Bus travel is not as cheap in Colombia as it is in neighbouring Ecuador or Venezuela. As a rule of a thumb, the corriente bus costs between US$2 and US$2.50 for every 100 km. Pullmans cost about 20% more than corrientes and the air-con buses 15% more than pullmans.

If various companies service the same route, the fare is much the same with all of them. The standard, however, may differ from one company to another, and you'll soon become familiar with which are better than others.

When you get on a bus somewhere on the road, you pay the fare to the *ayudante* (driver's sidekick) and rarely get a ticket. The ayudantes sometimes tend to charge gringos more than the actual fare or at least round the price up to the nearest thousand pesos. Ask other passengers beforehand to be sure of the correct fare.

On the main roads buses run frequently, so there is little point in booking a seat in advance. You just go to the terminal, find which company has the next bus due to depart, buy your ticket and board the bus.

The only time you need to book is during the Christmas and Easter periods, when hordes of Colombians are on holiday. In some places off the main routes, where there are only a few buses daily, it's better to buy a ticket several hours before departure.

All seats on long-distance climatizados, pullmans and (usually) corrientes are numbered; when you buy a ticket at the terminal it usually has a seat number. At intermediate points, you just grab an unoccupied seat if there are any, or wait for the next bus.

## CHIVA

Apart from conventional buses, there is one more peculiar kind – the chiva. This Disneyland-type vehicle was the principal means of transport a few decades ago. Today, the chivas have almost disappeared from the main roads but they still play an important role on outback roads between small towns and villages. There are still a few thousand of them and they are most common in Antioquia, Huila, Nariño and on the Caribbean coast. Chivas take both passengers and any kind of cargo, animals included. If the interior is already completely packed, the roof is used for everything and everybody who doesn't fit inside. Chivas usually gather around markets, from where they depart for their journeys along bumpy roads. They are rare guests at the bus terminals.

The chiva – in some regions called *bus de escalera* – is a piece of popular art on wheels. The body is made almost entirely of wood and has wooden benches rather than seats, and each bench is accessible from the outside. The body is painted all around with colourful decorative patterns, each different, with a main painting on the back. There are native artists who specialise in painting chivas. Ceramic miniatures of chivas are to be found in just about every handicraft shop all over the country.

Recently, night tours by chiva have become popular. They are organised by travel agents in several larger cities. There is usually a group playing traditional music aboard, and a large stock of aguardiente to create the proper atmosphere.

## COLECTIVO

The *colectivo*, a mode of transport quite widespread in Colombia, is a cross between a bus and a taxi. They are usually large, US-made cars from the 1950s and 1960s, less often minibuses, jeeps or pick-up trucks. They cover fixed routes, and charge roughly 50% more than buses. The colectivo service came into being on roads where buses didn't run or offered infrequent service. Although they mainly cover short-distance routes, there are some medium or even long-distance services.

Colectivos have their own timetables – they simply depart when all seats are filled. In the case of cars, it's quite easy to determine – usually five or six passengers. As for pick-up trucks etc, it largely depends on the driver's mood: when he feels there are enough passengers – he departs. The frequency of service varies largely from place to place. At some places there can be a colectivo every five minutes, but elsewhere you can wait an hour or longer until the necessary number of passengers has been collected. Colectivos are a good option if you have a long wait for a bus, or if you want more speed. In some cities they depart from and arrive at the bus terminal but in smaller towns they usually flock in the main square.

## TRAIN

In the previous edition of this book I wrote: 'the Colombian railway (Ferrocarriles Nacionales de Colombia) is in its death throes so you'd better be quick if you want to take a train ride'. You no longer have to hurry: the train has died.

There have been several short-term campaigns launched to bring the train back to life but nothing much has come of it. Actually, it would mean rebuilding the railway from scratch, as the abandoned railtrack has been largely dismantled by locals and enterprising trade operators.

There are no longer trains operating passenger services apart from the Medellín-Barrancabermeja line and the short stretch between Bogotá and Nemocón, which has been turned into a tourist attraction.

## CAR & MOTORCYCLE

Travelling by an independent means of transport (either owned or rented) is a comfortable and attractive way of getting around the country. The advantages are schedule flexibility, access to remote areas, and the ability to seize fleeting photographic opportunities, to name just a few.

Unfortunately, Colombia is not the best country for travelling by car or motorcycle. The major problem is the security. Car theft is a well established business and yet more common is stealing the accessories and anything of value left inside. Although the major highways are usually in a good shape, there are not that many of them and the signposting is sporadic. As soon as you turn into back roads however, you'll immediately understand what Colombian unpaved roads really are. A jeep is the best (or the only) kind of vehicle to drive on these roads. Here is where the next problem appears. Some obscure areas are noted for insecurity – caused either by guerrillas or by common criminals – and cars are obvious tempting prays. You will easily pass by such regions undisturbed if you travel by a public transport, but a nice jeep won't get through unnoticed.

In the cities, on the other hand, the traffic is heavy, chaotic and mad. Driving manners are wild and unpredictable. It takes some time to get used to the local style of driving but even if you master it, the risk of an accident still remains pretty high.

There has been quite a confusing legal jumble regarding motorbikes over the past decade. Since the *sicarios* (paid killers) began to use them as the most suitable means of transport for their killing raids, the authorities set about introducing new bike rules. The regulations included a ban on carrying a passenger, prohibition of using crash helmets (intended to make it easier to recognise the rider), a ban on riding at night, limitations on importing high-powered bikes etc. In most departments they have been abandoned after the number of murders committed from motorbikes decreased. Some have been declared unconstitutional and put down by the court. However, given the volatile situation, one can't rule out further changes.

To sum up, driving a car or a motorcycle in Colombia is a bit risky and not recommended. If you come with your own vehicle, try to keep to the major roads and to the safe regions. In the large cities, leave your vehicle somewhere safe and go sightseeing by taxi or other means of local transport.

All the internal problems aside, note that there is no way of bringing your vehicle to South America other than shipping it by sea or air. This involves time, costs and further risks (read the Bringing Your Own Vehicle section).

Renting a car is perhaps a better solution. Firstly, it saves you the money you would spend on getting in your own car. Secondly, it will have Colombian registration plates so it won't stand out from local vehicles and won't attract such attention. Furthermore, it's not your car after all, so it's likely to let you move around with less trauma. Check carefully all the clauses about the insurance and responsibility before you sign the rental contract.

### Car Rental

There are a few international car rental companies, including Hertz, Avis and Budget, and a number of local operators in Colombia. They have offices at some major airports and in the city centres. Any top-class hotel, tourist office or travel agent will give you information about where to look for them.

Rental agencies will require you to produce your driver's licence and a credit card (Visa, MasterCard and American Express are the most common and universally accepted). You need to be at least 21 years of age to rent a car, although renting some cars (particularly luxury models and 4WDs) may require you to be at least 23 or even 25 years of age.

Car rental is not cheap in Colombia – the prices are comparable to full-price rental in Europe or the USA – and there are seldom any discounts. The local companies are cheaper than international operators, but

their cars and rental conditions may leave something to be desired.

When you get rental charges quoted, make sure they include the insurance in the price. Otherwise, you'll have to pay for it on top of the quoted price, as it's compulsory. Some companies allow a set number of free km per day or week, but others don't, and will apply a per-km rate from the moment you take the car.

As a rough guide only, a small car per day will cost around US$50 to US$60, while the discount rate for a full week will be about US$300 to US$350. A per-km rate is around US$0.25. A 4WD vehicle is considerably more expensive and harder to obtain.

When renting a car, read the contract carefully before signing it. Pay close attention to any theft clause, as it may load a large percentage of any loss onto the hirer. Look the car over carefully and insist on making a note of any defects (including scratches) on the rental form. Check the spare tyre to make sure it's not flat and take a note of whether there is a jack.

### Bringing Your Own Vehicle

Bringing your own vehicle into Colombia is expensive. Since there is no road along the Darién Gap, it's impossible to drive all the way from Central to South America; any vehicle has to be shipped or flown in. From the USA or Canada you can continue by road as far as Panama, from where the only way to move your vehicle any further south is by sea or air.

The cheapest way will probably be the boat from Colón to Barranquilla or Cartagena. To find a cargo boat heading that way, go to the docks in Colón and ask what ships are going.

Smaller cargo boats depart from Coco Solo pier in Colón. They may offer you a relatively low price, but may not be able to help you with the paperwork you need to enter Colombia. These smaller vessels are sometimes contraband boats, and their service may be risky. Prices are very negotiable; they might start out asking US$1500 and come down to half or even less that. You might feel it's better to go with a more established shipping company. As a general rule, you can expect to pay a minimum of about US$700 to ship a car from Colón to Cartagena or Barranquilla but it could easily cost US$1000 or more. Prices are extremely variable.

The price apart, the procedure is time-consuming, as there's a lot of paperwork involved at both ends. The whole operation will perhaps require a lot of time and patience, and there's still another problem – the safety.

The security of shipping is minimal so take every possible precaution and the best insurance you can. Stealing vehicles being shipped is a big business. Outside mirrors, radio/cassette player, wipers, tools etc, are the first accessories to go. And, of course, your belongings. Remove everything removable and take everything of value out of the interior. The only sure way of avoiding a theft is to stay with your vehicle every minute but, unfortunately, it is difficult to arrange a passage for the driver with the vehicle.

Motorcyclists may consider the air option, which is safer, easier and faster than boat, but obviously more expensive. Start by asking the cargo departments of the airlines that fly to Colombia (like Copa), or at the cargo terminal at Tocumen international airport in Panama City. Travel agents can sometimes help. If money is not a problem, you can also have your car flown over. Cargo planes do have size limits, but a normal car, or even a Land Rover, can fit.

Another possibility is to ship your vehicle from the USA to Venezuela, and then continue overland to Colombia. You thus avoid the corrupt Panamanian and Colombian shippers and arrive in one of Venezuela's ports, most probably in La Guaira, Puerto Cabello or Maracaibo. The cheapest point of departure from the USA will probably be Miami. Prices are variable, so call several places before committing yourself; look in the Yellow Pages under 'Automobile Transporters' for toll-free 800 numbers. You usually need to give one or two weeks' notice to the shipping company, and expect it to take a month or more from the date of sailing. The cost of shipping a car is likely to be somewhere between US$1200 and US$2000.

Shipping a car from Europe is still more expensive (roughly US$2500 to US$5000) and probably only makes sense if it's a vehicle specially prepared for an overland expedition across South America, or for another particular purpose.

Drivers of cars and riders of motorbikes will need the vehicle's registration papers, liability insurance and an International Driver's Permit in addition to their domestic licence. You will also need a Carnet de Passage en Douane, known in Spanish as Libreta de Pasos por Aduana. The carnet is a bond guaranteeing that you won't sell your vehicle in South America – you post a bond to get the carnet, and it's partly refunded when you get back and show that you still have the vehicle.

You don't need the carnet for travel in Central America, but you will need it as soon as you arrive on South American soil. You should arrange it before you arrive in South America. If you don't have a carnet, you and your vehicle could be halted and refused admission at any border in South America. Contact your local automobile association and relevant consulates for details about all documentation.

According to several travellers, the best way to obtain a carnet is through the Touring y Automóvil Club de Venezuela, where it costs only US$300, with US$150 of that being refundable. The Club has their head office in Caracas (☎ 914879, 9106039, 914448, 916373), Centro Integral Santa Rosa de Lima, Planta Baja, Local 11 and 12, Avenida Principal Santa Rosa de Lima, on the corner of Calle A. It may be better to get the carnet here than in your home county, not only because it will be far cheaper, but also because it will be issued by a South American country, so the documents will be in Spanish and thus more easily recognised and accepted throughout South America.

You can arrange a carnet through local automobile associations in Canada or the

UK, but it is very expensive: travellers have had to post bonds for more than the full value of their vehicle, coming to thousands of dollars.

In the USA, the American Automobile Association (AAA) used to issue the carnets but they no longer do so. Don Montague at the South American Explorers Club (see Useful Organisations) in the USA has some information on carnets, and his most recent advice was to go through the Venezuelan Automobile Club.

Anyone who is planning to take their own vehicle with them needs to check in advance what spares and petrol are likely to be available. Lead-free is not on sale worldwide, and neither is every little part for your car or motorcycle.

Colombia has a reasonably developed automobile industry. Various foreign makes are assembled locally and include Mazda (323, 626), General Motors (Sprint, Swift, Trooper) and Renault (R 9, R 19, Étoile). Most spare parts for these models are available locally. However, spare parts for cars other than those assembled in Colombia are difficult to obtain and expensive, so bring along a good supply.

Petrol stations in the large cities and along the main roads are in good supply. They sell diesel fuel and leaded petrol in two octane levels (*corriente* and *extra*), and some also sell unleaded petrol. Petrol is sold in US gallons; one gallon of ordinary/super petrol costs US$1/1.20; diesel goes for US$0.90 per gallon.

An alternative to bringing your own car from overseas is to purchase a vehicle in South America, but here, again, the price and paperwork are two major drawbacks. Cars in Colombia (both new and used) are expensive, even those which are assembled locally. Furthermore, you can't buy a car in Colombia if you don't have a Colombian *cédula*, the national identity card, which you can only get if you come to study or work in Colombia, or are a resident of this country. Reputedly one of the best places on the continent to buy a vehicle, be it motorbike or car, new or second-hand, is Santiago de Chile.

## Driving in Colombia

Traffic in Colombia is not exactly what you've been used to at home. It's wild, chaotic, noisy, polluting and anarchic. You may still find some similarities if you're coming from, say, Italy or Spain, but if you're a fresh visitor from Australia, Germany or Canada you're in for a shock. It's not that road rules don't exist; it's just that nobody respects them and they're not enforced.

Whether you bring your own vehicle or hire one from a rental company, drive carefully and defensively. Don't expect local drivers to obey the rules. Don't assume, for example, that a vehicle will stop at a red light or stop sign. Using indicators before making a turn is rare.

When you drive in Bogotá and other big cities, it's best to have the doors locked and windows closed (or almost closed), to prevent unexpected theft at red lights or in traffic jams. If you can't stand windows closed, don't have handbags and packets lying around on the seats, and wear your watch on the hand away from the window.

Car security is a problem, so never leave valuables in the vehicle and lock it securely. Always leave the vehicle in a guarded car park (*parqueadero vigilado*). There are so many of them (which is the best indicator of the problem) that you really don't need to look around much. Leaving your vehicle unattended on the street would mean that you don't want to see it again (and probably will not, or at least some of the accessories and belongings).

If your car is stolen, report the theft immediately to the police, where a written report known as a *denuncia* will be produced. It is essential for claiming on your insurance or for the car rental company. Don't expect that the car will ever be found.

## BICYCLE

Cycling is a cheap, convenient, healthy, environmentally sound and above all a fun way of travelling. All this sounds terrific, but Colombia is certainly not a paradise for bikers. There are no bike tracks, bike rental or any other facilities. Cycling is unsafe because of the mad traffic, unpredictable drivers and Colombia's endemic security problems. Foreign travellers with their own bikes are virtually unknown.

Despite all that, cycling is popular among locals and is even one of Colombia's national sports.

## HITCHING

Hitching is never entirely safe in any country in the world, let alone in Colombia. Predictably, hitch-hiking in Colombia is uncommon and difficult. Given the complex internal situation, drivers don't want to take risks and simply don't stop on the road. Apart from that, the idea of hitching is not well understood; most drivers think that you must be a beggar or a hippie to use such a form of transport. People rich enough to have cars don't stoop so low as to pick up 'poor' travellers, while the trucks usually ask for money for the ride.

As the bus transport is fast, efficient and relatively cheap, it's probably not worth wasting time on hitching and taking a potentially serious risk. If you decide to hitch, be prepared for long waits and even then don't count on reaching your destination.

## BOAT

With some 3000 km of Pacific and Atlantic coastline, there is a considerable amount of shipping. This consists mostly of irregular cargo boats which may also take passengers.

Boats along the Caribbean coast are of little interest (except for the Golfo de Urabá), as road transport is faster and cheaper. On the Pacific coast, however, where there are no roads, boats are the main means of transport, with Buenaventura being the main port.

Rivers are important transport routes in the regions such as the Chocó and the Amazon where there is no other way of getting around. The Atrato and San Juan rivers are the main water routes of Chocó. In the Amazon, the Putumayo and Caquetá rivers are the major waterways.

Very few riverboats run on any regular schedule, and as most are primarily cargo boats, they are far from fast. Conditions are primitive and food (if provided) is poor. The fares are a matter of discussion with the captain. On certain stretches of rivers there are semi-regular passenger boats which are very fast but very expensive.

The Magdalena River was once the principal waterway of the central part of the country but no longer has much importance as far as the river transport goes. Some passenger boats service parts of its lower course where the roads are few and far between. The only boats you are likely to use on the Magdalena are in the Mompós area.

## TOURS

Tours are an established and steadily growing business among local travel agents. There is a number of tour operators in most major touristy cities, including Bogotá, Medellín, Cali and Cartagena. They mostly cater for local demand as there are simply not many foreign visitors taking tours. This is, in many ways, a reflection of the structure of international tourism in Colombia. The well-off tourists (who would be those potentially interested in tours) are few in Colombia, as they usually prefer less dangerous countries. On the other hand, budget backpackers who come to Colombia, prefer to travel independently rather than to take tour excursions.

What travel operators offer is rather conventional: it usually includes city tours, one-day excursions to the neighbouring towns and other nearby attractions, and a night trip by chiva around the city night spots. Longer, more adventurous tours to remote regions are thin on the ground, due to both the fear about safety and a lack of demand.

Over the past few years, some more ambitious operators have begun to emerge on the market, some of whom focus on ecotours. The number of independent guides who can provide escorts for treks in the mountains, trips to caves and other unconventional projects, is also on the increase.

## LOCAL TRANSPORT
### Bus
Buses are the main means of getting around the cities. Almost every urban centre of over 100,000 inhabitants has a bus service, as do many smaller towns. The standard, speed and efficiency of the buses varies from place to place but on the whole they are slow and crowded. City buses have a flat fare, so the distance of the ride makes no difference. You get on by the front door and pay the driver or his assistant, if any, on entering. You never get a ticket.

In some cities or in some streets there are bus stops (*paraderos* or *paradas*), while in most others you just wave down the bus anywhere you happen to be. To let the driver know that you intend to get off you simply say, or shout, *por aquí, por favor* (here, please), *en la esquina, por favor*, (at the next street corner, please) or *el paradero, por favor* (at the coming bus stop, please).

There are lots of different types of buses, ranging from old post-war wrecks all the way through to the modern air-con vehicles. One very common type among them is the buseta, or a small bus, which has become a dominant means of urban transport in some cities, like Bogotá and Cartagena.

An increasingly popular kind of service is the so-called *servicio ejecutivo* which means that the bus (or buseta) takes only as many passengers as it has seats. The bus fare is somewhere between US$0.15 and US$0.40, depending on the city, type of bus and kind of service.

Some cities (Bogotá being one) also have minibuses called *colectivos*. They ply several main routes and are more comfortable and faster than buses, and charge about US$0.30.

A bus or buseta trip, particularly in the large cities such as Bogotá or Barranquilla, is not a smooth and silent ride but rather a sort of breathtaking adventure and a taste of the local folklore. You'll have an opportunity to be saturated with the blasting tropical music, understand the Colombian meaning of traffic road rules, and see the driver in

action while he desperately tries to make his way through the ocean of vehicles.

Following is an observation taken from the letter of a traveller:

Where in the world except Colombia can a driver do all these things all at the same time:

- Drive his bus
- Continually blow his horn
- Change gear in the most inconvenient place
- Take your fare
- Count out your change
- Even count his takings
- Tune his radio to the loudest salsa station
- Have a conversation with all and sundry, who might be on the other side of the road

### Taxi
Taxis are an inexpensive and a convenient means of getting around, especially if you are travelling with a few companions. The price will usually be the same, regardless of the number of passengers, though some drivers may demand more if you have a lot of luggage. Taxis are particularly useful when you arrive in an unfamiliar city and want to get from the bus terminal or the airport to the city centre to look for a hotel.

A taxi may also be chartered for longer distances. This is convenient if you want to visit places near major cities which are outside local transport areas but too near to be covered by long-distance bus networks.

In most cities, taxis are painted yellow or yellow-black. In major cities they have meters, though drivers are not always eager to switch them on, preferring to charge a gringo fare, obviously far higher than it would be according to the meter. It's always advisable to ask a few people beforehand (a shop keeper for example) what the usual taxi fare to your destination would be. Then, ask the taxi driver for the expected fare, and if they quote you a significantly higher fare, bargain and agree on a price. If you are not satisfied, try another taxi.

Due to permanent price rises, the taxi meters are not always adjusted to the latest tariff and the driver can legitimately ask more than is shown on the meter. Taxis are officially obliged to display the additional legal tariff but often don't.

In provincial towns, taxi meters are a rare sight and instead there are commonly accepted fares on given routes. Always fix the price beforehand.

Don't take taxis with a driver and somebody else inside. Taxi drivers sometimes have a friend along for company or for their security, but it may be insecure for you; some cases of robbery have been reported.

**Metro**

Over the past 20 years Bogotá drew and redrew plans and studies for building a metro for the city. A decision was finally taken in 1987 but nothing came out of it. The project was ultimately abandoned.

Meanwhile, Medellín set about constructing its fast city train and the design is steadily becoming reality. The construction is well under way and the first stretch of the metro is planned to open in 1995. Thus, Medellín will be the first (and for some time yet the only) city in Colombia to have a metropolitan train.

# Bogotá

Bogotá is the quintessence of all things Colombian. It's a city of futuristic architecture, universities, intellectuals, artists, splendid colonial churches, brilliant museums and all the latest in styles and gadgets, offering a vibrant and diversified cultural life. Yet it is also a city of shantytowns, street urchins, beggars, bootblacks, lottery vendors, thieves, drug dealers, busetas, traffic jams and graffiti.

It is not a handsome, pleasant or peaceful place but rather a bizarre mixture of everything from oppressive poverty to sparkling prosperity, which gives newcomers an impression of visual and mental disarray – perhaps more so than most other large capital cities on the continent. A *despelote* (chaos) – as its inhabitants would charmingly summarise their town.

It's all easily seen and felt as soon as you arrive at the city centre. The spontaneous architecture, with shabby shacks sitting next to ultramodern towers, seems to have sprung up beyond all rational rules of urban planning. Streets are the battlefield of wild traffic – everything from mules to Maseratis, which all struggle to impose their own right of way. The pavements are crammed with a human mosaic crawling between countless street stalls and vendors selling just about everything. Although the population is essentially mestizo, every colour of skin can be found in this huge cosmopolitan melting pot.

Over the past 50 years Bogotá has grown 20-fold to its present population of between six and seven million. Before the end of the century it is expected to pass the 10 million mark.

The size and status of the capital city makes Bogotá the major focus of political, economic, cultural and intellectual life. It's a bustling, noisy and aggressive metropolis – amazing but awful, fascinating but dangerous. You may love it or hate it, but it won't leave you indifferent.

## HISTORY

Long before the Spanish conquest, the Saba-

na de Bogotá, a fertile highland basin, which today has been almost entirely taken over by the city, was inhabited by one of the most advanced pre-Columbian cultures, the Muisca Indians.

The Spanish era began when Gonzalo Jiménez de Quesada and his expedition arrived at the Sabana. Quesada set off from Santa Marta in April 1536 with about 750 men and reached the Sabana one year later, accompanied by only 166 soldiers. On 6 August 1538 he founded a town near the Muisca capital of Bacatá. The town was named Santa Fe de Bogotá, a combination of the traditional name and Quesada's hometown in Spain, Santa Fe. Nonetheless, throughout the colonial period the town was simply referred to as Santa Fe.

At the time of its foundation Santa Fe consisted of 12 huts and a chapel where a mass was held to celebrate the town's birth. During the early years Santa Fe was governed from Santo Domingo (on the island of Hispaniola, the present-day Dominican

Representation of Bogotá's original coat of
arms, presumably lost in the fire of Las
Galerías in 1900

After independence the Congress of
Cúcuta shortened the town's name to Bogotá
and decreed it the capital of Gran Colombia.
The town developed steadily and by the
middle of the 19th century it had 30,000
inhabitants and 30 churches. In 1884 the first
tramway began to operate and soon after
railway lines were constructed to link
Bogotá to Zipaquirá, Sibaté and Facatativá.
The latter line was then extended to La
Dorada and Girardot thereby providing
Bogotá with access to the ports on the Magdalena River. At the beginning of this century
the population had not yet reached 100,000;
and by 1938 the 400-year-old city had
330,000 inhabitants.

Rapid progress came only in the 1940s
with industrialisation and the consequent
peasant migrations from the countryside into
the city. On 9 April 1948, the popular leader
Jorge Eliécer Gaitán was assassinated,
sparking off the uprising known as El
Bogotazo. The city was partially destroyed;
136 buildings in central Bogotá were burnt
to the ground and 2500 people died.

In 1954 the surrounding towns of Bosa,
Engativá, Fontibón, Usme, Suba and
Usaquén were annexed for the city's metropolitan area, forming the so-called Distrito
Especial (DE), encompassing an area of
1587 sq km. In recent decades the city has
continued to expand rapidly to become a vast
metropolis.

In 1991 the city reverted back to its traditional name, though no one can agree on how
to spell it (you'll find Santa Fe, Santa Fé or
Santafé de Bogotá). In any case, people are
used to calling it just Bogotá.

## CLIMATE

Bogotá is the third-highest capital in South
America, after La Paz and Quito. It sits at an
altitude of between 2600 and 2650 metres,
and at this height altitude sickness can occur.
If you come by air from the lowlands you
may feel a bit dizzy for the first day or two.
Take it easy – this soon goes away.

The city's average temperature is 14°C all
year round, dropping to about 9°C at night
and rising to around 18°C (higher on sunny

Republic), but in 1550 it fell under the rule
of Lima, the capital of the Viceroyalty of
Peru and the seat of Spain's power for the
conquered territories of South America.

Santa Fe became an important staging
point for countless expeditions in search of
El Dorado and soon began to develop. The
Muisca religious sites were destroyed and
replaced by churches. By 1600, 13 religious
buildings were constructed, among them
five churches.

In 1717 Santa Fe was made the capital of
the Virreynato de la Nueva Granada, the
newly created viceroyalty comprising the
territories of present-day Colombia,
Panama, Venezuela and Ecuador. Despite its
political importance, the town's development was hindered by earthquakes and
smallpox and typhoid epidemics which
plagued the region throughout the 17th and
18th centuries. The first census of 1778
showed only 16,002 inhabitants (52% of
whom were whites). The Indian Chibcha
language was banned in 1783.

days) during the day. In the rainy season there is less difference between day and night-time temperatures.

The main dry season lasts from December to March, and there is also a second, less dry period with only light rainfall from July to August or September. The wettest months are April and October. The mean annual rainfall is about 1020 mm. By and large, the mornings are usually clearer and drier than the afternoons, so plan on doing some outdoor sightseeing before midday and leave the museums for the afternoon.

## ORIENTATION

The city, set in the Sabana de Bogotá, has grown along its north-south axis and is bordered to the east by a mountain range. Having expanded up the mountain slopes as far as possible, Bogotá is now rapidly filling the savannah to the west and north.

The central city area divides the metropolis into two very different parts. The northern sector consists mainly of elegant residential districts dotted with modern commercial centres and posh restaurants. The further north you go, the more modern and luxurious the districts become – they are the home of the upper-class Bogotanos. In contrast, the southern part of the city is a vast spread of undistinguished brick architecture culminating in the extreme poverty of the southernmost outskirts. The western part, away from the mountains, is the most heterogeneous and is more industrial. Here is where the airport and the bus terminal are located.

The downtown area is not uniform and can be roughly divided into three parts. The southern one (south of Avenida Jiménez), La Candelaria, is the partly preserved colonial sector, the heart of the original town. The northern part (north of Calle 26), the Centro Internacional, is a small Manhattan where most of the city's skyscrapers have sprung up. Sandwiched between these two is the city centre, the area full of office buildings, restaurants, shops and cinemas.

The carreras run north-south, parallel to the mountains, with Carrera 1 at the foot of the mountains and numbers increasing towards the west. The calles run east-west with a dual numbering system. Calle 1 is next to Calle 1 Sur and numbers increase towards the north or south respectively. Thus the addresses in the southern part of the city are, for example, Calle 35 Sur No 15-23 or Carrera 12 No 42-50 Sur (Sur is often abbreviated to S), while those to the north (which includes central Bogotá) are denominated simply by a number, eg Calle 128 No 86-17.

The main thoroughfares, either calles or carreras, are called avenidas or autopistas and usually bear names like Avenida Boyacá or Autopista del Norte.

Carrera Séptima (Carrera 7) is one of the main streets running parallel to the mountains along the entire length of the city. In the centre it links the Plaza de Bolívar with the Centro Internacional. It is alive with commerce, cafés, restaurants and cinemas.

Avenida Jiménez is a business and financial street with a mishmash of architecture and, unusually, it is curved as a result of it having been built over a riverbed. Carrera Décima (Carrera 10) is the busiest traffic artery of the centre, crowded with busetas and countless street vendors. It roughly cuts the centre into the less dangerous area to the east and the 'heavy' zone to the west. Finally, Avenida Caracas (Carrera 14) is the major road linking the centre with the north and south, the principal bus route and an example of air pollution at its worst. It's best avoided – it can be dangerous.

## INFORMATION
### Tourist Offices

Bogotá has three tourist bureaux. The CNT office (☎ 284 3761) is at Calle 28 No 13A-59, on the ground floor. It is easy to find, as it's in Bogotá's highest skyscraper, with the Banco Cafetero logo on the top. The office is open Monday to Friday from 9 am to 12.15 pm and 2 to 5 pm. They still have some free brochures, left over from their good times, which are available in English, French and German. It's a good idea to stock up here with all the brochures you're likely to need as they can be hard to find elsewhere around

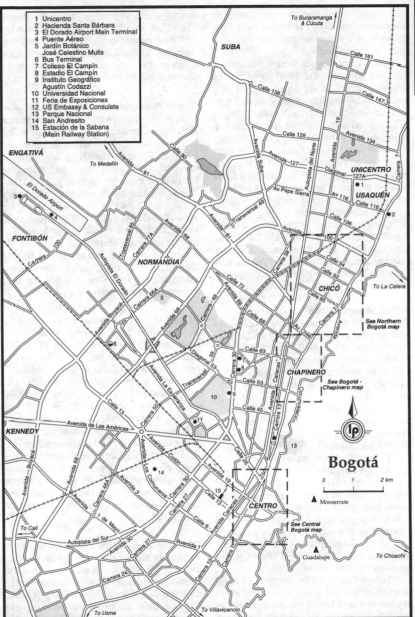

1 Unicentro
2 Hacienda Santa Bárbara
3 El Dorado Airport Main Terminal
4 Puente Aéreo
5 Jardín Botánico
  José Celestino Mutis
6 Bus Terminal
7 Coliseo El Campín
8 Estadio El Campín
9 Instituto Geográfico
  Agustín Codazzi
10 Universidad Nacional
11 Feria de Exposiciones
12 US Embassy & Consulate
13 Parque Nacional
14 San Andresito
15 Estación de la Sabana
  (Main Railway Station)

To Bucaramanga
& Cúcuta

SUBA

Calle 161

Calle 147

Calle 138

ENGATIVÁ

Calle 90

Calle 81

To Medellín

Avenida

Avenida Suba

Avenida 127

Calle 129

Avenida 134

Autopista del Norte

Avenida 7

Diagonal 127A

UNICENTRO
1

Av Pepe Sierra

USAQUÉN

El Dorado Airport

3

Av 116

Calle 116

FONTIBÓN

Carrera 100

Transversal 85

Carrera 7A

Avenida 68

Avenida 81

Transversal 49

Calle 106

Avenida

100

2

Calle 94

Calle 92

NORMANDIA

Autopista El Dorado

Carrera 66A

Calle 72

Avenida 68

Carrera 48

Carrera 68

Calle 68

Avenida 36

CHICÓ

Calle 85

To La Calera

Avenida Boyacá

5

Diagonal 39

Avenida La Esperanza

Transversal 93

Calle 13

6

10

Avenida 68

Calle 63

7
8

Calle 53

9

Carrera 30

Calle 45

Caracas

Avenida Chile

Av Chile

Carrera 7

Carrera 9

CHAPINERO

See Northern
Bogotá map

See Bogotá -
Chapinero map

Avenida 13

Circunvalar

KENNEDY

Avenida de Las Américas

Calle 13

11

Avenida Colón

Avenida 68

Avenida Boyacá

Avenida 48A

Avenida Los Comuneros

Carrera 30

14

Avenida 19

Avenida 1

Carrera 27

Calle 13

15

12

13

Carrera 13

Carrera 7

CENTRO

See Central
Bogotá map

Bogotá

0        1        2 km

Monserrate

1 de Mayo

To Cali

Autopista del Sur

Avenida 30

Carrera 27

Carrera 24

Carrera 30

Carrera 10

Avenida Caracas

Guadalupe

To Choachí

To Usme

To Villavicencio

the country or they won't be free. They also sell posters and books and have their own library with a variety of tourist publications (most in Spanish only).

If you fly into Bogotá, there is a branch of the CNT office on the 1st floor of the El Dorado Airport in the departure hall. It's open Monday to Friday from 7 am to 8 pm, Saturday and Sunday from 7 am to 2 pm.

The Instituto Distrital de Cultura y Turismo (☎ 334 6010, 286 5554) is the city tourist board, which focuses on Bogotá itself. The office is on the corner of Plaza de Bolívar and is open Monday to Friday from 8.30 am to 5 pm. They, too, have an outlet at the airport (ground floor), open from 7 am to 8 pm Monday to Saturday.

The Corporación de Turismo de Cundinamarca (☎ 284 0600, 284 8452, 284 2194), at Calle 16 No 7-76, deals with the Cundinamarca department, the region surrounding Bogotá. The office is open Monday to Friday from 9 am to noon and 1 to 5 pm.

### Useful Organisations

**Inderena** The government body which deals with national parks, Inderena (☎ 283 0964), is at Carrera 10 No 20-30, Oficina 805. This is the place to get permits for the parks, as well as information about them, including a good English-language guidebook on the parks (US$4).

Inderena, though, is in the process of liquidation. By the time you arrive there may already be a new government body, the Unidad Administrativa Especial del Sistema de Parques Nacionales, managing Colombia's national parks, but the addresses are likely to remain the same. Refer to the National Parks section in the Facts about the Country chapter for further details.

In theory, you need a permit to enter each park, though in most of them nobody will ask you for it. Some parks have established admission fees (usually about US$1), while the entry to others is free.

When you apply for the permit, you must state when you are going to visit the park, pay the entrance fee (if applicable) and the accommodation fee (if the park has these

facilities, and you are going to use them). The office receives applications on Monday and Wednesday from 9 am to noon and 2 to 4 pm, and on Tuesday and Friday from 9 am to noon. The permits can be picked up on Tuesday and Friday between 2 and 4 pm.

**Red de Reservas Naturales** This is an association which keeps track of private nature reserves, collecting (and providing) information about their location, features and facilities. There are already 53 reserves affiliated with the association, and there are likely to be more by the time you read this. The association has its office in Cali (there's not one in Bogotá), Carrera 35A Oeste No 3-66 (☎ 542294, 542300). The information about the Red is included in this section, as the reserves are scattered throughout the country (some of which are in the Bogotá region) and you may want to know about them to plan your itinerary. See the Cali section for further details.

**Alcom** Alcom (Albergues de Colombia para el Mundo) is the Colombian youth hostel association. Their office (☎ 280 3125, 280 3202) is at Carrera 7 No 6-10. Here you can get the youth hostel card (US$15) and information about the Alcom youth hostels. The office is open Monday to Friday from 8.30 am to 12.30 pm and 2 to 5.30 pm.

Strictly speaking, there's only one genuine youth hostel in Colombia, which is at the same address as the Alcom office (see the Places to Stay section for more information). However, Alcom has arrangements with several regular hotels and recreational centres throughout the country which give special discounts to the holders of the youth hostel card.

**COA** The Corporación Colombiana para la Amazonía Araracuara is a corporation which deals with various issues (geography, economy, ethnography, peoples) of the Colombian Amazon. Their office (☎ 285 6755) at Calle 20 No 5-44 has an extensive library focusing on the region. The library is open to the general public Monday to Friday from 8 am to noon and 1 to 5 pm.

If you have a particular interest in some topics, you can consult specialists who work in the Centro de Documentación of COA, at the same address.

**Sal Si Puedes** Sal Si Puedes is an association of hiking enthusiasts, which organises weekend walks to the countryside. These are essentially one-day excursions around Bogotá and the Cundinamarca department, but longer hikes to other regions are also arranged during long weekends and holiday periods. Foreign travellers are warmly welcomed. Some members of Sal Si Puedes are foreigners living in the city or Bogotans who speak foreign languages, so you are likely to find company for some English, French or German conversation. The club office (☎ 283 3765, 341 5854) is at Carrera 7 No 17-01, Oficina 640, and stocks a brochure with detailed information about the association's programme.

Created in 1979 as an informal group of walkers led by Justo Alfonso Gamboa Bohórquez, Sal Si Puedes acquired legal status as a foundation in 1988. They put much emphasis on ecological preservation and are very active, organising over 100 trips annually.

**Corporación Ecofondo** This is the place to get information about NGOs (nongovernment organisations) which deal with environmental issues. There are about 500 such organisations in Colombia, 300 of which are recorded by the Corporación Ecofondo, together with their addresses, activities etc. Their office (☎ 249 7590, 310 0026, 310 0097) is at Carrera 12 No 70-96.

Fundación Natura (☎ 616 9262, 616 9263, 218 0471), Avenida 13 No 87-43, is another environment-focused body and can also be useful.

**Tours & Guides**
There are loads of travel agencies organising tours, but they usually cover the most popular tourist sites, such as San Agustín, San Andrés, Villa de Leyva, Cartagena and

Leticia. Most of these places you can easily visit on your own and it will work out much cheaper. The following are among the better-known agents:

Aviatur (☎ 282 7111, 286 5555), Calle 19 No 4-62, has a choice of tours to popular tourist destinations and is the only company which occasionally operates helicopter trips to Ciudad Perdida.

Punto Amazónico (☎ 248 7251, 212 0094), Carrera 24 No 53-18, Piso 2, specialises in the Amazon region but may also offer tours to other regions, such as Isla Gorgona or Serranía de la Macarena.

Colombia Viva (☎ 226 8182), Calle 95 No 11A-44, has a variety of tours, including Alta Guajira, Isla Gorgona and the Amazon.

Eco-Guías (☎ 212 6049; fax 212 7450), Carrera 8 No 63-27, is a new, alternative travel agency focusing on ecotourism. They organise individualised trips at reasonable prices to various regions of the country, including Ciudad Perdida, Leticia and most national parks. They are in touch with many social and ecological organisations and can provide advice to foreign travellers in Spanish, English or German. Their postal address is: AA 050 454, Bogotá.

Viajes Chapinero (☎ 612 7716; fax 215 9099), Avenida 7 No 124-15, offers a variety of services and may organise out-of-the-way tours for travellers interested in environmental issues. There is another office in Chapinero (☎ 235 5544; fax 211 6407), Calle 63 No 13-37.

City tours and excursions to nearby attractions, such as Guatavita and Fusagasugá, are offered by some of the top-class hotels, including Hotel Tequendama, and travel agents like TMA (see the Money section for addresses).

Hikers may be interested in hiring guides. Given the security problems of some regions, guides do offer a certain protection. They've learned a thing or two about the areas they go to and know which routes are safer than others.

Almacén Aventura (☎ 248 1679), Carrera 13 No 67-26, can provide guides for mountain hikes and cave exploration. Expect a guide to cost around US$50 a day per group. For information about mountain treks and mountaineering, you may also want to contact Centro Nacional de Montaña (☎ 214 0884), Transversal 10 No 106-35, which has some of the best Colombian *montañistas* (mountaineers) as members.

### Money

Bogotá's banks have different working hours from banks elsewhere in the country – they work without a lunch break from 9 am to 3 pm Monday to Thursday, and 9 am to 3.30 pm on Friday. However, they usually handle foreign exchange transactions only until 1 or 2 pm.

Check a few banks before changing your money, as the exchange rates may differ considerably, especially for cash.

Most of the useful banks are conveniently located within one or two blocks of the corner of Avenida Jiménez and Carrera 7. They include:

Banco Anglo Colombiano
    Carrera 8 No 15-60 (exchanges cash at a good
    rate and travellers' cheques at the best rate in
    town; possibly the most efficient bank)
Banco Popular
    Calle 17 No 7-43 (regular rate for travellers'
    cheques and very good for cash; perhaps the most
    crowded bank and sometimes runs out of money)
Banco Sudameris Colombia
    Carrera 8 No 15-42 (cash only, at variable rates)
Banco Unión Colombiano
    Carrera 8 No 14-45 (low rate for cash but good
    for travellers' cheques)
Banco Industrial Colombiano
    Carrera 8 No 13-55 (exchanges cash and gives
    cash advances on MasterCard)
Banco Colombo Americano
    Carrera 7 No 16-36, above the Avianca post
    office (Visa)
Credibanco of Banco de Bogotá
    Calle 14 No 7-73 (cash advances on Visa; has
    extended business hours: Monday to Friday from
    9 am to 5 pm, Saturday from 10 am to 4 pm)

There's another concentration of useful banks in the area of the Centro Internacional, about one km north.

There are plenty of casas de cambio in the city centre. They don't accept travellers' cheques but do change cash, paying slightly less than the banks. The advantage is that the whole operation takes a minute instead of the half an hour it takes on average in the banks. Another bonus is that they are open until 5

or 6 pm on weekdays and usually until noon on Saturday.

In the central area are Exprinter and Novatours, next door to each other on the corner of Avenida Jiménez and Carrera 6. There are more than a dozen casas de cambio in the large edifice at Carrera 7 No 17-01. Another four casas de cambio are at Carrera 7 No 26-62.

The most popular currency is US dollars. Some casas de cambio will also accept Deutschmarks, pounds sterling and French francs but the rates are poor. At all of these casas de cambio you can buy US dollars (and sometimes other popular currencies) for pesos. The selling/buying rate difference is about 1% to 2%.

The Tierra Mar Aire (TMA) travel agency, which represents American Express, has its office in the Centro Internacional, Carrera 10 No 27-91 (☎ 283 2955). They don't change travellers' cheques but it is the place to contact if your cheques are lost or stolen. TMA has several other offices scattered throughout the city, including three in northern Bogotá: at Calle 73 No 8-60 (☎ 217 1300); Calle 92 No 15-63 (☎ 218 5666); and Avenida 15 No 120-75 (☎ 215 0100). You'll also find TMA offices at both the El Dorado airport terminal and Puente Aéreo.

### Post

The Avianca main post office is at Carrera 7 No 16-36, open Monday to Friday from 7.30 am to 7 pm, Saturday 8 am to 3 pm. They also have a poste restante service in the *sótano* (basement).

Avianca has several branch post offices scattered throughout the city. In northern Bogotá, there are Avianca post offices at Carrera 15 No 90-45 and Carrera 13A No 93-36.

Adpostal has its main office in Edificio Murillo Toro, Carrera 7 between Calles 12A and 13. The post office is on the ground floor (entrance from both Carreras 7 and 8), but if you want to send a parcel, the package section is in the basement of the south-western corner of the building, which is accessible by a separate entrance. The office is open Monday to Friday from 8 am to 5 pm. There's also an Adpostal office at Carrera 7 No 27-54 in the Centro Internacional (open Monday to Friday from 9 am to 5.30 pm). You can send parcels from there as well. Refer to the Post & Telecommunications section in the Facts for the Visitor chapter for postal rates.

DHL Worldwide Express (☎ 217 2200) has its main office at Carrera 13 No 75-74 and a branch office in the Centro Internacional, in the building of San Diego Church, opposite the Hotel Tequendama.

### Telephone

The main office of Telecom is at Calle 23 No 13-49, and is open Monday to Saturday from 8 am to 7.45 pm. You can also make long-distance calls and send telegrams from any of the branch Telecom offices in the city. There's a conveniently located Telecom office on Carrera 13, opposite the Banco Popular in the Centro Internacional, and another one on Carrera 8 between Calles 12 and 12A, close to the Plaza de Bolívar.

The telephone area code for Bogotá is 91. If you are calling from abroad, drop the 9.

### Foreign Embassies & Consulates

All Latin American countries have their diplomatic representatives in Bogotá. There's no Australian embassy in Colombia; the nearest is in Caracas, Venezuela. Australians and New Zealanders can go to the UK embassy. The embassies and consulates of selected countries are listed below. The full list is given in the phone directory.

Argentina
    Embassy: Avenida 40A No 13-09, Piso 16 (☎ 288 0900)
    Visa section: Avenida 40A No 13-09, Piso 2 (☎ 287 2678)
Austria
    Embassy: Carrera 11 No 75-29 (☎ 235 6628)
    Visa section: Calle 70 No 5-60, Apto 703 (☎ 249 3139)
Belgium
    Calle 26 No 4A-45, Piso 7 (☎ 282 8881)
Bolivia
    Transversal 12 No 119-95, Oficina 101 (☎ 215 3274)

Brazil
    Calle 93 No 14-20, Piso 8 (☎ 218 0800)
Canada
    Calle 76 No 11-52 (☎ 217 5555)
Chile
    Calle 100 No 11B-44 (☎ 214 7926)
Costa Rica
    Calle 104 No 14-25 (☎ 619 0694)
Cuba
    Carrera 9 No 92-54 (☎ 257 3353, 257 3371)
Denmark
    Carrera 10 No 96-29, Oficina 611 (☎ 610 0798)
Dominican Republic
    Carrera 16A No 86A-33, Apto 301 (☎ 236 2588, 219 1925)
Ecuador
    Embassy: Calle 89 No 13-07 (☎ 257 0066)
    Visa section: Calle 100 No 14-63, Oficina 601 (☎ 257 9947)
El Salvador
    Carrera 9 No 80-15, Oficina 503 (☎ 212 5932)
Finland
    Carrera 7 No 35-33, Piso 7 (☎ 232 1202)
France
    Carrera 11 No 93-12 (☎ 618 1863)
Germany
    Carrera 4 No 72-35, Piso 6 (☎ 212 0511)
Guatemala
    Transversal 29A No 139A-41 (☎ 259 1496, 258 0746)
Honduras
    Carrera 21 No 93-40 (☎ 616 3376, 236 3753)
Iceland
    Carrera 10 No 92-56 (☎ 610 2149)
Israel
    Calle 35 No 7-25, Piso 14 (☎ 287 7783)
Italy
    Calle 93B No 9-92 (☎ 218 6604)
Jamaica
    Calle 100 No 8A-55, World Trade Center, Torre C, Oficina 811 (☎ 219 1842, 128 1351)
Japan
    Carrera 9A No 99-02, Piso 6, Edificio Seguros del Comercio (☎ 618 2800)
Mexico
    Calle 99 No 12-08 (☎ 236 4957, 616 3462)
Netherlands
    Carrera 9 No 74-08, Piso 6 (☎ 211 9600)
Nicaragua
    Carrera 13A No 97-35 (☎ 257 4153)
Norway
    Carrera 13 No 50-78, Oficina 506 (☎ 235 5419)
Panama
    Calle 92 No 7-70 (☎ 257 5067)
Peru
    Embassy: Carrera 10 No 93-48
    Visa section: Calle 90 No 14-26, Piso 4, Oficina 417 (☎ 257 3147)

Portugal
    Calle 71 No 11-10, Oficina 703 (☎ 212 4468)
Spain
    Calle 92 No 12-68 (☎ 236 2062)
Sweden
    Calle 72 No 5-83, Piso 9 (☎ 255 3777)
Switzerland
    Carrera 9A No 74-08, Oficina 1101 (☎ 235 9507, 255 3945)
UK
    Calle 98 No 9-03, Piso 4 (☎ 218 5111)
USA
    Calle 38 No 8-61 (☎ 320 1300, 285 1300)
Venezuela
    Embassy: Calle 33 No 6-94, Piso 10 (☎ 285 2035)
    Visa section: Avenida 13 No 103-16 (☎ 256 3015)

### Visa Extensions

A 30-day extension of your stay in Colombia can be obtained from the DAS office (☎ 610 7315 ext 214, 226 8220), Calle 100 No 11B-29. Only your passport is required (no photos, no onward ticket). The office is open Monday to Thursday from 7.30 am to 4 pm, and Friday from 7.30 am to 3.30 pm, but be there early, as you have to pay the US$18 fee at the bank. You get the extension on the spot.

### Guidebooks

There are several locally-published guidebooks to Bogotá. Perhaps the most complete is *Guía Turística: Bogotá y sus Alrededores* (Ediciones Mundo Turístico, Bogotá, 1987). This is a bilingual Spanish/English guide containing comprehensive descriptions of sights in and around the city, plus practical information. Unfortunately, it's outdated and hard to get.

*Guía Cultural y Turística: Bogotá, Capital Cosmopolita* (Edisoma, Bogotá, 1991) is another useful guide. It's much more up to date and is also bilingual, though not all the Spanish text has its English translation.

You may also like to use *Guía Turística: Colombia* (Norma, Bogotá, 1992), a bilingual guide covering the whole country, but its section on Bogotá is quite general.

Foreign guidebooks to Colombia or South America in general are almost unobtainable in Bogotá, let alone outside the capital. There is only one place which imports and sells the *South American Handbook* and the Lonely Planet series: Librería Aldina (see the Bookshops section). Their prices are high: the Handbook costs about US$60 and LP guides are sold at almost double the printed price. The Almacén Aventura (see the Trekking Equipment section) and Eco-Guías (see the Tours & Guides section) were planning to distribute LP guidebooks at more reasonable prices, so check them first.

### Newspapers & Magazines

*El Espectador* (founded in 1887) and *El Tiempo* (1911) are two leading Bogotá papers, and both give a good rundown of local and international politics, economy, culture and sport. Other Bogotá papers include *El Siglo*, *La Prensa* and *La República*. *Semana* is the major weekly magazine. They are all sold at countless street stalls.

If you don't read Spanish, but want to keep track of Colombian politics, buy *The Colombian Post*, the only English-language local paper published weekly. Only some major newsstands sell it.

Major foreign papers such as *The New York Times*, *The International Herald Tribune*, *Le Monde* and *Der Spiegel* are available but it's not all that easy to get them. Most widely distributed are two popular international weekly magazines, *Time* and *Newsweek*.

### Bookshops

There are plenty of bookshops both in the centre and in the northern part of the city. Most of the books they sell are in Spanish. Imported books in foreign languages are available but expensive and the choice is limited.

The Librería Nacional (☎ 284 4546), Carrera 7 No 17-51, offers a good selection of books on Colombia as does the Librería Mundial (☎ 341 8346), Carrera 7 No 16-74, and Librería Lerner (☎ 243 0567), Avenida Jiménez No 4-35.

Librería Buchholz has three bookshops, at Carrera 7 No 27-68 (☎ 245 2023), Calle 59 No 13-13 (☎ 235 1249) and Avenida 15 No

104-30 (☎ 610 1080); it's worth a visit as they have a number of foreign books. For imported books also check Librería Oma (☎ 610 3200), Carrera 15 No 82-54, and Librería Aldina (☎ 235 6465), Carrera 7 No 70-80.

Librería de la Academia Colombiana de Historia, Calle 10 No 8 87, has a selection of books referring to Colombia's history and politics from pre-Columbian times to the present.

Librería Francesa (☎ 249 0039, 255 8899), Carrera 8 No 63-41 has a choice of books in both French and English. They also sell French and English weekly magazines (*Time, Newsweek, L'Express*). There is another Librería Francesa (☎ 256 4618) at Calle 86A No 13A-44.

The cheapest place to buy books is at the collection of *casetas* (bookstands) on the corner of Carrera 10 and Calle 13, in a rather unsafe area called San Victorino; they have a hotchpotch of books, both new and second-hand, from rare antiques to the latest publications. Prices are cheaper than in the bookshops and are negotiable.

The best selection of postcards is to be found in the Banco de Fotografías Movifoto at Avenida Jiménez No 4-64. They offer about 2000 postcards from all over the country (US$0.20 each).

## Maps

The best general map of the country (*Mapa Vial de Colombia*, scale 1:2,000,000) and the Bogotá city map (*Plano de Bogotá*, scale 1:25,000) are produced by Rodríguez and distributed through some of the major bookshops (eg Librería Buchholz) and handicraft shops. Either costs about US$3. You'll also find country and city maps produced by other publishers, but they don't seem to be as accurate as those of Rodríguez.

The Instituto Geográfico Agustín Codazzi (IGAC), Carrera 30 No 48-51, next to the Universidad Nacional, produces and sells the widest selection of maps (see the Map section in the Facts for the Visitor chapter for details). There are direct busetas from the centre (passing along Carreras 10 and 7)

which will let you off near the entrance. The institute is open Monday to Friday from 8 am to 3.30 pm.

If the colour maps are unavailable (which is usually the case) they will make a B&W copy of the original, which can be collected the next working day. Maps which include the frontier areas and strategic installations (eg military zones) need a special permit from the military authorities, which takes a lot of time to process and is not always granted.

The cost of maps depends on their type and size and varies between US$1 and US$3 per sheet.

## Film & Photography

The cheapest place to buy film and photographic gear as well as video, hi-fi and TV equipment, computers, watches and cassettes among other things is San Andresito, Carrera 38 between Calles 8 and 9. Urban buses and busetas go there from the centre and you can catch them on Avenida Jiménez. San Andresito is a huge commercial centre with a couple of thousand stalls and has almost everything that can be bought in Colombia. Two recommended stalls to check out are Foto Islas (☎ 360 1732), Carrera 38 No 8-70, Locales 1 & 2, and Centro Cámaras 'La 38' (☎ 201 1716), Carrera 38 No 8A-08, Local 93.

Apart from San Andresito, one of the cheapest places selling film (mostly Fuji) is Surtidor Fotográfico Comercial (☎ 248 1782, 212 2863), Carrera 11 No 65-69, Oficina 201. Foto Graf (☎ 236 4855, 618 4014), Carrera 18 No 79-32, has the widest choice of Ilford film. In the city centre, a good selection of Ilford film is to be found in Poder Fotográfico, Carrera 5 No 20-60.

There are plenty of places throughout the city which process negative films. You can easily have your prints done within an hour or two, and the quality is usually acceptable. However, you should be more careful when processing slides. Although many photo laboratories offer this service, the result is not always satisfactory. The most reliable person is Fidel Anzola (☎ 249 2312), Carrera 19 No 50-59. Most local professional photographers have their slides processed here. His lab is in a private house, without any sign on the door. Call him before you come.

Audiocine Servicio Técnico (☎ 248 1111), Calle 61 No 15-42, is probably the most recommended place for camera repairs. They deal with most of the common brands of still cameras as well as with video equipment.

## Trekking Equipment

There's not much to choose from as far as trekking gear is concerned. Colombia produces little and what is produced is mostly poor quality and expensive. There is almost no imported equipment. The best place to check out is Almacén Aventura (☎ 248 1679), Carrera 13 No 67-26. They manufacture backpacks, the best available on the Colombian market, and also sell sleeping bags, jackets, stoves, tents and other hiking gear.

## Spanish Courses

Several universities run Spanish courses. The best place to check is the Centro Latinoamericano of the Universidad Javeriana (☎ 212 3009), Carrera 10 No 65-48. They have intensive courses going throughout the year. There are five different levels to choose from. Each course lasts four weeks and consists of 80 hours (Monday to Friday from 8 am to noon), and each costs US$180.

The Universidad de Los Andes (☎ 283 8679), Carrera 1 No 18A-70, also offers intensive four-week courses (Monday to Friday from 8 am to noon) but only in June, and the course costs US$440. Probably the cheapest is the Universidad Nacional (☎ 269 9111, 269 1700), but they only have extensive five-month courses (February to June or July to November, four hours a week), which cost about US$100.

## Dangers & Annoyances

Is Bogotá unsafe? One of the local brochures has an excellent answer: 'Bogotá is no more dangerous than was ancient Rome or than are contemporary New York or Istanbul'. I wouldn't jump to such grandiloquent conclusions, especially about ancient Rome.

Bogotá certainly does not have a good reputation for security. It's perhaps the least safe Colombian city, fiercely competing for this infamous title with Medellín and Cali. Violent crime, either common or politically motivated, is the city's most visible and alarming security problem, but theft, armed robbery, rape and traffic accidents are all common in the city.

Bogotá's security (or insecurity) varies greatly from one district to the next, or even between two neighbouring streets. Predictably, the poor barrios and the *tugurios* (shantytowns) are where the majority of crime is reported. Don't venture into these areas at any time of the day, and especially at night. Unfortunately, delinquency is spreading over the city centre and into the more affluent districts.

The whole of the city centre is increasingly unsafe, the area west of Carrera 10 being in general more dangerous than the area to the east of this street. There's no need to panic about strolling about during the daytime (though armed robbery can occur at any time, anywhere), but you should limit your walks after dark to a minimum. As a rule, do not carry money (except for an emergency wad of notes to satisfy muggers if you happen to be assaulted) or valuables when walking around, especially at night, and heed the precautions in the Danger & Annoyances section in the Facts for the Visitor chapter.

Although the northern districts are safer, it's best to observe some security precautions there as well. Some visitors prefer to stay in the north rather than in the centre. However, this is a viable proposition for more affluent tourists only, as both accommodation and restaurants are pricier in the north. The majority of tourist attractions are in the central area; you are likely to spend most of your time in the city centre anyway.

Bogotá's street traffic is heavy, fast, busy and wild – for God's sake be careful! Drivers don't obey traffic rules as they usually do in the West, and may run red lights or crawl against the flow on a one-way street if they feel like doing so. This is simply the land of the strong, and pedestrians are at the end of the chain. Crossing the street may involve some effort and risk; take it as a rule that no driver will stop to give way to you.

Air contamination is largely a by-product of the poor condition of many of the vehicles. They leave behind clouds of smoke reminiscent of steam locomotives. The pollution may be appalling to visitors from 'cleaner' countries, especially during windless weather.

## THINGS TO SEE

Bogotá has enough tourist sights to keep you busy for several days. It's particularly renowned for its museums and colonial churches. Almost all major tourist attractions are conveniently sited in the central city area, within easy walking distance of each other.

### Plaza de Bolívar

The usual place to start discovering Bogotá is the Plaza de Bolívar, the heart of the original town. In the middle of the square is a bronze statue of Simón Bolívar (cast in 1846), the work of an Italian artist, Pietro Tenerani. This was the first public monument erected in the city.

The square has changed considerably over the centuries and is no longer surrounded by colonial architecture; only the Capilla del Sagrario (see the Churches section for a description) on the eastern side of the plaza dates from the Spanish era. Other buildings are more recent and feature different architectural styles.

On the northern side of the square is the **Palacio de Justicia**, or the Supreme Court. The Palace of Justice has had quite a tragic history. The first court building on this site was erected in 1921, but was burnt down by a mob during El Bogotazo in April 1948. A modern building was then constructed, but, in November 1985, it was taken by M-19 guerrillas and then gutted by fire in a fierce 28-hour offensive by the army in an attempt to reclaim it. The ruins stood untouched for four years, until the authorities decided to take it down altogether and construct a new

building in a different style. The shell has already been put up, but it will be a few years before the building is completed. It roughly matches the style of the Capitolio on the opposite side of the plaza.

The whole western side of the plaza is taken over by the French-style **Edificio Liévano**, today home to the Alcaldía (mayor's office). The building was erected between 1902 and 1905.

On the southern side of the plaza stands a monumental stone building in classical Greek style, the **Capitolio Nacional**, the seat of Congress. It was begun in 1847 but due to numerous political uprisings it was not completed until 1926. The façade facing the square was designed by an English architect, Thomas Reed.

Behind the Capitolio is the **Palacio Presidencial**, also known as Palacio de Nariño. It was built at the beginning of the century but in 1948 it was sacked after the assassination of Jorge Eliécer Gaitán and only restored in 1979. Between the Capitolio and the Palacio is a spacious formal ground, where the change of the presidential guard is held on Monday, Wednesday, Friday and Saturday at 5 pm. On the western edge of the grounds stands the **Observatorio Astronómico**, commissioned by José Celestino Mutis and constructed in 1803. This is reputedly the first astronomical observatory built on the continent. It's closed to the public.

### La Candelaria

East of the Plaza de Bolívar stretches the colonial barrio of La Candelaria, the oldest part of the city. Some of the houses have been carefully restored, others are in a dilapidated state, but on the whole the neighbourhood preserves an agreeable old-time appearance, even though a number of modern edifices have replaced the original buildings. Possibly the best preserved part of the quarter is between Calles 9 and 13 and Carreras 2 and 5. It's a pleasant area for a stroll.

The largest modern building in La Candelaria is the **Biblioteca Luis Ángel Arango**, which occupies the whole block between Carreras 4 and 5 and Calles 11 and 12. The building houses a good library, a concert hall, several small auditoriums for video and music, a small exhibition of musical instruments, a museum of religious art (see Museums) and a cafeteria on the top floor.

Opposite the main entrance to the library, at Calle 11 No 4-41, is a restored colonial house known as **Casa Luis López de Mesa**, where temporary exhibitions are held.

Next door, at Calle 11 No 4-93, is **Casa de la Moneda**, a beautiful colonial house (note the doorway) which you can enter and look around. A permanent exhibition of paintings belonging to the Banco de la República is displayed in eight rooms of the house. The paintings date from colonial to modern times. The exhibition is open Tuesday to Saturday from 10 am to 6.30 pm, Sunday from 10 am to 4 pm. Entrance is free.

One block west, at Calle 10 No 5-32, is the Italian-style **Teatro Colón**, begun in 1885 and opened in 1892 for the 4th centenary of the discovery of America. It was designed by an Italian architect, Pietro Cantini, and is lavishly decorated inside. It is only open for performances. Concerts, opera and ballet are performed here.

Opposite the theatre is the massive building of **Palacio de San Carlos**, originally a Jesuit college (it's not open to the public).

It's worth including some of the museums and churches described in the following sections in your strolls around La Candelaria.

**Museums**

Bogotá has about 50 museums; several of the main ones are excellent and well worth a visit. The following list covers some of the most outstanding museums, all of which are in the central area of the city and within easy walking distance. Some of the other museums not described here are dedicated to important personages in the history of the nation (Nariño, Caldas, Gaitán) or to specific subjects (such as medicine, police, numismatics, the military). Contact the tourist office if you need information about them. Even if you hate museums, you shouldn't miss the Museo del Oro. Most of Bogotá's museums are closed on Monday.

**Museo del Oro** Installed in a modern building on the corner of Carrera 6 and Calle 16, on the eastern side of the Plaza de Santander, the Gold Museum is the most important of its kind in the world. It houses approximately 33,000 gold pieces from all the major pre-Columbian cultures in Colombia (5000 of these gold objects are on display). Most of the gold is displayed in a huge strongroom on the top floor – a breathtaking sight. There are hundreds of precious pieces of astonishing beauty. Taking photos with a flash (but not with a tripod) is permitted inside.

It's impossible to list all the highlights, but the poporos of the Quimbaya, pectorals of the Tolima, tunjos of the Muisca, men-birds of the Cauca and the figurines of the Tayrona are all extraordinary. Don't miss the famous Balsa Muisca and ponder the genius of the people who created that mysterious golden world several centuries ago. It is worth planning more than one visit to the museum, as it's impossible to appreciate it all in one go.

A part of the strongroom, the so-called Salón Dorado, is currently being refurbished; a further 8000 pieces of gold are to be put on display there.

Apart from the strongroom, the museum has a large exhibition presenting historical, geographical and social aspects of pre-Columbian cultures, which are well illustrated by artefacts including objects in stone, bone, clay, gold and textiles. You'll also find here explanations of gold production methods and the importance of gold in these cultures.

Tours are conducted a few times a day. Guides in English and French are available at no extra cost. If you want to book a foreign-language guide for your party, call beforehand on ☎ 342 1111 ext 5424. The museum is going to introduce a headphone commentary system in English, which may be available by the time you read this.

Several videos are shown every day (some of them with an English soundtrack), featuring various pre-Columbian cultures. Check the programme when you come to plan your visit accordingly.

The museum is open Tuesday to Saturday

from 9 am to 4.30 pm, and on Sunday from 10 am to 4.30 pm. Admission is US$1.20 (US$0.70 on Saturday and Sunday). There is a bookshop next to the ticket office, which has a good selection of books about art, architecture, nature and pre-Columbian cultures.

**Museo Arqueológico** If you want to see more artefacts from pre-Columbian cultures, go to the Archaeological Museum at Carrera 6 No 7-43. It is housed in the Casa del Marqués

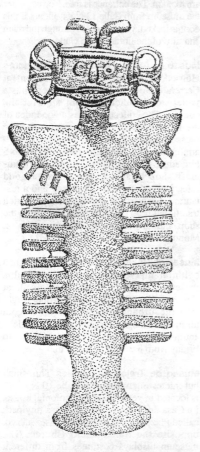

Bat-shaped pectoral from the Tolima area

de San Jorge, a beautifully restored 17th-century mansion and an outstanding piece of local colonial architecture (known as *arquitectura santafereña*). The museum has an extensive collection of pottery from the county's most outstanding pre-Columbian groups, confirming the high technical level and artistic ability achieved by the local Indian cultures. The museum is open Tuesday to Saturday from 9 am to 12.30 pm and 1.30 to 5 pm, and on Sunday from 10 am to 1 pm. The admission fee is US$1.20 (US$0.25 for students). Sometimes it's possible to have an English-speaking guide at no additional cost.

**Museo Nacional** The National Museum is at Carrera 7 No 28-66 in an unusual building known as El Panóptico. It was designed as the city prison by Thomas Reed (the same English architect who planned the Capitolio) and built of stone and brick on a Greek cross floor plan in the second half of the 19th century. The jail, which housed over 200 cells for both men and women, was eventually closed down in 1946, and after considerable internal reconstruction it was transformed into a museum in 1948.

The museum, comprising three sections, displays a wealth of exhibits ranging from pre-Columbian to contemporary art distributed in several halls on three floors. The section on archaeology and ethnography, on the ground floor, has Muisca and Tayrona art, and artefacts made by present-day Indians from different regions of Colombia. The section of history, on the 1st floor, traces the colonial and independence periods, and features a variety of exhibits including furniture, paintings, memorabilia, documents and weapons. The fine arts section, on the top floor, focuses on 19th and 20th-century Colombian painting including small collections of the best known national painters: Enrique Grau, Guillermo Wiedermann, Alejandro Obregón, Fernando Botero, Pedro Nel Gómez and Andrés de Santamaría.

The museum also puts on some temporary exhibitions, presenting both national and international artists. It is open Tuesday to

Saturday from 9 am to 4.30 pm, Sunday from 10 am to 3.30 pm. Entry costs US$0.80, US$0.40 for students.

**Museo de Arte Moderno** Opened in the mid-1980s in a modern, spacious building at Calle 24 No 6-00, the museum focuses on 20th-century art. There are no permanent collections on display; all rooms are given to frequently changing exhibitions by national and sometimes foreign artists. The museum is open Tuesday to Saturday from 10 am to 7 pm, Sunday from noon to 6 pm. Admission is US$0.70, (US$0.35 for students). There is a good bookshop at the entrance hall.

**Museo de Arte Colonial** This museum, at Carrera 6 No 9-77, was founded in 1942 in a fine colonial building and reopened to the public in 1986 after four years of restoration. The mansion, built at the beginning of the 17th century, was originally a Jesuit college (Colegio de la Compañía de Jesús), but after the expulsion of the Jesuits in 1767 it was used for diverse purposes, among them a national library, a museum of natural science, a university, and even a prison (Francisco de Paula Santander was jailed here in 1828).

The museum houses a large collection of colonial paintings, carvings, furniture, silverwork, books and documents, and has over 150 paintings and drawings (not all of which are on display) by Gregorio Vásquez de Arce y Ceballos (1638-1711), the most important painter of the colonial era. The museum also puts on temporary exhibitions. It is open Tuesday to Saturday from 9 am to noon and 2 to 5 pm, Sunday from 10 am to 4 pm. Admission is US$0.70 (US$0.35 for students).

**Museo de Arte Religioso** Housed in the building of the Biblioteca Luis Ángel Arango, this museum stages temporary exhibitions of religious art, which are usually well prepared and interesting.

The only objects on permanent display – and the pride of the museum – are two *custodias* (monstrances), exhibited in the strongroom on the 1st floor. The larger of the two, known as La Lechuga, comes from Bogotá's Iglesia de San Ignacio and dates from the early 18th century. It is 4902.60 grams of pure gold, encrusted with 1485 emeralds, one sapphire, 13 rubies, 28 diamonds, 168 amethysts, one topaz and 62 pearls. The other one, which has been brought from the Iglesia de Santa Clara La Real of Tunja, is slightly younger and has a marginally shorter list of precious stones.

The museum is open Tuesday to Friday from 9 am to 5 pm, Saturday and Sunday from 10 am to noon. The entrance is free. You can enter the museum from Calle 12 No 4-33, but if this door is locked, you can get in through the main entrance of the library, from Calle 11.

**Museo de Artes y Tradiciones Populares** Housed in an old Augustine convent at Carrera 8 No 7-21, this museum exhibits a variety of handicrafts from all over the country. The collection gives a good idea of the richness of Colombia's craftwork. The museum is open Tuesday to Friday from 8.30 am to 5.30 pm, Saturday from 9.30 am to 5 pm; admission is US$0.40. There is a handicraft shop attached, which has a good selection and is relatively cheap, and a restaurant, Claustro de San Agustín, with rich traditional food (see Places to Eat). Both the shop and the restaurant are also open on Monday.

**Museo de Desarrollo Urbano** Installed in a colonial house dating from 1650, this museum is just off Plaza de Bolívar, at Carrera 8 No 9-83. It provides a good insight into the urban development of Bogotá through old maps, photos, drawings, models, antiques and the like. It's open Monday to Friday from 8.30 am to 4.30 pm.

**Museo de Trajes Regionales** This small but interesting museum at Calle 10 No 6-44 is located in yet another fine colonial house, La Casa de los Derechos, facing a tiny park called Plazoleta de Don Rufino José Cuervo, opposite the San Ignacio Church. The museum displays costumes from different regions of Colombia. It's open Monday to

Friday from 10 am to 5 pm, Saturday from 10 am to 1 pm.

**Museo 20 de Julio** The museum, in a colonial house called the Casa del Florero, at Calle 11 No 6-94, is on the corner of Plaza de Bolívar next to the cathedral. It was here on 20 July 1810 that the Creole rebellion against Spanish rule broke out. The museum contains memorabilia (documents, paintings, furniture etc) recalling that important event, a milestone in the struggle for independence, which was achieved nine years later. The house is open Tuesday to Saturday from 9.30 am to 5.30 pm, Sunday from noon to 4.30 pm.

**Quinta de Bolívar** This villa at Calle 20 No 3-23 Este, at the foot of the Cerro de Monserrate, was a country house set in a garden built in 1800 and donated to Simón Bolívar in 1820 in gratitude for his services. Bolívar lived here for short periods on several occasions. After his death, the Quinta had multiple purposes, serving as a college, brewery, tannery and hospital. It was eventually taken over by the government, declared a national monument and turned into a museum. The house has been furnished in the style of Bolívar's day and filled with his possessions, documents, weapons, maps, uniforms and medals. It's open Tuesday to Sunday from 9 am to 5 pm; admission is US$0.80. Don't miss a stroll in the lovely, sloping garden.

**Other Museums** The Museo de Historia Natural in the Planetario Distrital features a collection of flora and fauna typical of Colombia. The Museo Militar, Calle 10 No 4-92, traces the evolution of Colombia's armed forces. The Museo del Siglo XIX, Carrera 8 No 7-93, focuses on the culture and art of the 19th century. Museo de la Policía, Calle 9 No 9-27, boasts a variety of objects related to the police, including a prison van from 1914. Museo del Cobre, Carrera 6 No 14-28 (Plazoleta del Rosario), exhibits various old objects made of copper and bronze.

## Churches

Having been the capital since the early days of Spanish rule and a centre of evangelisation of a vast colony, Bogotá boasts a good selection of colonial churches, most dating from the 17th and 18th centuries. Unlike the churches of the other viceroyalties' capitals, such as Lima or Mexico City, those of Bogotá are usually quite austere on the outside, though internal decoration is often very elaborate.

Two elements of decoration are particularly noticeable: the influence of the Spanish-Moorish style known as the Mudéjar style (mainly in the ceiling ornamentation), and paintings by Gregorio Vásquez, the best known painter of the colonial era, who lived and worked in Bogotá. Other noteworthy artists who left behind a good number of works in local churches, include two painters, Gaspar and (his son) Baltasar de Figueroa, and Pedro Laboria, possibly the most outstanding sculptor of the Spanish times.

**Iglesia de Santa Clara** This church, on the corner of Calle 9 and Carrera 8, is probably the most representative of Bogotá's colonial churches. Built between 1629 and 1674 as a part of the convent of the St Clare order, the church is a single-nave construction. The walls of the interior are covered with frescoes, and decorated with numerous paintings, images and altarpieces, all dating from the 17th and 18th centuries. The wooden figure of Santa Clara in the main retable is the oldest piece of artwork in the church. It's open as a museum, Tuesday to Saturday from 9 am to 1 pm and 2 to 5 pm, Sunday from 10 am to 4 pm; admission is US$0.60 (US$0.30 for students).

**Catedral** The cathedral on the Plaza de Bolívar is a monumental building in the neoclassical style. It stands on the site where the first mass was celebrated after Bogotá had been founded in 1538. Predictably, the original church where the event took place was just a small thatched chapel.

A more substantial building was erected in

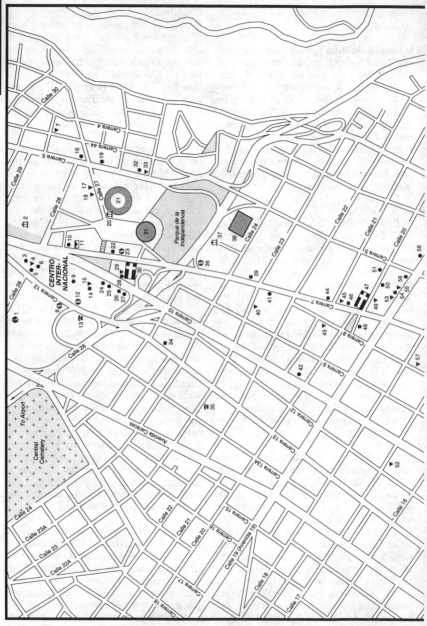

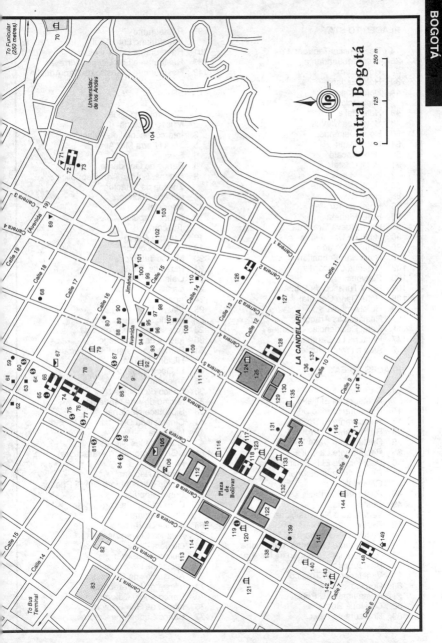

# Central Bogotá

0    125    250 m

## PLACES TO STAY

| | |
|---|---|
| 14 | Residencias Tequendama |
| 26 | Hotel Tequendama |
| 34 | Hotel Romar |
| 39 | Hotel España |
| 44 | Hotel Bogotá Internacional |
| 46 | Hotel Italia |
| 48 | Hotel Las Nieves |
| 50 | Hotel Menéndez |
| 54 | Hotel Dann |
| 56 | Hotel Bacatá |
| 61 | Hotel Cristal |
| 62 | Hotel Manila |
| 63 | Hotel Monserrate |
| 88 | Hotel Regina |
| 95 | Hotel del Turista |
| 96 | Hotel Planeta |
| 97 | Hotel Nueva Granada |
| 98 | Hotel La Candelaria |
| 99 | Hotel El Dorado |
| 100 | Hotel San Sebastián |
| 102 | Hotel La Concordia |
| 103 | Platypus |
| 107 | Hotel Turístico de Santafé |
| 108 | Hotel Dann Colonial |
| 109 | Hotel Ambalá |
| 110 | Residencias Aragón |
| 111 | Hotel Residencias Dorantes |
| 147 | Hostería La Candelaria |
| 149 | Alcom (Youth Hostel) |

## PLACES TO EAT

| | |
|---|---|
| 4 | Café Oma |
| 7 | Restaurante El Patio |
| 15 | Restaurante Piso 30 |
| 17 | Restaurante El Boliche |
| 18 | Restaurante Pierrot |
| 29 | Restaurante Casa Vieja |
| 33 | Restaurante La Orilla |
| 40 | Restaurante El Refugio Alpino |
| 43 | Restaurante Vegetariano Govinda's |
| 45 | Pastelería Florida |
| 49 | Restaurante Vegetariano Nuevos Horizontes |
| 52 | Restaurante Vegetariano Flaber |
| 53 | Restaurante La Fonda Antioqueña |
| 55 | Restaurante El Zaguán de las Aguas |
| 57 | Restaurante Vegetariano El Trópico |
| 69 | Dominó |
| 71 | Restaurante La Pola |
| 86 | Cafetería Romana |
| 89 | Restaurante Félix |
| 93 | Restaurante Vegetariano Loto Azul |
| 101 | Restaurante Casa Vieja |
| 137 | Restaurante Los Últimos Virreyes |
| 142 | Restaurante Claustro de San Agustín |

## OTHER

| | |
|---|---|
| 1 | CNT Tourist Office |
| 2 | Museo Nacional |
| 3 | Intercontinental de Aviación |
| 5 | TMA (Tierra Mar Aire) |
| 6 | Sam |
| 8 | Banco de Occidente |
| 9 | Satena, Sahsa, AeroRepública & Zuliana de Aviación |
| 10 | Librería Buchholz |
| 11 | Adpostal |
| 12 | Banco Popular |
| 13 | Telecom |
| 16 | Quiebra Canto |
| 19 | La Teja Corrida |
| 20 | Museo Taurino |
| 21 | Plaza de Toros |
| 22 | Galería Artesanal |
| 23 | Casas de Cambio |
| 24 | Aces |
| 25 | Viasa |
| 27 | Avianca |
| 28 | Artesanías de Colombia |
| 30 | Iglesia de San Diego |
| 31 | Planetario Distrital & Museo de Historia Natural |
| 32 | El Goce Pagano |
| 35 | Telecom |
| 36 | Banco de Bogotá |
| 37 | Museo de Arte Moderno |
| 38 | Biblioteca Nacional |
| 41 | Cinemateca Distrital |
| 42 | Inderena |
| 47 | Iglesia de las Nieves |
| 51 | COA (Corporación Araracuara) |
| 58 | Aviatur |
| 59 | Librería Nacional |
| 60 | Casas de Cambio & Sal Si Puedes |
| 64 | Banco Popular |
| 65 | Corporación de Turismo de Cundinamarca |
| 66 | Iglesia La Tercera |
| 67 | Avianca Correo Aéreo |
| 68 | Quiebra Canto |
| 70 | Quinta de Bolívar |
| 72 | Iglesia de las Aguas |
| 73 | Artesanías de Colombia |
| 74 | Iglesia de la Veracruz |
| 75 | Banco Anglo Colombiano |
| 76 | Iglesia de San Francisco |
| 77 | Banco Sudameris Colombia |

| 78 | Plaza de Santander |
| 79 | Museo del Oro |
| 80 | Auditorio de la Antigua Calle del Agrado |
| 81 | Banco Unión Colombiano |
| 82 | Book Market |
| 83 | Mercado de San Victorino |
| 84 | Banco Industrial Colombiano |
| 85 | Credibanco del Banco de Bogotá |
| 87 | Casas de Cambio Exprinter & Novatours |
| 90 | Banco de Fotografías Movifoto |
| 91 | Plazoleta del Rosario |
| 92 | Museo del Cobre |
| 94 | Teatro Popular de Bogotá |
| 104 | Media Torta |
| 105 | Edificio Murillo Toro & Adpostal |
| 106 | Telecom |
| 112 | Palacio de Justicia |
| 113 | Mercado Pasaje Rivas |
| 114 | Iglesia de la Concepción |
| 115 | Edificio Liévano |
| 116 | Museo 20 de Julio |
| 117 | Catedral |
| 118 | Capilla del Sagrario |
| 119 | Instituto Distrital de Cultura y Turismo |
| 120 | Museo de Desarrollo Urbano |
| 121 | Museo de la Policía |
| 122 | Capitolio Nacional |
| 123 | Museo de Trajes Regionales |
| 124 | Museo de Arte Religioso |
| 125 | Biblioteca Luis Ángel Arango |
| 126 | Teatro Libre de Bogotá |
| 127 | Teatro de la Candelaria |
| 128 | Iglesia de la Candelaria |
| 129 | Casa de la Moneda |
| 130 | Casa Luis López de Mesa |
| 131 | Teatro Colón |
| 132 | Iglesia de San Ignacio |
| 133 | Museo de Arte Colonial |
| 134 | Palacio de San Carlos |
| 135 | Museo Militar |
| 136 | El Son de los Grillos |
| 138 | Iglesia de Santa Clara |
| 139 | Observatorio Astronómico |
| 140 | Museo del Siglo XIX |
| 141 | Palacio Presidencial |
| 143 | Museo de Artes y Tradiciones Populares |
| 144 | Museo Arqueológico |
| 145 | Camarín del Carmen |
| 146 | Iglesia del Carmen |
| 148 | Iglesia de San Agustín |

1556-65 but soon after collapsed because of the precarious foundations. In 1572 the third church went up but the earthquake of 1785 turned it into ruins. Only in 1807 was the building of the eventual massive structure initiated and it was successfully completed by 1823. Today it's Bogotá's largest church but not its most beautiful.

The interior is spacious and solemn but has relatively little ornamentation. The tomb of Jiménez de Quesada, the founder of Bogotá, is in the second-last chapel off the right-hand aisle. The cathedral is open Monday to Saturday from 9 to 10 am and 6 to 7 pm, Sunday from 9 am to 2 pm.

**Capilla del Sagrario** The chapel stands on the same side of the Plaza de Bolívar as the cathedral. It was built in the second half of the 17th century and has preserved its mannerist-Baroque façade, which is considered to be one of the best examples of arte santafereño. The chapel boasts a Mudéjar vault and several paintings by Gregorio Vásquez. It is open Monday to Friday from 8 am to 1 pm and 3 to 6 pm.

**Iglesia de San Ignacio** San Ignacio, Calle 10 No 6-35, was begun by the Jesuits in 1610 and although opened for worship in 1635, it was not completed until their expulsion in 1767. It was the largest church during the colony and perhaps the most magnificent. Today it's one of the most richly decorated churches and houses a wealth of artwork, including more than a hundred colonial paintings. It has a typical Mudéjar vault and a fine main retable (carved in 1749 by Pedro Laboria), but more captivating are the dozen elaborate side retables, each different, lining both aisles. The best artists and artisans of the period contributed to the internal decoration.

Note the magnificent Baroque altarpieces by Juan de Cabrera, fine wood carvings by Pedro Laboria and paintings by Gregorio Vásquez. If you want to know more about the contents, go to the sacristy (at the head of the right-hand aisle) and buy a brochure describing the church's artwork. The church is open Monday to Friday from 9 to 11.30 am and 3 to 5 pm, Saturday 9 to 11.30 am, and Sunday 9 to 11 am.

**Iglesia de San Francisco** Completed in 1556, the church of San Francisco, on the corner of Avenida Jiménez and Carrera 7, is Bogotá's oldest surviving church. It is rather sober from the outside but the interior is elaborately decorated.

Of particular interest is the extraordinary 17th-century gilded retable in the presbytery. Carved by an unknown artist around 1622, the work reveals Flemish influences and is without doubt the best retable in Bogotá. Also note the intricate construction of the roof and the fine Mudéjar ornamentation of the ceiling under the organ loft. The long chapel to the right of the presbytery has a fine altar. The church is always full with worshippers, and the lighted candles create a special atmosphere. It is open Monday to Friday from 7 am to 7 pm, Saturday and Sunday from 7 am to 1 pm and 6 to 7 pm.

**Iglesia de la Veracruz** This church, on the corner of Carrera 7 and Calle 16 next to the San Francisco, is known as the National Pantheon because many of the heroes of the struggle for independence have been buried here. Of the 80 patriots executed by the Spaniards in Bogotá between 1810 and 1819, most have found their resting place in La Veracruz.

The church was largely destroyed in 1827 by an earthquake and reconstructed later in an altered style. It has a rather simple interior, covered with a typical panelled Mudéjar ceiling. There are four richly decorated old retables in the right-hand aisle, of which the impressive Señor de la Buena Esperanza, which has sat at the back of the aisle since colonial times, attracts the major number of faithful.

The tomb of the martyrs is in the nave in front of the high altar. In the niche in the left-hand wall, left of the tomb, is Cristo de los Mártires. This small Christ figure on the cross witnessed all the executions of the heroes buried in the church.

The church is open for mass only, at 8 am, noon and 6 pm.

**Iglesia La Tercera** Next to La Veracruz, Iglesia La Tercera was built between 1761 and 1780 and is remarkable for its beautiful stone façade. Inside, it has a coherent decoration noted for a number of retables and altarpieces carved in walnut and cedar. Have a look at the lateral chapel to the right of the high altar. The church is open daily from 7 am to 6 pm.

**Iglesia de San Diego** The church of San Diego, on the corner of Carrera 7 and Calle 26, is a lovely white-washed church built as part of a Franciscan monastery at the beginning of the 17th century. At that time it was well outside the town; today it is surrounded by the forest of high-rise buildings that form the Centro Internacional.

The statue of Nuestra Señora del Campo in the adjoining chapel, carved by the Spanish sculptor Juan de Cabrera, has become the patroness of the peasant farmers of the region. The church is open Monday to Friday from 7.30 to 8.30 am and 6 to 7.30 pm, Sunday from 8 am to noon; there is no fixed schedule on Saturday.

A part of the adjacent monastery building has been taken over by the Artesanías de Colombia (a handicraft shop) and the Casa Vieja restaurant.

**Iglesia de La Concepción** Built in 1583-95, this is the second-oldest existing church in Bogotá, after San Francisco. Without a bell tower, and completely undistinguished from the outside, the church is easy to overlook. It should not be missed, however: it has the best Mudéjar ceiling (brought from Seville and installed in the presbytery) of all of Bogotá's churches. Also note the highly ornamented arch separating the presbytery from the nave.

**Iglesia de La Candelaria** This church, on the corner of Calle 11 and Carrera 4, has a typical gilded main retable but it's not as inspiring as those in other old churches in the city. Of particular note is the Mudéjar decoration of the choir loft. The church is only open for mass, at 7 am and 6.30 pm; more masses are held on Sunday.

**Iglesia del Carmen** This is the most recent church in Bogotá's colonial quarter, only inaugurated in 1938. It's an impressive piece of architecture, which looks as if it belongs in a fairy tale. Resembling a colourful wedding cake, the church has recently been restored and it's a major landmark of this part of town. The interior, consistent in every detail, has fine stained-glass windows and a mosaic of the Virgen del Carmen over the high altar. The church, on the corner of Carrera 5 and Calle 8, is open for mass only, at 7 am and 6.30 pm, with additional masses on Sunday, at 11 am and 1 pm.

**Other Churches** Other colonial churches include Santa Bárbara, San Agustín, and a beautiful small church on the Plazoleta del Chorro de Quevedo, on the corner of Carrera 2 and Calle 13, which no longer operates as a church. Some historians argue that it was here, not on Plaza Bolívar, that the first mass was celebrated to honour the birth of the town.

### Cerro de Monserrate

This is one of the peaks (3190 metres) in the mountain range flanking the city to the east and overlooking the whole Sabana de Bogotá. It's easily recognisable by the church crowning its top. Monserrate has become a mecca for pilgrims, due to the statue of the Señor Caído (the Fallen Christ), sculpted in the 1650s by Pedro Lugo de Albarracín, to which many miracles have been attributed. The church, dedicated to the Christ figure, was erected several decades ago, after the original shrine was destroyed by an earthquake in 1917.

As the site is frequently visited by both pilgrims and tourists, several cafés and restaurants have sprung up around the church. The two best (but expensive) restaurants are *Casa San Isidro*, open Monday to Saturday from noon to midnight, and *Casa Santa Clara*, open Saturday and Sunday from 8 am to 4 pm. A small replica of a colonial town has also been built and it houses some handicraft shops. Plenty of food stalls are open on Sunday, the busiest day.

The view of the city from the top is superb. On a clear day you get a magnificent view of Los Nevados, the volcanic range in the Cordillera Central, 135 km away, noted for the perfectly symmetrical cone of the Nevado del Tolima, the Colombian Mt Fuji.

There are three ways to get to the top: by cable car (*teleférico*), funicular, or on foot along a path.

Both the cable car and the funicular operate Monday to Saturday from 9 am to midnight, and on Sunday from 6 am to 6 pm. The one-way ticket for either costs US$1.50; the return fare is US$3. If you want to do the trip on foot (one hour uphill), do it only on Sunday, when crowds of pilgrims go; on weekdays, take it for granted that you will be robbed. The lower stations of the cable car and the funicular are close to the city centre, but the access road leads through shantytowns, so it's better to take the bus marked 'Funicular' from Avenida Jiménez, or a taxi.

### Plaza de Toros de Santamaría

The Moorish-style bullring was built in 1927-31 and is one of the most stylish in the country. It has a capacity for 13,600 spectators, and on Sunday in January and February (the peak season) the ring is invariably full. Other minor corridas are held throughout the year, but mainly in the dry season. Young bullfighters practise their skills on weekdays. In the adjoining building is the Museo Taurino which displays posters, photos, dresses and other objects related to bullfighting. It's open Monday to Friday from 9.30 am to 12.30 pm and 2 to 5.30 pm, Saturday from 10 am to 2 pm.

### Jardín Botánico José Celestino Mutis

The botanical gardens, at Carrera 66A No 56-84, have a variety of national flora from different climatic zones, some in gardens and others in greenhouses. It is open Tuesday to Friday from 8 to 11 am and 1.30 to 3.30 pm,

Saturday and Sunday from 10 am to 4 pm. To get there take any bus running along the Autopista El Dorado, eg the one to the airport (from Carrera 10), which will let you off near the gardens.

### Other Attractions

Bogotá is a vibrant, somewhat mad metropolis where walking about the city centre, observing people, street scenes, avalanches of busetas, extravagant stores and roadside stalls is as fascinating as contemplating the serene atmosphere of the colonial churches and museums. Give yourself some time for this kind of exploration.

Hang around the south-western corner of Avenida Jiménez and Carrera 7 to see the flourishing street **emerald market** where dozens of *negociantes* buy and sell stones. If you are approached by one of them, look at the stones but don't get involved in any business.

Stroll about the **Plaza de Santander** where something is almost always going on: illusionists presenting their tricks, clowns mimicking passers-by, magicians walking on crushed glass, amateur groups playing music, jugglers, fire-eaters and miracle-makers. Watch the photographers with their antique cameras, and have your sepia snap taken.

Visit the lovely campus of the **Universidad de los Andes**, beautifully located on the slopes of Monserrate. This is one of Colombia's most exclusive universities and certainly the most expensive. Make sure you ascend to its upper section which is the most beautiful.

On Sunday don't miss going to the **Mercado de las Pulgas**, a colourful flea market on Carrera 3 between Calles 19 and 23. It opens about 8 am and goes well into the afternoon, but it's probably at its best around noon. According to the most recent news, it has moved one block, to the area of the Iglesia de las Aguas.

The **Media Torta**, at the far upper end of Calle 18 (have your wits about you when you walk there), is a popular open-air amphitheatre where often on Sunday mornings there are concerts by visiting national and sometimes international groups. The Media Torta is unique in that there is never an entrance charge. Under Colombian law, all foreign acts have to give a free performance or pay a fine. The Media Torta is the normal place for such concerts.

Also on Sunday, it's worth going to the **Parque Nacional**, Carrera 7 between Calles 35 and 38, where *teatro callejero* (street theatre) groups often present their plays.

All these places are in the city centre but it's also worth seeing what the rest of Bogotá looks like, particularly the more elegant northern districts. The north is safer, cleaner, greener and more modern. It's a pleasant area to stroll around, dotted with posh restaurants, commercial centres, parks, art galleries and boutiques. Pop into two new commercial complexes: the **Centro Andino,** on the corner of Carrera 11 and Calle 82, and the **Hacienda Santa Bárbara**, on the corner of Carrera 7 and Calle 116.

Of the few colonial buildings left in northern Bogotá, you can visit the **Museo El Chicó**, Carrera 7 No 93-03, located in a fine 17th-century *casona*, surrounded by what was once a vast hacienda, today little more than a garden. It features a collection of old objects of decorative art, mostly from Europe, and is open Monday to Friday from 8.30 am to noon and 2.30 to 5 pm, Saturday from 9 am to noon, Sunday from 9 am to 4 pm; admission is US$0.70.

If you happen to be in the area on a full moon, go to the Parque de las Flores, around the corner of Calle 88 and Carrera 20, where a **poets' meeting** is held every month on that very evening from 9 pm onwards.

### FESTIVALS & EVENTS
#### Feria Taurina

Like most other big cities, Bogotá has its feria taurina, or bullfighting season, when the major corridas take place. Famous international matadors are invited, mostly from Spain and Mexico. The feria is celebrated in January and February, with corridas held almost every Sunday.

### Festival Iberoamericano de Teatro
The theatre festival, featuring groups from all of Latin America and beyond, takes place in March/April of every odd year. Many of the local groups present their latest achievements, so it's a good time to taste what's going on in Colombian theatre.

### Feria Internacional del Libro
The international book fair, attended by publishers from all over the world, is held in late April and early May.

### Festival de Jazz
Still young and very modest, the festival is held for a few days in June.

### Feria Internacional de Bogotá
This international fair, featuring industrial and consumer goods, takes place in July and/or August of every even year.

### Expoartesanías
This show of handicrafts produced by various regions of the country, is organised in December. The crafts can be bought.

## PLACES TO STAY
Bogotá has loads of places to stay in every price bracket. The vast majority of hotels are concentrated in the city centre. This is the most convenient area to stay in, as most tourist attractions are here. The alternative area is the northern part of the city, but there are virtually no budget hotels here. Hotels (even the cheap ones) are usually safe.

The accommodation listed below has been arranged by price bracket and location. The central city area has been further divided into La Candelaria (south of Avenida Jiménez), downtown (between Avenida Jiménez and Calle 26) and Centro Internacional (north of Calle 26).

### Places to Stay – bottom end
The bottom-end accommodation includes anything that costs up to about US$12 for a double.

There's a variety of budget hotels scattered throughout the city centre, usually grouped in certain areas or along certain streets. The most numerous group of cheapies is west of Avenida Caracas, where the bus companies were once located before they all moved in 1984 to the central bus terminal, but forget about staying in this area – it's one of the most dangerous parts of the city.

There's a good choice of budget accommodation in La Candelaria, and this is the most popular area with foreign travellers. You will also find cheap hotels in the downtown area, but there are not many of them and they are not popular with foreigners. Don't waste time looking for a cheap room in the Centro Internacional, let alone in the northern districts of the city.

**La Candelaria** Two budget hotels in this area deserve a special mention. They are at opposite ends of La Candelaria and perhaps not ideally located, but otherwise are perfectly all right.

Since opening in the mid-1993, the *Platypus* (☎ 341 2874, 341 3104), at Calle 16 No 2-43, has swiftly become a favourite place among foreign backpackers, even though it hasn't yet managed to put its sign on the door. This small travellers' guest house, located in a colonial house, has two six-bed dormitories and several singles and doubles. Although conditions are quite simple and only a few rooms have private baths, the hostel is clean and pleasant and has hot water in communal baths. A bed in the dormitory costs US$4, while rooms go for US$5 per person. You can use the kitchen to cook, and there's a cosy dinning room to eat, read and have a tinto, which is provided free of charge. The hostel is run by a friendly Colombian-German couple who can even pick you up from the airport or bus terminal. They also offer a poste restante service (your name, AA 3902, Bogotá, Colombia) and plan on organising ecological walks for visitors.

The other place is the *Alcom* youth hostel (☎ 280 3125, 280 3202), at Carrera 7 No 6-10, four blocks south of Plaza de Bolívar. It has spotlessly clean six and eight-bed dormitories. There are only shared baths, but they are clean, and there is hot water in the morning. The hostel, set in an old house with a pleasant patio, also operates a good, cheap restaurant. Holders of a hostel card pay US$3.50 per bed, while nonmembers can stay for US$5 (or they can buy a hostel card here and stay at members' rates). The members also get a discount on meals. The hostel keeps the door open from 6 am until midnight.

It's hard to find any other cheapie that will offer you more for your money than the two mentioned above, but there are some other acceptable places. Of these, the *Residencias Aragón* (☎ 342 5239, 284 8325), at Carrera 3 No 14-13, is one of the cheapest at US$3.50 per person. Although the rooms don't have private baths, they are quite spacious and have large windows, which is uncommon in Bogotá's budget hotels. There's hot water in communal baths.

The recently refurbished *Hotel El Dorado* (☎ 334 3988), at Carrera 4 No 15-00, has smaller rooms, and some of them have private baths. It costs US$4.50/5.50 per person in a room without/with bath.

There are several more budget hotels in La Candelaria but they are either more basic or more expensive. You can try, for example, the *Hotel La Concordia* (☎ 342 9102), at Carrera 3 No 15-64, which has claustrophobic, cell-like rooms with private bath costing US$3 per person.

The *Hotel La Candelaria* (☎ 2439857), at Carrera 4 No 14-87, has rooms with bath and hot water (US$6 per person), but they vary in size and value, so look at a few.

**Downtown** There are several cheap (but not attractive) hotels close to the corner of Carrera 7 and Calle 20, midway between La Candelaria and the Centro Internacional. The *Hotel Menéndez* (☎ 341 3542), at Calle 20 No 5-85, is one of the cheapest options. It offers simple but acceptable singles/doubles with bath and hot water for US$6/9.

The *Hotel Las Nieves* (☎ 334 8181), at Calle 20 No 7-27, is a small family-run place, which has rooms with TV, private bath and hot water. Expect to pay US$8/10/14/16 for a single/couple/double/triple.

A few paces away, the *Hotel Italia* (☎ 342 5965), at Carrera 7 No 20-40, is a large (110-room) unkempt and basic hotel whose only advantage, perhaps, is that you can be pretty sure of getting a room. It costs US$8/12/15/16 for a single/double/triple/quad without bath – not good value. Add US$4 if you need a room with bath.

Two blocks north, you'll find another basic shelter, the *Hotel España* (☎ 342 1705, 342 1396), at Carrera 7 No 23-20. It's in a dilapidated state and costs US$5/8 for a single/double without bath and US$6/10 with bath.

**Places to Stay – middle**
Accommodation listed in this section includes hotels costing somewhere between US$12 and US$25 for a double. As with cheapies, the best choice in this price range is to be found in La Candelaria. There are also some in the downtown area, but not in Centro Internacional, or further north.

**La Candelaria** One of the cheapest hotels in this price bracket is the *Hotel Turístico de Santafé* (☎ 342 0560, 342 0932), at Calle 14 No 4-48. Neat, airy rooms with private bath and hot water cost US$10/13/17/20 for a single/double/triple/quad. You can eat in the hotel restaurant, which is cheap and has acceptable food. For the same price, you also can stay in the small *Hotel del Turista* (☎ 342 0649), at Avenida Jiménez No 4-95.

The marginally more expensive *Hotel Residencias Dorantes* (☎ 334 6640, 334 1776), at Calle 13 No 5-07, is in a fine old house and offers much the same as the Santafé. Have a look at rooms first to choose the best.

The *Hotel Ambalá* (☎ 341 2376, 281 7124), at Carrera 5 No 13-46, in the same area, is yet another option offering good value. Rooms are rather small but comfortable and all have TV. They cost US$12/14/17 for a single/couple/double.

The *Hotel Planeta* (☎ 2842711), at Carrera 5 No 14-64, has larger rooms but they are more expensive (US$16/22/28 a single/double/triple).

**Downtown** One of the good options in this area is the *Hotel Manila* (☎ 243 9010), at Calle 17 No 8-23, which has unusually large rooms with bath and hot water, all equipped with three or four beds. You pay US$14/18/23/27 for a single/double/triple/ quad.

If you want to be close to the Centro Internacional (which is reputedly a safer area), try the small *Hotel Romar* (☎ 281 3468), at Carrera 13 No 24-68. Spacious singles/matri-monios/doubles with bath and TV go for US$18/21/26. Don't walk further south along Carrera 13, as this is a red-light district.

**Places to Stay – top end**
Any accommodation that costs more than US$25 for a double is included in this section. Hotels in this price range can be found in all sectors of the city centre and in the north.

Bogotá has plenty of posh hotels, particu-larly in the northern part of the city, but they obviously cost far more than US$25. If money is not a problem, you can have stan-dards and facilities comparable to top-class hotels in the West.

**La Candelaria** As in all other categories, La Candelaria has quite a lot to offer in this price bracket. Although there's nothing extremely posh here, at least the prices are reasonable.

One of the cheapest is the *Hotel San Sebastián* (☎ 334 6042), at Avenida Jiménez No 3-97. It has fairly good, airy rooms with TV and private bath, which cost US$20/30/40 for a single/double/triple.

The *Hotel Regina* (☎ 334 5135), at Carrera 5 No 15-16 (not exactly in La Can-delaria but just over Avenida Jiménez), offers much the same for the same price.

The *Hostería La Candelaria*, also known by the name of its restaurant, Café de Rosita (☎ 342 1727, 286 1479), at Calle 9 No 3-11, is possibly the most charming place to stay in La Candelaria. It's a beautiful colonial house with three pleasant patios. Rooms are furnished to match the old-time style and cost US$20/30 for singles/doubles – very good value. The hotel's restaurant serves good food at reasonable prices. If there's

anything to object to, it's the location. The hostería is in the far end of La Candelaria, so you have to tramp across the whole district to get to and from the centre. It's best to use a taxi after dark.

The *Hotel Dann Colonial* (☎ 3411680), at Calle 14 No 4-21, is modern, not colonial, despite its name. Nonetheless it's a good and pleasant hotel, offering singles/doubles/ triples for US$33/44/55.

The high-rise *Hotel Nueva Granada* (☎ 286 5877), at Avenida Jiménez 4-77, is the best of what La Candelaria has to offer. Choose a room on one of the upper floors and you'll have an excellent view over the city and less noise from the busy Avenida Jiménez. Expect to pay US$60/70/85 for a single/ double/triple.

**Downtown** There are two inexpensive but rather undistinguished hotels on Calle 17, just off Carrera 7. The *Hotel Cristal* (☎ 243 0030), at Calle 17 No 7-92, and just across the street the *Hotel Monserrate* (☎ 341 0659), at Calle 17 No 7-71, both charge US$28/35/40 for a single/double/triple. Slightly better is the *Hotel Bogotá Internacional* (☎ 341 9513), at Carrera 7 No 21-20, offering singles/doubles/triples for about US$32/ 42/54.

If you need somewhere really posh in the downtown area, choose between the *Hotel Dann* (☎ 284 0100), at Calle 19 No 5-72 (US$70/105/130), and the *Hotel Bacatá* (☎ 283 8300), at Calle 19 No 5-20 (US$115/140/160).

**Centro Internacional** Possibly the cheapest and quite a good choice in this area is the *Residencias Tequendama* (☎ 286 8111), at Carrera 10 No 27-51 (don't confuse it with Hotel Tequendama just a few steps away). It consists of two towers, Torre Norte and Torre Sur, the latter being slightly cheaper. Both have a range of mini-apartments equipped with a kitchen, for one to three persons. The minimum period to stay is five days, in which case you pay US$55/80/90 per day for a single/double/triple. The longer you stay the cheaper the price per day becomes.

The *Hotel Tequendama* (☎ 286 1111, 283

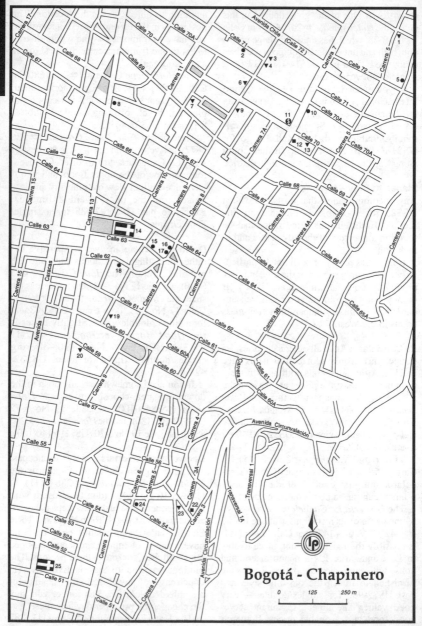

**Bogotá - Chapinero**

0    125    250 m

---

**PLACES TO STAY**

12 Casa Medina
22 Hotel Las Terrazas

**PLACES TO EAT**

1 Restaurante Típico La Embajada
   Antioqueña
3 Hamburguesas El Corral
4 Restaurante O'Sole Mio
6 Los Primos
7 Restaurante Le Poivre
9 D'Arte Gusto
13 La Petite Sensation
19 Restaurante Vegetariano Los
   Vegetarianos
20 Restaurante Vegetariano El Vega
21 Restaurante Giuseppe Verdi
23 Restaurante La Poularde

**OTHER**

2 Teatro Nacional
5 German Embassy & Consulate
8 Almacén Aventura
10 Librería Aldina
11 Banco Colombo Americano
14 Iglesia de Lourdes
15 Teatro Experimental La Mama
16 Librería Francesa
17 Eco-Guías
18 Teatro Libre de Bogotá
24 Teatro La Baranda
25 Iglesia de Chiquinquirá

---

7740), at Carrera 10 No 26-21, is perhaps the poshest place to stay anywhere in the central area, but it's quite costly: the cheapest single will cost about US$150. The hotel has most facilities you might need, including sauna, jacuzzi, hairdressers, two restaurants, two bars etc. Even if you don't stay here, pop into the foyer to have a look at the mural by Luis Alberto Acuña.

Another top-class (and top-price) option in the Centro Internacional is the *Hotel Orquídea Real* (☎ 285 6020), at Carrera 7 No 32-16. It's the tallest hotel in Bogotá (previously the Hilton), offering excellent views from its top floors.

**The North** There are no inexpensive hotels in the northern part of Bogotá except for

some places west of Avenida Caracas, but these are of marginal interest for travellers.

The *Hotel Las Terrazas* (☎ 255 5777), at Calle 54A No 3-12, is close to Chapinero, roughly halfway between the city centre and the north proper. It's a bit inconvenient as there's no public transport passing nearby, but otherwise it's OK and relatively inexpensive: US$33/44/56 a single/double/triple.

The *Hostal Bonavento* (☎ 218 3612, 218 4814), at Calle 93 No 18-11, is one of the cheaper options in northern Bogotá, costing US$55/66/75 for a single/double/triple. It's a small, quiet place with nine rooms only, some of which face a fine interior garden. The hostel has its own restaurant.

The *Hotel Country 87* (☎ 617 0787, 257 9206), at Carrera 15 No 87-06, is comfortable and reasonably priced. Singles/doubles go for US$72/85.

The *Hotel La Bohème* (☎ 617 1177, 236 1840), at Calle 82 No 12-35, is a new, topclass hotel right in the middle of the Zona Rosa. A double suite will cut about US$200 out of your budget. The hotel has a classy French restaurant, La Terrasse, with prices to match.

If you want somewhere cheaper in the Zona Rosa area, try the *Hotel Charleston* (☎ 257 1100), at Carrera 13 No 85-46, where a double room will cost around US$150. It, too, has a good but expensive restaurant, La Biblioteca, with an international menu.

The *Casa Medina* (☎ 217 0288, 249 3170), at Carrera 7 No 69A-22, is one of the best and most atmospheric places to stay in town. Installed in a meticulously restored old building, it has much of the old-time charm plus modern facilities. Suites for one or two people go for about US$200. The hotel has its own, excellent restaurant, specialising in French cuisine. In 1993 a large extension was built, adding 32 new suites to the 26 existing ones. Have a look at a few rooms before deciding, as all are different.

There are several expensive hotels on Avenida 100. They include the *Hotel Bogotá Royal* (☎ 218 9911) in the World Trade Center, *Hotel El Belvedere* (☎ 257 7700),

*Hotel Bogotá Plaza* (☎ 257 2200) and the *Hotel Cosmos 100* (☎ 257 4000).

## PLACES TO EAT

The Bogotá phone directory lists about 1000 restaurants and that's not all: there are markets, food stalls and other establishments serving meals, such as hospedajes, supermarkets, transport terminals, universities, clubs and societies. Almost every foreign cuisine is available and, of course, a full range of regional Colombian dishes. On the whole, the city centre is better for budget eating while the north certainly takes pride in fine dining.

### Cheap Eats

If you are on a tight budget you will be stuck with the regular set meals – almuerzo and comida – which are the staple offerings of hundreds of cheap restaurants scattered throughout the city. They cater for office employees and do much of their business at lunch time, between noon and 2 pm, then stay empty or close. Some of them also serve a set dinner, roughly between 6 and 8 pm. A set meal costs somewhere between US$1 and US$2, rarely more.

By and large, these restaurants are not attractive places – just have your meal quickly and move on. Perhaps the best thing you could do is just drop into the first one on your way, see what people are eating, and stay or move on to the next one.

Eating only comidas may become boring after a while, but there are, fortunately, many ways to diversify your menu and still remain within a reasonable budget.

There are a number of barbecued-chicken restaurants, where a half chicken with potatoes or chips makes a really filling meal for about US$3. *Kokoriko* and *La Brasa Roja* are the most popular pollo-asado chains, both with about 20 outlets throughout the city, and there are many others. Should you prefer pizza, there are plenty of pizzerias.

There are also several big international fast-food chains, including *Wimpy* and *Burger King*, which have their outlets scattered throughout the city; easy to come across.

**City Centre**  The restaurants serving set meals are particularly numerous in the downtown area and La Candelaria. They thin out in the Centro Internacional, but there are some, especially on Carrera 13.

There are so many of these places that it's not easy to make a selection. For example, on the corner of Calle 17 and Carrera 4 there are nearly a dozen, all of the same basic standard; several of them are run by Chinese and serve meals continuously from about 11 am to 10 pm.

Carrera 10 is densely dotted with chicken outlets, but there are also many pollo asado venues on other streets. You will find several pizzerias conveniently grouped on Calle 19, between Carreras 3 and 7.

For something more Colombian go to *Restaurante Las 7 Sopas*, at Calle 30 No 6-70, which serves a choice of soups. For about US$2, you get a large clay bowl of hearty ajiaco, mondongo or sancocho. The place is open only on weekdays, from noon to 3 pm.

*La Fonda Antioqueña*, at Calle 19 No 5-98, has good Antioquian food at reasonable prices.

Pop into *Pastelería Florida*, at Carrera 7 No 20-82, for good chocolate santafereño (hot chocolate with cheese, accompanied by pan de yuca or almojábanas).

*Dominó*, at Carrera 3 No 18-55, is one of the best places for empanadas; it has empanadas chilenas (with onions, olives and raisins), plus empanadas de queso (with cheese) and empanadas de carne (with meat); all are delicious and cheap (US$0.50 each).

*Crepes & Waffles*, at Carrera 10 No 27-91, Piso 2 (Centro Internacional), has delicious crêpes with a range of fillings, for US$4 at the most. There are several of this chain's outlets in the north (see the following section).

There's quite a choice of vegetarian restaurants in the city centre. They are all simple, virtually without décor, and serve inexpensive, straightforward food. Most of them operate from Monday to Friday only, and close in the mid-afternoon. All offer set lunches for US$1.50 to US$2. They include *Govinda's*, at Carrera 8 No 20-55, *Nuevos Horizontes*, at Calle 20 No 6-37, *El Trópico*, at Carrera 8 No 17-72, *Flaber*, at Calle 17 No 10-51, and *Loto Azul*, at Carrera 5 No 14-00.

**The North** There are plenty of restaurants serving cheap set meals in Chapinero, but further north, especially past Avenida Chile (Calle 72), they are not so numerous and not so cheap. However, like in the city centre, there are other options to keep your stomach filled at a moderate cost.

*D'Arte Gusto* (☎ 249 2269), at Carrera 9 No 69A-26, is a restaurant of Cooperartes (an association of artists), serving rich, reasonably priced almuerzos, and is frequented by artists.

*Hamburguesas El Corral* (☎ 210 4006), at Carrera 9 No 71-24, is a simple, unpretentious place that serves some of the better hamburgers in town. There's another outlet of the same chain at Carrera 15 No 85-58.

*Los Primos*, at Carrera 9 No 70-55, is the place for great hamburgers and sandwiches. The walls are decorated with images of cats (the owner is a cat fan).

*Crepes & Waffles* has several outlets including one at Carrera 9 No 73-33 and another at Carrera 11 No 85-79.

*Dominó* offers its famous empanadas at two locations in the north: at Carrera 9 No 72-81 and at Calle 79 No 14-14.

There are a few fast-food venues on the upper floor of the Centro Comercial Unilago, Carrera 15 No 78-77 (the commercial centre specialising in computer goods). They include *Spaghetti & Co*, which does inexpensive spaghetti (US$2), and *A Todo Taco*, which serves cheap Mexican food. You'll find another A Todo Taco at Avenida 82 No 11-24.

*Desayunadero de la 42*, on the corner of Avenida Caracas and Calle 42, is open round the clock and is known city-wide for its hearty food, typical of Santander. If you happen to return from a night drinking session, its caldo will certainly put you back on your feet.

Vegetarians might be interested in two simple but cheap restaurants in Chapinero: *El Vega* at Calle 59 No 10 59 and *Los Veg etarianos* at Carrera 10 No 60-44. There's a better vegetarian outlet, *El Integral Natural* (☎ 256 0899), at Carrera 11 No 95-10. This small restaurant, open daily till 9 pm, offers a set lunch for US$2.50 and a varied menu (different each day) at around US$4 per dish.

### Mid Range

This section includes restaurants where the average main course is likely to cost somewhere between US$4 and US$6.

**City Centre** The *Claustro de San Agustín* (open Monday to Friday till 5 pm), in the Museo de Artes y Tradiciones Populares, has delicious local food (served until 3 pm only). It has a different menu every day of the week.

*La Pola* (☎ 341 1343), at Calle 19 No 1-85, has a list of fine regional dishes, including a puchero sabanero which is second to none. *Félix* (☎ 341 7211), at Avenida Jiménez No 4-80, is well known for its paella valenciana.

In the evening, go to *El Boliche*, at Calle 27 No 5-64, for reasonably priced Italian food and a good atmosphere. Next door, *Pierrot* (☎ 334 4292) is plusher and more expensive, and often has live music.

*La Orilla* (☎ 282 4703), at Carrera 5 No 26-04, is a small place that does good comida de mar at affordable prices. Ask for the bandeja La Orilla (US$4) or festival marino (US$6).

*El Patio* (☎ 282 6141), at Carrera 4A No 27-86, is a cosy, bohemian place with only a few tables. It is becoming one of the trendiest restaurants for a lunch or dinner in the city centre. It serves excellent Italian food.

**The North** *Restaurante O'Sole Mio* (☎ 248 2085), at Carrera 9 No 71-12, is a good place for pizzas, spaghetti and other Italian fare at mid-range prices (US$4 to US$7 per dish).

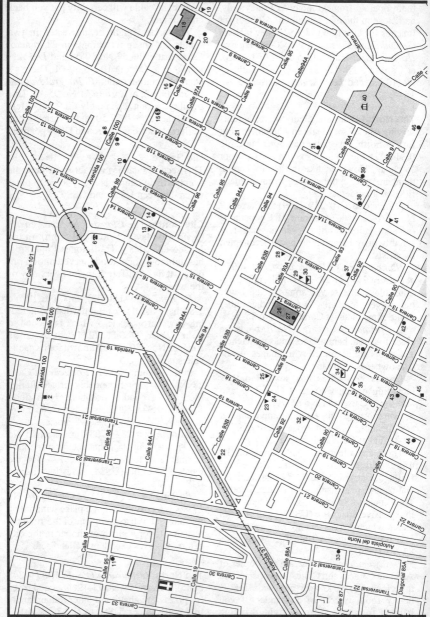

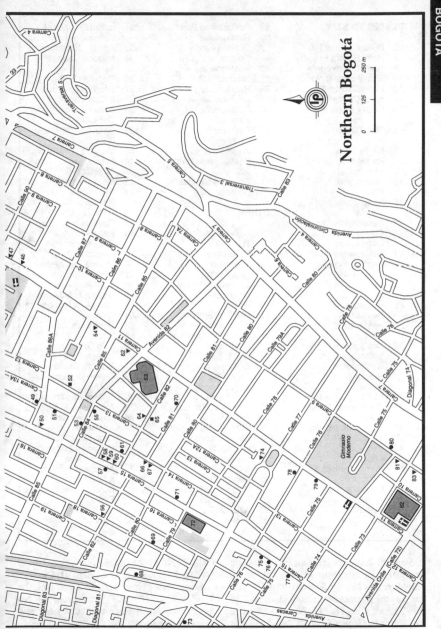

Northern Bogotá

BOGOTÁ

## PLACES TO STAY

2 Hotel Cosmos 100
3 Hotel Bogotá Plaza
4 Hotel El Belvedere
24 Hostal Bonavento
45 Hotel Country 87
52 Hotel Charleston
65 Hotel La Bohéme

## PLACES TO EAT

1 Restaurante Hatsuhana
12 Piccolo Café
13 Restaurante Shila
16 Restaurante Il Fogolar
19 Restaurante Las Cuatro Estaciones
21 Restaurante Vegetariano El Integral Natural
23 Restaurante Il Giardino
25 Houston's Restaurant
28 Restaurante Hatsuhana
29 Restaurante Al Salam
32 Restaurante Rincón de la China
35 La Cuisine Suisse
41 Restaurante China Town
47 Restaurante Casa Vieja
48 Restaurante Khalifa
50 Hamburguesas El Corral
54 Crepes & Waffles
56 Restaurante Chez Stefan
58 Café Oma

59 Restaurante Pimm's
60 Restaurante Shakespeare y Compañía
62 Restaurante Tandoor
64 Restaurante Bourbon Street
66 Restaurante Na Zdarovia
67 Restaurante Japonés Welcome
74 Restaurante Gran China
81 Crepes & Waffles
83 Dominó

## OTHER

5 Railway Station
6 Telecom
7 Ecuadorian Consulate (VisaSection)
8 Chilean Embassy & Consulate
9 DAS
10 Mexican Embassy & Consulate
11 Teatro Nacional La Castellana
14 Nicaraguan Embassy & Consulate
15 Banco Anglo Colombiano
17 Japanese Embassy & Consulate
18 World Trade Center
20 UK Embassy & Consulate
22 Honduran Embassy & Consulate
26 Centro 93
27 Brazilian Embassy & Consulate
30 Avianca Correo Aéreo

31 Italian Embassy & Consulate
33 Fundación Natura
34 Avianca Correo Aéreo
36 Peruvian Embassy
37 Spanish Embassy & Consulate
38 French Embassy & Consulate
39 Peruvian Consulate (Visa Section)
40 Museo El Chicó
42 Ecuadorian Embassy
43 Flower Market
44 Dominican Republic Embassy & Consulate
46 Panamanian Embassy & Consulate
49 Librería Francesa
51 Ramón Antigua
53 Saint Amour
55 Galería El Museo
57 Galería Café Libro
61 Salomé
63 Centro Andino
68 Aires
69 Foto Graf
70 Galería Café Libro
71 Quiebra Canto
72 Centro Comercial Unilago
73 Gallera San Miguel
75 Artesanías El Balay
76 Artesanías Sinú
77 Artesanías Lana Lana CueroCuero
78 Canadian Embassy & Consulate
79 Austrian Embassy & Consulate
80 Dutch & Swiss Embassies & Consulates
82 Centro Granahorrar

Several Chinese restaurants may be included in the mid-priced category, although this largely depends on what you eat. Try the *Restaurante China Town* (☎ 236 0993), at Carrera 11 No 91-58, the *Restaurante Gran China* (☎ 249 5938), at Calle 77 No 11-70, or the *Rincón de la China* (☎ 618 3441), at Carrera 18 No 91-15.

Somewhat exotic on Colombian soil, the *Tandoor* (☎ 218 9698), at Carrera 11 No 84-53, is a small place that serves hot and spicy Indian food.

*Restaurant Típico La Embajada Antioqueña* (☎ 249 4616), at Carrera 5 No 73-98, does typical paisa food at moderate prices.

## Top End

Although the best choice of top-class restaurants is in the northern part of the city, central Bogotá also has a good selection. Expect to pay from US$6 upwards for a main course.

**City Centre** *Casa Vieja* is acclaimed for its regional food. It has two outlets in the city centre: at Avenida Jiménez No 3-73 (☎ 334 6171) and at Carrera 10 No 26-50 (☎ 284 7359) in the building adjoining the San Diego Church. Both have the same prices and menu, including delicious ajiaco, cuchuco and sobrebarriga. There's a third Casa Vieja in the north (see the following section).

*El Refugio Alpino* (☎ 284 6515), at Calle 23 No 7-49, serves rich, European food at up-market prices. It's particularly known for its fondue. *La Fragata* (☎ 243 2959), in the Centro Internacional, is one of the best places in the city centre for seafood, though it has probably seen better days. There's another La Fragata in northern Bogotá.

*Restaurante Los Últimos Virreyes* (☎ 342 6580), at Calle 10 No 3-16, is in the Fundación Gilberto Alzate Avendaño, which also has an art gallery staging mainly temporary exhibitions of modern art. The restaurant is on the 1st floor overlooking a beautiful patio. It's one of the best restaurants in La Candelaria, doing international and local food, for about US$6 to US$8 per dish. It's open till midnight.

*El Zaguán de las Aguas* (☎ 241 2336), in a fine colonial house at Calle 19 No 5-62, is a well-appointed restaurant serving Bogotan dishes. Hour-long shows of folk dancing are presented on Wednesday, Thursday and Friday evenings (at no additional charge). Its ajiaco (US$7) is considered one of the best in the city.

There's an attractive *Restaurante Piso 30* (☎ 286 8570) on the top floor of the Torre Norte of Residencias Tequendama, Carrera 10 No 27-51, in the Centro Internacional. It

serves French food and you can enjoy the panoramic view of the city centre. It's open till midnight.

**The North** It's here that one can find the cream of the city restaurants, specialising in various cuisines from around the world.

French food is well represented. Among the most authentic French restaurants are *Chez Stefan* (☎ 236 1082), at Carrera 18 No 82-10, and *Le Poivre* (☎ 249 8198), at Carrera 10 No 69-38. Other places to consider include *La Poularde* (☎ 249 5368), at Carrera 4 No 54-88, and *La Petite Sensation* (☎ 212 3374), at Calle 70 No 6-37. Don't forget about excellent French restaurants in the *Hotel La Bohème* and *Casa Medina* mentioned under Places to Stay. One more place to try for French specialities is the *Restaurant Bourbon Street* (☎ 257 0953), at Calle 82 No 12-36 (1st floor), in the heart of the Zona Rosa. Live piano jazz is usually played in the evening.

There's also a lot of Italian cuisine to choose from, including *Giuseppe Verdi* (☎ 249 5368), at Calle 58 No 5-35, *Il Fogolar* (☎ 257 7114), at Calle 98 No 10-08, *Il Giardino* (☎ 236 1937), at Calle 93 No 18-25, and *Piccolo Café* (☎ 257 3394), at Carrera 15 No 96-55.

Probably the two best Middle-Eastern restaurants in Bogotá are *Al Salam* (☎ 236 2380), at Carrera 13A No 93-52, serving Syrian-Lebanese food, and *El Khalifa* (☎ 236 1374), at Carrera 11 No 88-46, run by a Palestinian. The latter has belly-dancing shows on weekends.

A curiosity is *Na Zdarovia* (☎ 218 5072), Carrera 14 No 80-71, the only Russian restaurant in town. Try the beef stroganoff (US$10) and borscht (US$4.50).

Next door to Na Zdarovia is the *Restaurante Japonés Welcome* (☎ 256 4790), at Carrera 14 No 80-65, which does good but expensive Japanese food. Possibly a better place for Japanese specialities (but also more expensive) is *Hatsuhana* (☎ 236 3379), at Carrera 13 No 93A-27. You'll find another Hatsuhana (☎ 610 3056) at Transversal 21 No 100-43. One more Far Eastern restaurant is the *Shila* (☎ 256 6821), at Carrera 14 No

97-21, which serves fine Korean and Japanese food.

North Americans will find themselves at home in *Houston's Restaurant* (☎ 236 5417), at Carrera 17 No 93-17. *La Cuisine Suisse*, at Calle 90 No 15-65, is renowned for its delicious fondues.

*Las Cuatro Estaciones* (☎ 256 9309), at Carrera 8A No 98-38, has a varied international menu, including a mouthwatering paella.

*La Fragata* (☎ 222 8806), set on the rotating top floor of the World Trade Center on Calle 100, serves exquisite seafood in its nautical-styled interior, and one can enjoy a 360° panoramic view of the city while enjoying a delightful cazuela de mariscos.

*Shakespeare y Compañía* (☎ 616 6175), at Carrera 15 No 82-22, is a pleasant restaurant-cum-bar, serving international food (around US$7 for an average dish) and a large variety of drinks and cocktails. It's open from 10 am until midnight (longer on weekends).

Just a few paces away, *Pimm's*, at Carrera 15 No 82-46 (☎ 236 5265), is a restaurant-cum-coffee shop, noted for rich crêpes (about US$5 a plate), steaks (US$8), and excellent espresso coffee. It's also open till midnight.

If you prefer to keep to the local cuisine, there's perhaps nothing better than the *Casa Vieja* (☎ 236 3421), at Carrera 11 No 89-08, a beautiful place with excellent food.

### Coffee Shops

You can get tinto everywhere but not all places serve good coffee. Cheap cafeterias, fast-food outlets and restaurants sometimes serve a reheated muck hardly reflecting the taste of coffee, let alone the delicious mild Colombian coffee. Better establishments (such as those listed in the Top End section) won't usually disappoint you.

*El Viejo Café* is a chain of cheap coffee stalls scattered throughout the city. They have good tinto and carajillo (tinto with liqueur). There are several outlets in the city centre, including one on the ground floor of the commercial centre Terraza Pasteur, on

the corner of Carrera 7 and Calle 24, and another one on the corner of Calle 19 and Carrera 5.

*Cafetería Romana*, on the corner of Avenida Jiménez and Carrera 6A, is one of the best places for a cup of coffee. *Café Oma* in the Centro Internacional, Edificio Bavaria, torre B, is also noted for its coffee, though it may have bad days. There is another Café Oma in northern Bogotá, Carrera 15 No 82-58.

## ENTERTAINMENT

Bogotá has far more cultural activities than any other city in Colombia. *El Tiempo* or *El Espectador*, the two leading local newspapers, will tell you what's going on. Universities are a source of interesting events and also present concerts and films. The Universidad Nacional (main entrance from the corner of Carrera 30 and Calle 45) is the city's biggest university and has the most active cultural life.

### Cinema

Bogotá has about 60 cinemas screening the usual commercial fare, mainly from the USA. If you need something with more artistic content check the programmes of the cinematecas (art cinemas). Regular cinemas of that type are the Cinemateca Distrital, Carrera 7 No 22-79, and the Museo de Arte Moderno which has its own cinema hall (entrance from Calle 26). Other places, which operate daily or several days a week, include the Teatro Popular de Bogotá (TPB), Carrera 5 No 14-71, the Auditorio de la Antigua Calle del Agrado, Calle 16 No 4-75, and Teatro El Camarín del Carmen, Calle 9 No 4-93. Several universities have *cineclubes* (film clubs) which show films on campus or utilise the cinema halls of institutions such as the Planetario Distrital or Comfenalco.

It's worth checking the programmes of cinematecas and cineclubes as they often have interesting films which are not seen elsewhere – such as local and other Latin American films which never make it to the commercial cinemas. All films are shown with the original soundtrack and almost all have Spanish subtitles (except, of course, the Spanish-language films).

## Theatre

There are a dozen regular groups with their own theatres, and many more that put on their productions wherever they can. Over the past two decades the Teatro de la Candelaria, Calle 12 No 2-59, has been one of the most inspiring venues in town. It gained fame for its play first performed in 1975, *Guadalupe Años Sin Cuenta*, about La Violencia, and confirmed its high profile with several subsequent mature works. Next to Teatro de La Candelaria is the Seki Sano, which hires out its rooms to various amateur groups. Another place to check is the Teatro Libre de Bogotá, Calle 13 No 2-44, although most of its productions are now presented in its new theatre in Chapinero, Calle 62 No 10-65.

The Teatro Popular de Bogotá (TPB), Carrera 5 No 14-71, may occasionally have an interesting performance. Other theatres worth checking include the Teatro La Baranda, Carrera 6 No 54-04, Teatro Experimental La Mama, Calle 63 No 9-60, and Teatro Nacional in its two locations, at Calle 71 No 10-25 and Calle 95 No 30-13.

The Taller de Investigación de la Imagen Dramática is a new experimental theatre which has already gained some international attention. Look in the Universidad Nacional to find out if and where it currently performs.

## Classical Music

Check the programme of the Biblioteca Luis Ángel Arango which runs concerts in its own concert hall. Concerts by international artists are usually presented on Wednesday at 7.30 pm (tickets are rather expensive) while young local artists are scheduled on Monday (nominal fee). Another regular stage for invited orchestras is the Auditorio León De Greiff in the campus of the Universidad Nacional, which usually has concerts on Saturday (tickets cost US$1.50).

## Spectator Sports

Soccer fans may like to attend some matches; it's Colombia's national sport. The principal venue is the Estadio El Campín, on the corner of Carrera 30 and Calle 55. Matches are held from March to November, usually on Sunday afternoons and Wednesday evenings – a great spectacle for around US$3 to US$5.

Bullfighting is extremely popular, with bullfights held during the Feria Taurina. They traditionally take place on Sunday afternoon and bring the area around the city bullring, Plaza de Toros de Santamaría, to a standstill. The bullring itself invariably fills to capacity, or beyond, with men, women and children alike.

Another breakout of emotions takes place at the Gallera San Miguel, Calle 77 No 19-65. This is Bogotá's principal cockfight ring, open on Monday from 3 pm to 1 am, and from Friday 2 pm to Saturday 8 am. The entrance fee is US$1.50, and the betting can reach astronomical levels. This is definitely a spectator sport for men, and it's taken seriously; go accompanied by a local who knows the rules of the game. Watching the excited patrons is perhaps as memorable a spectacle as looking at the fighting cocks.

## Nightlife

Bogotá is alive 24 hours a day and there's a lot of activity going on at night. There are plenty of nightspots offering a variety of music, from Western rock to salsa. The latter is perhaps the most popular among the hot-blooded Bogotanos, and a worthwhile experience for *forasteros* (outsiders).

Salsa has become fashionable (for ages it was seen as a vulgar, lower class rhythm), and now there are many disco-type places, the *salsotecas* or *salseaderos* which play predominantly or exclusively salsa.

Salsa includes a variety of musical styles, from the authentic old Cuban *son* all the way to synthesised Latin jazz. However, the son cubano, the original Cuban rhythm, which was one of the main roots of the whole salsa family, is the trendiest beat. Many salsotecas pepper their programmes with this genre, and they are the most 'in' places. Some of the best are listed in this section. Don't miss trying one, if only to listen to the music and watch people dancing.

The salsotecas are usually open every night except Monday, though Thursday, Friday and Saturday, especially around midnight, are when things are hottest. On weekends there may be live music in some places. There's usually no cover charge on weekdays but there may be on the weekend. This may or may not include a voucher to the value of a few beers or *tragos* (drinks) of aguardiente. Salsotecas don't usually serve any snacks or meals, so come after your dinner.

Don't take handbags or cameras, as you will have to keep a constant eye on them; these places are often crowded and thieves never sleep.

There are several salseaderos around the corner of Carrera 5 and Calle 27, the best-known of which is La Teja Corrida, Carrera 5 No 26A-54, which often has good salsa groups.

Other places to try in the area are the Quiebra Canto, at Carrera 5 No 27-14, and El Goce Pagano, at Carrera 5 No 26-42. There are half a dozen more places around. Quiebra Canto has several other outlets (with much the same hot atmosphere and music) including the ones at Carrera 5 No 17-76, Carrera 7 No 45-77, and one in the Zona Rosa (read below).

In La Candelaria, you have El Son de los Grillos, Calle 10 No 3-60, which is pleasant, relatively quiet, and sometimes has groups playing.

The city centre is gradually losing its popularity in favour of the increasingly trendy Zona Rosa, in the northern sector of the city, which has become the new focus of night entertainment among Bogotá youth. The area sits between Carreras 11 and 15, and Calles 81 and 84, Calle 82 being its main axis. There's a maze of music spots, bars, restaurants, cafés and snack bars which become particularly vibrant on weekend nights. This is the best time to hang around

and see Bogotá's more affluent revellers in action.

Salomé, at Carrera 14A No 82-16, is the place with possibly the best son cubano in town, as it's run by the renowned collector and connoisseur of that genre, César Pagano.

Galería Café Libro, at Carrera 15 No 82-87, and its younger (and more pleasant) offspring, at Calle 81 No 11-92, are two of the best salseaderos and they, too, focus on son cubano. Live music is often staged on weekends.

Quiebra Canto, at Carrera 15 No 79-28, is another good salsa spot, with music going daily except Sunday, from 6 pm until 1 am (longer on Friday and Saturday night). Like other Quiebra Canto outlets, it usually has plenty of old Cuban music.

Saint Amour (☎ 256 8772), at Calle 84 No 14-00, has a varied programme, including salsa (live and from discs), recitals, poetry etc. On weekends (Thursday to Saturday) there's a US$3 entrance fee. Ramón Antigua, Carrera 14 No 85-57, is one more spot for dancing to salsa rhythms.

The Zona Rosa is not the only nucleus of night-time *rumba* (partying); there are others further to the north, including one on Avenida Pepe Sierra. La Calera, high on the mountain slopes overlooking northern Bogotá is becoming the trendiest area these days. The road to La Calera is rapidly becoming packed with a variety of posh restaurants, night bars and discos.

## THINGS TO BUY

For handicrafts go to Artesanías de Colombia, Carrera 3 No 18-60 next to the Iglesia de las Aguas, or Carrera 10 No 26-50 attached to the Iglesia de San Diego. Close to the latter, on Carrera 7, is an interesting, cheap craft market, the Galería Artesanal. The shop at the Museo de Artes y Tradiciones Populares, Carrera 8 No 7-21, is also worth a visit. The Pasaje Rivas market, on the corner of Carrera 10 and Calle 10 is a good place for cheap buys.

There are more handicraft shops in the northern districts, several of which are on

Carrera 15 between Calles 72 and 85. Artesanías El Balay, Carrera 15 No 75-63, is one of the largest craft shops in this area. Also try two nearby shops, Artesanías Sinú, Carrera 15 No 75-25, and Artesanías Lana Lana Cuero Cuero, Carrera 15 No 74-49.

Emeralds can be bought in plenty of *joyerías* scattered throughout the city centre and the northern districts. There are some good (but expensive) jewellers in the Centro Internacional. Before you set off on your emerald-shopping spree, read the following letter, sent by one traveller:

The best place to purchase emeralds is at one of the shops in the international sector. Buying one from a street vendor is probably a very poor idea. I purchased mine at a shop called Palacio de Esmeralda that I found in the commercial complex beneath the Hotel Tequendama. The good news is that an emerald purchased at one of the upscale stores comes with a certificate of authenticity guaranteed by the Colombian government (what exactly that guarantees is probably another matter). The bad news is that unless you know exactly what you're doing, it's doubtful you'll get a very good deal. I purchased a loose stone after bargaining the price down approximately 40%. Upon returning to Seattle, a city not necessarily known for cheap emeralds, I spoke with a gem wholesaler who informed me that I had actually paid a price slightly less than the retail price in the US, and substantially more than the wholesale value of the stone. In other words, I didn't get much of a steal. It is very difficult for an amateur (like myself) to judge the value of an emerald because minute differences in the colour, cut and clarity of a stone can mean extraordinary differences in its worth. I purchased the stone with the hope of reselling it in the US for a profit. Obviously, I didn't make any money. It was a very educational experience, though not a very happy one.

The Centro Internacional also boasts some of the best shops selling pre-Columbian pottery (try Precolombinos San Diego or Galería Cano). They are, of course, very expensive but you can be pretty sure about their authenticity. Copies are sold on the street, in the handicraft shops and at the Mercado de las Pulgas.

For top-quality leather goods try shops on Calle 19 between Carreras 4 and 7; more shops of that kind are on Carrera 10, in the Centro Internacional and further north.

## GETTING THERE & AWAY
### Air
**Airport** Bogotá has one airport, Aeropuerto El Dorado, which handles all domestic and international flights. It is 13 km north-west of the city centre.

There are two passenger terminals. The main one, El Dorado, has snack bars, restaurants, handicraft shops and two tourist offices (see the Tourist Offices section for details), but no luggage lockers or left-luggage counter. There's a branch of the Banco Popular on the ground floor, between the departure and arrival sectors, which is open daily from 7 am to 10 pm; it changes both cash and travellers' cheques, at the same rate as the bank's branches in the city.

Another terminal, Puente Aéreo, is about one km from El Dorado towards the city. It handles Avianca's international flights to the USA, and domestic ones to Cali, Medellín and a few other destinations. Make sure to check which terminal your flight departs from.

About 200 metres before El Dorado terminal are two cargo buildings, Edificio de Carga No 1 and No 2, which house two dozen freight companies. Their planes depart from there.

**International Flights** There are international flights to all South and Central American capitals, the USA and Europe, serviced by both domestic and international carriers. See the Getting There & Away chapter for further details.

**Domestic Flights** There are plenty of domestic flights from Bogotá to destinations all over the country. Some of the major routes and their approximate fares (in US$) with the main airlines are given in the following table. They include the US$3.50 domestic airport tax, which you'll usually pay when buying your ticket.

Use the listed fares as guidelines only. They were correct at the time of writing but may change any time. If you plan on flying

**Domestic Flights from Bogotá**

| Destinations | Avianca | Sam | Aces | Intercontinental | Satena |
| --- | --- | --- | --- | --- | --- |
| | | *Airlines & Fares (inUS$)* | | | |
| Armenia | – | – | 48 | – | – |
| Barranquilla | 104 | 104 | 104 | 73 | – |
| Bucaramanga | 72 | – | – | – | 64 |
| Cali | 66 | 66 | 66 | 42 | 46 |
| Cartagena | 104 | 104 | 104 | 73 | – |
| Cúcuta | 83 | 83 | 82 | 58 | 59 |
| Leticia | 127 | – | – | – | 104 |
| Manizales | – | – | 48 | – | – |
| Medellín | 58 | 58 | 58 | 46 | 48 |
| Pasto | 92 | – | – | 7 | – |
| Pereira | 52 | 52 | – | 4 | – |
| Popayán | – | – | – | 54 | – |
| San Andrés | 147 | 147 | 147 | 109 | – |
| Santa Marta | 108 | 108 | – | – | – |
| Valledupar | 101 | – | – | 74 | – |

to San Andrés or Cartagena, check the fares of the two young airlines, AeroRepública and Isleña de Aviación, which may offer considerable discounts. It's also a good idea to consider noncommercial and cargo flights.

Satena has noncommercial passenger flights to San Andrés, roughly one per month (about US$60). These flights are heavily booked in advance, but it's sometimes possible to get on one: call the Satena office a couple of days before the scheduled departure date (as they may 'bump' passengers who haven't reconfirmed the flight), or go directly to the airport on flight day (as there may be some 'no-shows').

Aerosucre has cargo flights to various destinations, including San Andrés (once or twice weekly) and Leticia (almost daily). Its planes depart from its office/warehouse in the Edificio de Carga No 1, close to the El Dorado terminal. They sometimes take passengers, charging roughly two-thirds of the commercial airfare.

These flights don't have any fixed schedule, nor can you be sure of getting on board as not all pilots take passengers. It'll probably take some time and effort (and more than one trip to the airport) before you eventually arrange the flight. It's usually easier to get on these flights at the opposite end (see the Leticia and San Andrés sections for details).

Other cargo carriers may sometimes be useful though they don't fly as often on these routes as does Aerosucre. Ask around if you are there as most freighters are in the same or the neighbouring cargo building.

**Airlines** Following is the list of the airlines of Colombia and neighbouring countries. For the full list, see the Bogotá phone directory, contact the tourist office or any travel agency. A good part of the offices are in the Centro Internacional.

Aces
  Carrera 10 No 26-53 (☎ 281 7211)
AeroRepública
  Carrera 10 No 27-51, Local 303 (☎ 281 5199, 281 5511)
Aires
  Avenida 13 No 79-56 (☎ 257 3000, 610 9653)
Avianca
  Carrera 7 No 16-36 (☎ 241 5497)
Copa
  Calle 100 No 8A-49 (☎ 226 9550, 226 9525)
Intercontinental de Aviación
  Carrera 10 No 28-31 (☎ 283 3015)
Lacsa
  Calle 72 No 10-03, Oficina 703 (☎ 210 4428)
Sahsa
  Carrera 10 No 27-51, Local 209 (☎ 286 7771, 286 7898)

Sam
  Carrera 10 No 27-91 (☎ 282 1647)
Satena
  Carrera 10 No 27-51, Local 211 (☎ 286 2701, 281 7094)
Viasa
  Carrera 10 No 26-49 (☎ 283 8200)
Zuliana de Aviación
  Carrera 10 No 27-51, Local 206 (☎ 282 5666)

## Bus

**Bus Terminal** The new bus terminal at Calle 33B No 69-13 (☎ 295 1100) came into operation in 1984. It is large, modern, functional, well organised and efficient, and is home to more than 50 bus company offices. It has restaurants, cafeterias, showers and left-luggage rooms, plus a number of well-dressed thieves who will wait for a moment's inattention to grab your stuff and disappear.

The terminal has three departure halls: Norte (from which all buses towards the north depart), Oriente & Occidente (handling all buses towards the east and west) and Sur (servicing southbound buses). If one bus company operates buses in various directions, it has separate offices in the relevant halls. The terminal handles buses to just about every corner of the country, except for some short-distance regional buses which depart from other points of the city.

See the following Getting Around section for details on how to get to and from the terminal.

**Bus Routes & Fares** On the main roads, buses run frequently almost round the clock. For example, for Medellín, Cali or Bucaramanga, you can expect departures every half an hour throughout most of the day, by one or another of several companies which operate these routes. The usual type of bus on long-distance routes is the climatizado.

The main destinations, distances, fares and the approximate times of the journeys are given in the following table. Fares are for climatizados, except for the San Agustín pullman fare, as no climatizados ply this route.

| Destination | Distance (km) | Fare (US$) | Time (hours) |
|---|---|---|---|
| Armenia | 296 | 11 | 8 |
| Barranquilla | 999 | 37 | 20 |
| Bucaramanga | 429 | 16 | 10 |
| Cali | 481 | 19 | 12 |
| Cartagena | 1127 | 41 | 23 |
| Cúcuta | 630 | 24 | 16 |
| Ipiales | 948 | 37 | 24 |
| Manizales | 292 | 12 | 8 |
| Medellín | 440 | 17 | 9 |
| Neiva | 309 | 10 | 6 |
| Pasto | 865 | 33 | 22 |
| Pereira | 340 | 13 | 9 |
| Popayán | 617 | 24 | 15 |
| San Agustín | 529 | 16 | 12 |
| Santa Marta | 966 | 35 | 19 |
| Tunja | 147 | 5 | 3 |

## Train

The train station, Estación de la Sabana, is in the city centre on the corner of Calle 13 and Carrera 18, but you won't get far from here. The only passenger service still in operation is the *Tren Turístico* to Nemocón (refer to the Nemocón section for details).

## GETTING AROUND
### To/From the Airport

There are three ways of getting from the city centre to the airport (or vice versa): by a buseta (US$0.20), colectivo (US$0.30) or taxi (US$4). In the centre, you catch busetas and colectivos marked Aeropuerto El Dorado on Calle 19 or Carrera 10. At the airport, they park next to the El Dorado terminal. They all pass by Puente Aéreo en route. Urban transport to the airport stops at about 8 pm. If going by taxi, you pay a surcharge (*sobrecargo*) of US$1.

### To/From the Bus Terminal

The new terminal for long-distance buses is a long way from the centre and the urban bus service is relatively poor and stops around 9 pm. During rush hours it may take an hour to get to the terminal from the city centre.

There are both buses and colectivos running between the terminal and the city centre. From the centre, take the northbound colectivo marked 'Terminal' from Carrera 10 anywhere between Calles 19 and 26. You can also take a bus or colectivo from Calle 13 west of Avenida Caracas but this is an unsafe area best avoided. The best and fastest way is a taxi (US$2.50).

The same applies if you are going from the terminal to the city centre: you can take a bus or colectivo but it's best to go by taxi. The terminal has an excellently organised taxi service.

Upon arrival, follow the 'Taxi' signs which will lead you to a taxi booth at the exit of the terminal. In the booth you get a computer printout which indicates the plate number of your taxi and the expected fare to your destination. You then take the allocated taxi which waits at the door. The fare to anywhere within the central city area shouldn't be higher than US$2.50.

### Local Bus & Buseta

As there are no city trains or tramways, Bogotá's public transport is operated by buses and busetas (small buses). The collection of these vehicles – perhaps 10,000 of them altogether – includes everything from WW II relics to the newest air-con models. They all run the length and breadth of the city, usually at full speed if the traffic allows. Accidents are a way of life but considering the condition of these crates, their wild speeds and the drivers' carefree manners, the accident rate is relatively low.

Except on a few streets, there are no bus stops – you just wave the bus or buseta wherever you happen to be. You get on through the front door, pay the driver or the assistant but you don't get a ticket. In buses you get off through the back door, where there's a bell to ring to let the driver know to stop. In busetas there's usually only a front door through which all passengers get on and off. When you want to get off tell the driver *por acá, por favor* (here, please) or *en la esquina, por favor* (at the corner, please).

The traffic police have recently established bus stops on certain routes, most importantly on Carrera 7 and Avenida Caracas. It really has made transport faster and more efficient but naturally has aroused the protest of the Bogotanos unaccustomed to having to move themselves 100 metres to

a bus stop. Bus stops are being introduced in more streets.

Each bus and buseta displays a board on the windscreen indicating the route and number. For the locals they are easily recognisable from a distance but for the newcomer it can be a nightmare. They all run at breakneck speed using the whole width of the street, so it is difficult to decipher the route description quickly enough to wave down the right bus. It will probably take you several days to learn to recognise busetas and buses; Carrera 10 is a classic example of traffic chaos – practise there and within a week you will be an expert.

The fare ranges from US$0.15 to US$0.40 depending on the class and generation of the vehicle, and is slightly higher at night (after 8 pm) and on Sunday and holidays. The fare is always posted by the door or on the windscreen. The fare is flat, so you will be charged the same to go one block as to go right across the city.

Many buses and busetas now offer a so-called *servicio ejecutivo*, which means that they theoretically can only take as many passengers as they have seats. This service costs about 30% more than the ordinary service.

The buses and busetas operate with less frequency after 8 pm and stop running after 11 pm and midnight. On some principal routes such as Avenida Caracas, they run round the clock, although infrequently. However, it's better to use taxis at night because there have been a number of armed robberies in night buses and busetas.

There are also minibuses, called colectivos, which operate on the major routes. They are faster and cost about US$0.30.

### Taxi

Bogotá's taxis are mostly of relatively recent vintage. They all have meters and the drivers usually use them, though occasionally the sight of a gringo can make them reluctant to do so. Insist or take another taxi. They also should have stickers with day and night-time fares.

Taxis are a convenient and inexpensive means of getting around. A 10-km ride (eg from the Plaza de Bolívar to Avenida 100 in northern Bogotá) shouldn't cost more than US$3.

You can either wave down a taxi on the street or request one by phone from any of the numerous companies that have radio service, eg ☎ 211 1111, 411 1111 or 288 8888. They all have a fixed *recargo* (surcharge) of about US$0.40 for this service, and will usually arrive at the requested address within 15 minutes (this may take longer on weekend nights).

### Car Rental

The major international and national car rental companies operating in Bogotá include:

Avis
    Avenida 15 No 101-45 (☎ 610 4455)
Budget
    Avenida 15 No 107-08 (☎ 213 6383, 213 6020, 612 5040)
Dollar
    Diagonal 109 No 14-61 (☎ 620 0362, 620 0043)
Hertz
    Avenida 15 No 107-24 (☎ 214 9745, 214 4228)
    Aeropuerto El Dorado (☎ 266 9200)
    Puente Aéreo (☎ 263 1779)
National Car Rental
    Calle 100 No 14-46 (☎ 612 5635, 620 0055)
Renta Car
    Calle 71 No 9-39 (☎ 212 1592, 212 0664, 235 4824)
Rentamos
    Calle 100 No 11B-95 (☎ 616 0657, 256 7259, 257 8548)
Rentautos
    Carrera 7 No 46-41 (☎ 285 9648, 285 7339, 287 9601)

# Around Bogotá

Cundinamarca, the department surrounding Bogotá, has much to offer. Thanks to its varied topography, it provides every kind of environment, from hot lowlands in the west to freezing páramos in the east. Within a two-hour bus ride from Bogotá, you may experience significant differences in temperature and landscape. You will find lakes,

waterfalls, forests, mountains and a maze of small towns and villages, many of which still conserve some of their colonial fabric.

The western slopes of the Cordillera Oriental, running gently down to the Magdalena River, are dotted with old market towns such as Anapoima, Anolaima, Apulo and La Mesa, and are very picturesque. The area east of Bogotá, by contrast, where the Cordillera reaches its greatest heights, is rugged and sprinkled with tiny lakes, many of which were once sacred ritual centres of the Muiscas. This is good territory for some trekking.

If you prefer to relax in a warm climate in the company of Bogotanos, go to Melgar, their favourite weekend destination. The main road passing through Melgar is densely packed with hotels and cabañas, most of which have swimming pools and restaurants with a good supply of cold beer.

On the whole, the road network in Cundinamarca is dense and transport is frequent. Most buses leave from the Bogotá bus terminal.

If you plan on exploring the region go to the Corporación de Turismo de Cundinamarca (☎ 284 0600), Calle 16 No 7-76 in Bogotá, where you can get a brochure on the department in Spanish and English. You may also want to buy maps in the IGAC: the map of the Sabana de Bogotá (excellent) for shorter trips and the map of Cundinamarca department (not so good) for longer excursions.

Contact the Grupo de Caminantes 'Sal Si Puedes' (see Bogotá's Information section). It organises Saturday and Sunday hikes around Cundinamarca and know virtually every corner of the department.

### ZIPAQUIRÁ
• *pop 60,000* • *2650 m* • *14°C* • ☎ *(91852)*
Zipaquirá, 50 km north of Bogotá, takes pride in having the richest salt mines in Colombia. They are in the mountain just west of the town. Although the mines date back to the Muisca period and have been intensively exploited, they still contain vast reserves; it is virtually a huge mountain of rock salt.

BOGOTÁ

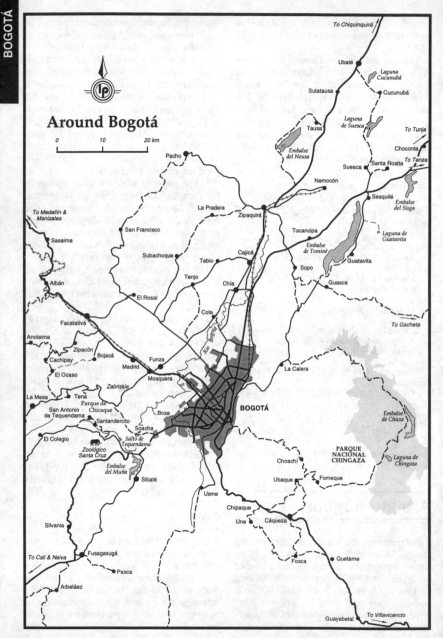

**Around Bogotá**

0      10      20 km

In the heart of the mountain, a unique underground cathedral was carved out of the solid salt and opened for visitors in 1954. The interior is some 25 metres high and is capable of holding 10,000 people. However, as the walls began to crack a few years ago the cathedral was closed down. A new one, with supposedly similar characteristics, is being hewn out of rock on a lower level, and is going to open to visitors in the 'near future'. Check with Bogotá's tourist offices for news. The entrance to the mine (and the cathedral) is a 20-minute walk uphill from the centre of town.

Although Zipaquirá was founded in 1606 and still has some colonial buildings, the town itself is of little interest. You can have a quick glance at the central plaza with its church and chapel and then return to Bogotá, or give yourself the rest of the day for a visit to nearby Nemocón or Tausa (see the following sections).

### Getting There & Away

Buses to Zipaquirá depart every 10 minutes from the corner of Calle 13 and Carrera 30 in Bogotá. They can be caught further north along Carrera 30. They cost US$0.80 and the trip takes 1¼ hours.

## NEMOCÓN

• *pop 6000* • *2585 m* • *14˚C* • ☎ *(91854)*

Nemocón, 15 km north-east of Zipaquirá, is believed to have been founded in 1537 (before Bogotá) by the expedition of Jiménez de Quesada which arrived in the Sabana basin. Until then it was an important Muisca centre where tribal elders gathered to give themselves up to laments over misfortunes and the dead and to perform their mournful rituals. According to local sources, the name Nemocón means 'lion's lament' in Chibcha, but how the Muiscas could have known about lions is not quite clear.

The Spaniards, and later the Colombians, perhaps had no reason to lament here since they exploited salt reserves on which the town sits. The salt mine, along with an underground chapel built by miners, is today the main attraction for tourists who come mostly on weekends.

### Getting There & Away

Nemocón is linked to Bogotá by railway, and this is the only passenger line operating out of the capital. The so-called *Tren Turístico* (Tourist Train), which uses the last surviving steam locomotives, has been put into operation, and runs on Saturday, Sunday and public holidays. The train departs at 8.30 am from the Estación de la Sabana and reaches Nemocón at noon. It then leaves at 3 pm and arrives back at Bogotá at 6.30 pm. The train stops en route at the station in northern Bogotá (off the corner of Calle 100 and Carrera 15), so you can get on and off there.

Tickets can be bought in advance from the TMA offices (see the Bogotá Money section for addresses) or directly from the station before departure. The return fare is US$9.

There are also buses to Nemocón, if you want to get there at other times, and they are cheaper at US$1.20 one way.

## TAUSA

Tausa is 20 km north of Zipaquirá along the road to Chiquinquirá, plus one km west by a side road. It is just an uninspiring small village, but climb the nearby hill along a rough road to see Tausa Viejo, an impressive ghost town consisting of the abandoned ruins of the old village with its church and thatched huts.

### Getting There & Away

Frequent buses depart from Bogotá terminal to Chiquinquirá and will let you off near Tausa. All these buses go via Zipaquirá, where you can catch them on the main road. From Tausa, you can make your way back along a dirt road passing the Embalse del Neusa, an artificial lake surrounded by reforested highlands. A few buses run daily along this road.

## GUATAVITA

• *pop 2500* • *2680 m* • *14˚C* • ☎ *(91857)*

Guatavita, also called Guatavita la Nueva, is a new town built from scratch in the late

1960s when the old, colonial Guatavita, dating from 1542, was flooded by the waters of a hydroelectric reservoir, the Embalse de Tominé. Guatavita is somewhat artificial but impressive. The architects took the best of the colonial style and added modern designs to obtain an interesting blend of old and new.

Although the town is a lovely architectural creation, it has failed as a social experiment. The traditional rural mentality hasn't accepted the radical leap into modernity; the inhabitants of old Guatavita were reluctant to settle in modern homes. As only a handful of peasants live in the town, it has become a weekend haunt for Bogotanos and tourists who come to look at its architecture. Among the things to see are the museum of religious art, the bullring, the church (don't miss its beautiful altar) and the market on Sunday, which is best in the morning.

There are a couple of simple places to stay and eat in Guatavita. More restaurants open on Sunday when tourists come.

### Getting There & Away
Buses to Guatavita depart from the corner of Calle 19 and Carrera 30 in Bogotá, and run north along Carrera 30 (where you can wave them down). They leave every hour on weekdays and every 15 minutes on Sunday; the fare is US$2 and the journey takes two hours.

### LAGUNA DE GUATAVITA
• *3000 m* • *11°C*
The sacred lake and ritual centre of the Muisca Indians, the Laguna de Guatavita is the cradle of the myth of El Dorado. It was here half a millenium ago that the Zipa, the Muisca cacique coated with gold dust, would throw precious offerings into the lake from his ceremonial raft and then plunge himself in the waters to obtain god-like power.

The famous golden piece representing the ceremonial raft, *Balsa Muisca*, is the best evidence of the elaborate Indian rituals held in the lake. You can see the raft in the Gold Museum in Bogotá.

Don't bring along scuba gear or diving equipment; instead, enjoy the beauty of this perfectly circular lake with its emerald waters, nestled in a crater-like ring covered with greenery. As both the lake and the town of Guatavita are near one another it's convenient to do them in one trip from Bogotá.

### Getting There & Away
To get to the lake from Bogotá, take a bus to Guatavita la Nueva but get off 11 km before there (six km past Sesquilé), where there is a sign directing you to the lake (drivers will let you off at the right place). From the road, continue seven km up along a dirt road to the lake. There are several farms around so ask for directions if in doubt. At weekends there are occasional private jeeps so it's sometimes possible to get a lift. You will arrive at the lake shore after passing through a deep, V-shape cut in the lake's bank that is the legacy of the ill-fated efforts to drain it. Don't miss the walk around the lake.

### SUESCA
Suesca is a small town several km north of the Bogotá-Tunja road. The turn-off to Suesca is close to the Guatavita turn-off. The town dates from the time of early Spanish conquest; it was reputedly founded by Jiménez de Quesada two weeks before he gave birth to Bogotá.

The main square boasts a small colonial church dating from the early 17th century, and there are several other buildings around remembering the Spanish era.

There are spectacular rocky cliffs just out of the town, which have become a favourite place for Bogotá's rock climbers. They often come here on weekends. The rail track heading west from the rocks will lead you to the small hamlet of Santa Rosita and a spectacular gorge.

About eight km north of Suesca is the Laguna de Suesca. North of the lake is the tiny village of Cucunubá and, beyond it, yet another lake, the Laguna Cucunubá.

Suesca is a good one-day excursion out of Bogotá. It's best to do it on Sunday when you're likely to meet some intrepid montañistas. Suesca is serviced regularly by buses from Bogotá. If you don't want to return the same

## The Treasures of Laguna de Guatavita

The Muiscas had many sacred lakes such as Tota, Siecha, Iguaque and Chingaza, but Guatavita was presumably the most important, supposedly because of its astral origins. Everything seems to suggest that the lake was made by a giant meteor which fell some 2000 years ago and left a huge circular hole shaped like a volcanic crater. The Indians interpreted the phenomenon as the arrival of a golden god who lived thereafter at the bottom of the lake. The lake became an object of worship, where gold pieces, emeralds and food were offered to ensure abundant crops and protection against misfortunes.

When the Spaniards saw the Indians throwing gold into the lake, they believed incalculable treasures were to be found at the bottom and they made numerous attempts to salvage the riches. In fact, no other lake in Colombia, and perhaps on the whole continent, experienced as many desperate efforts to get to its bottom as did the Laguna de Guatavita.

One of the best known early expeditions was directed in the 1560s by a rich merchant, Antonio de Sepúlveda, who succeeded in getting a permit from the Crown to drain the lake. With a large Indian labour force, he cut into one side of the crater to drain off the water. The result of this enormous effort was 232 pesos and 10 grams of fine gold. Sepúlveda died bankrupt.

In the 19th century, after Colombia achieved independence, the attempts to retrieve the legendary treasures intensified. Initially, the most viable way to do so appeared to be to enlarge the former cut in the ridge to drain the lake. Several successive operations succeeded in lowering the water level (though not in draining the lake completely) but the gold didn't materialise as expected. Other methods were then tried, such as a siphon construction and an underground channel, but all in vain.

Despite these failures, the lake continued to draw in new challengers. By the turn of the century an English company, Contractors Ltd, arrived with a load of machinery including the new high-tech invention of the day, a steam pump. The company managed to drain the lagoon almost completely and even washed out most of the mud from the bottom. However, the 20-odd gold objects plus some emeralds and ceramics found during eight years of exploration didn't compensate for the £40,000 invested in the whole operation. The company went broke.

The rains refilled the muddy basin and peace and quiet returned to the lake. Not for long, however: new treasure hunters began to search the lake with more determination. In the 1940s a Colombian miner, Gustavo Jaramillo Sánchez, set about installing a dragline. Soon after North American divers arrived with sophisticated metal detectors. As so many times before, very little was found.

Yet another attempt was planned in 1965 by a US-Colombian company. By that time, however, the Colombian authorities decided to ban further excavations in the lake. Thus, after four centuries of digging, draining, dragging, pumping and diving, the lagoon has finally been left in peace.

Legend has it that the bottom still retains its treasure, but the more cautious historians have some doubts. First of all, there are no historic records of the amount of gold the Indians actually deposited in the lake. By all rational estimates there couldn't have been much; the Muiscas had emeralds and salt but no gold mines of their own. Given the number of sacred lakes, the gold offerings are likely to have been distributed over plenty of ritual sites, and not lakes alone. Caves, for example, were also places where ritual sacrifices were made.

Furthermore, it's not quite clear whether it was the Laguna de Guatavita that served as the major centre of gold-offering. It was just the lake where the Spaniards had the opportunity to witness the Muisca ceremony. Some sceptics believe that the Indians simply played a sort of theatre for the Spaniards in order to confuse them and divert their attention from the places where genuine rituals were held.

The Balsa Muisca, considered to be the Muiscas' most elaborate gold object, and the ultimate proof of their ceremonies, was found (in 1856) in Laguna de Siecha, not in Guatavita. Another Balsa (the one displayed today in the Bogotá's Gold Museum), only found in 1969, doesn't come from Guatavita either, but from a cave near the village of Pasca.

Regardless of whether the Laguna de Guatavita contains Muisca treasures, it is certainly full of mystery and beauty. ■

way, walk to Nemocón from where you can catch a bus back to the city.

Should you wish to stay in the area longer, there are Cabañas La Esperanza on the road to the Laguna de Suesca. There doesn't seem to be any accommodation in town.

## PARQUE NACIONAL CHINGAZA

The closest national park to Bogotá, Chingaza lies about 50 km east of the capital and covers 504 sq km of the highlands of the Cordillera Oriental. Like most Andean parks, it's noted for its rough topography, with rolling hills, high mountains and deep gorges. The highest altitudes reach nearly 4000 metres at the Cerro de San Luis. The climate is determined by the elevation; the average annual temperatures range from 5°C to 12°C in most of the park area. The rainfall is high, exceeding 3000 mm per year, with most of rains falling during the long wet season from April to November.

The vegetation ranges from Andean mountain forests at lower altitudes to desolate páramos in the highest reaches. The frailejón, a plant typical of páramos, is represented by a number of species, including the *Espeletia uribei*, the tallest existing species of the family, which grows up to 12 metres and is endemic to the region. Seven condors have recently been brought from California and let free in the park. You may occasionally spot them.

The park is sprinkled with small mountain lakes, some of which were once sanctuaries or ceremonial sites of the Muiscas. Laguna de Siecha might have been the major sacred lake within the park. As with Guatavita, various attempts were carried out here to retrieve the alleged treasures, rewarded with the finding of the famous Balsa Muisca. The Laguna de Siecha is in the northernmost part of the park at an altitude of 3673 metres. It is a half an hour's walk uphill from the road.

Apart from the natural lakes, there's a large artificial lake, the Embalse de Chuza. It has been formed by a dam constructed, together with a network of tunnels and pipelines, by the Bogotá aqueduct company. The

system provides a large portion of Bogotá's water supply.

At the northern end of the reservoir is the water company's camp, Campamento Chuza. About one km south of the camp is the Inderena visitors centre, Monte Redondo. Inderena has opened two scenic paths for visitors, La Arboleda and Laguna Seca, which allow you to observe the local flora, including frailejones, mosses, ferns and native grasses. La Arboleda is five km south of the visitors centre, while Laguna Seca is 10 km to the north; both are close to the road. There are also a few *miradores* (viewpoints) from which the mountainous scenery of the area can be enjoyed.

The region south of the Laguna de Chingaza (the largest natural lake in the park, nestled amidst steep slopes at 3270 metres) maintains its natural beauty pretty much intact. There is a scenic walk from the lake to the small hamlet of San Juanito, passing several small lakes on the way. Give yourself a whole day to complete the return trip at a leisurely pace.

East of the reservoir, just outside the park's boundaries, is the Reserva Biológica Carpanta, a small nature reserve encompassing 12 sq km, run by the Fundación Natura. There's a cabaña by the entrance to the reserve. Contact the foundation's Bogotá office (☎ 616 9262, 218 0471) to visit the reserve.

The best time to visit the park is the relatively dry season from December to February. Don't forget to take your permit from Inderena, who will also give you details about transport, lodging and eating facilities.

### Places to Stay & Eat

Inderena is in the process of constructing some accommodation for visitors. As yet, it only offers camping facilities (US$7 per tent) at Monte Redondo. There's no restaurant so take your own provisions.

Sometimes it's possible to stay with the aqueduct workers in the Campamento Chuza. In this case you will probably be allowed to eat in their canteen as well.

# Parque Nacional Chingaza

0        2.5       5 km

Lagunas de Siecha

Lagunas de Bulfrago

To La Calera & Bogotá

Sendero Natural Laguna Seca

Laguna Verde

Laguna Seca

Río Chuza

Campamento Chuza

Centro de Visitantes Monte Redondo

Embalse de Chuza

Sendero Natural La Arboleda

Reserva Biológica Carpanta

Río La Playa

Mirador Montes Negros

Presa de Golillas

Río Chuza

Río Blanco

To Bogotá

Choachí

Mirador Alto del Cristal

Laguna de Chingaza

La Unión

Río Negro

Río Frío

Laguna del Medio

Laguna Larga

Fómeque

Laguna del Guájaro

Río Guájaro

San Juanito

Quebrada   Negra

Río Guatiquía

## Getting There & Away

There are two access roads from Bogotá to the park: from the north and south. These roads join in the park so it's possible to make the whole loop, providing you have your own transport. This loop can be easily done in a day trip from Bogotá.

The north route leads through La Calera and is used by all trucks and jeeps servicing the installations and Campamento Chuza. Public transport to La Calera departs frequently from the corner of Avenida Caracas and Calle 72 (Avenida Chile) in Bogotá, but there are no regular buses further on to the park. Hitching is possible up to Chuza where most transport stops.

The south route leads through Fómeque, which can be reached in two hours by bus from the Bogotá terminal. Again, there's no public transport further on. From Fómeque you have to walk 28 km uphill along a dirt road to the entrance of the park (a 1500-metre ascent); there's virtually no traffic on this road. In the rainy season, the road may be in poor shape and only passable by jeeps. It's sometimes blocked by landslides.

Inderena may offer guided trips in its bus, which is the only easy way of visiting the park for people without their own vehicles.

## SALTO DE TEQUENDAMA

This waterfall, 135 metres high, is about 30 km from Bogotá on the road to El Colegio, off the Girardot road. The falls overlook a magnificent rock-wall cirque often covered in mist. However, there are some drawbacks to this magnificent scenery. During the dry season the waterfall is pretty faint and the water is filthy. This is, after all, the Río Bogotá, probably one of the most polluted rivers in the world. If the wind blows from the wrong direction the smell can be putrid.

## Getting There & Away

Take a bus from the Bogotá terminal to El Colegio. They depart every half an hour and pass by the waterfall (US$1).

## ZOOLÓGICO SANTA CRUZ

This is a private zoo housing about 100 species of animals typical of Colombia and beyond, including mammals, reptiles and birds. It is open daily from 8 am to 5 pm; entrance costs US$1.

The zoo is on the road to El Colegio, about 10 km past the Salto de Tequendama. The El Colegio bus will drop you off nearby (US$1.20). It's

Green Toucan

best to visit the two sights, the zoo and the falls, in one trip.

## FUSAGASUGÁ
• *pop 57,000* • *1730 m* • *19°C* • ☎ *(91)*

Commonly known as Fusa, this town on the Bogotá-Cali road is known for its gardens. Thanks to its mild climate, a wide variety of decorative plants are grown in the region. In the town itself, you can visit the pleasant, though recently unkempt garden of the Casa Municipal de la Cultura, on Calle 11 opposite the petrol station.

The best known garden in the surrounding area is La Clarita, noted for its orchids. The seasons are in May and December, but there may be some orchids in bloom at other times of the year. The garden is open daily from 8 am to 5 pm; entry fee is US$1. The señora will guide you around. The garden is on the road to Bogotá via Sibaté, about five km from Fusa.

Most of the other gardens are *viveros* (nurseries) where plants are cultivated for sale. There are many viveros scattered around Fusa, including La Negrita, off the main Bogotá-Girardot road, and Tocarema, next to La Negrita. There are also some on the Sibaté road, near La Clarita.

### Places to Stay
There are quite a number of hotels in town. If you want to be close to the main square, you'll find several budget places on Carrera 6 near the church, including *Hotel Buenos Aires*, Carrera 6 No 4-40, and *Hotel Calipso*, Carrera 6 No 4-53. Either costs US$4 per person.

### Getting There & Away
Plenty of buses, operated by Autofusa and Cootransfusa, run to Fusa from the Bogotá terminal. The trip takes about two hours and costs US$2. Fusa can be visited as a one-day excursion from Bogotá, or you can just stop here en route to Armenia, Neiva, Cali etc.

## ZABRISKIE
Zabriskie got its name for its similarity to the setting used in Antonioni's film *Zabriskie Point*. It is an arid area where erosion has sculpted strange, colourful rock and sand formations. Zabriskie is some 25 km from Bogotá on the Mosquera-La Mesa road and is a pleasant place to escape from the city rush.

### Getting There & Away
Take one of the frequent buses to Facatativá (marked Faca) from Bogotá train station on Calle 13. Get off in Mosquera and catch any bus going to La Mesa. About five km on you will see Zabriskie on your right. Alternatively, take a bus from the Bogotá terminal going to La Mesa, Anapoima, Tocaima or Girardot (via Mosquera) which will drop you at Zabriskie.

## PARQUE DE CHICAQUE
The Parque de Chicaque is a private nature reserve not far from Zabriskie. Most of its three-sq-km area is covered with cloudforest *(bosque de niebla)*. Walks along the paths of the reserve (about eight km long altogether) will give you an opportunity to enjoy the forest's flora and fauna, particularly the birds. The reserve is open to visitors daily from 8 am to 4 pm; admission fee is US$1.50. You can rent horses (US$5 per hour) and are allowed to camp (US$2 per person). Construction of a cabaña has begun which will provide accommodation for visitors.

### Getting There & Away
The reserve is a few km off the Soacha-La Mesa road. To get there, take a bus, colectivo or taxi to the plaza in Soacha, where a colectivo directly to the administrative centre of the reserve can be contracted for US$5 (up to five passengers).

Eco-Guías (see Tours & Guides earlier in this chapter) is planning to introduce tours to the reserve. The five-hour trip is expected to cost about US$10 per person with a minimum of three persons required; the price includes return transport, entrance fee to the reserve, and guided walks.

From the reserve, you can walk along a *camino de herradura* (old Spanish path) to the small village of San Antonio de Tequendama. Ask the management for details.

## BOJACÁ
• *pop 3700* • *2600 m* • *14˚C* • ☎ *(91846)*

Bojacá is a small town about 35 km from Bogotá off the Facatativá road. It dates from the early years of the Spanish era and its colonial church, built in 1720, boasts an image of the Virgin of Health, renowned for miraculous powers. Predictably, the Virgin draws pilgrims.

The best day to visit is Sunday when the faithful come from Bogotá and surrounding villages for the morning mass. The central plaza fills at that time with photographers and their assortment of backdrops – saints and models of horses predominate. This is the right place to turn up to if you happen to need that evangelical happy snap to send home. Or perhaps you'd prefer an equestrian pose (Mexican sombreros provided).

A pleasant four-hour walk can be taken from Bojacá down to El Ocaso. It is a scenic 1200-metre descent from the cold climes of the eucalyptus forests to the mandarin and orange orchards at an altitude of 1400 metres. Follow the dirt road, and where it divides, take the left-hand fork (the one to the right climbs to Zipacón).

### Getting There & Away
Buses from Bogotá to Bojacá leave from Carrera 18 near the train station (US$0.80). Buses from El Ocaso back to Bogotá run until about 6 pm (US$1.20).

## FACATATIVÁ
• *pop 52,000* • *2590 m* • *14˚C* • ☎ *(91)*

Faca, 48 km north-west of Bogotá on the main road to Honda, has grown rapidly as a satellite town. It's not the town itself that is a tourist attraction, but the Parque Arqueológico Piedras de Tunja, one km north of Faca. This is a big recreational park with paved alleys, a small artificial lake and spectacular rocks.

The site was once an important centre of the Muiscas, who left behind a number of still-undeciphered petroglyphs. Today, the rocks are indeed covered with inscriptions, but not of the Muisca variety. They are mainly names, dates, broken hearts and even some artistic attempts including a colourful abstract painting. This contemporary 'art' left by tourists has covered many of the original petroglyphs that had already suffered from the ravages of time. Of about 70 Muisca sites marked with numbers, only a few are of any interest.

At weekends the park turns into a picnic spot and fills with cars, people and music. It is open daily from 8 am to 6 pm; entry for visitors is free but cars are charged US$1.

### Getting There & Away
Frequent buses to Facatativá leave from next to the train station in Bogotá. They cost US$0.80 and the trip takes an hour, though may take twice as long at rush hours.

## GUADUAS
• *pop 10,000* • *990 m* • *23˚C* • ☎ *(91)*

Guaduas is an example of a colonial town in Cundinamarca, though not as good as some of the lovely towns in Boyacá or Santander. The most interesting part of town is around the central square, the Plaza de la Constitución, with the statue of Policarpa Salavarrieta in its middle. La Pola, as she is affectionately referred to, was the heroine of the war of independence, executed by the Spaniards in 1817, at only 22 years of age. A visit to the **Casa de Policarpa Salavarrieta**, the restored house where she was born, Calle 2 between Carreras 4 and 5, will provide more information about her life.

Another museum, the **Museo del Virrey Ezpeleta**, on the corner of the plaza, Calle 4 No 4-14, houses a variety of objects related to the country's history. The museum was named after José de Ezpeleta de Galdeano, a Spanish general who was the governor of Cuba (1785-89) and the viceroy of Nueva Granada (1789-97). Both museums are open Tuesday to Friday from 8 am to noon and 2 to 5 pm, Saturday from 8 am to noon.

Guaduas is a popular weekend spot for Bogotanos, who come here to warm up from

Ráquira street vendors

Colonial-style hotels in Puntalarga, near Duitama

the cold metropolis. There are stalls on the Villeta-Guaduas road selling baskets and other handicrafts.

### Places to Stay & Eat
The loveliest of the town's several hotels is the *Hostería Colonial* (☎ 846 6041) on the main square next to the church. It's a 200-year-old colonial house with a marvellous patio full of flowers. At US$3.50 per person for rooms with bath, it's good value. The hotel's restaurant serves just about the best set meals in town.

Other lodging options at a similar price include *Hotel Central Plaz* on the main square, which also has its own restaurant, *Hotel Morgan*, Calle 4 No 2-84, just off the plaza, and *Residencias La Posadita*, Calle 4 No 5-48.

### Getting There & Away
Guaduas is on the main Bogotá-Honda road and there is frequent transport operated by several companies. It's probably better to include Guaduas as a stop on the way to Medellín or Manizales rather than to do it as a round trip from Bogotá.

## SALTO DE VERSALLES
If you stay in Guaduas don't miss the Salto de Versalles, a beautiful 40-metre-high waterfall 10 km away on the side road to Caparrapí. The waterfall is set amidst green hills and there is a natural pool at the bottom where you can have a refreshing shower. You can also climb to the top of the waterfall along a path on the left facing the falls. You can camp at the base of the falls.

### Getting There & Away
Flota Santa Fe operates buses from Guaduas to Caparrapí approximately every two hours. Its Guaduas office is in the Restaurante Santa Fe, on the corner of Calle 4 and Carrera 9, just off the main road. Get off when you see the large sign (drivers know where to drop you) and walk two km to the waterfall. The 20-minute bus ride costs US$0.50.

# Boyacá, Santander & Norte de Santander

The three departments of Boyacá, Santander and Norte de Santander cover the northern part of the Cordillera Oriental to the north of Bogotá, between the Magdalena River in the west and Los Llanos in the east. Like all other parts of the Andean region, the topography varies from hot lowlands to perpetual snow.

The region offers a great variety of landscapes, such as the verdant Valle de Tenza (southern Boyacá), the arid Cañón del Chicamocha (Santander) and the snowy peaks of the Sierra Nevada del Cocuy (northern Boyacá), to name just a few.

Once the territory of the Muiscas (Boyacá) and the Guane Indians (central Santander), the region was one of the first to be conquered and settled by the Spaniards. Many colonial towns have been preserved to this day in remarkably good shape. Villa de Leyva, Barichara and Girón are among the best examples.

Boyacá and the Santanders were also the cradle of Colombia's independence. Socorro was the site of one of the first rebellions against Spanish rule, and Simón Bolívar fought decisive battles at Pantano de Vargas and Puente de Boyacá. The first constitution was signed in Villa del Rosario, and there are many more reminders of that turbulent period.

Of the three departments, Boyacá is perhaps the safest, easiest and most pleasant in which to travel. It is also the most traditional province, widely known for its handicrafts, particularly pottery, basketwork and weaving.

Boyacá's craftwork has a long tradition dating back to pre-Columbian times. The Muisca forms and patterns, developed by their descendants and backed by the techniques introduced by the Spaniards, have resulted in a wide variety of good-quality handicrafts.

## Boyacá

### TENZA
• *pop 2000* • *1540 m* • *20°C* • ☎ *(987)*

Tenza is a small town set in the Valle de Tenza in southern Boyacá. It's noted for its mild climate, uncommon in Boyacá, and its fine if modest old architecture. There is nothing of particular interest in the town – no museums or monuments, and even its large church is not an architectural gem – but despite that, the town as a whole is one of the loveliest in Boyacá. It has been whitewashed throughout, and it's well kept, clean and quiet. It is a pleasant place to rest for a while and use as a base for short excursions into the surrounding Valle de Tenza.

Tenza is an important regional centre for basket weaving. Its main street, Calle 5, is dotted with handicraft shops which sell an

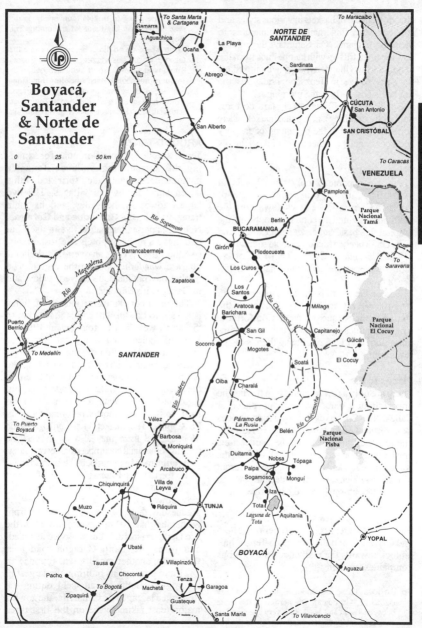

BOYACÁ

amazing choice of baskets in various styles and colours, from fingernail-sized miniatures to metre-high giants. On Saturday, the market day, the town fills up with campesinos from the neighbouring villages, who bring their baskets for sale. Arrive in Tenza on Friday, as the market is best early in the morning.

Small as it is, Tenza has a plaza de toros bullfighting(bullring), next to the market, where corridas are held at the beginning of January and occasionally at other times of the year.

### Places to Stay

There are apparently only three hotels in Tenza. The *Casa del Campesino*, the cheapest, is on Carrera 4, one block down from the main plaza, behind the church and opposite the hospital. It's basic but clean and pleasant, and costs US$3 per bed (a couple would squeeze in).

The *Albergue*, at Carrera 7 No 4-63, offers rooms with private baths and charges US$5 per person.

Top of the range is the large *Hotel Tenza* (☎ 540397), at Carrera 5 No 5-35, next to the church in the parque principal. Comfortable singles/doubles overlooking the hotel swimming pool cost US$20/28, and there's also a restaurant.

### Places to Eat

There are only a few restaurants in town. The one without a name on the main plaza, at Calle 6 No 5-70, serves a good comida, as does *Restaurante La Llamarada*, at Calle 6 No 7-20, one block off the square. In the market area, you have the budget *Restaurante Social*, on the corner of Calle 5 and Carrera 10. The restaurant of the *Hotel Tenza* is a more decent place to eat but it's obviously more expensive.

### Getting There & Away

Flota La Macarena, on the corner of Calle 5 and Carrera 9, and Flota Valle de Tenza, half a block towards the market, are the two bus companies servicing Tenza.

**To Bogotá** There are about eight buses a day (US$3.75, 4½ hours). The portion of the route between Tenza and Machetá is very spectacular; choose a seat by the left-hand window of the bus

if you are going to Bogotá (conversely, grab a seat on the right-hand side when coming from Bogotá).

**To Tunja** There are no direct buses. You can either take the Bogotá bus, get off on the main Bogotá-Tunja road near Chocontá and catch one of the frequent northbound buses heading for Tunja, Sogamoso, Bucaramanga etc; or go to Garagoa, from where several buses a day go to Tunja by an unpaved, rough but spectacular road via Chinavita.

## AROUND TENZA

Tenza is a good jumping-off point for exploring the surrounding Valle de Tenza, a picturesque, verdant valley sprinkled with a dozen small towns and villages. The two largest towns in the valley, and its main transport hubs, are **Guateque** and **Garagoa**. Neither is particularly attractive in itself but both have a range of hotels and restaurants, so either may serve as an overnight shelter if you are wandering around the region. The market day in Guateque is Wednesday, and in Garagoa it's Sunday.

The most popular excursion out of Tenza is a walk to **La Capilla**, a village five km to the north-west. It was founded in 1793 by Virrey Ezpeleta, and is a local centre for apiculture and tomato growing. A few buses a day go by an unpaved road to La Capilla, but perhaps the most pleasant way to enjoy the scenery is by walking. There's an old *trapiche* (traditional sugarcane mill) off the road (to the right) shortly before arriving in La Capilla. The market in the village is on Monday, and there may also be a vegetable (mainly tomato and cucumber) market on Friday.

A rough road (without public transport) continues for 13 km to **Pachavita**, a town founded in 1793 and known for its handicrafts, particularly straw hats. The best time to visit is Wednesday, the local market day. A road from Pachavita winds 10 km down northwards to the Río Garagoa (sporadic buses service this road) and joins the Tunja-Garagoa road near **Chinavita**, another small town, founded in 1821 and proud of its bullring, the largest in the region. Bullfights are held during the Romería a la Virgen de Chinavita, the town's major feast taking place on the first three days of the year.

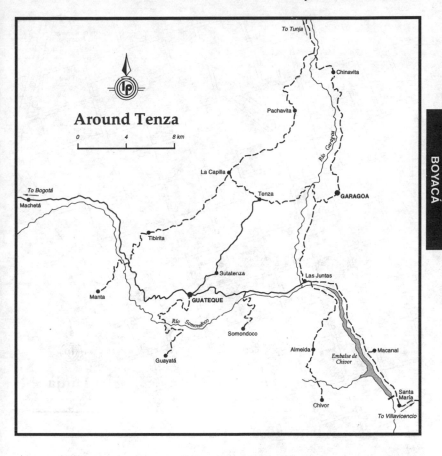

**Around Tenza**

0    4    8 km

*To Tunja*

Chinavita

Pachavita

*Río Garagoa*

La Capilla

Tenza

**GARAGOA**

*To Bogotá*

Macheté

Tibiritá

Sutatenza

Las Juntas

Manta

**GUATEQUE**

*Río Somondoco*

Somondoco

Guayatá

Almeida

*Embalse de Chivor*

Macanal

Chivor

Santa María

*To Villavicencio*

South of Tenza, on the southern slopes of the valley, are two spectacularly located small towns, **Somondoco** and **Guayatá**. You will see them from the road when coming from Bogotá, shortly before reaching Guateque. There's infrequent transport from Guateque to both Somondoco and Guayatá.

East of Somondoco is yet another sloping town, **Almeida**. A rough road from Almeida continues south to the town of **Chivor**, noted for the emerald mines nearby.

Further east is the **Embalse de Chivor**, a reservoir for a hydroelectric project, which provides electricity to the region and

beyond. The reservoir, set in a deep, steep-sided gorge, is long and narrow, and very spectacular. The road from Las Juntas to Santa María (where the dam is) skirts around the lake and passes through several tunnels. There are some marvellous views.

## TUNJA
• *pop 120,000* • *2820 m* • *13°C* • ☎ *(987)*

Tunja, the capital of Boyacá, is an old colonial town founded by Gonzalo Suárez Rendón in 1539 on the site of Hunza, the capital of the Zaque domain, the northern

BOYACÁ

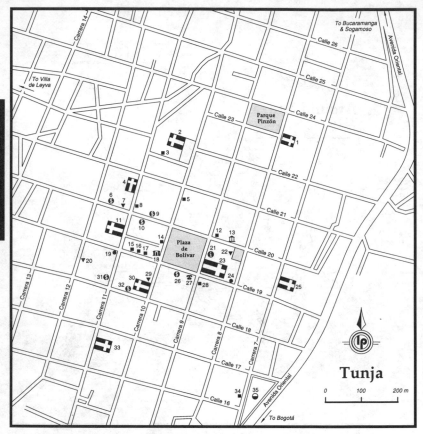

Tunja

0        100        200 m

part of the Muisca empire. The town developed as the starting point for expeditions to Los Llanos, where the Spaniards hoped to find the legendary El Dorado. Within a short time Tunja became an important religious centre.

Though almost nothing is left from the Indian period, much colonial architecture remains. The central sector has been carefully restored for the town's 450th anniversary, and many old public houses have recovered their original splendour. Unfortunately, the streets further off the main square are slowly losing their colonial character, as modern buildings and apart-

ment blocks mushroom between fine old mansions. Tunja is a city of churches: several imposing examples from the 16th century are almost untouched by time.

Tunja is the highest and coldest departmental capital in the country. Lying at an altitude of 2820 metres, it has a mountain climate, characterised by a considerable difference between day and night-time temperatures. Make sure you bring enough warm clothing.

### Information
**Tourist Office** The regional tourist office (☎ 422924) is in the Casa del Fundador, on

## PLACES TO STAY

3 Hotel Hunza
5 Hostal El Cid
8 Hostería San Carlos
12 Hotel El Conquistador
14 Hotel Don Camilo
15 Hotel Dux
16 Hotel Lord
17 Hotel Saboy
28 Hotel San Francisco
34 Residencias Bolívar

## PLACES TO EAT

7 Restaurante Estar de Hunzahua
20 Saloon Ejecutivo Kevin's
22 Restaurante Pila del Mono
29 Restaurante El Bodegón de los Frailes

## OTHER

1 Iglesia de San Agustín
2 Iglesia de San Francisco
4 Iglesia de Santa Clara La Antigua
6 Banco Popular
9 Banco de Bogotá
10 Banco Industrial Colombiano
11 Iglesia de Santo Domingo
13 Casa de Don Juan de Vargas
18 Casa de la Cultura
19 Casa del Capitán Luis Mancipe
21 Tourist Office & Casa del Fundador Suárez Rendón
23 Catedral
24 Casa de Don Juan de Castellanos
25 Iglesia de Santa Clara La Real
26 Casa de Cambio
27 Telecom
30 Iglesia de San Ignacio
31 Banco del Estado
32 Banco de Occidente
33 Iglesia de Santa Bárbara
35 Bus Terminal

the Plaza de Bolívar. It's open daily from 8 am to noon and 2 to 6 pm, and the staff are helpful and knowledgeable.

**Money** Only the Banco del Estado will change cash dollars. The Banco del Estado and Banco de Bogotá both change travellers' cheques, but the latter pays a better rate. Both these banks and the Banco Popular give cash advances on Visa card, while the Banco de Occidente and the Banco Industrial Colombiano will honour your MasterCard. Cash and travellers' cheques are changed only from 8 to 10 am. If you are stuck without pesos, the casa de cambio on the southern side of the Plaza de Bolívar changes cash dollars (at a poor rate) until 6 pm, and on Saturday until noon.

**Inderena** The Inderena office (☎ 423996) is at Calle 17 No 9-53.

### Historic Houses & Museums
**Casa del Fundador Suárez Rendón** One of the finest architectural gems of Tunja, this house, on the eastern side of the Plaza de Bolívar (previously the Plaza de Suárez Rendón), was built in the mid-16th century as the home of the founder of Tunja. At the time of its construction, it was considered to be one of the most splendid aristocratic residences in what is now Colombia. Today it is a museum containing some colonial artefacts, but the star attraction are the ceilings which are covered with intriguing paintings depicting mythological scenes, human figures, animals and plants, coats-of-arms etc. The paintings were done after the founder's death in 1583, most likely between 1585 and 1605.

The mishmash of motifs taken from very different European traditions makes for an astonishing decoration. Read the following Casa de Don Juan de Vargas section for further details on these curious paintings. The house is open daily from 8 am to noon and 2 to 6 pm; admission is US$0.30.

**Casa de Don Juan de Vargas** Once home to Juan de Vargas, this house, at Calle 20 No 8-52, dates from the end of the 16th century and has also been converted into a museum. It has many colonial artworks on display, including some interesting paintings. However, here again, most captivating are the ceilings which are also covered with paintings, similar to those in the Casa del Fundador, and equally enigmatic.

The explanation of this mystery is that Juan de Vargas was a scribe and had a large

BOYACÁ

library with books on classical and European art, which were the source of motifs for the anonymous painters of the ceiling decoration in both houses. It's interesting to note that the original illustrations were in black and white, so the colour is the product of the imagination of the unknown artisans. Curiously enough, they also introduced elements of local origin, particularly the native flora and fauna. Zeus and Jesus amidst tropical plants, elephants, rhinos and monkeys – chances are that such a composition is unlike anything you have ever seen before. This kind of decoration exists nowhere else in Latin America.

They are not frescoes, as was initially thought. They are all painted *al temple* (in tempera) on dry plaster. Even though this technique doesn't usually assure extreme durability, the paintings remain in remarkably good shape and colour, despite the 400 years since their execution.

The museum is open Tuesday to Friday from 9 am to noon and 2 to 5 pm, Saturday and Sunday from 10 am to 4 pm. Admission is US$0.30 and all visits are guided.

**Casa de Don Juan de Castellanos** This house, at Calle 19 No 8-14, is yet another early colonial structure dating from the closing decades of the 16th century. It was commissioned by Juan de Castellanos, one of the most famous chroniclers of the period, particularly remembered for his *Elegías de Varones Ilustres de Indias* (1589). He was a good friend of Juan de Vargas, so it's little wonder that Vargas adorned the ceiling of his friend's home as well. The house is today a public library but you can enter to see the paintings on the ceiling, similar to, though maybe not as diverse as those in the two previous houses. The library is open Monday to Friday from 8 am to noon and 2 to 6 pm.

**Casa de la Cultura** Yet another spacious 16th-century mansion, this house on the western side of the Plaza de Bolívar, Carrera 10 No 19-17, is today home to the Instituto de Cultura y Bellas Artes de Boyacá. There's a Museo de Museos in part of the house, which stages temporary exhibitions. It's open Monday to Friday from 8 am to noon and 2 to 6 pm.

**Casa del Capitán Luis Mancipe** Again a 16th-century colonial construction, at Calle 19 No 11-13, this house has been taken over by Granahorrar (a banking corporation) and extensively restored. It now houses commercial establishments and the offices of the company. Of particular interest are the original stone columns on the 1st floor, including one beautifully decorated with carvings (in 1597).

## Churches

Tunja has one of Colombia's best collections of colonial churches, only to be compared to those in Bogotá, Popayán and Cartagena. Even if churches are not your cup of tea, don't miss entering Santa Clara La Real and Santo Domingo – you'll hardly find more impressive interiors anywhere in the country.

Tunja's churches are noted for their Mudéjar art, an Islamic-influenced style which developed in Christian Spain between the 12th and 16th centuries. It is particularly visible in the ornamented coffered vaults.

**Iglesia y Convento de Santa Clara La Real** The Church and Convent of Santa Clara, Carrera 7 No 19-58, was founded in 1571 and is thought to be the first convent in Nueva Granada. In 1863 the nuns were expelled and the convent was used for various purposes, among them as a hospital. The church, however, continued to provide religious services. In the 1980s the church and a part of the convent were extensively restored and opened as a museum.

The single-naved interior of the church is wholly impressive. There's a wealth of colonial artwork distributed over the walls. They all come from the 16th to 18th centuries. The vault is, typically, in the Mudéjar style and the splendid, three-tier, 17th-century main retable is an excellent example of local Baroque woodcarving. Note the golden sun above it, a Spanish trick to help the Indians convert to Catholicism (the sun was the principal god of the Muisca people). The pulpit is reputedly one of the oldest objects, dating back to around 1572. Don't miss the wall paintings at the side altar, directly opposite as you enter the church.

The interesting wall-paintings in the church choir were discovered during the restoration after the outer plaster layer was removed. Some of them are preserved in admirable shape. They reveal similar features to those made in the Casa del Fundador and other historic houses, and they may have been executed by the same team of artisans.

Next to the choir is the cell where Madre Francisca Josefa, a mystic nun looked upon as Colombia's St Teresa, lived for 53 years (1689-1742). The museum is open daily from 8 am to noon and 2 to 5.30 pm. Admission is US$0.30 and includes a guide service.

**Iglesia de Santo Domingo** This church, at Carrera 11 No 19-55, looks pretty undistinguished from the outside, but don't be put off, the inside is quite remarkable. Built in the mid-16th century, it has one of the most richly decorated interiors in Colombia. To the left as you enter is the large Capilla del Rosario, referred to as 'La Capilla Sixtina del Arte Neogranadino'. Decorated by Fray Pedro Bedón from Quito, the chapel is exuberantly rich in gilded woodcarving and wonderful in every detail – a magnificent example of Hispano-American Baroque art, possibly the most impressive chapel in Colombia. The statue of the Virgen del Rosario in the altar niche is encrusted in mother-of-pearl and clad with mirrors, another typical Spanish trick to attract Indians. The church is usually open from 8.30 to 11.30 am and 2.30 to 6 pm.

**Iglesia de San Francisco** Yet another masterpiece of colonial religious art, the San Francisco church, Carrera 10 No 22-23, was built between 1550 and 1572. Once inside, your eyes will immediately be captured by the fascinating main retable, framed into an elaborate gilded arch at the entrance to the presbytery.

There are more treasures worth seeing here, though. At the beginning of the left-hand aisle is an impressively realistic sculpture of Christ (carved in 1816), Cristo de los Mártires. At the other end of this aisle you'll come to the Capilla de la Virgen de las Angustias, with a filigree carved black cedar altar. It's known as the Altar de los Pelícanos, after the birds on both sides (note the delicate carving). It's thought that the altar was made in Quito and brought to Tunja by the Franciscans.

In the opposite, right-hand aisle, you'll find several side altars, among which is the Camarín de la Inmaculada Concepción and the famous statue of San Francisco. The church tends to open from 6 am to 12.30 pm and 2.30 to 7 pm.

**Iglesia de Santa Bárbara** This church, at Carrera 11 No 16-62, was completed in 1599. The highlight here is the Capilla de la Epístola with its outstanding Mudéjar ceiling. The chapel is to the right of the main altar. The church is open irregularly, usually for mass only, early in the morning and late in the afternoon on weekdays, with more masses on Sunday.

**Catedral** The cathedral, on the Plaza de Bolívar, is Tunja's largest church and stylistically the most complex. Its construction was begun in 1554, but many interruptions delayed its completion until the end of the 19th century. It was started in Gothic style, but every fashion since has left its mark. Note its amazing stone façade, dating back to around 1600.

Once inside, walk along the aisles to see the side chapels, made in different periods, of which the large Capilla de la Hermandad del Clero, dating from 1647, is perhaps the most magnificent. It is the second chapel to the right after you enter the church and it boasts a gold-plated Baroque retable and colonial paintings on both sides.

The cathedral is open Tuesday to Sunday from 9 am to noon and 2 to 5 pm. The entrance for visitors is through the side door, from Calle 19. The main door from the Plaza de Bolívar is usually only open for mass. The Despacho Parroquial, next door to the cathedral, may still have a brochure on the cathedral's history and its artwork.

**Other Churches** There are several other colonial churches which you might like to visit (see the map for locations).

**Iglesia y Convento de San Agustín**, facing the Parque Pinzón (thought to be the place where the heart of Hunza, the Muisca capital, once was), were built at the end of the 16th century. In 1828 the convent became home to the newly founded Universidad de Boyacá and was later turned into a jail. It served as a city prison until 1966. Today the convent houses the offices of various cultural institutions, while the church is a library. It's worth popping in anyway, to see the recently discovered fragments of old frescoes.

**Iglesia de San Ignacio**, just off the Plaza Bolívar, erected by the Jesuits in the 17th century, no longer serves religious purposes either. It is now used as a concert hall. There are no original furnishings or decorations inside.

**Iglesia de Santa Clara La Antigua** (not to be confused with La Real) has an amazing doorway but there's not much to see inside.

**Capilla de San Lázaro**, high on the hill on the outskirts of Tunja, was built in 1587 in thanksgiving for the relief of a plague. The chapel is closed but the site provides a good view over the town. Take some basic safety precautions when you walk there. It's about two km north-west of the city centre, off the road to Villa de Leyva.

### Muisca Sites

**Cojines del Zaque** This is an Indian ritual site presumably used in sun-worshipping ceremonies. There's a large, plain rock here, with two protruding circular stone 'cushions' carved out of the same rock. In fact, there's not much to see here. The site is one km north-west of the Plaza de Bolívar, a 15-minute walk.

**Pozo de Donato** This is a pond, thought to be one of the Muiscas' sacred waters where they made their offerings. Predictably, the

Muisca votive offering

gold-hungry Spaniards rushed to sack the treasures and, predictably, they didn't find anything. The site was named after one of these Spaniards, Jerónimo Donato de Rojas. The pond is at the campus of the Universidad Pedagógica y Tecnológica de Colombia, on the road to Sogamoso, about 2.5 km from the city centre. Urban buses go there from Carrera 9 in the city centre.

### Festivals & Events

**Semana Santa** Boyacá is one of the most traditional departments, so religious celebrations in the countryside and Tunja itself are observed with due solemnity. Processions circle the city streets on Maundy Thursday and Good Friday.

**Festival Internacional de la Cultura** This cultural festival, which takes place in the last week of May and the first week of June, includes theatre performances, concerts (held, among other sites, in the Iglesia de San Ignacio) and exhibitions.

**Aguinaldo Boyacense** This popular/religious feast goes for a week or two in December, almost until Christmas. It features contests, fancy dress parades, *desfile de carrozas* (procession of floats), music, dances and the like.

### Places to Stay – bottom end

There are several hotels on Carrera 7, just off the bus terminal, but they are very basic and not worth a look, unless you're really hard up. If this is the case, the *Residencias Bolívar* seems to be the cheapest (US$2.50/4 a single/double), though hot water is unknown here. Check how many blankets you have on your bed and ask for more if you think you might get frozen solid. The same advice applies to other budget hotels listed below.

It's much more pleasant to stay in the heart of the city, around the Plaza de Bolívar. The cheapest hotel there, and quite reasonable, is the *Hotel Saboy*, at Calle 19 No 10-40, which costs US$3/4 per person in rooms without/ with bath. A few paces on along the same street you'll find the *Hotel Lord* (☎ 423556), at Calle 19 No 10-64, which has singles/doubles without bath for US$3.50/6.50 and rooms with bath for US$6.50/8. Next door is the *Hotel Dux* (☎ 425736), at Calle 19 No 10-78, which offers much the same, and for a similar price, as the Lord.

All three – Saboy, Lord and Dux – are installed in pleasant old houses with glass-roofed patios. The Saboy claims to have hot water 24 hours a day (check it personally), the other two can provide hot showers only in the morning. It's best to have a look at all three before deciding.

Right on the Plaza de Bolívar is the small, family-run *Hotel Don Camilo* (☎ 426574). Rooms don't overlook the plaza and are rather simple; they cost US$4.50/7 for a single/double. Hot water is available in the morning only.

Located in a fine colonial house but slightly unkempt, the *Hotel El Conquistador* (☎ 423534), at Calle 20 No 8-92, has large rooms, without bath, lined around a warm, glass-covered patio. Singles/doubles cost US$7/11, more than they actually should. For marginally more, the *Hotel San Francisco* (☎ 426645), at Carrera 9 No 18-90, has smaller rooms but with bath attached. Both hotels have hot water in the morning only.

### Places to Stay – middle & top end

The *Hostal El Cid* (☎ 423458), at Carrera 10 No 20-78, claims on its business card to have 'the most comfortable rooms in town'. It's not exactly true but nonetheless they are clean and have private baths, and cost US$10/15 a single/double. Given that hot water is only available in the morning (a typical shortcoming of almost all inexpensive hotels in this cold city), this is perhaps not a great deal.

Going up the price scale, there's the pleasant (if overrated) *Hostería San Carlos* (☎ 423716), at Carrera 11 No 20-12, for US$16/24. It seems to have 24-hour hot water, and has its own restaurant serving inexpensive meals (nothing extremely special) and mid-priced à la carte meals.

The town record for overpricing is held by the *Hotel Hunza* (☎ 424111), at Calle 21A No 10-66, which charges US$55/75 for a single/ double. The management seems to be aware of the unrealistic nature of these prices, and immediately offers a 20% discount. To be fair, the hotel is far better than anything listed above, and you can be pretty sure of a hot shower any time of the day or night. The hotel has its own restaurant, not cheap but pretty good, and there is also a small swimming pool and sauna.

### Places to Eat

Plenty of restaurants serve inexpensive set meals and you'll find them easily while you're tramping the backstreets. There are even some within a block or two of the Plaza de Bolívar, such as *Restaurante San Ricardo*, at Calle 19 No 8-38, just behind the cathedral, or *Restaurante Doña Cecilia*, at Carrera

8 No 18-18. The set meal in either of them will cost at most US$1.50.

One of the best places for set meals (only at lunch time) is the *Estar de Hunzahua*, at Calle 20 No 11-30, which also has some typical regional dishes. For trout, go to either *El Bodegón de los Frailes*, at Carrera 10 No 18-45, or the *Pila del Mono*, at Calle 20 No 8-19. Both have a range of other dishes as well as an assortment of wines to wash your dinner down.

The name of the latter restaurant comes from the fountain in front of the establishment, crowned with a small stone figure of *el dios del silencio* (the god of silence) commonly referred to as the *mono de la pila* (monkey of the fountain). The fountain was initially on the main plaza, but in 1886, when the authorities set about erecting the monument to Simón Bolívar, the 'monkey' was moved here.

You will find many more reasonable restaurants in the central city area, especially to the west of the Plaza de Bolívar (such as *Saloon Ejecutivo Kevin's* at Carrera 12 No 18-48), but if they don't satisfy you go to the restaurant at the *Hotel Hunza*.

### Getting There & Away

The bus terminal is on Avenida Oriental, just a few blocks from the Plaza de Bolívar.

**To Bogotá** Buses run every 10 to 15 minutes during the daytime and there's also regular transport for most of the night. Climatizados cost US$5, pullmans US$4.50; the journey time largely depends on the traffic in Bogotá, and ranges between 2½ and 3½ hours.

**To Bucaramanga** Climatizados (all coming through from Bogotá) leave every half an hour or less (US$11, seven hours).

**To Sogamoso** Buses run frequently till late (US$2, 1½ hours). They all pass Paipa (US$1, 45 minutes) and Duitama (US$1.40, one hour).

**To Villa de Leyva** Buses leave every two to three hours (US$1.25, one hour). For marginally more, you can get there faster by taxi colectivo; they depart from Carrera 7, next to the Residencias Bolívar, and from Calle 22, next to the corner of Carrera 16. They stop running somewhere between 4 and 5 pm.

## PUENTE DE BOYACÁ

The Puente de Boyacá is an important historic site where the decisive battle for Colombia's independence was fought on 7 August 1819. On the republican side was an army of 2850 soldiers under the command of Simón Bolívar. The Spanish troops, numbering 2670 men, were led by General José María Barreiro. The battle began at 2 pm and, after a massive attack by patriots led by General Francisco de Paula Santander, the royalists surrendered. Barreiro tried to escape but was captured and later executed in Bogotá. Colombia's independence was sealed.

Several monuments have been erected on the site of the battlefield in the course of the past century. The main structure is the **Monumento a Bolívar**, an 18-metre-high composition topped by the statue of this great man accompanied by five female figures symbolising the so-called *países bolivarianos*, the countries liberated by Bolívar – Venezuela, Colombia, Ecuador, Peru and Bolivia. The monument is the work of German sculptor Ferdinand von Müller, and was erected in 1939.

The **Obelisco de la Libertad** is the oldest (1896) and highest (24 metres) monument built on the site. There's also the **Monumento a Santander** and the **Arco de Triunfo** (from 1954) on whose pedestal the verses of the national anthem have been carved.

The **Ciclorama** constructed on the site presents audiovisual shows of Bolívar's campaign, Tuesday to Sunday from 10 am to 3 pm, given there are at least eight visitors interested to see one. Opposite the Ciclorama is a tourist kiosk selling publications related to the event.

The **Puente de Boyacá**, the bridge which gives its name to the entire site, and over which Bolívar's troops crossed to fight the Spaniards, is just a small, simple bridge reconstructed in 1939.

The site is on the main Tunja-Bogotá road, 15 km south of Tunja, so any bus passing along this road will drop you off. The monuments are scattered on both sides of the road over an area of about one sq km. There's also a restaurant nearby.

## VILLA DE LEYVA

• *pop 4000* • *2140 m* • *18°C* • ☎ *(987320)*

Villa de Leyva is a beautiful, small colonial town almost untouched by the 20th century. The town was declared a national monument in 1954, so it has been restored and preserved, and is free of modern architecture. Today it looks little different than it did three centuries ago, and is one of the finest architectural gems in the country.

The town was founded in 1572 by Hernán Suárez de Villalobos, and named Nuestra Señora de la Villa Santa María de Leyva. Ever since its early days, it has attracted many famous politicians, artists and clergymen who have come and settled here. It continues to draw people, and many Colombians and some foreigners have chosen to live here.

As Villa de Leyva lies relatively close to the capital, it has become a trendy weekend spot for Bogotanos. This has made the town somewhat artificial, with a noticeably split personality – on weekdays, it is a quiet, sleepy, bucolic village, but on weekends and holidays, it comes alive, crammed with tourists and their cars. It's up to you to choose which of the town's faces you prefer, but don't miss it. It is one of the loveliest places in Colombia, full of history, museums and sightseeing opportunities. Villa de Leyva experiences the healthy, dry and mild climate of the arid valley in which the town sits.

### Information

**Tourist Office** The tourist office (☎ 411), on the corner of the main plaza, is open Tuesday to Sunday from 10 am to 1 pm and 2 to 6 pm. The staff are friendly and knowledgeable.

**Money** Come prepared, as you can't change cash or travellers' cheques in Villa de Leyva. The Banco Popular, on the main plaza, may accept your Visa card. The nearest money-changing facilities are in Tunja.

**Tours** The Villa Tour agency, on the main plaza, operates chiva tours to the attractions in the vicinity of the town. The tour includes El Fósil, the Convento del Santo Ecce Homo,

El Infiernito and a few other places, and costs US$6 per person. The 3½-hour tour departs on Saturday and Sunday, and on request on weekdays if there are at least six people.

### Things to See

Villa de Leyva is leisurely place in which to wander around the cobbled streets, enjoying the lazy rhythm of days gone by. As you wander about you are sure to find interesting places and fine houses other than those listed here.

Most museums are set in historic mansions and are open Wednesday to Sunday from 10 am to 1 pm and 3 to 6 pm.

**Plaza Mayor** The centre of town is dominated by the Plaza Mayor, an impressive central square different from any other, paved with massive cobblestones and lined with whitewashed colonial houses and a charmingly simple parish church.

Measuring nearly 120 by 120 metres, this is reputedly the largest main square in the country; yet it seems even larger as it is surrounded by unpretentious, at most, two-storey houses. The vast plain is only interrupted by a small Mudéjar fountain in its middle, which provided water to the village inhabitants for almost four centuries. Unlike all other cities and towns where the main squares were renamed 'Plaza de Bolívar', 'Plaza de Santander' or 'other hero plaza', this one is traditionally and firmly called Plaza Mayor.

**Churches** Villa de Leyva has four churches, all of which date back to the town's early years. The **Iglesia Parroquial**, the parish church facing the main square, was built in 1608 and has hardly changed since. It boasts a marvellous Baroque main retable.

The only other church in religious service is the **Iglesia del Carmen**, which is worth entering if only to see the paintings hanging in the presbytery and the wooden structure supporting the roof. It's open for mass only, usually at 7 am weekdays. It's easier to find it open on Saturday and Sunday.

The **Iglesia de San Francisco** is closed

BOYACÁ

BOYACÁ

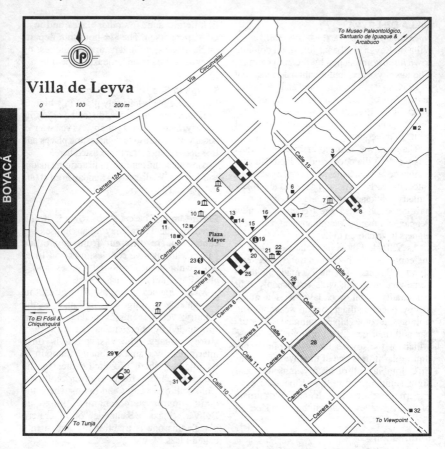

Villa de Leyva

To Museo Paleontológico,
Santuario de Iguaque &
Arcabuco

To Museo Paleontológico,
Santuario de Iguaque &
Arcabuco

To El Fósil &
Chiquinquirá

To Tunja

To Viewpoint

and the adjoining monastic building is now home to the Colegio Verde, a private institution focusing on ecological issues and environmental conservation. The **Iglesia de San Agustín** is currently under thorough restoration.

**Museo del Carmen** Located in the convent of the same name, next to the church, this is one of the best museums of religious art in the country. It contains valuable paintings, carvings, altarpieces and other religious objects dating from the 16th century onward. The museum is only open on Saturday and Sunday, from 10 am to 1 pm and 2 to 5 pm.

**Museo de Luis Alberto Acuña** This museum on the main square displays a collection of works of art by this noted painter, sculptor, writer and historian who was inspired by influences ranging from Muisca mythology to contemporary art.

**Museo Paleontológico** The Museum of Palaeontology is one km out of town on the Arcabuco road. It has a collection of fossils collected in the region and dating from the period when the area was a sea bed some 100 to 150 million years ago.

**PLACES TO STAY**

| | |
|---|---|
| 1 | Hostería La Candelaria |
| 2 | Hostería del Molino La Mesopotamia |
| 6 | Hospedería El Mesón de los Virreyes |
| 11 | Hospedería Colonial |
| 12 | Hospedería El Mesón de la Plaza Mayor |
| 14 | Hostería La Roca |
| 17 | El Hostal |
| 18 | Hospedería La Villa |
| 24 | Hostería El Zaguán de los Héroes |
| 32 | Hospedería Duruelo |

**PLACES TO EAT**

| | |
|---|---|
| 3 | Restaurante Rincón de Bachué |
| 15 | Restaurante La Dicha Buena |
| 16 | Restaurante Nueva Granada |
| 20 | Restaurante El Estar de la Villa |
| 26 | Restaurante de la Calle Real |
| 29 | Restaurante El Parrillón de los Caciques |

**OTHER**

| | |
|---|---|
| 4 | Iglesia del Carmen |
| 5 | Museo del Carmen |
| 7 | Casa de Antonio Ricaurte |
| 8 | Iglesia de San Agustín |
| 9 | Museo Prehistórico |
| 10 | Museo de Luis Alberto Acuña |
| 13 | Villa Tour |
| 19 | Tourist Office |
| 21 | Casa de la Real Fábrica de Licores |
| 22 | Telecom |
| 23 | Banco Popular |
| 25 | Iglesia Parroquial |
| 27 | Casa de Antonio Nariño |
| 28 | Market |
| 30 | Bus Terminal |
| 31 | Iglesia de San Francisco |

**Casa de Antonio Nariño** Antonio Nariño was a patriot and fighter for human rights (he translated Thomas Paine's *Rights of Man* into Spanish). Known as the forefather of independence, he lived here and died in 1823. His home has been converted into a museum which contains colonial objects and memorabilia related to this great personage.

**Casa de Antonio Ricaurte** This is the house where Antonio Ricaurte was born in 1786. He fought under Bolívar and is remembered for his heroic act of self-sacrifice in the battle of San Mateo (near Caracas in Venezuela) in 1814. Defending an armoury and closely encircled by the Spaniards, he let them in, then set fire to the gunpowder kegs and blew up everybody including himself. The battle was won. The house is now a museum which displays furniture and weapons of the period as well as some related documents.

**Casa de la Real Fábrica de Licores** Once the ancient royal distillery of aguardiente, the first of its kind in the Nuevo Reino, the building is now in the process of restoration and adaptation for the Museo Colonial. See the doorway topped with a carved Spanish coat of arms.

**Hostería del Molino La Mesopotamia** This exceptional mansion, built as a flour mill in 1568, now functions as a hotel. It is without doubt one of the loveliest treasures of Villa de Leyva. Even if you don't stay there, the management is friendly and will allow you to look around the grounds and the public rooms (see Places to Stay for more details).

**Other Attractions** Give yourself a couple of hours to wander about the charming cobbled streets, and climb the hill behind the Hospedería Duruelo for a marvellous bird's-eye view of the town. The market, held on Saturday on the square three blocks uphill from Plaza Mayor, is very colourful. Go there early in the morning.

**Festivals & Events**
The **Festival de la Cometa** (Kite Festival) is held in mid-August. Locals and some foreign kite fans compete in this colourful event. The **Festival de las Luces** (Firework Festival) takes place in the evening of 8 December, when a firework show is presented.

**Places to Stay**
The town has over a score of places to stay, and except for the bottom end, the hotels are

BOYACÁ

particularly charming. If there is a place to splurge in Colombia, it's probably Villa de Leyva. Keep in mind, however, that the accommodation gets scarce on *puentes* (long weekends) and during Easter week.

**Places to Stay – bottom end** There are only two really cheap places in town: the *Hospedería La Villa*, on the corner of the main square (around US$3 per person), and the *Hospedería Colonial*, a few steps from La Villa (marginally more expensive but with cleaner toilets). Both places are simple and have rooms of varying quality, so have a look before paying. Bargains are possible in either place if you come in a larger party on weekdays.

The *Hostería La Roca*, on the main square, has a nice patio but is otherwise not significantly better than the above two, though it charges US$6 per person.

**Places to Stay – middle & top end** There is a range of lovely hotels, almost all set in colonial mansions with beautiful patios. One of the best value-for-money options is the small *Hostería La Candelaria*, run by a Spanish family (US$16/25 a single/double).

If you are ready to pay up to US$35 for a double, choose between the *Hostería El Zaguán de los Héroes* (☎ 476), the *Hospedería El Mesón de la Plaza Mayor* (☎ 425), *El Hostal* (☎ 668) and the *Hospedería El Mesón de los Virreyes* (☎ 497). All are charming places with an old colonial flavour.

At the top of the range, you have the famous *Hostería del Molino La Mesopotamia* (☎ 235), installed in an amazing 400-year-old flour mill set in a lovely garden. If you want to sleep in a canopied bed, request the old section. The restaurant is situated in the original mill and the bar is to the side. It is all decorated with taste and full of antiques. Prices are US$35/50 for singles/doubles, US$20 for each additional person. Add US$14 per person for full board which includes three well-prepared meals with efficient service. Though La Mesopotamia seems a little unkempt lately, it's still good value for money.

Another recommended top-end option is

the beautifully cared for, hacienda-style *Hospedería Duruelo* (☎ 222). It costs much the same as La Mesopotamia and also has its own excellent restaurant.

Three km out of Villa de Leyva on the road to Arcabuco is the pleasant *Nido Verde* (☎ 674) that is run by a friendly Danish-Colombian couple. They have two cabañas, both of which have two bedrooms, dining-living room, bathroom and a fully equipped kitchen. The larger one has beds for up to eight people and costs US$60 per day. The smaller cabin sleeps up to five guests and costs US$40. It's quite a good deal if you are in a larger party.

You can cook for yourself or have the meals served (breakfast for US$2.50, lunch or dinner for US$6), but let them know in advance. English, Danish, French and Spanish are spoken. Check for vacancies by phone.

**Places to Eat**
A rash of restaurants has opened in Villa de Leyva over the past few years, so there's a lot to choose from. The cheapest set meals (US$1.50) are probably found in the *Nueva Granada*. For about US$2, you'll get better almuerzos and comidas at *El Estar de la Villa*. Tasty vegetarian dishes, though a bit expensive, are served at *La Dicha Buena*. This is also a pleasant place for an evening drink.

*El Parrillón de los Caciques*, diagonally opposite the bus terminal, has cheap churrasco and sobrebarriga, while the *Rincón de Bachué* is a good and pleasant place for the comida típica. The *Restaurante de la Calle Real* (open only on Saturday and Sunday) is noted for its ajiaco.

Among the hotel restaurants, those deserving a special mention are El Zaguán de los Héroes (comida criolla), La Candelaria (Spanish specialities), El Hostal, La Mesopotamia and El Duruelo.

**Things to Buy**
Inspect the handicraft shops noted for fine basketry and good-quality woven items, such as sweaters and ruanas. There are some

artisan shops on the Plaza Mayor and several more in the side streets. A number of weavers have settled in town and their work is of excellent quality and their prices are reasonable. Quite a number of shops are closed on weekdays.

The locals and their children have fossils for sale. Prices are a matter of negotiation and usually drop considerably.

### Getting There & Away

All buses and colectivos arrive at and depart from the bus terminal, just three blocks south-west of the Plaza Mayor.

**To Bogotá** There are half a dozen buses daily (US$5, four hours). They are operated by several bus companies and go either via Tunja or Chiquinquirá. One or two additional buses are put into service on Sunday and holidays in the late afternoon.

**To Tunja** There are eight buses daily (US$1.25, one hour). Taxi colectivos ply this route more frequently and are faster (US$1.50).

**To Chiquinquirá** Buses depart every couple of hours (US$1.50, 1¼ hours). They will get you close to El Fósil and may also be useful if you want to go to Ráquira.

**To Ráquira** There are only two buses a day, at 2.30 and 6.30 pm. Alternatively take any Chiquinquirá bus, get off at Tres Esquinas and walk the remaining five km.

**To Santa Sofía** The Santa Sofía buses are useful for visiting Ecce Homo, as they pass within one km of the convent. However, there seems to be only one morning bus a day, at 9.30 am.

### AROUND VILLA DE LEYVA

Villa de Leyva is a perfect base for short excursions into the surrounding area, which offers a variety of attractions. The region abounds with fossils.

You can move around the area on foot and use local buses. The Villa Tour agency in Villa de Leyva operates chiva tours, providing an easy way to visit some of the sights.

All three sites listed are on the tour's route. If you want to visit the area's attractions on

**BOYACÁ**

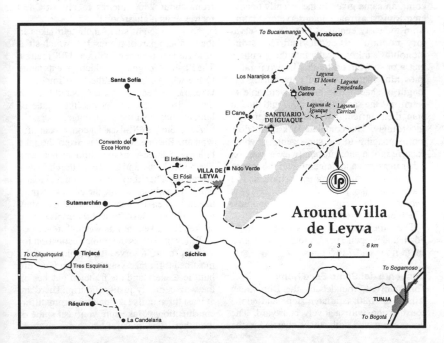

Around Villa de Leyva

your own, the tourist office will give you details on sights, their opening hours, and the public transport you need to get there.

### El Fósil

This is a reasonably complete fossil of a kronosaurus, a prehistoric marine reptile, vaguely resembling a crocodile, which is about 110 million years old. The fossil is seven metres long (the animal was about 12 metres long but its tail hasn't survived). It's a baby kronosaurus (the adult animals were far larger) and it remains in the place where it was found.

The fossil is off the road to Chiquinquirá, six km from Villa de Leyva. You can walk there by a path in one hour, or the Chiquinquirá buses will drop you off one km from the fossil. The site is open from 8 am to noon and 1 to 5 pm except Monday and Thursday.

### El Infiernito

El Infiernito (literally 'the little hell') is the common name given to the recently uncovered Muisca astronomic observatory dating from the early centuries AD. The observatory contains 30-odd cylindrical stone monoliths sunk vertically into the ground a metre or so from each other in two parallel lines nine metres apart. By measuring the length of shadow the Indians were able to determine the season of the year and thus to plan their agricultural and other activities accordingly. The complete lack of shadow (corresponding to the sun's zenith), which occurred for a short instant twice a year, on a day in March and September, is thought to have been the time for great festivities. The place was also a ritual site, noted for a number of large, phallic stone monoliths, which are scattered around the grounds.

The Infiernito is about two km from El Fósil, and is open Tuesday to Sunday from 8 am to noon and 2 to 5 pm.

### Convento del Santo Ecce Homo

This convent, founded by the Dominican fathers in 1620, is a large stone and adobe construction with a lovely courtyard. The floors are paved with stones quarried in the

region, so they contain ammonites and fossils, including petrified corn and flowers. Also look out for fossils in the base of a statue in the chapel. See the magnificent gilded main retable with a small image of Ecce Homo and the original wooden ceiling.

The convent is 13 km from Villa de Leyva. The morning bus to Santa Sofía will drop you a 15-minute walk from the convent. It's open Tuesday to Sunday from 8 am to noon and 2 to 5 pm. A nun will show you around, pointing out the most important treasures that are kept inside the convent.

## SANTUARIO DE IGUAQUE

A mountain range stretches north-east of Villa de Leyva up to Arcabuco. Most of this highland area was declared a nature reserve in 1977, the Santuario de Fauna y Flora de Iguaque. The reserve encompasses 67.5 sq km and covers the 22-km-long portion of the range. The altitude within the reserve ranges from about 2400 metres to almost 3800 metres at its highest point.

There are eight small mountain lakes in the northern part of the reserve, which sit at an altitude of between 3550 and 3700 metres. The Laguna de Iguaque, which gave its name to the whole reserve, is the most important lake, mostly because it was a sacred lake for the Muiscas. Iguaque means 'the cradle of humankind' in Chibcha language.

According to Muisca legend a beautiful woman, Bachué, walked out from the lake holding a three-year-old child in her arm. She built a house and lived until the child was grown up. Then they married and had many children, and that is how the earth was populated. When they reached old age, they returned to the lake, turned themselves into snakes and dived into its waters forever.

Today the lake is the prime destination for visitors to the reserve. It's perhaps not the most beautiful lake you've seen in your life but the scenery and the frailejón patches on the way certainly justify the trip. There are at least three trails leading there from different directions. Make sure you visit some of the other lakes, most of which are no more than an hour's walk away. These side trails may be faint but it's pretty easy to get around.

Keep in mind that it gets pretty cold here, so come prepared. The average temperature at these altitudes ranges between 10°C and 12°C. The mean annual rainfall in this area is about 1700 mm. The wettest months are April, October and November, but March and September are not ideal months for hiking either. It's best to come here between January and February or between June and August.

### Places to Stay & Eat
Inderena has its visitors centre in Carrizal, at an altitude of 2950 metres, three km off the Villa de Leyva-Arcabuco road. It offers accommodation for up to 60 people (US$7 per bed) and camping facilities (US$6 per tent). The entrance fee to the park is US$0.60. There's also a restaurant in the centre.

### Getting There & Away
The usual starting point for the reserve is Villa de Leyva. Take a bus to Arcabuco (there is only one a day, at 6 am), get off 12 km from Villa at a place known as Los Naranjos, where a rough road branches off to the right and leads to the visitors centre. Walk three km uphill to the centre. The walk from here up to the Laguna de Iguaque will take you between two and three hours.

There are other access routes to the reserve. One is El Cane, eight km from Villa de Leyva by the Arcabuco road, from where you walk five km along a side road branching off to the right to the Inderena post at Chaina. You then continue by path uphill to Laguna de Iguaque.

You may want to get your permit to the reserve in Bogotá or Tunja, though it's possible to get it from the park on arrival.

### RÁQUIRA
• pop 1000 • 2150 m • 18°C
Ráquira is a small village 25 km from Villa de Leyva which is known nation-wide for its pottery. You can see and buy a great variety ranging from excellent kitchenware to fine copies of indigenous pots. The Handicraft Centre just off the main square displays and sells pottery. There are also several small workshops in the village where you can see the production process.

The Museo de Artes y Tradiciones Populares on the plaza is worth seeing for its regional handicrafts as well as for some ancient pottery. Don't miss El Rancho on the road to Ráquira, about one km before the village. It is a nice house with a small garden marvellously decorated with hundreds of beautiful ceramic items made by a local artisan.

### Places to Stay & Eat
There is a hotel and a restaurant on the main square, and a couple of budget hospedajes in the side streets, none of which have names.

### Getting There & Away
Ráquira is five km off the Chiquinquirá-Tunja road, down a dirt road branching off at Tres Esquinas. Only two or three buses daily go along this road to Ráquira (and continue on to La Candelaria). All come from Bogotá, and go through either Tunja or Chiquinquirá. Buses on the Chiquinquirá-Tunja road run every two or three hours, so you can get off at Tres Esquinas and walk one hour to Ráquira.

### LA CANDELARIA
This tiny hamlet set amidst arid hills, seven km beyond Ráquira, is noted for its Monasterio de La Candelaria. The monastery was founded in 1597 by Augustine monks and completed about 1660. Part of it is open to the public. The young monks will show you through the chapel (note the 16th-century painting of the Virgen de la Candelaria over the altar), a small museum, the library, and the courtyard flanked by the cloister with a collection of 17th-century canvasses hanging on its walls. Some of them were allegedly painted by Vásquez de Arce y Ceballos and the Figueroa brothers. The monastery is open for visitors daily from 9 am to 5 pm.

BOYACÁ

BOYACÁ

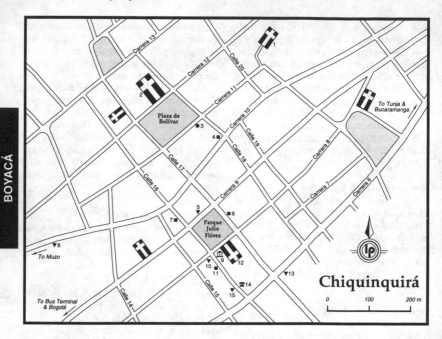

Chiquinquirá

0        100        200 m

### Places to Stay & Eat

The *Parador La Candelaria*, close to the monastery, is the only place to stay. This lovely small hotel set in a colonial house has neat, pleasant rooms with private baths and hot water, facing a beautiful flowering patio. Singles/doubles cost US$15/20. The hotel has its own restaurant.

### Getting There & Away

Only two buses a day call at La Candelaria; both come from Bogotá. Alternatively, you can walk from Ráquira to La Candelaria along a path which is considerably shorter. The path begins behind the museum, winds up the hill to a small shrine at the top and then drops down and joins the road to La Candelaria.

### CHIQUINQUIRÁ

• *pop 40,000* • *2590 m* • *14°C* • ☎ *(98726)*
Chiquinquirá is the religious capital of Colombia. It's here that the image of the Virgen de Chiquinquirá, the nation's patron saint, is kept. She attracts pilgrims from all corners of the country.

The image of the Virgin was painted around 1555 in Tunja by a Spanish artist, Alonso de Narváez. It was made with ordinary vegetable dyes on a cotton cloth manufactured by Indians. The colours soon faded away and the painting wandered around the region from home to home. Nobody, it seems, had any major interest in owning it. It finally reached Chiquinquirá where its fortunes changed.

According to legend the picture miraculously recovered its bright colours and full splendour on 26 December 1586 before the eyes and prayers of a humble campesina, María Ramos. From then on its fame swiftly grew and the miracles attributed to the Virgin multiplied. On 9 July 1919 the Virgen de Chiquinquirá was solemnly crowned and proclaimed the patroness of Colombia.

The painting, measuring 113 by 126 cm,

1   Iglesia do Santa Bárbara
2   Basílica de la Virgen de
     Chiquinquirá
3   Rafael Norato's Shop
4   Hotel Río
5   Restaurante El Escorial
6   Hotel Alcarraza
7   Hotel Real Muisca
8   Kokopico
9   Museo Centro Mariano
10  Restaurante La Fogata
     Antioqueña
11  El Gran Hotel
12  Iglesia de la Renovación
13  Pescadería La Otra... Casa
14  Telecom
15  Asadero El Parrón

depicts the Virgin accompanied by San Antonio de Padua and San Andrés Apóstol, and is the oldest documented Colombian painting. There have been innumerable copies, which can be found in churches and museums all over the country.

### Basílica de la Virgen de Chiquinquirá
Dominating the Plaza de Bolívar, this monumental basilica houses the holy image of the Virgin. Construction of the huge neoclassical church began in 1796 and was completed in 1812. The spacious three-naved interior, 80 metres long and 35 metres wide, boasts 17 chapels and an elaborate high altar where the painting is displayed.

The faithful flock to the church all year round, and you'll see some of the more devoted pilgrims approaching the holy image on their knees to pay respect to the Virgin. The church witnesses the largest crowds on 26 December, the anniversary of the day when the miracle happened.

### Iglesia de la Renovación
Overlooking the Parque Julio Flórez (named after a locally born poet), this is a relatively new church, constructed on the site where the miracle of the Virgen de Chiquinquirá occurred, replacing a chapel which previously stood here. The painting of the Virgin displayed on the main altar is a copy.

Down a narrow staircase in front of the altar is a holy cave formed gradually over the centuries as many pilgrims took away a handful of the sacred earth to keep the supposedly miracle-making substance at home. Next to the church is the Museo Centro Mariano, which has a collection of religious art.

### Places To Stay
There are plenty of hotels scattered throughout the centre of town, but none around the bus terminal.

The *Hotel Río* (☎ 2832), at Carrera 10 No 17-93, is the best budget bet in town. Run by a friendly manager, the hotel has comfortable rooms with bath and hot water, which cost US$3.50 per person. The hotel also offers rooms without private bath at US$3 per person.

Possibly the best up-market option is the new *El Gran Hotel* (☎ 3700, 3713), at Calle 16 No 6-97, which costs US$12 per person. Alternatively, try the *Hotel Real Muisca* (☎ 4647), at Calle 16 No 9-22, which offers much the same for a bit more. The *Hotel Alcarraza* (☎ 3733, 2389), at Calle 17 No 8-44 (Parque Julio Flórez), is marginally cheaper but perhaps not as good as the above two.

### Places to Eat
*La Fogata Antioqueña*, on the corner of Parque Julio Flórez, serves some of the cheapest set meals in town (US$1.20), but the food is only so-so. Better set meals can be had in *Pescadería La Otra... Casa*, at Carrera 6 No 17-02, which also has good trout for around US$3.

*Asadero El Parrón*, at Calle 16 No 6-11, is an ordinary-looking place but the carne asada for less than US$2 is good value. The best chicken in town is reputedly to be found in *Kokopico*, at Carrera 10 No 12-10.

*El Escorial*, in Parque Julio Flórez, is one of the better eateries in town. Try the churrasco (US$5) or conejo (US$6), the specialities.

### Things to Buy
Apart from its religious importance, the town is noted for its handicrafts, particularly min-

iatures carved in *tagua*, a very hard, ivory-like nut of the tagua palm. Stringed instruments, such as guitars, *bandolas*, *requintos* and, particularly, *tiples*, are the town's other speciality. There are several craft shops on the Plaza de Bolívar; Rafael Norato's shop, Carrera 11 No 17-100, is considered the best for musical instruments.

## Getting There & Away

All buses operate from the bus terminal, a 10-minute walk from Parque Julio Flórez, south along Carrera 9.

**To Bogotá** Buses depart every 15 minutes (US$3.50 corriente, US$4 pullman, three hours).

**To Bucaramanga** There are two buses only, at 5 and 11 am (US$9.50, seven hours). They go north by a largely unpaved road to Barbosa, where it joins the main Tunja-Bucaramanga road.

**To Tunja** Buses leave every hour or two (US$2.75 corriente, US$3.25 pullman, two hours). Some of these buses pass through Villa de Leyva.

**To Muzo** There are about 10 buses daily (US$3.75, 3½ to four hours).

## MUZO

• *pop 5000* • *810 m* • *24°C* • ☎ *(987)*

Muzo is a magical word which electrifies many Colombians. This town, about 80 km west of Chiquinquirá, takes pride in having the world's richest emerald mines. Muzo is not the only emerald town in Boyacá but its mines are the largest, and the stones from here are famous for their beauty.

Before the Spanish conquest, the region was inhabited by the Muzos, an Indian group of the Carib linguistic family. The Spaniards soon pinpointed the emerald-rich area and founded Muzo in 1541. The town was destroyed three times by the Indians fiercely defending their territory, before it was permanently re-founded in 1558.

The mines are about 10 km west of the town. They are in the upper end of a river gorge and are well guarded; you probably won't be allowed to visit them. What you can see is the impressive spectacle in the two-km-long gorge below, where hundreds of *guaqueros* dig the length and breadth of the

river bed searching for emeralds. Many of them live there for years, dreaming of the day when a large precious stone will materialise. But until that happens (if ever), they are obliged to sell imperfect, inexpensive pieces to the *negociantes*, the middlemen of Muzo, who then sell the stones in Bogotá and other commercial markets.

The guaqueros live in primitive shacks scattered over the slopes of the gorge. A small shantytown has grown up with basic eateries and drinkeries.

Obviously, they will try to talk you into buying emeralds, but it's best not to get involved, even though it's a cheap place to buy. Don't make purchases unless you have come with someone who knows the locals, or you have bodyguards to protect you.

Note that the mines are far from safe. The emerald dream attracts fortune hunters and shady adventurers from the four corners of the country. Many people have guns and don't hesitate to use them.

## Places to Stay

Muzo has a dozen or more hotels, none of which are anything posh. Many are pretty basic and will cost US$5 to US$7 per person. The prices are not stable, inflating in periods of 'emerald fever'. Although it is generally not difficult to find a bed, it's worth checking in early.

## Getting There & Away

There are about 10 buses daily from Chiquinquirá to Muzo, between 5 am and 3 pm. The fare is US$3.75 and the trip takes nearly four hours. The road is very rough but the almost 1800-metre descent provides spectacular scenery. There are also a few direct buses from Bogotá.

Frequent jeeps leave for the mines area, when full, from the market in Muzo, two blocks from the main square (US$1.50, 45 minutes). This road is even rougher and dustier, and a large bandana will come in handy.

The last bus from Muzo back to Chiquinquirá leaves at 2 pm.

## PAIPA
• *pop 8000* • *2520 m* • *16°C* • ☎ *(987)*

This town on the Tunja-Duitama road has become a popular destination thanks to its *termales*, the hot mineral springs renowned for their curative properties. The springs are about three km from the town, on the side road to Pantano de Vargas. It is here, not Paipa itself, that the tourists come. Several posh hotels have been built in this area, most of which have small thermal plunge pools piped in from the springs. If your purse isn't up to all that, your alternative is the unattractive municipal thermal pools, open daily from 6 am to 9 pm; the entrance fee is US$3.

### Places to Stay
Budget hotels can only be found in the town, but of course these places don't have thermal baths. There are about half a dozen cheap hotels there. All are clean and pleasant and all cost much the same: US$3.50/4 per person in rooms without/with bath.

Possibly the most agreeable is *La Posada* (☎ 850073), at Calle 4 No 4-39, in an old colonial house. If you prefer something modern, try the *Hotel Turístico* (☎ 850154), at Carrera 4 No 4-57.

Other options include the *Hotel Posadero La Casona* (☎ 850176), at Calle 5 No 3-23, the *Hotel Nayarid* (☎ 850124), at Calle 6 No 3-31, and the *Mi Hotel Capri*, at Calle 6 No 2-79. All of these hotels have hot water in the morning.

*Hotel Zuhé* (☎ 850604), Calle 6 No 2-34, is the only top-end place in town, costing US$32/42 for a single/double.

In the spring area there are only top-class hotels with thermal baths, swimming pools, TV, sauna etc. The most pleasant is *La Casona El Salitre*, an old colonial hacienda, carefully restored and turned into a charming hotel. Simón Bolívar slept here for two nights, a few days before his triumph in the battle of Puente de Boyacá. The Casona has its own excellent restaurant.

### Getting There & Away
Buses pass through Paipa every 10 to 15 minutes and can take you to Duitama (US$0.40, 15 minutes), Sogamoso (US$1, 40 minutes), Tunja (US$1, 45 minutes) or Bogotá (US$6, four hours).

It is a half-hour walk to the springs, or you can take a taxi (US$1).

## PANTANO DE VARGAS
This is where one of the most crucial battles for Gran Colombia's independence was fought on 25 July 1819. This battle largely undermined the morale of the Spaniards, which led to their defeat 13 days later, on 7 August, at the battle of Boyacá.

The battlefield is 10 km from Paipa, seven km beyond the hot springs. The Monumento a Los Lanceros, an imposing bronze sculpture by Rodrigo Arenas Betancur, was erected here in homage to the valiant lancers who won the battle. Betancur is Colombia's number one monument designer and this is considered among his best works.

### Getting There & Away
There is a paved road from Paipa to Pantano de Vargas but public transport is scarce. You can walk but it takes two hours. A return taxi trip from Paipa, including waiting time for a look at the monument, won't cost more than US$7.

## DUITAMA
• *pop 75,000* • *2530 m* • *15°C* • ☎ *(987)*

Duitama is an industrial town which has little to show tourists, but there are two interesting places nearby, in the area known as Puntalarga, on the road to Belencito.

### Museo de Arte Religioso
The museum was founded in 1969 in the Hacienda San Rafael, a fine mansion built towards the end of the 18th century. It has a good collection of religious objects, including altarpieces, sculptures, retables, paintings etc, collected from the parishes of Boyacá. The oldest exhibits date from the 16th century. The museum is open daily except Tuesday, from 8 am to noon and 2 to 5 pm. Admission is US$0.60 and includes a guide service. The museum is six km east of Duitama, on the road to Belencito.

## Viñedo de Puntalarga

Set amidst the rolling hills of Puntalarga, at an altitude of about 2500 metres, this is reputedly the world's highest commercial vineyard. Interestingly enough, the wines coming from here are among the best produced on the continent, comparable to some renowned European wines.

The vineyard was established in the mid-1980s by a local entrepreneur, Marco Quijano. A chemistry graduate, he analysed the conditions of various European vineyards and found important similarities to the local conditions. This led him to believe that the region could successfully produce wine.

The harmonious blend of light, warm days and cold nights is such that the region experiences various seasons within a single day. The conditions are roughly similar to the Alsace and Rhine regions (in summer), and so are the wines. The difference is that Puntalarga has that climate year round, so the crop can be harvested twice a year.

The vineyard is pretty small, just four hectares (about 10 acres), allowing for production of 15,000 bottles a year at most. Nine varieties of wine are currently produced, including reds and whites, and work on further varieties is under way. The focus of attention is on quality rather than quantity.

The Puntalarga vineyard is about seven km from Duitama on the road to Belencito (1.5 km past the Museo de Arte Religioso), just uphill from the Complejo Turístico. The owner is proud of his wines and welcomes connoisseurs and novices alike, allowing them to taste some of his achievements. You can buy the locally produced wines here, though they are not cheap: prices range from US$6 to US$150 a bottle, depending on the variety.

The successful experiments of Marco Quijano have encouraged locals. Several small vineyards have already been established in the region and new ones are likely to appear in the future.

Colombia has almost no wine tradition. Although the first vineyards were introduced by Nikolaus Federmann in the early days of the Spanish conquest, and later continued by the Jesuits, the decree of Phillip II effectively put an end to them. Those who challenged the ban on wine production faced death. Vineyards only appeared again in the present century. Most production today comes from the Valle del Cauca, but these wines are of poor quality.

### Places to Stay

If you are on a tight budget, you'll have to stay in Duitama, which has lots of cheap hotels. If money is not a problem, you may prefer to stay in Puntalarga which is certainly a more pleasant place than the town.

**Duitama** There are a dozen cheap hotels around the bus terminal square. There are not many to recommend, though some are better than others. Try, for example, the *Hotel Sander*, at Carrera 18 No 18-11, which is clean and OK and costs US$4 for a couple, or the *Hotel del Parque* (☎ 602254), at Calle 18 No 17-59, a small family-run hospedaje with neat doubles/triples without bath for US$6/9.

The cheapest accommodation in the vicinity of Plaza de los Libertadores (the main square) is the *Hotel Tabacoa's* (☎ 602213), at Calle 15 No 16-74, just one block from the plaza. Doubles without/with bath cost US$5/6. None of those listed above has hot water.

Round the corner from the Hotel Tabacoa's is the appreciably better *Hotel Castilla* (☎ 602837), at Carrera 17 No 15-39, which has good rooms with bath and TV and costs US$7.50/10 for a single/double. Hot water is available in the morning.

Still better is the *Hotel Suarel* (☎ 600297), at Carrera 17 No 17-30, which has singles/doubles for US$15/24. Again, you can only have a hot shower in the morning.

The *Hotel Azuay* (☎ 602862), overlooking the bus terminal, at Carrera 18 No 17-53, costs much the same as the Suarel.

**Puntalarga** There are two very good places to stay in Puntalarga. The *Hostería San Luis de Ucuengá* (☎ 603260) is a lovely colonial country mansion, 1.5 km beyond the museum. It has been transformed into a enchanting hotel, with its rooms – each different – arranged and decorated in colonial style. Look around and choose the one you like best. Singles/doubles cost US$35/50 while suites for up to three people go for US$80.

Directly opposite is the *Complejo Turístico Puntalarga* (☎ 605841), another charming old-time place, though not kept in as genuinely a colonial style as the Hostería. Singles/doubles cost US$20/35. There's a beautiful chapel on the grounds with a service on Sunday at noon, but it's open at other times and is well worth a visit. You can also visit the workshop where they make furniture in colonial style, set in the upper end of the complex. Almost all furniture for the hotel comes from this workshop. Up the hill from the hotel is the vineyard.

### Places to Eat

There are plenty of budget restaurants in Duitama in the area of the cheap hotels. *Asadero San Jorge*, at Carrera 18 No 17-45, is probably a bit better than the others, for both the set meals and chicken. Next door, at Carrera 18 No 17-37, is the *Panificadora Real Danesa*; good for an early breakfast.

*Asadero Zaguán del Cuacuy*, at Calle 17 No 17-37, and *Brasas & Brasas*, at Carrera 18 No 16-26, have good, reasonably priced food such as cuchuco, mondongo, cordero al horno or cerdo asado.

Both the Hostería San Luis de Ucuengá and Complejo Turístico Puntalarga have their own well-appointed and pleasant restaurants.

The *Asadero El Manicomio* is reputedly the best place around for carnes a la brasa. It's on the Duitama-Sogamoso road, about half a km past the turn-off to Belencito.

### Getting There & Away

The bus terminal is in the centre of Duitama, on the square between Carreras 18 and 19 and Calles 17 and 18.

**To Bogotá** Buses by Rápido Duitama and Coflonorte Los Libertadores run every 15 minutes between 5 am and 7 pm and then every hour or so until 11 pm (US$6, four hours). All these buses pass through Tunja (US$1.50, one hour).

**To Sogamoso** There are buses every 15 minutes (US$0.60, 20 minutes).

**To Güicán & El Cocuy** Four or five buses a day run to El Cocuy, then continue on to Guicán. Most depart at night. The trip to Güicán costs US$8 and takes about eight hours. The fare to El Cocuy is marginally cheaper.

**To Belencito** Minibuses depart every half an hour and can drop you near the museum and, 1.5 km further on, at the door of the two hotels in Puntalarga.

## SOGAMOSO
• *pop 70,000* • *2570 m* • *14°C* • ☎ *(987)*

Sogamoso is a nondescript industrial town which has no tourist attractions except one: an excellent archaeological museum. Sogamoso is also the usual starting point for visits to its attractive environs, including the beautiful Laguna de Tota and the picturesque old town of Monguí.

Sogamoso was founded on what was the religious capital of the Muiscas, known as Suamox (meaning the 'land of the sun' in Chibcha language). Suamox was centred around the Templo del Sol (Temple of the Sun), the most sacred sanctuary, where Sugamuxi, the Muisca 'pope', resided.

The Spanish conquerors led by Gonzalo Jiménez de Quesada arrived at Suamox in August 1537 and burned down the temple. According to the chronicles, the Spaniards had no intention of burning it. It appears that the building went up in flames by accident when the invaders inspected its dark interior, illuminating it with torches.

Today, after 450 years, the temple stands again. It has been recently reconstructed in the archaeological park.

### Museo y Parque Arqueológico

The museum and park were established in the 1950s on what was once Suamox. The museum features an extensive collection of Muisca artefacts, including gold objects, stone carvings, pottery pieces and weavings, making it the best-displayed and most complete exhibition of Muisca culture. There's

BOYACÁ

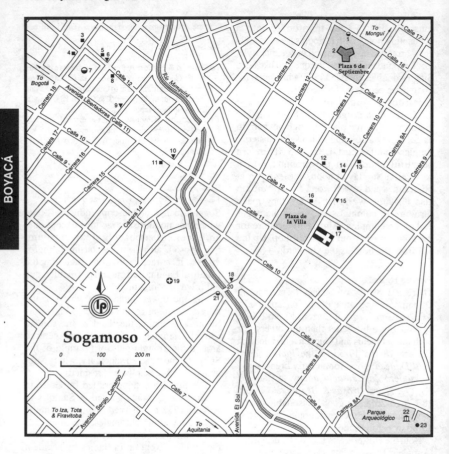

Sogamoso

0    100    200 m

To Monguí

Plaza 6 de Septiembre

To Bogotá

Avenida Libertadores (Calle 11)

Río Monquirá

Calle 12

Calle 10

Calle 9

Calle 13

Calle 14

Calle 15

Calle 16

Calle 17

Plaza de la Villa

Calle 11

Calle 10

Calle 9

Calle 8

Calle 7

Avenida Sergio Camargo

Avenida El Sol

To Iza, Tota & Firavitoba

To Aquitania

Parque Arqueológico

also an introductory section on prehistory and the evolution of humans on the continent.

Next to the museum building is the Templo del Sol, a great circular structure topped with a conical thatched roof, supported by a central, massive trunk of guayacán tree. The temple was built with the same natural fibre that the Muiscas are believed to have used in the original construction. The interior wasn't completed at the time of writing this book, but it's likely to be finished by the time you come. Originally, the temple housed the mummies of the tribal elders and some important ritual objects.

The museum is on the south-eastern outskirts of the town, a 10-minute walk from the Plaza de la Villa, the main square. It's open Tuesday to Sunday from 9 am to noon and 2 to 5 pm. Admission is US$0.60.

About 100 metres east of the entrance to the park is the Fuente de Conchucua, a small spring where Sugamuxi is said to have taken his ritual baths.

### Places to Stay – bottom end

There are a dozen inexpensive hotels clustered around the bus terminal. If you don't need a private bath, try the *Residencias Santa*

BOYACÁ

## PLACES TO STAY

3   Residencias Santa Marta
4   La Posada del Rey
5   Residencias Embajador
8   Residencias El Terminal
11  Hotel Bochica
12  Hotel Tobacá
13  Hotel Bachué
14  Hotel Sogamoso Real
16  Hotel Litavira
17  Hotel Astoria

## PLACES TO EAT

6   Asadero El Terminal
9   Restaurante Susacá
10  Asadero Tocaima
15  Restaurante Colombia 500 Años
18  Asadero El Morichal

## OTHER

1   Colectivos to Monguí
2   Administración Municipal de
    Sogamoso & Telecom
7   Bus Terminal
19  Hospital
20  Puente de Pesca
21  Colectivos to Iza, Firavitoba &
    Aquitania
22  Museo Arqueológico
23  Templo del Sol

*Marta* (☎ 704771), at Carrera 18 No 11A-15, which has airy rooms for US$3 per person. Much the same is offered at the *Residencias Embajador*, at Calle 12 No 17-24. Possibly the best of the lot in this area is *La Posada del Rey* (☎ 702899) at Carrera 18 No 11-83. Neat rooms with their own bath and hot water cost US$7/8/10/12 for a single/double/triple/quad. Avoid the *Residencias El Terminal*, which is simply a dirty, basic, sex hotel.

If you prefer to stay in the town centre, the cheapest place around the Plaza de la Villa is the *Hotel Astoria*, at Calle 12 No 9-95 (US$5 for a matrimonio with bath). It's rather basic.

### Places to Stay – middle & top end

The *Hotel Bochica* (☎ 704140), at Calle 11 No 14-33, halfway between the bus terminal and the Plaza de la Villa, is perhaps the best value for money. Comfortable singles/doubles with bath, hot water and TV go for US$8/14. Another good option is the *Hotel Bachué* (☎ 702512), at Carrera 10 No 13-68, costing about US$15/25/30 for a single/double/triple.

There's quite a choice of top-end hotels, including the *Hotel Litavira* (☎ 702585), at Calle 12 No 10-30 (US$22/30 a single/double), the *Hotel Sogamoso Real* (☎ 707645), at Carrera 10 No 13-11 (US$24/34), and the best, the *Hotel Tobacá* (☎ 705316) at Calle 13 No 10-68 (US$26/35).

### Places to Eat

There are several cheap asaderos in town where a plate of sliced, spit-roast beef or pork makes a tasty meal for US$2 to US$3. Try *Asadero El Morichal*, on the corner of Carrera 11 and Calle 9, or *Asadero Tocaima*, on the corner of Carrera 14 and Calle 11. If you don't mind a short trip, reputedly the best asadero, *El Bosque*, is three km out of town on the road to Iza. One km further along the same road is another good asadero, *Los Techos Rojos*.

*Restaurante Susacá*, at Carrera 16 No 11-35, is a pleasant restaurant. Try the trucha (trout) or conejo (rabbit). *Restaurante Colombia 500 Años*, at Carrera 10 No 12-46, also has a choice of local specialities, including cuchuco and viudo, as well as cheap set meals.

### Getting There & Away

The bus terminal is on Carrera 17 between Calles 11 and 12. It handles all bus transport. Colectivos to Firavitoba, Iza and Aquitania depart from the Puente de Pesca, on the corner of Carrera 11 and Calle 9.

**To Bogotá** Buses run every 15 minutes or so until around 7 pm, and then every hour until 11 pm (US$6.25, 4½ hours). All these buses pass via Tunja (US$2, 1½ hours).

**To Monguí** Buses depart every couple of hours (US$0.60, half an hour). They pass through Plaza 6 de Septiembre, where you can catch them.

There are also colectivos which leave from the Plaza.

**To Aquitania** Buses leave approximately every hour (US$1, one hour). A few buses a day go along the indirect, largely unpaved road via Iza and Tota (US$1.20, 1½ hour).

## MONGUÍ
• *pop 4000* • *2920 m* • *12°C* • ☎ *(987)*

Monguí is a small, cold town picturesquely set on a mountain slope 20 km east of Sogamoso. The first missionaries appeared in the region around 1555 but the town was not founded until 1601. It then began to grow as a catechetic centre of the Franciscan monks. Construction of the convent further strengthened the religious importance of the town, until 1821 when it was closed down by government decree. The Franciscans returned in 1876 and reopened the convent for a time.

Monguí is also known as a manufacturer of basketballs and soccer balls, which are sold all over the country and to neighbouring Ecuador and Venezuela. They are made by several small workshops, and are reputedly of high quality. The market day in Monguí is Sunday.

### Things to See & Do
The Iglesia y Convento de San Francisco occupy a good part of the upper side of the sloping main plaza. The construction was begun in 1694 and completed by 1760. It's quite an imposing piece of architecture, all made of red stone from a nearby quarry. Give yourself a while to inspect the façade of the church.

The three-nave interior boasts a richly gilded main retable; note the image of the Virgen de Monguí, crowned in 1929 as the patron saint of Boyacá. There's another interesting retable at the head of the right-hand aisle. Among the 30-odd canvasses distributed over the walls, mostly in the transept, there are some painted by Gregorio Vásquez de Arce y Ceballos.

Enter the adjoining monastic building to see the old painted decoration on the porch ceiling. You may be lucky enough to find the door to the courtyard open and be able to look around the cloister. There are plans to open a museum of religious and colonial art in the old convent building.

Stroll about the backstreets, particularly those uphill behind the church, and along Carrera 3. Further down Carrera 3, on the outskirts of town, you'll find an interesting old stone bridge.

If you want to do a longer hike, the most popular walk is up to the páramo in the mountains east of town. Reserve the whole day for this excursion. Ask around for Juan Florencio Agudelo, commonly known as Pacheco, who is perhaps the best guide to take you there.

### Places to Stay & Eat
Accommodation is thin in Monguí. The only regular place to stay is *La Cabaña*, a fine cottage outside town, a five-minute walk beyond the stone bridge. It costs US$4 per person. To arrange a bed there, go to Panadería La Lomita, at Carrera 3 No 2-87, and ask for Miriam who manages the cabaña.

Alternatively, go to Calle 5 No 2-36. La señora who lives there rents out one double room at US$3 per person.

There seems to be only one restaurant in town, on the lower corner of the main plaza. You can buy good bread and cheese in shops and panaderías (bakeries).

### Getting There & Away
Buses to Sogamoso depart every hour or two from the main plaza (US$0.60, half an hour). There are also colectivos.

## TÓPAGA
• *pop 1200* • *2900 m* • *12°C*

Tópaga is a small village noted principally for the Iglesia de Tópaga, a well-preserved church on the main square, built by the Jesuits in 1642. The interior has fine wooden altars including the extraordinary Altar de Los Espejos, richly adorned with mirrors to attract the Indians.

### Getting There & Away
The village lies two km off the Sogamoso-

Monguí road; buses between these two towns will drop you off at the turn-off.

## LAGUNA DE TOTA
• *3015 m* • *11°C*

About 12 km long and five km wide, Laguna de Tota (also called Lago de Tota) is one of the largest lakes in Colombia. This Sea of Boyacá – as it's sometimes referred to – is also one of the deepest, reaching 60 metres at its deepest point. The shoreline is convoluted, forming several bays and peninsulas, and half a dozen picturesque islands add to the scenery. The lake is beautifully set in the mountains south of Sogamoso and has become a centre of tourism, with people coming from as far away as Bogotá on long weekends.

The largest village on the lake's shore is Aquitania. It's not very inspiring, but if you climb the nearby hill, you will get a magnificent view over the entire lake. You can walk to Playa Blanca further along the lake shore, where there is a camping site.

### Places to Stay & Eat
There are a few budget hospedajes in Aquitania (eg the *Residencias Venecia*, one block off the main plaza), but a more pleasant option is one of several hotels which have sprung up right on the lake shore, particularly along the eastern bank on the Sogamoso-Aquitania road. The *Hotel Cabaña Rocas Lindas*, *Hotel Camino Real* and *Hotel Turístico Santa Inés* are some of the better known and their restaurants serve the local speciality, trout, which comes fresh from the lake. Camping is possible, but keep in mind that it gets cold at night at this high altitude.

### Getting There & Away
There are hourly buses from Sogamoso to Aquitania along the eastern shore, with beautiful views from the road as you drop down to the lake after El Crucero. The bus trip costs US$1 and takes one hour. A few buses daily run along the western shore through Iza and Tota; perhaps the best idea is to go one way and come back the other.

# Sierra Nevada del Cocuy

Although little known outside of Colombia, the Sierra Nevada del Cocuy is one of the most spectacular mountain ranges in South America. It is the highest part of the Cordillera Oriental, formed by two parallel ranges that run north-south for about 25 km. A chain of beautiful valleys is sandwiched in between. The western range is the higher, and its highest peak, Ritacuba Blanco, reaches 5330 metres. There are more than 15 peaks over 5000 metres.

Because of its climate and topography, the Sierra Nevada del Cocuy has a striking abundance of flora. It is especially noted for its frailejones, and many varieties are unique to the region. The entire mountain range has been declared a national park. Administratively, it lies in the northern end of Boyacá department.

The mountains are quite compact, relatively easy to reach and ideal for trekking, though rather more suited to experienced hikers. The starting points for these hikes are the villages of Güicán and El Cocuy, which are connected to each other by road, and both of which provide accommodation and food facilities.

## GÜICÁN
• *pop 2000* • *2960 m* • *12°C*

Güicán is a cold village at the foot of the Sierra Nevada. It's a good starting point for trekking up into the mountains, and it is more popular among hikers than the larger and warmer El Cocuy.

### Places to Stay & Eat
There are two cheap hospedajes on the main square, both of which cost US$3 per person. One more place is the *Hotel Brisas del Nevado*, at Carrera 5 No 4-57, which costs US$8 for a double. All three places serve meals. On Thursday, which is market day, you can also eat at the market, on the corner of Carrera 4 and Calle 2.

BOYACÁ

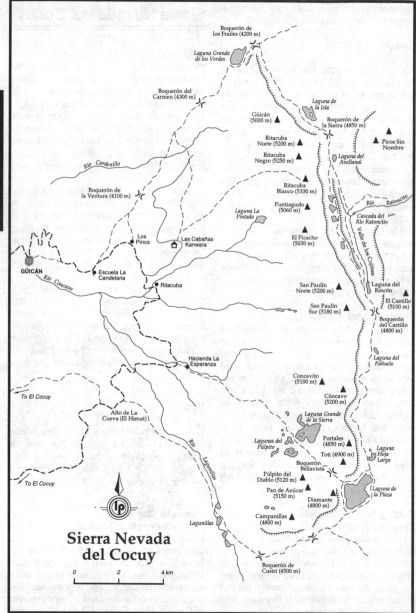

Boquerón de
los Frailes (4200 m)

Laguna Grande
de los Verdes

Boquerón del
Carmen (4300 m)

Laguna de
la Isla

Güicán
(5000 m) ▲

Boquerón de
la Sierra (4850 m)

Ritacuba
Norte (5200 m) ▲

▲ Picos Sin
Nombre

Ritacuba
Negro (5250 m) ▲

Laguna del
Avellanal

Río Cardenillo

Ritacuba
Blanco (5330 m) ▲

Boquerón de
la Ventura (4100 m)

Río Ratoncito

Puntiagudo
(5060 m) ▲

Cascada del
Río Ratoncito

Laguna La
Pintada

Valle de los Cojines

El Picacho
(5030 m) ▲

Los
Pinos

Las Cabañas
Kanwara

GÜICÁN

Escuela La
Candelaria

San Paulín
Norte (5200 m) ▲

Laguna del
Rincón

Río Cóncavo

Ritacuba

San Paulín
Sur (5180 m) ▲

El Castillo
(5100 m)

Boquerón
del Castillo
(4800 m)

Hacienda La
Esperanza

Laguna del
Pañuelo

To El Cocuy

Concavito
(5100 m) ▲

Cóncavo
(5200 m) ▲

Alto de La
Cueva (El Himat)

Laguna Grande
de la Sierra

Río Lagunillas

Lagunas del
Púlpito

Portales
(4850 m) ▲

Laguna
Hoja
Larga

Toti (4900 m) ▲

To El Cocuy

Boquerón
Bellavista

Púlpito del
Diablo (5120 m)

Pan de Azúcar
(5150 m)

Laguna de
la Plaza

Diamante
(4800 m) ▲

Campanillas
(4800 m) ▲

Lagunillas

# Sierra Nevada
# del Cocuy

0        2        4 km

Boquerón de
Cusiri (4500 m)

## Getting There & Away

There are four or five buses daily to Bogotá (US$13, about 13 hours), all of which pass through El Cocuy and Capitanejo. Buses leave from the main plaza.

If you don't plan on going south to Bogotá but intend to head north, stop in Capitanejo, from where buses go north to Cúcuta (US$10) and north-west to Bucaramanga (US$9). Basic accommodation and food are available in Capitanejo.

## EL COCUY

• *pop 3500* • *2700 m* • *14°C* • ☎ *(987)*

Although this is basically just a starting point for exploring the Sierra Nevada del Cocuy, the town itself is pleasant enough to stroll about for a couple of hours. The area up from the main square is the best preserved, with the balconies of many old houses bedecked with flowers; Carrera 3 is particularly fine. Some basic trekking supplies can be bought in town, though the choice is minimal.

## Places to Stay & Eat

The simple *Hospedaje El Nevado*, at Carrera 5 No 9-65, two blocks from the main plaza, is one of the cheapest places to stay, costing US$3 per person. The *Hotel Granada*, just around the corner from the El Nevado, is better and the staff are friendly. Rooms cost US$4 per person. Avoid the rooms facing the hotel restaurant. It's a very popular place to eat and for that reason it can be noisy.

The *Residencias Cocuy*, at Calle 7 No 3-60, one block up from the main square, has acceptable, clean double rooms for US$8. The staff will tell you they have hot water but check before you take a room. The *Hotel Gutiérrez*, at Carrera 4 No 7-30, costs US$10 for doubles. It is clean and does have hot water.

All of these hotels have restaurants and there are a few more restaurants in town.

## Getting There & Away

The only direct bus connections are to Bogotá (through Capitanejo) and Güicán. There are four or five buses a day to Bogotá (US$12, 12 hours) and the same number to Güicán (US$0.80, one hour). For other places in the north (Bucaramanga, Cúcuta) change in Capitanejo. Buses arrive at and leave from the main plaza.

## GÜICÁN-EL COCUY TREK

This is one of the most spectacular treks the Colombian mountains have to offer. On the way, you'll see more than 20 snow-capped peaks, a dozen beautiful mountain lakes, marvellous frailejón-filled valleys, waterfalls, glaciers and abundant flora.

You'll need six to seven days to complete the whole circuit as described below, but of course it's up to you how long you wish to walk and where you want to camp. Keep in mind that the changeable weather may affect your plans considerably.

The trek can be done from Güicán to El Cocuy or vice versa; the time and difficulty are more or less the same in either direction. The most difficult pass is in the middle of the route, so turning round and coming back the same way takes just as long. The route described is from Güicán to El Cocuy.

There are many shorter hikes, but if you want to get to the heart of the mountains, and the beautiful valleys between the two ranges, you will need at least four or five days. These shorter hikes are essentially portions of the circular route.

There are some accommodation facilities closer to the mountains than Güicán and El Cocuy (read the Places to Stay section), but they are all on the western slopes of the western range, still quite some distance from the valleys.

If you don't have a tent and trekking gear, the only way to explore the mountains is in a series of short, one-day walks from a base at one of these places. This, however, will give you just a taste of these magnificent mountains.

## Warnings

The trek is not easy and those without previous trekking experience should not attempt it. The average altitude is between 4000 and 4600 metres and there is a glaciated pass on the way. There are no people living along the route, nor are there many other walkers, so

BOYACÁ

you must be absolutely self-sufficient. There are no short cuts, and very importantly, the weather is unpredictable so you must be prepared for rain or snow at any time.

Allow enough time to acclimatise to the altitude, bearing in mind the fact that once you are beyond the first high pass, Boquerón del Carmen, there is little opportunity to descend in case of altitude sickness. Although you can descend to the north or east, you have to climb back up the same way. Don't plan on trekking down to Los Llanos as the region is dangerous because of guerrillas.

The guerrillas have unfortunately ascended the mountains. Since the late 1980s the ELN groups have shown their presence in the southern part of the Sierra (eg Laguna de la Plaza), while the FARC have occasionally appeared on the trekking routes in the north. The north is reputedly more secure. Travellers haven't experienced any major problems, but a potential danger does exist, especially if you have a US passport: guerrillas don't love that nation and hassle americanos more than others.

Quite recently another danger has appeared: the army. It was sent into the hills to squelch the guerrillas, but this only made the situation more tense and explosive. Furthermore, the soldiers are suspicious about hikers, suspecting them of collaborating with the guerrillas and some unpleasant confrontations have been reported.

Bearing this in mind, you may want to consider taking a guide, either from Bogotá (see Tours & Guides in that chapter) or a local, who can offer some protection. The same can be said about a local muleteer, if you are going to hire mules.

### Places to Stay

Apart from Güicán and El Cocuy, the only regular accommodation in the mountain area is in *Las Cabañas Kanwara*, a few cabins located at the foot of the Ritacuba peaks. They cost about US$8 per person and there is hot water and a restaurant. If you have your own tent you can camp there (US$5 per tent) and use the facilities. You can also hire

horses and guides. Bookings can be made in Bogotá through Almacén Aventura (☎ 248 1674), at Carrera 13 No 67-26.

Other overnight options in the area are in private homes, in the *Finca Los Pinos*, *Ritacuba*, *Hacienda La Esperanza* and *El Himat* in Alto de la Cueva. All these places are connected with Güicán and El Cocuy by an eastern upper road. Occasional trucks and jeeps use this route and the *lechero* (milk truck) comes up every morning, but there is no regular transport.

### When to Go

The only period of reasonably good weather is from December to February. The first half of March is usually OK but the second half may be unstable. The rest of the year is rainy and there is snow at high altitudes and on the highest passes. This can make them harder to cross, and you will need more time than is given in the following description. The weather changes frequently in the space of a single day and the Sierra is known for its strong winds.

### What to Bring

High-mountain trekking equipment is needed, ie a tent, good sleeping bag, sturdy shoes, down jacket, ski hat, gloves and enough warm clothes. Don't forget reliable rain gear, good suntan cream and sunglasses. Cooking equipment is a must as firewood is scarce. The French Camping Gaz Bluet 206 stoves are the most used in Colombia and you can get gas canisters in Bogotá (eg in Almacén Aventura) and a few large cities. You cannot buy them in Güicán or El Cocuy. Take extra food because the weather can cause unexpected delays.

Although there is a glaciated pass on your route, you can cross over it without any special mountaineering equipment such as crampons or an ice axe. A length of rope may be useful to link trekkers in pairs while crossing the areas noted for crevasses.

Maps are a great help. You can buy maps in the Instituto Geográfico Agustín Codazzi in Bogotá. Plancha (sheet) No 137 entitled *El Cocuy* and plancha No 153 entitled *Chita*,

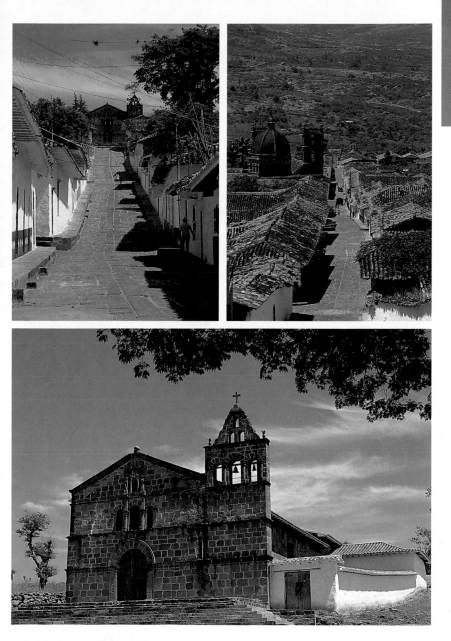

Left, Right: Barichara streets
Bottom: Iglesia de Santa Bárbara, Barichara

Top: Morning light on Ojeda Peak, Sierra Nevada de Santa Marta
Middle: Trekking in Sierra Nevada de Santa Marta
Bottom: Pink Flamingos on the Guajira coast

both to the scale 1:100,000 cover the whole route. The maps are not up-to-date and lack the names of the peaks but the topography is correct.

As the Sierra Nevada is a national park, you are required to obtain a permit from Inderena, though nobody is likely to ask for it.

### Horse & Mule Rental

Horses or mules can be hired in Las Cabañas Kanwara, Los Pinos, La Esperanza and Alto de la Cueva. They will go only as far as the Laguna del Avellanal on the northern side or up to the Laguna de la Plaza in the south. The animals do it in one day so you must walk quickly to keep up. The price depends on the route and the conditions, but is roughly US$10 to US$12 a day per animal and the same price again for the *arriero* (horseman or muleteer), who can handle up to three animals. When negotiating, make sure to state clearly that you will not be responsible for the animals (sickness, death or accidents).

### Days 1 & 2: Güicán to Laguna Grande de los Verdes

This part can be done in a single day, but it would be a hard walk and a rapid ascent to high altitudes, which may result in soroche (altitude sickness). It's recommended that you do this first leg over two days. Take it easy at the beginning and allow yourself time to acclimatise. Most hikers do so, using Las Cabañas Kanwara as an overnight stop.

Kanwara can be reached by road, though there's no public transport and traffic is sporadic. You might be able to hire a jeep in Güicán, or catch a lift with the morning lechero up to the turn-off past Los Pinos and walk the remaining bit (one to 1½ hours).

Alternatively, you can walk the whole way in about four hours. Leave Güicán by Calle 6 uphill and take the trail branching off to the right at the outskirts of the village. After about an hour you will join the road – follow it uphill until you get to the turn-off to Las Cabañas Kanwara, and continue along the side road to the cabins.

A few excursions can be made from Kanwara, the most popular being the one to the top of the Ritacuba Blanco up its gently sloping back face. The ascent takes five hours from Las Cabañas, but start very early because the top tends to cloud over by about noon.

The management will inform you of the possible walks out of Las Cabañas and give you instructions about the next leg of your trek, to Laguna Grande de los Verdes.

You first walk to the Río Cardenillo (a creek rather than a river) along either a rough road or a path (about a two-hour walk either way). Once you cross the creek there is a steady two-hour ascent to the Boquerón del Carmen pass (4300 metres).

Keep to the right-hand side of the valley as you descend from the pass. The trail then crosses the valley and continues along the left-hand slope just below the cliffs, finally arriving at the Laguna Grande de los Verdes (3900 metres). There are a lot of good camping sites around the lake, including a fabulous, white sandy beach right on the lake shore.

If you arrive at Las Cabañas early enough (eg by vehicle) and don't plan on side trips, you can walk up to Laguna Grande de los Verdes the same day. It's not that difficult (a six-hour walk), though bear in mind the potential acclimatisation risks.

**Alternative Route** A more strenuous route (less used by hikers) to Laguna Grande de los Verdes leads via the Boquerón de la Ventura. You begin from Güicán along the same way as in the previous route until you get to a school building, the Escuela La Candelaria, on your right. About 400 metres further on, a footpath branches off to the left. This is the path which heads to the pass. You can also continue by the road to Los Pinos, from where another path to the pass begins. The two trails join into one which heads steeply uphill to the Boquerón de la Ventura (4100 metres), noted for a stone wall and cross at the top. From there, the trail descends to the Río Cardenillo. Cross the river on a bridge made of frailejones 100 metres downstream, then continue up the path which joins the one from Las Cabañas and leads to the Boquerón del Carmen.

The total walking time from Güicán to the lake is about eight hours. It may be too much for one day (the first day), so you might want to do this over two days and camp at Río Cardenillo.

### Day 3: Laguna Grande de los Verdes to Laguna del Avellanal

The average walking time between these two lakes is about seven hours. The trail skirts around the eastern side of the Laguna Grande de los Verdes and heads up to the Boquerón de los Frailes pass (4200 metres). From here onwards, up to Laguna de la Plaza and even further, you'll be enjoying magnificent views of snowy peaks.

After a short descent the trail divides. Take the right-hand branch which heads south along the foot of rocky cliffs. After about three hours you will arrive at the Laguna de la Isla, passing high above its western side. There are no good campsites around the lake; the only reasonable one is below the laguna (at its northern end).

Continue up to the Boquerón de la Sierra pass (4850 metres). It's often covered with snow in the rainy season, and sometimes has snow in the dry period as well, but the trail is usually easy to find. From the pass, if the weather is clear, you will see the Laguna del Avellanal below and the long, magnificent Valle de los Cojines beyond, lined on both sides by snowy peaks. The trail drops down to the lake where you can camp, although the lake shore is quite rocky. There is a cave a few hundred metres west of the lake where enormous rocks have formed a tent-like roof. It offers some natural accommodation, though during the rainy season the ground can be wet.

### Day 4: Laguna del Avellanal to Laguna del Pañuelo

This leg will require about seven hours of constant walking, stops and photo sessions not included. From the Laguna del Avellanal the trail descends slowly, following the river into the Valle de los Cojines. You will pass a few small waterfalls on your right before reaching the most spectacular of all, the Cascada del Río Ratoncito. Here the main trail turns eastward and follows the river down into Los Llanos, but this is not the right route. Use this trail down to see the falls only, but then climb back up again to the point where it turns east.

Cross the creek and continue south along the Valle de los Cojines, keeping close to its right-hand (western) side, just above the wide, plain bed of the valley. The trail here is faint and disappears, but don't worry: just head on to the far end of the valley, sticking all the time to the right-hand slope. During the driest period, it may be easier to walk on the stones along the river bed, but most times the valley is boggy and can be dangerous, particularly in the rainy season. Once you reach the end of the valley you begin to ascend. From there you will get to the Laguna del Rincón (4400 metres) within half an hour.

From the lake you climb up to the glacial pass, the Boquerón del Castillo (4800 metres). There is no trail as such, so just head up to the lowest point between the ranges. Walk carefully checking the surface, as there are hidden crevasses in the glacier. It's best to use a rope, especially during bad weather. The walk to the pass is actually not very steep or very long, so you should reach it in one hour from the lake. From the pass, if the weather is clear, you will have breathtaking views on both sides. You will also see the small Laguna del Pañuelo, which can be reached after an hour's descent and where you can camp. Descend carefully and don't hurry, as there are crevasses on this slope as well.

The pass is often hidden in clouds and fog in the rainy (snowy) season, usually from late morning or noon on. Even in the dry season it may be clouded, particularly in the afternoon. If this is the case, don't attempt to cross – it's too dangerous. Camp at the Laguna del Rincón and cross over the pass the following morning.

**Alternative Route** There's another way from the Laguna del Avellanal to the Laguna del Rincón; it goes on a terrace high above the Valle de los Cojines, just below vertical walls of the western range. By taking this route you miss the Cascada del Río Ratoncito, but you pass by a few beautiful, small lakes and get a splendid panorama of the valley. To take this route, don't follow the trail that goes down from the Laguna del Avellanal into the valley, but instead head up to the right and keep close to the cliffs. There is no trail in this part, so you just follow the lakes.

### Day 5: Laguna del Pañuelo to Laguna de la Plaza

This bit may be quite difficult as there is no trail as such and you might lose your way and end up in a cul-de-sac far below where you should be. The walking time can be somewhere between six and eight hours, depending on how well you find your way. The best advice is to keep close to the rocky walls on your right at all times and stay at roughly the same altitude. Do not descend. Pay special attention when passing El Cóncavo where there are several rock terraces; you should follow the upper ones. Previous trekkers have left behind piles of stones to mark the right trail and you will probably find these helpful signs on the way.

If all goes well, you should reach the Laguna Hoja Larga within five hours. You will arrive at the marvellous, large Laguna de la Plaza after one hour's more walking. Here you can pitch your tent. There are other good camping sites on the far southern end of the lake.

### Day 6: Laguna de la Plaza to Lagunillas

Follow the path from the southern end of the Laguna de la Plaza, and you will soon get to the well-defined trail leading to Alto de la Cueva. It's a three-hour walk to the last pass, the Boquerón de Cusiri (4500 metres), then an hour's descent to the lovely chain of lakes, Lagunillas, where you will find lots of charming campsites. If you are here early enough, you can continue on to the Alto de la Cueva.

**Alternative Route** There is a somewhat adventurous route to the Laguna Grande de la Sierra and on to Hacienda La Esperanza. This is a difficult route; you have to pass over the crest of the range through a glacial pass, the highest of all on the route. Crampons and an ice axe are a must in some periods though at other times you won't really need them.

The almost nonexistent trail heads from the shore of the Laguna de la Plaza up to the Boquerón Bellavista pass (4900 metres). The climb is steep, long and strenuous, but the view from the top is breathtaking: you will see the two biggest lakes of the Sierra Nevada and a famous rock formation, the Púlpito del Diablo (5120 metres).

Descending, follow an imaginary line going between the lakes and watch out for crevasses. You can camp on the lake shore, or continue for three or four hours along the valley to the Hacienda La Esperanza. Accommodation and food are available here and so is occasional transport (mostly in the mornings) to El Cocuy or Güicán.

### Day 7: Lagunillas to Alto de la Cueva

From Lagunillas you have an easy four-hour walk beside the Río Lagunillas to the Alto de la Cueva, where the Himat meteorological station is located. And so, you are back on the road. Hitch (transport is scarce) or walk along the road for another four hours to El Cocuy. There are also footpaths to both El Cocuy and Güicán.

# Santander

## SOCORRO

• *pop 25,000* • *1230 m* • *22°C* • ☎ *(977)*

Socorro is known as the birthplace of the so-called Revolución Comunera, the first massive revolt against Spanish rule. The rebellion broke out in 1781, initially in protest against tax rises levied by the Crown, but it soon spread over the region and took on more pro-independence tones. In effect, Socorro was one of the first towns in Nueva

Francisco de Paula Santander

Granada to declare independence, on 10 July 1810. Colonial rule was again brutally established in 1816, but only three years later Simón Bolívar sealed the independence of the country.

Socorro has some attractions worthy of breaking the Tunja-Bucaramanga journey, if time permits. The town has preserved pretty much of its colonial character, visible in the old houses lining many of its streets.

## Information

The tourist office is in Pasaje Popular, a pedestrian passage which branches off Carrera 15 between Calles 13 and 14 next to the Banco Popular.

If you need a guide for a comprehensive tour around the town's sights, a recommended person is Iván Ángel Malagón Plata. You'll find him either in the Casa de la Cultura (☎ 272096), where he regularly runs the museum tours, or at his home (☎ 273031), at Calle 15 No 16A-16. His city tour includes a dozen sights, takes about four hours and costs around US$15 per group. He can also put together a tour to San Gil, Villanueva, Barichara and Guane. This is a full-day

excursion which costs US$25 per group, transport not included.

### Casa de la Cultura

This lovely 300-year-old colonial house, with its attractive façade (note the doorway) and a charming patio, is at Calle 14 No 12-31. It has been turned into a museum which features an archaeological collection of objects of the Guane Indians, the group that originally inhabited the region (from Barbosa in the south to Bucaramanga in the north) and who became extinct in the 18th century. There are some pottery pieces, a mummy and a funeral urn, but perhaps most interesting are the deformed skulls of the males, intentionally disfigured in their youth. The reason is not entirely clear but it was most likely for strictly utilitarian purposes: to carry loads on the head in a comfortable manner. Other exhibits include documents and objects related to the town's history, mostly dealing with the Revolución Comunera. Don't miss the balcony at the back of the house for the beautiful view it offers across the tiled roofs of the old part of the town.

The museum is open Monday to Saturday from 8 am to noon and 2 to 6 pm, and Sunday from 8 am to noon. The entrance fee is US$0.50. All visits are guided, with the commentary in Spanish. Some guides speak a bit of English.

### Plaza de la Independencia

The main square boasts two statues erected to commemorate the heroes of the Revolución Comunera. In the middle of the square is the monument to José Antonio Galán, the leader of the movement, who was hanged in Bogotá by the Spaniards in 1782. In the north-eastern corner of the plaza is the statue of Antonia Santos, a heroine executed on 28 July 1819, just 10 days before independence became a reality.

### Catedral

The massive Iglesia de Nuestra Señora de Socorro, commonly referred to as the Catedral, on the eastern side of the main square, took 70 years to build (1873-1943) and yet the work inside continued for several more

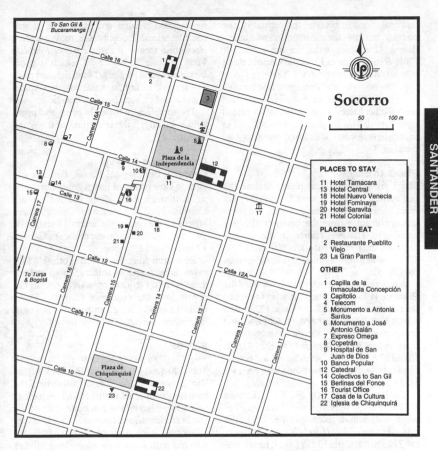

Socorro

0      50      100 m

**PLACES TO STAY**

11 Hotel Tamacara
13 Hotel Central
18 Hotel Nuevo Venecia
19 Hotel Fominaya
20 Hotel Saravita
21 Hotel Colonial

**PLACES TO EAT**

2 Restaurante Pueblito Viejo
23 La Gran Parrilla

**OTHER**

1 Capilla de la Inmaculada Concepción
3 Capitolio
4 Telecom
5 Monumento a Antonia Santos
6 Monumento a José Antonio Galán
7 Expreso Omega
8 Copetrán
9 Hospital de San Juan de Dios
10 Banco Popular
12 Catedral
14 Colectivos to San Gil
15 Berlinas del Fonce
16 Tourist Office
17 Casa de la Cultura
22 Iglesia de Chiquinquirá

SANTANDER

years. There is an image of the Virgen del Socorro, the patron saint of the town, over the high altar.

### Iglesia de Chiquinquirá

Of all of the town's churches, the Iglesia de Chiquinquirá, on the corner of Carrera 14 and Calle 10, is the most interesting for both its sober stone façade and its interior. When built in 1765, the entire interior was in stone but later some brick additions were made, which are now planned to be removed. The church is open irregularly, mostly for morning and evening mass.

### Other Attractions

Wander about the town's centre to see some of the relics of the colonial past. The sector uphill from the main square (to the east) is possibly the most interesting area. A number of charming single-storey houses line its sloping streets.

Near the main square, have a look at the beautiful former **Hospital de San Juan de Dios** (the first hospital in town, built in 1775), Calle 14 No 15-41, and the intriguing ruins of the **Capitolio**, on the corner of Carrera 14 and Calle 16. The Capitol building was begun in 1872, a time when Socorro had ambitions to become the capital of the country, but later the construction was abandoned. One block west, on the corner of Calle 16 and Carrera 15, is the **Capilla de la Inmaculada Concepción**. It's referred to as the Panteón de los Próceres Socorranos because it was here that Antonia Santos and several other heroes of the revolutionary period were buried. This is the earliest church still in existence in Socorro. It's closed awaiting restoration.

### Places to Stay

There are several budget places around the bus offices, on and around Carrera 17, the main thoroughfare. These hotels are very cheap but noisy from the heavy traffic day and night. The best choice in this area is probably the *Hotel Central*, at Carrera 17 No 13-13, which has doubles and matrimonios for US$3.

A more pleasant area to stay is south of the Plaza de la Independencia. It's best to go to the corner of Carrera 15 and Calle 13, around which you'll find four hotels, all good and inexpensive. Possibly the most agreeable of them is the *Hotel Saravita* (☎ 272282), at Carrera 15 No 12-64. Set in a colonial house, this friendly place offers rooms with bath for US$3 per person.

The *Hotel Fominaya* (☎ 272708), at Carrera 15 No 12-73, opposite the Saravita, has rooms without/with bath, costing US$2.50/4 per person. The *Hotel Nuevo Venecia* (☎ 272350), at Calle 13 No 14-37, has rooms at similar prices. The brand-new *Hotel Colonial* (☎ 272842), at Carrera 15 No 12-45, has doubles with bath and TV for US$10.

The *Hotel Tamacara* (☎ 273515), at Calle 14 No 14-45 (on the main square), is the best in town and, accordingly, it is the most expensive (US$24/33 a single/double).

### Places to Eat

There's a choice of restaurants throughout the central area, serving inexpensive set meals and à la carte dishes. Both the *Hotel Saravita* and *Hotel Fominaya* have their own restaurants.

*La Gran Parrilla* on Plaza de Chiquinquirá serves good parrillas and churrascos at reasonable prices. Probably the most pleasant place for a meal is the *Restaurante Pueblito Viejo*, at Calle 16 No 15-39, which is good, inexpensive and pleasant. Meat, fish and pasta are served, including some of the typical regional dishes, such as carne oreada.

The top place in town, in price and probably in quality, is the restaurant of the *Hotel Tamacara*.

### Getting There & Away

Copetrán, Berlinas del Fonce, Brasilia and Omega have plenty of buses going north and south through town along the main road, Carrera 17. Copetrán and Omega have offices on the corner of Carrera 17 and Calle 14, while Berlinas is on the corner of Carrera 17 and Calle 13.

Buses run frequently to Bogotá (US$11, seven hours), and to Bucaramanga (US$5, three hours). Frequent colectivos to San Gil depart from the corner of Carrera 17 and Calle 13 (US$1.20, 25 minutes). They will take you to the San Gil bus terminal.

### SAN GIL

• *pop 30,000* • *1110 m* • *22˚C* • ☎ *(97724)*

This 300-year-old town on the bank of the Río Fonce has one special attraction, the riverside Parque El Gallineral. The park is set on two islands between three arms of the Quebrada Curití, and measures four hectares (10 acres). Almost all of its 1867 trees are covered with *barbas de viejo*, long silvery fronds of tillandsia that form spectacular, transparent curtains of foliage. The park is on the road to Bucaramanga, a 10-minute walk from the town centre. It is open every day from 8 am to 5.30 pm, and entry costs US$0.40.

San Gil also has a pleasant Parque Principal (main square) with huge old ceibas and a handsome 18th-century stone cathedral. Have a look at the Casa de la Cultura, a fine 18th-century mansion with two patios, at Calle 12 No 10-31, just off the main square.

These attractions apart, there's not much to see in town, but the neighbouring region is interesting and worth exploring. In particular, don't miss Barichara (see the following section), a beautiful colonial town. You may also want to take a short trip to Curití, a quiet village only 10 km away, noted for its 17th-century church.

## Information

Oficina de Turismo de San Gil (☎ (97724) 4372, 4617) is at the entrance to the Parque El Gallineral, with the same opening hours as the park.

## Places to Stay – bottom end

Possibly the best budget place to stay is the *Residencias Villas del Oriente*, at Calle 10 No 10-47. It has simple matrimonios without bath (US$3) in its old section, and comfortable double rooms with bath in the newly constructed extension at the back (US$6). It's probably the cleanest of the cheapies.

The *Hotel San Gil* (☎ 2542), at Carrera 11 No 11-25, has doubles without bath for US$3, but it's more basic than the Villas, and the noise from the busy traffic on the street may be disturbing.

The *Residencias El Águila* (☎ 2170), at Carrera 10 No 13-17, is conveniently located on the corner of the main square. It was probably a good hotel decades ago, but most rooms have since been divided by hardboard partitions to increase the hotel's capacity. Doubles without/with bath cost US$4/5 but inspect the rooms before booking in.

The *Hotel Victoria* (☎ 2347), at Carrera 11 No 10-40, has neat doubles with bath and fan for US$8. The *Residencias El Viajero* (☎ 4817), at Carrera 11 No 11-07, may be an alternative, with doubles going for US$9.

## Places to Stay – middle & top end

If you need something better, go to the friendly *Hostal Isla Señorial* (☎ 4442), at Calle 10 No 8-14. This is possibly the best hotel in the city centre, offering comfortable singles/doubles/triples with TV for US$11/17/23.

The *Residencias Capri* (☎ 4218), at Calle 10 No 9-31, is apparently the only mid-priced competitor to the Hostal. It offers doubles with TV for US$20.

The best place is the expensive *Hotel Bella Isla* (☎ 2971), out of town on the road to Bucaramanga.

## Places to Eat

A good number of the cheapest restaurants are along Carrera 11, all the way from the market to the Parque El Gallineral, and on Calle 10 between Carreras 10 and 11. To name a few: *Restaurante Santandereano* at Calle 10 No 10-24, *Restaurante El Pasaje* at Carrera 11 No 12-38 and the restaurant in the *Hotel San Gil*.

The *Restaurante Fonda*, on the southern side of the main square, is one of the most pleasant restaurants in the town centre. The food is quite acceptable and reasonably priced. Next door is *Dusi's King*, the place to go for snacks, such as hot dogs, hamburgers and sandwiches.

The restaurant in the Parque El Gallineral is among the best in town, and its menu of local food (such as mute, cabro or carne oreada) is not that expensive.

## Getting There & Away

San Gil has a new bus terminal, built two km west of the town centre, on the road to Bogotá. Urban buses shuttle between the terminal and the centre approximately every half an hour. You can also take a taxi (US$0.60), or you can walk (20 minutes).

San Gil lies on the Bogotá-Bucaramanga road which sees some of the busiest bus traffic in the country. Keep in mind that long-distance buses don't stop in the town centre (although they pass through, just two blocks from the main square).

**To Bogotá** Buses, operated by several companies, leave every hour or less (US$12, 7½ hours). All come through from Bucaramanga or further north.

**To Bucaramanga** You can expect at least one bus per hour (US$4, 2½ hours). In addition, Cotrasangil operates half-hourly minibuses (US$4.50, two hours).

**To Barichara** Buses are operated by Cotrasangil and depart every 1½ hours or so (US$0.80, 40 minutes) from the company's city office, Carrera 10 No 14-82. Buses to Villanueva (US$0.80) and Curití (US$0.40) also leave from here.

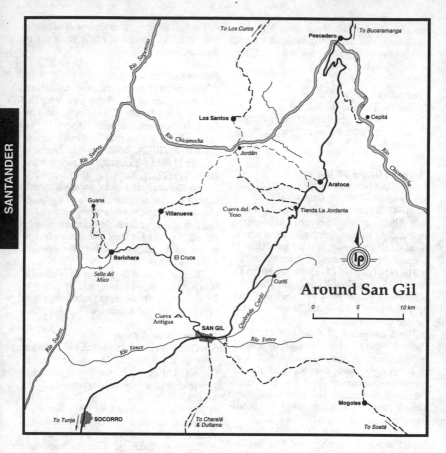

**Around San Gil**

0      5      10 km

## BARICHARA

• *pop 3000 • 1340 m • 22°C •* ☎ *(97724)*

Barichara is a small, well-preserved colonial town, set amidst arid hills on the rim of the canyon of Río Suárez. Founded in 1741 and named Villa de San Lorenzo de Barichara, the town was laid out on a chessboard grid. Its streets were paved with massive, flat slabs and lined with modest single-storey adobe houses. Four stone churches were built, including a massive cathedral.

Despite the 250 years that have passed since its foundation, Barichara is almost untouched by time; its paved streets, adobe houses and stone churches are all still there. In 1975 the town was declared a national monument, and much work has gone into its restoration. Although there are no outstanding individual sights, the town's charm lies in its beauty as a whole and its lazy, old-world atmosphere. Authentic, clean and well kept, it's one of the most beautiful and homogeneous colonial towns in Colombia.

The name Barichara comes from Barachalá, a Guane Indian word (the original inhabitants of this territory) which means 'a good place for a rest'; absolutely right. Whether you are going to sightsee this small colonial pearl or just want a place to rest, Barichara won't fall short of your expectations. Don't miss it.

## Things to See

As you stroll about the streets, take a look at the churches. The 18th-century stone **Catedral** is the largest and most elaborate single piece of architecture in town, looking somewhat too big for the town's needs. Its golden stonework (which turns deep orange at sunset) contrasts with the whitewashed houses surrounding it. The doorframe of the main entrance is designed so that when open it appears that the arched entrance has no doors, giving an impression of space and airiness. The building has a clerestory (a second row of windows high up above the nave) which is unusual among Spanish colonial churches.

Also interesting is the **Iglesia de Santa Bárbara** at the northern end of town, which has recently been carefully reconstructed (only the façade survived).

The cemetery chapel, the **Capilla de Jesús Resucitado**, unfortunately lost a part of its bell tower when it was damaged by lightning. Do visit the cemetery, next to the chapel, noted for a number of interesting tombs elaborated in stone. Also have a look at the **Capilla de San Antonio**, the youngest of the town's churches, dating from 1831.

The **Casa de la Cultura**, on the main square, houses a museum featuring a small collection of fossils and antiques. It's worth dropping in just to see the interior, laid out around a fine patio. The museum is open Wednesday to Saturday from 8 am to noon and 2 to 6 pm, and Sunday from 8 am to 1 pm.

The **Casa de Aquileo Parra Gómez** is a small, humble house where an ex-president lived, but there's not much to see inside. If you want to check it out, la señora in the house around the corner will open it for you.

Barichara is a good jumping-off point for a couple of short excursions, particularly to Guane (see the following section) and the **Salto del Mico** (Monkey's Falls). This waterfall, over 50 metres high, drops into a beautiful semicircular cirque and is spectacular, especially in the wet season after heavy rains. It's about two km south-west of the town; a half-hour walk.

If you are looking for a guide and a good companion for these trips, contact José Rafael Pradilla, the manager of the Hostal Misión Santa Bárbara. This friendly fellow may be able to guide you around, if he has no important tasks to do in the hotel.

## Places to Stay

There are five hotels in Barichara. All are good and all have private baths, but they are not that cheap: the bottom line is US$6 per person.

At that price, it's probably best to start off with the *Hotel Coratá*, at Carrera 7 No 4-02. This colonial house, which was turned into a hotel, has spacious rooms and its own restaurant. The *Hotel Bahía Chala* (☎ 7036), at Calle 7 No 7-61, offers pretty much the same, and also costs US$6.

The *Hotel Posada Real* (☎ 7002), at Carrera 6 No 4-69, has modern rooms and costs the same as the two above.

The *Hostal Misión Santa Bárbara* (☎ 7163), at Calle 5 No 9-12, is a charming place. Set in a colonial house, the rooms have been decorated accordingly and cost US$20/30 a single/double plus US$8 for an additional person. The hotel has a swimming pool and its own restaurant. Booking is available in Bucaramanga (☎ 351432) and in Bogotá (☎ 618 4373, 618 4383).

The recently opened *Posada del Campanario* (☎ 7261), at Calle 5 No 7-53, is an alternative up-market choice to the Hostal. The rooms are also in colonial style, though with some more modern additions. A double costs about US$35 plus US$15 for an additional person. You can book the Posada in Bogotá (☎ 282 6546, 610 5446).

## Places to Eat

For a town of its size, Barichara offers a wide choice for lunch or dinner. All of the hotels listed above have their own restaurants. The *Posada Real* is the cheapest and has some local dishes. The *Bahía Chala* also serves local food but for marginally more. The best

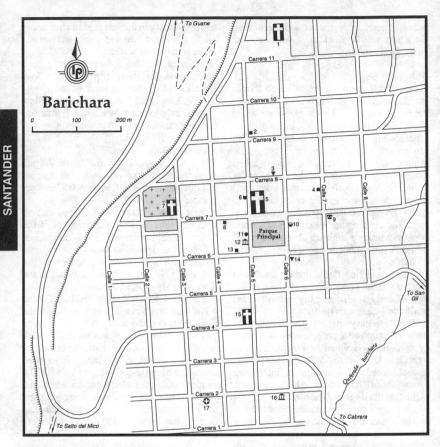

Barichara

0    100    200 m

To Guane

Carrera 11

Carrera 10

Carrera 9

Carrera 8

Carrera 7

Carrera 6

Carrera 5

Carrera 4

Carrera 3

Carrera 2

Carrera 1

Calle 1

Calle 2

Calle 3

Calle 4

Calle 5

Calle 6

Calle 7

Calle 8

Parque Principal

To San Gil

To Cabrera

To Salto del Mico

Quebrada Barichara

for regional cuisine is the *Coratá*, though it's the most expensive of the three.

The *Hostal Misión Santa Bárbara* does good comida casera (home-cooking), which includes some regional specialities. The *Posada del Campanario* has international cuisine at probably the highest prices in town.

There is also a range of other restaurants. *La Casona*, off the south-eastern corner of the main plaza, is good for comida típica.

The specialities of the region include cabro (goat), mute and the famous hormiga culona, a giant fried ant which appears mainly in March and April. Barichara is also well-known for its arequipe; there are several outlets selling it, reputedly the best being the *Arequipe Barichara* on Carrera 8 behind the cathedral. The local drink is the chicha de maíz (an alcoholic maize drink).

### Getting There & Away

The best way to get to Barichara is via San Gil. There are buses operated by Cotrasangil every one or two hours between these towns (US$0.80, 40 minutes). In San Gil, the buses depart from the Cotrasangil office in the town centre, Carrera 10 No 14-82. In

1   Iglesia de Santa Bárbara
2   Hostal Misión Santa Bárbara
3   Arequipe Barichara
4   Hotel Bahía Chala
5   Catedral
6   Posada del Campanario
7   Capilla de Jesús Resucitado
8   Hotel Coratá
9   Telecom
10  Cotrasangil Office
11  Alcaldía & Police
12  Casa de la Cultura
13  Hotel Posada Real
14  Restaurante La Casona
15  Capilla de San Antonio
16  Casa de Aquileo Parra Gómez
17  Hospital

**SANTANDER**

Barichara, the buses arrive at and depart from the main square.

Two unreliable lecheros are supposed to depart for Guane at around 7 am and 2 pm (US$0.35). You can also walk to Guane, either by road (a good two-hour walk) or, preferably, by the path (which is more direct and takes half an hour less). Ask for directions, or tag along with a local.

## GUANE

Guane is a tiny village 10 km north of Barichara along a rough road. The Iglesia de Santa Lucía, built between 1785 and 1816, is worth a visit, as is the museum which contains a large collection of locally found fossils and Guane Indian artefacts. There are some charming little houses just off the plaza.

### Getting There & Away

The only reliable lechero tends to leave for Barichara around 7 am, so you may have to stay overnight in Guane. If so, ask for rooms in the Cooperativa on the square. Alternatively, walk back along the road or take the trail.

## CUEVA DEL YESO

There are several caves in the region. The best known are the Cueva Antigua, five km from San Gil on the road to Barichara; the Hoyo del Aire, near the village of La Paz; the Cueva de Los Pájaros, near Mogotes, inhab-

ited by *guácharos* (oilbirds); and the Cueva del Yeso.

If you have seen the caves in eastern Antioquia then you probably won't want to visit these. They are more difficult to explore, don't seem to be as impressive and are not very well known even among the locals. Nevertheless, if speleology is your thing, they may prove interesting.

Walking inside the Cueva del Yeso is difficult. You have to go along a long tunnel, which is narrow in parts before it reaches a wider section. There are side corridors so you have to be careful not to get lost. A rope is a must, and obviously you'll need a torch. It's not easy to find anyone in the nearby huts who knows the cave and is willing to guide you; the locals just ignore it.

### Getting There & Away

The Cueva del Yeso lies about 20 km north of San Gil. Take the bus along the main road to Bucaramanga and get off seven km before Aratoca at the Tienda La Jordania, a roadside house on your left that has a shop. From here, follow a dirt turn-off which divides 400 metres further on. Take the left-hand fork for about four km until it finally drops to a stream in the valley. The cave is nearby in a small rocky cliff on the slope on the opposite side of the stream.

## ARATOCA

This small, picturesque village, just off the San Gil-Bucaramanga road, 28 km north of San Gil, is spectacularly set in a valley among green hills. You will get a marvellous bird's-eye view of Aratoca from the road, two km before you reach the turn off to the village. If you want to get a closer feel, it's a 15-minute walk from the turn-off to the village, though it looks more impressive from a distance. There are a couple of basic places to stay and eat.

## CAÑÓN DEL CHICAMOCHA

This spectacular, winding canyon formed by the Río Chicamocha stretches along most of the river's length, with considerable changes of scenery. In the upper reaches of the river, the canyon is narrow with steep, rocky cliffs. Below Capitanejo, the river expands and the canyon widens. It is deepest in the lower course of the river, downstream from Pescadero, where it reaches a depth of about 700 metres.

There are various ways to see and explore the canyon; the easiest is from the main Bogotá-Bucaramanga road which crosses the gorge at Pescadero. Past Aratoca the road begins to zigzag down the steep slopes to Pescadero, with impressive views of the canyon and the river below. Although the road is in good shape it is dangerous, illustrated by the numerous crosses which dot it, put there in memory of those who went over the edge.

If you're not in a hurry, get off the bus at the turn-off to Cepitá, between Aratoca and Pescadero, and walk 12 km along the snaking, rough road down to the village set on the opposite side of the Río Chicamocha. Cepitá is a pleasant village, which can only be accessed by a pedestrian bridge across the river. It is noted for the aniseed grown in the area that is used for flavouring aguardiente.

The upstream part of the gorge can be seen from the road between Susacón and Capitanejo, which you will pass on the way from Bogotá to the Sierra Nevada del Cocuy. Further on, past Capitanejo toward El Cocuy, the road skirts alongside the river in a deep narrow gorge.

### Villanueva-Los Santos Trek

The walk described here provides an opportunity to get close to one of the most spectacular parts of the canyon, in the lower reaches of the Río Chicamocha. The route leads from Villanueva to Los Santos, crossing the river at Jordán. This can be done leisurely within a day, but start early.

Villanueva is an unremarkable village, easily accessible by bus from San Gil. If you are coming from Barichara, change buses at El Cruce. From Villanueva, walk seven km along a dirt road to get to the edge of the canyon. This road may be difficult to follow as it divides and joins with other roads leading to the *fincas* (farms) scattered around. Ask for directions about the 'camino a Jordán' along the way and confirm them at every opportu-

nity. Once you get to the rim of the canyon, you will find a well-marked trail leading down to Jordán. It's a very scenic (but hot) two-hour descent.

Jordán was founded in 1830 and had its prosperous times, but it has since died because it lacks a road connection. Only a few families still live here. Most houses have been abandoned, and left open to the ravages of time. The main church has not been used since its roof fell in. Walk around the village and see the hospital chapel, the cemetery and the bridge.

However, the situation is changing. A new road to Jordán is being constructed from the west and only a couple of km are still missing. The village is beginning to revive.

From Jordán, a well-preserved *camino de herradura* (old Spanish bridle path) climbs to Los Santos on the other side of the canyon; the walk up will take two hours. A few buses daily (the last one around 1 pm) depart from Los Santos to Los Curos, back on the main road (US$2, 1½ hours). Two or three families in Los Santos rent out rooms in their houses; ask around.

## BUCARAMANGA

• *pop 480,000* • *960 m* • *23°C* • ☎ *(976)*

Bucaramanga, the capital of Santander, is a fairly modern, busy commercial and industrial centre with a very agreeable climate. It is noted for its parks, cigars and the famous hormiga culona, a large ant which is fried and eaten.

The city was founded in 1622 but very little of its colonial architecture remains. The old town developed around what is today the Parque García Rovira, and some colonial buildings still survive in this area.

There is not much to see in Bucaramanga, although it may be a stopover on the long route from Bogotá to Santa Marta or Cúcuta. If you stop here, don't miss taking a side trip to Girón, 10 km away (see the following section).

### Information

**Tourist Office** The tourist office is in the Hotel Bucarica, on the corner of Carrera 19 and Calle 35.

**Money** Banks which might deal with your cash, travellers' cheques and credit cards (Visa or MasterCard) are marked on the map. They are packed within a small central area. Shop around, as the rate varies from one to another.

### Things to See
The **Casa de Bolívar**, Calle 37 No 12-15, contains the Museum of Ethnography and History. It is open Tuesday to Friday from 8 am to noon and 2 to 6 pm, and on Saturday from 9 am to 1 pm. The **Casa de la Cultura**, in a colonial house at Calle 37 No 12-46, diagonally opposite the museum, sometimes has art exhibits. One block east, you'll find another of the few surviving colonial relics, the **Casa de Perú de la Croix**, Calle 37 No 11-18, which also stages art exhibitions.

The **Capilla de los Dolores**, in the Parque García Rovira, is the oldest chapel in Bucaramanga. It's no longer operating as a church and is seldom open, but you won't be missing much.

The city has pleasant botanical gardens, the **Jardín Botánico Eloy Valenzuela**, noted for a variety of fine trees, a small pond and a replica of a Japanese garden. The gardens are in the suburb of Bucarica, and are open daily from 8 to 11 am and 2 to 5 pm. To get there, take the Bucarica bus from Carrera 15, in the city centre.

On weekend evenings, stroll around the Hotel Chicamocha, where a string of live-music bars and discos attract young locals.

### Places to Stay – bottom end
Budget accommodation is centred near the Parque Centenario, particularly on Calle 31 between Carreras 19 and 21, where you'll find a single/double for under US$3/5. They are mostly basic, though some have private baths. The best of the lot seems to be the clean and friendly *Hotel Elena* (☎ 428845), at Carrera 21 No 30-55 (US$3 a single without bath, US$6 a double with bath).

If the Hotel Elena is full (as often happens), try the nearby *Residencias ABC* (☎ 337352), at Calle 31 No 21-44, or the *Residencias Amparo* (☎ 304098), at Calle 31 No 20-29, both just around the corner and

costing much the same. Similar prices and value are offered by the *Hotel Tamaná* (☎ 304726), at Carrera 18 No 30-31, though the area is less pleasant. Avoid strolling on and around Calle 31 east of the Parque Centenario – this is the red light district, and can be dangerous, especially at night.

### Places to Stay – middle
The *Hotel Balmoral* (☎ 426232), at Carrera 21 No 34-85, is pleasant and friendly. Singles/doubles/triples with private bath and hot water go for US$10/13/16.

If you need something a bit more flash, go to the *Hotel Morgan No 2* (☎ 424732), at Calle 35 No 18-83, just off the Parque Santander. Clean, ample rooms with own bath (but with cold water only) cost US$13/18/23; choose one with a window facing the street. Don't confuse this hotel with the *Hotel Morgan No 1*, a few paces down Calle 35, which is marginally cheaper but not as good.

The *Hotel Farallones* (☎ 428739), at Calle 34 No 17-73, is one of the cheaper options that provides rooms with air-con, for US$14/18 a single/double. But the hotel is otherwise undistinguished and not particularly clean.

### Places to Stay – top end
If you want something more up-market and not too expensive, try the *Hotel Andino* (☎ 303319), at Calle 34 No 18-44, which is OK and costs US$30/40 a single/double in rooms with air-con, private bath and hot water.

At the top of the scale, you can choose between the *Hotel Bucarica* (☎ 301592) in the Parque Santander, and the *Hotel Chicamocha* (☎ 343000) at Calle 34 No 31-24, in the more easy-going residential district, one km east. Either hotel will bill you about US$60/70 for a single/double.

### Places to Eat
Local dishes include mute and cabrito. The legendary hormiga culona is not a dish you order in restaurants but a kind of snack you buy by weight in shops (about US$30 a kg). The ants are sold in several delicatessens and

SANTANDER

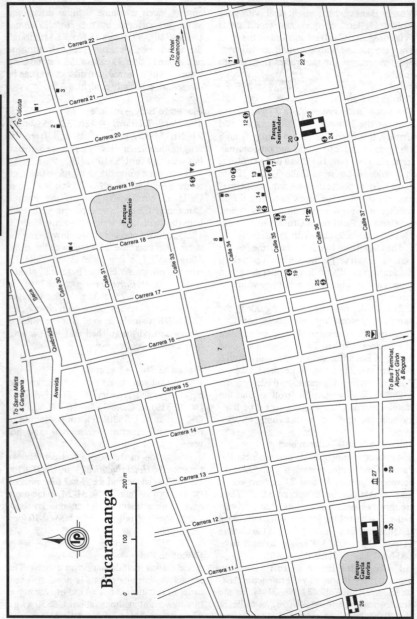

Bucaramanga

## PLACES TO STAY

1 Hotel Elena
2 Residencias Amparo
3 Residencias ABC
4 Hotel Tamaná
8 Hotel Farallones
9 Hotel Andino
11 Hotel Balmoral
13 Hotel Morgan No 2
14 Hotel Morgan No 1
17 Hotel Bucarica

## PLACES TO EAT

6 Restaurante El Consulado
  Antioqueño
22 Restaurante El Paisa

## OTHER

5 Banco Sudameris Colombia
7 Market
10 Banco Unión Colombiano
12 Banco Popular
15 Banco Industrial Colombiano
16 Tourist Office
18 Banco de Colombia
19 Banco de Bogotá
20 Colectivos to Airport
21 Telecom
23 Catedral
24 Banco Anglo Colombiano
25 Banco de Occidente
26 Capilla de los Dolores
27 Casa de Bolívar
28 Avianca Correo Aéreo
29 Casa de la Cultura
30 Casa de Perú de la Croix

in the Sanandresito La Isla shopping centre, on Diagonal 15 between Calles 55 and 56.

There are plenty of cheap restaurants around, some attached to the budget hotels, where you can grab a set meal for US$1.50 or less. There are virtually no really good restaurants in the city centre, save perhaps the expensive one in the *Hotel Bucarica*. More affordable prices are found in *El Paisa*, at Carrera 21 No 36-28, and *El Consulado Antioqueño*, at Carrera 19 No 33-81, both serving local and Antioquian food.

A better area for dining is the eastern district of the city, particularly the areas on

and around Carreras 27 and 33. Try, for example, *La Pampa*, at Carrera 27 No 42-27, serving Argentine food, or the *Casona de Chiflas*, on the corner of Carrera 33 and Calle 36, noted for its parrillada and other meat dishes (choose a table upstairs, where it's much more pleasant).

*Señora Bucaramanga* and *El Mesón de los Búcaros* are two popular, reasonably-priced places that serve hearty, local food. They are opposite one another on the corner of Carrera 27 and Calle 22, and both are open till late.

### Getting There & Away

**Air** The Palonegro airport is on a *meseta* (plateau) high above and overlooking the city, off the Barrancabermeja road. The landing here is breathtaking. The airport and the city centre are linked by very infrequent local buses (every hour or two) marked 'Aeropuerto'. In the city centre, you can catch them on Carrera 15. It's much faster to go by colectivo (US$1.50); you will find them in the Parque Santander, opposite the cathedral.

Avianca has flights to Bogotá (US$72), Cúcuta (US$34), Medellín (US$76) and San Andrés (US$142). For other cities, you have to change in either Bogotá or Medellín. Satena flies to Bogotá for US$64.

**Bus** Bucaramanga has a brand-new, well-organised bus terminal. It's quite a distance from the city centre, off the road to Girón, but you can easily get to and from there on the frequent city buses marked 'Terminal'. In the centre, you catch them on Carrera 15.

**To Bogotá** There are plenty of buses with various companies (US$16 climatizado, US$14 pullman, 10 hours).
**To Barranquilla & Cartagena** At least two dozen buses (with Copetrán and Brasilia) depart daily to Barranquilla (US$21 climatizado, US$18 pullman, 10 to 11 hours); some of them continue on to Cartagena (US$25 climatizado, 14 hours).
**To Santa Marta** There are several buses a day (US$19 climatizado, nine hours).
**To Cúcuta** Copetrán or Berlinas del Fonce have buses every hour or two (US$8 climatizado, US$7 pullman, six hours). A very scenic road

winds up to the páramo at 3400 metres and then drops down to Cúcuta. If you sit on the right-hand side of the bus, you will have a splendid view as you leave Bucaramanga and again when you arrive at Pamplona. Travel by day if possible and have a sweater handy.

## GIRÓN

• *pop 42,000* • *780 m* • *24°C* • ☎ *(976)*

San Juan de Girón is a pretty colonial town 10 km from Bucaramanga. It was founded in 1631, and in 1963 it was declared a national monument to protect its character. Its central area has been largely restored and preserves much of its colonial flavour.

The town has become a trendy place, and is home to several artists. Due to its proximity to Bucaramanga, Girón fills up at the weekends with city dwellers.

### Things to See

Girón is a nice place to stroll around its narrow cobbled streets, looking at the fine houses, charming patios and a few small bridges. Don't miss the **Plazuela Peralta**, which is perhaps the most charming spot in town. Also enchanting is the **Plazuela de las Nieves** with its simple, but noble, 18th-century **Capilla de las Nieves**.

The **Catedral** on the main plaza was begun in 1646 but not completed until 1876, so it's stylistically eclectic. Also on the main square is the **Mansión del Fraile**, a beautiful colonial house which is 350 years old. It now houses a restaurant (see Places to Eat), a craft shop and a museum displaying objects related to the town's history. The museum was closed recently but should reopen in the future.

### Places to Stay

Girón is just a day trip from Bucaramanga, but if you wish to stay longer, there is the good, pleasant *Hotel Las Nieves* (☎ 468968), on the main square. It has large, comfortable rooms – most with three beds – apparently

To Bucaramanga

Calle 33

Calle 32

To Airport &
Barrancabermeja

Calle 31

Carrera 27

Carrera 26

Carrera 25

Carrera 24

Carrera 23

## Girón

0        100        200 m

1    Parque
     Principal

2

3

Calle 30

4    5

9

8

6

Calle 28

7

10

Río de Oro

1  Plazuela Peralta
2  Catedral
3  Hotel Río de Oro
4  Hotel Las Nieves
5  Mansión del Fraile
6  Restaurante Antón García
7  Restaurante El Carajo
8  Plazuela de las Nieves
9  Capilla de las Nieves
10 Restaurante La Casona

intended for well-off families and charging accordingly (US$30 to US$40 per room). If you come on weekdays, when the hotel is half empty, you may be charged less.

A cheaper alternative is the *Hotel Río de Oro*, also on the main square. It's a poorly kept, slowly decaying old mansion with a certain old-world charm. The price seems to be negotiable; count on around US$10 per double. For a couple of dollars more you can fit four or five people into these large rooms.

### Places to Eat
*Antón García*, at Calle 29 No 24-47, and *El Carajo*, at Carrera 25 No 28-08, are two places for cheap food. More up-market are *La Casona*, at Calle 28 No 27-47, and *Mansión del Fraile*, on the main square. Both are pleasant and serve good local food.

On weekends, several stalls open at the riverside and offer a choice of regional dishes.

### Getting There & Away
There are frequent city buses from Carrera 15 in Bucaramanga, which will deposit you on the main square of Girón in half an hour.

---

# Norte de Santander

## PAMPLONA
• *pop 40,000* • *2290 m* • *16˚C* • ☎ *(978)*

Pamplona, the only town of note on the Bucaramanga-Cúcuta road, is spectacularly set in the deep Valle del Espíritu Santo in the Cordillera Oriental. It was founded by Pedro de Orsúa and Ortún Velasco in 1549, making it the oldest town in the region. Soon after its foundation, five convents were established, and the town swiftly developed into an important religious and political centre.

The only Spanish dot on the map for hundreds of kilometres around, Pamplona became the base for various expeditions that set off to conquer the region and to found new cities. Bucaramanga, Cúcuta, San Cristóbal and Mérida (the last two in present-day Venezuela) were all founded from

Pamplona and, ironically, they are all far larger and more important than their mother town today.

On 4 July 1810 Pamplona heeded the Grito de Independencia (Cry for Independence) proclaimed by Agueda Gallardo de Villamizar, which made it one of the forerunners in the move to independence. By then, it was a stately, fair-sized town, dotted with churches and noble mansions.

Unfortunately, an earthquake in 1875 wiped out a good part of the colonial architecture. The most representative buildings were restored or reconstructed in their previous style but most of the houses were replaced by new ones. Since then the construction of modern buildings has changed the colonial character of the town even further.

Pamplona was a schooling and catechistic centre from its early days, and the traditions have not been lost. Today the town is home to the Universidad de Pamplona, and the large student population is very much in evidence. Pamplona has a distinctly cultured air, and boasts more museums than Cúcuta and Bucaramanga combined.

### Information
**Tourist Office**  The Oficina de Turismo (☎ 681250) is at Carrera 5A No 6A-19, right behind the cathedral, and is open Monday to Friday from 8 am to noon and 2 to 6 pm.

**Money**  Don't plan on changing money in Pamplona. The Banco de Bogotá in the Parque Agueda Gallardo (the main square) may give a cash advance on Visa credit cards but that's about it.

### Museums & Historic Houses
Pamplona has quite a collection of museums and almost all are set in restored colonial houses.

Have a look at the market building, just off the main square. It was constructed in the 19th century and has preserved its original style.

### Museo de Arte Moderno Ramírez Villamizar  Set in an old mansion known as the Casa de las Marías, the museum features

NORTE DE SANTANDER

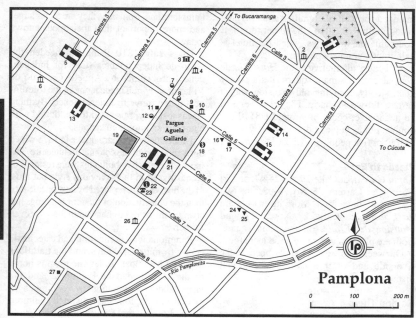

**Pamplona**

0    100    200 m

about 30 works by Eduardo Ramírez Villamizar, one of Colombia's most outstanding artists, who was born in Pamplona in 1923. The collection gives a good insight into his artistic development from expressionist painting of the 1940s to geometric abstract sculpture in recent decades. The museum is open Tuesday to Friday from 9 am to noon and 2 to 6 pm, Saturday and Sunday from 9 am to 6 pm. Admission is US$0.70 (US$0.40 for students).

**Museo Arquidiocesano de Arte Religioso**
This museum has an interesting display of religious art, comprising paintings, statues, altarpieces and the like, collected from the region. It's open Monday to Saturday from 10 am to noon and 3 to 5 pm, Sunday from 10 am to noon. Entry costs US$0.40.

**Casa Anzoátegui** This beautiful, restored colonial house, at Carrera 6 No 7-48, is named after General José Antonio Anzoátegui, the

Venezuelan hero of the independence campaign, who fought under Bolívar and whose strategic abilities largely contributed to the victory in the Battle of Boyacá. He died in this house on 15 November 1819, at the age of 30 years. The house has recently been turned into a museum presenting a modest collection of arms and other exhibits related to the crucial historical events of the period. It's open daily from 9 am to noon and 2 to 5.30 pm.

**Casa Colonial** This fair-sized mansion built around an ample patio, at Calle 6 No 2-56, has also been converted into a museum. The collection includes pre-Columbian pottery, colonial sacred art, artefacts of the Motilones and Tunebos (the two Indian groups living in Norte de Santander department) plus a variety of antiques, old photos and banknotes. The museum is open Tuesday to Sunday from 8 am to noon and 2 to 6 pm; admission is US$0.30.

**PLACES TO STAY**

9   Hotel Orsúa
11  Hotel Imperial
17  Hotel El Álamo
21  Hotel Lincoln
27  Hotel Cariongo

**PLACES TO EAT**

16  Restaurante y Tienda Vegetariana
24  Restaurante La Casona
25  Restaurante El Portón de la
     Frontera

**OTHER**

1   Iglesia del Humilladero
2   Museo Fotográfico
3   Casa de las Cajas Reales
4   Museo Arquidiocesano
    de Arte Religioso
5   Iglesia del Carmen
6   Casa Colonial
7   Copetrán
8   Cotranal
10  Museo de Arte Moderno
    Ramírez Villamizar
12  Extra Rápido Los Motilones
13  Iglesia de las Clarisas
14  Iglesia de San José
15  Iglesia de Santo Domingo
18  Banco de Bogotá
19  Market
20  Catedral
22  Tourist Office
23  Telecom
26  Casa Anzoátegui

**Casa de las Cajas Reales** Yet another colonial building, on the corner of Carrera 5 and Calle 6, this casa is today the office of SENA (Servicio Nacional de Aprendizaje), a national training institution. You can enter and have a look at its patio and a sculpture by Ramírez Villamizar.

**Museo Fotográfico** A curiosity rather than a museum, this house at Carrera 7 No 2-44 has a hotchpotch of old photos. It also operates as a funeral parlour so don't be put off by a collection of coffins at the entrance.

**Churches**

There are perhaps 10 old churches and chapels in the town centre, reflecting Pamplona's religious status in the colonial days, though not many of them have preserved their past splendour.

The 17th-century **Catedral** was extensively damaged in the earthquake of 1875 and altered in the reconstruction. The wide, five-nave interior (the two outer aisles were added in the beginning of the present century) is rather austere except for the magnificent main retable which somehow survived the disaster. It was made in two stages, in 1628 and 1795. The central figure of San Pedro was made in Spain in 1618.

The **Iglesia del Humilladero**, at the entrance to the cemetery, boasts the famous Cristo del Humilladero, an impressively realistic sculpture of Christ brought from Spain in the 17th century. The **Iglesia de Santo Domingo** has a fine doorway but it's not very interesting inside.

**Festivals & Cultural Events**

The town is known nationwide for its solemn Holy Week celebrations (the week before Easter Sunday). Another important annual event is the Fiestas del Grito de Independencia, also called the Fiestas de Pamplona. The feast is celebrated for about two weeks preceding 4 July, and features a variety of activities, including concerts, exhibitions, bullfights and – never to be missed on such occasions – the beauty pageant.

**Places to Stay**

The *Hotel Orsúa* (☎ 682470), on the main square, is one of the cheapest places to stay, but it's rather basic. Rooms without/with private bath go for US$3.50/4 per person. Appreciably better is the *Hotel El Álamo* (☎ 682137), at Calle 5 No 6-68. Singles/doubles with own bath and hot water in the morning cost US$5.50/8.

The *Hotel Lincoln* (☎ 682056), next to the cathedral, offers reasonable rooms with private bath and hot water for US$6/10 a single/double. Much the same is the *Hotel Imperial* (☎ 682571), also on the main plaza.

*Hotel Cariongo* (☎ 681515, 681100), on the corner of Calle 9 and Carrera 5, two blocks south-west of the plaza, is Pamplona's top-end accommodation, at US$20/25 a single/double.

## Places to Eat

There are quite a number of restaurants scattered throughout the central area. Some of the cheapest set meals can be had in the restaurant of *Hotel Orsúa*, which is as simple as the hotel itself. As almost everywhere in the country, the market serves cheap local food.

For cheap vegetarian meals (but only between noon and around 1.30 pm) go to *Restaurante y Tienda Vegetariana*, at Calle 5 No 6-60.

*Restaurante La Casona*, at Calle 6 No 7-58, has quite good, reasonably priced food, and is probably a bit better than *Restaurante El Portón de la Frontera* next door.

Possibly the best food, though also the most expensive, is served in the restaurant of the *Hotel Cariongo*.

## Getting There & Away

Pamplona sits on the Bucaramanga-Cúcuta road, and buses pass by regularly to both of these destinations. Climatizados to Bucaramanga cost US$5 and take 4½ hours, while to Cúcuta they cost US$3 and take 1½ hours.

Two colectivo companies, Extra Rápido Los Motilones and Cotranal, both on the main plaza, operate shared taxis to Bucaramanga (US$6, 3½ hours) and Cúcuta (U$3.50, 1½ hours).

## CÚCUTA

• *pop 520,000* • *320 m* • *27°C* • ☎ *(975)*

The capital of Norte de Santander, Cúcuta was founded in 1733 but completely destroyed by the earthquake of 1875. The town was rebuilt from the ground up, and in the 100 years since has evolved into a busy commercial city influenced by its proximity to Venezuela, with a modern centre and vast suburbs. The climate is hot and dry.

Unless you're travelling to or from Vene-zuela, there's little reason to come here as the city doesn't have any significant tourist attractions. If you happen to pass through, you may want to visit the nearby Villa del Rosario (see the following section).

Note that there's one hour's time difference between Colombia and Venezuela. Move your watch one hour forward when crossing from Colombia into Venezuela.

## Information

**Tourist Office** The tourist office (☎ 713395) is at Calle 10 No 0-30. It's open Monday to Friday from 8 am to noon and 2 to 6 pm.

**Money** At the time of writing, no banks in Cúcuta were interested in changing cash dollars, and only the Banco del Estado and Banco Industrial Colombiano would change travellers' cheques. Other banks marked on the map may give advances on Visa or MasterCard.

There are plenty of casas de cambio, at the bus terminal and in the city centre. They will change dollars, Colombian pesos and Venezuelan bolívares. There's also a rash of casas de cambio in San Antonio del Táchira (the Venezuelan border town), paying much the same as in Cúcuta.

**Venezuelan Consulate** The Venezuelan consulate is on the corner of Calle 8 and Avenida 0. The office is officially open Monday to Friday from 8 am to 3 pm but it closes for almuerzo. Regardless of your nationality, you do need a visa for an overland crossing into Venezuela.

This seems to be the only Venezuelan consulate in Colombia which issues tourist visas for non-Colombians. It usually gives visas valid for a 30-day stay, but this seems to be up to the whim of the officials. All other Venezuelan consulates in Colombia (and perhaps in other South American countries) can only issue a 72-hour transit visa, which cannot be extended no matter what the consulate tells you. The only viable alternative is to fly into Venezuela, in which case you'll automatically be granted the 60-day tourist card issued by the airline. There are direct flights to Venezuela from Cartagena, Medellín and Bogotá, but not from Cúcuta.

To get your visa in Cúcuta, you need your passport and one photo, and you have to fill in a form. The visa costs US$30. You may be lucky enough to get it the same afternoon but start queuing early, as you have to pay the fee at the bank (not at the consulate), and this can only be done before 11 am.

**Immigration** DAS (where you have to get an exit/entry stamp in your passport) has three offices in the area. The city's main office is at Avenida 1 No 28-57, in the suburb of San Rafael, across the city from the bus terminal. The office is theoretically open daily from 8 am to noon and 2 to 8 pm. To get there, take the city bus marked 'San Rafael', or a taxi. Taxi drivers wait at the bus terminal for incoming tourists, to take them to the DAS office and then straight to the DIEX (the Venezuelan counterpart of DAS) office in San Antonio del Táchira, for a fat fare, naturally.

There's another, more convenient DAS office right on the border, about half a km before San Antonio. It's open daily from 7.30 am to noon and 2 to 6.30 pm. By stamping your passport here, you avoid the side trip to the San Rafael office.

There's also a DAS office at Cúcuta airport, but you can only have your passport stamped there if you fly into Cúcuta and head straight to Venezuela.

The DIEX has its office in San Antonio, on Carrera 9, between Calles 6 and 7; it's supposed to be open daily from 6 am to 9 pm. This is where you have your passport stamped when leaving or entering Venezuela. There's also a DIEX office at San Antonio airport, but it only seems to be open around incoming and outgoing flights, and even then not always.

### Things to See
The **Museo de Arte e Historia de Cúcuta**, at Calle 14 No 1-03, is just about the only real place of tourist interest. It opened in 1987 in a well-restored old house and features an extensive private collection of documents and objects relating to the town's history. You can see photos of the devastation caused by the earthquake of 1875 and learn about many foreign inventions which reached Cúcuta (through Maracaibo) earlier than elsewhere in Colombia. The museum also has a small collection of paintings by national artists. It's open Tuesday to Saturday from 8 am to noon and 2 to 6 pm.

The **Casa de la Cultura**, at Calle 13 No 3-67, was being thoroughly restored when this book was researched, but may be open by the time you come. It will probably stage temporary exhibitions, as it used to.

### Places to Stay – bottom end
There are plenty of residencias around the bus terminal, particularly along Avenida 7, but they range from basic to ultra-basic. Most double as love hotels, and some are genuine brothels. The area is far from attractive and gets dangerous at night. The only positive comment which can be made about these hotels is that they are cheap, and you can find a single/double for less than US$3/4. The *Hotel Casa Real* (☎ 728932), at Avenida 7 No 4-45, is one of the few acceptable places. Doubles with bath and fan go for US$4.50.

It's safer and much more pleasant to stay in the city centre, though the hotels here are not as cheap. All those listed below have rooms with fan and private bath. Among the cheapest, at US$4/6 for a single/double, are the *Hotel Central* (☎ 713673), on the corner of Avenida 5 and Calle 9, and the *Hotel Su Familia* (☎ 710354), at Avenida 3 No 11-41. For a dollar more, you have a range of fairly decent places, including the *Hotel La Bastilla* (☎ 712576) at Avenida 3 No 9-42, *Hotel Daytona* (☎ 717927) at Avenida 5 No 8-57, and perhaps the best for that price, *Hotel Colonial* (☎ 712661) at Avenida 5 No 8-62.

### Places to Stay – middle
If you are prepared to pay US$7/13 for a single/double, there's possibly nothing better in town than the *Hotel Internacional* (☎ 712718), on Calle 14 No 4-13, which has

NORTE DE SANTANDER

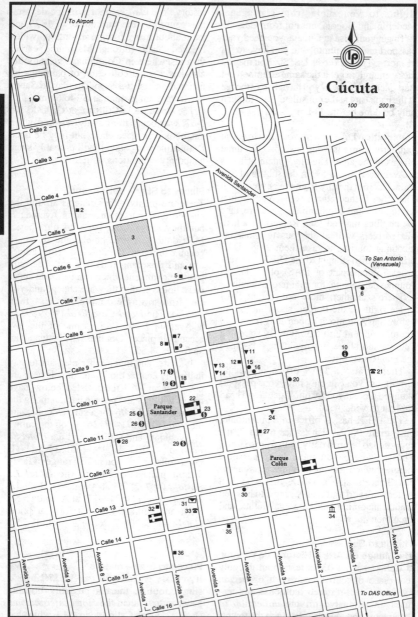

Cúcuta

0    100    200 m

To Airport

Calle 2

Calle 3

Calle 4

Avenida Santander

Calle 5

3

Calle 6

To San Antonio
(Venezuela)

4

5

6

Calle 7

Calle 8

7

8    9

11

Calle 9

13    12    15

14        16

10

17

19    18

21

20

Parque
Santander

22

23

25

26

24

Calle 11

28

27

29

Parque
Colón

Calle 12

30

Calle 13

31

32    33

34

35

Calle 14

36

Calle 15

Avenida 10

Avenida 9

Avenida 8

Calle 16

Avenida 7

Avenida 6

Avenida 5

Avenida 4

Avenida 3

Avenida 2

Avenida 1

Avenida 0

To DAS Office

## PLACES TO STAY

| | |
|---|---|
| 2 | Hotel Casa Real |
| 5 | Hotel Don Paco |
| 7 | Hotel Daytona |
| 8 | Hotel Colonial |
| 9 | Hotel Central |
| 12 | Hotel La Bastilla |
| 18 | Hotel Amaruc |
| 27 | Hotel Su Familia |
| 32 | Hotel Louis |
| 35 | Hotel Internacional |
| 36 | Hotel Casa Blanca |

## PLACES TO EAT

| | |
|---|---|
| 4 | Restaurante Vegetariano Salud y Vida |
| 11 | Restaurante Don Pancho |
| 13 | Restaurante Doña Pepa |
| 14 | Restaurante La Mazorca |
| 24 | Restaurante Mi Cabaña |

## OTHER

| | |
|---|---|
| 1 | Bus Terminal |
| 3 | Market |
| 6 | Venezuelan Consulate |
| 10 | Tourist Office |
| 15 | Intercontinental de Aviación |
| 16 | Sam |
| 17 | Banco del Estado |
| 19 | Banco de Colombia |
| 20 | Aces |
| 21 | Telecom (Main Office) |
| 22 | Catedral |
| 23 | Banco de Occidente |
| 25 | Banco Industrial Colombiano |
| 26 | Banco de Bogotá |
| 28 | Satena |
| 29 | Banco Popular |
| 30 | Casa de la Cultura |
| 31 | Avianca (Airline & Post Offices) |
| 33 | Telecom |
| 34 | Museo de Arte e Historia de Cúcuta |

spacious, clean rooms, a fine patio and a swimming pool.

If you need somewhere with air-con at a reasonable price, choose between the *Hotel Louis* (☎ 730598), at the corner of Avenida 6 and Calle 13, and *Hotel Don Paco* (☎ 731902), at Calle 7 No 4-44. Both cost

around US$10/14; the latter is more pleasant, but the surrounding area isn't.

### Places to Stay – top end
The *Hotel Amaruc* (☎ 717625), overlooking the main square from the corner of Avenida 5 and Calle 10, and the *Hotel Casa Blanca* (☎ 721455), at Avenida 6 No 14-55, are options for those who don't need to count every peso. Both have good singles/doubles with air-con for US$25/32. In both hotels, ask for a room on one of the upper floors.

### Places to Eat
There are several cheap restaurants around the corner of Calle 9 and Avenida 6, but they are not terrific. Better set meals, and local specialities, are served at *Restaurante Doña Pepa*, at Avenida 4 No 9-59, or next door at *Restaurante La Mazorca*. The *Restaurante Don Pancho*, at Avenida 3 No 9-21, does good parrillada and cabrito al vino at reasonable prices.

For vegetarians, the *Restaurante Vegetariano Salud y Vida*, on Avenida 4, is the budget place to go, while the pleasant restaurant on the top floor of the *Hotel Amaruc* has vegetarian food at more up-market prices.

*Restaurante Mi Cabaña*, at Calle 11 No 2-53, is one of the best restaurants in town, noted particularly for its churrasco and róbalo.

### Getting There & Away
**Air – within Colombia** The airport is five km north of the city centre. Urban buses, which you catch on Avenida 3 in the centre, will drop you nearby.

Domestic flights to and from Cúcuta are handled by almost all major Colombian airlines. They all have offices in the city centre; their locations are marked on the map.

There are flights to most major Colombian cities, including Bogotá (US$83 with Avianca and Sam, US$82 with Aces, US$59 with Satena, US$58 with Intercontinental); Medellín (US$78 with Avianca, Sam and Aces); Bucaramanga (US$34 with Avianca); San Andrés (US$142 with Avianca and Sam); Pereira (US$115 with Sam and Aces,

NORTE DE SANTANDER

US$88 with Intercontinental); Santa Marta (US$81 with Sam); and Riohacha (US$88 with Intercontinental).

**Air – to Venezuela** There are no direct flights to Venezuela – you must go to San Antonio. San Antonio's airport is two km north of town, accessible by local colectivos. From San Antonio, there are four flights a day to Caracas (US$72 with Avensa, US$68 with Aeropostal), one to Mérida (US$34) and one to Maracaibo (US$51).

## Getting There & Away

**Bus – within Colombia** The bus terminal is on the corner of Avenida 7 and Calle 1. It's very dirty and very busy – one of the poorest in Colombia. Watch your belongings closely.

All the routes listed below pass over the Cordillera Oriental and are very spectacular; daytime travel is recommended.

**To Bogotá** Copetrán and Berlinas del Fonce have at least a dozen air-con buses daily (US$24, 16 hours).

**To Bucaramanga** Buses operated by Copetrán and Berlinas del Fonce depart regularly throughout the day (US$8 climatizado, US$7 pullman, six hours). There are also taxi colectivos with Extra Rápido Los Motilones, departing every half an hour to one hour (US$9.50, five hours).

**To Ocaña** There are about six buses daily with Trans Peralonso (US$6, eight hours).

You may be approached by well-dressed English-speaking characters who will offer to help you buy a bus ticket (particularly if you've come from Venezuela). Ignore them – they are conmen. Buy your ticket directly from the bus company office. Read this story sent by a traveller:

There's a very well-organised and efficient gang of conmen working at the bus terminal; they've been operating with impunity for so long it's frightening. Upon arrival you're approached and asked if you want to buy a bus ticket, which of course you do, and you're led to a small office which you take to be the bus ticketing office. A ticket is issued (though they actually just go round the corner to buy it from the official people); you are then told that the bus company has an insurance scheme for your money, since so many buses have been robbed. There's a huge record book of people's names, signatures, nationalities, and the amount of money each had, so the whole thing appears completely genuine. After showing your money (feeling completely safe because you think you're in the bus company office), it's given back to you in a white plastic bag which, as instructed, you place in your shoe ('for security'). While my money was being placed in the bag then was a slight distraction which caused me to momentarily look away; in this moment half the money was moved away. I lost nearly US$100 and since I was halfway to Bogotá by the time I realised, there was nothing I could do. They even had the audacity to overcharge for the bus ticket by altering the price. Having just arrived in the country I was unfamiliar with the currency, and so paid up without realising how expensive it was. The head conman speaks fluent English and is a real charmer; one of his henchmen also speaks some English.

**Bus – to Venezuela** Cúcuta lies about 12 km from the Venezuelan frontier on the Río Táchira. Just past the bridge over the river is the Venezuelan border town, San Antonio del Táchira.

There are no direct buses from Cúcuta to Caracas; you need to go to San Antonio from where you can easily proceed further into Venezuela. Plenty of buses and shared taxis run from Cúcuta's bus terminal to San Antonio (US$0.30 and US$0.50 respectively, paid in either pesos or bolívares).

Don't forget to get off just before the bridge to get your exit stamp from DAS (if you haven't done it in the Cúcuta office), and then walk the remaining half a km over the bridge to San Antonio. Be careful when walking, as some cases of robbery have been reported. The favourite scam is that someone 'accidentally' bumps you, throwing you off balance, your backpack is meanwhile torn off and thrown over the barrier down from the bridge, where accomplices take care of it. It's perhaps better to take another bus from the DAS office to San Antonio. Make sure to pay a visit to DIEX in San Antonio.

San Antonio has no central bus terminal; each company has its own office. They are all close to each other on or just off Carrera 4. Four companies – Expresos Mérida, Expresos Los Llanos, Expresos Alianza and Expresos San Cristóbal – operate buses to Caracas, with a total of seven buses daily. All depart in the late afternoon or early evening and all go via the El Llano route, reaching their destination in about 14 hours. The ordinary fare is US$15. Los Llanos and Mérida also have air-con buses for US$16.50.

There are no direct buses to Mérida; go to San Cristóbal and change. Colectivos to San Cristóbal leave frequently from Calle 5 (US$1, one hour).

## VILLA DEL ROSARIO
Villa del Rosario, a town 10 km from Cúcuta on the road to the Venezuelan border at San Antonio, played an important role in Colombia's history. It was here, in 1821, that the so-called Congress of Cúcuta drew up and passed the constitution of Gran Colombia.

Gran Colombia, the union of Venezuela, Colombia (then Nueva Granada) and Ecuador, was brought to life in Angostura (today Ciudad Bolívar in Venezuela) in 1819. It was largely a concept of Simón Bolívar, who insisted on creating a strong, centralised republic made up of the provinces he was liberating. In practice this didn't happen; Gran Colombia was, since its birth, a weak, vast state incapable of being governed by a central regime. It gradually disintegrated before splitting into three separate countries in 1830. Bolívar's dream came to an end before he died.

Apart from its historical importance, Villa del Rosario is a rapidly developing recreational tourist centre.

### Things to See
The site where the constitution was signed has been converted into a park. It embraces some old buildings which witnessed the historic event and a few monuments erected since. The most important places are described below.

**Casa de Santander** This large country house was the birthplace of Francisco de Paula Santander and his home for the first 13 years of his life. The house was damaged by the earthquake of 1875 and restored in a partly altered style. It now houses a museum

displaying some documents and photos relating to Santander's life and to the Congress. It's open daily from 8 am to noon and 2 to 6 pm.

**Templo del Congreso** This is the church (erected in 1802) where the sessions of the Congress were held. The Congress was installed on 6 May and debated in the sacristy of the church until 14 October, only then agreeing on the final version of the bill. Also in this church, the inauguration ceremonies of Bolívar and Santander as president and vice-president of Gran Colombia took place on 3 October.

The church was almost completely destroyed by the earthquake of 1875, and although some efforts were made to reconstruct it, only the dome was rebuilt (in quite a different style from the original). A marble statue of Bolívar has been placed in the rebuilt part of the church.

**Casa de la Bagatela** This old house, just across the road from the Templo, has been confusingly named after a revolutionary newspaper, *La Bagatela*, founded in 1812 in Bogotá by Antonio Nariño. The house actually served as a government seat and a vice-presidential residence. It, too, suffered from the earthquake. Today it houses a collection of pre-Columbian pottery from various regions. It's open Tuesday to Saturday from 8 am to noon and 2 to 6 pm, Sunday from 9 am to 1 pm.

### Getting There & Away
Frequent city buses and colectivos shuttling between Cúcuta's terminal and San Antonio pass next to the park and the historic buildings.

## OCAÑA
• *pop 55,000* • *1200 m* • *22°C* • ☎ *(974)*
Ocaña is mainly known to Colombians for the Convention of Ocaña, the assembly held here in 1828, during which separatist tendencies came to the fore that largely contributed to the dissolution of Gran Colombia two years later.

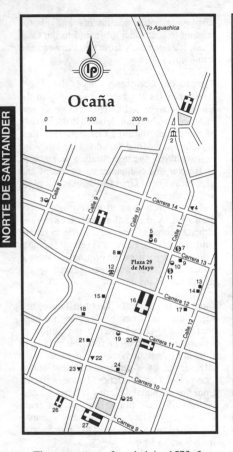

Ocaña

**PLACES TO STAY**

| | |
|---|---|
| 5 | Hotel Los Estoraques |
| 8 | Hotel Hacaritama |
| 9 | Hotel Sevilla |
| 14 | Hotel Real |
| 15 | Hotel Astoria |
| 17 | Hotel Vicamor |
| 18 | Hotel El Viajero |
| 21 | Hotel Atlántico |
| 24 | Hotel Rincón Colonial |

**PLACES TO EAT**

| | |
|---|---|
| 4 | Yalon's Pizza |
| 22 | Daniel's Restaurante |
| 23 | Restaurante El Faraón |

**OTHER**

| | |
|---|---|
| 1 | Iglesia de San Agustín |
| 2 | Casa de la Cultura |
| 3 | Colectivos to La Playa |
| 6 | Cootransunidos |
| 7 | Banco de Bogotá |
| 10 | Cooperativa de Transportadores Hacaritama |
| 11 | Banco de Colombia |
| 12 | Telecom |
| 13 | Aces |
| 16 | Catedral |
| 19 | Omega |
| 20 | Copetrán |
| 25 | Trans Peralonso |
| 26 | Iglesia de Santa Rita |
| 27 | Iglesia de San Francisco |

The town was founded in 1572 from Pamplona and prospered during the Spanish times. Today, however, little remains from the colonial era, apart from a few churches and a handful of other buildings. These alone probably wouldn't justify a special trip to Ocaña. But there is Los Estoraques, the fascinating rock formations nearby, for which the town is the most convenient base (see the following section).

**Things to See**

The **Catedral** on the main square, Plaza 29 de Mayo, has a fine façade and an unusual bell tower, and it's worth visiting for the interesting retable over the high altar. This is the only church open regularly during the daytime.

While you are on the main plaza, have a look at the **Columna de Los Esclavos** in the middle of the square. This column was raised in 1851 to commemorate the abolition of slavery in Colombia, though in many regions slavery continued well into the present century.

The **Iglesia de San Agustín**, on the corner of Calle 10 and Carrera 15A, dates from about 1596. Its interior lacks decoration but have a look at the wooden ceiling, a good example of the style of construction commonly used at that time.

Opposite the church, at Calle 11 No 15-97, is the **Casa de la Cultura**. This colonial house has been converted into a historical museum displaying a modest collection of mostly religious artefacts. The museum is open Monday to Friday from 2 to 6 pm, Saturday from 2.30 to 5 pm.

The **Iglesia de San Francisco**, on the corner of Calle 11 and Carrera 9, is currently closed for restoration. It was here that the Convention meetings were held in 1828.

### Places to Stay – bottom end

Ocaña has lots of hotels throughout the town centre. The residencias in the market area, around the corner of Calle 8 and Carrera 14, are not attractive, nor is the area itself. It's better to stay in the vicinity of Plaza 29 de Mayo.

The cheapest basic places near the plaza include the *Hotel Astoria*, at Calle 10 No 11-47, which has matrimonios and doubles without bath at US$3 for either, and the *Hotel Atlántico*, at Calle 10 No 10-49, offering singles/doubles/triples without bath for US$2/3/4, and rooms with private baths for a dollar more. One more bottom-end place, the *Hotel Los Estoraques*, is right on the main square, at the back of the Cootransunidos office, at Carrera 13 No 10-51. Doubles without/with bath cost US$3/4.

Probably the best bet among the cheapies is the *Hotel El Viajero*, at Carrera 11 No 9-17, which has clean and quiet doubles without/with bath for US$4/5.

The *Hotel Sevilla*, at Carrera 13 No 11-16 just off the main plaza, has a variety of rooms of different standards, some of them separated by only thin hardboard partitions. Doubles without/with bath go for US$4/5 but be sure to have a look at the room before you book in.

The *Hotel Rincón Colonial* (☎ 622252), at Carrera 10 No 10-79, is probably not worth the US$4/5/6 for a single/double/triple.

Appreciably better than all the above is the *Hotel Vicamor* (☎ 622702), at Carrera 12 No 11-64. It doesn't look very attractive from the outside but it has good, large singles/doubles/triples with bath for US$8/12/14.

### Places to Stay – middle & top end

The *Hotel Real* (☎ 622740), at Calle 12 No 12-39, looks more impressive from the street than it is inside. The rooms are adequate but rather small and cost US$14/20/23/27 for singles/doubles/triples/quad.

The *Hotel Hacaritama* (☎ 625232), on the main plaza at Calle 10 No 12-57, is the best place in town, for US$24/32 a single/double. Rooms are equipped with satellite TV and fridge, and there's a swimming pool for guests.

### Places to Eat

Almost all hotels listed above have their own restaurants, whose value and price roughly correspond to the class of the hotel. Accordingly, the cheapies will keep you going with comida corriente for about US$1.50, while the *Hotel Hacaritama* has one of the best restaurants in town.

There are also plenty of self-contained restaurants in the town's centre. Those worthy of a mention include the inexpensive *Restaurante El Faraón*, at Calle 10 No 9-63, set around a beautiful patio, and *Yalon's Pizza* on the corner of Calle 11 and Carrera 14, which serves unpretentious but tasty pizzas until 10 pm. *Daniel's Restaurante*, at Calle 10 No 10-06, is a rather nondescript place that has good mute on Sunday.

### Getting There & Away

Ocaña has no bus terminal. Buses arrive at and depart from the bus company offices scattered throughout the central area.

**To Aguachica** Frequent colectivos to Aguachica, on the main Bogotá-Barranquilla road, depart from the plaza (US$2.75, 1½ hours). From Aguachica there are plenty of buses going north and south.

**To Cúcuta** There are about half a dozen departures a day with Trans Peralonso, Calle 11 No 9-48. The trip costs US$6, and takes eight hours on a partly unpaved road but the scenery is magnificent. There are also colectivos operated by Cootransunidos, Carrera 13 No 10-51, on the main square (US$10, six hours).

**To Bucaramanga** There are three buses with Copetrán, on the corner of Carrera 11 and Calle 11, and another three with Omega, Carrera 11 No 10-46 (US$8.25, five hours). Cootransunidos, on the main square, has colectivos every hour or two (US$9.75, 4½ hours).

**To Bogotá** Omega has three buses a day and Copetrán another two (US$24, 15 hours).

**To La Playa** Colectivos leave in the morning from the market area, on the corner of Calle 8 and Carrera 13 (US$1.40, one hour).

## LOS ESTORAQUES

Los Estoraques are a group of intriguing rock formations caused by erosion. The rocks stretch along the dirt road to the village of La Playa, which branches off from the Ocaña-Cúcuta road 16 km from Ocaña. The most breathtaking scenery is just beyond the village. Walk about 500 metres along the road and turn to the left where you will see a stream (often dry in summer). Shortly afterwards you will enter a maze of rocks – some of which are up to 100 metres high – that bring to mind medieval castles. It's a very impressive sight.

### Getting There & Away

Colectivos leave from the market in Ocaña mostly in the morning (US$1.40, one hour). Come early as there are no residencias in La Playa and the last colectivo back to Ocaña leaves from La Playa around 2 pm.

# Caribbean Coast

The Colombian Caribbean coast extends over 1600 km from the dense jungles of the Darién in the west, on the Panamanian border, to the desert of La Guajira in the east, near Venezuela. El Caribe, or La Costa, as the Caribbean region is locally known, stretches to the south up to the foot of the Andes. Administratively, the area falls into seven departments: La Guajira, Cesar, Magdalena, Atlántico, Bolívar, Sucre and Córdoba. The northern parts of Chocó and Antioquia are also included in this chapter as they belong geographically to the Caribbean coast.

The Colombian Caribbean coast was inhabited long before Columbus crossed the Atlantic. Two major Indian groups evolved into highly developed cultures: the Tayrona in the Sierra Nevada de Santa Marta, and the Sinú in what are now the Córdoba and Sucre departments. Neither of the two cultures survived the Spanish conquest, but other Indian groups – either descendants or migrants – today live in the region: the Cunas (or Kunas) in the north-western tip of the coast (though most of them live in Panama), the Kogis and Arhuacos in the Sierra Nevada de Santa Marta and the Guajiros (or Wayú) in La Guajira.

The coast was the first region conquered by the Spaniards. Santa Marta (founded in 1525) and Cartagena (1533) are the oldest Colombian cities still in existence. Halfway between them sits Barranquilla, which is much more recent. It's the largest city of El Caribe and Colombia's biggest port.

The coastline is not, as local brochures suggest, 'an endless ribbon of golden beaches shaded by coconut groves', but there are some amazing sand stretches. The loveliest beaches are probably in the Parque Nacional Tayrona, though those around Cabo de la Vela in La Guajira and Sapzurro on the Golfo de Urabá are not bad either.

Parts of the coast are bordered by coral reefs. There are five main coral reef areas: the north and middle of La Guajira, some bays of the Parque Nacional Tayrona, the

north-east of the Golfo de Morrosquillo, the western coast of the Golfo de Urabá and the Islas del Rosario. The latter are the largest and by far the most magnificent, comparable to those in San Andrés and Providencia.

El Caribe has a lot more to offer than just beaches and reefs. Here is the unique Sierra Nevada de Santa Marta, the tallest coastal mountain range in the world, topped by Colombia's highest peaks. Hidden deep in the lush tropical forest on the slopes of the Sierra Nevada is Ciudad Perdida, the lost city of the Tayronas, the Colombian Machu Picchu.

The coast has one of Latin America's most beautiful colonial cities, Cartagena. Away from the coastline is another small gem of old architecture, the town of Mompós.

The region has seven national parks, of which the Parque Nacional Tayrona is the most popular among foreign visitors. If you prefer somewhere less invaded by tourists, try the Parque Nacional Los Katíos, which is one of the loveliest Colombian nature reserves.

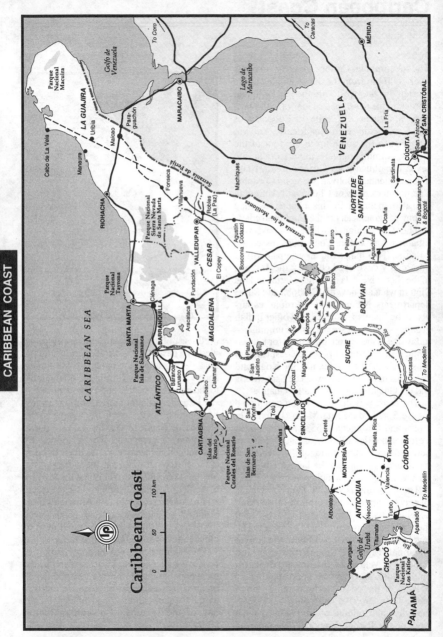

Other highlights of the coast include the mud volcanoes in Arboletes and near Barranquilla, flamingos near Manaure, the Arhuacos' fairy-tale town of Nabusímake, the arid bay of Taganga and the Islas de San Bernardo, to list just a few.

The coast is steeped in sun, rum and tropical music. Its inhabitants, the costeños (predominantly mulattos), are lively, energy-filled, fun-loving folks with much of the hot African spirit who give the coast a carnival atmosphere. El Caribe stages what is generally acclaimed as the most colourful and wild Colombian feast, the Carnaval de Barranquilla. The Festival de la Leyenda Vallenata in Valledupar and the Festival de Música del Caribe in Cartagena are not far behind.

# Cesar

## VALLEDUPAR

• *pop 250,000* • *170 m* • *27° C* • ☎ *(955)*

Valledupar is the capital of Cesar, the only Caribbean department that doesn't touch the coastline, but it lies within the coastal plains and is close enough to the coast to be considered a part of El Caribe.

Neither the department nor its capital offer much to tourists. It is an important cattle and cotton region, for which Valledupar is the major centre. It's just a hot, dusty and busy city. It was founded in 1550 but don't expect to find much here of the past.

You may wish to come here if you are a fan of vallenato music and want to attend the local festival, or you plan on hiking into the Sierra Nevada de Santa Marta.

## Information

**Tourist Office** The tourist office (☎ 730271, 732272) is in the Casa de la Cultura, on the corner of Carrera 6 and Calle 16A. It is open Monday to Friday from 8 am to 12.45 pm and 2.45 to 5.45 pm.

**Money** Most major banks are close to each other in the city centre; their location has been marked on the map. The Banco Indus-

trial Colombiano and Banco Popular may change cash and travellers' cheques, but not always.

There are several casas de cambio in the same area, particularly on Calle 16 between Carreras 8 and 9. They are open until 5 or 6 pm on weekdays and until noon on Saturday, and change cash at a rate slightly lower than banks, but they don't accept travellers' cheques.

## Things to See

There are still several colonial houses on and around the Plaza Alfonso López Pumarejo, the main square named after one of the Colombian presidents. On the same square is the oldest city church, the **Iglesia de la Concepción**, which has a fine main retable and a side retable, in similar style, in each aisle.

Possibly the most interesting attraction in the city is the **Museo Arqueológico**, in the Escuela de Bellas Artes, on Calle 15 near the corner of Carrera 12. Its collection of pottery of the indigenous peoples from the region, and includes some marvellous funeral urns of the Chimila, the community once living south-west of Valledupar, on the border of the present-day Magdalena department. The museum is open Monday to Friday from 8 am to 12.30 pm and 2.30 to 5.30 pm.

## Festival de la Leyenda Vallenata

This festival, the main annual event of Valledupar, is celebrated between 27 and 30 April. On these days the town blasts out with vallenato, a local kind of music which has its origins in Cesar and La Guajira and is now popular all over Colombia. Vallenato is usually sung and accompanied by a small band of three or four instruments. The accordion and the *guacharaca* (a percussion instrument) are central elements of this music.

The best known vallenato musicians include Alfredo Gutiérrez, Alejo Durán and Nicolás 'Colacho' Mendoza. If you want to hear the roots of vallenato, look for the records or CDs of Rafael Escalona, one of the originators of the style. Also, get a CD of the group Bovea y sus Vallenatos, which has

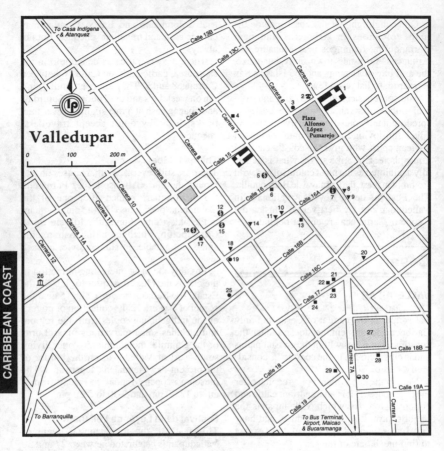

some beautiful, classic vallenatos. If you are interested in what is going on with this musical style today, listen to the music of Carlos Vives, who has introduced some new elements into the genre. His music is based on the original rhythms, but has quite a different sound. His recordings are currently the top sellers on the local market.

### Places to Stay – bottom end

The cheapest residencias are near the market, particularly on Carrera 7 between Calles 18B and 19A. However, the area is frequented by prostitutes who use some of the basic hotels.

One of the cheapest places that is not a brothel is the super-basic *Residencias Tequendama*, at Calle 18B No 7-27. It costs US$1.50 per person in rooms without bath.

One of the better hotels in the market area is the *Hotel Majestad*, at Carrera 8 No 18-82. It has fairly acceptable singles/doubles/triples for US$5/6/8.

Towards the north, or the city centre proper, the price of accommodation rises. About the cheapest in this area is the *Hotel Roma*, at Calle 16 No 7-23. The rooms are basic but have their own bath and fan, and cost US$5 for a double.

## PLACES TO STAY

| | |
|---|---|
| 4 | Hotel Central |
| 6 | Hotel Roma |
| 13 | Vajamar Hotel |
| 17 | Hotel Sicarare |
| 21 | Apartamentos Duque |
| 22 | Apartamentos Karim |
| 23 | Apartamentos Éxito |
| 24 | Hotel Londres |
| 28 | Residencias Tequendama |
| 29 | Hotel Majestad |

## PLACES TO EAT

| | |
|---|---|
| 8 | Restaurante Bella Isla |
| 9 | Restaurante Típico Mi Viejo Valle |
| 10 | Restaurante El Rancho de Tato |
| 11 | Merendero La Bella |
| 14 | Patacón Pisao |
| 18 | Restaurante Caribe |
| 20 | Restaurante La Pirámide |

## OTHER

| | |
|---|---|
| 1 | Iglesia de la Concepción |
| 2 | Telecom |
| 3 | Aerocorales |
| 5 | Banco de Occidente |
| 7 | Tourist Office & Casa de la Cultura |
| 12 | Banco Popular |
| 15 | Banco de Bogotá |
| 16 | Banco Industrial Colombiano |
| 19 | Intercontinental de Aviación |
| 25 | Avianca |
| 26 | Museo Arqueológico |
| 27 | Market |
| 30 | Colectivos to Pueblo Bello |

Perhaps the best budget bet, and well located, is the *Hotel Central* (☎ 730191), at Carrera 7 No 14-51. It has clean, quiet doubles with bath for US$8.

There are several undistinguished but relatively inexpensive hotels on Calle 17. In ascending order of price and value they are: the *Apartamentos Karim*, at Calle 17 No 7-32 (US$5/7/8 a single/matrimonio/ double); *Hotel Londres*, at Calle 17 No 7A-77 (US$6/8 a couple/double); and *Apartamentos Duque*, at Calle 17 No 7-30 (US$6/10/13 a single/ double/triple). All have private baths.

### Places to Stay – middle & top end

For somewhere with air-con, try the *Apartamentos Éxito* (☎ 732140), at Calle 17 No 7A-19. Comfortable singles/doubles go for US$14/18.

The city's best hotels include the *Vajamar Hotel* (☎ 731125), at Carrera 7 No 16A-30 (US$50/60/70 a single/double/triple); and the *Hotel Sicarare* (☎ 732137), at Carrera 9 No 16-04 (US$55/70 a single/double).

### Places to Eat

The city centre is packed with budget restaurants serving set almuerzos and comidas. They include: *Restaurante Caribe*, at Calle 16A No 8-52; *Merendero La Bella*, at Calle 16A No 7-64; *El Rancho de Tato*, at Calle 16A No 7-44; *Restaurante La Pirámide*, at Calle 17 No 6-54; *Patacón Pisao*, at Carrera 8 No 16-45; *Restaurante Bella Isla*, at Carrera 6 No 16A-25; and *Restaurante Típico Mi Viejo Valle*, at Carrera 6 No 16A-39. The last of the list is probably the best of the lot.

There doesn't seem to be a great choice of stylish, well-appointed restaurants in the city. The restaurants of the *Hotel Sicarare* and the *Hotel Vajamar* are among the best in the central area.

### Getting There & Away

**Air** The airport is five km south of the city centre, on the road to Robles. Take a taxi for US$2, or an urban bus to the bus terminal from where it's a 20-minute walk to the airport terminal.

Avianca (office at Calle 16B No 9-46) flies to Bogotá (US$101) and Riohacha (US$34). Intercontinental de Aviación (Carrera 9 No 16A-03) has flights to Bogotá (US$74), Riohacha (US$27) and Medellín (US$78).

Aerocorales, at Calle 15 No 5-64, is a new regional carrier servicing some of the cities and towns along the coast. It operates flights to Barranquilla (US$39) and Cartagena (US$53), and also used to have flights to Mompós which have been temporarily suspended because of upgrading work to the Mompós airstrip.

CARIBBEAN COAST

**Bus** The new bus terminal is 3.5 km south of the city centre. Urban buses between the centre and the terminal run frequently, or you can take a taxi (US$1.50).

**To Barranquilla** There are plenty of buses with Copetrán, Brasilia, La Costeña and other companies (US$10.25 climatizado, US$9 pullman, five hours).

**To Bucaramanga** Copetrán and Brasilia operate this run (US$16.75 climatizado, US$14.75 pullman, nine hours).

**To Maicao** There are frequent buses with Copetrán, Cootracegua and a few other companies (US$8.25 climatizado, US$7 pullman, four hours).

**To Riohacha** Several buses depart daily (US$8.50 climatizado, US$7.25 pullman, 4½ hours).

**To Pueblo Bello** Jeeps leave from Carrera 7A near the market (US$1.75, 1½ hours). See the Nabusímake section for further details.

# La Guajira

La Guajira is Colombia's north-easternmost department, part of which lies on the Península de la Guajira, the country's largest peninsula. The region is often divided into Alta Guajira (the Upper Guajira, or the peninsula proper) and Baja Guajira (the Lower Guajira, or the mainland part of the department).

Alta Guajira is different from the rest of Colombia in its climate, flora, fauna and people. A large part of the peninsula is semi-desert with occasional cactus-like vegetation. The climate is harsh, hot and dry. The rainfall does not exceed 500 mm per year (less than anywhere else in the country). The region is sparsely inhabited, mostly by the Guajiro Indians.

Most of the Alta Guajira is hardly accessible, as there are no roads, only a maze of sandy jeep trails, and virtually no transport. The region is not safe, and Maicao is particularly noted for its lawlessness. Be careful taking pictures of the Guajiros; they believe that it takes away some of their soul.

**The Guajiros**

The Guajiros (also called Guayú, Wayú or Wayuu after their native-language name) are the largest Indian group in both Colombia and Venezuela. There are about 80,000 of them living in Colombia and another 150,000 over the border in Venezuela. They belong to the Arawak linguistic family. Traditionally they have had a matrilineal society and have been stratified by caste. There has been no central authority. Power was divided among the heads of local clans.

The Guajiros have a subsistence economy based on fishing and goat herding, which forces them into a semi-nomadic way of life in search of fresh pastures. Water was traditionally obtained from *casimbas*, holes in the sand dug by hand.

They live in primitive huts made from thistle, palms and other local plant material. Instead of using furniture they keep everything in sacks hanging from the ceiling and they sleep in *chinchorros*, handmade cotton hammocks. When circumstances require it, they pile their humble goods and chattels on mules and donkeys, and take off for better pastures.

The Guajiro women are much more traditional in their dress than the men. They commonly wear the *manta guajira*, a long, loose-flowing dress, usually in bright colours. Many still paint their faces with *paipa*, a dark-coloured vegetal ointment used as a protection from the sun. The men originally wore the *guayuco*, a small loincloth tied with a belt, but today they mostly wear Western clothes.

The Guajiro Indians are increasingly losing their customs and culture. This is mainly due to the forces of contraband trade and drug trafficking (both well-developed in the region), which offer better opportunities than their austere traditional lifestyle. They have adapted quite easily to some aspects of civilisation such as cars, guns and alcohol. The enormous Cerrejón coal-mining project, which went into operation in the 1980s, has also contributed a great deal to their cultural destruction (or assimilation, if you prefer).

Some remote areas of the peninsula are still almost intact and the people there live the traditional way of life. You might even be lucky enough to witness their well-known dance, the *chichamaya*. ∎

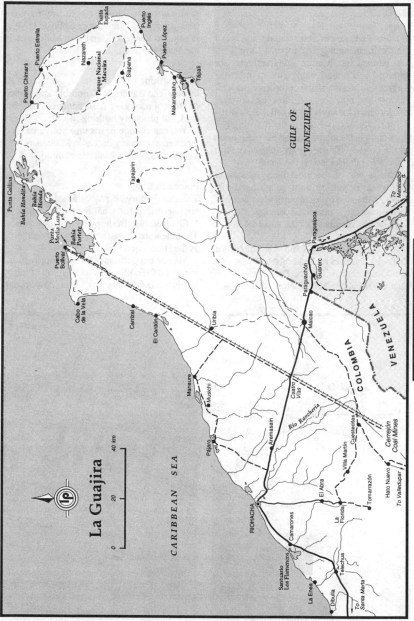

CARIBBEAN COAST

## MAICAO

• *pop 55,000* • *50 m* • *28°C* • ☎ *(954)*

Maicao is a centre of contraband trade and a highly unsafe smugglers' town, 12 km from the Venezuelan border. Most streets are unpaved and unbelievably full of rubbish. Aggressive and intensive commerce goes on indoors and outdoors, and hordes of street vendors hunt for anybody to sell them everything. Trade is very busy in the morning but stops early in the afternoon and the place turns into a cowboy-film set with only adventure seekers and drunks left on the scene.

This is one of the most likely places in Colombia for getting your gear ripped-off. Don't be deluded by local pamphlets describing the town as a 'commercial paradise', 'a show window of Colombia' or 'the supermarket of the world'.

If you are coming from Valledupar or Riohacha and plan on heading north-east into Alta Guajira, get off at the crossroads called Cuatro Vías, about 22 km before Maicao, and

continue on to Uribia (there are frequent pick-up trucks), Manaure or Cabo de la Vela. If going to Venezuela, arrive in Maicao early and leave the same day.

### Information

**Money** The Banco de Colombia and Banco de Bogotá may give peso advances on Visa card, but probably nothing more.

You can change pesos into bolívares (and vice versa) at many hotels in Maicao as well as at the numerous casas de cambio.

### Places to Stay

There are plenty of places to stay but most are overpriced for what they offer and tend to fill up early with shoppers and their goods. The hotels are almost as busy with commerce as the streets outside.

Maicao has permanent water-supply problems, and the common shortcoming of many hotels is a lack of running water. Always ask

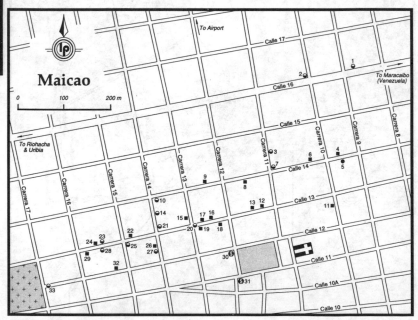

## PLACES TO STAY

| 4 | Hotel Don Blas |
| 6 | Hotel Gallo |
| 8 | Residencias San José |
| 9 | Hotel Avenida |
| 11 | Hotel El Dorado |
| 12 | Hotel Cartagena |
| 13 | Hotel Buenos Aires |
| 15 | Hotel Venecia |
| 16 | Residencias Yolimar |
| 17 | Residencias Colonial |
| 18 | Hotel Helda |
| 19 | Hotel Riohacha |
| 22 | Residencias Oasis |
| 24 | Hotel Latino |
| 26 | Hotel Kacumay |
| 29 | Residencias El Banco |
| 32 | Buen Hotel |

## OTHER

| 1 | Rápido Ochoa |
| 2 | Expreso Brasilia |
| 3 | Transportes Maicao |
| 5 | Maicao Tours |
| 7 | Cootracegua |
| 10 | Unitransco |
| 14 | Expresos Gran Colombia |
| 20 | Colectivos to Riohacha |
| 21 | Coolibertador |
| 23 | Transporte Torcoroma |
| 25 | Cootragua |
| 27 | Agencias Unidas |
| 28 | Copetrán |
| 30 | Banco de Bogotá |
| 31 | Banco de Colombia |
| 33 | Pick up Trucks to Uribía & Manaure |

about this, or better still, check for yourself before booking in.

Most of the bottom-end residencias are grouped along Calle 13, with several others on Calles 12 and 14. The price for a double room (usually with private bath and fan) runs between US$6 and US$8. In that price bracket are the *Buen Hotel*, *Residencias El Banco*, *Hotel Latino*, *Residencias Oasis*, *Hotel Kacumay*, *Hotel Riohacha*, *Residencias Colonial*, *Residencias Yolimar*, *Hotel Buenos Aires*, *Hotel Cartagena*, *Residencias San José*, *Hotel Gallo* and *Hotel Don Blas*. The Residencias El Banco is probably the best of the lot. The

Buen Hotel is possibly the least overrun by shoppers, so you may have more chance of getting a room there than elsewhere. The hotel also has a cheap restaurant so you can avoid walking about the streets.

Marginally better than those listed above is the *Hotel Helda*, where singles/doubles/triples/quads cost US$7/11/13/16. Further up the price scale is the *Hotel Venecia*, offering doubles with fan/air-con for US$12/20. The *Hotel Avenida* (☎ 268426) has slightly better double rooms for US$17/25.

One of the better places in town is the *Hotel El Dorado* (☎ 267242), where air-con singles/doubles/triples go for US$28/34/44.

### Getting There & Away

There's no central bus terminal. Each company has its own office and they are all scattered throughout the town centre. The only purpose-built and well-organised terminals are those of Expreso Brasilia and Rápido Ochoa. All the others are just shabby, busy cubbyholes with buses standing outside on the street, adding to the overall chaos.

**Within Colombia** Bus traffic is very busy – the hustlers with their smuggled goods have to get around somehow – but it dies completely before 5 pm. It's impossible to get out of town after that time.

**To Santa Marta, Barranquilla & Cartagena** There are plenty of buses to Santa Marta with Expreso Brasilia, Rápido Ochoa, Copetrán, Coolibertador, Torcoroma and Unitransco (US$8.25 climatizado, US$7 pullman, four hours) and to Barranquilla (US$12 climatizado, 5½ hours); some buses go as far as Cartagena (US$18 climatizado, eight hours).

**To Riohacha** All the above-listed buses pass through Riohacha (US$2.50, 1¼ hours). There are also frequent colectivos to Riohacha departing from the corner of Calle 13 and Carrera 13 (US$2.50, one hour).

**To Valledupar** There are frequent buses with Copetrán, Cootracegua and some other companies (US$8.25 climatizado, US$7 pullman, four hours).

**To Uribia & Manaure** Pick-up trucks depart from the corner of Calle 12 and Carrera 17. They usually wait until they get truly overloaded with passengers. The transport to Uribia operates until around 3 pm (US$1.75, 1¼ hours); to Manaure, it stops around noon (US$2.25, 1¾ hours).

**To Cabo de la Vela** There is no public transport. You can pay for an expreso but it probably won't be cheaper than about US$40 per jeep.

**To Venezuela** The border is at Paraguachón, 12 km east of Maicao on the road to Maracaibo. The DAS and DIEX immigration authorities will issue exit/entry stamps at the border.

All tourists need a visa to enter Venezuela overland. The border post does not issue visas so you will have to get one beforehand. The nearest Venezuelan consulate is in Riohacha but you probably won't get a visa there either. Refer to the Visas & Embassies section in the introductory Facts for the Visitor chapter for more information.

Cuna Indian woman

There are four buses daily from Maicao to Maracaibo operated by Expresos Gran Colombia (US$3.50, four hours); and also hourly taxi colectivos operated by Agencias Unidas and Transportes Maicao (US$7, three hours). They depart until around 3 pm from their respective company offices. The Expreso Brasilia office sells tickets for Transportes Maicao colectivos, and you board them directly from the Brasilia terminal.

## URIBIA
• *pop 5000* • *32 m* • *28˚C*

Once Guajira's capital, Uribia is now an unpleasant, dusty town in the middle of the semi-desert of Alta Guajira. It is characterised by a scarcity of everything – shops, restaurants, accommodation and places of interest. Nevertheless, the place is much quieter and safer than Maicao and can serve as your stopover before heading elsewhere, to Manaure or Cabo de la Vela for example.

### Places to Stay & Eat
There are only a few places to stay, including the basic *Residencias Olinda* (US$5 per person) and the better (but considerably more expensive) *Hotel Princesa del Desierto*. Two restaurants near the church serve basic meals.

### Getting There & Away
There are regular pick-up trucks to Maicao (US$1.75, 1¼ hours) and less frequent ones to Manaure (US$1.25, 45 minutes) and to Media Luna (US$2, 1½ hours).

There is no regular transport to Cabo de la Vela, though occasionally jeeps depart when they collect enough passengers. You can hire a jeep, and it will be considerably cheaper from here (about US$25) than from Maicao. Alternatively, take a pick-up truck to Media Luna (this is how Puerto Bolívar is commonly known) and ask the driver to let you off at the turn-off to Cabo de la Vela. It will be a very hot three-hour walk from the turn-off to Cabo. See under Tours in the Riohacha section for a more comfortable way to visit the region.

## MANAURE

• *pop 5000* • *3 m* • *28°C*

Manaure, a small town on the northern coast of La Guajira, is noted for its two special attractions, the *salinas* and flamingos.

### Salinas

Salinas are shallow seaside pools used for obtaining salt from the sea water. The water enters the pools at high tide and is trapped when the tide goes out. Thanks to the intensive sun, the water evaporates leaving behind a dense, salty mass. The salt is then collected into piles and taken away. The pools are refilled and the whole process begins again. Working conditions are very primitive; people collect salt by hand using basic tools.

What is particularly amazing here, is the unbelievable pink colour of the water. Since the pools are in different stages of evaporation, there's an incredible variety of tones, ranging from creamy pink to deep purple. The colouration of the water is due to the presence of artemia, a kind of microscopic shrimp which live in very warm brine.

The salinas extend for several km along the coast west of Manaure. The installations where the salt is stored, sorted and distributed are in the town itself. The salinas of Manaure are the largest in the country, and produce some 700,000 tonnes of salt per year.

### Flamingos

Walk about 10 km further along the coastal dirt road to Musichi (sporadic trucks can be waved down on this road) and you will come to one of very few flamingo habitats. These amazing pink birds are here all year round, fishing in the sea near the shore or in coastal lagoons. They are not always in the same place, so it may take some time to track them down. See the Santuario Los Flamencos section later in this chapter for more about flamingos. There are many other birds here as well. Allow a full day for this pleasant excursion and start early to avoid walking in the baking heat of the day. If you wake up early (at 5 am or so), you might catch one of the salt trucks which can take you to Musichi.

### Places to Stay & Eat

There are two residencias in Manaure, both of which are fairly basic but acceptable, and both serve meals. There are two or three restaurants in town, if you prefer to dine out.

### Getting There & Away

Pick-up trucks regularly go to Uribia (US$1.25, 45 minutes) and Maicao (US$2.25, 1¾ hours). One or two early-morning jeeps go via the coastal road to Riohacha (US$2, 1½ hours). Otherwise go through Cuatro Vías.

To Cabo de la Vela, you must go back through Uribia. Theoretically, you can walk there along coastal paths and jeep tracks, but it's about 50 km.

## CABO DE LA VELA

This cape is one of the most beautiful places of Alta Guajira and perhaps of all the Colombian coast. The coast here is rocky and spectacular with high, brown cliffs and golden, sandy beaches below. If you climb the cone-shaped hill with a statue of the Virgin at the top, there is a good view around.

To the south of the hill, right on the beach, is the small hamlet of Cabo de la Vela – just a collection of houses and a church, surrounded by Indian huts.

### Places to Stay & Eat

There are a few simple residencias in the hamlet, including *El Caracol* which costs US$8 a double. If you prefer, they can give you a hammock for US$1.75 per day; leave your things at reception. The hotel has its own restaurant with good seafood at reasonable prices. Try the lobster. There are a few other places to eat, offering much the same fare for similar prices.

### Getting There & Away

There is no regular transport to Cabo de la Vela, but occasional pick-up trucks and jeeps, mostly from Uribia, call here once or twice a day. If you are not on a strict schedule, just wait until a vehicle turns up, and you'll get a lift back to Uribia or Maicao for a negotiable, but usually low, fare. If you have a taste for desert-hiking, walk for three hours to the Puerto Bolívar-Uribia road where vehicles pass by regularly.

## PARQUE NACIONAL MACUIRA

The Serranía de Macuira is a small mountain range, in the easternmost part of Alta Guajira. It is about 35 km long and 10 km wide, and reaches altitudes of up to 850 metres. Owing to their location and elevation, the mountains catch the humid ocean air brought by the north-east winds. The result is that the upper parts of Macuira are dripping with moisture which is then absorbed into the habitat.

In contrast to the xerophytic vegetation of the lowland Guajira, the plant life of Macuira is made up of species characteristic of humid climates, such as epiphytes, ferns, bromeliads and orchids. The fauna is also different from elsewhere on La Guajira and includes such mammals as wildcats, peccary and deer. As a result, in the middle of the desert, is an island of cloudforest, roughly similar to the Andean forest at altitudes of about 3000 metres.

The mountain range and the adjoining area were declared a national park in 1977; it covers 250 sq km. There are no tourist facilities in the park. The village of Nazareth at the north-eastern foot of the mountain is the usual starting point for tour-group walks into the mountains.

### Getting There & Away

You have little chance of getting here if you are travelling on your own. A jeep or truck (a 4WD is recommended) is a must. So is a guide because the region is cut by a maze of sandy trails and it's easy to lose your way. Alternatively, if money is not a problem, tours are available (see the Riohacha section).

## RIOHACHA

• *pop 110,000* • *3 m* • *28°C* • ☎ *(954)*
Nuestra Señora de los Remedios del Río de la Hacha was founded in 1545 by Spanish settlers from Isla Cubagua (near Isla de Mar-

garita, in present-day Venezuela), who moved here after Cubagua's fabulous pearl fisheries were depleted. From its birth the town's growth was hindered by Guajiro Indian attacks and frequent 'visits' by pirates. Riohacha was reputedly sacked and burnt down no less than 16 times. Of these, the raid by Sir Francis Drake in 1596 was perhaps the most destructive.

Riohacha was the birthplace of Almirante José Prudencio Padilla, one of the heroes of the war of independence. The admiral is remembered for the victory of the republican fleet over the Spaniards in the important naval battle on Lago de Maracaibo in July 1823.

Today Riohacha is the capital of La Guajira and a minor seaport. It's a rather undistinguished town without any significant tourist attractions.

### Information

**Tourist Office** Cortuguajira, or the Corporación Departamental de Turismo de la Guajira (☎ 272482), is on the waterfront and is open Monday to Friday from 8 am to noon and 2 to 6 pm.

**Money** There are only a few banks in town but none will change cash or travellers' cheques. The Banco Popular is the only bank which gives advances to Visa credit card holders. Cash dollars can be exchanged in the Casa de Cambio El Dollar, but the rate is poor.

**Venezuelan Consulate** The consulate is in the El Ejecutivo building, at Carrera 7 No 3-08. The official working hours are Monday to Friday from 9 am to 1 pm, but it often closes earlier.

**Tours** If there's anything to do in town it's to arrange a tour around Alta Guajira. The tour market has exploded over the past few years, and now there are four tour operators with self-contained offices and a few guides operating independently. They all specialise in jeep tours around the Península de la Guajira.

The standard tour is a one-day trip to Musichi (flamingos), Manaure (salinas) and Cabo de la Vela. A usual minimum is four people, in which case the price of the tour is between US$30 and US$35 per person. Food is not included but the tours all stop for lunch, usually in Cabo de la Vela.

A more adventurous trip, offered by almost all operators, is the four-day/three-night tour to the tip of the peninsula. The trip includes all the above-mentioned attractions, plus Nazareth and Macuira National Park. Again, four people are necessary to set off, or the price per person is considerably higher. Agents can either provide the transport and guide service only (about US$40 per person per day), or include food and accommodation in hammocks (chinchorros, of course), for an additional fee of around US$10 a day.

You should collect information from at least a few agents (including freelancers) and then compare their offers and prices. Given the competition, negotiating is part of the game, so don't hesitate to do it.

The established tour operators are: Administradores Costeños (☎ 273393), Calle 2 No 5-06; Guajira Tours (☎ 273385), Calle 3 No 6-39; Guajira Viva (☎ 273784), Calle 1 No 8-75 (in the Hotel Arimaca); and Viajes Iguarán (☎ 272000), Calle 3 No 6-07.

Ramiro Vanegas is the best known independent operator. You can ask for him in either the Hotel Gimaura or Hotel Miramar, or call (☎ 273119) or visit him at home, at Calle 18 No 8-25.

Some agents also offer other excursions, such as a visit to the Cerrejón coal mines and shopping in Maicao.

### Things to See
The city's central area, near the seashore, is quiet and pleasant for strolls, though don't expect many colonial relics. Walk along the waterfront boulevard, bordered by the sandy beach and some of the better restaurants.

Call at the **Parque Padilla**, the town's main square with the statue of the hero in the centre. On the eastern side of the square stands the **Catedral de Nuestra Señora de los Remedios**. The much venerated image of the Virgin has been here, in the high altar, since colonial times. She is the patron saint of Riohacha, and her day, 2 February, is solemnly celebrated. Padilla was buried in the church; his tomb is in the southern aisle.

The district further inland is dominated by the **market** on the corner of Carrera 7 and Calle 13, which spreads over the neighbouring streets. This area is very dirty and very busy – this is, after all, the first stopover for smuggled goods coming from Maicao.

Guajiro Indians come to town and you can see women in their traditional dresses, the manta guajira. Riohacha's market is a good place to buy Guajiro handicrafts, above all their famous chinchorros.

### Places to Stay
If you are only in Riohacha overnight it is more convenient to stay in the market area, near the Maicao-Santa Marta road. One of the options here is the *Hotel Internacional*, at Carrera 7 No 12A-31, 200 metres north of the main road. All rooms have baths, fans and comfortable beds, and cost US$5/9/12 for singles/doubles/triples.

Other hotels in the market area include: the *Residencias Aremasain*, at Calle 12 No 7-40 (US$5/9 a single/double); the *Residencias Yalconia*, at Carrera 7 No 11-26 (US$6/11); and the *Hotel Tunebo* (☎ 273326), at Carrera 10 No 12A-02 (US$11/14). All are acceptable, but the Tunebo is the best and the only one with air-con rooms.

If you plan on spending more time in Riohacha it is far more pleasant to stay downtown. The cheapest place here, the *Hotel Los Delfines* (☎ 272567), at Calle 2 No 9-74, is quite good and costs US$7/10/16 for a single/double/triple with bath. Marginally more expensive is the *Hotel Los Peces* (☎ 274426), at Calle 7 No 10-02.

For about US$9/12/16 you can stay in the *Hotel Musichi* (☎ 273967), at Calle 2 No 10-16, the *Hotel Miramar* (☎ 273382), on the corner of Calle 1A and Avenida de Circunvalación, or in the *Hotel Almirante Padilla* (☎ 272328), at Carrera 6 No 3-29. The Musichi is the most pleasant of the three.

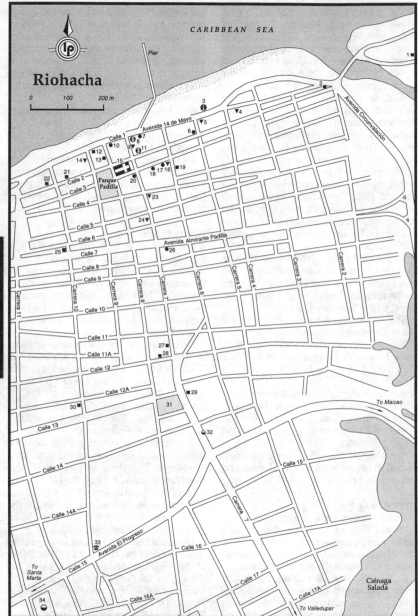

## PLACES TO STAY

1 Hotel Gimaura
2 Hotel Miramar
12 Hotel Arimaca
13 Hotel Taguara
19 Hotel Almirante Padilla
21 Hotel Los Delfines
22 Hotel Musichi
25 Hotel Los Peces
27 Residencias Yalconia
28 Residencias Aremasain
29 Hotel Internacional
30 Hotel Tunebo

## PLACES TO EAT

4 Restaurante El Rincón Guajiro
5 Leonardo's Pizza
9 Restaurante La Fragata
14 Ruben's Express Pizzería
16 Restaurante Moisy
23 Restaurante Maysi
24 Restaurante El Patio

## OTHER

3 Cortuguajira Tourist Office
6 Administradores Costeños
7 DAS
8 Banco Popular
10 Intercontinental de Aviación
11 Casa de Cambio El Dollar
15 Catedral de Nuestra Señora de los Remedios
17 Viajes Iguarán
18 Guajira Tours
20 Venezuelan Consulate
26 Avianca
31 Market
32 Jeeps to Manaure
33 Telecom
34 Bus Terminal

Yet another good, reasonably priced place is the *Hotel Taguara* (☎ 274573), at Carrera 8 No 1-32, just off the main square. It costs US$11/14/18 for a single/double/triple.

Should you need something appreciably better, choose between *Hotel Gimaura* (☎ 272234, 274587) on Avenida La Playa, which has cabañas and rooms for US$32/40 a single/double, or the central high-rise *Hotel Arimaca* (☎ 273481, 273515), at Calle 1 No

8-75 (US$40/52/64 a single/double/triple). Both hotels have air-con rooms, a restaurant, bar and a swimming pool.

### Places to Eat

The cheapest places to eat are in the market area, where there are several shoddy restaurants serving set meals for about US$1.50. The central part of town near the seaside has recently diversified as far as gastronomic matters go, and a range of new places has emerged.

Budget restaurants include *La Fragata, Maysi, Moisy* and *El Patio*. However, at US$2, the set meals are relatively expensive when compared to other cities.

For pizzas, choose between *Ruben's Express Pizzería* and *Leonardo's Pizza*. Good regional food is served at *El Rincón Guajiro*.

Possibly the best restaurants are at the top-end hotels, the Gimaura and Arimaca.

### Getting There & Away

**Air** The airport is about three km south-west of the town centre. There are flights to Bogotá (US$116 with Avianca, US$88 with Intercontinental), and to Valledupar (US$34 with Avianca, US$27 with Intercontinental).

**Bus** The bus terminal is on the corner of Avenida El Progreso (the road to Santa Marta) and Carrera 11A. All buses pass through the town near the market but only the corrientes will stop there, and not even all of them.

**To Maicao** There are frequent buses (US$2.50, 1¼ hours) and colectivos (US$2.50, one hour).

**To Santa Marta** There are plenty of buses, all coming through from Maicao (US$5.75 climatizado, US$5 pullman, three hours). Many buses continue on to Barranquilla, and some up to Cartagena.

**To Valledupar** Several buses leave daily (US$8.50 climatizado, US$7.25 pullman, 4½ hours).

**To Manaure** Jeeps leave from Carrera 7 in the market area around 7 am and rarely later (US$2, 1½ hours). They go via Musichi (flamingos) and then pass through the salinas before reaching Manaure. If you have light luggage, it's convenient to stop at Musichi and then walk the remaining bit to see both attractions on the way.

## SANTUARIO LOS FLAMENCOS

The Santuario de Flora y Fauna Los Flamencos is a nature reserve about 25 km west of Riohacha. It encompasses a few coastal lagoons supporting a variety of birds, including the flamingos.

The flamingos live in the reserve mainly during the rainy season. In the dry season, particularly from January to April and July to August, they are often forced to migrate as the water and vegetation dry up. Some small colonies may stay all year gathering in more hospitable areas, such as Punta Pecaro near Enea, at the western end of the reserve.

### Getting There & Away

The starting point for the reserve is the small village of Camarones, just off the Riohacha-Santa Marta road, 22 km from Riohacha. Get off at the turn-off to Camarones and walk for 10 minutes, passing through the village to the cemetery where the road divides. Take the right-hand branch which skirts around the lagoon and then passes several Indian huts, finally reaching the Boca de Camarones, where the lagoon joins the sea; this takes 45 minutes. There you will find a small house, the Cabaña del Inderena, and, if you are lucky enough, flamingos as well.

# Sierra Nevada de Santa Marta

The Sierra Nevada de Santa Marta is the highest coastal mountain range in the world. This surprising, three-sided pyramid rises abruptly from the lowland of the Caribbean coast, reaching up to nearly 5800 metres. The highest twin peaks, Simón Bolívar and Cristóbal Colón (both 5775 metres), are only about 45 km from the sea. They are the highest peaks in Colombia.

The Sierra Nevada is geographically isolated from the Andes. Geologically, it is a separate formation, independent of the Andes, though some investigators maintain that it is a structural continuation of the Andean Cordillera Oriental. The massif was

### The Pink Flamingos

The *flamenco rosado (Phoenicopterus ruber)* is characterised by its pink plumage. The birds have very long legs, a hooklike neck and downward-bent bill. Their diet is basically vegetable material combined with small animals such as molluscs, crustaceans and insects.

The flamingos inhabit brackish coastal waters. They often live in colonies of up to several hundred. Almost all day they stay immobile in shallow sea water just off the shore or in coastal lagoons. During their mating period, in March, some of them fly away to their nests, which can be hundreds of km away, while others stay in the area to prepare their unusual mud nests. Hatching takes place during April and May.

The flamingos originate from Eurasia where, from early times, they intrigued people. They appeared in legends and on primitive cave paintings. In the Americas the birds have found their home in the Caribbean basin and on the Galápagos Islands. In Colombia, they inhabit several sites on the northern coast of La Guajira – their favourite places seem to be Santuario Los Flamencos and Musichi near Manaure. They also visit several other sites in La Guajira including the bays of Portete and Honda further to the north-east. They have also been seen in Parque Nacional Tayrona and Ciénaga Grande de Santa Marta, and even occasionally in the Cartagena region. The Guajiro Indians refer to flamencos in their native language as *chiclocos* or *tococos*. ∎

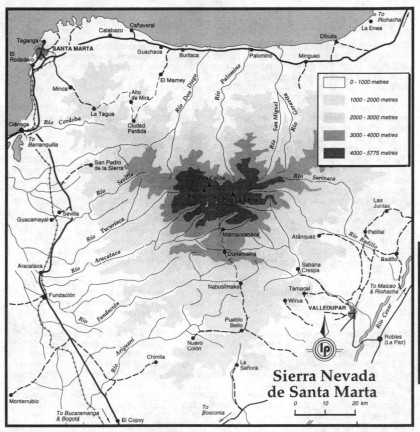

Sierra Nevada
de Santa Marta

0    10    20 km

shaped in the Jurassic period, some 170 million years ago.

On a relief map, the Sierra Nevada really looks like a well-shaped pyramid set on a regular triangular base, with the coast forming one side. A closer look reveals a more complex pattern. The Sierra is topped by a narrow, 25-km-long crest running east-west, with several snow-capped peaks over 5000 metres. This range is a barrier dividing the region into two parts, quite different in their topography, climate, flora, fauna and inhabitants.

The northern slopes, cut by several north-south river valleys dropping into the sea, are much wetter and covered by dense rainforest in large parts. The southern part is drier and made up of several ranges with their intervening valleys, oriented roughly east-west. On this side the forests only cover the lower altitudes and they are not so dense or humid. On the other hand, páramos are more extensive on this southern face.

Virtually the whole range of climates is present in the Sierra and, consequently, an almost complete spectrum of tropical habitats can be found. There is an astonishing variety of flora and fauna, and many species are unique to the region.

As the Sierra has been an isolated outcrop

## The Inhabitants of the Sierra Nevada de Santa Marta

**Tayrona Culture** In the past, the Sierra Nevada was home to various indigenous communities, of which the Tayrona, belonging to the Chibcha linguistic family, was the dominant and most developed group. The Tayronas (also spelt Taironas) are believed to have evolved into a distinctive culture since about the 5th century AD. A millennium later, when the Spaniards came, the Tayrona had developed into an outstanding civilisation, based on a complex social and political organisation and advanced engineering.

The Tayronas lived on the north-western slopes of the Sierra Nevada, where they constructed hundreds of settlements, all of a very similar pattern. Despite their different sizes and layouts they were usually situated on slopes centred over ridges.

Due to the rugged topography, a large number of stone terraces supported by high walls had to be built as bases for their houses. Although the terraces varied in shape, the thatched wooden houses were almost always round with a diameter of four to 12 metres. The groups of terraces were linked by a network of paths and stairways, all made of stone slabs. Ingenious technical know-how and an enormous amount of physical effort were required in the construction of their stone terraces, paths, stairways, bridges, irrigation canals and drainage systems.

Recent surveys have pinpointed the location of about 300 Tayrona settlements scattered over the slopes, once linked by stone-paved roads. Of all these, the Ciudad Perdida (Lost City), discovered in 1975, is the largest and is thought to have been the Tayrona 'capital'.

Tayrona was the first advanced indigenous culture encountered by the Spaniards in the New World in 1499. It was here, in the Sierra Nevada, that the conquerors were for the first time astonished by the Indian gold, and the myth of El Dorado was born. Predictably, the obsessive search for gold took off to become the principal driving force behind the conquest for at least the next century.

The Spaniards crisscrossed the Sierra Nevada but were met with brave resistance by the Indians. The Tayronas defended themselves fiercely but were almost totally decimated in the course of 75 years of uninterrupted war. A handful of survivors abandoned their homes and fled into upper reaches of the Sierra. Their traces have been lost forever.

**Indian Groups Living Today** At present, three Indian groups live in the Sierra Nevada: the Kogi (also spelt Kogui), the Ijka (or Ika, but better known as Arhuacos) and the Sanká (also referred to as Arsarios or Malayos). The total population of the three communities is estimated at 20,000 to 25,000 people. They all belong to the Chibcha linguistic family, though they speak different dialects. Their cultures are basically similar and feature many common elements in their complex religious, social and political world.

Their highest traditional authorities are the Mamas, who are the guardians of their culture and responsible for the social and spiritual order of the tribe. Combining the functions of witch doctor, judge and priest, the Mamas decide on all matters and activities at individual, family and community levels.

The Kogis (numbering approximately 5000 to 7000) inhabit the northern slopes of the Sierra along the valleys at altitudes between 1000 and 2000 metres. They don't live in these settlements

for millions of years – a sort of continental island – the flora and fauna have developed independently. Accordingly, there are many endemic species, particularly in the upper parts. By and large, endemism increases with altitude. Although not many studies have been made of the area, it's considered that the number of endemic plants accounts for nearly half of the total species recorded in the region.

The Sierra Nevada is one of Colombia's most significant regions as far as its historical, archaeological and cultural aspects go. Before the Spanish conquest it was inhabited by one of the most advanced cultures, the Tayrona. Numerous artefacts found in the area stand as the best proof of the high level of cultural development of the group. The discovery of the Ciudad Perdida, the ancient Tayrona city, confirmed their greatness as architects and urban planners.

Today the region is inhabited by a few

permanently, but are spread out in sparsely scattered farms, coming to the villages for collective meetings or significant events. They have a subsistence economy based mainly on agriculture. Coca has traditionally played an important cultural role.

The origins of the Kogi are not very clear; some investigators claim that the Kogis are the direct descendants of the Tayronas, while others maintain that they were separate tribes living close to each other. The similarities in their cultures (though little is known about the Tayronas) are evident in their dwellings: round huts with thatched conical roofs. Today, the almost untouched Kogi traditions are used in the study of Tayrona culture.

The Arhuacos (approximately 15,000 to 18,000) mainly inhabit the south-eastern slopes of the Sierra, with their traditional centre being Nabusímake. Like the Kogis, they don't live permanently in their villages and use them only for community meetings, ceremonies and feasts. Although their traditional culture is still very much alive, the influences from the 'civilised world' are felt here more strongly, principally due to the easy access to their territory. Capuchin missionaries and colonists have helped to change their traditional socio-religious system.

On the other hand, the Arhuaco culture was more diversified and didn't have such a clear identity as that of the Kogis. In contrast to the Kogis, who carefully avoided external contacts by isolating themselves, the Arhuacos reacted openly to outside influences, confronting the problems, refusing (sometimes violently) the new culture but also accepting some of its elements. Some Arhuacos have adopted the 'advantages' of modern civilisation. They have left their traditional way of life and moved to the lowlands, where they live mainly off trading. Nonetheless, those who still live in the Sierra have maintained much of their traditional culture. This can be seen in their customs, beliefs, clothing and artefacts.

The Sanká is the smallest and least significant group, numbering at most 2000 people. They live in the eastern and north-eastern part of the Sierra Nevada.

**Colonisation** Apart from the Indians, the Sierra Nevada is inhabited by a number of settlers, today greatly surpassing the total Indian population and estimated at roughly 100,000. The colonisation of the Sierra began during the colonial era, but it is only since modern times, from the 1950s, that it has intensified. This fast, spontaneous and uncontrolled settling of the area has resulted in the Indians being encircled and pushed further up into the poorer lands of the Sierra.

Many of the *colonos* (colonists), particularly those living on the northern slopes, turned into *guaqueros* (pre-Columbian tomb robbers) or *marimberos* (marijuana growers). In the early 1980s marijuana gradually gave way to coca cultivation, which was more profitable than cannabis. Some of the northern parts of the Sierra are today controlled by the drug lords. By the early 1990s marijuana was slowly reclaiming ground, and it's cultivation is expanding over new areas gained by deforestation.

There has been an increasing guerrilla presence (FARC), who also want to share of control over the region. In the late 1980s the FARC launched several armed attacks on the colonos, pushing the conflict to the brink of open war. Fortunately, the situation has calmed down over recent years. Although the guerrillas haven't gained much control of the Sierra, they are one of its most unwanted intruders. ■

CARIBBEAN COAST

Indian groups, one of which, the Kogi, is considered by some ethnologists as the most authentic surviving civilisation of pre-Columbian America.

The entire mountain range, together with its foothill borderland, was made a national park in 1977. It comprises an area of 3830 sq km.

## Orientation

Except for its fringe areas, the Sierra is little explored. Access into its heart is quite diffi-cult and requires some time and effort. The northern face of the Sierra, with the exception of Ciudad Perdida, is virtually inaccessible for tourists, as it is boarded by the jungle belt dotted with the colonists' ranchos and marijuana patches. Visitors have little chance of seeing the remote, untouched Kogi areas (that's why they are intact!).

Just about the only place you can visit on this northern side is Ciudad Perdida, which has become popular among foreign visitors.

Figure from Santa Marta

All routes to Ciudad Perdida begin in Santa Marta.

The southern part, Arhuaco territory, is easier to get to for various reasons. The region is drier, so the terrain in large parts is open and not covered by the impregnable forests of the north. The guaqueros and marimberos (the biggest danger for tourists) have not settled here because conditions aren't favourable for their 'work'. Finally, the Arhuacos have been more tolerant to newcomers than the Kogis, though this seems to be changing.

The region provides good opportunities for hiking, though it's more suited to experienced trekkers. The most popular route goes from the amazing village of Nabusímake to the mountain lakes at the foot of the highest peaks of the Sierra. It offers some special attractions, including a glimpse of the Arhuaco culture and the magnificent mountain scenery of the Sierra. The main gateway for excursions to the southern Sierra is Valledupar.

### Books

*La Sierra Nevada de Santa Marta* (Mayr & Cabal, Bogotá, 1984) is a wonderful, glossy book with general information and marvellous photography. English, French and German editions are also available.

*Los Kogi – una Tribu de la Sierra Nevada de Santa Marta* by Gerardo Reichel-Dolmatoff (Procultura, Bogotá, 1985) is a very comprehensive two-volume study of the Indians of the Sierra.

*The Heart of the World* by Alan Ereira (Jonathan Cape, London, 1990) relates the story of a visit to the Kogi land to film a documentary for the BBC.

### CIUDAD PERDIDA

Ciudad Perdida is one of the largest pre-Columbian towns discovered in the Americas. It was built by the Tayrona Indians on the north-western slopes of the Sierra Nevada de Santa Marta. During the conquest, the Spaniards burned the wooden dwellings of the Tayronas, leaving only the stone structures, which disappeared without trace under the lush tropical vegetation. Ciudad Perdida lay hidden for four centuries, until its discovery in 1975.

Ciudad Perdida literally means the Lost City, and this is how it's commonly known to Colombians and English-language speakers, respectively. It has more names, however. For archaeologists it's known as Buritaca 200, and the guaqueros call it the Infierno Verde, or the Green Hell. Its indigenous name is Teyuna.

Ciudad Perdida was built over a long period of time, most probably during the 13th and 14th centuries, though its origins are much older. It's estimated that its population was somewhere between 2000 and 4000 people, but it could have been far larger in its heyday. Spreading over an area of about two sq km, it was most probably the largest urban centre of the Tayrona.

Ciudad Perdida lies on the relatively steep

## The Discovery of Ciudad Perdida

Ciudad Perdida was found in 1975 by the guaqueros, who earned their living by seeking and plundering Indian tombs for gold and other antique objects. It was Florentino Sepúlveda, together with his sons Julio César and Jacobo, who discovered the Lost City. He was born in the Norte de Santander department but, like many other colonists, had come to the Sierra Nevada and settled in the 1950s with dreams of a better life. He divided his time between trading with the Indians and hunting for gold.

Life was not easy. The guaqueros were numerous and it became necessary to penetrate further and further into the Sierra to make new finds. During one such expedition, a long, strenuous march up the Buritaca River, the Sepúlvedas found the city. They were astonished by the long stone stairways which they had to climb to get to the dozens of terraces, all buried beneath rich tropical vegetation. It was the tombs that primarily interested them but they didn't find the gold they were after, only some necklaces made of colourful stones which they sold on their return to Santa Marta.

The news spread like wildfire. Other treasure hunters soon located the ruins and the Indian tombs fell victim to looting. A war for the Lost City broke out, with shooting between rival gangs of grave robbers. Not without reason the guaqueros named the place the Infierno Verde or the Green Hell.

The government woke up to the guaqueros' find in 1976 and sent out an expedition to examine it. Soon after, an archaeological base was established on the site, as well as an army post to protect the ruins. Nevertheless, the looting of graves continued and gangs of guaqueros rivalled for supremacy. In one of these clashes Julio César was killed and buried at the foot of the Infierno. Four years later his father brought his son's remains down to Guachaca where he lived. The finder of one of the greatest discoveries of our times, Florentino Sepúlveda died recently in his mid-70s in misery and oblivion. Actually, he never found any gold in Ciudad Perdida, but other guaqueros did. ■

slopes of the upper Buritaca River valley at an altitude of between 900 and 1300 metres. The central part of the city is set on a ridge from which various stone paths lead down to other sectors on the slopes. Although the wooden houses of the Tayronas are long gone, the stone structures, including terraces and stairways, remain in remarkably good shape.

There are about 150 terraces, most of which once served as foundations for the houses. The largest terraces are set on the central ridge and these were used for ritual ceremonies (they now serve as a heliport). Originally, the urban centre was completely cleared of trees but it was reclaimed by the jungle. Today, the city has been cleared of shrubs and brushwood except for tall trees and palms giving a somewhat mysterious atmosphere to the ruins.

Archaeological digs have uncovered some Tayrona objects (fortunately, the guaqueros didn't manage to take everything), mainly various kinds of pottery (both ceremonial and utensil), goldwork and some unique necklaces made of semiprecious stones. Some of these objects are on display in the Museo Arqueológico in Santa Marta and the Museo del Oro in Bogotá. It's a good idea to visit the museum in Santa Marta before going to Ciudad Perdida. You can see the superb model of the city and get a rough idea of what it's like.

### Getting There & Away

Ciudad Perdida lies about 40 km south-east of Santa Marta as the crow flies. It's hidden deep in the thick forest amidst rugged mountains, far away from any human settlements, and without access roads.

There are two ways of getting there: by helicopter or by foot. Both begin from Santa Marta; the former takes less than three hours, the latter takes a week. Both are operated on a tour principle and are expensive.

Yet, there may be more drawbacks. The Kogi Indians have repeatedly protested against tourists visiting Ciudad Perdida, which they consider their sacred city. As a result the Lost City has closed and reopened several times in the past few years. A longer-term agreement seems to have been

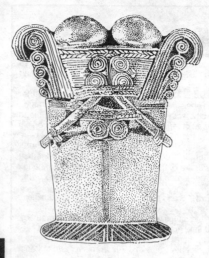

Sinú pendant cast in gold

eventually reached, and the city is currently open. This, however, may change at any time.

**Helicopter** The Aviatur travel agency has irregular helicopter tours during Christmas and Easter periods, and sporadically at other times if there's sufficient demand. It is a 20-minute flight from Santa Marta airport to Ciudad Perdida, followed by a two-hour guided visit. In all, it takes about two hours and 40 minutes and costs US$350 per person. If you are captivated by this whirl-wind speed, and are not deterred by the price, contact the Aviatur office in any of the major cities.

**Walking** There are basically two hiking routes leading to the Lost City: through La Tagua and Alto de Mira; and through El Mamey and up along the Río Buritaca. The sections between Santa Marta and La Tagua and between Santa Marta and El Mamey are done by jeep (three hours either trip).

Either route normally takes three days uphill to Ciudad Perdida, and two days back

down, plus one day at the site. The La Tagua trail is more demanding, with up and down-hill sections, but is supposedly more spectacular. The total walking time one way up to the city is about 18 hours. The El Mamey route is shorter, about 13 hours, and is mostly uphill.

Neither trail is very difficult, though this depends on the weather: if it's wet (as it is most of the year), the paths are pretty muddy. The only fairly dry period is from late December to February or early March. There are several creeks to cross on the way; be prepared to get your shoes wet and carry a spare pair.

Quite like the war between guaqueros two decades ago, a similar sort of battle has been fought over recent years for the right to let tourists into Ciudad Perdida and, more importantly, touring them there. Various groups and institutions, including Inderena, the tourist office, tour operators, the Institute of Anthropology and the Kogis, have clashed. Now it seems that the parties have reached an agreement. This has unfortunately resulted in the fixing of non-negotiable prices at around US$200 per person for an all-inclusive tour. All tours have to be led by one of the licensed guides, and all cheaper ways of visiting the Lost City have been suspended. You cannot now, for example, take a guide-only service (which was possible and much cheaper), even if you are fully equipped with trekking gear and food. Nor can you hire an independent, unregistered guide. And you can't do it on your own.

The effect of this policy is that the number of travellers has drastically dropped, and so have the profits of the travel operators and guides. Again everybody is unhappy and the situation is volatile – expect further changes.

The tour includes transport, food, accommodation (in hammocks), porters, guides and all necessary permits. You carry your own personal belongings. Take a torch, water container and insect repellent. Treks in groups of up to 10 people usually take six to seven days for the round trip. The route can be chosen by the group, though most guides prefer the El Mamey trail up and down. It's easier, shorter and supposedly safer (there has been some occasional guerrilla activity on La Tagua trail).

The major tour operator in Santa Marta is Jairo Portillo, the manager of the Hotel Miramar. He has the most frequent tours, using most of the registered guides, and his tours may be a bit cheaper than those organised through other agents.

Don't attempt to do this trip on your own. Apart from the strictly practical reasons (you can easily get lost), the region is a marijuana and coca growing area. There are also guerrillas operating in the zone, though as yet they haven't shown much of a presence on the trails to Ciudad Perdida. Besides all this, you'll probably be stopped and turned back by locals at some stage of the route. If you did manage to get the whole way undisturbed, it is likely that you would be refused entrance to Ciudad Perdida by the guards.

## NABUSÍMAKE
Whereas Ciudad Perdida is the most spectacular city of the Tayronas, Nabusímake takes the prize for being the loveliest town of the Arhuacos, the largest Indian community living today in the Sierra. Nabusímake is the Arhuaco 'capital', or at least their largest settlement. It is set at the bottom of a beautiful, verdant valley on the southern slopes of the Sierra Nevada. It's oval in shape and comprises about 50 thatched huts, almost all of which are laid out on a rectangular plan.

There is an open, grassy square at the southern end of the village with a simple, small stone church and a free-standing bell tower. The church was founded by the Capuchin missionaries who came here at the end of the 19th century. They changed the name of the village to San Sebastián de Rábago (which is how it is still shown on many maps). In 1982, after a serious protest by the Arhuacos against the 'civilising' programmes of the missionaries, the mission was expelled, the church closed down and the village returned to its original name.

At the opposite end of the village you will find Cancurua (or Kancurua), a small circular thatched hut where the community meetings are held. The whole village is circled with a low stone wall with a wooden ceremonial entrance gate. Climb the surrounding slopes for a lovely bird's-eye view of the whole village.

The Arhuacos don't live permanently in the village but gather here for meetings and occasional visits. You will probably find it almost empty, giving the impression of a ghost town.

Only 10 km away the power line passes by. When the government offered to provide the village with electricity the Mamas met to discuss the proposal and eventually decided against the idea. Among the reasons they gave was that the proposed line would have passed over ancient tombs, thus profaning the souls of their ancestors.

Nabusímake is essentially a starting point for the hike up into the mountains (see the following section), so if you plan on hiking you'll pass through the village and are most likely to camp somewhere nearby. A special trip to Nabusímake alone is either expensive or involves a long walk.

### Places to Stay & Eat
Down along the valley from the Arhuaco village is a collection of loosely scattered houses, a product of colonisation. One of them, a five-minute walk down along the river, has a small shop where you can buy basic food (bread, canned fish, sugar etc). The shop is also the place to ask for mules if you plan on hiking up the mountain.

A couple of hundred metres downstream from the shop is a bridge over the river. One of the houses on the other side is a small hospedaje without a name. This pleasant family-run place has one big room with seven beds and a modern bathroom (but with cold water only), and costs US$3 per person. The hotel serves meals (US$2.50), but let them know in advance.

There are plenty of places along the river to pitch your tent; always ask permission in the neighbouring house.

## Getting There & Away

The jumping-off point for Nabusímake is Valledupar. Jeeps from Carrera 7A in the market area depart for Pueblo Bello, from early morning till around noon. They normally charge locals US$1.75 but usually ask more from travellers with large backpacks (US$2.50 to US$3). The trip takes 1½ to two hours.

Pueblo Bello is an uninspiring, small town inhabited by an Indian/mestizo population. There are several hospedajes and restaurants.

In Pueblo Bello look for a jeep to Nabusímake. The 25-km road is very rough and steep, and transport is almost nonexistent. You may be lucky enough to find a jeep which has already collected some passengers and is about to depart, but chances are rather slim. More likely, you'll have to negotiate an expreso with a jeep driver, who can ask for anything between US$60 to US$100 per jeep. The trip itself takes 2½ hours. Alternatively, you can walk, but it's a strenuous six to seven-hour hike.

## NABUSÍMAKE-PICO COLÓN TREK

This is just about the most spectacular high-mountain trek anywhere in Colombia, comparable only to the hikes in the Sierra Nevada del Cocuy. The description which

---

### The Arhuacos

Even though many people in Colombia have no idea about the Arhuacos, they surely know their *mochilas*. These are a kind of shoulder bag traditionally made and used by the Arhuaco Indians. Today, these fine, bucket-shaped bags with geometrical designs are used by people all over the country and fetch exorbitant prices in exclusive shops. The mochilas are made by various Indian tribes and not only those of the Sierra Nevada, but those of the Arhuacos have gained the best reputation.

The mochilas of the Arhuacos have traditionally been made with natural brown and white wool, sometimes mixed with goat's hair spun by hand. Today, synthetic fibres and artificial dyes are slowly making their way into the mochilas, though their use is still limited. Mochilas are made exclusively by women and this activity occupies a great deal of their time. They seem to be continually at work on their craft, even when they are walking.

While it is the women who make mochilas, it's the men who use them. Arhuaco men carry three mochilas, one on either side crossed over each other, and the third, hanging from the neck down the back, used to keep coca leaves and the *poporo*.

The poporo is another typical Arhuaco utensil, also common among other Indian groups in the Sierra. It is a small, pear-shaped gourd for carrying lime, open at the neck to allow a stick to enter to crush the sea shells into lime powder. The powder is added to the coca leaves which they chew to help extract the coca juice. Only the men use coca; the women, however, harvest it.

The Arhuacos are very traditional in their dress. The men wear a *ruana*, a kind of long poncho, handwoven from undyed wool mixed with cotton, tied around the waist with a wide, rolled cloth belt. The Arhuaco men look very striking with their long black wavy hair and white, fez-shaped hats on their heads. The women wear white tunics and, around their necks, the *chaquira*, strands of beads made of glass or dried seeds.

You will meet many Arhuacos while hiking in the Sierra; your first contact with them will probably be in Pueblo Bello, where some live. In Nabusímake, other than during one of their meetings (you might be lucky), you will see few. On the trail up into the mountains, you will pass several of their farms. A family has usually more than one farm, often in different climatic zones to allow the cultivation of a wider range of crops. This is why you will find some farms looking closed and unused. You will meet Arhuacos on the trail, moving from one farm to the other: the women continuously working on mochilas, the men with coca leaves in their cheeks, all in their typical dress. If you're lucky, you might even meet the Mama, recognised by his white mochilas without any design.

The Arhuacos are somewhat suspicious about strangers and are not very open. Mostly, you will find them to be quite indifferent towards you, but sometimes they can be hostile. Try to understand this attitude; for them, the snowy peaks are the home of their gods and the lakes are sacred.

The Arhuacos don't like to be photographed; respect this and never take pictures without permission. Above all remember that this is their land. Be a guest and not an intruder. ■

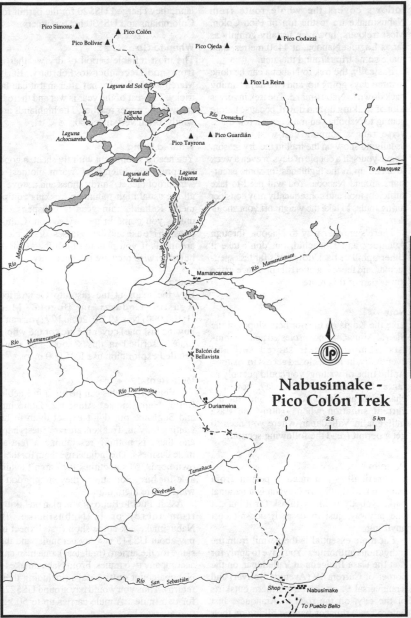

Pico Simons ▲

Pico Bolívar ▲  ▲ Pico Colón

▲ Pico Ojeda  ▲ Pico Codazzi

Laguna del Sol  ▲ Pico La Reina

Laguna Naboba  Río Donachuí

Laguna Achocuareba  ▲ Pico Guardián
Pico Tayrona ▲

To Atanquez

Laguna del Cóndor  Laguna Usucaca

Río Mamancduacua

Río Mamancanaca

Quebrada Guachuncopuramena  Quebrada Yepocimeina

Mamancanaca  Río Mamancanaca

Río Mamancanaca

Balcón de Bellavista

Río Duriameina

Duriameina

**Nabusímake –
Pico Colón Trek**

0    2.5    5 km

Tamañaca

Quebrada

Río San Sebastián

Shop  Nabusímake

To Pueblo Bello

CARIBBEAN COAST

follows covers the whole route from Nabusímake up to the top of Pico Colón. Most trekkers, however, usually go only as far as Laguna Naboba, at 4450 metres, then make some trips around the area.

Basically, the trek to Naboba can be done in three days going up, and two days coming back down to Nabusímake. The trek involves a lot of walking up and down, because before getting to Naboba you must cross a few transverse ranges running east-west. There is usually no snow on the trail in the dry season. Leave yourself a couple of days or even a week to spend up in the highlands for some excursions around Naboba. You will need to take sufficient food and consequently may consider hiring mules to take the weight off your shoulders.

There's another way to Naboba, through Atanquez and Donachuí, but don't take it either uphill or back down. It's far less spectacular and there is a guerrilla presence in the lower part of this route.

### Note
Like the Kogis on the northern slopes of the Sierra, Arhuacos, too, protested against tourists trampling their sacred soil and eventually, in 1994, closed access to visitors. At the time of writing, you could get only as far as Nabusímake. This may, however, change at anytime. You will find out the current situation when visiting the Casa Indígena in Valledupar, where you need to get a permit (read the following section).

### Permits
Theoretically, you need a permit from Inderena, as the Sierra Nevada is a national park. Nobody is likely to ask for it but get one anyway, just in case. It doesn't cost anything.

Far more essential is the permit from the indigenous authorities. You have to apply for it at the Casa Indígena in Valledupar, on the corner of Carrera 19 (Avenida Bolívar) and Transversal 9, on the far northern outskirts of the city, on the road to Atanquez. Just before the Arhuacos banned hiking on their

land, they charged US$20 for the permit for Colombians and US$30 for foreigners.

### When to Go
The most reliable period of dry weather is from mid-December to February. Early March is usually dry but after that it can be tricky. The rest of the year is wet and there is snow in the upper reaches. The highlands are windy, often very much so.

### What to Bring
You need a strong tent with fly sheet, a good sleeping bag, plenty of warm clothes, a windproof jacket, sturdy shoes and a stove – all the usual high-mountain trekking equipment. Reliable rain gear is indispensable unless you come in the dry season. Crampons, an ice axe and dark glasses (or goggles) are musts if you plan to climb Pico Colón, but otherwise they are not necessary.

### Maps
Buy the maps at the Instituto Geográfico Agustín Codazzi in Bogotá. Map (1:100,000) Nos 19, 20, 26 and 27 (you can't buy the last one) cover the area of the whole route described in this section. For more detailed exploration use 1:25,000 maps.

### Mule Rental
Theoretically, mules can be hired in Pueblo Bello, Nabusímake, Atanquez, Donachuí and Sogrome but don't expect them to be waiting for you. Trekkers are rare guests here and there is nothing resembling a rent-a-mule business. The Indians use them for their own needs, so sometimes they aren't available for hire. Sometimes they simply don't want to hire them out.

Ask in Pueblo Bello (if you plan on hiking from there) or in Nabusímake. In Nabusímake ask at the shop first. Expect to pay about US$15 per day per mule, and the same for the arriero (muleteer); one man can accompany two mules. From Nabusímake to Naboba count on five days (including their return). Thus you would pay around US$225 for two mules. A mule carries up to 50 kg, two average backpacks.

### Day 1: Nabusímake-Duriameina (seven hours)

From the shop in Nabusímake walk 200 metres down along the river, cross over the bridge and continue for 10 minutes downstream on a dirt road until you see a path branching off to the right and heading uphill. This is the trail. You have about five hours of steady climbing over an extensive, eroded mountain ridge before you get to the pass.

The first half hour will bring you to a stream with a few Indian huts beyond. From here the trail begins to climb steeply. After about two hours it becomes easier until finally reaching the pass at 3600 metres. The path is well marked, so you shouldn't get lost.

It can be quite hot by noon, so start early to get past the first steep rise before the sun is high. Shortly beyond the pass you will get to some Indian huts; past them the path ascends a bit, then turns to the right and drops down into the Duriameina Valley. Before descending, look carefully at the opposite side of the valley to see which way the trail goes; you have to follow it the next day.

Going down into the valley keep to the right-hand side. After reaching the river, continue upstream for 15 minutes to the hamlet of Duriameina (3300 metres). It's just a few huts encircled by a stone wall. The descent from the pass to Duriameina won't take you more than two hours. You can camp next to the river, though the site is open and windy.

### Day 2: Duriameina-Quebrada Yebosimeina (five hours)

This is an easier day, with a shorter walk and not much climbing. You start by ascending a steep range for two hours to get to the pass, the Balcón de Bellavista (3900 metres). In front of you is a panoramic view of the highest peaks of the Sierra – a breathtaking sight!

From the pass it is an easy descent of about two hours down into the Mamancanaca Valley, where there is a small Indian settlement at 3400 metres, the last huts on your way. Descending, keep to the slope on the right, then cross the stream and climb the opposite slope following the path. An hour later you get to the beautiful Quebrada Yebosimeina, where you will find a lovely place to camp next to the stream, with the snowy El Guardián in the background. If you have hired mules you won't be able to continue past here on the same day, as the mules stay overnight in Mamancanaca. But if you don't have mules, it's worth pressing on to cut down on the long trek the next day.

### Day 3: Quebrada Yebosimeina-Laguna Naboba (eight hours)

This leg is a long walk and more difficult than either of the previous days', so start early. If you have mules, you'll perhaps prefer to follow them; the route they tread is the shortest but it is rather unattractive. This would probably be wise, as the trekkers' trail to Laguna Naboba is not well marked and you might not reach it on the same day. You wouldn't want to spend the night without your tent and sleeping bag.

If you are carrying all your gear with you, go instead via the spectacular route through the lakes. Firstly, cross the range to the west (on your left facing Pico El Guardián) and drop into the next valley, the Quebrada Guiachinacopunameina. Follow the valley up as it snakes to the left, and then later to the right. After about three or four hours you will get to the first lake, Laguna Usucaca. Skirt the lake along its western shore, and carry on for half an hour more to the Laguna del Cóndor, a lovely lake surrounded by high, precipitous cliffs.

At the far end of the lake you will see the pass (4250 metres), which you get to by keeping to the right-hand side of the lake. The views from the pass are superb, with more magnificent lakes to the north. Sometimes you can see condors here (the Sierra Nevada de Santa Marta has the largest population of condors in Colombia).

The trail drops down towards the lakes but soon after turns to the right and goes about 50 metres above the big lake. The trail is faint here, occasionally marked by piles of stones left by earlier trekkers. When you get to the gorge which heads up to your right (about a one-hour walk from the pass), cross the creek and climb the opposite ridge. Keep an eye out for the piles of stones that mark the way: don't follow the stream. You will pass some small ponds, and shortly afterwards will see a small lake (actually it is a part of the big lake that you have already passed) with waterfalls at the far end. Follow the trail which heads up above the waterfalls until you finally see the Laguna Naboba (4450 metres), easily recognised by a small island on its eastern side.

The campsite is on the eastern shore of the lake, facing the island. It is not, however, an ideal place, as it is bare, open and windy. It is well worth walking 20 minutes east to the next small lake and camping at its far end. This lake is known to hikers as the Laguna del Helicóptero; a wrecked helicopter lies nearby.

The helicopter, as well as two others, crashed in the late 1970s in a rescue operation. This type of helicopter can only fly up to 4000 metres and the elevation here is 4500 metres. Who knows why they sent the helicopters on this mission. One helicopter, however, survived the operation, but only because it had been damaged earlier in Mamancanaca and couldn't make the final stage.

### Around Laguna Naboba

Laguna Naboba sits in the heart of the Sierra. To the north-west you have the highest peaks, Bolívar and Colón (you must climb a little up the southern slope of the lake to see them). To the south-east stretches a perfect view over El Guardián and Tayrona, and to the east is the majestic peak of La Reina, particularly spectacular at sunset. It is unlikely that you will want to just turn round and head back. Give yourself a few more days for short excursions around, to discover the lovely places and lakes nearby. There are several lakes to the west of Naboba, the largest being the Laguna Achocuareba. You can walk there and back in a day.

### Laguna Naboba-Pico Colón

This trek, or rather climb, to the top of Pico Colón (5775 metres) can be done in two days from Naboba (or more leisurely in three). The trail begins at the rocky cliff just north of the campsite on the Naboba lakeshore. It is faint and disappears in parts but you have the stone piles to guide you.

After passing a big lake (on your left), the trail turns to the right and skirts around another lake, the Laguna del Sol (4600 metres). Further on, there is no trail as such, just head up north-west towards Pico Colón. Ascend as much as you can to reduce some of the heavy climbing the next day. There are good places to pitch your tent on the *lajas*, the flat stone terraces at about 5000 metres, just below the snowline. You can get to this point without any mountaineering gear, and the trek is worth the effort even if you are not planning to conquer the peak. The views from the lajas are marvellous, particularly at sunrise and sunset.

From here upwards you'll need crampons, an ice axe and sunglasses. Start very early, and keep close to the rocky wall on your left (it is the east face of Pico Bolívar) heading straight to La Horqueta (5500 metres), the saddle between the Bolívar and Colón peaks. The climb is steep, and the terrain is icy in the morning, but later it's softened by the sun, making it difficult to walk on. From La Horqueta, if the weather is clear, you'll have a miraculous view to the north, stretching over all the northern slopes, as far as the sea. You can even see the beaches on the coastline! This view is obscured after the morning by a carpet of cloud below.

The walk from La Horqueta to the top of Colón is surprisingly easy. It should take four to six hours of climbing from the lajas to the top, taking you to the highest point in Colombia. Before you is a breathtaking panorama stretching all around, over almost all the other peaks of the Sierra Nevada. They are all below your feet, except for Pico Bolívar, to the south-west, which has the same altitude as Colón but is far more difficult to climb.

The descent from Colón down to Naboba is possible within the same day and takes about six hours.

# Magdalena

## SANTA MARTA

• *pop 280,000* • *2 m* • *27°C* • ☎ *(954)*

Founded in 1525 by Rodrigo de Bastidas, Santa Marta is the oldest surviving colonial town in Colombia. The site was chosen at the foot of the Sierra Nevada de Santa Marta to serve as a convenient base for the reputedly incalculable gold treasures of the Tayrona. Bastidas had previously briefly explored the area and was aware of the Indian riches to be found. However, as soon as the plundering of the Sierra began, so did the resistance of the locals, and clashes followed. By the end of the 16th century the Tayronas were eventually wiped out and many of their gold objects – melted down for rough material, of course – were in the Crown's coffers.

Santa Marta was also one of the early gateways to the interior of the colony. It was from here that Jiménez de Quesada set off in 1536 for his strenuous march up the Magdalena Valley, to found Bogotá two years later.

Engaged in the war with the Tayronas and repeatedly ransacked by pirates, Santa Marta didn't have many glorious moments in its colonial history, and was soon overshadowed by its younger, more progressive neighbour, Cartagena. If there's an important date remembered nationwide in Santa Marta's history, this is 17 December 1830, the day when Simón Bolívar died here, after bringing independence to six Latin American countries.

Today, Santa Marta is Colombia's third largest seaport and the easy-going, pleasant capital of Magdalena. It still has some fine old buildings, but its colonial character has virtually disappeared and what is left is increasingly being obscured by modern architecture.

Avenida Rodrigo de Bastidas (Carrera 1C) lining the beach is the principal tourist boulevard, alive till late at night. It provides a nice view over the bay with a small rocky island, El Morro, in the background. Almost all the tourist activity occurs between the waterfront and Avenida Campo Serrano (Carrera 5), the main commercial street.

The climate is hot but the sea breeze, especially in the evening, cools the city, making it agreeable to wander around, or sit over a beer in one of the numerous open-air waterfront cafés.

Santa Marta has become a popular tourist centre not for the city itself but for its surroundings. Nearby El Rodadero is one of Colombia's most fashionable beach resorts, though its beach and water are becoming dangerously polluted by the Santa Marta port. Taganga and the Parque Nacional Tayrona can be visited from Santa Marta, and it's also the place to arrange a tour to Ciudad Perdida.

### Information

**Tourist Office** The Oficina de Turismo del Magdalena (☎ 212425), the departmental tourist office is in the former Convent of Santo Domingo, at Carrera 2 No 16-44. It's open Monday to Friday from 8 am to noon and 2 to 6 pm.

**Money** The Banco Popular and the Banco Industrial Colombiano will change your travellers' cheques and cash. Other banks marked on the map deal only with credit cards. There are several casas de cambio (cash only), including one in the Hotel Sompallón, on the corner of Carrera 1C and Calle 10C. TMA (Tierra Mar Aire), the representative of American Express, is at Calle 15 No 2-60 (☎ 234190).

**Inderena** Inderena (☎ 236265, 236355), Carrera 1C No 22-75, is open Monday to Friday from 8 am to noon and 2 to 5 pm.

**Tours** Santa Marta's tour market revolves around Ciudad Perdida, the major attraction in the region, and the most profitable one. Prices and conditions for visiting Ciudad Perdida have been fixed recently, so you should find a similar offer whoever you talk to. It's perhaps best to start shopping around in the Hotel Miramar (see Places to Stay), which has the most frequent tours and may

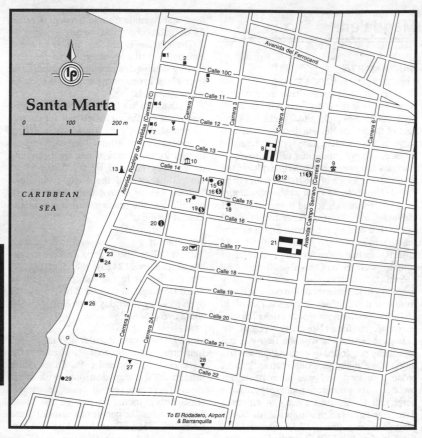

Santa Marta

CARIBBEAN
SEA

CARIBBEAN COAST

To El Rodadero, Airport
& Barranquilla

be slightly cheaper than other operators. Refer to the Ciudad Perdida section for further details on tours.

Another popular destination is Parque Nacional Tayrona. Here, again, the Hotel Miramar is one of the major operators and possibly the cheapest. It has chiva trips to Bahía Concha and Cañaveral, for about US$7 return each. If you want to go to Bahía Neguange, enquire at the Sol Hotel Inn, which is perhaps the cheapest for tours on this route (US$10).

Also check with TMA, at Calle 15 No 2-60, and Correcaminos, at Calle 15 No 3-

42, which may have tours to Ciénaga Grande de Santa Marta.

**Museo Arqueológico Tayrona**

The museum is in the Casa de la Aduana, a fine colonial mansion on the corner of Calle 14 and Carrera 2. It has an interesting collection of Tayrona objects, mainly pottery and gold, as well as artefacts of the Kogi and Arhuaco Indians. Don't miss the impressive model of the Ciudad Perdida. The museum is open Monday to Friday from 8 am to noon and 2 to 6 pm; the entrance fee is US$1. The museum has a choice of short documentary

**PLACES TO STAY**

| | |
|---|---|
| 1 | Hotel Sompallón |
| 2 | Hotel Miramar |
| 3 | Casa Familiar |
| 4 | Hotel Tayrona Mar |
| 6 | Hotel Yuldama |
| 24 | Hostal Miramar |
| 25 | Park Hotel |
| 26 | Sol Hotel Inn |

**PLACES TO EAT**

| | |
|---|---|
| 5 | Restaurante La Casa Vieja |
| 7 | Restaurante Rincón Paisa |
| 23 | Restaurante Panamerican |
| 27 | La Real Parrilla |
| 28 | Restaurante Oriental |

**OTHER**

| | |
|---|---|
| 8 | Iglesia de San Francisco |
| 9 | Telecom |
| 10 | Museo Arqueológico Tayrona |
| 11 | Banco Industrial Colombiano |
| 12 | Banco de Bogotá |
| 13 | Monumento a Rodrigo de Bastidas |
| 14 | Sam |
| 15 | Banco de Colombia |
| 16 | Banco Popular |
| 17 | Tierra Mar Aire |
| 18 | Correcaminos |
| 19 | Banco de Occidente |
| 20 | Tourist Office |
| 21 | Catedral |
| 22 | Avianca & Post Office |
| 29 | Inderena |

videos on indigenous cultures which are presented on request.

### Catedral

This massive whitewashed building on the corner of Carrera 4 and Calle 17 claims to be Colombia's oldest church, but it was not actually completed until the end of the 18th century, and thus reflects the influences of various architectural styles. It houses the ashes of the town's founder (just to the left as you enter the church). Simón Bolívar was buried here, but in 1842 his remains were taken to Caracas, his birthplace. The church is open for mass only, usually at 7 am, noon and 6 pm, with an additional mass at 10 am on Sunday.

### Quinta de San Pedro Alejandrino

This is the hacienda where Simón Bolívar spent his last days and died on 17 December 1830. Today it's a national monument. The hacienda was established at the beginning of the 17th century and was engaged in cultivating and processing sugarcane. The main house is furnished in the style of Bolívar's days. To one side of the house is the trapiche, the sugarcane mill.

Several monuments have been built on the grounds in remembrance of Bolívar. The most imposing is a monumental central structure, the Altar de la Patria. Next to it is a museum, part of which holds some historic paintings and other exhibits from the era. The other section features contemporary art donated by artists from Colombia, Venezuela, Panama, Ecuador, Peru and Bolivia, the countries liberated by Bolívar. Some works are related to Bolívar, others aren't, but all are worth seeing.

In the tourist season, the Quinta is open daily from 9.30 am to 4.30 pm; at other times it is closed on Monday and Tuesday. Admission is US$1.50. The Quinta is in the distant suburb of Mamatoco, about four km southeast of the city centre. Take the Mamatoco bus from the seafront (Carrera 1C); it's a 20-minute trip to the hacienda.

### Other Attractions

If you've read the *Fruit Palace* by Charles Nicholl, you might like to know that the famous Palacio de las Frutas which gave the book its title was at Calle 10C No 2-49. It no longer exists; now it's the Tienda El Progreso.

### Places to Stay

The legendary *Hotel Miramar* (☎ 214756), at Calle 10C No 1C-59, is the most popular budget place to stay. It offers the cheapest accommodation in town, and has become an archetypal gringo hotel, where you're likely to meet only foreign backpackers. The rooms are rather basic but have fans and some even have private baths. They cost about US$1.50 per person. If the rooms are full, the friendly manager, Jairo Portillo, can give you a hammock or a mattress (US$1 for either), or will find somewhere nearby for you. If you have your own hammock, you can string it up for a nominal fee. The hotel has its own café serving breakfast, fast food, snacks, soft drinks and beer.

The Miramar is a good place to pick up the latest travel news from other travellers. The manager is also a good source of information about the city and the region. He organises treks to Ciudad Perdida and runs tours to the Parque Nacional Tayrona in his own chiva. He will also store your gear free of charge.

The hotel is invariably full of backpackers and for some it may have too much of the Woodstock atmosphere. If you find the Miramar too noisy or too freak-filled, go to the *Casa Familiar* (☎ 211697), at Calle 10C No 2-14, a few steps east of the Miramar. It's smaller, quieter and cleaner and costs US$2.50 per person in rooms with bath. It's increasingly popular with gringos and the staff are friendly. They do excellent breakfasts but no other meals, and have information on tours to Tayrona, Ciudad Perdida etc.

Don't venture further east along Calle 10C. Most of the residencias there are used for prostitution and the area is not safe, especially at night.

If you need more comfort (but less atmosphere), there are several fairly good, modern places on the waterfront (Carrera 1C). In ascending order of price (and possibly value) they are: the *Sol Hotel Inn* (☎ 211131), at Carrera 1C No 20-23, at US$8/10 a single/double; the *Park Hotel* (☎ 211215), at Carrera 1C No 18-67, at US$9/12; the *Hostal Miramar* (☎ 214751), at US$12/16 (don't confuse it with the above-mentioned Hotel Miramar); and the *Hotel Sompallón* (☎ 214195), on the corner of Carrera 1C and Calle 10C, at US$10/18.

For something with a more individual style, go to the *Hotel Tayrona Mar* (☎ 212408), at Carrera 1C No 11-41, in an old house with a fine wooden interior and beautiful decorative tiling. It costs US$8 per person in a room with bath. The *Hotel Yuldama* (☎ 210063), at Carrera 1C No 12-19, is the top-end place in the area (US$22/30/35 a single/double/triple).

## Places to Eat

There are plenty of cheap restaurants around the Hotel Miramar, particularly on Calles 11 and 12 near the waterfront, where you can get an unsophisticated set meal for about US$1.25. The *Rincón Paisa*, next to the Hotel Yuldama, and *La Casa Vieja*, at Calle 12 No 1C-58, perhaps have slightly tastier food than the others.

The waterfront (Carrera 1C) is packed with restaurants offering almost everything from snacks and pizzas to local cuisine and seafood. The *Panamerican*, on the corner of Calle 18, is one of the best places.

*La Real Parrilla*, at Calle 22 No 2-28, does good grilled meats. *Restaurante Oriental*, at Calle 22 No 3-43, is recommended for Chinese food.

Several thatched restaurants between Calles 26 and 28, close to the beach, are noted for good fish. Choose between the *Terraza Marina* and *El Gran Manuel*.

## Getting There & Away

**Air** The airport is 16 km out of the city on the road to Barranquilla. City buses marked 'El Rodadero-Aeropuerto' will take you there from Carrera 1C (45 minutes).

Only Avianca and Sam operate flights to/from Santa Marta. You can book and buy tickets from their city offices, or from travel agents. There are flights to Bogotá (US$108), Medellín (US$91), Cúcuta (US$81) and Pereira (US$111).

**Bus** The spanking new bus terminal is on the south-eastern outskirts of the city, on the Troncal del Caribe (the Barranquilla-Riohacha road). Frequent urban buses go there from Carrera 1C in the city centre.

**To Bogotá** There are at least half a dozen direct buses (all go via Bucaramanga) with Copetrán and Expreso Brasilia (US$35 climatizado, 19 hours).

**To Medellín** There are four or five buses daily with Brasilia and Rápido Ochoa (US$27 climatizado, about 15 hours).

**To Barranquilla & Cartagena** There are plenty of buses to Barranquilla operated by several companies. La Veloz is the cheapest (US$2.25 pullman, two hours). The road goes through some spectacular scenery (see Isla de Salamanca for details).

Many of the climatizados continue on to Cartagena, but not so the cheaper pullmans. If you want to save money, go with La Veloz to Barranquilla and change to any of their frequent buses to Cartagena (see the Barranquilla section for more information).

**To Riohacha** Buses run frequently but only until mid afternoon (US$5.75 climatizado, US$5 pullman, three hours). All these buses continue on to Maicao (add US$2.50). Take any of these buses if you plan on going to Cañaveral in Parque Tayrona.

**Train** The train station is on the northern edge of the city centre but there are no longer passenger trains departing from there.

## EL RODADERO

El Rodadero, five km south of Santa Marta (formally within the city's administrative boundaries), is one of Colombia's most fashionable beach resorts. It has luxury hotels, posh restaurants, casinos, discos and nightclubs catering to the affluent Colombians who spend their holidays here. However, the bright days of El Rodadero have faded recently, as the bay and shore are becoming increasingly polluted. The beach itself is nothing extraordinary, and in the peak season (from Christmas to late January) it is dirty and crowded. If you like sunbathing in a sardine tin or are looking for a bit of nightlife this is the place. Otherwise go elsewhere, to the nearby Parque Nacional Tayrona for example, where you will find far more beautiful beaches.

### Information

The CNT tourist office is in a kiosk on the beach opposite Calle 8. It's open daily from 7.30 am to 6 pm.

### El Acuario y Museo del Mar

The aquarium and museum are on the shore a few km north-west of El Rodadero. The uninspiring aquarium has sharks, dolphins, turtles, seals and other marine species, all kept in small concrete tanks. The attached museum displays an odd variety of objects, ranging from copies of Inca ceramics to the propeller of an aeroplane which crashed nearby. They are both open daily from 8 am to 4 pm. The admission of US$3 makes this one of the most overpriced tourist sites in Colombia. You can get there by boat from the beach in El Rodadero; tickets can be bought on the corner of Carrera 1 and Calle 8 for US$3.50 including entrance fee. Otherwise you can walk there in one hour along the shore but you won't save much money, as you'll have to pay the entrance fee anyway.

### Places to Stay

El Rodadero is a creature made for large-scale tourism and it's certainly not cheap. The waterfront is lined with hotels but not the backpacker type. Less costly accommodation can be found further inland along the main road towards the south, but it is still not cheap. It's better to stay in Santa Marta and make a one-day trip to El Rodadero. Urban buses to and from Santa Marta are frequent and the trip takes only 15 minutes.

### Entertainment

The most famous local disco is La Escollera at the northern end of El Rodadero. It's open nightly from 8.30 pm to 4 am. Entry costs US$4. Have your dinner beforehand because no food or even snacks are available, and no beer. Spirits, however, are in good supply, and so is the music, at full volume of course.

### Getting There & Away

See the Santa Marta section for information about air and long-distance bus transport.

## TAGANGA

Taganga is a small fishing village set in a beautiful, deep, horseshoe-shaped bay, five km north of Santa Marta. The waterfront is packed with boats and is worth a stroll. Boat excursions along the coast can be arranged with locals, or you can walk around the surrounding hills, which offer splendid views.

Don't miss the Playa Grande, a magnificent bay north-west of the village. Either walk there (20 minutes) or take a boat from Taganga (US$0.50). The Playa Grande beach is lined with palm-thatched restaurants serving good fish. You can walk further along a path which winds around the slopes of the hilly coast up to the Playa Granate.

There's also the little-used path which heads up the arid hills to the Bahía Concha in the Parque Nacional Tayrona. It will take three or four hours to get there.

### Places to Stay & Eat

There's a choice of accommodation in Taganga. The best budget deal seems to be the *Hotel El Delfín* (US$4 per person). The *Hotel Playa Brava* offers more comfort but is far more expensive (US$15 a double, US$20 with air-con). The *Hotel La Ballena Azul* caters for more affluent tourists (US$30 a double) and has a good (though not cheap) restaurant. All three hotels are on the waterfront.

### Getting There & Away

Urban buses between Santa Marta and Taganga run every 20 minutes; you catch them on Carrera 1C in Santa Marta.

### PARQUE NACIONAL TAYRONA

This is probably the most popular national park in the country. It is set on the jungle-covered coast at the foot of the Sierra Nevada de Santa Marta. The park stretches along the coast from the Bahía de Taganga near Santa Marta to the mouth of the Río Piedras, 35 km to the east. The scenery varies from white sandy beaches to tropical rainforest at an altitude of 600 metres on the southern limits of the park. The extreme western part is arid, with light-brown hills and succulent vegetation. In contrast, the central and eastern parts are covered by lush forest. Many animals live in the park but most stay out of sight, deep in the forest.

The region was once the territory of the Tayrona Indians and some archaeological remains have been found in the park. The

Macaw

most important of these is the ancient town of Pueblito. Apart from the famous *caminos de piedra* (stone paths) and the stone foundations of several houses, not much is left, but nonetheless it's worth seeing, especially if you aren't planning a trip to Ciudad Perdida. The walk to Pueblito offers splendid rainforest scenery.

Perhaps the park's biggest attraction is its beaches, set in deep bays shaded by coconut palms. They are not wide or long but they are truly marvellous. Some of them are bordered by coral reefs which offer good snorkelling, but you need to be careful of the treacherous offshore currents.

The western part of the park is dry almost all year round except for a little rain in October and November. The eastern part is

CARIBBEAN SEA

**Parque Nacional Tayrona**

0      2.5      5 km

Ensenada de Guachaquita

Ensenada de Cinto

Ensenada de Gayraca
Ensenada de Chengue

Bahía Neguange

Arrecifes

Pueblito

Cañaveral

Gayraca

Los Naranjos

Isla de la Aguja

Bahía Concha    Concha

Ensenada de Granate

El Zaíno

Calabazo

Río Piedras

To Riohacha

Taganga

Pájaro

Palangana

Bahía de Taganga

To Santa Marta

wetter, particularly from May to June and from September to November. The upper parts get more rain than the coastline.

The park was closed in February 1994 for an indefinite time, but recent letters from travellers indicate that there are ways around this. Tour organisers in Santa Marta, including the manager of the Hotel Miramar, will surely know the current situation.

### Places to Stay & Eat

Inderena has a colony of cabañas known as the *Ecohabs* and a campsite in Cañaveral. The cabañas, made in the style of Tayrona huts, are spectacularly set on a coastal hill. The six-bed cabañas cost US$40, while the four-bed bungalows go for US$30.

The spacious campsite costs US$7 per tent and has baths, water facilities and a restaurant. You should book and pay for the cabañas or campsite in the Inderena office (Bogotá or Santa Marta) before you arrive in the park. It's best to book the cabañas well in advance in the high season (Christmas, January, Holy Week). There is also a restaurant in the complex.

In Arrecifes, two local families monopolise the accommodation facilities. They have

been living there since before the park was created, but now that tourists are coming, they are expanding the facilities. Both *Finca El Paraíso* and *Cañamar* have cabañas (about US$4 per person) and rent undercover hammocks (US$1.50), and both have restaurants. El Paraíso also has a camping area (US$1.50 per person).

In Bahía Concha, there's the *Restaurante Boconó* on the beach, and camping facilities for US$3 per tent.

### Getting There & Away

There are three separate roads leading to three different areas in the park – Bahía Concha, Bahía Neguange and Cañaveral – but these areas are not connected, by road or path, within the park.

Only Cañaveral is easy to get to on your own. Take one of the many buses that run along the coastal Santa Marta-Riohacha road and get off at El Zaíno, the main entrance to the park, 35 km from Santa Marta. It is open daily from 8 am to 5 pm; admission is US$0.50. You don't need a permit if you are only here for a day's visit.

Walk four km along the paved road to

Cañaveral on the shore. Here you'll find the park's administrative centre and Inderena's cabañas and campsite. The beaches are good here but there is no shade and the sea has dangerous offshore currents. You can walk to Los Naranjos (one hour) on the easternmost tip of the park, or west to Arrecifes (50 minutes) where the beaches are spectacular, with huge rocks both on and off the shore, adding a peculiar beauty. Remember, however, that sea currents here are just as dangerous as those in Cañaveral.

From Arrecifes, a scenic walk to Pueblito takes two hours along a path through the splendid tropical forest. There have been some cases of robbery on this route, so don't walk alone. Inderena organises free guided walks to Pueblito on Monday, Wednesday and Friday at 7.30 am. Enquire at the cabañas in Cañaveral. Don't continue down to Calabazo – this route is even more dangerous.

The western part of the park is accessible by two roads. One goes from Santa Marta through Pájaro to Bahía Concha, about 10 km. The other follows the main road to Riohacha for 12 km, then branches off to Gayraca and Bahía Neguange. There is no public transport on these roads. You can walk, hitch with difficulty or take a tourist bus from Santa Marta. See Tours in the Santa Marta section for information about transport to the park.

## ISLA DE SALAMANCA

Salamanca Island stretches along the coast between the town of Ciénaga in the east and the mouth of the Magdalena River in the west, and is bordered on the south by the lagoon of Ciénaga Grande de Santa Marta. The island has been declared a national park. Much of the area is (or rather was) covered by *manglares* (mangroves).

Mangroves are a kind of plantlife made up of various species of shrubs and trees which grow in the flat tropical and subtropical littorals. Their favourite habitats are brackish coastal waters, so they develop particularly well in estuarial areas of rivers. They grow rapidly and their fallen leaves decompose to provide a diet for fish and other water life.

Mangroves also attract other animals, mainly fowl.

You can find mangroves along most of the Colombian coast around river mouths. Isla de Salamanca is the most exceptional and tragic example of these. The Santa Marta-Barranquilla road constructed along the shoreline has formed an artificial barrier that has cut the fresh-water circulation and thus upset the ecological balance of the area. The coastal side, cut off from fresh water, has turned into a dead mangrove forest. Conversely, the mangroves on the other side of the road have also suffered due to a lack of salt water. A large part of the island is now a dead mangrove woodland which, though it looks extremely spectacular, is an ecological disaster. Work is now being carried out to reintroduce water circulation by opening drainage channels under the road to link the two parts.

There are basically two sites to visit in the park, Los Cocos and Cangarú.

### Los Cocos

Los Cocos, 10 km east of Barranquilla, is the administrative centre of the park. The mangroves in this area are less affected due to their proximity to the Magdalena River. A suspended wooden footpath has been built for visitors and it twists over the mangroves and ciénagas for about one km (a further 5000-metre stretch is under construction). It's a pleasant walk which provides an opportunity to see some of the birds in the park. You can also see the *criadero* (hatchery) behind the administrative house where the *babillas*, a species of a small spectacled cayman (*Caiman crocodilus fuscus*), are bred.

### Cangarú

Cangarú is 15 km east of Los Cocos by the road towards Santa Marta. The local tourist brochures rave about its beaches, but they are not very exciting. It is, however, the most damaged area of mangroves and worth seeing for that reason. You will see it passing along the road but stop if you want to get a closer look at this bizarre scene.

Colonial street in Girón, near Bucaramanga

Some of the old charms of Cartagena

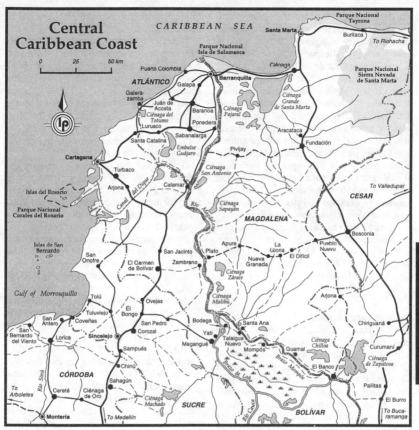

## Getting There & Away

It's very easy to get to both Los Cocos and Cangarú from either Barranquilla or Santa Marta as they are both on the main road and buses are frequent. On the other hand, it is difficult to get out by bus from Cangarú: buses don't like stopping here to pick people up. There is no problem in getting away from Los Cocos; local minibuses run between Barranquilla and the site called 'Km 13', passing through Los Cocos.

## CIÉNAGA GRANDE DE SANTA MARTA

The Ciénaga Grande was once a coastal bay at the mouth of the Magdalena River, but later on the Magdalena changed its course and moved further to the west. With time, the sea currents and waves built up a sand barrier (now the Isla de Salamanca) which sheltered the bay from the open sea and formed a vast, still body of water. Ciénaga Grande is Colombia's largest lagoon, some 25 km long and 20 km wide. It is shallow, on average one to two metres deep, with the deepest part near the sea.

To the south-west of the Ciénaga Grande there are several smaller lagoons linked to each other by an array of caños. Fertilised by silt deposited by the former course of the Magdalena River, this area is rich in vegetation, especially mangroves. It was made a nature reserve, the Santuario de Fauna y Flora Ciénaga Grande de Santa Marta, even though it doesn't include the lagoon after which it was named. The reserve occupies 230 sq km of swamps, lagoons and channels, and half of it is covered by mangroves. Aquatic resources and the mangrove forests provide a suitable habitat for a large animal population, particularly local and migratory birds. About 150 bird species, including ducks, egrets and herons, have been recorded in the area. Reptiles are represented by babillas (spectacled cayman), iguanas and turtles, and even boas have been seen here.

There are several fishing settlements scattered around the region, most of which are built on stilts. Nueva Venecia, in the middle of the Ciénaga Pajaral, is the most picturesque of all. However, it is more spectacular seen from the air than from the water.

### Getting There & Away

The Ciénaga is difficult to explore, as the only means of getting around is by boat and there is no regular transport. If you want to visit on your own, ask the fishermen in Ciénaga, Pueblo Viejo or Tasajeras to take you fishing, or negotiate an excursion. Otherwise contact Correcaminos in Santa Marta which can organise a tour to the Ciénaga Grande. They don't go as far as Nueva Venecia, and usually visit another village on the water, Trojas de Cataca.

# Atlántico

## BARRANQUILLA

• *pop 1,030,000 • 10 m • 28°C • ☎ (958)*

With a population of just over a million, Barranquilla is Colombia's fourth largest city and the capital of the Atlántico department. It's the country's main seaport and the most important industrial and commercial centre on the coast. It has a hot, damp

climate, with an average temperature of about 28°C.

The town was founded in 1629 but did not gain importance until the middle of the 19th century. Despite its potential as a port on the country's main fluvial artery, navigation problems at the mouth of the Magdalena River hindered development. Most of the merchandise moving up and down the Magdalena passed through Cartagena, using the Canal del Dique which joins the river about 100 km upstream from its mouth.

Only at the end of the 19th century did progress begin. The opening of the pier in Puerto Colombia and later, the regulation of the river mouth by the construction of breakwaters, boosted the development of the town, both as a fluvial and sea port.

By the turn of the century, Barranquilla was one of the major ports from which local goods, primarily coffee, were shipped overseas. It also came to be the gateway through which foreign influences and innovations first arrived into the country. It was here that Colombian aviation was born when the Sociedad Colombo-Alemana de Transporte Aéreo (SCADTA) was founded in 1919. South America's first commercial airline commenced scheduled flights into the interior in 1920. Twenty years later, it became Avianca, Colombia's national airline.

Progress attracted both Colombians from other regions and foreigners, mainly from the USA, Germany, Italy and the Middle East. This, in turn, gave the city an injection of foreign capital and accelerated its growth. It also brought about the city's cosmopolitan character.

Today, Barranquilla is a vast concrete sprawl without any obvious charm or many tourist attractions. The numerous industrial estates don't add much to its grace (more to its pollution), nor does the sweltering heat invite strolling about the streets. The sticky, still air is frequently refreshed by torrential rains which invariably turn most streets into rushing rivers, washing out litter, garbage, people and cars alike. This seems to be the only regular form of city cleaning.

The local tourist brochure on the city is

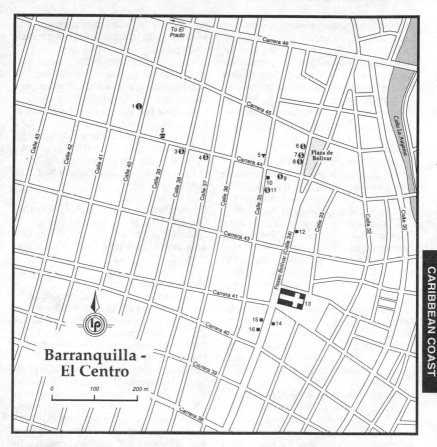

Barranquilla - El Centro

0    100    200 m

entitled *Barranquilla – Qué Maravilla!* (What a Marvel!), but few foreigners are likely to share this enthusiasm. However, for many Colombians (not just the city's inhabitants), Barranquilla does have great style and character. It embodies the costeño nature at is best (some would say craziest), and this is palpable in the city's ardent atmosphere and in the animated temperament of its dwellers. It all explodes during the four-day Carnaval de Barranquilla, the maddest of all Colombian fiestas.

Even though Barranquilla is thin on tourist sights it's an important place for coming to grips with the national psyche. It's here that

| | |
|---|---|
| 1 | Tourist Office |
| 2 | Telecom |
| 3 | Banco Popular |
| 4 | Banco Industrial Colombiano |
| 5 | Restaurante El Hogareño |
| 6 | Banco Sudemeris Colombia |
| 7 | Banco Anglo Colombiano |
| 8 | Banco Unión Colombiano |
| 9 | Banco de Bogotá |
| 10 | Hotel Victoria |
| 11 | Banco de Colombia |
| 12 | El Famoso Hotel |
| 13 | Iglesia de San Nicolás |
| 14 | Hotel Embajador |
| 15 | Hotel Hispano Americano |
| 16 | Hotel Niza |

you might start getting closer to Colombian magic realism, so puzzling for outsiders. Gabriel García Márquez (who lived here for a time at the beginning of his journalistic career) seems to have taken some of this from Barranquilla to weave into his novels.

If you decide to come here to feel the vibrant costeño pulse, keep in mind that, like every big city, Barranquilla can be unsafe.

## Orientation

Barranquilla sits on the left (west) bank of the Río Magdalena, about 10 km upstream from its mouth. The city plan is roughly oval, 12 km long from north to south and eight km wide. Its limits are marked by a ring road, Vía Circunvalación. Close to the river is the city centre (where the town was first settled), along the Paseo Bolívar. Most of this district, especially the area between the Paseo and the river is inhabited by wild street commerce – it's actually one vast market. It's busy, noisy and unbelievably littered.

Three km to the north-west is El Prado, Barranquilla's new centre, and possibly the most pleasant district of the city. Midway between the two is the cathedral. The bus terminal is off the southern edge of the oval, beyond Vía Circunvalación. The airport is still further south.

Urban transport is poor, wild and chaotic, a typical costeño affair. The buses still move around the outer suburbs but invariably get trapped in traffic jams as soon as they reach the central area. The use of car horns seems to be more common here than in other cities.

## Information

**Tourist Office** The tourist office, the Fondo Mixto de Promoción Turística (☎ 415055), is in Edificio Cámara de Comercio, Calle 40 No 44-39, Piso 5. It's open Monday to Friday from 8.30 am to noon and 2 to 5.30 pm.

**Money** There are several useful banks in the Paseo Bolívar area. Banco Unión Colombiano, Banco Anglo Colombiano, Banco Sudameris Colombia and Banco Industrial Colombiano all change American Express travellers' cheques. The Sudameris only

occasionally provides this service (some cajoling might be useful), but when it does, it will probably pay the best rate.

You can change cash in the Banco Industrial Colombiano. Banco Popular will also change cash but it is as inefficient here as it is elsewhere in Colombia.

Advance pesos on Visa card are given by Banco de Colombia, Banco de Bogotá, Banco Unión Colombiano and Banco Anglo Colombiano, while MasterCard is accepted by Banco Industrial Colombiano.

TMA (☎ 345152) is at Calle 74 No 52-34, in El Prado.

**Consulates** The Venezuelan consulate (☎ 582832) is in the Centro Comercial El Prado, Calle 70 No 53-74, Piso 4. The Panamanian consulate (☎ 451987) is at Calle 81 No 57-23.

## Things to See

The two areas you might want to visit are the city centre and El Prado. They are just a few km away but a world apart from each other.

The central sector is cut in two by the Paseo Bolívar. Halfway along it is the mock-Gothic Iglesia de San Nicolás, worth entering for its main altarpiece and the pulpit. To the east of the church is the sprawling market which spreads down to the river. It's fervent, crowded and perhaps reminiscent of oriental markets, but more so because of the noise, dirt and business fever rather than the colour and variety of products for sale. Contraband items, presumably coming here from Maicao, are plentiful.

El Prado is quite a different story. It's cleaner, greener and safer than the Paseo Bolívar area, and has a far calmer atmosphere. Calle 72 is the district's principal shopping street, lined with restaurants, snack bars, fancy shops and boutiques – a hell of a difference to the shabby street stands of Paseo Bolívar. There are a handful of high-rise buildings around but they are neither very high nor very inspiring.

Strolling around, you'll find some architectural relics from the turn of the century, the time when El Prado began its life. Note the buildings in the Muslim style, the effect of Middle-Eastern migration. You'll find a few of them on and just off Carrera 54. Include in your trip the attractions detailed below, all of which are in El Prado or its vicinity.

**Catedral** The modern cathedral, only completed in 1982, is on the corner of Calle 53 and Carrera 46. Don't be put off by its squat, heavy, somewhat bunker-like exterior – go inside. It's open from 4 to 8 pm, but if you knock on the door of the adjoining building to the left (south) at any other reasonable time of the day, someone will probably let you in. The interior has a number of large stained glass windows and mosaics of María Reyna y Auxiliadora (patron saint of the cathedral) and of San José, on the side walls. Each mosaic is composed of about 400,000 pieces of coloured glass imported from Germany. Both the stained-glass windows and the mosaics are the work of Mario Ayala, a Cali artist.

The sculpture of Cristo Libertador over the high altar is even more impressive. This unusual, 16-metre-high work in bronze, weighing 16 tons, was made by Rodrigo Arenas Betancur, Colombia's pre-eminent monument designer. If you are interested in the symbolism of the sculpture, read the plaques beneath the mosaics.

**Museo Romántico** Ironically named the Romantic Museum, this is actually a museum of the city's history. Scores of objects related to the city's past are displayed in several rooms. Some rooms are dedicated to migrant communities – German and Jewish among others – that have influenced the region. The museum is at Carrera 54 No 59-199 and is open Monday to Friday from 9 to 11 am and 2 to 5 pm; admission is US$0.70.

**Museo de Antropología** This museum, on the corner of Calle 68 and Carrera 54, displays a small collection of pre-Columbian ceramics from different regions, including several extraordinary pieces from the Calima, Tumaco and Nariño cultures (on the

1st floor). In the ground-floor hall is an interesting exhibition dedicated to the symbols, weaving and use of the mochila of the Arhuaco Indians living in the Sierra Nevada de Santa Marta. The museum is open Monday to Friday from 8 am to noon and 2.30 to 5 pm; entry is free.

**Jardín Zoológico** The zoo, at Calle 77 No 68-70, was perhaps once the best in Colombia but has recently suffered from neglect. Tightly packed in a small area, there are some 2000 animals belonging to about 300 species, including plenty of birds and several ligers (a cross between a lion and a Bengal tiger). There is also the small Museo de Historia Natural within the zoo grounds.

The zoo is open Monday to Friday from 9 am to noon and 2 to 6 pm, and on Saturday, Sunday and holidays from 10 am to 6 pm. Admission is US$1.25. The ticket office stops selling tickets one hour before closing time. To get to the zoo from the city centre, take the bus marked 'Vía Cuarenta' from the Plaza de Bolívar.

**Carnaval de Barranquilla**
With a century-long official history (but with traditions dating back much further), this four-day fiesta preceding Ash Wednesday (February or March) is when the whole city goes wild. All normal city activities such as urban transport and commerce are totally paralysed by street dances, music, parades and masquerades.

The Carnaval begins on Saturday with La Batalla de Flores (the Battle of Flowers), a float parade. It continues on Sunday with La Gran Parada, when thousands of people don fancy dresses and disguises and file through the streets. On Monday there is El Festival de Orquestas, a marathon concert of Caribbean music groups. The Carnaval concludes on Tuesday with a symbolic burial of Joselito Carnaval.

Apart from the official programme, it is a round-the-clock rumba, fuelled by large quantities of spirits. There is an estimated 100,000 cases of rum and aguardiente sold during these four days. Although it is getting more commercialised and lacks some of the spontaneity of years ago, it is still probably the most colourful and undoubtedly maddest of all of Colombia's carnivals. Unfortunately, as always, it's a focus for all sorts of local and visiting *ladrones* (thieves) and *atracadores* (robbers). Be on guard, especially if you plan to photograph or film the event.

### Places to Stay

The centre of budget accommodation is on and around Paseo Bolívar (Calle 34). This area is not that safe at night, so limit your evening strolls and keep your eyes open during the day. Since the bus offices operating buses to Santa Marta and Cartagena moved from the Plaza de Bolívar to the new terminal, the Paseo has lost much of its convenience. Yet if you are after a genuinely cheap room, this is the place to look.

Outside the Paseo there are no other concentrated areas of budget hotels. El Prado is a more pleasant area to stay in, but it is a rather upper-class district and the hotels there are more expensive.

During the Carnaval it is unlikely you will find a room in any of the budget or mid-range hotels, despite the fact that the prices are much higher.

**Paseo Bolívar & Around** There are lots of hotels all the way along the Paseo and in the adjacent streets, but not that many to recommend. Most double as sex hotels or are brothels, and the standard is generally poor or very poor.

One of the cheapest and good value for money is *El Famoso Hotel* (☎ 316513), at Calle 34 No 43-42. It's anything but famous, but has clean, airy rooms with private bath and fan that cost US$2.50 per person.

Other acceptable budget places, costing much the same as the Famoso, include the *Hotel Niza* (☎ 317080), at Calle 34 No 40-53, and diagonally opposite, the *Hotel Embajador* (☎ 517874), at Calle 34 No 40-66. The latter also has air-con rooms but they are far more expensive.

The *Hotel Victoria* (☎ 410055), at Calle 35 No 43-140, was perhaps one of the poshest hotels half a century ago, as you can see by its imposing balconied façade, antique lift and high, spacious corridors. These days it doesn't fly so high, but nonetheless it's still a comfortable place to stay and not expensive: US$8/10/12 for a single/double/triple with bath and fan, and US$10/12/15 for air-con rooms.

For much the same price you can stay in the *Hotel Hispano Americano* (☎ 515154), at Calle 34 No 40-73. It hasn't the old-time style of the Victoria but offers fairly good standards. Avoid rooms facing the Paseo, as it is noisy till late at night.

**El Prado** One of the cheapest in this area is the *Hotel Astor* (☎ 322318), at Carrera 53 No 55-129. It only has matrimonios (a sign that it doubles as a 'love hotel'), either with fan or air-con, costing US$10/12, respectively.

The prices of the more respectable hotels in El Prado normally begin at about US$20/25/30 for a single/double/triple – not very cheap by Colombian standards. For this price, or slightly more, you can choose between the *Hotel Caribeño* (☎ 560995, 451094), at Carrera 46 No 70-17, *Hotel Arenosa* (☎ 450600, 450071), at Carrera 48 No 70-136, *Hotel Davega* (☎ 561213), at Carrera 44 No 70-242, and *Hotel Las Brisas* (☎ 414107) at Calle 61 No 46-41. All have rooms with air-con and TV.

If you are prepared to pay a little more, perhaps the best choice is the *Aparta Hotel Sima* (☎ 341028, 450055), at Carrera 49 No 72-19. It has large rooms with air-con and TV, costing US$25/32 for a single/double. Some of the rooms also have an electric stove.

The *Hotel Majestic* (☎ 511542, 514271), at Carrera 53 No 54-41, is one of the most stylish places to stay, with something of a Moorish air. Singles/doubles/triples cost US$43/52/62 in air-con rooms with all the usual facilities. The hotel has a small swimming pool and a good restaurant.

The slightly more expensive *Hotel Dos Mundos* (☎ 581322) is strategically located on the main commercial artery of new

Barranquilla at Calle 72 No 47-59. Alternatively, for a bit more still, stay in the high-rise *Royal Hotel* (☎ 565533, 567125), at Carrera 54 No 68-124. Take a room on one of the upper floors for a good view of the city.

Half a block away at Carrera 54 No 70-10 is the large, old-style *Hotel El Prado* (☎ 565122). Built in 1928, it's traditionally considered one of the best in the city, with its own swimming pool, restaurant, bar and the like. However, this pleasure will cost you at least US$120/150 a single/double, and still more if you feel like staying in a suite.

### Places to Eat

The central city area, along and off Paseo Bolívar, is full of cheap restaurants which offer set meals for around US$1.50. *Restaurante El Hogareño*, on Calle 35 next to the corner of Carrera 44, is just an example, and you'll find plenty of others nearby. Look around and take your pick. There are several budget pseudo-Chinese restaurants on Calle 35 between Carreras 41 and 44.

You can also eat in the street or in the market – the centre is actually one huge market. Many stalls sell delicious arepas de huevo (a fried maize dough with an egg inside), the local speciality. You can get good fish in the market proper, towards the river; just point to the one you want and they will fry it in front of you.

El Prado is rather more for finer dining but there are a number of budget eateries to choose from as well. The *Italian Pizza*, at Calle 75 No 53-30, is one of them. It doesn't serve pizzas but does serve filling set meals for US$1.50 until 5 pm.

*Restaurante El Calderito*, at Carrera 52 No 72-107, does good costeño food at reasonable prices. *Restaurante El Tinajero*, at Carrera 47 No 69-97, is another good place for Colombian cuisine (a main course will cost somewhere between US$5 and US$7), and has tables arranged in its pleasant patio-garden.

*Restaurante La Plaza*, at Carrera 53 No 70-150, is an Antioquian venue, with both paisa food and décor. It's one of the loveliest places in the city; you feel as if you're on the plaza of some imaginary Antioquian town. Go and see the place, even if you are not after its hearty bandeja paisa.

The *Centro Gastronómico Internacional de Barranquilla*, at Carrera 46 No 64-14, houses a choice of up-market establishments, including *Restaurante El Mesón de Morgan*, recommended for seafood, and *Restaurante Bismark*, serving German and other European specialities.

*Restaurante Devis'*, at Carrera 56 No 72-110, is one of the best addresses to call at for French delicacies, though they are not cheap by any definition. An alternative place to go for French food is *Restaurante La Fourchette*, at Carrera 49C No 76-144.

The international menu of the *Hotel El Prado* probably won't disappoint you, though it won't be the cheapest dinner in town.

*Pastelería Repostería Dulcerna*, at Carrera 53 No 75-30, has excellent espresso coffee plus a choice of tempting high-calorie cakes and pastries.

### Getting There & Away

**Air** The airport is about 10 km south of the city centre and is connected to the centre by urban buses. Almost all main Colombian carriers land in Barranquilla and fly to most major cities. The main destinations include Bogotá (US$104 with Avianca, Sam and Aces; US$73 with Intercontinental), Medellín (US$90 with Avianca, Sam and Aces), Cali (US$118 with Avianca, Sam and Aces; US$78 with Intercontinental) and San Andrés (US$102 with Avianca, Sam and Aces).

Aerocorales, a new coastal carrier, flies light planes (daily except weekends) to Valledupar (US$39) and Cartagena (US$30), and is expected to reintroduce its flights to Mompós as soon as Mompós airport is refurbished.

Aerosucre (the cargo carrier) flies once or twice a week to the island of San Andrés. It occasionally takes passengers, for roughly half the commercial fare. Its office and warehouse are just before the main passenger

CARIBBEAN COAST

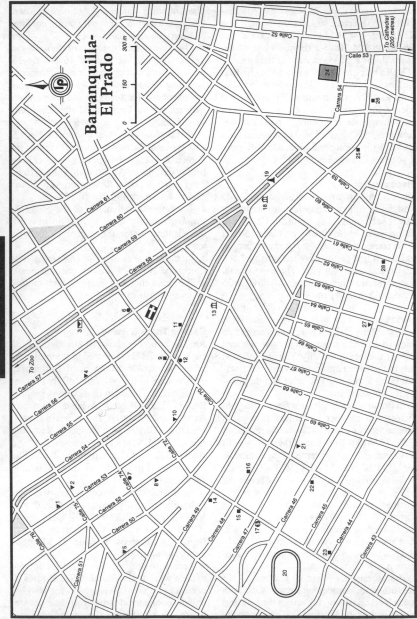

Barranquilla–
El Prado

## PLACES TO STAY

9  Hotel El Prado
11  Royal Hotel
14  Aparta Hotel Sima
15  Hotel Dos Mundos
16  Hotel Arenosa
22  Hotel Caribeño
23  Hotel Davega
25  Hotel Astor
26  Hotel Majestic
28  Hotel Las Brisas

## PLACES TO EAT

1  Pastelería Repostería Dulcerna
2  Restaurante Italian Pizza
4  Restaurante Devis'
5  Restaurante La Fourchette
8  Restaurante El Calderito
10  Restaurante La Plaza
21  Restaurante El Tinajero
27  Centro Gastronómico
    Internacional de Barranquilla

## OTHER

3  Avianca & Post Office
6  Copa
7  Tierra Mar Aire
12  Venezuelan Consulate
13  Museo de Antropología
17  Banco Anglo Colombiano
18  Museo Romántico
19  Monumento a los Héroes
    de la Aviación
20  Estadio Municipal Romelio
    Martínez
24  Teatro Amira de la Rosa

terminal, on your right going towards the airport.

Copa, the Panamanian airline, has two flights a week to Panama City (US$118 plus 19% Colombian tax). Lacsa, the carrier of Costa Rica, flies three times a week to Caracas (US$161 plus 19% tax).

**Bus** The new bus terminal came into operation in 1993 on the southern outskirts of Barranquilla, about seven km from the city centre. It's nowhere near or nowhere convenient, and nothing special in itself. For example, the builders haven't provided a left-luggage room.

Urban transport between the terminal and the city centre leaves a lot to be desired. As yet, there are infrequent buses, some of which go via the backstreets of the poor southern barrios, and can take up to one hour to complete the route (if it's not raining, of course). This may improve in the future when the urban bus companies realise that they have a new terminal.

A taxi from the city centre or El Prado to the terminal will cost US$4, and that's more than an intercity bus fare to Santa Marta.

**To Bogotá** There are a dozen buses daily with Copetrán and Brasilia (US$37 climatizado, 20 hours).

**To Bucaramanga** Brasilia and Copetrán have at least 20 buses daily (US$24 climatizado, US$18 pullman, 10 to 11 hours).

**To Medellín** Brasilia and Rápido Ochoa have about 10 buses a day; they don't pass through Cartagena but go via a shorter route through Calamar (US$27 climatizado, 13 hours).

**To Cartagena** Buses by one or another of several companies depart every 10 minutes or so. Brasilia and La Costeña are the most expensive (US$4.50 climatizado, 2½ hours), whereas Coolibertador, Unitransco and La Veloz are the cheapest (US$3.25 pullman, three hours).

**To Santa Marta** Buses to Santa Marta are operated by the same companies as those to Cartagena, and they run frequently. The expensive operators charge US$3 in their climatizados, while the pullmans of the cheap carriers cost US$2.25. The journey takes 1½ to two hours, depending on the traffic in Barranquilla. Watch out for the dead mangroves along the way.

**To Valledupar** Brasilia and La Costeña have buses leaving every hour (US$10.25 climatizado, US$9 pullman, five hours).

**To Mompós** Unitransco has one morning and one evening bus to Mompós via Magangué. The trip costs US$11, involving a ferry across the Río Magdalena, and can take up to 10 hours.

## AROUND BARRANQUILLA
### Puente de Pumarejo

Spanning the Río Magdalena some 20 km upstream from its mouth, the Puente de Pumarejo, built in 1974, is the longest bridge in Colombia. It provides a panoramic view of the entire city of Baranquilla and the river.

You will cross over it on the road to Santa Marta or Bogotá but otherwise it's not worth a separate trip.

### Bocas de Ceniza

Literally the Mouth of Ashes, this is the mouth of the Magdalena. The name refers to the colour of the river water at its opening to the sea. The mouth is bordered by two eight-km-long *tajamares* (breakwaters) built in 1937 to enable ships to enter the river. There are railway tracks along the west breakwater, but the tourist train which used to ply this route seems to be out of action. You can walk and enjoy the scenery of the blue sea on one side and the grey river on the other. Preferably, for safety reasons, don't wander around on your own.

### Puerto Colombia

Puerto Colombia, set on the coast 15 km west of Barranquilla, was previously the city's port, built to resolve the continuous problems of the unreliable and dangerous entrance into the mouth of the Magdalena. The nearly two-km-long wooden muelle (pier) was constructed in the 1890s to enable ships to dock. It was reputedly the world's longest pier at that time. Ships from Europe and the USA pulled in here and this pushed forward the city's development.

The pier was faced in concrete in the 1920s but soon began to lose its importance as currents and waves gradually deposited more and more sand around the shore and large ships were no longer able to anchor. The regulation of the river mouth and the construction of a new wharf in Barranquilla marked the end of the pier's service.

When the ships disappeared, the tourists came (attracted by the pier and sand) and Puerto Colombia enjoyed a short life as a trendy seaside resort. The area still draws city dwellers on the weekends, although little of its former splendour remains – except for the pier, the solitary remnant of its brisk period of prosperity.

Puerto Colombia is Barranquilla's main beach, though it's not too exciting. It's deserted on weekdays but has a flow of city holiday-makers on Saturday and Sunday. On these days, shack restaurants open to serve freshly caught fried fish and other local dishes to visitors.

Urban buses run regularly between the city centre and Puerto Colombia, or you can go by taxi (around US$8).

### Galapa

Galapa, 12 km from Barranquilla on the road to Cartagena, is a village noted for its craft traditions. For decades local artisans have manufactured elaborate masks which are then used in the Carnaval de Barranquilla. The masks, depicting animal heads, are carved in wood and painted in bright colours. They are also made for sale to tourists.

### VOLCÁN DE LODO EL TOTUMO

About 50 km south-west of Barranquilla, on the bank of the large but shallow Ciénaga del Totumo, one can find an intriguing 15-metre-high mud mound, looking like a miniature volcano. It's indeed a volcano but instead of lava and ashes, it eructs mud.

Legend has it that the volcano once belched fire but the local priest, seeing it as the devil's malicious games, frequently sprinkled it with holy water. He not only succeeded in extinguishing the fire but also in turning the insides into mud to drown the devil.

Mud volcanoes have nothing to do with traditional volcanoes. The phenomenon is due to gases emitted by decaying organic matter underground. The gases produce pressure which forces the mud upwards. It gradually accumulates to form a conical mud monticule with a crater at the top. The volcano continues to grow as long as mud is being pushed up to spill over the edge of the crater.

There are a number of mud volcanoes in Colombia. They are spread along the Caribbean coastline from the mouth of the Magdalena to the Golfo de Urabá. The biggest and best known are El Totumo and the one in Arboletes (see that section for details). The majority of others are just holes in the ground with occasional mud emissions.

El Totumo is the highest of all; it's reputedly one of the largest mud volcanoes in the world. It's conical in shape and really quite beautiful. Lukewarm mud fills its crater with the consistency of cream. You can climb to the top and have a refreshing mud bath. You may at first feel a bit uncomfortable about stepping into the unappetising thick sludge, but don't be put off. It's a unique experience. Surely volcano-dipping is something you haven't already tried! The mud contains minerals acclaimed for their therapeutic properties. Once you've finished your session, go down and wash the mud off in the ciénaga.

### Getting There & Away

El Totumo is on the border of the Atlántico and Bolívar departments, roughly equidistant between Barranquilla and Cartagena. You can get to the volcano from both of these cities, though in both cases you'll have to walk the last part of the way.

**From Barranquilla** Take the bus to Juan de Acosta from the corner of Calle 35 and Carrera 39 in the city centre. At the time of writing, Barranquilla's tourist office was planning to introduce a one-day tour to the volcano, so ask them for news.

**From Cartagena** Take the bus to Galerazamba. It goes along the Barranquilla road up to Santa Catalina and shortly after turns north onto a side road. Get off at Loma de Arena (US$1.50, one hour) and walk along the ciénaga's shore to the volcano.

# Bolívar

## CARTAGENA

• *pop 680,000* • *5 m* • *28°C* • ☎ *(953)*

Cartagena de Indias is legendary both for its history and its beauty. It has been immortalised on countless canvases, glorified in hundreds of books and had its every detail photographed; it really deserves all of these tributes. It is Colombia's most fascinating city and unique in South America. You surely wouldn't want to miss it. Don't come here in a hurry, intending to skip over the 'places of interest' and slip away. It is impossible! The charm of the city will keep you here for several days or perhaps even a full week.

### History

Cartagena was founded in 1533 by Pedro de Heredia. It quickly grew into a rich town but in 1552 an extensive fire destroyed a large number of its wooden buildings. Since that time only stone, brick and tile have been permitted as building materials. Within a short time the town blossomed into the main Spanish port on the Caribbean coast and the gateway to all of northern South America. It was the storehouse for the treasure plundered from the Indians until the galleons could ship it back to Spain. No wonder then that Cartagena became a tempting target for all sorts of buccaneers marauding the Caribbean Sea.

In the 16th century alone the town suffered five dreadful sieges by pirates, the most famous (or infamous) of which was headed by Sir Francis Drake. He sacked the port in 1586 and 'mercifully' agreed not to burn the town to the ground once he was presented with a huge ransom of 10 million pesos, which he shipped back to England.

It was in response to pirate attacks that the Spaniards decided to make Cartagena an impregnable port and constructed elaborate walls encircling the town, and a chain of outer forts to protect it. These fortifications made the city unique in South America and helped to save Cartagena during the fiercest and biggest attack of all, headed by Edward Vernon in 1741. He launched an offensive with a fleet of 186 ships, over 2000 cannons and about 25,000 men. The defence was commanded by Don Blas de Lezo.

If there is one man who stands out in Cartagena's heroic history it is probably Blas de Lezo. He was born in Spain of noble parents and entered the service of the king, but as a young officer he lost his left leg in the Battle of Gibraltar. He remained in service but misfortune followed him. In Toulon he lost his left eye and later on, in the Battle of Barcelona, lost his right arm. Nev-

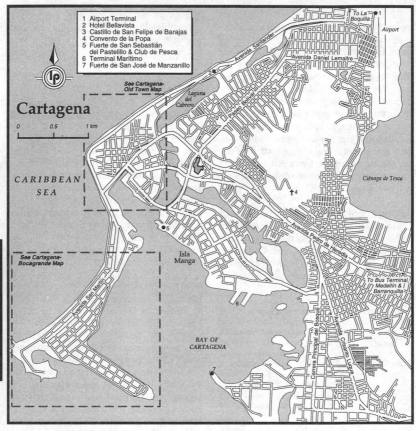

Cartagena

1 Airport Terminal
2 Hotel Bellavista
3 Castillo de San Felipe de Barajas
4 Convento de la Popa
5 Fuerte de San Sebastián
   del Pastelillo & Club de Pesca
6 Terminal Marítimo
7 Fuerte de San José de Manzanillo

ertheless, his tenacity and courage had made him a legend and when the Spaniards heard about a planned assault on Cartagena, they engaged Blas de Lezo to defend the city.

He had only 2500 men, including black slaves and Indians brought from the interior, and five warships. And he succeeded! The English were so sure of their imminent victory that they coined commemorative medals before the siege had ended. Such was their arrogance that one coin depicted Blas de Lezo on his knees in surrender to Vernon. The English apparently felt it ungallant to conquer half a man so they gave him back

his arm and leg in the scene depicting his capitulation which never took place.

Don Blas, however, was wounded again in the battle, this time in his remaining leg, and died shortly after the withdrawal of Vernon's fleet. His statue stands at the entrance to the San Felipe fortress.

In spite of the high price it had to pay for the pirate attacks, Cartagena continued to flourish. The Canal del Dique, constructed in 1650 to connect Cartagena Bay with the Magdalena River, made the town the main gateway for ships to the ports upriver, and a large part of the merchandise shipped inland passed through Cartagena. The town was also granted a royal monopoly as a slave-trading port. During the long colonial period, Cartagena was the most important bastion of the Spanish overseas empire and influenced much of Colombia's history.

The indomitable spirit of the inhabitants was rekindled again at the time of the independence movement. Cartagena was one of the first towns to proclaim independence from Spain, early in 1810, which prompted Bogotá and other cities to do the same. The declaration was signed on 11 November 1811, but the city eventually paid dearly for it. Spanish forces under Pablo Morillo were sent in 1815 to reconquer and 'pacify' the town and finally took it after a four-month siege. Over 6000 inhabitants died of starvation and disease.

In August 1819 Simón Bolívar's troops defeated the Spaniards at Boyacá and brought freedom to Bogotá. However, Cartagena had to wait for its liberation until October 1821 when the patriot forces eventually took the city from the sea. It was Bolívar who gave Cartagena its well-deserved name of 'La Heroica', the Heroic City.

Cartagena soon began to recover and was shortly once again the trading and shipping centre of South America. The city's prosperity attracted foreign immigrants, and many Jews, Italians, French, Turks, Lebanese and Syrians settled here. Today their descendants own many of the hotels and restaurants, particularly in Bocagrande.

Over the past decades Cartagena has expanded dramatically and is now surrounded by vast suburbs. Its population grew from 490,000 in 1985 to 660,000 in 1993. It is today Colombia's second largest port and an important industrial centre specialising in petrochemicals. Nevertheless, the old walled town has changed very little. It is a living museum of 16th and 17th-century architecture.

### Climate

Cartagena's climate is typically Caribbean, with its average annual temperature of 28˚C,
changing very little throughout the year. Although the days are hot, a fresh breeze blows in the evening making it a pleasant time to stroll around the city. The dry season lasts approximately from November to April; the rest of the year is wetter. Mean annual rainfall is about 900 mm.

### Orientation

The heart of the city is the old town, facing the sea to the west and almost entirely separated by water from the mainland to the east. The old town was built in two sections, creating an inner and outer town. Both were surrounded by walls and separated from each other by a channel, the Caño de San Anastasio. The channel was filled up to make way for the construction of the sharp, wedge-shaped, modern district, La Matuna.

The inner walled town, towards the west, is bigger than the outer one. It consists of El Centro, in the south, where traditionally the upper classes lived, and San Diego, in the north, previously occupied by the middle classes. The outer walled town, Getsemaní, once inhabited by the lower end of the social ladder, is smaller and understandably poorer, with more modest architecture. Outside the walled town several monumental fortresses still stand.

Stretching south of the old town is an unusual, L-shaped peninsula, occupied by three districts: Bocagrande, Castillo Grande and El Laguito. These are relatively new suburbs but are developing fast.

The coastline of the peninsula has limited the city's spread so growth has turned vertical, and today the area boasts a collection of high-rise buildings. Bocagrande and El Laguito have developed into up-market holiday resorts, becoming the main destinations for affluent Colombians and international charter tours. These areas are now packed with top-class hotels, posh restaurants, boutiques and nightspots.

The seafront of Bocagrande is lined with a beach, but it is neither attractive nor clean. Furthermore, it was closed for bathing in November 1994 after high levels of waste bacteria were found in the surrounding waters.

## Information

**Tourist Offices** The CNT office (☎ 647015, 647019) is in the Casa del Marqués de Valdehoyos, in El Centro. It's open daily from 8 am to noon and 2 to 6 pm.

The local tourist board, the Empresa Promotora de Turismo de Cartagena, has three offices: at the airport; at the Muelle de los Pegasos (☎ 651843), outside the walls of the inner town; and in Bocagrande (☎ 654987), on the corner of Carrera 1 and Calle 4. All three are open Monday to Friday from 7 am to 7 pm, and on Saturday and Sunday from 7 am to noon.

**Money** Three banks currently change travellers' cheques and cash: Banco Sudameris Colombia (best rate for cheques), Banco Industrial Colombiano (best rate for cash) and Banco Unión Colombiano. Most major banks will accept your Visa card, while MasterCard may be honoured only by Banco Industrial Colombiano and Banco de Occidente.

There are plenty of casas de cambio, particularly on or just off Plaza de los Coches. They are open daily except Sunday till 6 pm, and change cash (at slightly lower rates than the banks) but not travellers' cheques.

If your American Express travellers' cheques have been lost or stolen, contact the Tierra Mar Aire office (☎ 651062) in Bocagrande, Carrera 4 No 7-196.

Cartagena is probably the only Colombian city where you will get plenty of offers in the street (sometimes persistent ones) to change money at a very attractive rate, considerably higher than the bank rate. Give the street changers a big miss – they are all conmen.

The ploy goes something like the following. The changers hand you a bundle of peso notes, supposedly the exact equivalent of the dollars you want to change. You count them but it appears that some money is missing, sometimes only one or two small notes. They pretend to be surprised as if it was a genuine mistake and then take the bundle back, count

it out again, admit you're right, and top it up with the missing notes. At the same time they skilfully remove the largest bills, and give you back the 'correct' amount of money.

If you're determined to try your luck with these conmen, make sure you count the notes out again and don't hand over your dollar bills until you're satisfied. And remember that they have a full range of other tricks in case you happen to be wise to this one. They operate in gangs and are very clever with their hands.

**Consulates** The Venezuelan consulate (☎ 650382, 650353) is at Avenida Piñango (Calle 5A) No 10-106 in Castillo Grande. A traveller reported that he managed to get a tourist visa here for an overland crossing to Venezuela (US$35) on the basis of a confirmed flight out of Caracas on his onward ticket.

The Panamanian consulate is on the corner of Carrera 5 and Calle 67 in Crespo, near the airport. The visa is usually issued within 10 minutes and costs US$10 to US$15, depending on your nationality. This consulate has been known to issue visas for travellers planning an overland trip to Panama via the Darién without an onward ticket. If this is the case, get the consul to write a note in your passport specifying that you are travelling overland to North America. Otherwise, you'll be turned back in Puerto Obaldía. It's much safer to have an onward ticket anyway.

## Old Town

Obviously, the old city is the principal attraction, particularly the inner walled town. It is a real gem of colonial architecture, packed with churches, monasteries, plazas, palaces and noble mansions with their overhanging balconies and shady patios.

Getsemaní, the outer walled town, is less impressive and not so well preserved, but has some charming places and is well worth exploring. It is less tourist oriented and more authentic. However, take extra precautions – this part of the city is not that safe.

The old town is surrounded by thick walls,

the **Murallas**, built to protect it against enemies. Construction began towards the end of the 16th century after the attack by Francis Drake (until that time Cartagena was completely unprotected) but the project was to take two centuries to complete due to repeated damage from storms and pirate attacks. Only in 1796 was it finally finished, 25 years before the Spaniards were eventually expelled.

The Murallas are an outstanding piece of military engineering and they are well worth visiting. Only a handful of the walls of walled cities in the world are preserved in such good condition as those of Cartegena. A part of the wall facing La Matuna was unfortunately demolished several decades ago by 'progressive' authorities.

Most of the major tourist attractions are within the inner walled town, particularly in El Centro. The best approach is to wander leisurely, savouring the architectural details, rich street life and local snacks along the way. Don't just seek out the sights detailed below – there are many other interesting places which you will find while walking around. Almost every street is worth strolling down.

The following attractions have been listed in a sequence to conveniently connect them in a walking tour.

**Puerta del Reloj** Formerly called the Boca del Puente, this was the main gateway to the inner walled town and was linked to Getsemaní by a drawbridge over the moat. The side arches of the building, which are now traffic thoroughfares, were previously used as a chapel and armoury. The clock tower was added in the 19th century. The statue of the founder of the town, Pedro de Heredia, stands in front of the tower.

**Plaza de los Coches** Previously known as the Plaza de la Yerba, the triangular square just behind the Puerta del Reloj was once used as a slave market. It is lined with old balconied houses with colonial arches and walkways. Today these walkways are lined with confectionary stands (the so-called El Portal de los Dulces).

**Plaza de la Aduana** This is the largest and oldest square in the town and was used as a parade ground. In colonial times all the important governmental and administrative buildings were here. The old Royal Customs House was restored and is now the City Hall. A statue of Christopher Columbus stands in the centre of the square.

**Museo de Arte Moderno** The Museum of Modern Art, installed in a part of the former Royal Customs House, presents temporary exhibitions. It is open Monday to Friday from 9 am to noon and 3 to 7 pm, and Saturday from 10 am to 1 pm. Entrance fee is US$0.50 (US$0.25 for students).

**Iglesia y Convento de San Pedro Claver** This convent was founded by the Jesuits, originally under the name of San Ignacio de Loyola but later the name was changed in honour of the Spanish-born monk Pedro Claver (1580-1654), who lived and died here. Called the 'Apostle of the Blacks' or the 'Slave of the Slaves', he spent all his life ministering to the slaves brought from Africa. He was the first person to be canonised in the New World (in 1888).

The convent, built in the first half of the 17th century, is a monumental three-storey building with a triple-tier arched cloister surrounding the patio. The grounds are filled with mighty trees and inhabited by macaws and toucans.

A part of the convent has been opened to visitors and there is a museum exhibiting religious art and some pre-Columbian ceramics. The cell where San Pedro Claver lived and died can be visited and you can also climb a narrow staircase to the choir loft of the church. In the tourist season there is usually someone hanging around the choir loft to let visitors onto the roof (there are good views) for a small tip.

The convent is open daily from 8 am to 5 pm; admission is US$1.20 (half-price for students). Guides, should you need one, are waiting at the entrance and charge US$3 for a tour for up to six people (a tour in English is available for US$5).

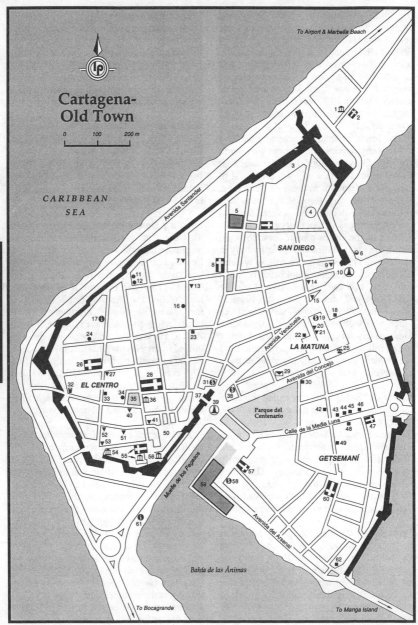

# Cartagena-
# Old Town

0    100    200 m

CARIBBEAN
SEA

CARIBBEAN COAST

To Airport & Marbella Beach

Avenida Santander

SAN DIEGO

Avenida Venezuela

LA MATUNA

Avenida del Concejo

EL CENTRO

Parque del
Centenario

Calle de la Media Luna

GETSEMANÍ

Muelle de los Pegasos

Avenida del Arsenal

Bahía de las Ánimas

To Bocagrande

To Manga Island

## PLACES TO STAY

18  Hotel del Lago
22  Hotel Montecarlo
23  Hotel Bucarica
30  Hotel San Felipe
33  Hostal Santodomingo
42  Hotel Viena
43  Hostal Valle
44  Hotel El Refugio
45  Hotel Holiday
46  Hostal Baluarte
48  Hotel Doral
49  Hotel Familiar
62  Aparta Hotel Portón del Baluarte

## PLACES TO EAT

7  Restaurante Novedades del Tejadillo
9  Nautilus Restaurant
13  Restaurante Jardines Turísticos
14  Restaurante Vegetariano Govinda's
15  Restaurante El Dragón de Oro
20  Restaurante Kon Nam
21  Restaurante La Tinaja
27  Paco's
40  Café Restaurant La Crêperie
41  Restaurante y Bar La Quemada
51  El Bodegón de la Candelaria
52  Restaurante Classic de Andrei
53  La Escollera de la Marina

## OTHER

1  Casa de Rafael Núñez
2  Ermita del Cabrero
3  Las Bóvedas
4  Plaza de Toros de la Serrezuela
5  Convento de Santa Clara
6  Buses to La Boquilla
8  Iglesia de Santo Toribio de Mangrovejo
10  Monumento a la India Catalina
11  Universidad Jorge Tadeo Lozano
12  Teatro Heredia
16  Universidad de Cartagena
17  CNT Tourist Office & Casa del Marqués de Valdehoyos
19  Banco Anglo Colombiano
24  Copa Airlines
25  Telecom
26  Iglesia de Santo Domingo
28  Catedral
29  Avianca & Post Office
31  Banco Unión Colombiano
32  Bar La Vitrola
34  Palacio de la Inquisición
35  Plaza de Bolívar
36  Museo del Oro y Arqueología
37  Plaza de los Coches & Puerta del Reloj
38  Banco Industrial Colombiano
39  Monumento a Pedro de Heredia
47  Iglesia de San Roque
50  Plaza de la Aduana
54  Museo Naval del Caribe
55  Iglesia y Convento de San Pedro Claver
56  Museo de Arte Moderno
57  Iglesia de la Santa Orden
58  Banco Sudameris Colombia
59  Centro de Convenciones
60  Iglesia de la Santísima Trinidad
61  City Tourist Office

**CARIBBEAN COAST**

The church alongside was built long after the convent and completed in the first half of the 18th century. It has an imposing stone façade and fine stained-glass windows. The remains of San Pedro Claver are kept in a glass coffin beneath the high altar, which is made of Italian marble.

**Museo Naval del Caribe** Opened to commemorate the 500th anniversary of Columbus' discovery, the Naval Museum has a rather modest collection related to the city's maritime history. It's open daily except Monday, from 9 am to noon and 3 to 6 pm; admission costs US$0.70.

**Casa de la Candelaria** This is one of the typical mansions built in the early Spanish colonial style. It has been carefully restored and decorated and is now a restaurant, El Bodegón de la Candelaria (see Places to Eat). You can visit the house without eating and go up to the bar, El Mirador, in the tower for views of the town. It is open Monday to Friday from noon to 3 pm and 7 to 11 pm, Saturday and holidays from 7 to 11 pm. It is closed on Sunday except on long weekends.

**Plaza de Bolívar** Formerly the Plaza de Inquisición, this plaza, or rather a tiny park, is surrounded by some of the city's most elegant balconied colonial buildings. As one might expect, a statue of Simón Bolívar stands in the middle of the plaza.

**Palacio de la Inquisición** The Palace of the Inquisition is one of the finest buildings in the town. Although the site was the seat of the Punishment Tribunal of the Holy Office from 1610, the palace wasn't completed until 1776. It is a good example of colonial architecture, noted particularly for its magnificent Baroque stone gateway topped by the Spanish coat of arms, and the long balconies on the façade.

On the side wall, just around the corner from the entrance, you'll find a small window with a cross on top. Heretics were denounced from here, and the Holy Office would than instigate proceedings. The principal 'crimes' were magic, witchcraft and blasphemy. When culprits were found guilty they were sentenced to death in a public auto-da-fé. Five autos-da-fé took place during the Inquisition until independence in 1821. About 800 people were condemned to death and executed. The Inquisition did not judge the Indians.

The palace has been converted into a museum. On the ground floor the instruments of torture used by the Inquisitors are on display. There is also a good model of Cartagena from the beginning of the 19th century, as well as an interesting collection of old maps of the Nuevo Reino de Granada from various periods.

The rooms on the upper levels house two sections: the archaeological section displays pre-Columbian art, mostly pottery, while the historical section features objects from the colonial and independence periods, including arms, paintings, furniture and several church bells.

The palace can be visited Monday to Friday from 8 to 11.30 am and 2 to 5.30 pm, and Saturday and Sunday from 10 am to 5 pm. Entrance is US$0.60. A half-hour tour in English can be arranged for around US$3 to US$4 per group.

**Museo del Oro y Arqueología** This is one of Banco de la República's 10 or so Gold Museums, which are scattered around the country, and, like most of the others, it's interesting and informative. It has a good collection of gold and pottery of the Sinú people (also known as Zenú) who inhabited the region of the present-day departments of Bolívar, Córdoba, Sucre and northern Antioquia before the Spanish conquest. There is also a model of a hut, complete with household utensils and artefacts, representing a dwelling of the Indians living in the region today.

The museum is open Monday to Friday from 8.30 am to noon and 2 to 6 pm. In the tourist season (December, January, June and July) it is also open on Saturday from 9 am to 12.30 pm. Entrance fee is US$1.

**Catedral** The cathedral was begun in 1575, but in 1586, while still under construction, it was partially destroyed by the cannons of Francis Drake, and not completed until 1612. Considerable alterations were made between 1912 and 1923 by the first archbishop of Cartagena, who covered the church with stucco and painted it to look like marble. He also commissioned the dome on the tower. Recent restoration has uncovered the lovely limestone on the building's exterior. Apart from the tower's top, the church has basically preserved its original form. It has a fort-like appearance and a simply decorated interior with three naves and semicircular archways supported on high stone columns. The main retable, worked in gold leaf, dates from the 18th century.

**Iglesia de Santo Domingo** The Santo Domingo Church, built towards the end of the 16th century, is reputedly the oldest in the city. Its builders gave it a particularly wide central nave and covered it with a heavy roof, but it seems they were not too good at their calculations and the vault began to crack. Massive buttresses had to be added to the walls to support the structure and prevent it from collapsing. The builders also had problems with the bell tower, which is distinctly crooked. However, legend has it that it was the work of a devil who knocked the tower.

The interior is spacious. The legendary figure of Christ carved in wood is set in the Baroque altar at the head of the right-hand aisle. Note the floor which is paved with old tombstones mostly dating from the 19th century. They are particularly concentrated in front of the high altar and in the two transepts.

The Convent of Santo Domingo is right beside the church and you can see its fine courtyard through the windows of the right-hand aisle of the church. You can enter it through the main door from the street.

**Casa del Marqués de Valdehoyos** This splendid colonial mansion, dating from the 18th century, was once the home of the Marquis of Valdehoyos, who made a fortune dealing in flour and, particularly, in slaves. Simón Bolívar stayed here for several days in 1830. There is a museum set in a part of the house that displays some historical objects and stages temporary exhibitions. The house is probably worth seeing more for its architecture than for its contents. There is a viewing terrace in the tower from which the marquis once looked out to sea waiting for the slave ships to arrive. From there you can look over the surrounding part of the old town. The house is open Monday to Friday from 8.30 to noon and 2 to 6 pm; admission is free. The CNT tourist office is located in the entrance hall.

**Iglesia de Santo Toribio de Mangrovejo** Compared to the other churches, this one is relatively small. It was erected between 1666 and 1732 and its ceiling is covered with Mudéjar panelling. During Vernon's attack on the city, a cannon ball went through a window into the church when it was filled with worshippers, but very fortunately there were no casualties. The ball is now on display in a glassed niche in the left wall.

**Bóvedas** The Bóvedas are 23 dungeons built between 1792 and 1796 in the city walls, which are more than 15 metres thick in this part. It was the last major construction carried out in colonial times and was destined for military purposes. The vaults were used by the Spaniards as storerooms for munitions and provisions. Later, during the republican era, they were turned into a jail. Today they are tourist shops. The Peña Taurina, at Bóveda No 16, is a bar decorated with photos and posters of bullfights.

**Plaza de Toros de la Serrezuela** This wooden bullring was built in the 19th century but closed down when a new bullring was constructed on the outskirts of the city on the road to Barranquilla.

**Monumento a la India Catalina** This lovely bronze statue of an Indian woman was forged in 1974 by Eladio Gil, a Spanish sculptor living in Cartagena. It stands at the main entrance to the old town from the mainland.

**Casa de Rafael Núñez** This house just outside the walls of the Bóvedas was the home of the former president, lawyer and poet. He wrote the words of Colombia's national anthem and was one of the authors of the constitution of 1886, which was in force (with some later changes) until 1991. The modest wooden house is now a museum featuring some of Núñez' documents and personal possessions. The chapel opposite the house, known as the Ermita del Cabrero, holds his ashes. The museum is open daily from 8 am to noon and 2 to 6 pm. The chapel only opens for mass, early in the morning and late afternoon.

**Muelle de los Pegasos** Back at the point from where you began your tour, Muelle de los Pegasos is the lovely old port of Cartagena on the Bahía de las Ánimas. It is invariably full of fishing, cargo and tourist boats. Sip a fruit juice from any of the stalls while watching the easy-going port life. The new harbour where big ships dock is on Manga Island.

**Centro de Convenciones** Across the Muelle is the large convention centre, looking somewhat out of place in this setting. It was built on the site of the old market, which was reputedly very lively, picturesque and colourful, until it was moved to Avenida Pedro de Heredia far from the old city. The edifice is supposedly one of the most modern convention centres in South America. But why on earth did they plump this massive, gloomy building, reminiscent of the Mao Zedong Mausoleum, right here in the middle of the beautiful, old colonial city?

There are free guided tours operated Monday to Friday at 10 am and 4 pm, if there are no events going on in the centre.

**Spanish Forts**
The old city is a fortress in itself, yet there are more fortifications built in strategic points outside the city. Some of the more important ones are included below.

**Castillo de San Felipe de Barajas** This is undoubtedly the greatest and strongest fortress ever built by the Spaniards in their colonies. The original fort was constructed between 1639 and 1657 on top of the 40-metre-high San Lázaro hill, and was quite small. In 1762 an extensive enlargement was undertaken which eventually resulted in the entire hill being covered over with this powerful bastion. It was truly impregnable and was never taken despite numerous attempts to storm it.

The fortress is an outstanding piece of military engineering. The batteries were arranged so that they could destroy each other if the fort fell to the enemy. A complex system of tunnels connects strategic points of the fortress to distribute provisions and to facilitate evacuation. The tunnels were constructed in such a way that sounds reverberate all the way along them, making it possible to hear the slightest sound of the approaching enemy's feet, and also making it easy for internal communication.

Some tunnels are lit and are open to visitors – a walk not to be missed. Take a guide if you want to learn more about the curious inventions of Antonio de Arévalo, the engineer who directed the fortress' construction. The view over old Cartagena from the top of the bastion is superb.

The fortress is open daily from 8 am to 5 pm; the entrance fee for foreigners is US$3 (US$1.75 for students). A bilingual English/Spanish brochure (US$0.70) about the fort is available from the ticket office. There is a statue of Blas de Lezo in front of the fortress.

From the old town, it's a 20-minutes walk to the fortress, or better still, take a local bus from the Parque del Centenario.

**Fuerte de San Sebastián del Pastelillo** This fort, on the western end of Manga Island, was originally constructed in the middle of the 16th century as one of the town's first defence posts. It's quite small and not particularly inspiring, but it's quite close to the old town – just across the bridge from Getsemaní. Today the fort is home to the Club de Pesca which has a marina where local and foreign boats anchor.

**Fuerte de San Fernando** San Fernando is on the southern tip of the Isla de Tierrabomba at the entrance to the Bahía de Cartagena through the Bocachica strait. On the opposite side of the strait stands another fort, Batería de San José (of little interest), and together they guarded the entrance to the bay. A heavy chain was strung between them to prevent surprise attacks.

Originally, there were two entrances to Cartagena Bay, Bocachica and Bocagrande. Bocagrande was partially blocked by a sand bank and two ships which sank there. An undersea wall was constructed after Vernon's attack to strengthen the natural barrage and to make the channel impassable to ships. It is still impassable today and all ships and boats go through Bocachica.

The fort of San Fernando was built between 1753 and 1760 on the site where the San Luis fortress previously stood but which was completely destroyed by Vernon's cannons. The new fort was designed to withstand any siege. It had its own dock, barracks, sanitary services, kitchen, infirmary, storerooms for provisions and arms, two wells, a chapel and even a jail, much of which can still be seen today.

The fortress can only be reached by water. Boats leave daily from the Muelle de los Pegasos between about 8 and 10 am, and return in the afternoon. The tour costs US$9 including lunch and entrance to the fort. Some boats charge US$5 for the journey only, but you must pay the US$1 for admission to the fort. The most famous boat running this route regularly is *Ferry Dancing*, but the crew play music at an unbelievable volume, which makes the ride a torture (or a delight if you enjoy loud salsa and vallenato).

### Convento de la Popa

This convent is perched on top of a 150-metre hill one km beyond the San Felipe fortress. Its name means literally the Convent of the Stern, named after the hill's similarity to a ship's poop. It's actually the Convento de Nuestra Señora de la Candelaria. It was founded by the Augustine fathers in 1607 but at that time it was little more than a wooden chapel. The chapel was replaced by a stouter construction and the hill was fortified two centuries later, just before Pablo Morillo's siege.

After independence the convent was used as a military headquarters, and was then abandoned for a long time. It has been recently restored by the same order of Augustine monks and today it is open for visitors. A beautiful image of La Virgen de la Candelaria, the patroness of the city, can be seen in the convent's chapel, and the flower-filled patio is exceptionally beautiful. The views stretch all over the city. The patron saint's day is 2 February (see the following section).

Theoretically, you can get to the convent by taking a bus from the Parque del Centenario, getting off at the foot of the hill and walking up. There is a zigzagging road to the top (no public transport) as well as paths cutting the bends of the road. It takes half an hour to get to the top. However, it's better not to walk. There has been an increasing number of reports of armed robbery on this way. Instead go by taxi (US$2.50). The convent is open daily from 9 am to 5 pm. Admission is US$1.

### Manga Island

While Cartagena is principally noted for its Spanish colonial architecture, other styles have also left their mark. Walk around the residential sector on Manga Island to see some interesting houses there dating mainly from the turn of the century – a real hotch-potch of styles. The most noticeable feature is the Islamic influence brought by immigrants from the Middle East.

### Festivals & Events

**Feria Taurina** The bullfight season takes place in the new bullring on Avenida Pedro de Heredia during the first week of the year.

**Fiesta de Nuestra Señora de la Candelaria** On the day of the patron saint of the city, 2 February, a solemn procession is held, during which the faithful carry lit candles. The celebrations begin nine days before, the so-called Novenas, when pilgrims flock to the convent.

**Festival Internacional de Música del Caribe** This festival takes place in the second half of March. It brings together local and foreign musical groups from around the Caribbean and lasts for three or four days. It's held in the Plaza de Toros. Tickets can be bought from either tourist office. Be careful of thieves in and around the plaza during this time.

**Festival Internacional de Cine** Cartagena hosts an international film festival in June.

**Reinado Nacional de Belleza** The National Beauty Contest is held in November to celebrate the independence day of the city. Miss Colombia, the beauty queen, is chosen on 11 November, the high spot of the event. The fiesta, which includes street dancing, music and fancy dress parades, begins several days prior to the contest. This is the most important annual event in Cartagena.

## Places to Stay – bottom end

Despite Cartegena's status as a popular tourist destination, budget accommodation is not very expensive here; the prices of residencias are much the same as in other cities. The peak tourist season is from late December to late January, but even then it's quite easy to find a room.

If you need something cheap, walk directly to Getsemaní, which is Cartagena's principal area of budget accommodation, mostly on or just off Calle de la Media Luna. Many places are dives that double as love hotels or brothels, but you have several clean and safe options to choose from.

The *Hotel Doral* (☎ 641706), at Calle de la Media Luna No 10-46, has a reputation as a travellers' lodge. It has spacious rooms surrounding a large, pleasant courtyard with several umbrella-shaded tables where travellers gather. The rooms on the 1st floor are more airy and pleasant but they don't have private baths; singles/doubles cost US$5/8. The ground-floor rooms have baths and cost US$1 more.

The same family which owns the Doral also runs two smaller hotels in the area: the *Hotel Familiar* (☎ 648374), at Calle del Guerrero No 29-66, and the *Hotel El Refugio* (☎ 643507), at Calle de la Media Luna No 10-35. The former has a nice patio and charges US$9 for a double; the latter offers much the same and is slightly cheaper.

Another place popular with foreign backpackers is the friendly *Hostal Valle* (☎ 642533), at Calle de la Media Luna No 10-15. It's small and fairly basic. Singles/doubles cost about US$5/8.

Appreciably higher standards are offered by the newly opened *Hotel Holiday* (☎ 640948), at Calle de la Media Luna No 10-47, opposite the Doral. Neat rooms without/with own bath cost US$4.50/5.50 per person. The manager is friendly and the place is well kept.

One more recommended place is the *Hotel Viena* (☎ 646242), at Calle San Andrés No 30-53. Run by a friendly Belgian, this hotel is unusual in that it allocates part of its profits to gamines (street children). Simple rooms cost US$4 per person, and there are cooking and laundry facilities, and a luggage store.

In El Centro, the heart of the old town, all the cheapies have apparently ended up as love hotels. If you do insist on staying there, the only tolerably 'clean' budget place is the *Hotel Bucarica* (☎ 641263), at Calle San Agustín No 6-08, which costs US$7/10 a single/double with private bath.

## Places to Stay – middle

**Old Town** There are several mid-priced hotels scattered throughout the walled city, most of which are in Getsemaní. All the hotels listed in this section have rooms with private bath.

Possibly the cheapest in this price bracket is the recently opened *Hostal Baluarte* (☎ 642208), at Calle de la Media Luna No 10-81. It has small but neat rooms costing US$7 per person.

The *Hotel San Felipe* (☎ 645439), on Avenida del Centenario, is one of the reasonably priced options that offers air-con rooms for US$16/22/28 a single/double/triple. It also has rooms with fan which are cheaper (US$13/19/25).

The *Hotel del Lago* (☎ 653819) in La Matuna is modern but otherwise undistinguished. It also offers a choice between rooms with fan and air-con, and costs marginally more than the San Felipe.

*Hotel Montecarlo* (☎ 645835) is another modern venue in La Matuna. It is slightly better than the Hotel del Lago and slightly more expensive.

More stylish but inconveniently sited in the far southern corner of Getsemaní is *Aparta Hotel Portón del Baluarte* (☎ 647035), Calle Larga No 10C-11, which costs US$10 per person in rooms with fan.

The *Hostal Santodomingo* (☎ 642268) is ideally located in El Centro, at Calle Santodomingo No 33-46. It has several doubles (US$22) and one five-bed room upstairs (US$35). The place is pleasant but quite simple, and the rooms have private baths and fans.

**Bocagrande** There are several mid-priced hotels in Bocagrande, though few independent foreign travellers opt to stay there. You'll find at least half a dozen small hotels along Carrera 3, between Calles 5 and 8. To name a few: the *Hotel Arrecife* (☎ 651546), at Carrera 3 No 5-66; *Hotel Residencias Mary* (☎ 652833), at Carrera 3 No 6-53; *Hotel Punta Canoa* (☎ 654179), at Calle 7 No 2-50; and *Hotel Leonela* (☎ 654761), at Carrera 3 No 7-142.

They all cost around US$20/25 for a double with fan/air-con, though the prices

may be higher during the major tourist peak, from Christmas to the end of January.

The *Residencias La Sultana* (☎ 655895), at Avenida San Martín No 7-144, is perhaps the cheapest hotel in Bocagrande (US$8 per person), but it's not pleasant. Appreciably better is the *Hotel Residencias Villa Mar* (☎ 654818), at Avenida San Martín No 9-183, which costs US$12/18 a single/double.

**Marbella Beach** If you don't mind staying outside the old town and Bocagrande, try the

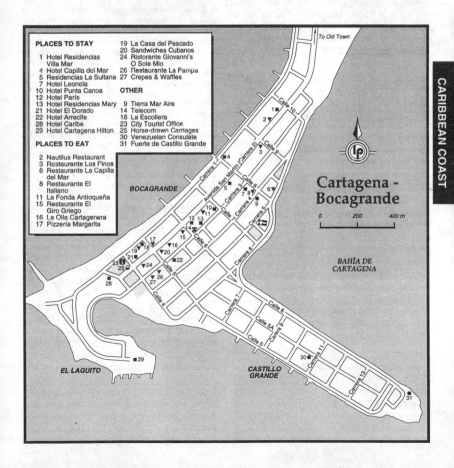

**PLACES TO STAY**
1 Hotel Residencias Villa Mar
4 Hotel Capilla del Mar
5 Residencias La Sultana
7 Hotel Leonela
10 Hotel Punta Canoa
12 Hotel París
13 Hotel Residencias Mary
21 Hotel El Dorado
22 Hotel Arrecife
28 Hotel Caribe
29 Hotel Cartagena Hilton

**PLACES TO EAT**
2 Nautilus Restaurant
3 Restaurante Los Pinos
6 Restaurante La Capilla del Mar
8 Restaurante El Italiano
11 La Fonda Antioqueña
15 Restaurante El Giro Griego
16 La Olla Cartagenera
17 Pizzería Margarita
19 La Casa del Pescado
20 Sandwiches Cubanos
24 Ristorante Giovanni's O Sole Mio
26 Restaurante La Pampa
27 Crepes & Waffles

**OTHER**
9 Tierra Mar Aire
14 Telecom
18 La Escollera
23 City Tourist Office
25 Horse-drawn Carriages
30 Venezuelan Consulate
31 Fuerte de Castillo Grande

Cartagena -
Bocagrande

0    200    400 m

BOCAGRANDE

BAHÍA DE CARTAGENA

EL LAGUITO

CASTILLO GRANDE

To Old Town

*Hotel Bellavista* (☎ 646411), on Avenida Santander No 46-50, a 10-minute walk from the walled city. It is not ideally located but it is a good and friendly place and some travellers stay there. Clean rooms with bath and fan cost US$7 per person. There are several more hotels in this area but they don't offer such good value.

### Places to Stay – top end
**Old Town** Surprisingly enough, the walled city has not a single top-class hotel. The Convento de Santa Clara (dating from 1621), which in modern times served as a hospital, is currently being extensively refurbished as a luxury hotel, and may become the town's poshest accommodation if and when the slow work is completed.

**Bocagrande** Almost all of Cartagena's best hotels are in Bocagrande and El Laguito. Many of them are along Avenida San Martín, while others are on Carrera 1 overlooking the beach.

The modern *Hotel Cartagena Hilton* (☎ 650666), in El Laguito, and the luxurious neo-colonial *Hotel Caribe* (☎ 650155) at Carrera 1 No 2-87 in Bocagrande, are both five-star hotels and very expensive.

If you are not up to that, there are several three-star establishments which will provide comfortable accommodation for a far more affordable price. For example, the *Hotel París* (☎ 652888), at Avenida San Martín No 6-40, and the *Hotel El Dorado* (☎ 650211), at Avenida San Martín No 4-41, both have air-con rooms and swimming pools and both cost around US$30/40 a single/double. There are many other options at similar prices scattered throughout Bocagrande.

### Camping
Cartagena has a campsite. *Camping La Boquilla* (☎ 654538) is three km north of the airport (six km from the walled city) on the road to La Boquilla. It costs US$4 per person in your own tent, and US$6 in a tent provided by the management. Note that camping here works out to be more expensive and less convenient than staying in a budget hotel in the city.

### Places to Eat
Cartagena is a good place for dining out. The upper range is particularly well represented, but even if you are on a minimum budget you won't starve here. The city has some culinary oddities which you shouldn't miss.

Before you set off for a dinner or beer, you may want to know about another of the local conmen's scam, as reported by travellers:

In the bank we met three people from Switzerland and walked to a restaurant to have a beer. When we entered, a man about 50 years of age walked in with us and when we sat down he asked us if we were going to eat. We thought he worked there and said that we only wanted a beer each. He walked over to the bar and a waiter brought us our drinks. We had two more beers and then asked for the bill. The Swiss noticed that the price of a beer on the bill was 50% more than what they had paid in the same bar/restaurant in the morning. When we complained, the waiter told us that he had to charge us extra as a guide had brought us there and he had to pay him his commission. We soon straightened him out on the point that we did not have a guide. The management then reduced the bill and threw the guide out, who was seated at another table waiting for his payoff.

**Cheap Meals** As everywhere in Colombia, the comida corriente is the cheapest way to fill up. There are plenty of budget restaurants serving set meals for around US$1.50.

Understandably, the cheapest restaurants are in Getsemaní, in the area of the bottom-end hotels. Calle de la Media Luna and the adjoining streets are packed with them. There's perhaps no point in listing them by name as they often close, reopen and change owners and names. See where others eat and how the food looks and decide for yourself.

There is also quite a choice of budget comida outlets in the inner walled town. The prices here are marginally higher, but the food may be tastier and the restaurants themselves may be more cheerful. For example, you can get hearty, filling set meals in the *Restaurante Jardines Turísticos* and *Restaurante Novedades del Tejadillo*. Both are near the Universidad de Cartagena, and there are several more places in this area.

*Restaurante Vegetariano Govinda's*, near the India Catalina in San Diego, serves cheap vegetarian meals.

Bocagrande is mostly an up-market district but some cheap eateries serving set meals can be found there. Several of them, including *Restaurante Los Pinos* and *Restaurante El Giro Griego*, are on Avenida San Martín.

**Snacks & Local Specialities** Plenty of cubbyholes throughout the old town serve a variety of snacks, such as arepas, empanadas and dedos de queso. Arepas de huevo – a maize dough fried with an egg inside – originated in Luruaco, a town midway between Cartagena and Barranquilla, and is now very popular along the central coast. And it's delicious.

A dozen stands along the Muelle de los Pegasos operate round the clock and serve an unbelievable choice of delicious fruit juices. The níspero, maracuyá, lulo, zapote and guanábana juices are just a few examples; they have a lot more and all are excellent. They also have plenty of local snacks.

Cartagena is a good place to try seafood cocktails. There are several stalls called ostrerías around the Parque del Centenario and along Avenida Venezuela, which serve cocteles de camarones, ostras, chipi-chipi, langostinos, caracoles and even something called la poderosa bomba submarina which is a sophisticated combination of the above.

Huevos de iguana (iguana eggs), cooked and threaded together like rosaries, are sold from small carts throughout the centre. The season for iguana eggs is from January to April. If you try them, try not to think too hard about the ecological havoc, or they won't taste so good.

Butifarras are a kind of small smoked meatball, only sold on the street by butifarreros, who walk along with big pots, striking them with a knife to get your attention.

Peto is a sort of milk soup made of maize, similar to the Antioquian mazamorra, sweetened with panela and served hot. It, too, is sold by street vendors.

If you are not after such exotic curiosities, you'll find enough places offering some familiar Western fare, such as hot dogs, hamburgers and sandwiches. Probably the best sandwiches are made by *Sandwiches Cubanos*, which has an outlet in El Centro and another one in Bocagrande.

*Café Restaurant La Crêperie* on Plaza de Bolívar does appetising crêpes and tortillas, while the restaurant at the *Hotel San Felipe* has some of the better inexpensive pizzas in town.

**Mid Range & Top End** Cartagena has many classy restaurants, though the prices seem to be a bit higher than what you'd pay for the same dish in Bogotá or Medellín. Most of the refined restaurants have gathered in Bocagrande, but the old city has a selection of well-appointed dining venues as well. As might be expected, seafood is the main local food and most restaurants have a list of seafood delicacies on their menus, particularly the cazuela de mariscos.

*Restaurante La Tinaja* in La Matuna is a pleasant open-air place specialising in grilled meats (roughly US$8 per average main course). It also does seafood but the *Nautilus Restaurant*, facing India Catalina, perhaps does it better. There's another Nautilus, with the same menu and prices, in Bocagrande.

*Restaurante La Quemada* in El Centro is not bad for seafood either, and has a nicer atmosphere. The attached bar usually stages live music on weekend evenings.

*El Bodegón de la Candelaria*, in a marvellous colonial mansion (see under Things to See), is also well known for its good cuisine, but it is expensive. Try the langosta caribeña, half lobster sautéed in coconut milk and flambéd with cognac, for US$20.

*Paco's*, on the Plaza de Santo Domingo, has a rather short menu, with the food being very good but not cheap. However, the restaurant has a special charm and its own style. It is probably the only top-end place in Cartagena where the waiters wear T-shirts instead of the official (and usually gloomy) uniforms. That makes the place warm, informal and friendly. On Wednesday, Thursday, Friday and Saturday nights, an ageing trio, Los Veteranos del Ritmo, play sentimental Caribbean music including some marvellous old Cuban boleros. There is no entry charge so drop in for a beer and have a listen to them.

A short walk south will lead you to the *Restaurante Classic de Andrei* and *La Escollera de la Marina*, two more top-class establishments, noted for their good style and food, and prices to match.

Should you fancy some Chinese cuisine, the *Kon Nam*, in La Matuna, and *El Dragón de Oro*, a few paces away, are the best for this fare, and both are reasonably priced.

Bocagrande has yet more to offer and has more ethnic variety. *La Pampa* is unbeatable for juicy churrasco (US$7), as is *La Capilla del Mar* for its cazuela de mariscos.

## Entertainment

A number of tabernas, discos and other venues stay open till late at night. In the old town, nightspots are concentrated along Avenida del Arsenal in Getsemaní, close to the Centro de Convenciones. On Friday and Saturday nights the street is closed to traffic, and fills with tables and chairs and bands of different styles.

La Vitrola, in El Centro, facing Las Murallas, is a nice bohemian restaurant-cum-bar with tables outside and classic Cuban music on tape. Paco's, already mentioned in Places to Eat, has a band that plays old Caribbean music (Wednesday to Saturday).

The place to go in Bocagrande is La Escollera on the corner of Carrera 1 and Calle 5. It's a disco in a large thatched hut, and throbs nightly till 4 am. It has three bars serving expensive spirits and soft drinks, but there's no beer or food. The cover charge is US$5. The music is played at extra-high volume, so don't plan on enjoying much conversation.

On the beach beside La Escollera there are plenty of vallenato bands that play music every night usually till dawn, depending on demand and mood.

The Hotel Cartagena Hilton has a Saturday-night buffet plus rock-salsa music show, for US$20.

## Things to Buy

Cartagena has a wide choice of tourist shops but the prices are generally high. They are worth looking at because the quality of their goods is usually high, but it's cheaper to buy elsewhere, perhaps in Bogotá or San Jacinto. The biggest tourist shopping centre in the old town is in Las Bóvedas, where they sell handicrafts, clothes, souvenirs and the like. There is a small but interesting and relatively cheap Almacén Artesanías at Avenida del Arsenal No 8B-55, opposite the Centro de Convenciones.

In Bocagrande there are several craft shops along Avenida San Martín. Artisans appear in the afternoon and spread their plastic sheets along the pavements to sell a variety of stuff. In El Laguito, the Centro Comercial Pierino Gallo has jewellery, leather goods and pre-Columbian art for sale.

## Getting There & Away

**Air** The airport is three km north-east of the old city, in El Crespo, and is serviced by frequent local buses from the centre. Avianca, Sam and Aces operate flights to most major cities, including Bogotá (US$104), Medellín (US$86), Cali (US$115), Pereira (US$103) and San Andrés (US$98). Intercontinental can fly you cheaper to Bogotá (US$73), Cali (US$88) and Pereira (US$79), but it doesn't operate flights from Cartagena to San Andrés or Medellín. Aerocorales is expected to fly every morning (except weekends) to Mompós and to return in the afternoon (about US$40 one way) when the refurbishment of the Mompós airport is completed.

Avianca flies to Miami and New York, while Viasa has direct Cartagena-Caracas flights (US$172 plus 19% tax). Copa, the Panamanian airline, has two flights weekly to Panama City (US$118 plus 19% tax). You can continue on with Copa to other

Central American capitals but it is more expensive than going via San Andrés with Sam or Sahsa (see the San Andrés section for further details).

**Bus** A new bus terminal came into operation in 1994 in the far eastern district of the city. A taxi to or from the old town will cost US$4, or you can go by local bus (US$0.20).

**To Bogotá** Brasilia and Copetrán service this route with a total of a dozen climatizados daily (US$41, 23 hours).
**To Medellín** Brasilia and Rápido Ochoa have about 10 departures daily (US$23 climatizado, 13 hours).
**To Sincelejo** Unitransco and Torcoroma have frequent corrientes (US$5, 3½ hours). Rápido Ochoa and Brasilia can drop you there in their climatizados (US$7, three hours) on their way to Medellín.
**To Barranquilla** There are plenty of buses with various companies (some continue on to Santa Marta). Coolibertador, Unitransco and La Veloz are the cheapest (US$3.25 pullman, three hours).
**To Tolú** Unitransco has five buses a day to Tolú via San Onofre (US$3.75, four hours). Alternatively, you can go there on a better but longer road via Sincelejo.
**To Mompós** Unitransco has one direct corriente bus daily at 5.30 am (US$9, eight hours). This bus goes via Magangué, then catches the Yati-Bodega ferry and continues on a dusty road to Mompós.
Alternatively go to Magangué, which is serviced regularly by Unitransco and Brasilia, with a total of at least 15 buses a day. Unitransco runs mainly corrientes (US$6.25, 4½ hours), while Brasilia has mostly climatizados (US$7.75) and is half an hour faster. From Magangué you either take the *chalupa* (boat) direct to Mompós (US$4, two hours) or go by boat to Bodega (US$1.75, 20 minutes) and continue by jeep to Mompós (US$2, one hour). See the Mompós section for more information.

**Boat** Cargo ships depart a few times a week from the Muelle de los Pegasos to San Andrés island but they don't take passengers. In the opposite direction, from San Andrés to Cartagena, you might occasionally get a lift for about US$35; it takes two to three days. You may also try your luck in the Club de Pesca on Manga Island, where private

sailing and motor boats dock, but again it's a long shot.

Small cargo boats (looking as if they could sink at any moment) depart from the Muelle de los Pegasos to Turbo. They usually take passengers and charge about US$15; the trip takes one to two days. Some of the boats continue on as far as Quibdó (about US$40, four to seven days). You shouldn't have to wait more than a few days to catch one of these vessels. Take a hammock and some of your own food as the crew's offerings leave a lot to be desired.

For boats to the Islas del Rosario see that section later in this chapter.

You may be approached by men offering fabulous trips around the Caribbean in 'their boats' for a little help on board. If you seem interested they will ask you to pay some money for a boarding permit or the like. Don't pay a cent – you'll never see the man or your money again. Don't be lured into this trick, even if they appear wearing sailor suits and speaking fluent English or French. It's amazing how innovative and skilful Colombian conmen can be.

**Car Rental** Car rental companies operating in Cartagena include:

Alquilautos
   Avenida San Martín No 6-96, Bocagrande (☎ 655786, 650968)
Avis
   Avenida San Martín No 6-94, Bocagrande (☎ 653259, 652427)
Budget
   Carrera 3 No 5-183, Bocagrande (☎ 651764, 656831)
Hertz
   Avenida San Martín No 6-84, Bocagrande (☎ 652852, 653359)
National Car Rental
   Calle 10 No 2-30, Edificio Torremolinos, Bocagrande (☎ 653336, 657145)

**Getting Around**
You are likely to spend most of your time in the old city, where everything is at hand and you don't need local transport.

Your most likely urban trip will perhaps be between the old town and Bocagrande, where buses shuttle frequently. If you want to do this trip in a more noble way, take a *paseo en coche* – a ride in a horse-drawn carriage. They depart from the corner of Avenida San Martín and Calle 4 in Bocagrande and go along the waterfront to the old town. After a short run around the main streets of the walled city, they return via either Avenida San Martín or the waterfront, whichever you prefer. They operate daily from 5 pm until midnight. The tour takes one hour and costs US$15 per coach for up to four people.

## AROUND CARTAGENA
### La Boquilla

This is a small, poor fishing village seven km north of Cartagena. It lies at the end of a narrow peninsula bordered by the sea on one side and the Ciénaga de Tesca on the other. The entire population is black and lives off fishing. You can see them at the ciénaga working with their famous atarrayas, a round fishing net that is very common in Colombia, particularly on the Caribbean coast.

Palm-thatched shack restaurants on the beach attract people from Cartagena on weekends. They are almost all closed at other times. The fish is fresh but not as cheap as you might expect here given the proximity of the ocean. It is usually accompanied by *arroz con coco*, rice prepared with coconut milk.

You can arrange a boat trip along the narrow channels cutting through the mangrove woods to the north of the village. Several locals offer canoe trips, taking around five people at a time. The asking price of about US$5 per person is largely negotiable. They will try to include lunch for a few dollars extra, which is most likely to be fresh, home-fried fish.

**Getting There & Away** Frequent city buses run to La Boquilla from India Catalina in Cartagena. They cost US$0.20 and take half an hour.

### Islas del Rosario

This archipelago of small coral islands is about 35 km south-west of Cartagena. There are about 25 islands altogether, including some tiny islets only big enough for a single house. The archipelago is surrounded by coral reefs, where the colour of the sea ranges from turquoise to purple. The whole area has been declared a national park, the Corales del Rosario.

The coral reefs around the Islas del Rosario are the largest and most magnificent on the Colombian Caribbean coast, comparable to those in San Andrés and Providencia. Marine life is abundant in the surrounding waters, making the area a paradise for snorkelling and scuba diving. The two largest islands have inland lagoons. An aquarium has been built on the Isla de San Martín.

The driest period in the region is from December to March, while the wettest is from September to October.

**Getting There & Away** The usual way of visiting the islands is on a day-tour. The cruise through the islands has become a well-established business, and tours operate daily all year round from the Muelle de los Pegasos in Cartagena. In the tourist season, there are plenty of boats running to the islands. They all leave between 7 and 9 am and return about 4 to 5 pm. The tour costs roughly US$12 to US$18 per person, including lunch, but bargaining is possible with smaller boats, especially at the last minute when some seats remain unoccupied.

The route is more or less the same with most operators – they go through the Bahía de Cartagena and into the open sea through the Bocachica strait, passing between two Spanish forts: the Batería de San José and, directly opposite, the Fuerte de San Fernando. They then take you to Playa Blanca on the Isla de Barú to let you rest and bathe for about two hours. The beach is pretty crowded as all tour boats stop there, and several food stalls have sprung up along the shore. Some locals sell shells and black coral items of poor quality. The boats then cruise among the islands and stop at one or two, and invariably call in at El Acuario on San

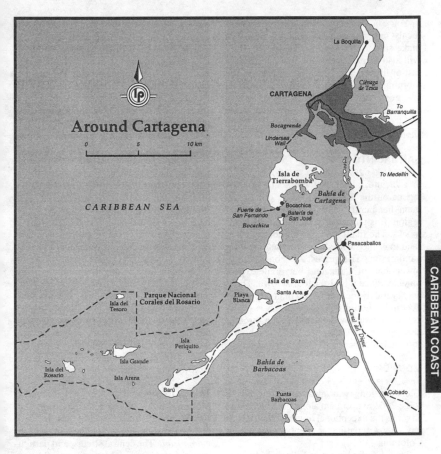

Around Cartagena

CARIBBEAN SEA

Martín. Entrance to the aquarium is US$1.50 and is not always included in the tour price – check beforehand. Small boats are able to pass nearer the islands and over the shallow coral fields. Some of these boats return through the Canal del Dique, entering it from the Bahía de Barbacoas near the village of Santa Ana.

If you want to stay longer on the islands or go diving, a charter trip is required, but you can expect to pay much more than for a tour. Some people rent out their houses or bungalows on the islands and provide their own transport or have arrangements with

boat owners. You can usually find the boats in the small round bay between Bocagrande and El Laguito. Fix exactly the conditions, time and price before departure.

Note that the coral reefs extend up to the western coast of the Isla de Barú, which is accessible by road from Cartagena (with a ferry across the Canal del Dique). If snorkelling is all you want to do, you need not go to the Islas del Rosario; it is much cheaper to go by land to the Isla de Barú. It's possible to stay with local families there but take a hammock, some food and your snorkelling gear.

You can also stay at Playa Blanca where locals rent out hammocks for US$3, but make sure to ask for a mosquito net. They will also prepare meals for US$7 for breakfast or dinner. The beach is crowded in the morning, but by 2 pm or so all the tour boats are gone and the place becomes pretty deserted. The snorkelling is excellent – the coral reefs begin just a few metres off the shore.

## SAN JACINTO
• *pop 16,000* • *240 m* • *27°C* • ☎ *(952)*

San Jacinto, about 100 km south of Cartagena on the Medellín road, is one of the main handicraft centres of the Caribbean region. It is particularly known for its hammocks. The main road passing through San Jacinto is lined with shops and stands selling handicrafts. The prices are considerably lower than in Cartagena but don't expect miracles since it is also a tourist town. There are several residencias if you plan on staying overnight, though it is not necessary as transport is frequent, with buses passing through heading north to Cartagena (US$3, two hours) and south to Sincelejo (US$2, 1½ hours).

## MOMPÓS
• *pop 25,000* • *33 m* • *28°C* • ☎ *(952)*

Tucked a long way away from the coast, some 200 km upstream along the Magdalena River, is the exceptional town of Mompós. It has its own particular identity, unique in Colombia.

Traditionally known as Villa de Mompox, the town was founded in 1537 on the eastern branch of the Magdalena, which in this part has two arms, Brazo Mompós and Brazo de Loba. Mompós actually lies on an island, the Isla Margarita. The town's name comes from Mompoj, the name of the last cacique of the Kimbay Indians, who inhabited the region before the conquest.

Mompós soon became an active port and important commercial centre, through which all the merchandise from Cartagena passed via the Canal del Dique and the Magdalena up to the interior of the Nuevo Reino de Granada. When Cartagena was attacked by pirates, Mompós served as a refuge for the families of the city's defenders.

The town flourished; several fair-sized churches and many luxurious mansions were built. In 1810 Mompós proclaimed its independence from the Virreynato de la Nueva Granada, the first town to do so. Simón Bolívar, who stayed here for a short time during his liberation campaign, said: 'While to Caracas I owe my life, to Mompós I owe my glory'.

Towards the end of the 19th century, shipping on the Magdalena was diverted to the other branch of the river, the Brazo de Loba, bringing the town's prosperity to an end. Mompós has been left in isolation, living on memories of times gone by. Little has changed; yesterday's air is still very much in evidence, as is the old architecture which reflects the town's glorious past.

Mompós has a long tradition in hand-worked filigree gold jewellery of outstanding quality. Nowadays the gold is gradually being replaced by silver. Another speciality of the town is furniture. Despite the scarcity of timber in the region, several workshops still continue the tradition, making *muebles momposinos*, particularly rocking chairs, which are known nationwide.

### Things to See

Mompós' colonial character has been preserved almost intact and it has its own distinctive style, known as the *arquitectura momposina*. The central streets, and particularly the main thoroughfare, Carrera 2 (or, as it's still traditionally called, Calle Real del Medio), are lined with whitewashed colonial houses. Their most characteristic feature is the elaborate wrought-iron grilles, invariably based on pedestals and topped with narrow, tiled roofs, that cover the windows. Some of the houses boast imposing carved doorways – a mark of the town's former glory and the wealth of its dwellers.

Like most old towns, the best way to get a feel for the local architecture and atmosphere is to wander through the streets. The colonial core is pretty small, so you'll soon be familiar with most of its charming

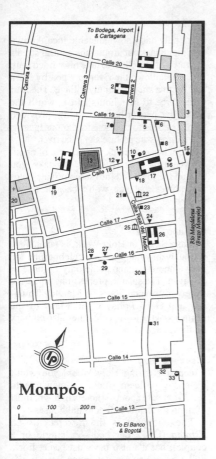

**PLACES TO STAY**

4   Residencias La Valerosa
5   Residencias Isleña
6   Residencias La Estrella
8   Residencias Solmar
19  Residencias Unión
21  Hostal Doña Manuela
23  La Posada del Virrey
30  Residencias Aurora
31  Residencias Villa de Mompox

**PLACES TO EAT**

10  Restaurante Tebe's
11  Restaurante Robin Hood
12  Restaurante Frío Carlis
18  Restaurante Milena Paola
24  La Pizzería
27  Asadero Pollo Rico
28  Piqueteadero Lo Sabroso

**OTHER**

1   Iglesia de San Francisco
2   Iglesia de San Juan de Dios
3   Market
7   Alcaldía
9   Aces Airlines
13  Colegio Pinillos
14  Iglesia de Santo Domingo
15  Boats to El Banco & Magangué
16  Plaza Real de la Concepción,
    Buses to Bosconia & Jeeps to
    Bodega & El Banco
17  Iglesia de la Concepción
20  Cemetery
22  Museo Cultural
25  Casa de la Cultura
26  Iglesia de San Agustín
29  Estadero Los Cobos
32  Iglesia de Santa Bárbara
33  Unitransco Office (Buses to
    Cartagena)

**Mompós**

0   100   200 m

CARIBBEAN COAST

corners. Include in your walking tour the churches and museums listed in the following sections. Go to the market which spreads along the waterfront to the north of the Plaza Real de la Concepción, and visit the cemetery with its collection of old tombstones.

Strolling about, you'll find several gold and silver jewellers, two of which are on Calle Real del Medio close to the Hostal Doña Manuela. The management of the hostal can give you the addresses of artisans who work at home.

In the evening, when the baking heat of the day has slightly cooled, you'll see many locals relaxing in front of their homes, sitting in – of course – the Mompós-made rocking chairs. Colonies of flying bats complete the scenery. At certain periods of the year there may be also plenty of mosquitoes around, so have the insect repellent at hand.

**Churches** Mompós has six churches, all of which date from the colonial days and all are fairly similar in style and construction. They are open only for mass which is usually once or twice a week, most likely at either 6.30 am or 5.30 pm. The Hostal Doña Manuela and the Casa de la Cultura may be able to tell you about the churches' current opening hours.

The most interesting and unusual is the **Iglesia de Santa Bárbara**, facing the square of the same name next to the river. Built in 1630, the church has an octagonal Moorish-style bell tower circled by a balcony – a unique feature in Colombian religious architecture. The church is open only on Thursday and Sunday at 5.30 pm, but a part of its interior can be seen through cracks in the main door. It may occasionally be open at other times, when, for a small donation, you can go up to the bell tower.

The **Iglesia de San Agustín** houses the famous, richly gilded Santo Sepulcro (in the back of the right-hand aisle), which is one of the most prominent objects carried around the streets during the Holy Week processions. The statues of the saints in this church are paraded as well.

The **Iglesia de San Francisco** is one of the oldest churches in town and has possibly the most interesting interior, particularly the lateral retables.

The **Iglesia de la Concepción** is the largest local church and is open more frequently than the others.

**Museums** There are two museums in the town, both set in colonial houses. The **Casa de la Cultura** displays memorabilia relating to the town's history. It's open Monday to Friday from 8 am to noon and 2 to 5 pm, Saturday from 9 am to noon and 3 to 5 pm, and Sunday from 9 am to noon; the entrance fee is US$0.40.

The **Museo Cultural**, installed in the house where Simón Bolívar once stayed, shows a small collection of religious art plus some objects related to Bolívar. It's open on Monday, Wednesday, Saturday and Sunday from 9.30 am to noon, and Tuesday, Thursday and Friday from 9.30 am to noon and 3.30 to 5 pm; admission is US$1.

## Tours

A friendly and knowledgeable local known as Chipi hangs out around the central streets in search of travellers to take his guided tour, by launch, down the river to a nearby finca and on to a small, friendly village. The tour takes three to four hours and is worth the US$8 per person he is charging, provided there are at least four persons for the tour. Iguanas and monkeys are profuse along the river.

Chipi has a sidekick named José of about 12 years of age. This boy can take you around the town and into some private colonial homes that you won't be able to see otherwise.

## Semana Santa

Semana Santa, or Holy Week, is taken very seriously in Mompós. The celebrations are very elaborate, comparable only to those in Popayán. The solemn processions circle the streets for several hours on Maundy Thursday and Good Friday night. Many of the saints from the town's churches also embark on these excursions.

## Places to Stay

Except for during Holy Week, you won't have any problem finding somewhere to stay. There are about 10 hotels in town, most of them set in pleasant colonial houses.

The cheapest is the *Residencias La Estrella* (US$2 per bed – a single or a couple), but it's also the most basic. For a dollar more, you can stay in the *Residencias Solmar* or *Residencias La Valerosa*. These are also rather basic, although La Valerosa is undergoing an extensive restoration process.

Somewhat better are the *Residencias Isleña* (☎ 855245), which costs US$4 per person in rooms with bath, and *Residencias Unión* (☎ 855723), which offers much the same for marginally more.

There are a few good, reasonably priced places to stay in town, including the *Residencias Villa de Mompox* (☎ 855208), at US$5 per person in rooms with bath; *Residencias Aurora*, at US$6 per person with bath; and *La Posada del Virrey* (☎ 855630),

Left: Old balconied house of Cartagena
Right: Middle-Eastern influenced Barranquillan architecture
Bottom: *Mola* of the Cuna Indians

Top: The main street in Mompós
Left: Colonial street in Cartagena
Middle: Stall selling iguana eggs, Cartagena
Right: Muelle de los Pegasos, Cartagena
Bottom: Bathing in the mud volcano, Arboletes

at US$6/7 per person without/with bath. All three are pleasant and friendly and serve good free tinto.

The best place in town is the *Hostal Doña Manuela* (☎ 855620), in a restored colonial mansion with two ample patios. Singles/doubles with bath and fan cost US$23/30 (US$29/36 with air-con). The hotel has a swimming pool, restaurant and bar, and the management can provide information about the town – worth noting as there is no tourist office in Mompós.

### Places to Eat
Food stands at the market along the riverfront provide cheap meals. There are four budget restaurants around the small square behind Iglesia de la Concepción: *Tebe's*, *Robin Hood*, *Frío Carlis* and *Milena Paola*. They all serve set meals for about US$1.75.

The *Piqueteadero Lo Sabroso* has inexpensive food (good mondongo). For chicken, go to the *Asadero Pollo Rico*, while for pizza, try *La Pizzería*.

The *Hostal Doña Manuela* has the best restaurant in town, and it's not that expensive.

### Entertainment
The Hostel Doña Manuela has a bar, El Mesón de la Villa, but perhaps a more pleasant place for an evening drink (and a dance if you wish) is the open-air Estadero Los Cobos, open from 8 pm till late. It plays good taped music.

### Getting There & Away
**Air** Aerocorales has daily flights (except weekends) to and from Cartagena (US$38) and Barranquilla (US$40). The Aces office in town takes bookings and sells tickets. The carrier doesn't provide transport to/from the airport. Take any of the jeeps heading to Bodega and ask them to drop you at the turn-off to the airport – a short walk.

At the time when this book was researched, the airport was closed for the airstrip upgrading, but is likely to be in operation again by now.

**Bus & Boat** Mompós is well off the main routes but can be reached relatively easily from different directions by dirt road and river. Whichever way you come, however, the journey is time-consuming. As Mompós lies on an island and there are no bridges across Magdalena in the region, any trip involves a ferry or boat crossing.

**To Cartagena & Sincelejo** There's one morning bus direct to Cartagena (US$9, eight hours). The bus goes by dirt road to Bodega, catches a ferry to Yati, then continues via Magangué (paved road from here) and San Jacinto to Cartagena.

Alternatively, go by jeep to Bodega – they depart frequently until about 3 pm (US$2, one hour) – where chalupas wait to take passengers to Magangué (US$1.75, 20 minutes). There are also direct Mompós-Magangué boats (US$4, two hours), though they don't depart as frequently as the jeeps. However, the trip is more comfortable as you avoid the often very dirty and overcrowded ride by jeep.

From Magangué, there are at least a dozen departures a day to Cartagena (US$7.75 climatizado, US$6.25 corriente, four to 4½ hours), and even more to Sincelejo (US$2.75 corriente, 2½ hours).

**To Bucaramanga & Bogotá** Take a jeep (US$4, two hours) or a chalupa (US$4.50, two hours) to El Banco. Jeeps shuttle more frequently and are marginally faster but, again, the trip is less comfortable and can be really dusty. From El Banco there are half a dozen buses a day to Bucaramanga (US$11 climatizado, seven hours), a few of which continue on to Bogotá. Alternatively, take another jeep from El Banco to El Burro on the main Barranquilla-Bucaramanga road (US$3, 1½ hours), where you can catch any of the frequent buses heading south to Bucaramanga.

**To Santa Marta & Valledupar** One or two buses (operated by La Veloz) depart from Mompós' main plaza early in the morning and go by a backwater road to Bosconia (US$7 corriente, five hours). These buses go for 25 km westward to Talaigua Nuevo, cross the Brazo Mompós to Santa Ana by ferry, and head north-east via La Gloria and El Difícil to Bosconia. They continue on to Valledupar, but get off and change in Bosconia if you are heading for Santa Marta. Most northward buses go to Barranquilla; take any of them and change again in Ciénaga – it will probably be faster than waiting for the less frequent bus direct to Santa Marta.

# Sucre & Córdoba

The departments of Sucre and Córdoba rarely make it into local tourist guides, and not without reason. The colonial heritage of the area is insignificant, and both departmental capitals, Sincelejo and Montería, are just unremarkable cities. The Sinú Indians who lived in the region before the conquest were one of the first pre-Columbian groups to be wiped out by the Spaniards.

There's a large, mountainous national park, the Parque Nacional Paramillo, in the southern end of Córdoba, but it's hardly accessible and has no tourist facilities. Probably the major tourist destinations in the region are two seaside resorts, Tolú and Coveñas, and the nearby archipelago of small islands, Islas de San Bernardo.

## SINCELEJO

• *pop 150,000* • *210 m* • *27˚C* • ☎ *(952)*

Sincelejo, the capital of Sucre, lies 185 km south of Cartagena on the road to Medellín. It's a hot, dusty city serving as a centre for cattle farming, the principal activity of the department.

Sincelejo was previously known for its *corraleja*, a sort of bullfight where anybody can enter the bullring and try their luck with the bull. Originating in Pamplona, Spain, these breathtaking, dangerous games were held annually in Sincelejo from the mid-19th century. They were indefinitely suspended after an accident in 1980 when a stand overcrowded with spectators collapsed. Local corralejas in the towns and villages of the region continue to be held, mostly in January.

There is very little to see or do in the city. However, you might need to stay here overnight before heading elsewhere, such as to Mompós or maybe Tolú.

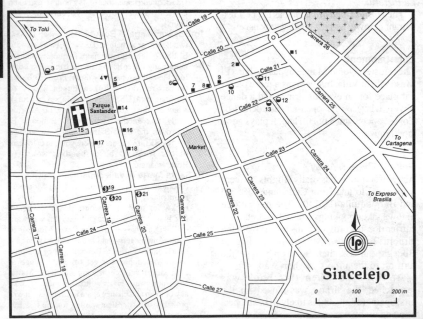

Sincelejo

## Information

There doesn't seem to be a tourist office in the city. Most banks are within a couple of blocks south of the Parque Santander. The most useful ones are marked on the map.

## Places to Stay

There are a dozen bottom-end residencias on Calle 22 in the market area, where a double room shouldn't cost more than US$5. Most of these places are suspicious dives, doing much of their trade on an hourly basis. If you are really hard up, look at several and take your pick. The *Hotel Marqués*, at Carrera 20 No 21-73, is better located and marginally cleaner than the others. Doubles without/with bath cost US$4/5.

Calle 21 is also packed with hotels; these are better than their neighbours one block south, but are usually noisy and nothing very special. The *Residencias Monserrate* is the cheapest on this street, at US$4 for a double with bath.

Among the better inexpensive places, check the *Hotel Santander* (☎ 825119), at Carrera 20 No 19-59, *Gran Hotel*, at Calle 21 No 22-21, and *Hotel Gloria*, at Calle 21 No 23-17. Any of these costs US$5 per person in rooms with bath and fan.

Appreciably better are the *Hotel Victoria* (☎ 820316), at Carrera 20 No 20-51 (on the main square), and the *Hotel Palacé* (☎ 823900), at Carrera 19 No 21-39. Both have singles/doubles with fan for about US$10/15 and air-con rooms for US$15/20.

The upper price bracket of the city accommodation includes the *Ancor Hotel* (☎ 821125), at Carrera 25 No 20A-45, *Hotel Majestic* (☎ 821872), at Carrera 20 No 21-25, and the *Hotel Marsella* (☎ 820729), at Carrera 24 No 20-38. In any of the three you can expect to pay around US$20/27/35 for a good air-con single/double/triple. The Marsella is the best and the only one which has a swimming pool.

## Places to Eat

There are plenty of budget restaurants in the vicinity of Parque Santander (the main square) and in the market area. *Restaurante La Olla*, Carrera 20 No 19-46, is a good example, recommended for its tasty and filling set meals. Possibly the best in town is the restaurant at the *Hotel Marsella*.

## Getting There & Away

Sincelejo hasn't got a central bus terminal. Most of the eight or so bus companies servicing the city have their own offices in the city centre from where their buses depart (indicated on the map). Expreso Brasilia is the only company which has built a terminal to speak of. It's about 1.5 km south-east of the city centre, on the corner of Carrera 25 and Calle 38 (the main Cartagena-Medellín road). Rápido Ochoa should have moved to a neighbouring location by the time you read this.

**PLACES TO STAY**

| | |
|---|---|
| 1 | Ancor Hotel |
| 2 | Hotel Marsella |
| 5 | Hotel Santander |
| 7 | Gran Hotel |
| 8 | Residencias Monserrate |
| 9 | Hotel Gloria |
| 14 | Hotel Victoria |
| 16 | Hotel Majestic |
| 17 | Hotel Palacé |
| 18 | Hotel Marqués |

**PLACES TO EAT**

| | |
|---|---|
| 4 | Restaurante La Olla |

**OTHER**

| | |
|---|---|
| 3 | Buses to Tolú |
| 6 | Rápido Ochoa |
| 10 | Unitransco &Copetrán |
| 11 | Cooperativa Torcoroma |
| 12 | Transportes González |
| 13 | Sotracor |
| 15 | Catedral de San Francisco de Asís |
| 19 | Banco Popular |
| 20 | Banco de Colombia |
| 21 | Banco de Bogotá |

CARIBBEAN COAST

**To Medellín** Expreso Brasilia and Rápido Ochoa have a dozen departures daily (US$19 climatizado, 10 hours).

**To Cartagena** Unitransco and Torcoroma have frequent corrientes (US$5, 3½ hours), while Rápido Ochoa and Brasilia offer climatizado services (US$7, three hours).

**To Magangué** This is the route you take to get to Mompós. Torcoroma, Sotracor and Transportes González have buses approximately every hour, from 4 am to 6 pm (US$2.75 corriente, 2½ hours).

**To Tolú** Torcoroma and Transportes González have departures every 20 minutes, from 6.30 am to 7 pm (US$1, one hour).

## TOLÚ & COVEÑAS
• *3 m* • *28°C* • ☎ *(952)*

Tolú and Coveñas, two seaside towns on the Golfo de Morrosquillo, have developed over the last decade into holiday beach resorts. They both cater for middle-class tourism, or *turismo marrón*, as the locals call it (literally 'brown tourism'). In the tourist season they fill up with Colombians from the interior, mostly from Antioquia, but are very quiet during the rest of the year. The peak tourist times are from late December to late January, Holy Week and, to a lesser extent, July.

With a population of about 15,000, Tolú is bigger than Coveñas and is linked to Sincelejo by a 42-km paved road. It is pleasant and has some fine old palm-thatched houses. The tourist area is along the beach and most of the hotels and restaurants have sprung up on the waterfront. The beach itself is not fabulous, being narrow and not particularly attractive. It's not golden but rather brownish or even blackish – the effect of contamination from the nearby port which is used for loading coal and cement.

Coveñas, 20 km south-west along a dirt coastal road, is not much more than a village, yet it is also geared towards tourists. Several cabañas have been built in the village but most accommodation and restaurants are spread along the road to Tolú. The beaches have a more natural colour and are a bit better than those in Tolú. Coveñas is the terminal for the *oleoducto*, a crude-oil pipeline coming here from Caño Limón in Arauca near the Venezuelan border.

You can pass a couple of days here enjoying the peace and tranquillity, or crowds of Colombian tourists on their holidays, depending on when you come. Once in Tolú, it's probably worthwhile taking a trip to the Islas de San Bernardo (see the following section).

### Places to Stay
Accommodation tends to fill fast during the tourist peaks and the prices rise on average by 50%. In the low season hotels are almost empty and most of the restaurants are closed. The prices given below are for the low season.

Tolú's seafront boulevard, Avenida 1, is lined with hotels catering to all budgets. The *Residencias El Turista* (☎ 885145), at Avenida 1 near the corner of Calle 11, is one of the cheapest, costing US$3 per person in rooms with bath and fan. It serves cheap meals. The *Hotel El Dorado* (☎ 885148), on the corner of Avenida 1 and Calle 21, is slightly better, but it costs US$5 per person (bargaining is possible).

The *Hotel Brisas del Mar* (☎ 885032), on the corner of Avenida 1 and Calle 16, is set in a pleasant house with rooms overlooking the sea, and costs US$6 per person.

There are several better hotels on the waterfront, including the *Hotel Playa Mar* (☎ 885125), at Avenida 1 No 22-22, *Hotel Caribe* (☎ 885115), at Avenida 1 No 18-82, and *Hotel Ibatama* (☎ 885110), at Avenida 1 No 19-45. All three are decent and cost about US$10 per person in rooms with private bath and fan. The Caribe and Ibatama also offer air-con rooms for about US$14 per person.

The *Hotel Alcira* (☎ 885036), at Avenida 1 No 21-151, is the best place in town but perhaps not good enough to justify its prices: US$60/75 a double/triple.

If you don't want to stay in town, take a bus to Coveñas, get off on the bridge some 10 km from Tulú and continue walking along the shore road which is lined with hotels and cabañas; take your pick.

### Getting There & Away
You can get to Tolú from Cartagena (through San Onofre); Unitransco has several depar-

tures daily (US$3.75, four hours). From Sincelejo there are buses every 20 minutes (US$1, one hour). From Montería, go through Lorica and Coveñas. The buses between Tolú and Coveñas run every two hours or so.

## ISLAS DE SAN BERNARDO

Islas de San Bernardo is an archipelago of nine small islands, scattered off the Golfo de Morrosquillo about 40 km north-west of Tolú. The islands were once inhabited by a community of Carib Indians but it's not known whether they were still living there when the Spaniards arrived. The conquerors were not interested in settling on the archipelago, and it was probably not until the late 19th century that some mestizo fishers found the islands a good base for their work. Today most of the islands are inhabited, with a total population of some 1000 people.

Isla Tintipán is the largest of these islands. It has a mangrove ciénaga in its middle with quite diversified birdlife. Next to Tintipán is El Islote, the smallest island in the archipelago but, curiously, the most heavily populated. About 700 locals live in a village which spreads over the whole of the tiny islet.

West of El Islote is the Isla de Múcura, which reputedly offers the best snorkelling and scuba diving. Some cachacos have built their holiday homes here.

Closer to the mainland is the Isla de Palma, which boasts the posh Hotel Isla de Palma, set in a huge, stylised palm-thatched hut. The hotel has a small zoo and an aquarium.

### Places to Stay & Eat

The *Hotel Isla de Palma* is by far the most outstanding place to stay, if you can afford US$100 per person a night. The hotel has its own restaurant and excursion boats for visitors. Information and bookings are available in Cartagena (☎ 656202) and Bogotá (☎ 614 5392).

The *Puntanorte*, on the Isla de Tintipán, is another established accommodation option and is cheaper. The price of US$50 per person includes full board and boat excursions. You can book the hotel in Bogotá (☎ 218 4581).

Other islands offer mostly informal accommodation – locals rent out rooms in their houses and they might also serve meals if there's no restaurant.

### Getting There & Away

The main jumping-off point for the islands is Tolú, and the usual way to visit them is on a one-day tour. There are three tour operators in Tolú: Club Náutico Altamar, Club Náutico Tolumar and Club Náutico Los Delfines. All three are on the waterfront (Avenida 1) near the corner of Calle 11, and all run tours to the archipelago. The routes may differ slightly, but the price is roughly the same: US$12 per person (US$14 in the tourist peaks).

The tour takes about seven hours and usually includes stops on four islands: Palma (zoo and aquarium, US$3 entrance fee extra), El Islote, Múcura (snorkelling, equipment provided free of charge) and Tintipán. They also stop at a restaurant on one of these islands for lunch (its cost is not included in the tour's price).

These tours require a minimum of six persons to set off. In the high season when there are plenty of holiday-makers, tours with one or other of the operators may go every day. However, in the off season, there may be tours on weekends only, unless you're prepared to pay for the empty seats.

If you want to stay longer on the islands, the cheapest transport option is to take a tour (at the tour price) and get off at one of the islands they call in at. They can pick you up again on a pre-arranged date, but only if a tour departs on that day. Don't forget to take some insect repellent and a torch.

Alternative routes and itineraries are possible with all operators, and are a matter of individual negotiation. They can provide scuba-diving equipment or take you water skiing, and they also have angling and windsurfing gear.

## MONTERÍA

• *pop 270,000* • *20 m* • *28°C* • ☎ *(947)*

Montería, the capital of Córdoba, is an important cattle centre on the Sinú River. There is no special reason to come here,

CARIBBEAN COAST

unless you need to pass through to change buses for Arboletes, Coveñas or elsewhere.

## Places to Stay

Most of the budget hotels are along Carrera 2 between Calles 34 and 37. This is a busy and dirty market area, and most of the bus companies are also located here.

The *Hotel Mónaco*, at Carrera 2 No 36-64, costs US$4/7 for singles/doubles with bath. It's OK but the surrounding area is noisy and not particularly pleasant, and feels unsafe after nightfall. The *Residencias Americano* (☎ 822984), at Calle 32 No 1-65, costs much the same and is quieter and better located. It also has some basic rooms without private bath, which are cheaper.

The *Hotel Better* (☎ 824269), at Carrera 2 No 36-26, is indeed better. It offers rooms with bath and fan/air-con for US$6/8 per person. Alternatively, try the *Hotel Imperial* (☎ 825497), at Carrera 2 No 35-20, which has rooms with bath and fan at similar prices.

For somewhere considerably better go to the *Hotel Alcázar* (☎ 824900), at Carrera 2 No 32-17, which has air-con singles/doubles with bath and TV for US$20/25.

## Getting There & Away

Montería hasn't got a central bus terminal; each company has its own office from where its buses depart. They are all close to each other, in the market area, except for Expreso Brasilia which is tucked away on Calle 41 on the corner of Carrera 6. Rápido Ochoa is on Carrera 2 No 38-54, and Unitransco and Sotracor have their bus depots next to each other on Calle 37 between Carreras 1 and 2.

**To Medellín** Expreso Brasilia and Rápido Ochoa service this route, with at least 10 departures daily (US$16.50 climatizado, nine hours).

**To Arboletes & Coveñas** Sotracor has hourly buses to both these destinations (US$2.50, three hours either trip).

**To Cartagena** Several companies, including Unitransco, Brasilia, Rápido Ochoa and Copetrán, service this route (US$10.50 climatizado, six hours). Unitransco also has a few cheaper pullmans (US$8.50).

**To Turbo** Jeeps depart in the morning from Calle 37 near the Sotracor office (US$10, six hours). Sotracor has one morning bus (US$8, seven hours). The trip is rough and can be unsafe because of the guerrillas in the region. The journey time listed above is for optimal conditions but may be longer due to a variety of developments on the road. Read the experience of a traveller journeying to Turbo:

I got a bus at 5.15 am to San Pedro (US$5.50), from where I was told I could get transport to Turbo. Well, the bus broke down after three hours of travelling on a bone-shaking road. We waited two hours by the roadside until the bus from Montería to Turbo (leaving supposedly at 7 am but it was late) picked us up. That bus also broke down an hour later but it took us only an hour to fix it this time. From San Pedro it is US$3.50 and supposedly two hours to Turbo. I wouldn't know for sure because shortly after leaving San Pedro, our bus got stopped by the guerrilleros of the 5th front of FARC. These charming fellows searched the bus (as well as a dozen other vehicles, trucks or jeeps) and went through my day-pack very thoroughly: they were very inquisitive about my tapes and my book (but they concluded that Thomas Hardy was not contra-revolutionary I suppose). They didn't steal anything but they let us simmer in the heat for two hours then gathered everyone on the road for a lecture on the virtues of the revolution. I can't say I agree with their method to get an audience but I suppose it's hard to sell tickets for that kind of performance...Thus, we were free to continue this journey into hell which was uneventful thereafter, apart from a brief moment when the bus got stuck in the mud. I arrived in Turbo around 6.30 pm, 13 hours after leaving Montería. I wouldn't say that it was a wonderful experience...

## ARBOLETES
• *pop 7500* • *4 metres* • *28˚C* • ☎ *(948)*

Arboletes is a seaside town on the border of the Córdoba and Antioquia departments (on the Antioquian side). It is slowly gaining popularity as a holiday spot, but is still quiet and unspoilt. The beaches are not particularly wonderful on this part of the coast, but Arboletes has one special attraction: the mud volcano, the most popular of its kind in Colombia.

The volcano is one km north-east of the town, a 10-minute walk along the beach. It's not as handsome as the Volcán de Lodo El Totumo (see that section for information about mud volcanoes) near Barranquilla, being just an inconspicuous, low hill. However, it has a larger crater than El Totumo, and is full of lukewarm, thick grey mud with bubbles rising to the surface indicating its permanent 'volcanic' activity.

The crater has been recently fenced off (suggesting that it's someone's private land) but tourists are admitted free of charge. Take the chance to wallow about like a hippo in the mud – it's supposed to be good for skin complaints and it does leave your hair silky smooth. The experience is unusual. When you've had enough, wash it all off in the sea only 100 metres away.

### Places to Stay
The most romantic, though very basic, place to stay is the *Residencias El Platanal*, on the seashore overlooking the beach. It's a rustic, thatched country cottage, slowly being eaten away by the high tides. Conditions are primitive and the beds are hard, but the view over the sea, especially at sunset, is lovely. There are no private baths, or fans (actually you don't need them thanks to the refreshing evening breeze), and the friendly owner charges US$2 per person.

If the standards of El Platanal are not what you are accustomed to, there are half a dozen budget residencias between the beach and the Parque Principal (the main square), including the *Florida*, *Arboletes*, *Tropical*, *Aristi* and *Julia*. All have clean rooms with private bath and fan. Most of them cost around US$3 per person; the Arboletes is slightly cheaper but poorer in quality.

The *Hotel Los Caracoles* near the beach is the best place to stay in town and has its own restaurant.

In the high season (end of December, January and the Holy Week), the prices may go up a little, but there's usually no problem finding a room.

### Places to Eat
There are several restaurants in town, of which *Restaurante Guido*, near the Residencias Arboletes, and *Restaurante Las Acacias*, in the main square, are both good options for filling set meals at US$1.75.

### Getting There & Away
Arboletes is linked to the outside world by poor, unpaved roads, but transport on these roads is fairly regular.

**To Montería** Buses operated by Sotracor leave every hour from the main plaza (US$2.50, three hours). The road is rough and very dusty in the dry season. It can be muddy and at times impassable during the rainy periods.

**To Turbo** There are three buses a day operated by Transportes Gómez Hernández and departing from their office two blocks south of the main square (US$6, five hours). Alternatively, take a jeep to Necoclí (which leave when full) – US$5, 2½ hours – then continue on to Turbo by bus or chiva. The unpaved road to Necoclí is in very poor shape, and there has been some guerrilla activity on this route.

# Urabá

Urabá is the westernmost part of the Colombian Caribbean coast, centred around the Golfo de Urabá. The region has grown into a major banana producer, primarily for export, with the town of Turbo as its major port and largest urban centre.

The region has a couple of places of great natural beauty, principally the Parque Nacional Los Katíos and the Capurganá area with its beautiful coast. Cuna Indians live in certain areas, mostly close to the border with Panama.

Urabá appears frequently on the front pages of the press but not for its nature spots. The region is notorious for its problems of public order and is infiltrated by guerrillas (they are now spreading over the border into Panama). Take extra precautions while travelling here.

See the Darién-Urabá Routes map, included in the Getting There & Away chapter at the start of this book, for general orientation.

### TURBO
• *pop 40,000* • *2 m* • *28°C* • ☎ *(948)*
Turbo is the main port on the Golfo de Urabá, from where bananas, cultivated in the region,

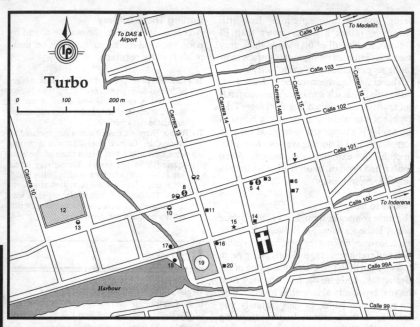

CARIBBEAN COAST

are shipped overseas. The main port facilities are outside the town. There's another harbour for smaller craft in a long inlet which cuts into the town's centre. This smelly body of water is covered in oil and rubbish and is full of the run-down wooden boats that look ready to sink at any moment.

The town itself perfectly complements this picture. It's ramshackle, dirty and noisy, and the putrid smell from the polluted caños (water channels) spreads for blocks around. The streets are full of suspicious characters and look unsafe, especially after dark. The electricity blackouts are a part of everyday life, as are water-supply shortages. Turbo is not an idyllic tourist destination.

However, it's virtually impossible to avoid passing through if you plan on visiting the region's highlights or doing the overland trip to or from Panama. Turbo is the only gateway to Capurganá and Sapzurro on the western coast of the Golfo de Urabá, and the most convenient starting point for Parque

Nacional Los Katíos. It's also an obligatory stopover to get an entry or exit stamp in your passport if you are coming from or heading to the Darién in Panama. See the introductory Getting There & Away chapter for description of the two possible routes via the Darién.

### Information

**Money** There are no banks in Turbo which change cash or travellers' cheques. Some shops and other establishments will change US dollars but they pay at a poor rate.

Try Banco de Bogotá or Banco Ganadero for a peso advance on your Visa credit card, but don't count too much on it.

**Inderena** This is where you can get a permit for Parque Nacional Los Katíos. The office is on the road to Medellín, a 15-minute walk from the town's centre, east along Calle 100

**PLACES TO STAY**

3   Residencias El Viajero
6   Residencias Turbo
7   Residencias Marcela
11  Hotel La Montaña
14  Hotel Castilla de Oro
20  Hotel Saussa

**PLACES TO EAT**

1   Restaurante El Paisa

**OTHER**

2   Jeeps to DAS & Airport
4   Banco Ganadero
5   Aces
8   Banco de Bogotá
9   Sotraurabá
10  Transportes Gómez Hernández
12  Plaza de Mercado
13  Buses to Necoclí & Jeeps to
    Montería
15  Police
16  Alcaldía
17  Cigarrería Carnaval
18  Boats to Acandí, Capurganá,
    Riosucio & Quibdó
19  Casa de la Cultura

to its end. It is open Monday to Friday from 8 am to noon and 1 to 5 pm. They are friendly, helpful and give good information on Los Katíos.

**Immigration** The DAS office (where you need to have your passport stamped when coming from or going to Panama) is at the Apostadero Naval in the Naval Base, on the bank of the Golfo de Urabá, a few km west of the town's centre, on the road to the airport, one km before the terminal. It would take you half an hour to walk there, but jeep-colectivos from Carrera 13 between Calles 101 and 102 will take you there in less than 10 minutes for around US$0.50.

The office is open daily from 8 am to noon and 1 to 5 pm. The formalities are usually over very quickly, but you have to beware of corrupt soldiers. A traveller reported:

One soldier asked US$1 from an Austrian tourist for having searched his luggage (!) while I was asked US$5 to be let out of the base. I flatly refused and walked past them, no problem.

The Panamanian immigration and customs posts are in Puerto Obaldía (if you head via the Caribbean coastal route) and in Boca de Cupe (if you trek through the jungle). Both posts will require you to have a visa, sufficient funds (US$400 or more) and an onward ticket. Make sure you meet all three requirements; otherwise you may be turned back.

**Panamanian Consulate** There's none in Turbo. There's a consulate in Capurganá, but it's unreliable. You are strongly recommended to get the visa beforehand, for example in Medellín, Barranquilla or Cartagena (see those sections for addresses).

**Places to Stay**
There are a few basic residencias between the port and the market, but they are not good. It's better to stay near the church where you'll find three budget hotels.

The friendly *Residencias Marcela*, at Carrera 14B No 100-54, is the best bet among the cheapies. Rooms don't have private baths but they do have fans, are clean and cost US$3 per person. If it's full (rather improbable), try the *Residencias Turbo*, next door at Carrera 14B No 100-78, or *Residencias El Viajero*, just round the corner at Calle 101 No 14-48. The Turbo offers much the same for marginally more money, while El Viajero is slightly cheaper but more basic. Neither has private baths but both have fans.

The *Hotel La Montaña* (☎ 682974), at Carrera 13 No 100-64, has rooms with their own bath and fan but otherwise it's not any better than the Marcela. Rooms should normally cost around US$4 per person, but the management may demand higher prices from gringos. Bargain, or go to the *Hotel Saussa* (☎ 682020) just a block away at Carrera 13 No 99A-28, which is better and costs US$6/9 for a single/double.

The best in town is the *Hotel Castilla de*

*Oro* (☎ 682466), at Calle 100 No 14-07. It has air-con singles/doubles with TV, private bath and hot water for US$20/32.

### Places to Eat
The *Hotel Saussa* has its own restaurant which serves filling set meals till around 6 pm for US$2. *Restaurante El Paisa*, Calle 101 No 14B-21, does set meals at lunch time (US$2) and has good mondongo (US$1).

You'll find several more cheap eateries around the central streets, but nothing particularly great.

### Getting There & Away
**Air** Aces has three flights a day to Medellín (US$52), and four flights a week to Acandí (US$25). Bookings can be made at its office in town at Calle 101 No 14-10. It provides free transport to the airport (which is about four km out of town), and also picks up passengers from the incoming flights – watch out for a navy-blue Land Rover. Otherwise, you can get from or to the airport by jeep-colectivo (US$1.50). In the town's centre, they park on Carrera 13 between Calles 101 and 102.

**Bus** There's no bus terminal. Two major companies, Transportes Gómez Hernández and Sotraurabá, have offices on Calle 101, diagonally opposite each other. Buses, chivas and jeeps of other local carriers all cram in front of the Plaza de Mercado, the market.

**To Medellín** There are three corriente buses daily with Gómez Hernández and another two with Sotraurabá (US$13, 13 hours along a rough road). Most depart in the late afternoon or early evening for the overnight trip.

**To Montería** Jeeps leave when full (10 passengers) between 6 am and noon from the Plaza de Mercado (US$10, six hours). Read the comments about this route in the Montería section.

**To Necoclí** Buses and chivas leave from the market every hour from 7 am to 5 pm (US$1.75, 1½ hours).

**To Arboletes** There are three buses daily with Gómez Hernández at 7, 9 and 11 am (US$6, five hours).

**Boat** Fast passenger motorboats cover the main water routes around the region. Tickets are sold in Cigarrería Carnaval, across the street from the wharf where they depart. Go to the port early to get your ticket as the boats may fill up fast, especially during the holiday periods. Better still, buy your ticket the previous day. Check the schedule of departures, as it changes frequently.

**To Riosucio** These are the boats you take to get to the Parque Nacional Los Katíos, as they pass through Sautatá, the entrance to the park. They depart daily at 8 am (US$10, 1½ hours to Sautatá).

**To Quibdó** Boats leave every morning for a fascinating, full-day trip (US$33, eight to 10 hours). Book the ticket one day in advance. See the Quibdó section for more details.

**To Acandí** One boat departs daily at 8 am (US$9, two to 2½ hours), and another one may go an hour or two later if there's the demand.

**To Capurganá** Boats leave about 8 am once they have gathered enough passengers (US$12, 2½ to three hours). Otherwise go to Acandí and change for another boat (which usually waits for that from Turbo to arrive) to Capurganá (US$4, one hour).

**To Puerto Obaldía** There are no direct boats all the way from Turbo to Puerto Obaldía, but it's sometimes possible to do the whole route in stages within a day. Go to Capurganá (either direct or via Acandí) and look for a boat to Sapzurro (US$2.50, 40 minutes). In Sapzurro, you may be lucky enough to catch a boat to Puerto Obaldía (US$4, 45 minutes). There are also irregular direct Capurganá-Puerto Obaldía boats.

Cargo boats ply regional routes and usually take passengers. They obviously don't have any fixed schedules, but you shouldn't have to wait more than a couple of days for a boat to Riosucio. It is more difficult to catch cargo boats to Quibdó but at least one or two go there each week. Sometimes you can find a cargo or fishing boat to Acandí or Capurganá. You can count on paying a little more than half of the passenger boat fare but the trip takes much longer. Cargo boats to Cartagena depart a few times a week and take one to two days; expect to pay about US$15.

There are occasional boats to Colón in Panama but some may carry contraband stuff or even drugs. If you have any doubts about the boat or the legitimacy of its cargo then don't get aboard.

## NECOCLÍ
• *pop 6000* • *20 m* • *28°C*

Necoclí is a small town on the Golfo de Urabá, about 50 km north of Turbo. It is praised in the local pamphlets for its beaches, which are in fact almost nonexistent. If you are looking for some fine coast, you can find it just across the Gulf, north of Acandí.

### Places to Stay
The *Residencias Caribe* and the *Hotel Las Palmas*, around the corner from each other, are both good and cost US$5/6 per person in rooms without/with bath.

### Getting There & Away
The Turbo-Necoclí road is unpaved but in relatively good shape. The road which continues on to Arboletes is very rough and can occasionally be impassable in the wet season.

**To Turbo** Buses and chivas run every hour (US$1.75, 1½ hours). Some Cuna Indians live along the way and sell fine *molas* (handmade, rectangular, colourful pieces of tapestry).

**To Arboletes** Jeeps depart when full (mostly in the morning), for a rough trip over a poor road (US$5, 2½ hours). Also, three buses a day pass through from Turbo (US$4.25, three hours).

## CAPURGANÁ, SAPZURRO & ACANDÍ
These three villages sit on a spectacular stretch of the Golfo de Urabá near the Panamanian border. It is a rugged coastal region with steep cliffs falling right down into the sea, and tropical forest further inland. Tiny islets and quiet bays with white sandy beaches add to the colour. The coast has still not been invaded by mass tourism and remains largely unspoilt.

The best time to visit the region is from December to March; August can be relatively dry, but not always. The rest of the year is wet, and the paths may be muddy.

### Capurganá
Capurganá is the main destination point for tourists. It is a pleasant village with typical one-storey wooden houses; its main square is just a grassy meadow. Capurganá has the widest choice of accommodation, including a few recently built colonies of cabañas. You can make a trip to El Cielo, a lovely nature spot an hour's walk upstream alongside the small river passing through Capurganá. Some hotels have horses for hire. A few establishments in the village will change your US dollars, though the rate is poor.

### Capurganá to Sapzurro
From Capurganá you can walk to Sapzurro in 1½ hours, but it is best done leisurely to take in the splendid scenery. There is no road, only a footpath. It doesn't skirt around the coast but climbs a high hill then drops down to Sapzurro, beautifully set on the edge of a bay. Descending, you will get a marvellous view of the bay and the cape, Cabo Tiburón.

### Sapzurro
Sapzurro is a fishing village, smaller than Capurganá and much quieter. The village is right on the shore and it is possible to stay there in a few hospedajes. The deep, horse-shoe-shaped bay in which Sapzurro sits has one of the nicest beaches in the area. It's narrow but white and clean, and shaded with coconut palms.

### Sapzurro to Puerto Obaldía
From Sapzurro you can walk to La Miel, the first Panamanian village over the border. It's only a half-hour walk one way, and it's worth doing just as a side trip (there are no guards on the border proper). This is also a part of the coastal route to Panama. The description of the whole route is included in the introductory Getting There & Away chapter. The following is an expansion of the La Miel-Puerto Obaldía leg, as this is the most confusing part of the way. If you can, try to tag along with a local who is walking this route.

The path from La Miel initially follows the beaches. Past them, the trail continues close to the sea, passing over the rocks. There are several paths branching off inland but don't follow them, otherwise you'll end up in some corn fields. After one-hour's walk

CARIBBEAN COAST

you will get to a farm house, the only one on the La Miel-Puerto Obaldía trail. Ask for further directions here.

Proceeding on, you'll cross a river twice before you get to the beach. Head for the lighthouse, visible from the beach, from where it's just a 15-minute walk to Puerto Obaldía.

Note that the La Miel-Puerto Obaldía trail is said to be unsafe because of the risk of robberies. Locals warn travellers and suggest that they take a boat rather than walk. So far, however, Lonely Planet hasn't received any alarming messages from travellers, although some have commented about the misleading side paths which made their walk longer than expected.

### Capurganá to Acandí

This is a lovely walk but you'll need to allow most of the day to get to Acandí. Start from Capurganá along the beach and follow the path, which doesn't always stick to the coast; at a few points it goes inland climbing the hills around the difficult coastal cliffs. One hour's walk will bring you to Aguacate, which is only a bunch of huts with a beautiful local-style house functioning as a hospedaje. Follow the footpath for a bit over an hour to Rufino, a cluster of houses. From there the path turns inland. It heads up the extensive coastal ridge, passes over it and descends into the Acandí River valley. It takes another hour to get to this point from Rufino. Follow the river downstream to Acandí – it is a leisurely three-hour walk. The path does not always follow the river and includes several crossings.

### Acandí

Acandí is a bigger village than Capurganá; in fact, it's almost a town. It is not as attractive but has a wider choice of shops, and the food is cheaper. You can change your cash dollars here, and you'll probably get a better rate than in Capurganá. Acandí's beaches are unremarkable.

### Acandí to Los Katíos

From Acandí you can go overland to Parque Nacional Los Katíos. You can shorten the walk by taking a boat to Titumate (some boats going to Turbo stop there) for US$5. From Titumate, it is a pleasant two to three-day hike. Unfortunately, guerrillas have appeared in this area, although so far travellers haven't reported any problems.

From Titumate, walk along the rough road to the Río Tanela (at most two hours), then continue by footpath to El Gilgal (three hours). This part of the route may not be very easy to follow and you may get lost. It's best to tag along with a local or contract a guide in Titumate. A man called Agapo is known to have guided travellers to El Gilgal for about US$10. From El Gilgal, a short walk on a dirt road will take you to Santa María where you can find basic accommodation and food.

Santa María was established on the site where one of the earliest Spanish settlements on the continent, Santa María La Antigua, once existed. Also known as Santa María del Darién, the original town was founded in 1510 by Francisco Pizarro and Martín Fernández de Enciso. It was repeatedly attacked by the Indians and eventually destroyed and abandoned in 1519.

From Santa María, a rough road goes to Puerta Negra on the Río Tigre (a three-hour walk) and continues on to Unguía. There are occasional jeeps on this road (US$2, 2½ hours). In Unguía you can stop for the night as there are a couple of restaurants and residencias (eg *Residencias El Viajero* and *Doña Julia*, both with private baths), or you can ask at INCORA (Instituto Colombiano de la Reforma Agraria), where they may allow you to sleep for free.

If you arrive in Unguía early enough, you can continue on the same day to Peyé, the entrance to Los Katíos (a four to five-hour walk). This part of the trail is also confusing and easy to lose, so you may be interested in hiring a guide. Ask about guides in the mayor's office in Unguía and they may help you to find one.

You can sleep for free in the Cabaña del Inderena in Peyé, but bring your own food. From Peyé, it is a four-hour walk to the park's administrative and visitors centre. It's worth stopping on the way to visit the Tilupo waterfall, which is near but off the trail; count on spending a few more hours to do this detour.

### Places to Stay & Eat

All three villages, Capurganá, Sapzurro and Acandí, have a choice of cheap accommodation as well as houses that take in guests. Even in the peak season (late December and January), it is relatively easy to find a place to stay, though the prices tend to rise. Camping is possible almost everywhere, but always ask permission if the land seems to be private property.

Food and drink are expensive. Obviously, fish dishes are the most prominent on the local menus.

**Capurganá** There are three budget residencias, the *Merce*, *Estela* and *El Uvito*, on the street near the beach where the boats anchor. They are basic but acceptable. Expect to pay between US$3 and US$4 per person in any of the three. The Merce has a restaurant which serves filling comidas for US$3, and there are a couple of cheaper eateries around.

The handicraft shop in the Estela has a wide choice of cheap, beautiful Cuna molas. The shop next door to El Uvito can change your dollars, but the rate is poor.

*Las Cabañas*, on the main square, costs US$25 for a double cabin with bath. It is pleasant and has a swimming pool and a good restaurant.

**Sapzurro** *El Retiro*, a house on the beach, rents small cabañas equipped with two beds for US$7. Hearty meals are available for guests. The owner is helpful and friendly. There are a couple of cheap hospedajes behind the church. Several restaurants open on the waterfront in the tourist season.

**Acandí** Residencias are scattered all over the town. The *Pilar*, at US$3 per person, is one of the cheapest, and there are several more nearby.

### Getting There & Away

**Air** Acandí and Capurganá have airstrips, both just a short walk from town. Flights are operated by Aces. From Acandí there are four flights a week to Medellín (US$75); all go via Turbo (US$25). From Capurganá there are two direct flights a day to Medellín (US$77).

**Boat** There are regular morning boats between Turbo and Acandí, some of which go via Titumate. They cost US$9 and take two to 2½ hours depending on sea conditions; it can be quite a rough ride at times. There are also daily boats between Acandí and Capurganá. They cost US$4 and take one hour (if the *motorista* doesn't feel like fishing on the way!).

Direct boats between Turbo and Capurganá run most days (US$12, 2½ to three hours); if there's none due to depart, go to Acandí and change.

Boats between Capurganá and Sapzurro run irregularly, depending on demand (US$2.50, 40 minutes). So do the Sapzurro-Puerto Obaldía boats (US$4, 45 minutes). The latter may demand more from foreigners, claiming that this is an 'international route'.

### PARQUE NACIONAL LOS KATÍOS

This national park lies at the extreme northwest end of Colombia, on the Panamanian border. Created in 1973 and covering 720 sq km, the park protects a very interesting stretch of land, noted for its rich animal and plant life and diverse geography. The Atrato River, which passes through the park, divides it into two wholly different parts. The eastern part is a swampy plain with a chain of four lakes, the Ciénagas de Tumaradó. By contrast, the western section is hilly, in parts mountainous with altitudes of up to 600 metres. It's covered by tropical rainforest and cut by a maze of streams with several waterfalls.

Originally, the region was inhabited by Cuna Indians but they were pushed out by Katío-Emberá groups, after whom the park has been named. Today, no people live in the park.

Parque Nacional Los Katíos

Los Katíos is one of the most beautiful parks in Colombia. Several footpaths cut through the woods which allow you to access marvellous waterfalls and enjoy the lush vegetation and wildlife. Birds and butterflies are particularly numerous. About 400 species of birds have been recorded in the park, which represents a quarter of all bird species to be found in the country.

There are tourist facilities in the park and the friendly rangers are very informative and may even take you around. The best time to visit the park is from December to March, which is really the only relatively dry period. August may be OK, but in other months it can rain a lot, making the paths muddy (at times impassable). The highest rainfall is usually in May, September and October. The average temperature is about 27°C (23° at the highest elevations).

You must get your permit for the park from Inderena before arriving. It can be obtained in Bogotá, Medellín or Turbo. While applying for the permit you'll also have to pay the entrance fee (US$0.75) and accommodation costs.

Los Katíos lies on the southern end of the adventurous Panama-Colombia trail through the Darién. Many travellers who do this trail stay in the park, either before setting off or after completing the trek. Refer to the introductory Getting There & Away chapter for the description of the whole route.

### Things to See & Do

**Salto del Tilupo** At nearly 100 metres, this is the highest and most spectacular waterfall in the park. It can be reached along a path, a 2½-hour walk from the visitors centre. The path can be muddy in parts even during the dry season, but you can clean up and take a refreshing shower in the pool at the foot of the waterfall.

**Salto del Tendal & Salto de la Tigra** These two waterfalls are close to each other. A well-worn but often muddy trail heads there over three river crossings (be prepared to get your shoes wet) before dividing. It's a 1½-hour leisurely walk to get to this point. El Tendal is only 10 minutes away along the left-hand branch.

The path to La Tigra is not as well defined; go down to the river following the right-hand branch, and then walk upriver for about 50 metres until you see a stream joining it from the opposite side. Cross the river and follow the stream up. After about 20 minutes you will get to a 10-metre-high waterfall, but don't stop there; that's not it. Climb up the waterfall on the left-hand side and from there you can see the beautiful La Tigra.

**Ciénagas de Tumaradó** These four lakes are on the opposite side of the Atrato River, and are only accessible by boat. The park has its own motorboats and sometimes rents them out to tourists, charging only for petrol. Ask the staff. This is a pleasant four-hour excursion.

**Cementerio de Sautatá** The cemetery is a 10-minute walk off the main path linking the boat wharf on the Atrato with the visitors centre. The cemetery dates back to the 1930s when a sugarcane mill operated on the site of the present park.

### Places to Stay & Eat
The park has a pleasant, spacious house with a capacity for about 20 visitors (US$6 per person). If you have your own hammock, you can string it under the roof for a nominal fee or even for nothing. Camping is also possible (US$2 per tent).

The park's kitchen serves breakfast, lunch and dinner for US$3 per meal, but only if there are not too many visitors. As everything has to be shipped in from Turbo, food is limited. It's best to bring your own food; you can cook it yourself, or ask to have it cooked for you. There are no soft drinks or beer, but there is good tinto.

### Getting There & Away
Access to the park is not as difficult as it seems, but it is expensive. From Turbo there are daily motorboats to Riosucio, passing Sautatá, the entrance to the park. They cost US$10 and take 1½ hours.

There are also large cargo boats from Turbo, irregularly going up the Atrato River. Look around in the Turbo port. The usual price is about US$6 and the trip can take a full day.

Another way to get to the park is from Quibdó (see the Quibdó section for details). One more option is the trek from Acandí (see the description in the Acandí section).

From the Sautatá wharf, it is a 20-minute walk to the administrative and visitors centre.

# San Andrés & Providencia

This archipelago of small islands in the Caribbean Sea lies about 750 km north-west of the Colombian mainland and only 230 km east of Nicaragua. The archipelago is made up of two groups of islands: the southern group, with San Andrés as its largest and most important island; and 90 km to the north, the group centred around the island of Providencia. There are also several small cays away from the main islands scattered over an area of 350,000 sq km. Of these, the Cayo Bolívar, 30 km south-east of San Andrés, and the Cayos de Albuquerque, 50 km south of San Andrés, are the best known.

The archipelago is a department in its own right, San Andrés y Providencia. Territorially, it's Colombia's smallest administrative unit, comprising an area of 44 sq km (52.5 sq km including the outer cays, reefs and sand banks).

The islands were reputedly discovered in 1527 by Spanish explorers but they remained unsettled. The first inhabitants were probably the Dutch, who came to live on Providencia towards the end of the 16th century. In 1631, however, they were expelled by the English who effectively colonised the islands. They brought in black slaves from Jamaica and began to cultivate tobacco and cotton. By then the Spaniards finally seemed to realise the importance of the islands. They attacked the archipelago in 1635 and gained control but were soon driven out.

Because of their strategic location, pirates often sheltered on the islands waiting to sack the Spanish galleons that were bound for home laden with gold and riches. In 1670 the legendary pirate Henry Morgan established his base on Providencia. From there he raided Panama and Santa Marta. Legend has it that his treasures are still on the islands, hidden in an underwater cave or in another secret place.

Shortly after independence, Colombia laid claim to the islands, although Nicaragua

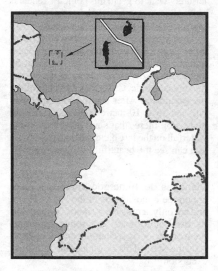

fiercely disputed its right to do so. The issue was eventually settled by a treaty in 1928 which confirmed Colombia's sovereignty over the archipelago. However, the islands didn't have any consistent form of transport or communication with the Colombian mainland until the 1950s. Until that time, the English heritage, reflected in the islands' language, religion and architecture, remained virtually intact.

The situation began to change when a regular domestic flight service was established, and when San Andrés was declared a duty-free zone in 1954. Commerce and tourism attracted mainlanders to the islands. Many of them, finding the conditions favourable, decided to settle, principally on San Andrés.

The population of San Andrés grew quickly, from 20,000 in 1973 to 55,000 in 1993, largely because of migration from the mainland. The Colombian mainlanders now account for around 60% of the total population of San Andrés. In the early 1990s, the local government introduced restrictions on migration to the islands in order to slow the rampant influx of people and preserve the local culture and identity.

The native inhabitants, descendants of the Jamaican slaves, still speak a thick Jamaican-English, but Spanish is now widely spoken throughout San Andrés and, to a lesser extent, in Providencia. Similarly, whereas Baptist congregations were once dominant, now Catholicism is more prevalent.

The tourist and commercial boom has accelerated the process of cultural change, and San Andrés is now a blend of Latin American and English-Caribbean culture. Much original culture has been lost, and Providencia is likely to suffer the same fate.

Nicaragua incessantly questions Colombian sovereignty over the islands. Of course, Colombia rejects all such suggestions and at the same time does what it can to keep the *isleños* (islanders) content. The government invests more money in the islands' development than it does on some other regions. Nevertheless, the islanders don't seem too happy about the government flooding them with Spanish culture, or with the avalanche of shoppers that come. Despite all this, the native population is very friendly, patient and open to visitors.

There is virtually no local industry and agriculture is scarce. Almost everything except fish and some fruit and vegetables has to be shipped in, which makes the islands quite expensive to visit.

The climate is typical of tropical islands, with average temperatures of 26° to 29°C. The rainy period is from September to December and (a less wet period) from May to June. The tourist peaks are from late December to late January, Holy Week and a quieter season from July to August.

The islands, especially Providencia, provide an opportunity to experience the ambience of the Caribbean. The crystal-clear, turquoise waters, extensive coral reefs and rich marine life are a paradise for snorkellers and scuba divers. The easy-going

life, friendly atmosphere, adequate tourist facilities and general safety make it a good place to escape from the outside world.

San Andrés lies on the cheapest and most convenient route between Central America and Colombia, and is quite a popular stopover for travellers. All visitors to San Andrés are charged US$15 on arrival and handed the so-called Tarjeta de Turista. This fee is a local government levy designed to improve the island's budget. In practical terms it's the entry ticket to the islands.

# San Andrés

• *pop 57,000* • *27°C* • ☎ *(9811)*

Shaped like a seahorse, San Andrés is the largest island of the archipelago, about 12.5 km long and three km wide. Its topography is relatively flat, with a small, low range crossing the island from north to south, and reaching an altitude of 85 metres at the highest point. The island is largely covered with coconut palms. There are no rivers, only some intermittent streams during the heavy rainy periods.

The town of San Andrés (known locally as El Centro) is the urban centre and the capital of the archipelago. It's in the extreme north of the island and has more than two-thirds of the population. This is the principal tourist and commercial area, packed with hotels, restaurants and stores.

There are also two small towns, La Loma, in the central hilly region, and San Luis on the eastern coast. Both are far less tourist oriented than San Andrés, and both have some fine English-Caribbean, wooden architecture.

There is a 30-km scenic, paved road circling the island, and a few more roads that cross inland. The island is bordered on the north-east by extensive *arrecifes* (coral reefs) and small cays.

The two things that draw people to San Andrés are its natural beauty and duty-free shopping. The island has become one of the main tourist attractions of Colombia.

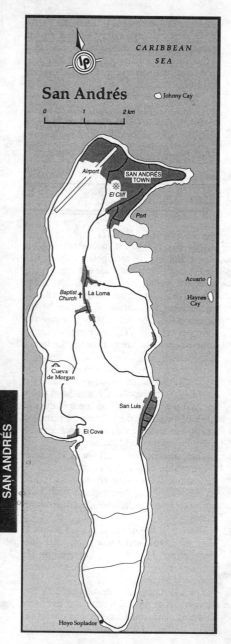

San Andrés

CARIBBEAN SEA

Johnny Cay

0    1    2 km

Airport

SAN ANDRÉS TOWN

El Cliff

Port

Acuario

Baptist Church   La Loma

Haynes Cay

Cueva de Morgan

San Luis

El Cove

Hoyo Soplador

SAN ANDRÉS

Snorkelling and scuba diving are good and equipment can be easily rented in El Centro. Contrary to what might be supposed, however, the island is not surrounded by beaches; there are none along the western shore and those along the eastern coast are nothing special (aside from the beach in San Luis). Possibly the best beach is at the northern end of the island bordering El Centro, but it's usually crowded. If you are looking for beaches, it's probably best to go to the islet of Johnny Cay just opposite El Centro, though it too fills with visitors on weekends.

The commercial aspect of San Andrés has been another magnet for Colombian visitors. El Centro is packed with several hundred shops selling everything from Chinese porcelain to liquor. Consumer goods such as TVs, cameras and audio and video gear dominate trade. Bargaining is the norm in most places, although in some stores prices are fixed.

However, measures to liberalise the economy, introduced in 1991, have caused San Andrés to lose a lot of its commercial attractiveness. Today, many products can be bought at competitive or even lower prices on the Colombian mainland. Despite this, the island continues to be overrun with shoppers who – as you can judge by their luggage at the airport – somehow manage to spend their money. On the whole, though, the duty-free bonanza seems to be over, and the main focus of local government is now tourism.

### Information
**Tourist Office** The CNT office (☎ 24230) is on Avenida Colombia, near the airport. It's open Monday to Friday from 9 am to 1 pm and 2.30 to 6.30 pm.

**Money** Travellers' cheques and cash can be changed at the Banco Popular (the best rate for both cash and cheques), the Banco Industrial Colombiano and the Banco del Estado. Plenty of shops and some hotels accept payments in cash dollars, and they also change dollars for pesos (but at a lower rate than the banks). MasterCard is accepted by Banco Industrial Colombiano, while Visa card will be honoured at the Banco Popular.

**Consulates** Costa Rica, Guatemala, Honduras and Panama have consulates in San Andrés, which are all located in shops. It's a good idea to get any visas you need on the mainland, as consuls do not always stay on the island and you may be stuck for a few days (or weeks) waiting for one to return. All consulates are open from Monday to Friday.

Costa Rica, in the Almacén Regina, next to the Calypso Beach Hotel on Avenida Colombia, is open from 9 am to 12.30 pm and 3 to 7.30 pm (☎ 25772).
Guatemala, in the Almacén El Hogar, Avenida de las Américas No 3-136, is open from 9 am to noon and 2 to 5 pm (☎ 26357).
Honduras, in the Almacén Lady Vanity, Avenida Atlántico No 1A-50, is open from 9 am to 12.30 pm.
Panama, in the Almacén Chévere, Avenida de las Américas No 3-131 (opposite the Guatemalan consulate), is open from 9 am to noon and 3 to 6 pm (☎ 26901).

## Things to See & Do
You will probably stay in El Centro, but you should take some time to look around the island. Refer to the Getting Around section for details on how to get to the listed attractions.

**El Cliff** This cliff, 50 metres high, is a 20-minute walk from the airport. It offers good views over the town and the surrounding coral reefs.

**Cueva de Morgan** This is an underwater cave where the Welsh pirate Henry Morgan is said to have buried some of his treasure. The cave is small and actually not very inspiring, yet the magic of alleged riches draws in plenty of tourists.

**Hoyo Soplador** The Hoyo Soplador, at the southernmost tip of the island, is a blowhole where the sea water spouts into the air through a natural hole in the coral rock. This phenomenon only occurs at certain times, depending on the tide and winds.

**La Loma** This small town, in the central part of the island, is one of the more traditional places. The first Baptist church established on the island was built here in 1847. In 1896 it was largely rebuilt in pine brought from Alabama.

**San Luis** Another small town, San Luis, lies on the east coast of the island and still boasts some fine traditional wooden houses. It has a good beach, and the sea just offshore is good for snorkelling. The town is becoming pretty touristy, and there's an increasing number of hotels and restaurants.

**Johnny Cay** Johnny Cay is a small coral islet, lying about 1.5 km north of San Andrés town. It is covered with coconut groves and surrounded by a lovely, white-sand beach. The sunbathing is good but be careful swimming here, because there are dangerous currents. The island is a popular picnic spot and, particularly on weekends, it fills up with food vendors serving seafood, and local musicians performing, sometimes accompanied by dancers.

**Acuario & Haynes Cay** Acuario and Haynes Cay are two small cays off the east coast of San Andrés island. The surrounding sea is perfect for snorkelling. Don't forget to bring your snorkelling gear when you come.

## Places to Stay – bottom end
Accommodation in San Andrés is expensive. There are only a few lower-priced places, and they are not particularly cheap. You'll pay roughly twice what you would pay for similar standards on the mainland.

The most popular budget place to stay is the *Hotel Restrepo* (☎ 26744), on the opposite side of the runway from the airport terminal. It has become a mecca for foreign backpackers; Colombians are rare guests here. It is basic but pleasant and friendly, and costs US$5 per person, regardless of what room you get – some have their own bath, others don't, but all rooms have fans. Some rooms are considerably better than others, so have a look at a few if there's any choice of vacancies. There is a dining room, where you can get breakfast, lunch and dinner (US$1.50 per meal). The hotel fills up early, so go there

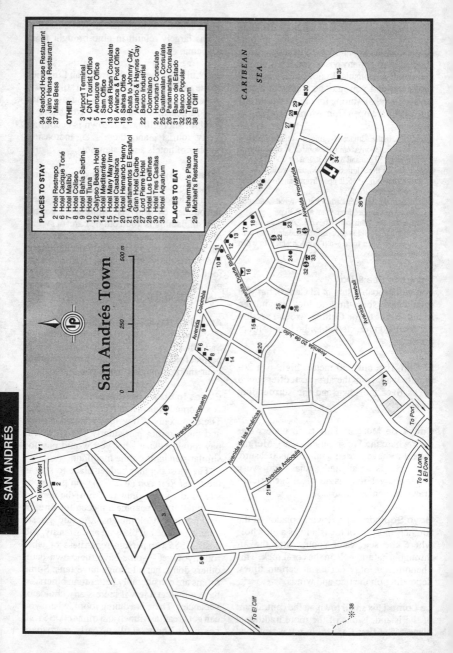

## San Andrés Town

**PLACES TO STAY**
2  Hotel Restrepo
6  Hotel Cacique Toné
7  Hotel Malibú
8  Hotel Coliseo
9  Hotel Bahía Sardina
10  Hotel Tiuna
12  Calypso Beach Hotel
14  Hotel Mediterráneo
15  Hotel Mary May Inn
17  Hotel Casablanca
20  Hotel Hernando Henry
21  Apartamentos El Español
23  Gran Hotel Caribe
27  Lord Pierre House
28  Hotel Los Delfines
30  Hotel Tres Casitas
35  Hotel Aquarium

**PLACES TO EAT**
1  Fisherman's Place
29  Michael's Restaurant
34  Seafood House Restaurant
36  Jairo Hansa Restaurant
37  Miss Bess

**OTHER**
3  Airport Terminal
4  CNT Tourist Office
5  Aerosucre Office
11  Sam Office
13  Costa Rican Consulate
16  Avianca & Post Office
18  Sahsa Office
19  Boats to Johnny Cay,
    Acuario & Haynes Cay
22  Banco Industrial
    Colombiano
24  Honduran Consulate
25  Guatemalan Consulate
26  Panamanian Consulate
31  Banco del Estado
32  Telecom
33  Banco Popular
38  El Cliff

CARIBBEAN SEA

as soon as you arrive on the island. If the rooms are full, and you don't mind mosquitoes (they are only a problem during certain periods, mostly in the wet season), ask for a hammock (US$3). You can string up your own, if you have one.

A steady and rather heavy flow of travellers makes the hotel a good source of travel information. If you've entered Colombia at San Andrés, you'll probably get a lot of up-to-date news about the country from visitors who've just finished travelling through Colombia and are leaving for Central America.

One of the few other low-budget hotels in San Andrés is the *Apartamentos El Español* (☎ 23337), one block south of the airport terminal. This is essentially a budget hotel for Colombians with hardly a foreigner in sight. It is not an attractive place to stay, but all rooms have private bath, and the price, by San Andrés standards, is a bargain – US$8 for a dark double, and US$10 for a considerably better room with a window facing the street.

If you can't get a room at either hotel, or you need more comfort, be prepared to pay at least US$15/20 for a single/double.

### Places to Stay – middle & top end

The more affordable places include the *Hotel Mediterráneo* (☎ 26722), which is simple but relatively inexpensive (US$20/25 a double/triple); the *Hotel Coliseo* (☎ 23330), which is similar (US$15/20 a single/double); the *Hotel Mary May Inn* (☎ 25669), a very good, small hotel (US$22 for the first person plus US$5 for each additional guest); and the *Hotel Hernando Henry* (☎ 23416), one of the best deals for a double (US$25 with breakfast included). The *Hotel Malibú* (☎ 24342) is another good choice for a double (US$30, without breakfast but with air-con). The *Hotel Los Delfines* (☎ 24083) is the cheapest hotel facing the sea (US$28/35).

Rooms in all of these places have private bath and fan, and some have air-con. Most of these hotels are crowded with Colombian shoppers busily packing and repacking the goods they have purchased.

If money is not a problem, San Andrés has a range of luxury hotels, most of which are on the Avenida Colombia. Some of the best in town are the *Hotel Cacique Toné* (☎ 24251), *Hotel Tiuna* (☎ 23235), *Calypso Beach Hotel* (☎ 23558), *Gran Hotel Caribe* (☎ 23026), *Lord Pierre Hotel* (☎ 25556) and the *Hotel Aquarium* (☎ 23120).

Most hotels listed in this section raise their tariffs by about 20% between 15 December and 31 January.

### Places to Eat

There is not much in the way of budget eating. The comida corriente is the most economical meal (US$2 to US$3), but not many restaurants serve it and it's the same plain meal which you can have all over Colombia. You may prefer to pay a little more for something typical of the island.

*Fisherman's Place*, on the beach near the Hotel Restrepo, has crab soup for US$2 and fried fish for US$3. *Miss Bess*, in the Coral Palace Centre, is an ordinary-looking place but serves filling meals, and good rondón (a local soup prepared with coconut milk, vegetables, fish and sea snails) for US$6, as well as other seafood dishes.

The top-end restaurants are not cheap but serve delicious food, particularly comida de mar (seafood). Among the places deserving recommendation are *Jairo Hansa Restaurant*, *Michael's Restaurant* (try the fiesta del mar) and *Seafood House Restaurant*. Most of the top-end hotels have their own restaurants.

### Entertainment

San Andrés has a choice of discos, including the Éxtasis, in the Gran Hotel Caribe, and Las Palmas, on the top floor of the Hotel Tiuna. The best place, however, is the Atlántida (formerly La Escollera), about seven km out of town, on the western coast near Morgan's Cave. It is an attractive, huge, two-storey open-sided hut, thatched with palm leaves. It plays good reggae, Caribbean, rock and salsa music. The place is open

SAN ANDRÉS

nightly, but Friday and Saturday around midnight are when things get hottest. The entrance fee is US$4. A free bus shuttles patrons between the disco and the town, stopping opposite the Hotel Tiuna. It runs every hour or so.

## Getting There & Away

Theoretically, there are two ways to get to and from the island: by air or sea. In practice though, almost all visitors arrive and leave by plane. The airport is in the San Andrés town, a 10-minute walk from the centre, or US$3 by taxi. The port is on the southeastern edge of the town (the same walking time and taxi fare).

**Air – international** Avianca and Sahsa (the Honduran airline) have regular connections between San Andrés and the USA, including Miami (US$260), New Orleans (US$270) and Houston (US$310).

All Central American capitals are covered by Sam and Sahsa, with flights to San José (US$85), Panama City (US$115), Tegucigalpa (US$117), San Salvador (US$150), Guatemala City (US$125) and Managua (US$168). On some routes, there are discounts for a 30-day return ticket. For example, a round trip to Tegucigalpa costs US$200; to Guatemala City, it's US$215. See the introductory Getting There & Away chapter for more details.

If you buy a ticket in San Andrés for any international flight, you pay a 5% Colombian tax on top of the price (2.5% on round-trip tickets). Elsewhere in Colombia the tax is 19% and 9.5%, respectively. The airport departure tax on international flights from San Andrés is the same as elsewhere in the country: US$17 if you have stayed in Colombia less than 60 days, and US$30 if you've stayed longer.

Flights from Central America (especially from Tegucigalpa and Guatemala City) to Colombia via San Andrés have become popular with travellers as a cheap and convenient way to bypass the Darién Gap. If you come this way, buy a ticket to San Andrés only, then another ticket on a domestic flight to the Colombian mainland (a ticket cover-ing the whole route will be more expensive). The same rule applies if you're going in the opposite direction.

**Air – domestic** San Andrés is a lucrative market for Colombian airlines, so most include the island on their routes. Avianca, Sam and Aces fly from San Andrés to most major Colombian cities and keep their fares high. Direct flights by these carriers include Bogotá (US$147), Cartagena (US$98), Barranquilla (US$102), Medellín (US$123) and Cali (US$142). They also offer indirect flights to Cúcuta (US$142), Bucaramanga (US$142), Pereira (US$132) and some other destinations.

Several other carriers, such as Intercontinental, AeroRepública and Isleña de Aviación, offer cheaper fares. At the time of writing, Intercontinental had flights to Bogotá (US$109), Cali (US$109) and Medellín (US$94), whereas AeroRepública could fly you daily to Cartagena for just US$57 – a significant saving. Treat these fares as guidelines only and make sure you shop around before committing yourself to any of the expensive carriers.

You will probably be asked by the airline to check in at the airport two or even three hours before your flight; you'll understand why when you see the crowds of Colombians, each with a huge pile of bags and boxes. If you don't have much luggage, someone may ask you to take one or two boxes of theirs as your free luggage allowance. Never do it, even if they offer to pay you for the favour. You don't know what's inside. Some desperate individuals may try to fly their stuff as yours behind your back, arranging matters directly with the attendant at the check-in desk. Have your eyes and ears open and check how many pieces of luggage they write onto your ticket.

There are two even cheaper ways to get to the mainland, with Aerosucre or Satena. Aerosucre (a cargo carrier) has one or two cargo flights a week to Barranquilla (usually on Monday and/or Tuesday) and Bogotá (Friday or Saturday). It sometimes takes passengers and charges about US$40 to Barranquilla and US$50 to Bogotá. Enquire at the Aerosucre office, near the passenger terminal. It's in the green-roofed building next to the building with the Marlboro cowboy advertisement on top. The entrance is on the right-hand side, not at the front.

Another option is to fly with Satena. It has irregular noncommercial passenger flights to Bogotá, roughly one per month (about US$60). These flights are in small, 26-seater planes and are heavily booked in advance, but there is always a chance of getting a seat; go to the airport before the flight and try your luck.

Sam and Satena have several flights daily to Providencia (US$31). Book in advance during the high season.

**Boat** There are no regular ferries or boats to the Colombian mainland or elsewhere. Cargo ships run to Cartagena every few days and occasionally take passengers (about US$35, including food, two to three days). Sporadic freighters go to Colón (in Panama), but they are hard to track down. Cargo boats for Providencia leave once a week, usually on Thursday night or Friday morning, and these do take passengers (about US$14, eight hours).

### Getting Around
**Bus** Local buses circle a large part of the island as well as ply the central road to El Cove. They are the cheapest way of getting around, unless you want to walk. Buses run every 15 to 30 minutes and the ride costs US$0.40. They can drop you down close to the major attractions.

A bus marked 'San Luis' goes from Avenida Colombia along the east-coast road to the southern tip of the island (this is the bus to take to San Luis and the Hoyo Soplador), and along the western shore to the point known as Km 7, from where it is a 10-minute walk to Morgan's Cave.

The bus marked 'El Cove' runs along the inner road to El Cove, passing through La Loma. You can catch it on Avenida 20 de Julio and it will drop you in front of the Baptist church (it also passes near Morgan's Cave).

**Taxi** Taxis can be hired for circle-tours of the island. They have a standard route that takes in the major tourist sites for US$12 (up to five people). The taxi drivers will be happy to show you around other sights, for a little extra.

**Other Road Transport** Another way of seeing the island is the Tren Blanco, a sort of road train pulled by a tractor dressed up like a locomotive. It leaves twice daily from the corner of Avenida Colombia and Avenida 20 de Julio to circle the island, stopping at several sites of interest, including Hoyo Soplador and Morgan's Cave (US$4, three hours).

Other popular ways of getting around the island are by bicycle, motorbike, scooter, minimoke (with bald tyres) and car, which are all easy to rent from various agencies in San Andrés town. Most of these are along Avenida Colombia. Bicycles cost about US$1.50 per hour or US$8 for a full day (9 am to 6 pm); motorbikes and scooters go for US$5 per hour or US$30 a day. Shop around, as prices and conditions can vary, and bargaining is possible in some places.

**Boat** Boats to the nearby cays are operated by the Cooperativa de Lancheros Native Brothers, which has its office on the main beach. Motor boats to Johnny Cay leave relatively frequently, taking 10 minutes to get there; the round trip costs US$3. There aren't as many boats to Acuario and Haynes Cay (US$4).

You can go by one boat and return by another, but make sure another boat is scheduled to do the run, otherwise you'll be spending the night out there. The combined trip to both places costs US$6. Individually designed boat trips (to the Cayo Bolívar or Cayos de Albuquerque for example) can also be arranged.

SAN ANDRÉS

# Providencia

• *pop 5000* • *27°C* • ☎ *(9811)*

Traditionally known as Old Providence, Providencia is located about 90 km north of San Andrés island. It is the second-largest island of the archipelago, seven km long and four km wide. It is a mountainous island of volcanic origin, much older than San Andrés. Its highest peak, El Pico, reaches 320 metres, and there are a few others slightly lower. The island has diverse forest, with coconut palms growing mainly along the shores.

An 18-km road skirts the island, and virtually the entire population lives along it in scattered houses or in one of the several hamlets. Santa Isabel, a village at the island's northern tip, is the local administrative centre. Santa Catalina, a small island facing Santa Isabel, is separated from Providencia by the shallow Canal Aury. A pedestrian bridge connects the two islands.

Providencia has been much less affected by tourism than San Andrés. English is still widely spoken and there's much of the Caribbean-English architecture still standing. The locals are even friendlier and more easygoing than in San Andrés, and the duty-free business fever is unknown.

Providencia has an image of a lost paradise, which unfortunately draws in an increasing number of tourists. Aguadulce, on the western coast, has already been converted into a small tourist centre packed with hotels and restaurants. You can hire such things as motorbikes and snorkelling gear here, and there is also a choice of boat excursions. Almost all the tourism is centred in Aguadulce, leaving the rest of the island largely unspoiled. But this situation is changing.

Providencia does not have good beaches. The principal ones are at Bahía Aguadulce, Bahía del Suroeste and (the best) at Bahía Manzanillo on the southern end of the island. There are also some tiny, deserted beaches on the island of Santa Catalina, which is worth a look if only to see Morgan's Head – a rocky cliff in the shape of a human face, best

seen from the water. There's an underwater cave at the base of the cliff. The shoreline changes considerably with the tides; the beaches during low tide are quite wide, but at high tide they are almost nonexistent.

On the other hand, the inner, mountainous part of the island, with its rich vegetation and abundant small animals, is amazing. Probably nowhere else in Colombia can you see so many colourful lizards scampering through the bushes. Be careful of a very common shrub with spectacular horn-like thorns; the ants living inside them have a painful bite. Unfortunately, mosquitoes also abound on the island.

A trip to El Pico should not be missed. The most popular trail begins in the south, in Casabaja or Aguamansa. Ask there for directions as several paths crisscross the lower part (further up there are no problems), or ask in Casabaja for a guide. Some locals will take you up and charge US$5 to US$8 a group, regardless of the number of people. It is a steady hour's walk to the top. Carry drinking water because there is none along the way.

Snorkelling and diving are the island's other big attractions. The coral reefs around Providencia are more extensive than those around San Andrés and the turquoise sea is beautiful. You can rent snorkelling gear in Aguadulce (or better, buy some in San Andrés and bring it along). Diving trips can be arranged with a couple of local operators in Aguadulce.

Boat excursions around the island are organised from the Aguadulce waterfront, and sometimes from the pedestrian bridge over Canal Aury. They pass close to Morgan's Head and usually call at Cayo Cangrejo, the most popular islet around.

Food, accommodation and tourist services are expensive on Provedencia, more so than on San Andrés.

## Information

There's a tourist office at the airport, theoretically open from 8 am to noon and 2 to 6 pm. The Banco Central Hipotecario in Santa Isabel might change cash (but not cheques)

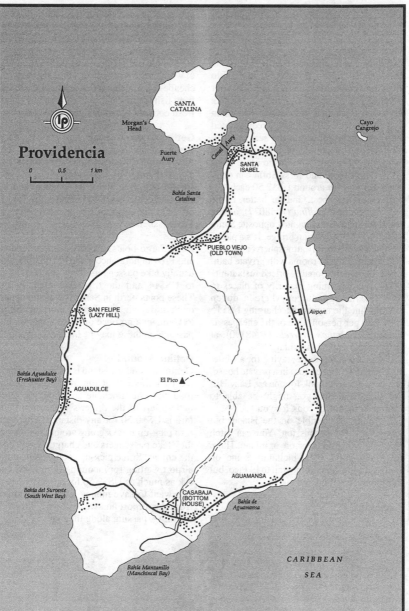

**Providencia**

0    0.5    1 km

SANTA
CATALINA

Morgan's
Head

Cayo
Cangrejo

Fuerte
Aury

Canal Aury

SANTA
ISABEL

Bahía Santa
Catalina

PUEBLO VIEJO
(OLD TOWN)

SAN FELIPE
(LAZY HILL)

Airport

Bahía Aguadulce
(Freshwater Bay)

AGUADULCE

El Pico ▲

AGUAMANSA

Bahía del Suroeste
(South West Bay)

CASABAJA
(BOTTOM
HOUSE)

Bahía de
Aguamansa

Bahía Manzanillo
(Manchincal Bay)

CARIBBEAN

SEA

PROVIDENCIA

at a very poor rate. It's best to bring enough pesos with you from San Andrés.

## Places to Stay
The only really cheap place to stay is the *Residencias Sofía* (☎ 48109), in Pueblo Viejo, two km south of Santa Isabel. Get your driver to stop at the SENA building, and take the rough track that branches off the main road (next to a two-storey, green-painted shop) and leads towards the seaside. The hotel is only a couple of hundred metres away, on the shore. This rustic place costs US$4 per person, and Miss Sofía can cook meals for you for around US$2.50 each.

The next cheapest, and far better, is the *Cabañas Santa Catalina* (☎ 48037), on the island of Santa Catalina, just opposite Santa Isabel, by the pedestrian bridge. It's a pleasant place with a family atmosphere, and costs US$9 per person in rooms with private bath. It has its own, reasonably priced restaurant.

The overwhelming majority of places to stay are in Aguadulce, where a dozen cabañas line the main road, charging US$15 to US$20 per person. One of the cheapest is the small *Cabañas Marcelo* (☎ 48190), at the southern end of the village.

If you are going to be staying for a while, it's cheaper to rent a room in a private house. The best places to look for one are Lazy Hill and Casabaja, and you might be able to arrange someone to cook for you.

Camping is possible on the island, but always ask for permission. You can pitch your tent either on the shore or inland. There are many good sites, including some on Santa Catalina and off the trail to El Pico, but take your own food and water.

## Places to Eat
Food is expensive, though usually good, particularly the seafood. Most restaurants are in Aguadulce. One of the cheaper places here is the *Restaurante Miss Elma*. It is good for comida isleña.

In Santa Isabel, there are three restaurants, of which the *Refresquería Junto al Mar* is the cheapest. Set meals go for around US$3, and fried fish is a dollar more. You can buy good, fresh coconut bread in some of the shops.

## Getting There & Away
**Air** Sam and Satena shuttle between San Andrés and Providencia several times per day (US$31). In the tourist season, you should buy your ticket in advance, and be sure to reconfirm return tickets at the Satena office at the airport, or at the Sam office in Santa Isabel.

**Boat** Cargo boats run between San Andrés and Providencia once a week, and they will usually take passengers. They charge US$12 to US$14 and the trip takes eight hours. These boats berth in Santa Isabel and depart on Saturday night or Sunday morning. Ships to Cartagena go once or twice a month, but passage on these may be harder to arrange.

## Getting Around
Getting around the island is quite easy. There are two chivas that run along the circular road with the timetable and direction more or less left to the driver's inclination. The fare is US$0.50 for any distance. There are also pick-up trucks going around the island; they take passengers and charge the same as the chivas. Some pick-ups congregate at the airport waiting for incoming flights and can ask as much as US$2.50 for any distance. If you want to save money, walk a bit further from the airport and wave down a chiva, or anything, passing along the road.

# The North-West

The north-west, as treated in this chapter, comprises the departments of Chocó and Antioquia except for their northernmost tips (which geographically belong to the Caribbean coast and are dealt with in that chapter), the three coffee-growing departments of Caldas, Risaralda and Quindío, and the northern part of Tolima.

In broad terms, the north-west is made up of two large regions, quite different in their geography, climate, people and culture. The first, the Chocó department, lies along the Pacific coast and is essentially an extensive stretch of low-lying rainforest. The region is sparsely populated, mainly by blacks. As there are almost no roads, transport is either by water or air, and is expensive. Difficult to access, scarce in facilities and lacking any obvious tourist attractions, the region is rarely visited by Colombians, let alone foreigners.

The other part of the north-west is comprised of the departments of Antioquia, Caldas, Risaralda and Quindío. It covers the rugged sections of the Cordillera Occidental and the Cordillera Central. This is picturesque mountain country, crisscrossed by roads and sprinkled with little towns with interesting architecture. This region is attractive and relatively easy to explore, and is inhabited by the greatest proportion of whites in the country. Medellín, the capital of Antioquia, is the major urban centre for the whole of the north-west.

## Chocó

Chocó is an immense green carpet of lush, tropical forest which has much in common with the Amazon. Yet there are some significant differences. First is the climate: Chocó is far wetter than the Amazon. Annual rainfall reaches 10 metres in some areas, making it one of the wettest regions in the world.

Accordingly, the flora and fauna also differ, and there are numerous species that have adapted to these extremely moist conditions.

The region is crisscrossed by many rivers. Two of the longest and most important are the Río Atrato, which flows northward and empties into the Golfo de Urabá, and the southbound Río San Juan with its mouth at the Pacific. The Río San Juan empties more water into the Pacific than any other river in South America.

A canal between the Pacific and Atlantic oceans (Canal Interoceánico del Atrato) is being planned to rival the Panama Canal. The proposed canal will follow the Atrato and Truandó rivers; however, it will probably be decades before construction begins, if ever.

The population of Chocó is small, and most people live in small settlements sparsely scattered through the region. There are no cities, and the only town to speak of is Quibdó, the department capital.

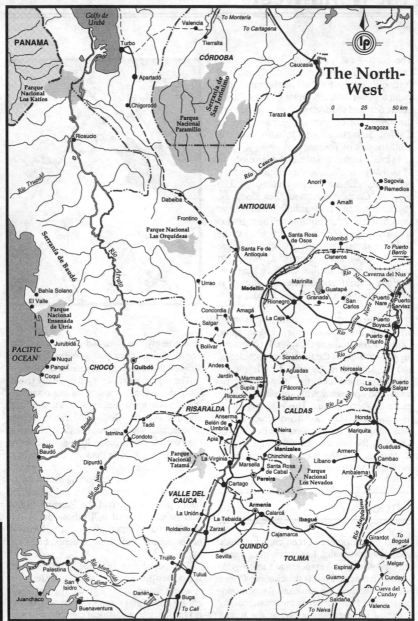

A large percentage of the population are black descendants of African slaves, relatively unmixed with other racial groups. They live mostly along the major rivers and the Pacific coast, having gradually pushed the indigenous inhabitants into more remote areas of the jungle.

Remnants of their African cultures and a common slave heritage have helped to reinforce a sense of identity. Chocoan music has a pronounced rhythmic beat carried by drums. Their funeral rites last nine days, include nightly prayers, betting games and the consumption of large quantities of alcohol. On the whole, however, remnants of African traditions and beliefs have survived only among small groups living in isolation.

The main Indian groups are the Chocó and Emberá, who inhabit the basin of the Río Atrato, and the Waunana and Cholo, who live in the basin of the Río San Juan.

Chocó is hardly a popular tourist destination. There are only a few places, principally Bahía Solano, El Valle and the Parque Nacional Ensenada de Utría (all of them on the coast), which receive visitors. The coast can only be reached by air, or by cargo boat from Buenaventura.

The Pacific coast is quite different from the Caribbean. Apart from some small areas, the beaches are not white or golden, but conspicuously dark. They are sandy and you may find them attractive, but they are not the fabulous beaches you know from postcards. They change with the tide, from narrow ribbons at high tide to surprisingly wide belts at low tide.

## QUIBDÓ

• *pop 60,000 • 40 m • 28°C • ☎ (949)*

The capital of Chocó, Quibdó is a hot, ramshackle town on the Atrato River. It was founded in 1690 by Antioquian explorers combing the region in search of gold. They did indeed find some in the area, and so Quibdó was born.

Today, Quibdó may be proud of the fact that it's over 300 years old, but it has few other reasons to be proud. The region has been ignored for centuries by the central government which has failed to provide it with decent access roads. The road that connects Quibdó with Medellín is rough and unpaved, and it's one of the very few roads in Chocó.

The department capital is set on the main fluvial artery of the region but has no genuine port. Nor has it any significant industry, and almost everything, save fish and some vegetables, has to be brought in, mostly from Medellín. The few crops which are grown in the region, mainly for local needs, include plantain, yucca, sugarcane and cacao.

Although the population of the region is predominantly black, the people of Quibdó are racially mixed, and include mestizos and mulattos, and there are also some zambos. Pure Indians are few in Quibdó and its environs, but they come to the town's market to sell their products and buy supplies.

Quibdó has an unusually high annual rainfall, around seven metres, so you can expect a lot of heavy rains. There are no dry seasons in the proper sense, but the period from December to March is least wet, with the rains being less intense and not so frequent.

Quibdó has no important tourist attractions, though it does have a certain charm as a backwater port from yesteryear – a bit like something out of a Joseph Conrad novel. Despite this, the town is not worth a special trip, unless you intend to explore the wilderness further afield, for which Quibdó is the major transportation hub. You can travel from here all the way down the Río Atrato to Los Katíos National Park and on to Turbo. From nearby Istmina you can go down the Río San Juan to the Pacific coast.

## Information

**Money** Bring enough pesos with you, as it's difficult to change cash dollars, and travellers' cheques are virtually worthless. The Banco Popular may be able to handle cash and travellers' cheques in the future, though it did not when this book was researched. It may, however, give advances on Visa card.

## Things to See & Do

There is not much to see in Quibdó. Parque

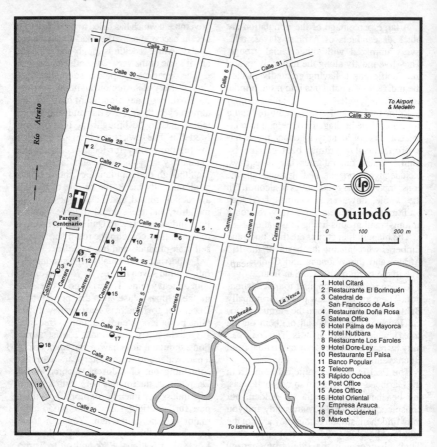

Quibdó

| | |
|---|---|
| 1 | Hotel Citará |
| 2 | Restaurante El Borinquén |
| 3 | Catedral de San Francisco de Asís |
| 4 | Restaurante Doña Rosa |
| 5 | Satena Office |
| 6 | Hotel Palma de Mayorca |
| 7 | Hotel Nutibara |
| 8 | Restaurante Los Faroles |
| 9 | Hotel Dore-Ley |
| 10 | Restaurante El Paisa |
| 11 | Banco Popular |
| 12 | Telecom |
| 13 | Rápido Ochoa |
| 14 | Post Office |
| 15 | Aces Office |
| 16 | Hotel Oriental |
| 17 | Empresa Arauca |
| 18 | Flota Occidental |
| 19 | Market |

Centenario, facing the river, is the town's main square. On its northern side stands the Catedral de San Francisco de Asís, possibly the most monumental construction in town, but otherwise rather undistinguished. The celebrations of the patron saint take place in late September and early October.

The colourful scene at the riverside market, when the campesinos arrive in their small boats laden with bananas, sugarcane and fruit for sale, is worth a look. Also worth seeing is the ritual before sundown, when the town's inhabitants go down to the river to bathe, wash their clothes and utensils or simply relax.

You might be able to arrange a half-day trip in an outboard motor boat with a local owner, who may take you to the nearby settlements along the Río Atrato and Río Quito, where sugarcane and bananas are grown and grain is still pounded by hand.

If you are interested in learning about the Indians living in the region, ask around for the office of Orewa (Organización Regional Emberá Waunana), where you can also buy some of their crafts.

### Places to Stay

Most budget accommodation is on Calle 26 between Carreras 3 and 6, and on Carrera 3 between Calles 24 and 27. They are all pretty rudimentary and the rooms often don't have private baths, but all have fans. Value varies from one to the other, so check a few before deciding.

The places to try include the *Hotel Palma de Mayorca*, at Calle 26 No 5-36, *Hotel Nutibara*, at Carrera 5 No 25-93, and *Hotel Dore-Ley*, at Carrera 3 No 25-32. They all cost about US$5/8 for a single/double.

The *Hotel Oriental*, at Carrera 3 No 24-08, costs marginally more but is pleasant, friendly and clean. Possibly the best in town is the *Hotel Citará*, at Carrera 1 No 30-63, which has air-con singles/doubles with bath for US$20/24.

### Places to Eat

Because so many products have to be brought in from Medellín, food is not cheap. Quibdó sits on the Río Atrato and the market is full of river fish, but for some reason sea fish are better represented on restaurant menus. Try local fruit and fruit juices, such as borojó juice, which allegedly has aphrodisiac properties.

*Restaurante Doña Rosa*, at Carrera 6 No 26-25, serves tasty almuerzo for US$2.50, as does *Restaurante Los Faroles*, at Carrera 3 No 25-78. *Restaurante El Paisa*, at Carrera 4 No 25-54, has some Antioquian dishes at modest prices.

*Restaurante El Borinquén*, at Carrera 1 No 27-18, is one of the best places in town, with good churrasco. Alternatively, go to the restaurant of the *Hotel Citará*, which is not bad either.

### Getting There & Away

**Air** The airport is two km east of the town's centre, off the road to Medellín. You can walk there in 25 minutes, or take a taxi (US$2). Only light planes can land here.

Flights in and out of Quibdó are operated by Satena, which has an office at Calle 26 No 6-09, and Aces, at Carrera 4 No 24-74. Aces flies three times a day to Medellín (US$34), once daily to Bogotá (US$66) and four days a week to Bahía Solano (US$28). Satena flies three days a week to Medellín (US$31),

Cali (US$42) and Bahía Solano (US$24), and once weekly to Bogotá (US$59).

**Bus** Buses leave from the bus company offices, scattered throughout the town's centre; most of them are on Carrera 1. Be prepared for a tough journey on an unpaved road whichever destination you head for. Buy your ticket several hours before departure (except for Istmina). Any journey southward to Istmina, Pereira or Cali involves a boat crossing over the Río Atrato, which is about an hour in a bus from Quibdó.

**To Medellín** Rápido Ochoa, Carrera 1 No 24A-38, has four buses daily (US$10.75 corriente, 11 hours).

**To Pereira** Flota Occidental, Carrera 1 No 22-28, has one corriente daily via a new road through Tadó (US$10.25, 11 hours).

**To Cali** There is one bus a day with Empresa Arauca, Calle 24 No 4-84 (US$16.50, 15 hours).

**To Istmina** There are buses every one to two hours with Empresa Arauca and Trans Progreso del Chocó (US$3.50, 3½ hours).

**Boat** There are high-speed passenger boats down the Atrato River to Turbo, daily at about 8 am. They cost US$33 and take eight to nine hours, unless the launch breaks down. Boats leave from the riverside in front of the Flota Occidental office. Arrive early to be sure of getting a ticket, or better still, book one the previous day.

This is a fantastic trip in a fast motor boat (locally known as an *expreso* or *panga*) through wild, tropical forest. The boat snakes from one bank to the other, avoiding floating tree trunks. Have a jacket handy, because the air is cold at jet speed. Rain storms are frequent and not all boats have roofs or other protection. If you do this trip, stop at Sautatá and visit Los Katíos National Park. The trip from Quibdó to Sautatá costs US$30 and takes seven to eight hours.

Some more adventurous travellers may prefer a cargo boat. They go down the Atrato every few days, but there may be only one boat a week from January to March when the river is low. Cargo boats usually go to Turbo, although some continue on to Cartagena. The amount of time that the journey takes depends on whether the boat has to stop on the way to load or unload. Count on three to five days to Turbo, and one to two days more to Cartagena. Many other factors such as fixing the engine, or visiting relatives and friends, may make the trip even longer.

The price is about US$25 to Turbo, and US$40 to Cartagena; negotiate with the captain before you decide to step aboard. Food is included, but it's unappetising and monotonous. The water that the crew drinks is from the river, but you should carry your own. You must have your own hammock, but they are difficult to buy in Quibdó. A mosquito net and repellent are recommended, and it's best to bring some of your own food. The trip is far from comfortable so be prepared for the primitive conditions and, above all, arm youself with patience. Despite all this, a river trip in a cargo boat is a memorable adventure.

## ISTMINA

Istmina is a small, poor jungle town about 75 km south of Quibdó. The only reason for coming here is to continue your journey down the Río San Juan. However, the lower reaches of the San Juan have recently become a risky area and some kidnappings have been reported. It's perhaps best not to go all the way to Buenaventura nowadays; instead you can do a trip downriver to Dipurdú which is supposed to be safe. Although this stretch is lamentably littered, the jungle scenery is lovely and there are many small islands and sand bars on the way.

If you want to do this overnight excursion, take the panga to Dipurdú which leaves from Istmina around midday. Dipurdú is a medium-sized village which has no hotels or restaurants, but ask around for Yolanda, who runs the village infirmary. She will fix you up with a bed and prepare you a good fish and rice-soup dinner. Expect to pay the standard cheap-hotel and cheap-restaurant prices for these services. There's nothing much to do in the village except stroll about.

Early the next morning, Yolanda will wake you for the Dipurdú-Istmina panga, which will take you on a daybreak trip with the sun rising over misty jungle. You can also catch the panga coming from San Miguel which passes through Dipurdú later in the day.

### Places to Stay & Eat

There are several ramshackle, basic residencias on Istmina's main street. Most of these will charge about US$4 per person. It's probably better to go straight to the *Hotel Orsan*, which is clean and comfortable and costs US$5 per person.

Downstairs is the hotel's café which does excellent, cheap fish fillets and a hearty eggs-and-bread breakfast.

### Getting There & Away

**Bus** Buses to Quibdó depart every hour or two until about 3 pm (US$3.50, 3½ hours). Expreso Occidental has one bus a day to Pereira via Tadó (US$9, nine hours).

**Boat** There are boats going down the San Juan River to San Isidro. They have no schedule and depart only when they have enough passengers to pay for the full fare of the boat, which is about US$300 per trip. A boat can carry up to about 10 people. The boats go down the San Juan River and then up the Calima River to San Isidro, from where there is a very rough road to Buenaventura serviced by chiva. The boat trip takes about seven to nine hours to San Isidro. The trip to Buenaventura through the San Juan mouth and around the coast would take at least three hours more, and cost much more money.

There are daily pangas to Dipurdú (US$3.50, three hours), which are supposed to depart around noon and return to Istmina very early the following morning. There are also pangas to San Miguel, an hour downstream from Dipurdú, but they are not always reliable.

The river in Istmina is not navigable for larger boats, which don't often go further up the San Juan than the Munguidó River.

## BAHÍA SOLANO & EL VALLE

Bahía Solano and El Valle are two seaside

settlements on the Pacific coast of Chocó which are gradually developing into beach holiday resorts. The creation of the new Parque Nacional Ensenada de Utría (see the following section), just south of El Valle, has aided this development. These places together are the only tourist area of Chocó's coast.

The whole region has a long history of neglect and has thus remained very poor. For years, the only transport links were boats plying the coast to Buenaventura, Panama City and other smaller coastal settlements. Then the airport in Bahía Solano was opened, providing a more convenient and efficient way to develop tourism. Facilities for tourists are not yet very sophisticated, although better-class accommodation can already be found in both Bahía Solano and El Valle, as well as outside these two towns.

Bahía Solano is bigger – it's perhaps the largest town on Chocó's Pacific coast. It's set in a deep bay, also called Bahía Solano, and has potential as a deep-water port, but the lack of a road link with the interior has hindered development. The town's only land connection is with El Valle, 18 km to the south over a dirt road.

El Valle is no more than a village, but it has become more popular with tourists because of its beaches. There is a fine beach, Playa Larga, which extends for 12 km to the south (its southern half is within the boundaries of the Parque Nacional Ensenada de Utría). At low tide, the beach is very wide and is often full of *cangrejos* (crabs). You can also spot turtles at times. The beach north of El Valle is rocky in parts but also pleasant. Like almost all beaches on the Pacific coast, the sand is not white but brownish. Take precautions while swimming as there may be treacherous offshore currents.

It is possible to organise boat excursions upriver to some of the tiny inland settlements (predominantly black) and taste some of the dense tropical jungle and wildlife. The most popular trip is up the Río Valle from the river's mouth at the village of El Valle. Some locals in El Valle have boats and will be happy to take you on such a trip. One of the

usual stops on the way is at the *alambique* (distillery) where aguardiente is produced from sugarcane. It's good stuff, worth buying, but don't drink it straight away. It's best after a couple of weeks, and served well chilled.

The boatmen will probably also take you to La Tienda del Saber, where the Asproval (Asociación Progresista del Valle) conducts a research programme on organic agriculture. Asproval is a small local association which aims at finding optimal agricultural techniques which would combine traditional practices with modern technology. You can contact it in El Valle through Villa Maga (see Places to Stay & Eat).

Indians no longer live in the lower reaches of the rivers, after having been pushed up by the blacks into the Serranía de Baudó, a mountain range running parallel to the coast 50 km inland. However, they come down to the coastal resorts and the national park to sell their crafts to tourists.

The cost of a trip up the Río Valle depends on the number of people and the time of the journey. A full-day trip in a boat for four to five passengers should cost around US$50. The village boatmen offer other excursions, as well as provide transport to the national park.

Remember that the region is very wet. The best time to come is between December and March when the weather is relatively dry.

### Places to Stay & Eat

Several hotels and cabañas have opened in Bahía Solano and El Valle, and others have sprung up on the beach outside these two villages. Locals also offer accommodation in their homes. A bed can be had from about US$4. Many hotels have their own restaurants.

Understandably, most of the local fare is based on fish and seafood, and it's usually fresh and well prepared, even in the cheapest restaurants. Meals are often accompanied by arroz con coco (coconut rice). Try the chocolate con coco.

Bahía Solano is not the most convenient or pleasant place to stay, but it does have a

THE NORTH-WEST

choice of places to stay and eat. The *Hotel Bahía* is one of the flashier options (around US$10 per person) and has its own restaurant.

It's better to head directly to El Valle, which has more to offer and attracts more tourists. The best budget place to stay here is *Villa Maga*, run by the friendly Doña Carmen Lucía. Her husband is an artisan, and it's worth looking at his carvings in tagua (hard palm nut) and paintings on tree bark. A modest but pleasant cabaña costs US$4 per person. The Villa Maga doesn't serve meals.

You can also stay at the *Hotel del Valle* in the village, or the *Cabañas El Almejal*, a 15-minute walk away. Both are more expensive and have their own restaurants.

Possibly the best budget place to eat is the restaurant known by the name of its owner, as *Doña Coty*, where you'll be served a copious meal of almuerzo or comida for US$3. *Punta Roca*, outside the village along the beach, has excellent food but it's expensive. You can also stay in its cabañas for US$15 per person.

If you are prepared to cook for yourself, go early in the morning to the mouth of the Río Valle, where a variety of freshly caught fish and seafood is sold.

### Getting There & Away

**Air** The airport is on the Bahía Solano-El Valle road (closer to Bahía), and is serviced by chivas and jeeps to and from both these villages. The chiva trip to Bahía costs US$0.60 and takes 20 minutes, while to El Valle it costs US$1.50 and takes 45 minutes. Jeeps are faster but twice as expensive.

Aces and Satena service Bahía Solano. Aces flies once a week to Bogotá (US$103), daily to Medellín (US$64) and four days a week to Quibdó (US$28). Satena flies three days a week to Medellín (US$55), Cali (US$64) and Quibdó (US$24).

If you have a couple of spare hours before your flight, go to the waterfalls which are a 20-minute walk from the airport (ask anybody for directions to *las cascadas*). You can have a refreshing bath in the pond at the base of the falls.

**Boat** Transport is provided by the unscheduled cargo boats which sail north and south along the coast every few days. Their main point of departure is Buenaventura, Colombia's largest Pacific port, so if you plan on getting to Bahía Solano by sea, shop around there. Most of these boats call in at small ports en route, so the trip between Buenaventura and Bahía Solano can take anything between three and five days. The negotiable fare of about US$25 includes meals, but you'd be better off taking some of your own provisions and a container of drinking water. A hammock is an essential piece of gear.

## PARQUE NACIONAL ENSENADA DE UTRÍA

This park, created in 1987, comprises 543 sq km of the Pacific coast and the adjoining stretch of ocean. Its northern boundary is just six km south of the village of El Valle.

The park was named after the deep cove, Ensenada de Utría, which cuts about eight km inland and barely exceeds one km at its widest point. At the mouth of the cove is a small island, known locally as Isla de Salomón. The island has a beach, Playa Blanca, justifiably named as it's probably the only truly white beach in the region.

The terrain of the park is rugged and covered with thick rainforest which virtually drops right into the sea. Opposite the island is the beautiful, greenish Río San Pichí. Turtles lay eggs at the mouth of this river in the breeding season.

There are some coral formations and the marine life is rich. Whales usually turn up near the coast from August to September, and dolphins can also be spotted at times.

Inderena has accommodation and food facilities within the park, which make it a good base for exploring the area. The park offers great walking, sunbathing, swimming and diving opportunities.

Just outside the southern boundary of the park is the small fishing village of Jurubidá. Almost all of its huts are built from a local material, *caña brava* (a reed), and the roofs are thatched with palm leaves. Its population, like that of all coastal settlements in the region, is almost entirely black. Indians live further inland and some don't seem to be happy about tourists visiting their settlements. Be careful and respectful.

### Places to Stay & Eat

Inderena has a visitors centre on the Ensenada de Utría, which provides accommodation (US$6 per person) and food (US$10 full board) for guests. You have to book and pay for this while applying for the permit to the park in Bogotá or Medellín. Indians bring their crafts to the centre and leave them to sell to visitors.

Alternatively, use the lodging and food facilities of El Valle and visit the park as a day trip.

You can also eat on Isla de Salomón where Señor Salomón (here is where the island's name comes from) will serve you exquisite, fried fish.

### Getting There & Away

The obvious starting point for the park is El Valle – read the Bahía Solano & El Valle section for how to get there. From El Valle, you can either walk the whole way to the visitors centre (nine km, 2½ hours) or take a boat (30 minutes, price negotiable depending on the number of passengers).

There's a semi-regular, but infrequent, passenger boat service between El Valle and Jurubidá (about US$2) which offers an opportunity to visit Jurubidá; it can drop you en route at Isla de Salomón and pick you up on its return.

---

# Antioquia

Antioquia is one of Colombia's largest, most populated and richest departments. It has well-developed industry and agriculture, and some important natural resources, including gold deposits. About 70% of Colombian gold comes from Antioquia, principally from its northeastern part.

Antioquia's inhabitants, commonly known as *paisas*, have traditionally been reluctant to mix with either blacks or Indians, and the results are still noticeable today. In contrast to the neighbouring 'black' Chocó, Antioquia has a high percentage of Creoles, and is popularly referred to as Colombia's 'whitest' department. The paisas have had a more regional outlook than other Colombians, and separatist attitudes have been expressed at various times during the region's history. They seem to have more respect for the time, a notion still largely ignored in some regions. And while almost all the nation parties to salsa and vallenato, the paisas opt for the nostalgic tango.

On the whole, the paisas are more hardworking and entrepreneurial than their countrymen, and have good business skills. In this context, it's perhaps not a coincidence that the cocaine industry was born and flourished so successfully in Antioquia.

Antioquia, or the *país paisa* (paisa country) as its inhabitants call it, comprises the northern parts of the Cordilleras Occidental and Central, along with the inner valleys and outer lowlands. It's a picturesque, rugged landscape garnished with *pueblos paisas* (paisa towns). They have a distinctive architecture, characterised by the richly carved wooden adornments of their doors and windows. If architecture is your particular interest, you can easily get lost for a week or two, exploring these lovely little towns. If this is the case, it's worth having a look at the excellent four-volume account of Antioquian architecture, *Arquitectura de la Colonización Antioqueña* by Néstor Tobón Botero (Fondo Cultural Cafetero, Bogotá). The books contain a photographic documentary of the most representative examples in Antioquia, Caldas, Risaralda and Quindío, along with short descriptions of the towns.

Most of the region has a mild climate, diverse vegetation and is pleasant for travel. There are several spectacular caves in the eastern part of Antioquia.

### MEDELLÍN
• *pop 1,800,000* • *1540 m* • *23°C* • ☎ *(94)*
The capital of Antioquia, Medellín, is Colombia's second largest city after Bogotá.

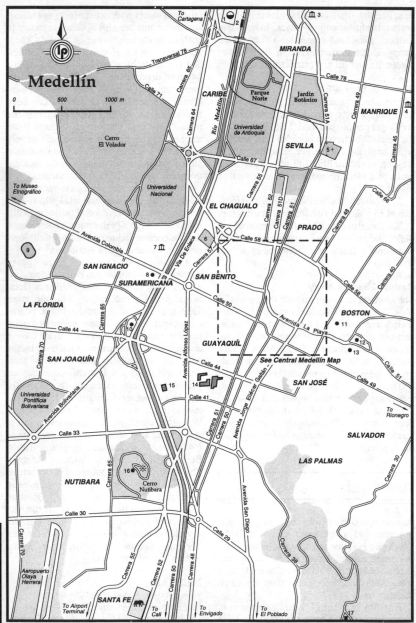

| 1 | Bus Terminal |
| 2 | Railway Station |
| 3 | Museo Pedro Nel Gómez |
| 4 | Casa Gardeliana |
| 5 | Cementerio de San Pedro |
| 6 | Plaza Minorista José María Villa |
| 7 | Museo de Arte Moderno de Medellín |
| 8 | Fuente a la Vida |
| 9 | Estadio Atanasio Girardot |
| 10 | Plaza de Toros La Macarena |
| 11 | Teatro Matacandelas |
| 12 | Teatro Pablo Tobón Uribe |
| 13 | El Pequeño Teatro de Medellín |
| 14 | Centro Administrativo La Alpujarra |
| 15 | Teatro Metropolitano |
| 16 | Pueblito Paisa |
| 17 | Hotel Intercontinental |

It's a thriving, dynamic industrial and commercial centre, pleasantly set in the Aburrá Valley in the Central Cordillera. The city has a modern centre dotted with a collection of skyscrapers and vast slum barrios perched all over the surrounding slopes.

The Spaniards first appeared in the valley as early as 1541, but the town was not founded until 1616, when another wave of colonists arrived and decided to settle. Historians maintain that most of the group were Spanish Jews fleeing persecution. Intermarriage with Indians and blacks was much less common than in other regions of the colony. The settlers divided the land into small haciendas which they farmed themselves, not following the common practice of using slaves. They were not really interested in having commercial contact with neighbouring regions, focusing instead on self-sufficiency as a way of life and development. The traditional values of the town's founders have endured till the present day.

The town was initially founded at what is now El Poblado and called San Lorenzo de Aburrá. In 1675 the name was changed to Villa de Nuestra Señora de la Candelaria de Medellín, and the settlement developed around the present-day Parque Berrío. By that time the town had 770 inhabitants.

Until the end of the 19th century there was little development, even though in 1826

Medellín replaced Santa Fe de Antioquia as the capital of the province. Only at the beginning of the present century did the town begin to expand rapidly, first as a result of the coffee boom, and then as the centre of Colombia's textile industry. Medellín became a large metropolitan city in a relatively short period of time.

Medellín's colonial architecture, apart from a couple of churches, was never significant, and the precious little that did exist has virtually disappeared in the frenzy of recent growth. The modern aspects of the city are not fascinating either. Yet, like any city of its size, Medellín does have an array of museums and other minor attractions, as well as a well-developed infrastructure of tourist facilities. With its three large universities and a few smaller ones, the city has a sizeable student population. Cultural activity is relatively varied and interesting, surpassed only by that of Bogotá.

Medellín is called the City of Eternal Spring, and the temperature is indeed very pleasant. There are, however, two rainy seasons, from March to May and September to November, and during these periods the weather can be unpleasant.

The mild climate stimulates a rich variety of flora, but contrary to the local tourist brochures, the central part of the city is not 'a gigantic garden with its flowering, perfumed tree-lined streets'. However, the vegetation of the surrounding region is fecund. Antioquia has a great variety of plants and flowers and is particularly renowned for its orchids.

The city is also known as the Capital of the Tango. It was here that Carlos Gardel, the legendary tango singer, died in an aeroplane crash in 1935.

## Orientation

The city has a rather compact modern centre, where you are most likely to stay and eat. Unlike in almost all other cities in the country, Medellín's central streets bear their proper names (not just their numbers) and are commonly known as such by the locals, especially in spoken language. In written lan-

THE NORTH-WEST

guage, in phone books or on business cards, the numerical system prevails.

Save for three churches and one museum, Medellín's tourist sights are scattered outside the central city area, so you need to use the local buses. Fortunately, the city transport is relatively efficient and well organised, and not as paralysed by traffic jams as is Bogotá or Barranquilla. A metro system is under construction and is expected to further ease the flow of city traffic.

## Information
**Tourist Offices** The Oficina de Turismo y Fomento (☎ 254 0800), at Calle 57 No 45-129, has information about the city. It's open Monday to Friday from 7.30 am to 12.30 pm and 2 to 6 pm.

Turantioquia (☎ 254 3335), at Carrera 48 No 58-11, with the same opening hours, focuses on the department, not the city itself, and has some tours on offer.

**Money** The Banco Popular and Banco Anglo Colombiano change travellers' cheques and cash. The Banco Unión Colombiano will also exchange your cheques, but not cash. All three banks pay advances on Visa. The Banco Industrial Colombiano will honour your MasterCard, and will change cash but not cheques. The Banco de Occidente may also give advances on MasterCard.

Tierra Mar Aire (☎ 242 0820), Calle 52 No 43-124, is the place to go if your American Express cheques are lost or stolen.

**Consulates** Medellín has a score of consulates, including:

Ecuador
    Calle 50 No 52-22, Oficina 802 (☎ 242 3638, 512 1193)
France
    Calle 52 No 14-200, Local 204 (☎ 235 8037)
Germany
    Calle 52 No 47-28, Oficina 1302 (☎ 251 6626)
Guatemala
    Carrera 42 No 33-173, Itagüí (☎ 277 1328, 277 6333)
Netherlands
    Carrera 52 No 51A-23, Oficina 401/2 (☎ 251 0314, 251 0324)

Panama
    Carrera 43A No 11-85, Oficina 201 (☎ 266 2390, 311 4273)
Spain
    Calle 17A No 54-100 (☎ 232 0037, 235 7282)
UK
    Calle 9 No 43B-93 (☎ 246 6427, 268 3806)
Venezuela
    Calle 32B No 69-59 (☎ 235 0359, 235 1020)

**DAS** The DAS office (☎ 341 4511, 341 5900) is at Calle 19 No 80A-40.

**Tours** There are plenty of travel agencies in the city centre, many of which also operate tours. You'll find a few of them, including Realturs, in the Parque de Bolívar. Also check the Viajes Veracruz, Carrera 50 No 54-06. It's perhaps best to start off at Turantioquia and see what they have on offer. Their tours may be cheaper than those with other operators.

One of the most popular tours is a three to four-hour night trip around the city in a chiva with a guide and a group playing local music. Routes vary but usually cover Pueblito Paisa, Envigado, Las Palmas and El Poblado. A few drinks of aguardiente and some local snacks are included. The tours are run mostly on Friday and Saturday, but may also go on other days of the week, if there are enough passengers. They cost roughly US$15 per person.

Another standard tour on offer is the so-called Circuito de Oriente (Eastern Circuit), to the south-east of Medellín. The area boasts a variety of cultural and natural attractions. See the Circuito de Oriente section later in this chapter.

The tour agents have some standard routes, or they can put together a tour to suit your interests. It's commonly a half or full-day trip, with lunch en route, and can be done by car or minibus, depending on the number of people. The price largely depends on the route and conditions; you can expect US$30 to US$50 per person, including lunch.

**Dangers** Few cities in the world have such bad press as Medellín. Repeatedly hitting the headlines of newspapers for more than a decade, Medellín has come to be known as the world's capital of cocaine trafficking, and home of Pablo Escobar and his violent Cartel de Medellín. It's no longer any of these; Escobar is dead, the cartel is virtually dismantled and the cocaine has largely moved to Cali. Yet Medellín still isn't the safest place on the globe. Like any large Colombian city, it has serious security problems and is notorious for crime. A strong presence of fully armed military police on the streets makes the city centre appear safe and quiet during the daytime, but keep your evening strolls to a minimum. If you want to try the nightlife, use taxis.

## Museums

Medellín has a choice of museums. Almost all are closed on Sunday.

**Museo de Antioquia** Formerly known as the Museo de Zea, this is the only important museum in the city centre, at Carrera 52A No 51A-29. It houses Colombia's largest single collection of paintings and sculptures by Fernando Botero, the most internationally famous Colombian contemporary artist, as well as works by other national artists, all on permanent display. There are also temporary exhibitions. The museum is open Tuesday to Friday from 10 am to 5.30 pm, Saturday from 9 am to 2 pm. Entry costs US$0.70 (US$0.40 for students). You can have lunch at the adjacent restaurant; it serves tasty set almuerzos at modest prices.

**Casa Museo Pedro Nel Gómez** Set in the house where this renowned Colombian artist lived, at Carrera 51 B No 85-24, this museum has an extensive collection (nearly 1500 pieces) of his watercolours, oil paintings, drawings, sculptures and murals. Pedro Nel Gómez is said to be Colombia's most prolific artist. The museum is open Tuesday to Saturday from 8 am to noon and 2 to 5 pm. Admission costs US$0.70 (students US$0.40) including a guide. Take the Aranjuez bus from the city centre, which will drop you at the entrance.

**Museo de Arte Moderno de Medellín** Often referred to as MAMM, this museum, at Carrera 64 B No 51-64, stages changing exhibitions of contemporary art. It is open Monday to Friday from 10.30 am to 7 pm, and Saturday from 10 am to 5 pm. Entry is US$0.50 (students US$0.25). Take any bus going west along Avenida Colombia from Parque Berrío, or walk for 15 minutes.

**Museo Etnográfico Miguel Ángel Builes** The Ethnographic Museum is at Carrera 81 No 52B-120, about four km west of the city centre, off the end of Avenida Colombia. The museum contains Indian artefacts from various regions of Colombia that were collected by missionaries. Objects from the Pacific coast and the Amazon are best represented. The museum is open Tuesday to Friday from 8 am to noon and 2 to 5 pm. There's no fixed fee, but leave a contribution in the box at the entrance. Brochures describing a few dozen Colombian Indian tribes are for sale. To get to the museum from the city centre, take the bus marked 'Circular 300/301' from Avenida Oriental in front of Turantioquia, or the Floresta-Estadio bus from Parque Berrío.

**Museo de Antropología** The Museum of Anthropology, in the Universidad de Antioquia at Calle 67 No 53-108, has a collection of pre-Columbian pottery from different regions of the country. It's open Monday to Friday from 8 am to noon and 2 to 6 pm. Entry is free. While you're here, take a look at the Monumento al Creador de la Energía, a sculpture by Rodrigo Arenas Betancur that is also at the university.

**Museo El Castillo** This mock-Gothic castle, at Calle 9 Sur No 32-269 in El Poblado, was built in 1930 and was home to an Antioquian landowner. After his death, it was donated to the state and turned into a museum. It contains all the original family belongings, furniture and art that came from all around the world. The museum is open Monday to Friday from 9 am to noon and 2 to 5 pm, and Saturday and Sunday from 9 am to 4.30 pm. All visits are guided and take about half an hour. Entry is US$1 and US$0.50 for students. There are usually concerts on Wednesday; check the local press for details.

The museum is five km south of the city centre. To get there, take the El Poblado-San Lucas bus from the Parque Berrío, get off at Loma de Los Balsos and follow the side street downhill for about five minutes to the museum. Instead of returning the same way, you might like to walk further down to Carrera 43A where there are plenty of buses going to the centre.

**Museo Filatélico** This museum, in the Banco de la República building, in Parque Berrío, has a collection of Colombian and foreign stamps. It's open Monday to Friday from 8 am to 6 pm. Entry is free.

### Churches
**Catedral Metropolitana** The gigantic neo-Romanesque cathedral, overlooking the Parque de Bolívar, is thought to be the biggest South American brick church. It was designed by a Frenchman, Charles Carré. Construction began in the 1890s and was completed 40 years later; 1,200,000 bricks were used. With its 3425 pipes, the organ, too, is believed to be the largest on the continent. It was commissioned in Germany. Don't be misled if the cathedral's front door is locked – check the side doors.

**Basílica de la Candelaria** This colonial church, facing the Parque Berrío, has an interesting gilded main retable. The image of the city's patron saint, Nuestra Señora de la Candelaria, watches over the faithful from above the high altar.

**Ermita de la Veracruz** Construction of this church, on the corner of Calle 51 and Carrera 52, was reputedly begun in 1682, but it was wholly rebuilt in a different style a century later. It has a fine stone façade.

### Jardín Botánico Joaquín Antonio Uribe
The botanical gardens are at Carrera 52 No 73-182, near the Universidad de Antioquia. In April and May every year, there is an orchid display in the Orquideorama. The good, but not cheap, Restaurante Salvatore is in the grounds. The gardens are open Monday to Saturday from 9 am to 5 pm, Sunday from 10 am to 5 pm. Entry is US$0.40.

### Zoológico de Santa Fe
The zoo, at Carrera 52 No 20-63, specialises in Colombian animals and birds, and in all about 180 species are represented. It's not the best zoo in Colombia; many cages are empty or without identifying names or other information. Don't come on Sunday when it's horribly overcrowded. The zoo is open daily from 9 am to 5 pm; entry costs US$1.20. Museo Santa Fe, inside the grounds, displays some colonial objects and antiques.

### Cerro Nutibara
The Cerro Nutibara is a hill quite close to the city centre which provides panoramic views over the city. The Pueblito Paisa, a replica of a typical Antioquian town, has been built on the top and is home to several handicraft shops. There are also a few food outlets, including the elegant, but not cheap, Restaurante La Mesa del Rey.

The Parque de las Esculturas (Sculpture Park) was established in 1984 on the slopes of the hill. It contains several modern abstract sculptures by South American artists, including such prominent names as Edgar Negret, Jesús Soto and Carlos Cruz Díez. The Guayabal bus from Avenida Oriental in the city centre passes by the foot of the hill, or go by taxi (US$2).

### Cementerio de San Pedro
Medellín's old cemetery, at Carrera 51 No 68-68, was established in 1842. It's an interesting collection of tomb architecture and well worth seeing, if such things interest you.

### Other Attractions
Medellín is a city of public monuments, particularly sculptures and murals. See the Fuente a la Vida (Fountain to Commemorate Life) by Rodrigo Arenas Betancur, in the Centro Suramericana, on Avenida Colombia at Carrera 64. Another impressive work by the same master, the Monumento a la Raza,

is in the Centro Administrativo La Alpujarra, on Calle 44. Another interesting sculpture by Betancur is the aforementioned Monumento al Creador de la Energía, in the Universidad de Antioquia.

Murals by Pedro Nel Gómez can be seen in the Palacio Municipal, Carrera 52 No 52-43; the Banco Popular, Calle 51 No 50-54; the Universidad Nacional and the Universidad de Antioquia; and the Biblioteca Pública Piloto, at Carrera 64 No 50-32.

There is also a controversial sculpture, commonly known as La Gorda, donated by Fernando Botero. It stands in front of the Banco de la República, in the Parque Berrío.

For a taste of local traditions, go to Carrera 48 between Calles 50 and 51. This stretch of the street is tightly packed with cafés where locals (almost exclusively men) gather for lengthy chats over endless cups of coffee.

You might like to have a look at the prison where Pablo Escobar was once interned. Read what a traveller reported:

People interested in political realities can have a look at Pablo Escobar's former prison, 'La Catedral', which was erected for him exclusively and housed him until his escape in July 1992. The name refers to a finca with the same name situated further down on the same slope. The prison itself was actually like a huge hotel complex with sports facilities including a football ground and a swimming pool, all surrounded by barbed-wire fences and several guard towers. It is not in a very good state but the scale of the complex is still clear. There is a marvellous view over the Aburrá valley with Medellín, Envigado, Bello and the surrounding mountains around.

To get there, take one of the buses to Parque de Envigado that leave every 15 minutes from the 'Éxito' warehouse at Carrera 47 in the city centre of Medellín. The trip costs US$0.20. They can also be caught at Carrera 46 further south. In Envigado take any bus to the barrio El Salado, and the driver will let you off at the road to La Catedral. There is little traffic from there, so it's better to walk, and the landscape is beautiful. After a 15-minute walk uphill there is a dirt road to the left leading through the remnants of a gate. This winding road goes up to a former military post which is now a farm. The walk should take about an hour and offers splendid views over Medellín. From there you will see La Catedral lying on the slope of the mountain. It is another 15-minute walk from there to the entrance, which is another huge, abandoned gate. You're not allowed to enter the former prison

and there's still a police post at the transmitter. If you want to take photos, do it from further away and nobody will mind.

## Festivals & Events
**Mercado de San Alejo** This handicraft market is held on the first Saturday of the month in Parque de Bolívar. It is good for cheap buys.

**Tangovía** This tango night kicks off on the last Friday of every month (from around 7 pm until midnight), and is the place to go to listen to and dance the tango. It takes place on Carrera 45 in the Manrique district, three km north of the city centre.

**Feria Taurina de la Candelaria** The bullfight season takes place in January and February at the Plaza de Toros La Macarena, the 11,000-seat, Moorish-style bullring built between 1927 and 1944. It's on Autopista Sur, on the corner of Calle 44.

**Feria de las Flores** Held in early August, this is the biggest event in Medellín. The highlight of the week-long festival is the Desfile de Silleteros, on 7 August, when hundreds of campesinos come down from the mountains and parade along the streets, carrying *silletas* full of flowers on their backs.

**Sinfonía de Luces en Navidad** This is a colourful Christmas illumination of the city, with thousands of lights strung across the streets and parks. The lights stay on from 7 December to 6 January.

## Places to Stay – bottom end
Medellín doesn't offer great budget lodgings. What is really cheap is poor, or of suspect reputation. The cheapest hotels are located around the street market, between Carreras 52 and 54 and Calles 47 and 50, but the area is dirty, noisy and unpleasant. One of the cheapest in this sector is the slowly disintegrating, basic *Nuevo Hotel* (☎ 512 2471), at Calle 48 No 53-29. It costs US$4 for a single or a matrimonio, US$5 for a double.

The best budget bet in the same area is the

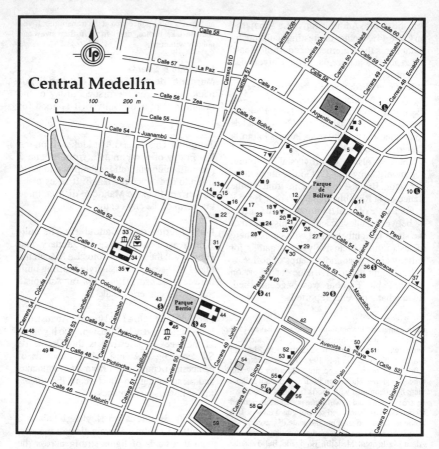

# Central Medellín

*Hotel Comercial* (☎ 512 9349), at Calle 48 No 53-102. This big, clean, well-run hotel has singles/doubles/triples without bath for US$5/7/9 (US$8/10/12 with bath).

It's more pleasant, and perhaps safer, to stay outside this area, closer to the Parque de Bolívar or on Avenida Oriental. There's the small *Hotel Residencias Gómez Córdoba* (☎ 513 1676), at Carrera 46 No 50-29, which is simple but clean, quiet and friendly. Rooms with bath cost US$6 for a single or matrimonio, and US$7 for a double. Next door, at Carrera 46 No 50-39, is the basic but cheap *Hotel Residencias Caldas* (☎ 513

1677), an option if you've run out of money. Some rooms have private bath, others don't, but all cost the same: US$3.50/4.50 for a matrimonio/double. Rooms are also rented for longer periods, so the hotel is often full.

Genuinely cheap accommodation close to the Parque de Bolívar is only available in the 'love hotels'. The *Hotel Americano*, at Calle 54 No 49-15, is ideally located, right on the edge of the square, but may not accept you for the whole night until after about 7 pm (never on weekends). It charges US$7 for a single or matrimonio. All rooms have one double bed, bath and TV. Next door, at Calle

## PLACES TO STAY

3   Hotel El Capitolio
4   Aparta Hotel El Cristal
6   Hotel Tropical
8   Hotel Cumanday
9   Hotel Veracruz
14  Aparta Hotel Santelmo
16  Hotel La Bella Villa
17  Hotel Eupacla
20  Hotel Plaza
21  Hotel Americano
22  Hotel Nutibara
23  Hotel Europa Normandie
24  Junimar Hotel
48  Hotel Comercial
49  Nuevo Hotel
52  Hotel Residencias Caldas
53  Hotel Residencias Gómez Córdoba

## PLACES TO EAT

7   Restaurante Los Toldos No 3
12  Restaurante La Estancia
18  Restaurante Chung Wah
19  Restaurante Los Toldos No 1
25  Café Versalles
26  Restaurante Aleros del Parque
27  Restaurante Los Toldos No 2
28  La Fonda Antioqueña
29  Restaurante La Posada de la
    Montaña
30  Restaurante Hato Viejo
31  Restaurante Vegetariano Palased
35  Restaurante Vegetariano Govinda's

37  Donizetti
40  Boulevard de Junín
50  Restaurante Vegetariano Paracelso

## OTHER

1   Turantioquia
2   Centro Comercial Villanueva &
    Copa Office
5   Catedral Metropolitana
10  Oficina de Turismo y Fomento
11  Aires Office
13  Intercontinental de Aviación
15  Minibuses to José María Córdoba
    Airport
32  Avianca & Post Office
33  Museo de Antioquia
34  Ermita de la Veracruz
36  Banco de Occidente
38  Sam Office
39  Banco Industrial Colombiano
41  Banco Industrial Colombiano
42  Crafts Market
43  Banco Anglo Colombiano
44  Basílica de la Candelaria
45  Banco Popular
46  La Gorda
47  Museo Filatélico
51  Tierra Mar Aire
54  Centro Popular del Libro
55  Aces Office
56  Iglesia de San José
57  Banco Unión Colombiano
58  Buses to Olaya Herrera Airport
59  Almacén Éxito

54 No 49-23, the *Hotel Plaza* (☎ 511 3900) has matrimonios and doubles, and is more tolerant of tourists, charging US$6/7 a matrimonio/double. Yet another love dive, the *Hotel Tropical*, at Calle 56 No 49-105, is cheaper but shabbier. It's only one block from the Parque de Bolívar but on the edge of the brothel area, so take care.

The *Hotel Cumanday* (☎ 512 4400), Calle 54 No 50-48, is a good 'clean' option in the area. Neat, quiet singles/doubles with bath cost US$7/10.

### Places to Stay – middle

The *Aparta Hotel El Cristal* (☎ 512 0001), at Carrera 49 No 57-12, is good value for money and is therefore often full. This clean

and pleasant place costs US$12/15/18 for a single/double/triple. All rooms have bath (with hot water), telephone, fan, colour TV and fridge. Some rooms are even equipped with a stove.

The *Aparta Hotel Santelmo* (☎ 231 2728), at Calle 53 No 50A-08, and the *Hotel La Bella Villa* (☎ 511 0144), at Calle 53 No 50-28, are two good, centrally located places. They are both very convenient if you fly into Medellín, as the airport minibuses deposit you just a few steps away. Both have comfortable singles/doubles with bath for US$15/20. The Bella Villa is slightly better. Much the same, for slightly less, is offered by the newly opened *Junimar Hotel* (☎ 512 5275), at Calle 53 No 49-76 in the same area.

THE NORTH-WEST

Other options in this price bracket include the *Hotel El Capitolio* (☎ 231 0970), Carrera 49 No 57-24 (US$16/22 a single/double), and the *Hotel Eupacla* (☎ 231 1844), at Carrera 50 No 53-16 (US$20/25).

## Places to Stay – top end

The *Hotel Europa Normandie* (☎ 512 4025), at Calle 53 No 49-100 (US$25/35), and the *Hotel Veracruz* (☎ 511 5511), at Carrera 50 No 54-18 (US$40/50), are both good and justifiably priced.

The *Hotel Nutibara* (☎ 511 5111), at Calle 52A No 50-46, is the best hotel in the central area and, predictably, the most expensive (about US$120 a double).

At the very top of the scale is the five-star *Hotel Intercontinental* (☎ 266 0680), at Calle 16 No 28-51. It's quite far from the city centre, in the hills of Las Palmas.

## Places to Eat

As is usually the case, the cheapest places are clustered around the budget hotels. You'll find plenty of undistinguished restaurants and cafés on Carreras 53 and 54 between Calles 48 and 49.

In the heart of the city, in the Parque de Bolívar, the self-service *La Estancia*, at Carrera 49 No 54-15, is perhaps the cheapest place to eat in town. It's not very clean or pleasant but does have filling set meals for only US$1. The attached bar serves drinks at extremely low prices, which makes the whole place noisy, crowded and rather bizarre.

There are many moderately priced restaurants and cafés on and around the pedestrian walkway Pasaje Junín (Carrera 49), between the Parque de Bolívar and Calle 52. For example, the two-level *Versalles*, at Pasaje Junín No 53-39, has a tasty menú económico, good cakes, fruit juices and tinto. The area on the 1st floor is more pleasant.

The *Aleros del Parque*, on a terrace overlooking Pasaje Junín and the Parque de Bolívar, is a popular rendezvous, where you can get typical Antioquian food or just sit with a beer and watch the world go by. If you just want to grab something quickly, go to the *Boulevard de Junín*, where several self-service places serve pizza, chicken, pastries, salpicón (fruit juice) and ice cream.

*Los Toldos* has reasonably priced Antioquian dishes. There are several branches: No 1 is at Calle 54 No 49-53; No 2 is at Calle 54 No 47-11; and No 3 is at Carrera 50 No 55-23. *Hato Viejo*, on the 1st floor of the Centro Comercial Los Cámbulos on the corner of Pasaje Junín and Calle 53, is pleasant, and a good place for regional dishes. *La Posada de la Montaña*, at Calle 53 No 47-44, has even better local food at affordable prices.

*Chung Wah*, at Calle 54 No 49-75, is a place serving Chinese food at modest prices. *Donizetti*, at Calle 54 No 43-102, has excellent home-made Italian food but it isn't cheap.

Vegetarians can have cheap set lunches (from noon till around 4 pm) at *Restaurante Vegetariano Govinda's*, on the 1st floor at Calle 51 No 52-17, and *Restaurante Vegetariano Palased*, at Carrera 50 No 52-35. The latter is also recommended for it's tamal vegetariano.

Somewhat more expensive is the *Restaurante Vegetariano Paracelso*, at Calle 52 (Avenida La Playa) No 45-06. It's more pleasant, has better food and is open until 7 pm.

There are plenty of expensive first-class restaurants on Variante Las Palmas, such as *Acuarius*, at Carrera 38 No 19-600; *Kevins*

Popular Colombian rum

(also a disco), 400 metres from the Hotel Intercontinental; and *Monserrat*, at Calle 16 No 30-187.

The suburb of El Poblado also has several top-line restaurants, including *Piemonte*, at Carrera 43A No 5A-170, and *La Bella Época*, at Calle 4 Sur No 43A-08.

### Entertainment
Check the local dailies, *El Colombiano* and *El Mundo*, for what's going on. Contact the universities which are the centres of often innovative and inspiring artistic activity.

**Cinema** Museo de Arte Moderno has a cinemateca with a diverse art-house programme. Films are screened here three times a day, except Wednesday when it's closed. Medellín has plenty of commercial cimemas serving up the usual fare.

**Theatre** El Águila Descalza, at Calle 40 No 74B-19, is a typical Antioquian theatre group with its own distinct brand of humour. Its last production, *Trapitos al Sol*, is an excellent portrait of paisa culture, spiced with humour and irony. This approach has characterised most previous works, including the famous *País Paisa*. It is well worth seeing one of the group's productions if you've mastered the language.

Other interesting theatre groups include El Pequeño Teatro de Medellín, at Carrera 40 No 50B-32 (or at its new home, Carrera 42 No 50A-12), and Teatro Matacandelas, at Carrera 42 No 53-31, which is one of Colombia's best experimental groups.

The largest and most modern city theatre, Teatro Metropolitano, at Calle 41 No 57-30, usually stages performances by visiting groups. Also check the programme of the Teatro Pablo Tobón Uribe at Carrera 40 No 51-24.

**Music** Medellín is known for its tangos. The best place to get a feel for these me`ancholic rhythms is the Tangovía (see Festivals & Events). In the same area is the Casa Gardeliana, at Carrera 45 No 76-50, which once had live tango, but now is only a small

museum. To get to the area, take the Manrique bus from the city centre.

A pleasant area to wander about on Friday or Saturday night is Carrera 70 between Avenida San Juan (Calle 44) and Circular 1, where there are several open-air bars, including Chócolo, Xochimilco and Panchovilla. Many small amateur groups play Caribbean music.

Other hot nightclub activity centres around El Poblado (mainly between Carreras 43 and 43A and Calles 9 and 10), Envigado and Variante Las Palmas.

Exploring Medellín by night is probably not the safest activity you've ever practised. The night chiva tour (see Tours) can be a convenient option, as it visits several hot nightspots.

The usual venues for concerts of classical music are the Teatro Metropolitano and the Teatro Gabriel Obregón Botero in the campus of Universidad de Medellín.

### Things to Buy
For handicrafts, a good and cheap place is the Mercado de San Alejo (see Festivals & Events). There are many handicraft shops in the city, including a few in the Pueblito Paisa on the Cerro Nutibara. *Carrieles*, the typical Antioquian leather bags, are best bought on the plaza in Envigado.

Medellín is Colombia's major textile producer, so there's a good choice of clothes and they are cheaper than elsewhere in the country. There are plenty of commercial centres and stores; the Almacén Éxito, on Calle 48 in the centre, is one of the cheapest.

If you are a bookworm, comb the second-hand book market, Centro Popular del Libro, at Carrera 48 No 49-38.

Plaza Minorista José María Villa is a huge, bustling market, comprising more than 2500 stalls under cover. It was established in 1984 to remove hawking vendors from the streets. It's open daily from 5 am to 6 pm, and Sunday from 6 am to 2 pm.

### Getting There & Away
**Air** The new José María Córdoba Airport was opened in 1985 near Rionegro, 35 km south-

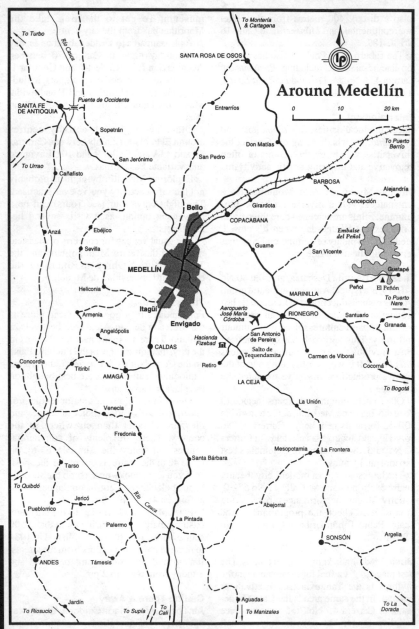

Around Medellín

east of Medellín. It handles all international and most domestic flights.

There's no tourist office at the new terminal, but a few travel agencies on the upper level (departure hall) may give you some information. There are branch offices of a few banks, though chances are that none of them will change your travellers' cheques. But they do change cash. Their usual working hours are Monday to Friday from 8 to 11.30 am and 2 to 4 pm. If you're really stuck for local currency, ask the porters, who often change cash dollars, but at poor rates. In this case, change only enough to get to the city.

Frequent minibuses shuttle between the city centre and the airport, passing via the bus terminal. In the centre, they depart from the corner of Carrera 50A and Calle 53 (US$1.50, one hour).

The old Olaya Herrera Airport is right inside the city, and operates regional flights on light planes. It has few tourist facilities, and is accessible from the city centre by the Guayabal bus from Avenida Oriental (next to Calle 49).

There are plenty of flights throughout the country with Avianca, Sam and Aces, including Bogotá (US$58), Cartagena (US$86), Cali (US$64), Cúcuta (US$78) and San Andrés (US$123).

Intercontinental is cheaper to Bogotá (US$46), Cali (US$48) and San Andrés (US$94), but it doesn't have direct flights to Cúcuta or Cartagena. All the above-listed flights depart from the new airport.

Medellín is the best point for flying to Chocó and Urabá. Aces has three flights a day to Quibdó (US$34) and Turbo (US$52), four flights a week to Acandí (US$75), two flights a day to Capurganá (US$77) and daily flights to Bahía Solano (US$64). Satena flies three days a week to Quibdó (US$31) and Bahía Solano (US$55). All these flights depart from the old airport.

There are flights into Panama City (US$115) with Sam and Copa. Zuliana de Aviación (a Venezuelan carrier) has daily flights to Maracaibo (US$81) and Caracas (US$122). Add 19% tax to the cost of international flights if you buy the ticket in Colombia.

The airlines' city offices have been marked on the Central Medellín map. Satena has its office at the Olaya Herrera Airport. You can also book and buy tickets at any of the travel agencies.

**Bus** All buses arrive at and leave from the central bus terminal, on Autopista Norte, on the corner of Calle 78, about three km north of the city centre. It takes 15 minutes to get there from the city centre by frequent urban buses. The terminal is large and well organised, and has a range of cafés and left-luggage facilities.

A new bus terminal, Terminal del Sur, is currently being built next to the Olaya Herrera Airport terminal and is planned to open in 1995. Local sources claim that it will be the most modern bus terminal in the country.

**To Bogotá** There are frequent buses by at least half a dozen companies (US$17 climatizado, nine hours).

**To Cartagena** Expreso Brasilia and Rápido Ochoa have about 10 departures daily (US$23 climatizado, 13 hours).

**To Cali** There are regular departures with several companies (US$18 climatizado, US$15.50 pullman, nine hours).

**To Pereira** The route is operated hourly by Flota Occidental (US$9.50 pullman, six hours).

**To Armenia** Flota Occidental has hourly buses (US$11.25 pullman, seven hours).

**To Manizales** Empresa Arauca has departures every two to three hours (US$7.75 pullman, five hours).

**To Turbo** Transportes Gómez Hernández and Sotraurabá have five departures a day between them (US$13 corriente, 13 hours).

**To Santa Fe de Antioquia** Sotraurabá operates minibuses approximately every hour from 6 am to 7 pm (US$4.25, 2½ hours).

**To Quibdó** Rápido Ochoa has four buses a day (US$10.75 corriente, 10 to 11 hours).

There are plenty of buses to Marinilla, Rionegro and La Ceja, as well as several buses daily to Sonsón, Abejorral, Jardín and Jericó.

**Train** The train station adjoins the bus terminal, and there is a daily morning train to

Barrancabermeja (US$8, 12 hours). It passes through Puerto Berrío (US$5.25, seven hours).

**Car Rental** The car-rental companies operating in Medellín include:

Avis
    Carrera 43A No 23-40 (☎ 232 4670, 232 3810)
Budget
    Carrera 43A No 23-52 (☎ 232 8203)
Hertz
    Carrera 43A No 23-50 (☎ 232 2307, 232 4874)
Renta Car
    Calle 58 No 49-50 (☎ 254 5766)

### Getting Around

**Bus** Urban transport is serviced by buses and busetas, and is quite well organised. All buses are numbered and display their destination point. There are bus stops on most routes, though sometimes buses will also stop in between. The majority of routes originate on Avenida Oriental and Parque Berrío, from where you can get to almost anywhere within the metropolitan area. Urban transport stops around 10 pm, leaving only taxis plying the streets at night.

**Metro** Medellín is Colombia's first (and for a long time will be the only) city to have the Metro or Tren Metropolitano, a fast metropolitan train. The 23-km north-south line, linking the city with Bello in the north and Envigado and Itagüí in the south, is in the final stage of construction and is planned to be opened in 1995. The train system operates on the ground except for a five-km stretch through the city centre, where it goes on a viaduct above the street (Carrera 51). A six-km western leg, from the centre to the suburb of San Miguel, is to be completed later.

### SANTA FE DE ANTIOQUIA

• *pop 11,000* • *550 m* • *26°C* • ☎ *(948)*

Usually called either Santa Fe or Antioquia for short, this is the oldest town in the region. Founded in 1541 by Jorge Robledo, it became the capital of the province in 1584, and was an important and prosperous centre during the colonial period. It was from here that Medellín was settled in 1616, but it wasn't until 1826 that Medellín took over the honour as the capital of Antioquia.

The town is a small gem of colonial architecture and should not be missed. Its old urban fabric has survived almost intact, with narrow cobbled streets, one-storey whitewashed houses and four churches. This is the only town in Antioquia which has truly preserved its colonial character. It is quite different from others in the region, where the more recent Antioquian architecture now dominates.

Give yourself a couple of hours to wander around the streets. See the decorated doorways of the houses, the windows with their carved wooden guards, and the patios in bloom. Walk to the outskirts of the town, where you will find some charming, rustic, thatched huts, and include in your walking tour the churches and museums detailed below. Also consider a short trip to the unusual Puente de Occidente (refer to the following section).

### Churches

Of the town's four churches, the **Iglesia de Santa Bárbara** is the most interesting. Built by the Jesuits in the second half of the 18th century, the church has a fine, wide Baroque stone façade. The interior, with its stone walls and brick arches, is also attractive, and boasts an interesting, if time-worn, retable over the high altar. The church is open from 10.30 am to noon and 2 to 6 pm, Sunday from 8.30 to 10.30 am and 2 to 6 pm.

The **Catedral**, in the Parque Juan del Corral (main plaza), is sometimes referred to as the Catedral Madre, as it was the first church built in the region. However, the original church was destroyed by fire, and the large building you see today was not completed until the beginning of the 19th century. Have a look at the *Last Supper* in the right transept and at an image of San Francisco de Borja with a skull in the opposite transept. The church is open daily for morning and evening mass, plus an additional service on Sunday at noon.

The two remaining churches, the **Iglesia de Chiquinquirá**, also known as La Chinca,

Typical San Andrés scene

Top: View over central Medellín
Middle: The roofs of Santa Fe de Antioquia
Bottom: Casa del Virrey, Cartago

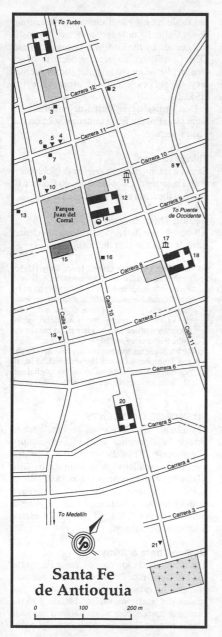

**Santa Fe de Antioquia**

0    100    200 m

**PLACES TO STAY**

2    Residencias Colonial
3    Hotel Mariscal Robledo
6    El Mesón de la Abuela
7    Hospedaje Toño
9    Hostal del Viejo Conde
13   Hospedaje Franco
16   Residencias Dally

**PLACES TO EAT**

4    Restaurante Pizzasbar
5    Restaurante Los Faroles
8    Restaurante Mi Ranchito
10   Taberna La Ceiba
19   Pilli Pollo
21   La Última Lágrima

**OTHER**

1    Iglesia de Chiquinquirá
11   Museo Juan del Corral
12   Catedral
14   Sotraurabá Office
15   Palacio Municipal
17   Museo de Arte Religioso
18   Iglesia de Santa Bárbara
20   Iglesia de Jesús Nazareno

and the **Iglesia de Jesús Nazareno**, both
dating from the early 19th century, are less
interesting. They are open Monday to Friday
at 7 pm only.

### Museums

The **Museo Juan del Corral** displays a
variety of historic objects collected in the
region, including pre-Columbian ceramics,
old religious artworks and the table on which
the Acts of Independence of Antioquia were
signed in 1813. The museum is open
Tuesday to Saturday from 9.30 am to noon
and 2 to 6 pm, and Sunday from 10 am to 5
pm. Entry is US$0.30. The staff can give you
information about the town.

The **Museo de Arte Religioso**, next door
to the Santa Bárbara church, has a collection
of regional religious objects. It is open Saturday and Sunday only, from 10 am to 5 pm.
Entry is US$0.40.

## Festivals

**Semana Santa** Like most traditional towns dating from the early days of the Spanish conquest, Easter Week is celebrated with much solemnity and attention.

**Fiesta de los Diablitos** This is the town's main popular festival, held annually over the last four days of the year (28 to 31 December). It includes music concerts, a handicraft fair and dancing, and – like almost every feast in the country – the *reinado de belleza* (beauty contest) and corridas.

## Places to Stay

The best budget place to stay is the *Residencias Colonial*, at Calle 11 No 11-72. Located in a nice, old mansion, it's quiet and friendly. The rooms on the upper floor are more pleasant and have a balcony. Doubles cost US$9. The hotel serves cheap set meals.

*El Mesón de la Abuela*, at Carrera 11 No 9-31, is in the same price range. It's quite simple, but clean and with a friendly atmosphere. It also has its own restaurant, which offers good breakfasts, lunches and dinners, but it is more expensive than the restaurant at the Colonial.

There are several cheaper residencias, including the *Franco*, at Carrera 10 No 8-67 (there's no sign on the door), and the *Dally*, at Calle 10 No 8-50. The basic *Hospedaje Toño*, at Carrera 11 No 9-40, opposite El Mesón de la Abuela, is probably the cheapest accommodation in town.

The best place to stay in Santa Fe is the *Hotel Mariscal Robledo*, at Carrera 12 No 9-70, which costs US$15 per person. It has a swimming pool (very useful in this climate) and a restaurant.

## Places to Eat

The cheapest place to eat is the market on the main square, where you can get a tasty bandeja for a little over US$1. Apart from the hotel restaurants listed above, there are at least half a dozen other places to eat. One of the best is *Los Faroles*, next to El Mesón de la Abuela. *Restaurante Mi Ranchito*, at Calle 12 No 9-63, is not bad either.

However, the best place to eat is an unremarkable looking and unmarked restaurant down Calle 10 near the cemetery, sarcastically called by the locals *La Última Lágrima* (The Last Tear), apparently because of its location between the hospital and the cemetery. It serves excellent almuerzos for US$2.50.

Don't miss trying pulpa de tamarindo, a local sweet made from tamarind sold on the main square.

## Things to Buy

Santa Fe is famous for its *orfebrería* (goldsmithery). There are a few workshops on Carrera 10 between the main plaza and Calle 11.

## Getting There & Away

All buses, minibuses and colectivos depart from or pass through the main plaza.

**To Medellín** There are several buses daily (US$3, three hours), most of which come through from Turbo. It's faster and more comfortable to go by the Sotraurabá minibus. They depart approximately every hour between 6 am and 7 pm (US$4.25, 2½ hours). Buy your ticket in the company's office (on the main plaza next to the cathedral) a couple of hours in advance.

**To Turbo** There are five buses a day with Sotraurabá and Transportes Gómez Hernández (US$10, 10 hours). All these buses come through from Medellín and might be full by the time they reach Santa Fe.

## PUENTE DE OCCIDENTE

The Puente de Occidente, or the Western Bridge, is a peculiar pearl of 19th-century engineering. This 291-metre-long bridge over the Cauca River was designed by José María Villa and constructed in 1887. When built, it was one of the first suspension bridges in the Americas. It carried general traffic until the 1960s, when it was declared a national monument.

## Getting There & Away

The bridge is six km east of Santa Fe, on the road to Sopetrán. Only pedestrians are now allowed to cross the bridge, and for that reason the traffic on the road leading to the bridge is scarce. Negotiate a round trip with a taxi driver in Santa Fe. Alternatively, do the

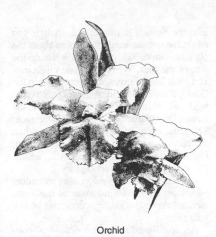

Orchid

steady hour's walk to the bridge, but avoid the unbearable midday heat.

## CIRCUITO DE ORIENTE

The Circuito de Oriente is a circular tourist route through the area south-east of Medellín. This popular trip offers an opportunity to visit a few picturesque pueblos paisas with their distinctive architecture, and enjoy en route the verdant, mountainous countryside with its haciendas. The standard loop usually includes Marinilla, Rionegro, Carmen de Viboral, La Ceja, Salto de Tequendamita, Retiro and the Hacienda Fizebad. It's a good route for getting a taste of Antioquia in a capsule.

The trip can be done as a super-express, one-day tour from Medellín (see the Medellín section for tour details), or you can do it more leisurely, choosing your own route and pace. It's worth including El Peñón in the same trip, which usually doesn't appear on the commercial tour routes because it's a bit off the track. You can put together your own tour from the information provided in the following sections. Accommodation and food are in good supply along the route, and transport is frequent.

Towns like Abejorral, Jardín, Jericó and Sonsón have some wonderful Antioquian architecture and are every bit as interesting as those on the standard tourist route. However, they are further afield and are linked to Medellín by unpaved roads, so they rarely see foreign tourists. You will find the information about these towns later in this chapter.

## MARINILLA
• *pop 12,500* • *2100 m* • *17°C* • ☎ *(948)*
Marinilla lies 46 km south-east of Medellín on the road to Bogotá. Dating from the first half of the 18th century, it's one of the oldest towns in the region. It was named after the cacique Mariní, who was the head of the Indian group which inhabited the area when the Spaniards arrived.

The town is a good example of Antioquian architecture, with a pleasant main square and adjacent streets. The Iglesia Parroquial on the main plaza was built between 1874 and 1901 and is not of particular interest, but make the effort to see the Capilla de Jesús Nazareno, on the corner of Carrera 29 and Calle 32. This fine colonial church was erected in the 1750s and has a beautiful brick façade. Its high altar and paintings on the side walls come from the period. At the time of writing, the church was about to close for restoration. Check it anyway, as it may be already open again.

The Semana Santa celebration in Marinilla is one of the most elaborate in Antioquia, with processions and concerts of religious music held in the Jesús Nazareno church.

If you're looking for a guitar, you're in the right place; Marinilla is known for manufacturing good-quality string instruments.

### Places to Stay
There are at least half a dozen hotels in town, all of which are on or just off the main plaza. The cheapest is the basic *Hotel California*, at Calle 31 No 29-44. The rooms have no private bath or hot water but cost only US$4/5 a single/double.

The *Casa del Turista*, at Carrera 30 No 29-26, is also on the basic side and nothing special. Matrimonios/doubles with bath cost

US$6/8, and there are also cheaper rooms without own bath.

The *Hotel Familiar*, at Carrera 31 No 30-59 (on the main plaza), is a better choice. It's also simple but clean and friendly. A matrimonio without bath costs US$5, while doubles with bath cost US$10.

The *Hostería del Camino Real* (☎ 754042), at Calle 30 No 29-41, is set in an old house with a nice patio, and is a pleasant place to stay. Singles/doubles with bath and hot water cost US$7/11. The hotel has its own restaurant serving inexpensive set meals.

Possibly the best standards are to be found in the brand-new *Hotel La Capilla* (☎ 755149), at Calle 31 No 29-30. Airy, bright doubles with bath, hot water and TV go for US$11.

### Getting There & Away

Buses to Medellín depart every 15 minutes from the main square (US$1, one hour). Frequent colectivos leave from the square to Rionegro (US$0.40, 15 minutes). Buses from Medellín to El Peñón pass via Marinilla every one to 1½ hours, but they don't call at the plaza. You have to walk five blocks along Calle 30 to catch them (US$1.50, 1¼ hours).

### EL PEÑÓN

El Peñón (literally, the Rock), is a huge, 200-metre-high, granite monolith, somewhat similar in shape to the famous Sugar Loaf of Rio de Janeiro. It sits on the bank of an artificial lake, the Embalse del Peñol, about 30 km east of Marinilla. The reservoir was formed by a dam built in the mid-1970s as part of a hydroelectric project to provide electricity for the region.

The waters of the reservoir have flooded several settlements in the area, including the early 18th-century town of Peñol. In order to provide a new home for its inhabitants, a modern town, bearing the same name, was built from scratch at a new location, on the road to the rock. There's an unusual church in the town, imitating El Peñón. Stop en route to the rock if you want to see it.

The rock itself, also referred to as El Peñol (after the flooded town) or La Piedra (liter-

ally, the Stone), is impressive, though you might have some aesthetic doubts about the gigantic letters 'GI' painted in white on the face of the rock. Why 'GI'?, one might ask. The rock lies on private property within the Guatapé district, and the owner, sponsored by local authorities, decided to have the name of the municipality placed on the rock. The project was stopped by Inderena when the second letter, 'U', was in production. Unfortunately, the inscription will 'adorn' the rock for at least several years.

A staircase leads to the top; after ascending 649 steps, one gets a magnificent bird's-eye view all around, with the spectacular lake at your feet.

An appalling four-storey, octagonal construction has been built on the top, which houses a restaurant. Access to the top of the rock is open daily from 8 am to 6 pm, for US$0.50.

### Places to Stay & Eat

You will probably make a day trip to the rock, but if you decide to linger and wander about, there is a wide choice of tourist facilities. The lake has become a popular weekend destination for Medellín's dwellers, and a number of estaderos and cabañas have sprung up on the road and the lakeside.

Estaderos provide accommodation in rooms and/or cabañas and food in their own restaurants. Some of them have boats to take tourists around the lake.

For budget rooms, ask at the *Estadero La Mona* (US$6 a double) or, right across the road, at the *Estadero El Mirador*. A five-minute walk down the road is the *Estadero Los Cisnes*, which has possibly the cheapest cabañas (US$10 for up to four people). All three estaderos are at the foot of the rock, on the Peñol-Guatapé road.

More luxurious options are also available, including multi-room houses complete with kitchen, dining room etc.

Accommodation tends to fill up in holiday periods and on puentes (long weekends), but at other times these estaderos are almost empty and the prices are negotiable.

## Getting There & Away

Buses to Medellín run approximately every 1½ hours (US$2.50, 2½ hours). They all pass via Marinilla (US$1.50, 1¼ hours).

## RIONEGRO

• *pop 37,000* • *2120 m* • *17°C* • ☎ *(94)*

Founded in 1663, Rionegro is the oldest town in the Medellín environs. It is also the largest, comprising a busy central district and, unfortunately, a wide ring of ramshackle barrios.

Rionegro is not a very pleasant or beautiful town, yet it has some attractions which you might like to see if you pass through. You'll probably do so, as the town is a regular stop on the Eastern Circuit route, and is a convenient jumping-off point for Carmen de Viboral.

## Things to See

The main plaza is adorned by the **Monumento a José María Córdoba**, a statue of the locally born hero of the War of Independence. This allegoric figure of the naked general is one of many unconventional works by Rodrigo Arenas Betancur.

The massive **Catedral de San Nicolás**, overlooking the plaza, was built between 1794 and 1804. Have a look at the impressive silver *sagrario* (tabernacle) in the high altar, and at the tomb of Juan del Corral in the chapel on the left. Juan del Corral was, for a short time, Antioquia's president after the province declared its independence in 1813. He died in Rionegro in 1814. The catedral houses the modest **Museo de Arte Religioso**, open daily except Saturday, from 1 to 5 pm.

The **Casa de la Convención**, at Calle 51 No 47-67, a few blocks from the plaza, is a colonial house where the Colombian constitution of 1863 was written during the government of Tomás Cipriano Mosquera. Known as the Constitución de Rionegro, this was the most liberal constitution in the country's history. The house has been converted into a historical museum that features a collection of documents and period exhibits related to the event. It's open daily except

Thursday, from 9 am to noon and 2 to 5 pm; entrance costs US$0.40.

One block from the Casa, on the corner of Calle 51 and Carrera 48, is the **Capilla de San Francisco**. Built in 1740, this is the oldest existing church in the town and has a fine rustic interior complete with a period altar.

Roughly similar in style, but with a more beautiful altar, is the **Capilla de San Antonio** in the village of San Antonio de Pereira, four km south of Rionegro. This tiny paisa village has a charming plaza and is worth the short trip. To get there from Rionegro, take a local bus from the corner of Calle 49 and Carrera 48.

## Places to Stay

Rionegro has plenty of hotels but the cheapest are not very good. Avoid the *Residencias Estrella*, at Carrera 51 No 50-03, unless you want to learn what 'very basic' can really mean (US$3.50 a matrimonio). The *Hotel Córdoba*, at Calle 49 No 51-58, may serve well as a further exposition of the same notion, and it's cheaper.

The cheapest acceptable accommodation seems to be in the small *Hotel Casa Vieja*, at Carrera 51 No 48-68, where a matrimonio costs US$5.

There's a satisfactory choice of better hotels within a few blocks of the main plaza, including the *Hotel Gutier* (☎ 271 0106), at Carrera 49 No 50-32, *Hotel El Oasis* (☎ 271 6005), at Carrera 50 No 46-23, *Hotel Dorado* (☎ 531 2030), at Carrera 50 No 46-124, and the *Hotel Casaloma* (☎ 531 3390), at Carrera 46 No 51-68. All of them have decent singles/doubles with bath, hot water and TV for around US$10/14, and all except for the Casaloma have their own restaurants. The Gutier is the closest to the plaza, but El Oasis is possibly the best of the lot.

There are also several hotels in the market area, including the *Hotel Onassis*, at Calle 55 No 45-61, *Hotel David* next door and the *Hotel Aymará*, at Calle 54 No 46-05. They are cheaper than the previously listed central establishments, but this area is far from attractive.

## Places to Eat

The cheapest restaurants in the vicinity of the main plaza are on Carrera 51 between Calles 48 and 49. One of these, *Restaurante Doña Berta*, at Carrera 51 No 48-66, serves filling comidas for US$1.50.

There are better options on the main square, such as the modestly priced *El Bosque*, on the 1st floor. Grab a table on the balcony for a good view over the busy plaza. Also on the square is *Los Cheffs*, which is one of the best in town, but understandably it's more expensive. You'll find several more eateries close by, or you can use the hotel restaurants.

## Getting There & Away

Buses and colectivos connect Rionegro to other cities and towns in the region.

**To Medellín** There are plenty of buses from the main square (US$1.25, 1¼ hours).

**To Marinilla** Colectivos depart from the corner of Calle 52 and Carrera 46 (US$0.40, 15 minutes).

**To Carmen de Viboral** Colectivos leave from the corner of Calle 49 and Carrera 49 (US$0.50, 20 minutes).

**To La Ceja** Colectivos leave from the corner of Carrera 50 and Calle 46 (US$0.70, 25 minutes).

## CARMEN DE VIBORAL

• *pop 14,000* • *2150 m* • *17°C*

Carmen de Viboral, a small town nine km south-east of Rionegro, is known nationwide as the main producer of hand-painted ceramics. There are a few large factories out of town (Continental, Capiro and Triunfo are the biggest), and several small workshops that are still largely unmechanised.

To find them, go along Carrera 31 for about 10 blocks from the main square, passing the hospital on your left, until you get to the bridge. Triunfo is about 500 metres further on, and 100 metres to the right. Continental is a few km further ahead. Ask the management to show you the production process. In most places they will, though you might wait some time until someone can take you around. Almost all Eastern Circuit tours from Medellín include a visit to one of the factories.

## Places to Stay & Eat

There are two hospedajes in the main plaza, as well as a few restaurants.

## Getting There & Away

Frequent colectivos run to Rionegro from the plaza (US$0.50, 20 minutes). There are only four direct buses a day to Medellín; instead of waiting for one, go by colectivo to Rionegro and change for one of the frequent buses to Medellín.

## LA CEJA

• *pop 24,000* • *2180 m* • *17°C* • ☎ *(948)*

La Ceja was founded in 1789 and has slowly developed into a handsome pueblo paisa. It has a pleasant, spacious main plaza lined with balconied houses – walk around to see the door and window decoration. Stroll about the adjoining streets for more examples of these delicate architectural details.

There are two churches on the plaza. The main church has a bright interior illuminated through a score of stained-glass windows. There's a fine tabernacle in the high altar. The church is open for most of the day.

The other church, or rather a chapel, is small and looks undistinguished from the outside, but don't miss it: it has possibly the most amazing interior of all the churches in the region. The showpiece is an extraordinary Baroque retable carved in wood. It's thought to be around 300 years old, and reflects the features of the *escuela quiteña* (Quito School). The chapel is open for mass only, daily at 11 am and additionally on Saturday and Sunday at 5.30 pm.

With haciendas nestled in the lush hills, the town's surroundings are beautiful. You'll see some of them on the road to Medellín, which winds spectacularly through pine forests.

Read the three following sections before you decide to go back to Medellín, as there are some other interesting places in the area.

## Places to Stay

There are only two hotels in town, both near the main square. The *Hotel Turín*, at Calle 19 No 21-55, is clean and friendly, and offers singles/doubles with private bath for US$6/9. It has its own restaurant which serves set lunches and dinners for US$2 each.

The *Hotel Primavera*, at Carrera 20 No 20-61, costs the same but has rooms without bath. Prices of both hotels may rise a little at weekends.

### Getting There & Away
Buses to Medellín depart from the main plaza every 15 minutes until 8 pm (US$1.25, 1¼ hours). Colectivos to Rionegro run frequently, also leaving from the plaza (US$0.70, 25 minutes).

## SALTO DE TEQUENDAMITA
Tequendamita is a waterfall nine km from La Ceja on the road to Medellín. There is a pleasant restaurant, *Parador Tequendamita*, ideally located at the foot of the falls. They serve good typical food at affordable, though not bargain prices. Try the plato típico antioqueño (US$5). Most tours organised from Medellín stop at the Parador for lunch.

## RETIRO
• *pop 5400* • *2180 m* • *17°C* • ☎ *(948)*
Retiro is a quiet, 200-year-old, tiny town – one of the nicest in the region. It's set in green hills 33 km from Medellín, four km off the road to La Ceja.

The main church, Iglesia de Nuestra Señora del Rosario, is perhaps not an architectural masterpiece, but the main square is a good example of Antioquian architecture. Walk around the surrounding streets to see some beautiful houses. The old chapel at the entrance to town, Capilla de San José, houses some valuable pieces of colonial art, but is seldom open.

A traditional festival, the Fiesta de Los Negritos, is held every year from 27 to 31 December, to commemorate the abolition of slavery in the region. It was here, in Retiro, that 126 slaves were liberated in the early 1810s, possibly the first case of its kind in the country's history.

### Places to Stay & Eat
The *Casa Campesina*, at Carrera 20 No 22-31, two blocks downhill from the main plaza, is the cheapest place to stay in town. It is basic and the beds are remarkably hard, but the staff are friendly. Singles/doubles cost US$3/4.

Softer (but more expensive) beds can be enjoyed in the *Hospedaje La Amistad*, *Hospedaje Don Pollo* and the *Hotel El Turista*.

The *Restaurante La Silla*, on the main square, is a nice place decorated with saddles, horseshoes and some Antioquian utensils and antiques. The food is good and inexpensive, and the management is friendly. A tasty comida costs US$2.

Drop into *La Montaña*, the bar next to the church, which resembles an antique shop. Another impressive collection of typical antiques is to be found at *Fonda Los Recuerdos*, about one km from Retiro on the only access road to the town.

### Getting There & Away
Buses to Medellín run every half an hour until around 8 pm (US$1.25, one hour). The road is spectacular. If you are coming from La Ceja, get off at the turn-off to El Retiro and catch the bus coming through from Medellín or walk the remaining four km. The walk is the better choice, as there are some lovely haciendas along the road.

## HACIENDA FIZEBAD
Fizebad is an old hacienda 27 km from Medellín on La Ceja road. The main house dates from 1825, and the original furniture and other period objects are on display. A replica of an Antioquian town, complete with chapel and shops, has been constructed, and about 150 species of orchids are grown on the grounds.

See the chapel altar decorated with orchids and a collection of old religious paintings on the walls. An archaeological museum is open in one of the houses and contains some pre-Columbian ceramics of various Colombian cultures, as well as pottery from Ecuador, Peru and Mexico. The hacienda is open Tuesday to Sunday from 10 am to 5 pm; the entrance fee is US$1.50 including a guide.

### Getting There & Away

Many buses from Medellín to La Ceja and Retiro pass by the hacienda on their way and will let you off at the entrance. Virtually all standard Eastern Circuit tours operated from Medellín call at the hacienda.

## SONSÓN

• *pop 17,500* • *2490 m* • *15°C* • ☎ *(948)*

Sonsón was founded in 1787 and developed unhurriedly in its isolated, mountainous setting. Although it has gradually modernised over the past decades, and some new buildings have replaced ancient casas, the old architecture still dominates the historic core of the town. The balconied houses lining the main plaza are lovely to look at, and you'll find more interesting houses in the backstreets. Unfortunately, a fine old church was destroyed during an earthquake in the 1960s, and a large, modern and uninspiring cathedral was built in its place.

### Places to Stay & Eat

The *Hotel Imperio*, on the main square, is an acceptable budget place to stay. Rooms with bath cost US$2.50 per person. The *Hotel Tahami*, also on the plaza, is the best in town. It costs US$9/14 a single/double with private bath and hot water.

There are several restaurants on and off the plaza, including the *Asadero de la Sexta* and *Restaurante La Meruza*.

### Getting There & Away

There are about 10 buses daily to Medellín operated by Sociedad Transportadores Sonsón Dorada and Expreso Sonsón Argelia. All buses depart from the square, the last leaving around 4 pm (US$3.75, 4½ to five hours). The first part of the journey is on a rough road but the scenery is splendid.

Buses to La Dorada depart at 5 am and 11 am (US$5.50, seven hours). This is an alternative route to Bogotá, if you don't want to backtrack via Medellín. The whole 160-km stretch is unpaved, but the landscape is beautiful, especially around Norcasia, where you pass the green Río La Miel.

## ABEJORRAL

• *pop 7000* • *2125 m* • *17°C* • ☎ *(948)*

Nestled among the green hills of southern Antioquia, Abejorral is connected to the outer world only by rough roads. It has preserved its old character pretty well and has a lazy rhythm of yesteryear. Founded in 1811, this tranquil town is worth a visit if you're in the region.

### Places to Stay & Eat

The *Casa Campesina*, the cheapest place in town, is at Carrera 51 No 49-19, a few steps from the plaza. Basic singles/doubles cost US$3/4. The *Hotel Colombia*, at Calle 52 No 51-10, one block from the plaza, costs US$4 per person (US$5 with bath). It is pleasant and friendly, and has a wonderful flowered patio. It also serves good meals for US$2.

### Getting There & Away

There are four or five buses a day to Medellín, operated by Expreso Sonsón Argelia and Transportes Unidos La Ceja (US$3.50, four to 4½ hours). The scenery is just as spectacular as that on the Sonsón route, and the road is equally rough. If you plan on visiting Sonsón from Abejorral, take the Medellín bus to the place known as La Frontera, just past Mesopotamia, and wait for the Medellín-Sonsón bus.

It is possible to get from Abejorral to La Pintada on the main Medellín-Cali road, and to Aguadas on the road to Manizales, but you have to change once or twice on the way.

## JERICÓ

• *pop 7000* • *1970 m* • *18°C* • ☎ *(948)*

Jericó is perhaps one of the most interesting small towns in the region, and quite an unusual one. It appeared on the map relatively late, in 1850, but progressed swiftly. It was the second town in Antioquia (after Medellín) to introduce electricity, in 1906. In 1915, Jericó was raised by Pope Benedict XV to a seat of the bishopric, which made it a focus of religious activity – a feature which is still very noticeable today.

The town has a massive, modern (though dull) cathedral, which apparently can accommodate the town's whole population. There is the Museo de Arte Religioso in the basement of the cathedral, which has, apart from some religious exhibits, contemporary paintings by local artists, pre-Columbian ceramics and antiques. Although there is much in quantity, the quality is questionable. The museum is open from 7 to 9 pm, on Sunday and holidays from 2 to 5 pm, and is closed on Tuesday.

This tiny town has at least half a dozen other churches and chapels, including Iglesia de San Francisco, Iglesia de Santa Clara and Capilla de la Visitación. There's also the Morro del Salvador, a 90-metre hill with a statue of Christ atop, just on the edge of the town. The view from the top will help you appreciate the religious status of the place and locate the churches for a closer look later on.

Back in town, walk around the plaza to see the beautiful balconied houses with the delicate carved decoration of their windows and doors. If you wander around the side streets you will find several more charming façades.

### Places to Stay

There are three hotels on the plaza, of which the *Hostería Piedras* is the best. It costs US$8 per person in rooms with baths and hot water.

### Getting There & Away

There are three buses daily to Medellín (US$4.25, 4½ hours). If you plan on heading to Jardín, take one of two chivas to Andes which depart at 7 am and 1 pm (US$2.50, 2½ hours). From Andes frequent colectivos go to Jardín.

### ANDES

• *pop 18,000* • *1360 m* • *21˚C* • ☎ *(948)*

Andes is a busy, uninteresting, dusty town which has one special attraction: chivas. There are plenty of them, all covered with colourful decorative patterns and usually with original paintings on the back. They park around the mercado, from where they depart for the surrounding villages. Most of the chivas were painted by one man, Alejandro Serna, a local artisan living in Andes.

### Getting There & Away

Andes is on the way from Medellín to Jardín (from where you can continue on to Riosucio). It is also the place to change buses for Jericó if you're coming from Jardín.

**To Medellín** There are four or five buses a day, operated by Transporte Suroeste Antioqueño (US$3.75, four hours).

**To Jardín** Three buses daily come through from Medellín (US$1, one hour). There are also frequent colectivos (US$1.50, 45 minutes).

**To Jericó** There are a couple of chivas which are supposed to depart early in the morning and around 2 pm (US$2.50, 2½ hours).

### JARDÍN

• *pop 6500* • *1800 m* • *19˚C* • ☎ *(948)*

Jardín is a clean, easy-going town set in a beautiful valley at the southern end of Antioquia. It is one of the most attractive examples of a pueblo paisa. Its pleasant main plaza is dominated by an impressive cathedral, an elaborate stone building reminiscent of a huge wedding cake. Its construction began in 1916 and took 16 years to complete. The striking interior has a high altar that was made from marble in Italy.

The main plaza is a beautifully homogeneous example of Antioquian architecture. All the houses that encircle it (except one) have typical paisa balconies. One of them, at Carrera 5 No 9-31 (on the southern side of the square), houses the Casa Museo de la Cultura. The exhibition features a hotchpotch of objects related to the town's history, including old photos, documents, furniture, images of saints and musical instruments – it's like a charming antique shop. It's open at different hours every day, but roughly from 9 am to 5 pm.

Stroll around the side streets for more fine houses and bucolic street life, where horses, horse carts and chivas are very much in

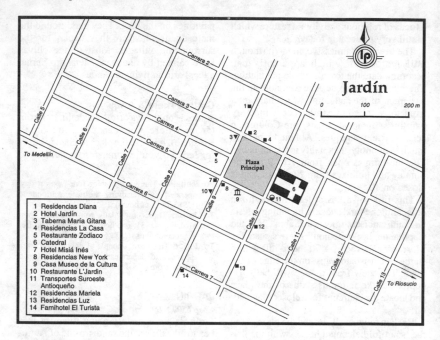

**Jardín**

1  Residencias Diana
2  Hotel Jardín
3  Taberna María Gitana
4  Residencias La Casa
5  Restaurante Zodiaco
6  Catedral
7  Hotel Misiá Inés
8  Residencias New York
9  Casa Museo de la Cultura
10 Restaurante L'Jardin
11 Transportes Suroeste
   Antioqueño
12 Residencias Mariela
13 Residencias Luz
14 Famihotel El Turista

evidence. Sunday is market day, held in the main plaza.

### Places to Stay

There are several places to stay in Jardín and most of them are clean, pleasant and friendly. All are inexpensive, though, as a general rule, prices rise at weekends.

The cheapest is *Residencias Luz*, at Calle 10 No 6-42, which is simple with shared bath facilities only, but acceptable at US$1.50 per person (US$3 at weekends). The *Residencias New York*, at Calle 9 No 5-14, costs US$2 per person (US$4 at weekends). It has a few good rooms with balconies overlooking the plaza, while others are small and basic. There are no private baths, but hot water in the shared facilities is available in the morning.

The *Hotel Jardín* (☎ 555651), across the square from the New York, at Carrera 3 No 9-14, is the most pleasant place to stay. This old house has a large balcony that is perfect

for sitting on and watching the life on the square pass by. The beautiful patio is full of flowers and the rooms are good, all with private bath and hot water, and cost US$4 per person (US$6 at weekends).

The only other place in town that has private baths is the modern *Residencias Diana* (☎ 555854), at Calle 9 No 2-39, costing US$4.50 per person (US$6 at weekends). This hotel provides good standards but it doesn't have the old-time charm of the Jardín.

Other hotels in town include the *Residencias Mariela*, at Calle 10 No 5-56, *Famihotel El Turista*, at Carrera 7 No 9-09, *Residencias La Casa*, at Carrera 3 No 9-46, and the *Hotel Misiá Inés* at Calle 9 No 5-13.

### Places to Eat

Perhaps the best place for a set meal or mondongo is *Restaurante Zodiaco*, at Carrera 4 No 8-63. *Restaurante L'Jardin*, at Calle 9 No 5-29, is not bad either, and also serves set meals and local dishes. One more recommended place for lunch or dinner is the restaurant of the *Hotel Jardín*.

The *Taberna María Gitana*, at Calle 9 No 3-03 (on the main square), is a pleasant, tastefully decorated place for a drink. Or you can just sit and enjoy a bottle of beer in one of several open-air cafés in the middle of the plaza.

### Getting There & Away
All buses, chivas and colectivos depart from the main plaza.

**To Medellín** Three buses a day depart at 6 am, noon and 5 pm (US$4.75, five hours). From Medellín they leave at 7 am, 2 and 5 pm. There are two additional buses in either direction on weekends.

**To Riosucio** There are three buses or chivas a day, at 7.30 am, noon and 3 pm (US$3.50, three hours). The route is very spectacular, but have a sweater at hand, as the rough road winds up to about 3000 metres. There's usually a stop near the top at a house where delicious *agua de panela con queso* is sold.

**To Andes** There are frequent colectivos (US$1.50, 45 minutes). Have a look at the colourful chivas before heading further on to Medellín or Jericó.

### RÍO CLARO AREA
The Río Claro is a relatively small river in eastern Antioquia, which flows from the eastern slopes of the Cordillera Central north-eastward down to the Río Magdalena. It crosses the Medellín-Bogotá highway on its way. About 18 km east of this point is the unremarkable roadside village of Doradal.

North of Doradal stretches the vast Hacienda Nápoles, the ex-property of Pablo Escobar, who had a private zoo on the grounds. It was the only zoo of its kind in the country, where animals from all over the world – including elephants, rhinos, hippos, zebras and camels – lived relatively freely in a fenced game park. In 1989, after the assassination of the presidential candidate Luis Carlos Galán, the government confiscated the hacienda, including the zoo. Only then did the authorities learn that the food for the animals had cost Escobar about US$5000 a day (entrance for the public was free), which the government couldn't afford. The animals

were said to have been distributed among the national zoos.

The zoo and several magnificent natural spots in the Río Claro area made the region a weekend tourist destination. Although the zoo is now closed, the area is indeed beautiful and worth visiting. The main attractions are the marble gorge along the Río Clara and three amazing caves.

If you are going to explore the caves, reliable bright torches are an absolute must. Wear your oldest clothes and comfortable shoes. Don't forget to take a flash if you intend to take pictures.

### Cañón del Río Claro
Cañón del Río Claro is a spectacular gorge stretching along the river south of the main road. From the bridge over the Río Claro, follow the rough side road heading south for about one km to the house at the end of the road. It's here that you pay your US$1 entrance fee.

From here, a path follows the river for 600 metres or so to El Refugio, a house beautifully located high above the river, overlooking a unique marble-slab river 'beach' below. The footpath continues past some overhanging rocks to the entrance of a cave, the Gruta de la Cascada, on the other side of the river. You can go further along the river, but the path ascends steeply into the lush tropical forest and gradually fades. It disappears completely a few hundred metres on.

### Gruta de la Cascada
This cave is nearly 500 metres long and pierces right through a mountain ridge, from the Río Claro on one side, to the hamlet of Jerusalén on the other. For the most part, the cave is a narrow and very high marble corridor which follows a stream. The scenery is extremely impressive.

It is possible to walk through the cave, but there are two difficult points. First is the entrance to the cave from the Río Claro, which is a high, rocky threshold with a waterfall spilling over it. The other problem is the series of deep pools in the cave through

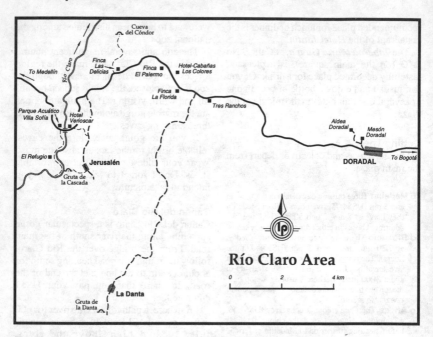

**Río Claro Area**

which you have to pass. You don't need a guide because there is only one way to go and you can't get lost.

You can explore the cave from either the Río Claro or the Jerusalén end. The dirt road to Jerusalén branches off from the main one two km from the Río Claro bridge; there's a big sign at the turn-off that reads 'Cementos Río Claro'. However, you don't need to follow the road because there's a path which shortens the way considerably (see the map); it is only a half-hour walk from the bridge to Jerusalén. Ask for directions to the cave in the last house in Jerusalén, the one with a statue of the Virgin outside.

The path leading to the cave begins a bit before the house and follows the stream down; it's a 10-minute walk to the entrance. The boys from the hamlet will probably accompany you. After passing through the cave you go down the waterfall, wade across the river and follow the path to El Refugio or back to the bridge.

## Cueva del Cóndor

This breathtaking marble cave is about 300 metres long and has huge halls full of fantastic stalactites and stalagmites. It is inhabited by guácharos, a species of nocturnal bird common in Colombian caves. Their largest colony is in the Cueva de los Guácharos (see that section for more information about the bird).

The starting point for the cave is the Finca Las Delicias, four km along the main road from the bridge. At the finca you will probably find local boys who will take you to the cave, but you can go without a guide. The cave is quite easy to find and explore. Descend from the finca to the stream and follow it directly to the cave. The stream goes right through it. It takes about 20 minutes to get to the cave's huge entrance.

The walk through the cave to another exit (following the stream all the way) takes 30 minutes or so. Wear proper shoes and clothing because you have to wade through the stream on several occasions. At some parts you'll be up to your knees in water. You can return the same way or by a path going over the ridge, but it's difficult to find this path without a guide.

### Gruta de la Danta

This is yet another cave, smaller than the Cóndor but also of outstanding beauty and containing magnificent stalactites and stalagmites. The cave is about 12 km off the main road, near the small village of La Danta. A jeep is supposed to leave at about 6 am from Doradal to La Danta, and this appears to be the only regular transport. The road is rough, and the traffic is sporadic, dying completely in the mid-afternoon. You can go on foot, but it is a steady 2½-hour walk from the main road; wear light clothes as it's hot.

In La Danta it is easy to find young locals who will guide you. It's worthwhile hiring them, as they know every corner of the cave and will show you all the interesting details. They charge a small fee. The cave is about one km beyond the village; there's a hut just before the entrance where, for about US$1, you can rent a *mechón* (a primitive petrol lamp made from a tin can). Be prepared to get your shoes wet in this cave too.

### Places to Stay & Eat

A number of hotels, cabañas and estaderos have sprung up along the road between the Río Claro bridge and Doradal. They usually offer both accommodation and food. Some will allow you to camp on their grounds and use their facilities. The prices fluctuate, rising at weekends when tourists come. On weekdays you may be able to negotiate prices in some places. Keep the prices listed below as guidelines only. During puentes (three-day weekends), accommodation tends to fill up.

The *Hotel Verioscar*, next to the bridge, is one of the cheapest options, but also one of the simplest. Expect to pay US$4/5 per person in a room without/with private bath.

*Parque Acuático Villa Sofía*, on the opposite side of the bridge, costs US$15 per person in cabañas, or US$25 with full board. It has a restaurant and a swimming pool with a slide. You can camp there for US$6 per person.

Probably the most romantic place to stay is *El Refugio*, which costs US$12 per person or US$20 with full board. The place is actually quite rustic, but neat and set in an idyllic spot amidst the lush vegetation.

*Tres Ranchos*, one km from the turn-off to La Danta, is a basic place to stay and eat. It costs US$3 per person to stay, and US$2 for a set meal. It may be unbearable at weekends due to the rumbas that last till morning. In the same area, there's the plush, but more expensive, *Hotel-Cabañas Los Colores*.

There's also a choice of accommodation and food options in Doradal, but since Escobar's zoo has gone, it's no longer a convenient place to stay.

The basic and noisy *Residencias Doradal*, on the main road, is the cheapest place (US$3 per person). Several paces back from the road, the *Residencias Las Brisas* is appreciably better and quieter (US$6 per person).

The *Mesón Doradal*, on the outskirts of the village, costs US$12/15/20 a single/ double/triple, all with bath and fan. It's a pleasant place with a garden, swimming pool and restaurant. You can get some information on the region here.

The *Aldea Doradal*, set on the hill 500 metres past the Mesón, is a modern, Mediterranean-style complex of buildings, which comprises a hotel, a restaurant and swimming pool.

### Getting There & Away

The Río Claro bridge is on the main Bogotá-Medellín highway, so all buses between these cities pass through. You can expect a bus to pass by every 15 minutes or so. They can drop you on the road near any of the sites, except for La Danta. The trip from the Río Claro to Bogotá costs US$11.50 in a climatizado and takes six hours; to Medellín, it costs US$7 in a climatizado and takes three hours.

Two corriente buses from Medellín pass over the Río Claro at around 9 am and 3 pm on their way to Puerto Nare. Also, a climatizado to Puerto Serviez passes by at around 10.30 am. These are the buses to take if you are heading to the Caverna del Nus.

## CAVERNA DEL NUS

Caverna del Nus is possibly the most beautiful cave in eastern Antioquia. It was discovered about 60 years ago, but it was not until the 1980s that it became known outside the region. Still, it is far from the main roads and usual tourist routes, and rarely visited.

The cave is partially marble and consists of several chambers, some of them lavishly ornamented with stalactites, stalagmites and columns. The cave runs 220 metres from north to south and is 50 metres wide.

The cave is managed by Blanca Aurora Jaramillo López, known locally as Blanquita or Blanjara. This charming, vigorous old woman lives in a small hut at the foot of the cave. She warmly welcomes all visitors and invites them to breakfast, passing around photos and articles about the cave. She or someone else will then guide you through the cave. Give yourself at least a couple of hours for the visit.

If you are on your own, you will pay a US$4 entry fee which includes a guide. If there are two or more of you, the price is US$2 per person. There are three primitive cabañas nearby where you can stay overnight free of charge. Bring your own food, and a torch is a must.

### Places to Stay

If you plan on a leisurely visit to the cave, you can stay at Blanquita's cabañas. If you want to do a day trip to the cave, stay in the village of La Sierra. There are about 10 budget hospedajes there, mostly along the railway track. All have fans and cost around US$4/6 for singles/doubles.

If you get stuck in Puerto Boyacá, there are a dozen residencias around the main square.

### Getting There & Away

Getting to the cave is complicated. You have to change your means of transport several

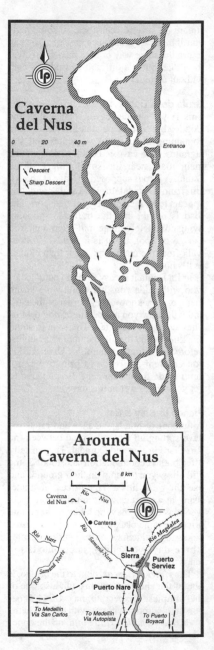

**Caverna del Nus**

0    20    40 m

Entrance

Descent

Sharp Descent

**Around Caverna del Nus**

0    4    8 km

Caverna del Nus

Río Nus

Canteras

Río Nare

Río Samaná Norte

Río Magdalena

La Sierra

Puerto Serviez

Río Samaná Norte

Puerto Nare

To Medellín Via San Carlos

To Medellín Via Autopista

To Puerto Boyacá

times and then walk. Basically, you can get there from Bogotá, Medellín or any intermediate point.

**From Bogotá** First, take a bus to Puerto Boyacá; there are about a dozen buses daily with Rápido Tolima, from 5.30 am until midnight (US$9, six hours). From Puerto Boyacá go to Puerto Serviez; there is one bus daily (coming through from Medellín) at around 12.30 pm (US$2.50, one hour), but it's much easier to take one of the relatively frequent jeep-colectivos which depart from the corner of Carrera 3 and Calle 13 until 5 pm (US$3).

In Puerto Serviez, cross the Magdalena River by one of the frequent canoes to La Sierra (US$0.40). From there, go by boat up the Samaná-Nare River to Canteras. Passenger boats depart five times daily, approximately every three hours (US$3, 30 minutes).

From Canteras, it's a one-hour walk to the cave. The path initially goes upstream along the river, but after about one km it swerves to the right, goes up a hill and then descends to a cattle farm. Up to this point things are pretty easy, but further on the path fades away. Ask for detailed directions at the farm; alternatively, ask around in Canteras for someone who could guide you to the cave.

**From Medellín** Take the Coonorte climatizado to Puerto Serviez, which departs at 7.30 am and goes via the Bogotá highway and Puerto Boyacá (US$9.50, six hours). Then continue as above.

Alternatively, take one of the two Coonorte corrientes to Puerto Nare (US$7.50, six hours). They depart at 6 am and noon, and also follow the Bogotá highway. From Puerto Nare there are frequent boats to La Sierra (US$0.70). Then follow the same route as above.

You can also get to Puerto Nare with Transportes Oriente Antioqueño. It has two corrientes a day, departing at 5.30 am and 10.45 am, which go via an unpaved road through San Carlos (US$6.75, seven hours).

# Zona Cafetera

Zona Cafetera, the region comprising the three small departments of Caldas, Risaralda and Quindío, lies just south of Antioquia. As its name suggests, it's Colombia's coffee growing heartland. The region provides nearly half of the total national coffee production, but covers only 1.2% of the country's area.

The region wasn't really settled until the mid-19th century, when Antioquia began to expand towards the south. It was essentially the paisas who colonised the region (the so-called *colonización antioqueña*), and they introduced the coffee plantations.

By 1905, the region had developed enough to become a department in its own right, Caldas. By the 1960s coffee accounted for half of Colombia's export earnings, and Caldas was its major producer. In 1966 conflicting economic interests within the department led to its split into three small administrative units.

The Zona Cafetera has much in common with Antioquia in terms of its people, culture, crafts and cuisine. The architecture too shows many similarities with Antioquian buildings, and one can find plenty of small towns reminiscent of pueblos paisas.

Although there are a lot of villages and towns scattered throughout the region, the only cities in Zona Cafetera are the three departmental capitals: Manizales, Pereira and Armenia.

Zona Cafetera is mostly a rugged, green land. Coffee plantations cover most mountain slopes between about 1300 and 1700 metres.

## MANIZALES
• *pop 380,000* • *2150 m* • *18°C* • ☎ *(968)*
Manizales, the capital of Caldas, was founded in 1848 by a group of Antioquian colonists looking for a tranquil place to escape the civil wars which plagued the country during that period. The group was reputedly composed of 20 families, including the family of Manuel Grisales, after whom the settlement was named.

Manizales' early development was painfully slow, hindered by two serious earthquakes in 1875 and 1878. It wasn't actually until the beginning of the present century that the town began to grow at a faster pace, partly because it became the capital of the newly created department, but mainly as a centre of coffee production. However, an extensive fire in 1925 razed the

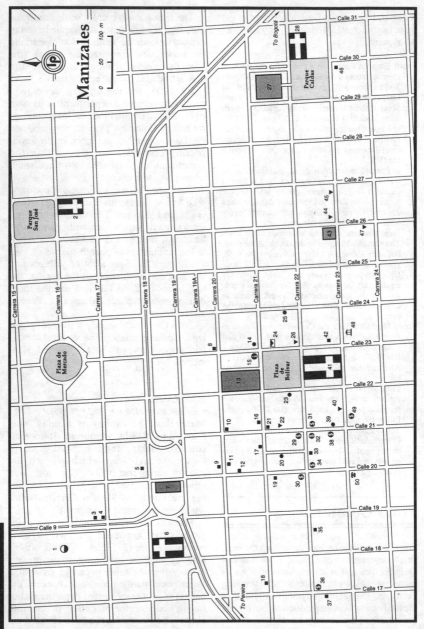

Manizales

THE NORTH-WEST

## PLACES TO STAY

3   Residencias Avenida No 3
4   California Hotel
5   Hotel Casablanca
8   Hotel Bolívar
9   Hotel Cónsul No 1
10  Residencias Avenida No 2
11  Hotel Cónsul No 3
12  Hotel Amarú
16  Hotel Cónsul No 5
17  Hotel Camino Real
18  Hotel Cónsul No 2
19  Hotel Cónsul No 4
21  Hotel Escorial
33  Hotel Las Colinas
35  Residencias Bonaire
37  Pensión Margarita No 2
42  Hotel Tama Internacional
46  Hotel Fundadores

## PLACES TO EAT

22  Restaurante El Pilón
26  Pollo Frito Frisby
40  Punto Rojo
44  Restaurante Chung-Mi
45  Salón de Té La Suiza
47  Restaurante CM

## OTHER

1   Bus Terminal
2   Iglesia de San José
6   Iglesia de los Padres Agustinos
7   Palacio Municipal
13  La Gobernación
14  Asociación Caldense de Guías
    de Turismo
15  Oficina de Fomento y Turismo
20  Turcaldas & Inderena
23  Manizales Tours
24  Avianca & Post Office
25  Aces
27  Centro Comercial Parque Caldas
28  Iglesia de la Inmaculada
    Concepción
29  Banco de Colombia
30  Banco de Bogotá
31  Banco Unión Colombiano
32  Banco Industrial Colombiano
34  Banco Popular
36  Banco Anglo Colombiano
38  Banco Sudameris Colombia
39  Tierra Mar Aire
41  Catedral
43  Centro Comercial La Casona
48  Museo del Oro
49  Banco de Occidente
50  Telecom

town, and the construction work had to start all over again.

Today, Manizales is a lively, modern city with a pleasant centre dominated by several high-rise buildings and a huge cathedral. Perched along a ridge of the Central Cordillera, Manizales' streets are hilly, a little like the streets of San Francisco, which gives the city additional charm. The temperature is pleasant but the rainy seasons, from March to May and September to November, can be slightly depressing.

### Information
**Tourist Office** The Oficina de Fomento y Turismo (☎ 846211) is by the Plaza de Bolívar opposite the cathedral, and is open Monday to Friday from 8.30 am to noon and 2 to 6 pm.

**Money** Banco Industrial Colombiano, Banco Unión Colombiano, Banco Anglo Colombiano and Banco Sudameris Colombia will all change your cash and travellers' cheques. The first listed pays the best rate for cash, while the last is the best for changing travellers' cheques. The Banco de Bogotá and Banco de Colombia, among others, handle Visa card operations, while the Banco Industrial Colombiano and Banco de Occidente handle MasterCard.

Manizales' TMA office (☎ 842277), at Calle 21 No 22-39, is not authorised to replace your lost or stolen American Express travellers' cheques but will help you initiate this process through its Bogotá head office.

**Inderena** If you plan on hiking in the Parque Nacional Los Nevados you will need a permit from Inderena. The office (☎ 848457, 848552) is on Piso 2 of Edificio Beneficencia, at Calle 20A between Carreras 21 and 22. The permit costs nothing and it takes one day to issue.

Camping in the park is permitted but you need your own camping equipment.

**Tours** Manizales sits on the north-western outskirts of the Parque Nacional Los Nevados, and the park is the focus of local tour activity. Access to the park is by the road which branches off from the Manizales-Honda road in La Esperanza, 31 km from Manizales. This road goes for about 10 km uphill to the border of the park, where it divides. The right fork leads to the Hotel Termales del Ruiz and continues back to Manizales. The left fork winds up to the snowline at about 4700 metres at the foot of the volcano of Nevado del Ruiz and continues down to Laguna del Otún. The road has been reopened for traffic since the volcano quietened down.

The most popular tour on offer is a full-day trip to the foot of the volcano. The tour includes transport there and back, a guide, a snack, a short walk up the volcano slope (but not to the top) and a bath in the hot springs of the Hotel Termales del Ruiz.

The tour can be organised through either the tourist office or Turcaldas (Corporación Departamental de Turismo de Caldas) and costs about US$14 per person with either operator. A minimum of eight persons is required to set off on a tour. Turcaldas has its main office in the Edificio Beneficencia, Oficina 501 (☎ 848124), on Calle 20A between Carreras 21 and 22 (open Monday to Friday from 8 am to noon and 2 to 6 pm), plus an outlet in the building of La Gobernación, on the corner of Calle 22 and Carrera 21 (open Tuesday to Friday from 9 am to noon and 2 to 6 pm, Saturday from 7 am to noon and 2 to 7 pm and Sunday from 7 am to noon). Some travel agents can organise the same tour but they will probably charge more.

Turcaldas can also book a room in the Hotel Termales del Ruiz, should you like to stay longer in the mountains. Set at 3500 metres, this is the highest hotel in the country. It has thermal pools and a restaurant. Singles/doubles/triples cost US$18/24/29

(20% more on weekends and holidays). There's no public transport to the hotel. Turcaldas operates a jeep or buseta to the hotel for US$4 return, but again, at least eight passengers are needed, or you pay for the empty seats.

Other tour options in the region include a visit to the Centro Nacional de Investigaciones del Café (Cenicafé) in Chinchiná, 22 km from Manizales on the road to Pereira. This trip can be arranged through Manizales Tours, at Calle 22 No 21-44, on the Plaza de Bolívar. The four-hour excursion includes transport, a guide, a snack and entrance to the Centro, and costs US$26/18/16 per person in groups of two/three/four people.

If you prefer to visit the Centro on your own, get a permit from the Comité de Cafeteros (☎ 841700), Edificio Leonardo Londoño, on the corner of Carrera 22 and Calle 18.

**Guides** The Asociación Caldense de Guías de Turismo (☎ 832500) is the departmental association of guides. The office is on the corner of the Plaza de Bolívar, across the street from the tourist office. Enter the building from Carrera 21 No 23-21, and go up the spiral staircase to Oficina 304.

The guides' standard offer is a trip to the top of the Cráter Arenas of the Nevado del Ruiz. It erupted in 1985 taking a toll of some 20,000 people. This is a one-day trip but you need to start as early as 4 am. You go by jeep to the foot of the volcano, then hike for three hours up to the rim of the crater. Time permitting, you can also go up the Cráter La Olleta. Good trekking shoes are recommended, as well as some sunglasses, but mountaineering equipment is unnecessary. Guides charge about US$70 for a group of up to six people. Transport (arranged by the guides) will cost another US$50 or so per group, but the prices are negotiable to a certain extent.

Longer hikes in the park can also be arranged with the guides. You can, for example, traverse the park from north to south, ending up in Ibagué, Pereira or Armenia.

## Plaza de Bolívar

The architecture around Manizales' central square is modern except for the fine 19th-century building of La Gobernación, which has been meticulously restored both inside and out to its original state. In the middle of the square stands an intriguing monument known as Bolívar-Cóndor. This is another work of Rodrigo Arenas Betancur, known for his unconventional designs.

## Catedral

The Manizales cathedral has had quite a chequered history. The existing building is the third church to be erected on this site. The first one, built in 1851, was destroyed by an earthquake in 1878. The next one, a handsome wooden church, went up in flames during the fire of 1925. There's an exact replica, the Iglesia de Nuestra Señora del Rosario, in the Chipre district, on the corner of Carrera 13 and Calle 12. The present cathedral has not escaped the misfortunes of nature either: during an earthquake in 1979 it lost one of its towers, but it has since been rebuilt.

The cathedral is a large, imposing piece of architecture, inspired by Gothic style. Its main tower is 106 metres high, and is possibly the highest church tower in the country. Begun in 1929, it took almost half a century to complete the cathedral. It was built out of reinforced concrete and was reputedly the first church in Latin America to be constructed this way. The grey concrete exterior has been left rough, giving the cathedral an unpolished, almost unfinished look. The three front bronze doors are covered with bas-reliefs which tell the history of the town and its earthquakes.

Don't be misled if these doors are locked (they are only open for Sunday mass); you can enter the cathedral by either of the side doors. They should be open Monday to Saturday from 6.30 to 9.30 am, 11.30 am to 12.30 pm and 5.30 to 6.30 pm; Sunday from 6.30 am to 1 pm and 5.30 to 9 pm.

The spacious interior is embellished with a number of lovely stained-glass windows in different styles. Some of them were commissioned in France and Greece, while others were made locally. The largest, at the back of the church over the main doors, has colourful folksy, rather than religious images. The richly ornamented baldachin over the high altar was carved in wood and gilded in Italy.

The walls and vault are a somewhat inconsistent combination of fine cream marble and rough concrete. Initially, the whole of the interior was to be laid out in marble, but the work was stopped after the engineers revealed that the structure wouldn't support such weight.

Underneath the church is a crypt housing the remains of the dead (either the ashes after cremation or bones brought from the cemetery). It's worth having a look inside if you are fortunate enough to be there when it is open. It's an eerie feeling walking around the shelves of this huge, bizarre 'library' lined with 8600 *nichos* (ossuaries).

The entrance to the crypt is from the Plaza de Bolívar through the door below the main church gate.

## Iglesia de la Inmaculada Concepción

This church, in the Parque Caldas, next to the ultra-modern Centro Comercial Parque Caldas, was built at the beginning of the present century and has a beautiful interior, which, including the columns, vault, pews, pulpit and other furnishings, is made of cedar wood.

## Capilla de la Enea

Manizales' oldest existing church, dating back to 1876, is in La Enea suburb, on the south-eastern outskirts of the city, about eight km from the centre. La Enea is actually the place where the town was originally founded, but it was soon after moved to the Plaza de Bolívar area. The church is small and not an architectural wonder, but if you want to see it, take a city bus to La Enea and walk the remaining distance to the church.

## Museo del Oro

The Gold Museum is in the Banco de la República, at Carrera 23 No 23-14, Piso 2. It has a small collection of Quimbaya gold and ceramic artefacts. It is open Monday to Friday from 8 to 11.30 am and 2 to 5.30 pm. Entry is free.

## Other Museums
There are two museums at the University of Caldas, in the eastern sector of the city. The **Museo Precolombino** (also known as the Arqueológico), at Carrera 23 No 58-65, has Quimbaya and Calima ceramics. The **Museo de Ciencias Naturales**, at Calle 65 No 26-10, has a few thousand animal species, including an extensive butterfly collection of particular interest. Both museums are open Monday to Friday from 9 am to noon and 2 to 6 pm.

## Torre El Cable
This wooden tower on the corner of Carrera 23 and Calle 65 is a relic of a cable-way constructed in 1922 between Manizales and Margarita. It was used for 15 years to transport coffee. The coffee was then carried overland to Honda, and shipped down the Magdalena River to Barranquilla and beyond.

## Festivals
**Feria de Manizales** With a history dating back to the 1950s, this is the city's major carnival, celebrated during the first week of the year. Costumed groups in colourful fancy dress take over the city, and the Plaza de Bolívar has nightly poetry meetings. A beauty contest is held in which the Coffee Queen is elected, and a handicraft fair draws in artisans from the region and beyond. The most important corridas take place during this period.

**Festival Latinoamericano de Teatro** Held since 1968, this is one of the two important theatre festivals in the country (the other is in Bogotá). There's always a good representation of leading Latin American theatre plus the cream of national groups. Half a dozen city theatres (including the modern Teatro de Los Fundadores, one of the best in the country) are used for the festival perfor-

mances, and free concerts are held nightly at the Plaza de Bolívar. Some years ago the festival was held in August, but in 1993 it was rescheduled for the end of September.

## Places to Stay – bottom end
All the hotels included in this section are in the central city area within a short walk of the Plaza de Bolívar, and all have hot water.

The main concentration of rock-bottom accommodation is north of Carrera 18, between the bus terminal and the market. The area is unattractive and not very safe at night. Avoid it or stay on its outskirts, for example on Carrera 18, where you'll find the *Hotel Casablanca* (☎ 823338) at No 20-17. Large rooms with a double bed (for a single or couple) without/with bath cost US$4.50/6, whereas doubles with bath go for US$7 – good value for money.

If you need somewhere cheap near the bus terminal, the *Residencias Avenida No 3* (☎ 842098), at Calle 19 No 16-35, is one option, costing a dollar more than the Casablanca. Next door is the new, modern *California Hotel* (☎ 824217), which costs US$9/11 a single/double.

It's more pleasant to stay south of Carrera 19, in the vicinity of the Plaza de Bolívar. Perhaps the cheapest here is the *Residencias Avenida No 2* (☎ 835251), at Calle 21 No 20-07. The rooms are rather small and don't have private baths, but the hotel is clean and pleasant. You pay US$3.50/4.50/6 for a single/matrimonio/double.

The budget accommodation in the centre has considerably improved after the opening of a chain of five Cónsul hotels just a few steps from each other. They include the *Hotel Cónsul No 1* (☎ 823720), at Carrera 20 No 20-25; *Hotel Cónsul No 2* (☎ 848674), at Carrera 21 No 17-21; *Hotel Cónsul No 3* (☎ 822719), at Carrera 20 No 20-30; *Hotel Cónsul No 4* (☎ 831385), at Calle 20 No 21-10; and the *Hotel Cónsul No 5* (☎ 844067), at Carrera 21 No 21-21.

They are all set in renovated old houses which are pretty small and offer satisfactory standards. Some rooms are better than others, so always look around before deciding. All the hotels charge more or less the same: around US$6/8 for singles or matrimonios/doubles without bath and about US$8/12 for rooms with bath. The Cónsul No 2 has only shared bath facilities and is slightly cheaper than the others.

The *Hotel Bolívar* (☎ 826599), at Carrera 20 No 23-09, costs much the same as the Cónsuls and its rooms are a bit better; choose one facing the street.

The *Pensión Margarita No 2* (☎ 834505), at Calle 17 No 22-14, is a little further away from the Plaza de Bolívar, but it's a pleasant, old-style hotel with clean rooms for US$5 per person.

The *Residencias Bonaire* (☎ 821936), at Carrera 22 No 18-38, is also a place with style. It has good, spacious rooms at similar prices to the Margarita, and the management is friendly.

### Places to Stay – middle

There's no shortage of mid-priced accommodation in the city centre. On the whole, the hotels offer decent standards including TVs in rooms, but they usually lack style. The *Hotel Tama Internacional* (☎ 847711), at Calle 23 No 22-43, is located in the large old building beside the cathedral. It does have style but its service leaves a bit to be desired. Singles/doubles/triples cost US$12/16/22.

The *Hotel Amarú* (☎ 843560), at Calle 20 No 20-19, is friendlier and better organised, and its singles/doubles/triples go for US$14/22/30.

The *Hotel Fundadores* (☎ 846490), facing the Parque Caldas, at Carrera 23 No 29-54, is rather undistinguished; small singles/doubles/triples cost US$19/25/31 – a bit more than they should.

### Places to Stay – top end

Perhaps the best of the more affordable options in this price bracket is the *Hotel Escorial* (☎ 847696), at Calle 21 No 21-11, which costs US$25/35 for a single/double. The *Hotel Camino Real* (☎ 845588), at Carrera 21 No 20-45, doesn't offer much more but is more expensive. At US$26/43/60 for a single/double/triple it's overpriced,

though the friendly staff are open to negotiation and apparently you can beat these prices down by 25%.

The *Hotel Las Colinas* (☎ 842009), at Carrera 22 No 20-20, is the poshest place to stay in the city centre, at around US$80/100/120 a single/double/triple. There are three cheaper options on Avenida Centenario: the *Hotel Europa* (☎ 822253), *Hotel Embajador* (☎ 831514) and *Hotel Castellano* (☎ 831384).

### Places to Eat

Predictably, the cheapest restaurants are clustered around the cheapest residencias but don't expect much from them. The Plaza de Bolívar area is better for eating but there are not many restaurants here which serve set meals. Particularly in the evening, it's not that easy to find a place for a budget comida corriente. If you can't track down anything, go to the Parque Caldas area, where you'll find a few budget eateries on Carrera 23 between Calles 30 and 32.

Carrera 23 is the main axis of gastronomic activity, tightly packed with restaurants, cafés and fast-food outlets. *Punto Rojo*, at Carrera 23 No 21-39, has self-service fast food. *El Pilón*, at Calle 21 No 21-21, is good for regional dishes (bandeja paisa, mondongo, sancocho, fríjoles) at modest prices. The restaurant in the Centro Comercial La Casona, on the corner of Carrera 23 and Calle 26, has inexpensive dishes (but not set meals), including plato montañero for US$3.

For Chinese food at reasonable prices, go to *Chung-Mi*, at Carrera 23 No 26-11. The classy *Restaurante CM*, at Calle 26 between Carreras 23 and 24, is one of the central restaurants. It has good international food where an average main course will cost US$6, and is open till midnight.

There are two pleasant places on Avenida Centenario, overlooking the valley, one km south-west of Plaza de Bolívar: *Los Arrayanes*, opposite the Hotel Embajador, and *Los Sauces* (the better of the two), 500 metres past the bullring. They both have good food at moderate prices, with a choice of fish and seafood.

THE NORTH-WEST

*Salón de Té La Suiza*, at Carrera 23 No 26-57, is good for cakes, fruit juices and tinto (it may sound like a paradox, but even in the heart of the coffee region, tinto is not always good). It closes at 7.30 pm.

### Getting There & Away

**Air** La Nubia Airport is about eight km south-east of the city centre, off the road to Bogotá; take the urban bus to La Enea, then walk for five minutes the rest of the way. Aces is the only airline operating flights to and from Manizales; it flies seven times a day to Bogotá (US$58), twice daily to Medellín (US$36) and once a day to Cali (US$44). Buy your tickets at the Aces office at Calle 24 No 21-34.

**Bus** The new bus terminal is a short walk from the Plaza de Bolívar.

**To Bogotá** Rápido Tolima has four busetas a day (US$10, eight hours). Expreso Bolivariano has six climatizados (US$12.50) and six more luxurious buses which they call *platinos* (US$13.75).
**To Cali** There are plenty of buses with Expreso Trejos and Expreso Palmira (US$11.75 climatizado, US$10.75 pullman, 5½ hours).
**To Medellín** Empresa Arauca and Expreso Sideral operate this route (US$7.75 pullman, five hours).
**To Pereira** Empresa Arauca has buses every 15 minutes until 8 pm (US$1.50, one hour).
**To Salamina** Expreso Sideral has a few buses a day (US$3, three hours), while Empresa Autolegal has colectivos approximately every half an hour (US$4, 2¼ hours).

## SALAMINA
• *pop 15,000* • *1775 m* • *19°C* • ☎ *(968)*
Founded in 1825, Salamina is one of the oldest towns in the region and possibly the best architectural example left from the Antioquian colonisation of Caldas. Many old houses with nicely decorated doors and windows can still be seen around the main plaza and in the adjacent streets.

The cathedral is an unusual construction, probably unique in Colombia. It was designed by an English architect and built between 1865 and 1875. The interior is a rectangular hall without columns, and has a flat, very wide wooden ceiling. The fine

wooden altar was made at the beginning of the present century. The cemetery chapel also has an interesting architectural design.

### Places to Stay

There are a few budget hospedajes in the market area on Carrera 6, where the buses stop. All are basic and cost around US$2.50 per person. More pleasant is the *Hotel Roma*, at Carrera 6 No 5-10, on the corner of the main plaza. It has small rooms but comfortable beds and costs US$4 per person.

### Getting There & Away

Buses stop on Carrera 6 between Calles 9 and 10.

**To Manizales** There are only a few buses departing for Manizales (US$3, three hours), but colectivos run regularly (US$4, 2¼ hours).
**To Medellín** There are a few buses daily via Aguadas and one bus via La Felisa. The latter is the bus you should take if you are heading for Riosucio.

## RIOSUCIO
• *pop 16,000* • *1780 m* • *19°C* • ☎ *(96859)*
Other than the Carnaval del Diablo, held at the beginning of January, this town doesn't have much to offer. It has two large squares just one block from each other, and both plazas boast large churches. The old one, Iglesia de San Sebastián, is on the upper plaza. The other, the modern Iglesia de la Candelaria on the square of the same name, is uninspiring.

### Places to Stay & Eat

There are a few budget hotels in the centre of the town. The *Hotel Palacio* (☎ 1832), on the street linking the two squares, Calle 8 No 6-18, is the cheapest and it's not too bad. You pay US$1.50/2 per person in rooms without/with bath.

The *Hotel Ingruma* (☎ 1802), at Carrera 6 No 6-21, 30 metres off the Plaza de San Sebastián, is definitely a place with style. It's set in an old house with wooden floors and a decorative wooden roof covering the central square hall. Note the wall paintings dating from 1930. Singles/doubles/triples without bath cost US$2/3.50/4.50, while rooms with bath go for US$3/4.50/7.

Marginally more expensive is the *Hotel Central* (☎ 1466) on the Plaza de San Sebastián, at Calle 7 No 5-40. It probably offers better standards than the Ingruma, but most of its rooms are without windows.

All the listed hotels are clean and have hot water in the morning. All have their own cheap restaurants, and there are several more eating establishments around.

Remember that during the carnaval, prices may double or even treble and rooms are hard to find. Some people rent out rooms in their homes, but you should come to Riosucio a day or two before to be sure of getting something.

### Getting There & Away

There are several bus companies servicing Riosucio, including Empresa Arauca, at Calle 9 No 4-71, Flota Magdalena, at Calle 9 No 3-51, and Flota Occidental, on the corner of Calle 9 and Carrera 4.

**To Medellín** Flota Occidental buses depart every one to 1½ hours (US$5.50 pullman, four hours; US$4.50 corriente, 4½ hours).

**To Manizales** Empresa Arauca and Flota Occidental together have nine corrientes a day (US$3, 2½ hours).

**To Pereira** Flota Occidental has buses and busetas departing every 20 minutes (US$3.50, three hours).

**To Belén de Umbría** Take the Pereira bus to Remolino (US$2.25), through which buses from Pereira to Belén pass approximately every hour.

**To El Jardín** Cootransrío, on the corner of Carrera 4 and Calle 10, has buses or chivas at 8 am, noon and 3 pm (US$3.50, three hours). The impressive scenery compensates for the very rough road. Halfway there, the buses stop at a house where very good cheese is sold.

### MARMATO
• *pop 1200* • *1050 m* • *23°C*

This village, set on the slopes of a mountain overlooking the Cauca Valley, is centred around gold mining and has the only important mines in Caldas (there are many more in Antioquia). There are dozens of mines in and around the village. They are just drifts dug

into the mountains (some are more than one km long), from which gold-bearing rock is hewn. The miners work in truly primitive conditions.

Most of the rock is sent elsewhere for processing, but some mines are mechanised and have crushing mills. You may be allowed to visit the mines, or at least the mills. If you wander around the mines you'll probably find a friendly miner who will show you around. Don't miss seeing the village itself. Marmato has only a network of steep paths. There are no streets except for the access road from Supía.

### Getting There & Away

The easiest way to get to Marmato is from Supía, a town on the Medellín-Cali road. Several chivas and jeeps head off down the rough but spectacular road to Marmato (US$2, 1½ hours).

If you don't mind walking, stop at the place where the dirt road branches off the Medellín-Cali road (about 20 km north of Supía) and heads up to Marmato (seven km). Walk along this road to the hamlet of El Llano and, just past a bridge behind the hamlet, take the path leading uphill to the right. You will pass several mines on the way before arriving at Marmato. The walk from the main road to the town should take about two hours.

### PEREIRA
• *pop 410,000* • *1410 m* • *21°C* • ☎ *(963)*

The capital of Risaralda, Pereira is an important centre for the surrounding coffee-growing region. The town was founded in 1863 and within little more than a century it had developed into a large, lively, modern city. It doesn't have many special tourist attractions, but you may want to visit, if you find yourself in the region.

You can take short trips from Pereira to Marsella and Termales de Santa Rosa. The city is also a starting point for the Parque Ucumarí, from where you can head further up the mountains into the Parque Nacional Los Nevados.

The rainy season in the region is from March to May and September to November.

THE NORTH-WEST

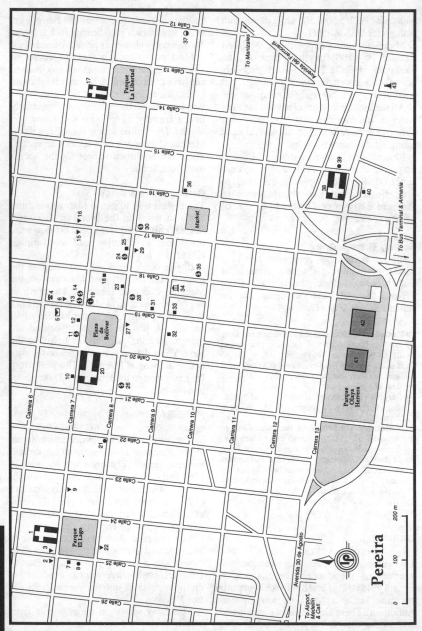

Pereira

## PLACES TO STAY

7   El Hotel
10  Hotel Bolívar
12  Hotel Soratama
18  Residencias Minerva
23  Residencias Confort
25  Hotel Colón
31  Hotel Cataluña
32  Residencias Ocmara
33  Gran Hotel
36  Hotel Fontana
40  Hotel Meliá Pereira

## PLACES TO EAT

2   Kokoriko
3   Pollo Frito Frisby
6   Pastelería Confitería Lucerna
9   Restaurante El Túnel
15  Restaurante El Vitral
16  Primo's Pizza
22  El Balcón de los Arrieros
27  Punto Rojo
29  El Balcón de los Arrieros

## OTHER

1   Iglesia El Claret
4   Telecom
5   Avianca & Post Office
8   Carder
11  Banco Popular
13  Banco Anglo Colombiano
14  Banco Industrial Colombiano
17  Iglesia La Valbanera
19  Tourist Office
20  Catedral
21  Sam
24  Banco de Colombia
26  Banco Unión Colombiano
28  Banco de Bogotá
30  Banco de Bogotá
34  Museo del Oro
35  Banco de Occidente
37  Transportes Florida
38  Iglesia del Carmen
39  Aces
41  Biblioteca Municipal
42  Gobernación del Risaralda
43  Monumento a Los Fundadores

In February 1995, a powerful earthquake shook the region of Pereira, and ruined a number of buildings in the city. At least 30 people were killed and about 200 others were injured. It's possible that some of the following information (which was gathered before the disaster) may be effected.

### Information

**Tourist Office** The Dirección de Fomento y Turismo (☎ 357132, 357172) is at Carrera 7 No 18-55, Piso 2, and is open Monday to Friday from 8 am to noon and 2 to 6 pm.

**Money** If you need to change cash or American Express travellers' cheques, the most reliable banks are the Banco Industrial Colombiano and the Banco Anglo Colombiano, next to each other on the corner of the Plaza de Bolívar (the former usually pays better rates). Cash can also be exchanged in the Banco Popular and travellers' cheques at the Banco Unión Colombiano. Visa credit cards are accepted by the Banco de Bogotá, Banco de Colombia and Banco Anglo Colombiano. MasterCard advances can be arranged at the Banco Industrial Colombiano and Banco de Occidente.

There's a number of casas de cambio. Several are clustered in the vicinity of the Banco de la República and others are scattered throughout the city centre. There's also one on the ground floor underneath the Banco Unión Colombiano.

**Carder** The Corporación Autónoma Regional del Risaralda (☎ 357819, 357888) is at Calle 25 No 7-48, Piso 11, at the Parque Lago Uribe Uribe (popularly known as Parque El Lago). Here is where you can arrange accommodation for La Pastora (see the Parque Ucumarí section) and get the permit for the Parque Nacional Los Nevados (it's not available from Inderena). The office is open Monday to Thursday from 8 am to noon and 2 to 4 pm, and Friday from 8 am to 2.30 pm.

### Museo del Oro

The Gold Museum is on the 1st floor of the Area Cultural of the Banco de la República, at Carrera 9 No 18-23, and is open Monday to Friday from 8.30 to 11.45 am and 2 to 5.45 pm. The collection features some amazing ceramics of the Quimbaya Indians who dominated the region before the Spanish conquest. There are also some gold pieces of the Quimbaya people, but they are not so impressive. There are usually exhibitions of modern art held on the 2nd floor of the building.

### Bolívar Desnudo
The 8.5-metre-high, 11-tonne bronze sculpture of the naked Bolívar on horseback, in the Plaza de Bolívar, is probably the most unusual monument to El Libertador. The sculpture is the work of Arenas Betancur, Colombia's most outstanding creator of public monuments, who donated it to the city in 1963, the bicentenary of Bolívar's birth.

Pereira has three other Betancur works: **Monumento a Los Fundadores** (Monument to the Founders) is on the corner of Carrera 13 and Calle 13; **El Prometeo**, dedicated to the local university professor Juan Manuel Mejía Marulanda, is in the Universidad Tecnológica de Pereira; and the controversial **Cristo sin Cruz** (Christ without the Cross) is in the Capilla de la Fátima, at Avenida 30 de Agosto between Calles 49 and 50.

### Zoológico de Matecaña
The zoo is just opposite the airport. It is particularly renowned for its *ligres (Pantera leotigris)*, a cross between an African lion and a Bengal tiger, bred here in Pereira. You can see lots of birds, including Andean condors, flamingos and tucans. You can even have a chat with the *papagayos* (macaws). The zoo is open daily from 8 am to 6 pm (entry until 5.30 pm). Tickets are US$1. Frequent urban buses marked 'Matecaña' run between the city centre and the zoo. The trip takes 20 minutes.

### Iglesia del Carmen
Of the city churches, the Iglesia del Carmen (also known as San José), on the corner of Calle 15 and Carrera 13, is probably the most interesting. It's a large neo-Gothic construction, a replica of the Catedral del Buen Pastor

in San Sebastián in Spain. It has lovely stained-glass windows.

### Places to Stay – bottom end
There is a large number of budget hotels on Calle 17 and in the area between the market and the Parque La Libertad. The cheapest accommodation costs about US$2.50/4 a single/double. However, most of these places are basic or ultra-basic and many of them, particularly in the market area, are used for prostitution.

There is not much to recommend in this area, except perhaps the *Hotel Fontana* (☎ 342061), at Carrera 9 No 15-71, which costs US$4/5.50 a single/double without bath and US$5/6/7 a single/double/triple with bath. It is relatively clean, and has hot water and its own restaurant.

It's safer and more pleasant to stay in the Plaza de Bolívar area. The cheapest place here is the *Residencias Confort*, at Carrera 8 No 18-30, but don't let the name confuse you. It's basic and has only shared baths, and costs US$4/5 a single/double.

Slightly better is the *Hotel Bolívar* (☎ 335141), at Carrera 7 No 20-50. Singles/doubles without bath cost US$4.50/7, while rooms with private bath cost US$6/10. Rooms vary largely in size and quality, so inspect a few before deciding.

The *Residencias Ocmara* (☎ 356675), at Carrera 9 No 19-25, has matrimonios without/with bath for US$6/9. Another undistinguished option is the *Hotel Colón* (☎ 356400), at Carrera 8 No 17-30, which costs US$6/10 for a single /double with bath. You may get the urge to sleep in a round bed. If so, go to the *Residencias Minerva* (☎ 334493), at Calle 18 No 7-32, where a matrimonio with TV and bath costs US$11.

### Places to Stay – middle
The pleasant and comfortable *El Hotel* (☎ 352217), at Calle 25 No 7-16 (Parque El Lago), is good value at US$10/15 a single/double with TV and bath. The hotel has only 14 rooms and tends to fill up.

The *Hotel Cataluña* (☎ 354527), at Calle 19 No 8-61, is a good clean place just off the Plaza de Bolívar. Choose one of the bright rooms facing the street, as the others are somewhat dark. Singles/doubles cost US$14/20. The hotel restaurant serves set meals (US$2.50) at lunch and dinner time.

### Places to Stay – top end

The two-star *Gran Hotel* (☎ 359500), at Calle 19 No 9-19, is a large establishment which costs US$35/50/60 for a single/double/triple. The three-star *Hotel Soratama* (☎ 358650), at Carrera 7 No 19-20, sits right on the Plaza de Bolívar and offers singles/doubles for US$50/60. The poshest place in town is the five-star *Hotel Meliá Pereira* (☎ 350770), at Carrera 13 No 15-73.

### Places to Eat

The cheapest restaurants are clustered around the budget hotels. The eating places in the centre are more expensive, but the food is usually better.

If you stay at the *Hotel Fontana*, you can eat in its restaurant, or you can go down to the market, just opposite, which offers a variety of food.

In the heart of the city, *Punto Rojo*, at Carrera 8 No 19-17 on the plaza, is a big, self-service, 24-hour restaurant, where you can put together your own meal for US$3 to US$4.

*El Balcón de los Arrieros*, at Carrera 8 No 17-23 and at Carrera 8 No 24-65 (both on the 1st floor), are pleasant paisa venues, which serve inexpensive regional dishes. *Restaurante El Túnel*, at Carrera 7 No 23-41, offers a variety of food from different regions (including lechona tolimense) and serves a menú del día for US$2.

As elsewhere, there is a choice of chicken outlets, including *Kokoriko* and *Pollo Frito Frisby*, next to each other on the corner of the Parque El Lago.

*El Vitral*, at Calle 17 No 6-60, is one of the city's classier restaurants (it's closed on Sunday). It's good for fish and steaks, but it's not cheap. Right across the street is *Primo's Pizza*, which has some vegetarian pizzas.

The *Hotel Soratama* has its own restaurant serving international food, as does the *Hotel Meliá Pereira* but expect five-star prices.

*Pastelería Confitería Lucerna*, at Calle 19 No 6-49, is the place to go for fresh cakes and pastries.

### Getting There & Away

**Air** The Matecaña airport is five km west of the city centre, 20 minutes by urban bus. Avianca, Aces, Sam and Intercontinental operate flights. Like elsewhere, Intercontinental offers cheaper fares than the others.

There are a few direct flights a day to Bogotá (US$52 with Avianca or Sam, US$41 with Intercontinental) and Medellín (US$46 with Aces). Flights to other destinations require a connection in either of the above-mentioned cities. They include Cartagena (US$103 with Avianca or Sam, US$79 with Intercontinental), Cali (US$36 with Avianca) and San Andrés (US$132 with Sam, US$101 with Intercontinental).

**Bus** The bus terminal is about 1.5 km south of the city centre, at Calle 17 No 23-157. Many urban buses will take you there in less than 10 minutes.

**To Bogotá** Expreso Bolivariano operates hourly buses, mostly climatizados, from 6 am until midnight (US$13.25 climatizado, US$11.25 pullman, nine hours). Several other companies, including Velotax and Flota Magdalena, also cover this route. All buses go via Armenia, not Manizales.

**To Medellín** Flota Occidental runs hourly pullmans (US$9.50, six hours).

**To Cali** Expreso Palmira and Flota Magdalena service this route, with buses departing approximately every two hours (US$8.50 climatizado, four hours). If you don't want to wait, go to Armenia and change for one of the frequent buses coming through from Bogotá.

**To Armenia** Flota Occidental has busetas every 15 minutes (US$1.50, one hour).

**To Manizales** Empresa Arauca and Expreso Alcalá operate busetas that depart every 10 minutes (US$1.50, one hour). All pass via Santa Rosa de Cabal (US$0.40).

**To Marsella** The Flota Occidental buses leave every hour (US$1, one hour).

**To Belén de Umbría** Buses leave about every hour (US$2, two hours).

**To El Cedral** This is the way to the Parque Ucumarí. Transportes Florida, at Calle 12 No 8-76, has chivas departing from its office (not from the bus terminal) at 9.10 am and 12.40 pm on weekdays, and at 7 and 9 am, noon and 3 pm on Saturday and Sunday (US$1, 1½ hours).

**To Quibdó** Flota Occidental has one morning bus (US$10.25, 10 to 11 hours). It goes by unpaved road via Tadó, and involves a ferry crossing over the Río Atrato.

## MARSELLA
• *pop 9000 • 1600 m • 20°C • ☎ (963)*

Set amidst the green coffee-growing hills, 29 km north-west of Pereira, Marsella is a pleasant, typical paisa town founded in 1860 by Antioquian colonists. It still has some old houses, including the Casa de la Cultura, a large three-storey casona laid out around a patio. The house is decorated with contemporary art pieces and there is a small collection of pre-Columbian Quimbaya pottery. The two-towered church, Iglesia de la Inmaculada Concepción, in the main plaza, Parque La Pola, boasts a huge statue of Christ between its towers. However, Marsella's two main attractions are the botanical gardens and the cemetery.

### Jardín Botánico Alejandro Humboldt
The botanical gardens are on a hill overlooking the town, just two blocks from the main plaza. Created in 1979, the gardens are still young and have no great variety of plant species, but they are very well run and maintained. The enthusiastic management does its best to make the gardens attractive and ecologically sound, and they're considered some of the best in the country.

A series of cobbled footpaths have been laid, passing over five charming, small bridges built of guadua wood (a sort of bamboo). The Parque de la Ciencia y la Tecnología has recently been established in the gardens, which consists of several simple mechanical devices to explain physical phenomena. Some of them are useful; for example, the windmill pumps water to the local toilet.

Another curiosity is the Museo de la Cauchera (Museum of the Slingshot), probably the only one of its kind in the world. The museum is the by-product of a campaign to protect birds. It was launched among local kids who were killing birds with slingshots. The kids deposited their *caucheras* in exchange for free entrance to the park and other allurements. The museum is in the administrative building in the gardens, along with a cafetería (which serves excellent tinto).

The gardens are open Monday to Friday from 8 am to 5 pm, Saturday and Sunday from 8 am to 6 pm. There are four guides, should you need someone to show you around. The entry fee of US$0.60 includes the guide service.

### Cementerio Jesús María Estrada
The cemetery is on the outskirts of town, a 10-minute walk from the plaza. Designed by Julio César Vélez and constructed in 1927, it is a masterpiece of funerary architecture. It has been built on a slope, and employs a system of terraces. Bodies are buried for a period of four years in the *gradas* (the terraced area of the cemetery), the *bóvedas* (concrete box-like constructions at the back) or *en tierra* (in the earth at the far right corner of the cemetery). After that time, the remains are permanently put to rest in the *osarios* (ossuaries), the openings in the cemetery's walls, which are then cemented over.

The osario is purchased to keep the bones of the entire family. The remains of those who can't afford an osario are deposited (after four years) in the *templetes*, two towers on each side of the front wall of the cemetery.

In the centre of the cemetery is a statue of Christ, under which are the remains of Jesús María Estrada (the *padre* of Marsella and the founder of the cemetery). Talk to the grave digger who looks after the site; he is a living encyclopaedia of the cemetery's history. It is open daily from 8 am to 6 pm.

### Getting There & Away
Buses to and from Pereira run every hour (US$1, one hour). The trip takes you through the spectacular coffee plantations.

## TERMALES DE SANTA ROSA
• *1950 m • 18°C • ☎ (963)*
Also known as Termales Arbeláez, these are

the most popular hot springs in the region. They are nine km east of Santa Rosa de Cabal, a town on the Pereira-Manizales road.

There's not much to see in the town except for the main square, Parque de las Araucarias, which is noted for its 11 huge araucaria trees.

A tourist complex, including thermal pools, a hotel, restaurant and bar, has been constructed near the springs amongst some splendid scenery at the foot of a 170-metre-high waterfall. The hot (70°C) water of the springs has cooled down to about 40°C in the main pool.

You can make a day trip to the termales (which are open daily from 8 am till midnight, entrance fee is US$4) or stay there for longer. The springs are fairly quiet on weekdays, but tend to fill up with city dwellers during weekends and holidays.

### Places to Stay & Eat
The *Hotel Termales* (☎ 641322, 641309) at the springs comprises two sections. The old hotel, Casa Vieja, has rooms to accommodate two to seven guests. The approximate price for two persons is US$80, plus US$30 for each additional guest. The price includes full board and the use of the pools.

The new hotel, La Montaña, offers cabañas with five/six/seven beds costing US$220 /270/320, food included.

The restaurant and bar are open for non-guests, but the food is expensive.

You can book the accommodation in Santa Rosa de Cabal, in the Servicio al Cliente del Hotel Termales at Calle 14 No 15-41. The office is open Monday to Friday from 8 am to noon and 2 to 5.30 pm, Saturday from 8 am to 12.30 pm. The staff will give you information about the springs and about the transport there and back.

In Santa Rosa de Cabal, there's the modest *Hotel del Café* on the plaza (US$18/30/40 a single/double/triple) and a few cheaper residencias in the side streets.

### Getting There & Away
Santa Rosa de Cabal is very easily accessible from both Pereira (15 km) and Manizales (36

km); buses between these two cities run every 10 or 15 minutes.

Transport to the springs is operated by Cooperativa de Transportadores Araucarias, at Calle 14 No 12-42 in the market area. Two chivas depart on weekdays from the office, at 7 am and 1.30 pm (US$0.60, 45 minutes). The morning chiva turns around and goes back to Santa Rosa immediately, and the other one is supposed to return at 5 pm, but often leaves earlier so keep a sharp look out. There are two or three additional departures on weekdays.

You can also go by jeep (they park in the same area), but they charge about US$6 one way. You can also contract them to pick you up in the evening (US$8).

## BELÉN DE UMBRÍA
• *pop 10,000* • *1560 m* • *21°C* • ☎ *(963)*
This small town, 75 km north-west of Pereira, has a most unusual museum, Museo Eliceo Bolívar. It contains about 1000 pieces of pre-Columbian pottery (mostly Quimbaya), ancient books, newspapers, photos, banknotes and even packets of cigarettes. Everything is displayed in a charming mess in one big room. You can touch the ceramics, read a newspaper printed at the beginning of the century or play the ancient piano.

Talk to the owner of the museum, Julian Jil Bolívar, who has many anecdotes about the collection. The museum is on the outskirts of town, 10 minutes on foot from the centre along Avenida Umbría. There are no regular visiting hours; just knock on the door to have it opened for you.

### Places to Stay
*La Casa del Viajero*, on the corner of the main plaza at Calle 6 No 9-60, is basic but acceptable and costs US$2 per person. The *Residencias Barú*, at Transversal 9 No 7-19, one block from the square on the way to the museum, is similarly primitive and costs the same. Possibly the best in town is the *Hotel Paraíso*, at Carrera 11 No 4-20, just off the plaza. Its rooms have no private baths, but are clean and pleasant, and cost US$3 per

person. The *Hotel Mediterráneo*, next door, costs the same but is not as good.

### Getting There & Away

Buses to Pereira are operated by two companies, Flota Occidental and Cooperativa de Transportadores Belén de Umbría, both in the main square. You can expect a bus to depart every hour or so (US$2, two hours).

If you don't want to return the same way, you can head on to Apía and Santuario, two more towns dating from the times of Antioquian colonisation. There are infrequent jeeps to Higuerón (US$1.50, 45 minutes), from where you take a connecting jeep to Apía (another US$1.50 and 45 minutes). From Apía, there are buses to Pereira.

## PARQUE UCUMARÍ

Parque Regional Natural Ucumarí is a nature reserve about 30 km east of Pereira. It was created in 1984 and is administered by Carder. The reserve is located just outside the western boundaries of the Parque Nacional Los Nevados, and covers about 42 sq km of rugged, forested terrain around the middle course of the Río Otún.

Carder has constructed the Refugio La Pastora (at 2400 metres) which offers accommodation and food. From there, you can explore the park and beyond. There's a *sendero ecológico* (ecological path) through the hills, where you can get amongst the lush vegetation and spot some of the park's rich wildlife. Birds are the park's most conspicuous inhabitants, and about 175 different species have been recorded there.

You can also make some longer excursions. The hike up the Río Otún, leading through a gorge to the Parque Nacional Los Nevados is the most popular of these. You can even get to the Laguna del Otún (3950 metres) but it's a steady, six-hour walk uphill. It's possible to do the return trip within one day, though it's a strenuous hike. If you have camping gear, it's better to split the trek into a few days, and do some side excursions up in the páramo.

### Places to Stay & Eat

The *Refugio La Pastora* can provide accommodation for 22 visitors (in two four-bed rooms, one six-bed dormitory and one eight-bed dormitory) for US$5 per person. The Refugio serves breakfasts (US$2), lunches and dinners (both US$3) for guests.

The lodging has to be booked and paid for in the Carder office in Pereira (refer to that section for details). If you plan on making a day trip to the park, you still have to visit the Carder office to get the free permit. Carder also issues fishing permits (angling is permitted from April to August in certain areas of the park).

About 10 km down the Río Otún from La Pastora is *La Suiza*, the centre of ecological research run by Inderena. It also offers accommodation (US$2 a bed) and food (US$2 per meal).

### Getting There & Away

The park is accessible from Pereira over a rough road. Chivas will take you up to El Cedral, 24 km from Pereira (see the Pereira section). El Cedral is nothing more than the Estación Piscícola (piscicultural station) where they breed trout.

From El Cedral, it's a pleasant two-hour walk uphill along the path following the Río Otún to La Pastora (1½ hours in the opposite direction).

La Suiza is a one-hour walk downhill along the road from El Cedral. A chiva can drop you at the entrance.

## CARTAGO

• *pop 95,000* • *920 m* • *24°C* • ☎ *(9656)*

Cartago is a large, rather uninspiring town sitting on the Pan-American Highway, roughly midway between Medellín and Cali. Although administratively it belongs to the department of Valle del Cauca, geographically it's within the Zona Cafetera. It's just 28 km from Pereira, but 190 km from its departmental capital, Cali.

The town was originally founded by Mariscal Jorge Robledo in 1540 on the site of present-day Pereira, and it grew around the exploitation of gold. However, the gold reserves thinned, and the brave Pijao Indians

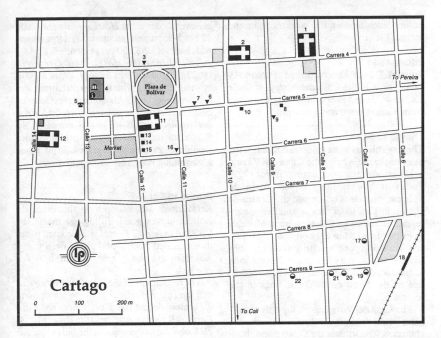

Cartago

0    100    200 m

To Pereira

To Cali

**PLACES TO STAY**

8   Hotel Mariscal Robledo
10  Hotel Don Gregorio
13  Hotel Sheraton
14  Hotel Villa del Río
15  Hotel Monserrate

**PLACES TO EAT**

3   Restaurante Mil Sabores
6   Pollo Frito Frisby
7   Kokoriko
9   Café París
16  Asadero El Portal

**OTHER**

1   Iglesia de Guadalupe
2   Iglesia de San Francisco
4   Casa del Virrey, Museum & Tourist
    Office
5   Telecom
11  Iglesia de San Jorge
12  Catedral de Nuestra Señora del
    Carmen
17  Expreso Alcalá
18  Railway Station
19  Expreso Trejos
20  Expreso Palmira
21  Empresa Arauca
22  Flota Magdalena

continually attacked the settlement. In 1691 the inhabitants decided to move the town to a quieter location 30 km west.

Cartago is famous for its *bordados*, decorative needlework designs made by hand on cloth. They feature colourful floral patterns, landscapes and other pictures. These embroideries are made on useful items such as tablecloths, bed sheets and clothing (particularly for children), or are just on pieces of cloth for decoration. There are reputedly 20,000 artisans, almost all women, working on bordados in over 100 workshops in and around the city.

## Information

**Tourist Office** Dirección de Turismo y Fomento is in the Casa del Virrey, at Calle 13 No 4-53, and is open Monday to Friday from 8 am to noon and 2 to 6 pm.

## Things to See

The city still has some colonial buildings, the most remarkable being the **Casa del Virrey**, a luxurious mansion dating from 1778. Today it houses the Conservatorio de Música, the tourist office and the Centro de Historia. The latter has a small museum related to the town's history, open Monday to Friday from 8 am to noon and 2 to 6 pm. It's also worth popping into the conservatory to have a look at its fine patio. Have a look at the façade of the house; it's regarded as one of the finest colonial buildings in the region.

The Casa del Virrey apart, the only significant relics from the colonial past are the churches. The **Iglesia de Guadalupe**, built in 1808, is a replica of the church of the same name in Mexico and has a fine brick façade. Other colonial churches include the **Iglesia de San Jorge** and **Iglesia de San Francisco**, both dating from the end of the 18th century, and both remodelled since.

The **Catedral de Nuestra Señora del Carmen** was built in the mid-20th century and is easily recognisable from the distance by its free-standing, slim bell tower. However, the church itself is uninteresting.

## Places to Stay

The cheapest hotels are around the bus company offices on Carrera 9 between Calles 7 and 9; all are basic and the area is unexciting. You would do much better staying in the centre near the Plaza de Bolívar, where you'll find several budget hotels around the market. The *Hotel Villa del Río*, at Calle 12 No 5-67, and the *Hotel Monserrate*, next door at Calle 12 No 5-75, are both acceptable and good value for money at US$3.50/5 a single/double with bath. Proba-

bly even better is the *Hotel Sheraton*, at Calle 12 No 5-55, which has unusually large rooms with bath for US$3.50 per person.

The three-star *Hotel Don Gregorio* (☎ 27491), at Carrera 5 No 9-59, is a good up-market option with its own restaurant and a swimming pool. Air-con singles/doubles cost US$30/36. The new, posh *Hotel Mariscal Robledo* (☎ 29461), at Carrera 5 No 8-105, costs US$50/70 a single/double. Double suites are available for US$90. It has a swimming pool, restaurant and disco.

## Places to Eat

*Restaurante Mil Sabores* on the Plaza de Bolívar serves good, filling set meals for US$2. *Asadero El Portal* is a pleasant place to eat grilled beef. *Pollo Frito Frisby* and *Kokoriko* are the places to call into for chicken.

The restaurants of the *Hotel Don Gregorio* and the *Hotel Mariscal Robledo* are options for a more decent lunch or dinner. The *Café París*, at the side entrance to the Hotel Mariscal Robledo, has just about the best espresso coffee in town. You can also have carajillo (coffee with coffee liqueur), café ruso (with vodka, of course) and café campesino (with aguardiente).

## Getting There & Away

**Bus** The bus company offices are on or just off Carrera 9, near the unused railway station.

**To Medellín** Empresa Arauca and Flota Magdalena together have about 10 buses a day (US$10.25 climatizado, US$9 pullman, six hours).

**To Cali** Expreso Palmira has buses every half-hour (US$7.50 climatizado, US$6.50 pullman, four hours).

**To Pereira** Expreso Alcalá runs busetas every 10 minutes until 9 pm (US$0.60, 40 minutes).

**To Manizales** Expreso Palmira operates busetas every half-hour (US$2.25, 1¾ hours).

**To Quibdó** Empresa Arauca has one pullman coming through from Cali at about 3 am (US$10, 10 to 11 hours).

**To Buenaventura** Expreso Trejos has one bus a day (US$8.50, 4½ hours).

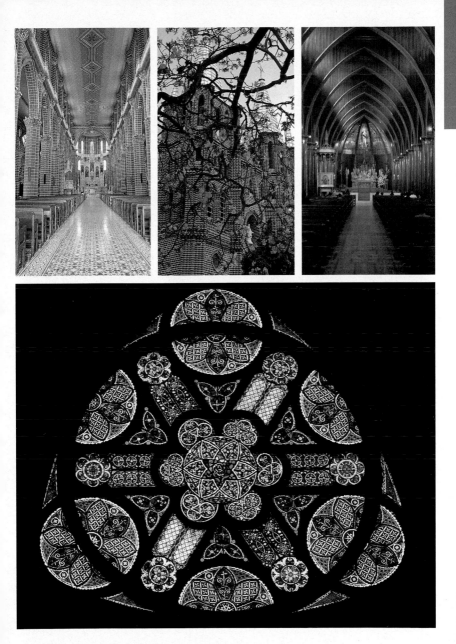

Left, Middle: Cathedral in Jardín, Antioquia
Right: Iglesia de la Inmaculada Concepción, Manizales
Bottom: Stained-glass window in Manizales' cathedral

Examples of Antioquian architecture

## ROLDANILLO

• *pop 17,000* • *970 m* • *23˚C* • ☎ *(922)*

Roldanillo, a small town in the north of the Valle del Cauca department, may be included in your coffee-region tour. It is noteworthy for its Museo Rayo, founded in 1981 by Omar Rayo, a Colombian painter. The museum displays drawings and prints only. It holds 2000 works by the founder and another 500 by several other Latin American artists. The displays of Rayo's work are changed every six months, and those of the other artists are changed every two months. The museum is located one block from the main plaza and is open daily from 9 am to 6 pm; entry fee is US$1.

The jumping-off point for Roldanillo is Zarzal on the Pan-American Highway, easily accessible from most major towns in the region. Busetas to Roldanillo depart from Zarzal every 20 minutes from the corner of Carrera 11 and Calle 9 (US$0.40, 15 minutes). Watch out for the art works by various Latin American muralists and sculptors displayed along the road.

## ARMENIA

• *pop 240,000* • *1550 m* • *22˚C* • ☎ *(967)*

Armenia was founded by Antioquian colonists as late as 1889. The town developed quickly around coffee production, and in 1966 it became the capital of the newly created department of Quindío. Today, Armenia is a modern though rather unexciting city. It does have an excellent museum and an interesting market, but the city is slim on other sights.

The city has a pleasant climate, although it rains quite often between March and May and between September and November. A handicraft fair is held during the second week of October.

Whereas the city itself is not a great attraction, the surrounding region is well worth exploring. Quindío, Colombia's smallest department (except for the San Andrés archipelago), covers a mere 0.16% of the country's area, but it has a lot to offer. It shares a part of the mighty Parque Nacional Los Nevados and has a number of smaller nature reserves

including the lovely Reserva Natural Acaime. The department also has several attractive towns founded by Antioquian settlers. They are all easily accessible from Armenia.

### Information

**Tourist Office** Corporación Municipal de Fomento y Turismo (☎ 410441, 410509), at Calle 20 No 15-31, is open Monday to Friday from 8 am to noon and 2 to 6 pm. You may also try the Dirección de Cultura, Artesanía y Turismo on the ground floor of the Gobernación del Quindío building on the Plaza de Bolívar. It opens for the same hours as the Corporación's office.

**Money** Cash can be exchanged at the Banco Popular and Banco Industrial Colombiano; the latter also changes travellers' cheques, and it's perhaps the only bank in the city to do so. Visa is accepted by the Banco de Bogotá, Banco de Colombia, Banco Popular and Banco del Estado, whereas MasterCard transactions are handled by the Banco Industrial Colombiano and Banco de Occidente.

**CRQ** Corporación Autónoma Regional del Quindío (☎ 412490, 412578, 412878; fax 410256), at Carrera 17 No 18-20, Piso 4, is a local government organisation which focuses on environmental conservation and promotes ecotourism. A number of nature reserves have been created in the department, some of which have tourist facilities. The following is a brief outline of selected reserves.

**Guayaquil** Guayaquil is the cabaña in the Reserva del Cañón del Alto Quindío. The reserve covers about 45 sq km of cloudforest around the upper course of the Río Quindío, just below the boundaries of Parque Nacional Los Nevados and above the Reserva Natural Acaime. Guayaquil, located at 3115 metres, offers accommodation for 25 visitors (US$6 per person), and has cooking facilities but you must bring your own food. A campsite is to be opened soon. There are different walking routes from the cabaña including an ascent to the páramo.

**Navarco** Navarco is a station for biological field study in the Reserva Navarco-Altamira. The

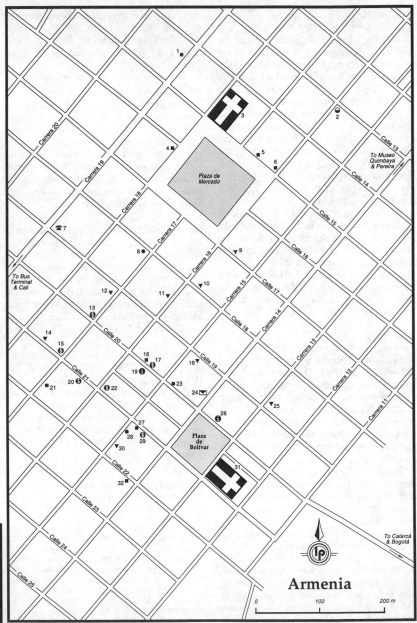

Armenia

## PLACES TO STAY

1 Hotel San Francisco
4 Hotel Hawaii
5 Residencias Centenario
6 Hotel Erasmo
16 Hotel Zuldemayda
21 Hotel Maitamá
23 Hotel Internacional
27 Hotel Palatino
32 Hotel Izcay

## PLACES TO EAT

9 Restaurante El Portón Quindiano
10 Restaurante Manjar Vegetariano
11 Restaurante Rincón Vegetariano
12 Restaurante El Rancho
14 Punto Rojo
18 Restaurante Rincón Quindiano
25 La Fonda Antioqueña
30 Pollo Frito Frisby

## OTHER

2 Minibuses to Circasia, Filandia & Salento
3 Iglesia de San Francisco
7 Telecom
8 Corporación Autónoma Regional del Quindío (CRQ)
13 Banco de Colombia
15 Banco de Bogotá
17 Banco Industrial Colombiano
19 Corporación Municipal de Fomento y Turismo
20 Banco Popular
22 Banco de Occidente
24 Avianca & Post Office
26 Dirección de Cultura, Artesanía y Turismo
28 Aces Office
29 Banco del Estado
31 Catedral

reserve lies about 20 km east of Armenia, next to the road to Ibagué, and encompasses 45 sq km. The station, set at 2920 metres, is a 45-minute walk from the road and has lodging for 14 visitors (US$6 per person).

**Bremen** Named by its former German owners, this six-sq-km finca, on the road to Pereira, past the turn-off to Salento, is now a reserve. Set at about 1900 metres, it's covered with partly natural forest, and partly reforested pine. There are various trails leading though the forest.

**El Jardín** This reserve lies about 50 km south of Armenia, in the southernmost tip of the Quindío department. It is an hour's rough ride by jeep south from Génova, a beautiful village picturesquely set in a deep valley. The reserve itself covers 2.25 sq km of land pitched between 2300 and 2650 metres. The diverse vegetation includes native forest and some spectacular ferns. A cabaña for eight visitors is under construction.

Trips to these and other nature reserves have to be organised with CRQ through its Armenia office. Read the Reserva Natural Acaime section for further ecotourism options.

### Plaza de Bolívar & Catedral

The Plaza de Bolívar is adorned with two monuments. One of them, predictably, is a monument to Bolívar, but unlike those in Pereira and Manizales, this statue is traditional. It was cast in Paris by a Colombian artist, Roberto Henao Buriticá, and unveiled on 17 December 1930, the centenary of Bolívar's death. The other monument on the square is the Monumento al Esfuerzo, yet another of many Arenas Betancur's extravaganzas.

The modern, tent-like Catedral de la Inmaculada Concepción houses the Byzantine-inspired mural of Christ and a series of abstract stained-glass windows.

### Museo Quimbaya

Also referred to as the Museo del Oro, this is one of the three Banco de la República's regional museums featuring the Quimbaya culture (the other two are in Pereira and Manizales). Armenia's museum is by far the best of these. There's a large collection of excellent ceramics and some extraordinary gold artefacts.

The museum is in the spacious, modern Centro Cultural, on the north-eastern outskirts of the city, five km from the centre, on the road to Pereira. To get there, take a local bus from behind the Gobernación del Quindío building, just off the Plaza de Bolívar, which will drop you in front of the museum. It is open Tuesday to Friday from

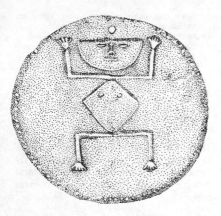

Quimbaya hammered-gold pectoral disc

10 am to 6 pm, Saturday and Sunday from 10 am to 5 pm. There are usually exhibitions of modern art held in the other part of the Centro Cultural building.

### Plaza de Mercado

Armenia has an unusually large and interesting market. Make sure you visit the basketry stalls, in the southern corner of the market building, where there's a surprising variety of baskets. It's hard to resist buying at least one.

The market also houses a series of herb stalls in the central part of the building. Watch out for El Remedio Botánico, the largest stand, claiming to have 3000 herb species! Even if it is not quite this number, you probably won't have seen such an impressive collection.

### Places to Stay – bottom end

If you are just passing through, it's probably most convenient to stay somewhere near the bus terminal, for example at the *Residencias El Viajero* (☎ 476692), at Carrera 19 No 34-21. It's basic but acceptable and costs US$4.50/7 for a single or matrimonio without/with bath. You can eat in its restaurant downstairs.

In the city centre, the majority of the budget hotels are clustered around the market. Some of them are bordellos, but you can usually recognise them by the prostitutes waiting at the entrance. Possibly the cheapest, acceptable option is the basic *Residencias Centenario* (☎ 455761), at Calle 15 No 16-38. Small, dark matrimonios without/with bath cost US$3/4, while doubles go for US$5/6.

Appreciably better is the *Hotel Erasmo* (☎ 456298), at Carrera 16 No 14-50, where bright, clean singles/matrimonios/doubles with own bath cost US$4/5/7. Alternatively, try the *Hotel Hawaii* (☎ 410724), at Carrera 18 No 16-10, which costs much the same. Inspect rooms before paying because they vary in size and quality. None of the hotels listed above have hot water.

The *Hotel San Francisco* (☎ 443600) is unattractively located on a busy thoroughfare in a rather shabby area, at Carrera 19 No 14-22. Nevertheless, it's not bad value for money. The rooms are rather small but they do have TV, video and bath with hot water, and cost US$8/11 a single or matrimonio/double.

### Places to Stay – middle & top end

The *Hotel Izcay* (☎ 410266), at Calle 22 No 14-05, is well located just one block from the Plaza de Bolívar, and is a good option. Ample, bright singles/doubles/triples cost US$22/28/35.

The *Hotel Palatino* (☎ 412730), at Calle 21 No 14-49, may be an interesting proposition if you're travelling in a larger party. It has rooms to accommodate one to five persons, costing US$22/28/34/40/46, respectively.

You may also want to check the *Hotel Zuldemayda* (☎ 410580), at Calle 20 No 15-38, though its rooms are rather small. Or try the *Hotel Maitamá* (☎ 410034), at Carrera 17 No 21-29, which is friendly but in urgent need of refurbishing.

The best central option is the *Hotel Internacional* (☎ 412921), at Calle 20 No 14-56. The airy singles/doubles cost US$40/55, but if you are in a group of three or four, enquire about the apartamento, which is a flat complete with kitchen and pots and pans, for US$60. Breakfast is included in these prices.

## Places to Eat

Food is quite inexpensive and good in Armenia. There's a number of restaurants which serve tasty set meals (US$1.50 to US$2) and a choice of regional food. To name a few: *El Portón Quindiano*, at Calle 17 No 15-40; *Rincón Quindiano*, at Calle 19 No 14-47; and *El Rancho*, at Carrera 17 No 19-10.

The newly opened *La Fonda Antioqueña*, at Carrera 13 No 18-55, is a pleasant place. Its interior is divided into several separate spaces, all laid out in guadua wood. It has set meals plus Antioquian specialities. The bandeja paisa shouldn't disappoint you.

The market offers some of the cheapest food in town. The stands serving meals are upstairs, right above the area where meat is sold.

For a vegetarian meal, choose between the *Rincón Vegetariano*, at Carrera 16 No 18-30, and *Manjar Vegetariano*, just 50 metres away at Calle 18 No 15-52. Both are on the 1st floor, serving set meals for US$1.75, and are open till 8 pm except Sunday.

There are several classier restaurants outside the central area in the northern residential district. One of the best of them is *La Fogata*, at Avenida Bolívar No 14N-39. It serves international food.

## Getting There & Away

**Air** El Edén Airport is 18 km south-west of the city, near the town of La Tebaida on the road to Cali. Aces has four flights a day to Bogotá (US$48), where connecting flights can take you to other cities. The Aces office is at Carrera 15 No 21-27.

**Bus** All long-distance buses arrive at and leave from the bus terminal on the corner of Carrera 19 and Calle 35. It is 1.5 km south-west of the centre and can be reached by frequent city buses which run along Carrera 19.

**To Bogotá** There are plenty of buses operated by several bus companies (US$11.25 climatizado, US$10 pullman, eight hours). Most of these come through from either Pereira or Cali.

**To Cali** A bus from one of several companies should depart every 15 to 30 minutes (US$7 climatizado, US$6 pullman, four hours).

**To Pereira** Flota Occidental runs busetas every 15 minutes (US$1.50, one hour).

**To Medellín** Flota Occidental pullmans depart every hour until late (US$11.25, seven hours).

**To Circasia** Nuevo Rápido Quindío has departures from the bus terminal every half an hour (US$0.35). Also, there are minibuses every 15 minutes from the corner of Carrera 16 and Calle 13 in the city centre.

**To Filandia** Buses with Nuevo Rápido Quindío depart hourly from the terminal (US$0.80, one hour), while minibuses from the centre run every 40 minutes (US$1.25, 45 minutes).

**To Salento** Expreso Alcalá has four buses a day from the terminal (US$1, one hour); minibuses from the centre depart hourly (US$1.25, 50 minutes).

**To Roldanillo** Nuevo Rápido Quindío has buses to Zarzal every 40 minutes (US$1.50, two hours), from where you catch frequent busetas to Roldanillo (US$0.40, 15 minutes).

## CALARCÁ

• *pop 40,000* • *1620 m* • *21°C* • ☎ *(967)*

The second-largest town of Quindío is Calarcá, just seven km to the east of Armenia. The two towns are separated by a deep narrow valley of the Río Quindío. Calarcá was founded in 1886 and was a handsome small town, but it has since experienced rapid growth as a satellite of the capital, losing much of its old character. Yet it still has some fine Antioquian houses, most of which can be found in the vicinity of the Iglesia de San José. The market is lively and colourful and is housed in an interesting old building.

Urban buses between Armenia and Calarcá run every few minutes, so it's a short and easy trip, and worth doing if you are already that close.

## CIRCASIA

• *pop 12,000* • *1770 m* • *19°C* • ☎ *(967)*

Circasia, just 12 km north of Armenia, was founded in 1884 by paisas from Sonsón, Abejorral and La Unión, and still has a collection of fine old houses around its main plaza and nearby streets. However, Circasia's major attraction is its Cementerio

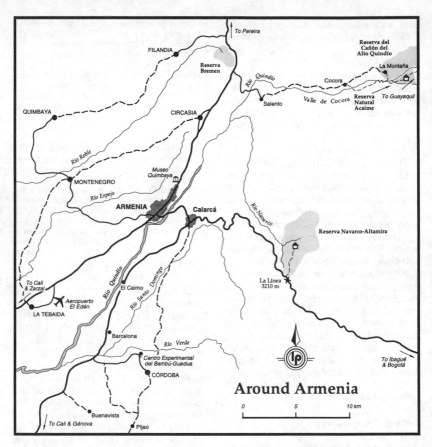

**Around Armenia**

0          5          10 km

Libre, founded in 1930. This was the first cemetery in South America to inter people of all religious persuasions.

The first three decades of the present century, known in Colombian politics as La Hegemonía, were a period of strong conservative rule, traditionally based around the Catholic Church. Despite constitutionally granted religious liberties, non-Catholics, or even Catholics who commited suicide, were virtually banned from burial in cemeteries. In an attempt to break with tradition, a group of free-minded citizens of Circasia took up the challenge of creating a 'Monumento a la

Libertad, la Tolerancia y el Amor' – as they called it.

The cemetery is small and immaculately kept. Engraved in the marble slab at the entrance is the *Himno de los Muertos* (Hymn of the Dead). Once you ascend a flight of stairs, you'll find the grave of Enrique Londoño, one of the founders of the cemetery. His is the oldest tomb, erected in 1930, and recognisable by the eagle on the top.

The cemetery is still in use. Anybody of any faith can be buried there, but the burial fee of US$150 is prohibitive to many people. After five years the remains are taken out of the grave and put into one of the four ossuaries, without any further costs. To this day, Catholics refuse to be buried in this cemetary regarding it as shameful to be interred next to non-Catholics.

The cemetery is nine blocks west of the main plaza, a 10-minute walk along Carrera 15. It's open daily from 10 am to noon and 4 to 6 pm. If it's closed, ask for the keys in the house with the red doors and windows, just by the right-hand side of the cemetery's gate.

Circasia is serviced by frequent buses and minibuses from Armenia.

## FILANDIA
• *pop 4500* • *1930 m* • *18°C* • ☎ *(967)*

Filandia, a small town 30 km north of Armenia, is probably the best example of a typical pueblo left behind by Antioquian settlers in Quindío. Filandia has preserved its character better than many other towns, and its traditional architecture still prevails, with only the occasional intrusion of modern buildings. Uninterrupted lines of brightly painted houses dating from the beginning of the century still stand on many streets.

There are two budget residencias on the main square. Buses/busetas between Armenia and Filandia run every hour/40 minutes, respectively. You can easily include a visit to Filandia and Circasia into a daytrip, and finish up with a visit to Armenia's Gold Museum, as they are all on the same route.

## SALENTO
• *pop 3000* • *1900 m* • *18°C* • ☎ *(967)*

Founded in 1850, Salento is perhaps the oldest town in Quindío, and it's just about the smallest. A local saying charmingly summarises it: *el pueblo de calles cortas y recuerdos largos* ('the town of short streets and long memories').

Salento is a lovely place which gives the impression that the 20th century got lost somewhere down the road. Its plaza and main street, Calle Real (Carrera 6), have some fine old houses, and its proximity to Los Nevados gives the town a noticeable mountain atmosphere and appearance.

However, the main attractions are outside the town, further to the east. Climb the Alto de la Cruz, a hill topped with a cross at the end of Calle Real, and you'll see the verdant Valle de Cocora with the mountains in the background. If the sky is cloudless (usually only early in the morning), you can spot the snow-capped tops of the volcanoes on the horizon.

### Places to Stay & Eat
The only hospedaje in town is at Calle 2 No 6-08. It's rustic but clean and pleasant and costs US$6 per double bed (single or matrimonio). There are two or three restaurants on Calle Real so you won't starve.

You can also stay and eat in *Los Bohíos*, two km of Salento on the road to Cocora.

### Getting There & Away
There are four buses daily to Armenia (US$1, one hour) and minibuses departing roughly every hour (US$1.25, 50 minutes).

A lechero comes through from Armenia and goes up the rough road to Cocora at about 7 am. It costs US$1 but takes about an hour because it frequently stops to collect milk. A jeep to Cocora departs at around 7.30 am (US$1, 35 minutes). It usually waits for the first bus to arrive from Armenia, but if it already has its fill of six passengers it won't wait. There may be later departures, but you either have to wait until six passengers have been collected or pay for the empty seats (US$1 each). Otherwise, you can hitch or do the very pleasant two-hour walk.

### COCORA
Cocora, 10 km east of Salento by dirt road, is just a collection of houses, two restaurants serving delicious trout, and the trout breeding station. The trout farm is open for visitors on Saturday afternoon and all day Sunday; the entrance fee is US$0.50.

All this may not sound alluring, but do come: Cocora is the best place in Colombia (and in the world) to see the 'forests' of *palma de cera (Ceroxylon quindiuense)*, a very particular palm. Literally the 'wax palm', this is perhaps the tallest palm species in the world, growing up to 60 metres. It has an unusually slim trunk and is the only palm that can grow at altitudes above 2500 metres. Some specimens have been seen as high as 3300 metres, but they also grow at low altitudes. In 1985, the palma de cera was declared Colombia's national tree.

Take the rough road heading downhill to the east of Cocora to the bridge over the Río Quindío (just a five-minute walk) and you will see hills covered with wax palms – a rare sight.

The palms have made Cocora a tourist destination, with visitors mainly arriving on weekends. On these days locals gather around the two restaurants to rent out horses (US$2.50 per hour). There doesn't seem to be any regular accommodation in Cocora.

See the Salento section for how to get to Cocora. On weekends it's quite easy to get a lift from Cocora in one of the tourists' cars; just hang around the area where they park and strike up a conversation.

## RESERVA NATURAL ACAIME

Reserva Natural Acaime is a nature reserve run by Fundación Herencia Verde, independently of CRQ. It lies on the slopes of Los Nevados between about 2600 and 3100 metres, above the Valle de Cocora, in a fork formed by the Río Quindío and Quebrada Las Mirlas. Most of the reserve's two-sq-km area is covered by cloudforest.

Acaime offers lodging and eating facilities in its cabaña, set at 2800 metres in the middle of the reserve. A guide service is provided free of charge on weekends (tipping is up to you).

There are paths through the forest which lead to several interesting spots, including El Mirador (a 20-minute climb from the cabaña) which offers good views over the Valle de Cocora. Other trails lead to a waterfall (15 minutes) and some old Indian tombs.

The 4.5-km access path from Cocora to the reserve goes through some spectacular and varied scenery along the Río Quindío. The path crosses the river seven times over a series of lovely small bridges. This is the Sendero de Interpretación del Bosque de Niebla Andino (Interpretation Path of Andean Cloudforest). The guides will give you a commentary as you tread the path.

The area is rich in flora and fauna, and birds are easy to spot. About 200 bird species have been identified in the reserve. Hummingbirds are fed around the cabaña and can be observed in detail. They make an amazing spectacle.

Uphill from Acaime is the CRQ-run Reserva del Cañón del Alto Quindío which stretches up to the borders of the Parque Nacional Los Nevados. You can walk to the Guayaquil cabaña in about 2½ hours. See CRQ in the Armenia section for further information.

### Places to Stay & Eat

The reserve's cabaña has lodging for 20 visitors and serves meals for guests for US$18 per person a day inclusive. It has to be booked and pre-paid in Salento, in the office of Herencia Verde (☎ 593142), at Carrera 6 No 2-17. Camping in the reserve is not permitted. Herencia's head office is in Cali, at Calle 4 Oeste No 3A-32 (☎ 808484, 813257).

### Getting There & Away

Acaime is 4.5 km east of Cocora. From Cocora's restaurants, take the road descending to the bridge over the Río Quindío (a five-minute walk). Cross the bridge and follow the path up the valley. The valley in this part is grassy and wide and the mountain slopes on both sides are covered with picturesque wax palms. The path runs roughly parallel to the river but at some distance from it. After a steady 50-minute walk uphill you enter the cloudforest. The valley becomes narrow and the path sticks to the river. You cross the river five times over five consecutive bridges before the path divides (another 30-minute walk to this point). The left fork leads uphill to La Montaña, the conservation station of CRQ. Take the right path which descends back to the river. It crosses the river twice more before ascending steeply up to the Acaime cabaña (a 25-minute walk from the fork to the cabaña). The walk back downhill to Cocora takes about 1½ hours.

You can also do this trip on horseback. The locals in Cocora hang around the restaurants and offer horse excursions (US$2.50 per hour). The round trip to Acaime, including an hour's wait in the reserve while you look around, costs about US$10 per person.

If you arrive at Salento during a weekend and book the cabaña at Herencia's office, you are likely to be accompanied by one of its guides all the way from Salento (where most guides live) to the cabaña.

## PARQUE NACIONAL LOS NEVADOS

Los Nevados, shared by the Caldas, Risaralda, Quindío and Tolima departments, covers 583 sq km of highlands of the Cordillera Central. Its axis is formed by a volcanic range, oriented north-south, and topped with several volcanic peaks. The main peaks, from north to south, are: El Ruiz (5325 metres), El Cisne (4750 metres), Santa Isabel (4950 metres), El Quindío (4750 metres) and El Tolima (5215 metres).

The Nevado del Ruiz is the largest and the highest volcano of the chain. Its eruption on 13 November 1985 took the life of over 20,000 people. Hot gases melted a part of the snow cap and swollen rivers of mud cascaded down the eastern slopes, sweeping away everything in their path.

Armero, a thriving town of about 25,000 inhabitants on the Río Lagunillas, disappeared entirely under the mud. Several other towns and villages in the region also suffered greatly. Even some distant regions, such as Boyacá, were covered with a thick layer of ash. El Ruiz had previously erupted in 1845 but the results were far less catastrophic.

Today, it seems that the volcano has returned to its slumber, and its activity is limited to an occasional puff of smoke hovering over the crater. It can wake up, however, at any time and several alerts have been raised over the past decade when the volcano's smoke was bigger than usual.

The Nevado del Tolima, the second highest volcano in the chain, is the most handsome of all with its classic symmetrical cone. On a clear day it can be seen from as far away as Bogotá. Its last eruption took place in 1943, but today it is considered almost extinct.

The park, stretching from about 2500 metres up to its highest peaks, covers various climatic zones and, consequently, its environments range from humid Andean cloudforest, through the páramos to perpetual snows.

There are several mountain lakes in the park, mostly in the páramos between 3800 and 4200 metres. The Laguna del Otún is the largest.

### Orientation

The only road access into the park is from the north. This road branches off from the Manizales-Honda road and winds up to the snowline at about 4700 metres at the foot of Nevado del Ruiz. The volcano actually has three craters: Arenas, Olleta and Piraña. The main one, Arenas (5325 metres), responsible for the 1985 disaster, has a diameter of 800 metres and is about 200 metres deep. It's a three-hour hike from the road up to the top. You walk on snow but the ascent is relatively easy and no special mountaineering equipment is necessary.

The extinct Olleta crater (4850 metres), on the opposite side of the road, is covered with multicoloured layers of sandy soil and normally has no snow. The walk to the top will take about 1¼ hours from the road, and it's possible to descend into the crater. See Tours and Guides in the Manizales section for information concerning the northern part of the park and the Nevado del Ruiz.

The road continues for another 38 km along El Cisne and Santa Isabel down to the Laguna del Otún, a large, beautiful lake at 3950 metres.

The southern part of the park is accessible only by foot. From Pereira, you can go to the Parque Ucumarí (see that section for details) and continue from Refugio La Pastora along a 15-km trail (partially through a spectacular canyon) to the Laguna del Otún. This is normally a two-day round trip. Add one day if you want to take a side trip to the Laguna La Leona (4050 metres). However, it sometimes dries up during the dry season. The

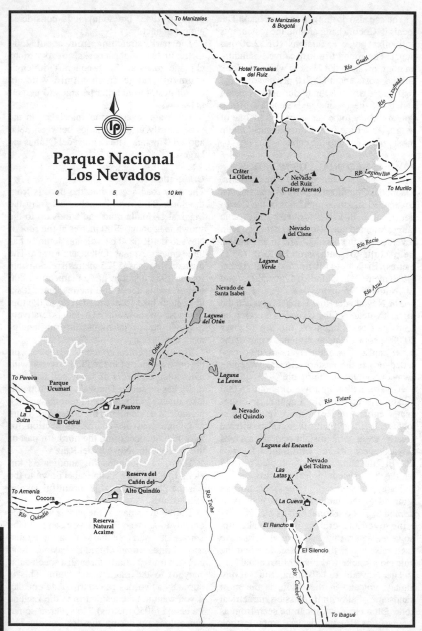

Parque Nacional
Los Nevados

0   5   10 km

water, when it's there, is sulphurous and there are no fish in it.

Another access route to the park is from the Reserva Natural Acaime (see that section) or the Reserva del Cañón del Alto Quindío (see CRQ in the Armenia section). From Guayaquil it's a three-hour walk up to the páramo, and you can continue on to the Nevado del Quindío. El Quindío volcano is considered extinct and you can camp in its crater.

The most spectacular trip in the southern part of the park is a trek to the top of the Nevado del Tolima. Although there are various routes, the most popular trail begins in El Silencio at the southern foot of the volcano; it is described below.

Some adventurous trekkers may consider a hike south to north (or vice versa) across the park over the whole chain of volcanic peaks. You should allow a week for this trek and buy 1:25,000 scale maps at the Instituto Geográfico Agustín Codazzi in Bogotá. Don't forget to get your permit from Inderena. Guides can be contracted in Manizales, and possibly in Pereira, Armenia and Ibagué as well.

### When to Go

The best months to trek in Los Nevados are January and February. December, March, July and August can be relatively good but you are less sure of good weather. The rest of the year is quite rainy and the volcanoes are usually hidden in the clouds, showing themselves only on occasional mornings.

### Nevado del Tolima Trek

The principal gateway for the trek to the Nevado del Tolima is Ibagué. A dirt road leads from there to Juntas, a village 20 km away. The road continues up to El Silencio (2600 metres), which is just a house and a small shop where basic food can be bought (you're better off shopping in Ibagué). The road between Juntas and El Silencio skirts around the edge of a magnificent, 200-metre-deep gorge of the Río Combeima and is a splendid scenic walk (three hours). Preferably, walk this stretch downhill after coming

back down from the volcano. There is virtually no transportation on this road except the morning lechero and the occasional cars of tourists visiting the thermal baths in El Rancho.

Three trails begin at El Silencio and go up to the top of Tolima. They are known to trekkers as the Camino del Inderena, the Camino del Filtro and the Camino de la Cueva; the latter is the shortest and the most popular. Plan on three days of walking to complete this trek (some hikers do it in two days, but it's strenuous). The trail has deteriorated over recent years and can be impassable during the rainy season. Be particularly careful in cloudy conditions – it's easy to get lost, especially in the upper parts. Don't attemp to climb the summit if it's clouded.

Camino de la Cueva leads from El Silencio to El Rancho along the river valley, an easy 45-minute walk. El Rancho (2600 metres) has thermal baths and a restaurant with basic food. You might be able to stay overnight. The baths are popular among tourists who come here mainly on weekends.

From El Rancho, a clear but often muddy trail climbs up the slope of the valley and enters the cloudforest. You need three to four hours to get to La Cueva (3800 metres). This is just a primitive wooden shelter built under the overhanging rock on the right-hand side of the trail shortly after you come out of the forest. The shelter is littered and has a dirt floor; be sure to bring a sheet of plastic with you if you want to stay overnight.

The trail enters the páramo and shortly afterwards merges with the Camino del Inderena, joining it from the right. The páramo stretches over quite a distance. Further up, the scenery changes to bare rock and the trail becomes faint, and finally disappears. Head up towards the big cross which is visible from a distance. It is known to hikers as Las Latas (4450 metres), and is the only acceptable place to camp around. Water is available from a nearby stream. It will take you three hours to get from La Cueva to Las Latas.

Next day, start out very early and head

directly towards the top of the volcano. There is no trail to follow. The snowline is at about 4800 metres, and you will probably need crampons from here on; sunglasses are also recommended. The first part of the climb on the snow is quite steep but later it flattens out. From Las Latas, you should be able to get to the top within four hours.

If the weather is clear, the view from the top is magnificent and stretches as far as the Nevado del Ruiz (about 25 km away). Be very careful when approaching the edge of the crater, which is a breathtaking hole about 100 metres deep and some 40 metres in diameter. The sulphur smell indicates that the volcano is 'breathing', although it hasn't done more than that in over 50 years. The hike back, straight to El Silencio, can be done in five to six hours.

### Getting There & Away
From Ibagué, Transportes La Ibaguereña, at Carrera 1 No 13-12, has chivas to Juntas every hour from 6 am (US$1, one hour). The lechero at 7.30 am goes as far as El Silencio (US$2, two hours).

# Tolima

## IBAGUÉ
• *pop 390,000 • 1285 m • 22˚C • ☎ (982)*
Ibagué appeared on the map as early as 1550, when the Spanish conquerors established a resting place on the trail between Bogotá and Popayán, after defeating the particularly fierce Panche Indians who lived in the region.

Today, Ibagué is a large commercial centre serving the agriculture and cattle farming in the region. It's the capital of Tolima and a quarter of the department's population lives here. Despite the city's long history, you won't find anything reminiscent of colonial architecture. In fact, there's not much to see or do at all.

Ibagué is known as the musical capital of Colombia; its Conservatory of Music was founded in 1906.

### Information
**Tourist Office** Turtolima is on the 1st floor in the pavilion on Carrera 3 between Calles 10 and 11, at the back of the cathedral. It is open Monday to Friday from 8 am to noon and 2 to 6 pm.

**Money** Most banks are on or just off Carrera 3. You will find their location on the map.

### Things to See
You can visit the Museo de Antropología and the Jardín Botánico Alejandro von Humboldt, although neither of these is of any special interest. The museum holds a small collection of pre-Columbian pottery, and the botanical gardens have about 500 species of trees and plants, but are poorly maintained. Both the museum and the gardens are located at the Universidad del Tolima, on the corner of Carrera 1 and Calle 41 in the Barrio Santa Elena. It's about three km south-east of the centre; take an urban bus marked 'Estadio' or 'Mirolindo' from Carrera 4.

### Festivals & Events
The International Polyphonic Competition is held in December of every second year. The Festival Folklórico Colombiano takes place at the end of June.

### Places to Stay – bottom end
Like most cities of its size, Ibagué has lots of hotels. Many of them are clustered in a two-block-wide belt (between Carreras 2 and 4), stretching between the Parque López de Galarza and Plaza de Bolívar. As a general rule, the prices and standards of hotels tend to rise the nearer they are to the Plaza de Bolívar.

There's at least a dozen bottom-end residencias between Carreras 3 and 4 and Calles 16 and 18. Most of them are basic and scruffy, and do much of their business on an hourly basis serving prostitutes. At the very bottom end you can expect to pay around US$3/4/5 for a single/couple/double with shared bath facilities. There's not much to recommend among these hotels; just have a look at a few of them and take your pick.

Perhaps slightly better than others in the neighbourhood is the *Residencias Acapulco* (☎ 632566), at Carrera 4 No 16-31. Singles/doubles without bath cost US$4/7 while rooms with bath go for US$7/8.

There are a few more decent hotels in the same area, of which the *Hotel Suiza* (☎ 611271), at Calle 17 No 3-19, is possibly the best. Good, airy rooms with private bath and hot water cost US$7/10/12. Alternatively, try the marginally cheaper *Hotel Bolivariano* (☎ 633487), at Calle 17 No 3-119, but it has cold water only.

### Places to Stay – middle

If you need somewhere inexpensive with a TV in your room, choose between the *Hotel Farallones* (☎ 633339), at Calle 16 No 2-88, and the *Hotel Cordillera No 1* (☎ 611084), at Calle 16 No 2-89, right opposite one another. The former costs US$10/13/16 a single/double/triple and has hot water; the latter is a dollar more expensive, and has better rooms but with cold water only. Yet another option for much the same price is the quiet *Hotel Cordillera No 2* (☎ 600180), at Calle 14A No 2-41.

There's no shortage of mid-priced hotels in the city centre, including the *Hotel Ambeima* (☎ 634300), at Carrera 3 No 13-32 (US$14/17/23), *Hotel Athabasca* (☎ 611092), at Carrera 2 No 14-68 (US$16/19/24), and *Hotel Bremen* (☎ 633514), at Calle 14 No 3-19 (US$15/18/23). The last of this list is the friendliest and the best of the lot.

The *Hotel Lusitania* (☎ 639166), at Carrera 2 No 15-55, is a motel with a swimming pool and costs US$18/23/28 for a single/double/triple.

### Places to Stay – top end

Top-end hotels include the *Nelson's Inn Hotel* (☎ 611810), at Calle 13 No 2-94 (US$25/30/35), and the *Hotel Pacandé* (☎ 610010), at Carrera 3 No 11-60 (US$40/50).

### Places to Eat

Many budget restaurants serve comidas for around US$1.50. For example, try *El Mesón*

Ubiquitous Colombian spirit

*Tolimense*, at Calle 16 No 3-95, which also has some inexpensive regional dishes.

Cheap food can also be found at the markets – the Plaza de la 21, on the corner of Calle 21 and Carrera 4, and the Plaza Chapinero, corner of Calle 14 and Carrera 1.

Carreras 2 and 3 are packed with various food establishments serving chicken, pizzas, snacks, sweets etc. Two of them are *Burger Pizza*, at Carrera 3 No 9-59 (Plaza de Bolívar), and *Pollo Frito Frisby*, at Carrera 3 No 12-33.

The *Restaurante Chamaco*, at Calle 13 No 2-60, has good, reasonably priced local food and is particularly renowned for its tamal tolimense. The *Restaurante Marcos* on the corner of Carrera 3 and Calle 12 (1st floor) has good Spanish-influenced food and a long list of fish and seafood.

Vegetarians have a choice between *Govinda's*, at Calle 13 No 1-57, and *Restaurante Tienda Vegetariana*, at Calle 14A No 2-24.

You should sample the local dishes such as lechona, tamales and viudo de pescado. Lechona is rarely available in the restaurants,

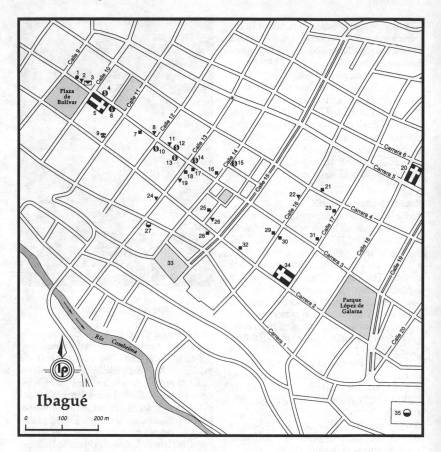

Ibagué

0      100      200 m

35 ⊖

but can be found at markets. On Sunday and holidays it's served from stalls which spring up along Calle 19 between Carreras 2 and 3.

## Getting There & Away

**Air** The Perales Airport is about 10 km east of the city centre, off the road to Bogotá. A taxi shouldn't cost more than US$5. All flights are operated by Aires. It flies six times a day to Bogotá (US$32), and once daily to Medellín (US$53), Cali (US$47), Neiva (US$35) and Florencia (US$67). Tickets can be bought from the Aires city office, at Carrera 3 No 9-43.

**Bus** The bus terminal is on the corner of Carrera 1 and Calle 20, an easy walk to the city centre and all hotels listed above. Set on the Bogotá-Cali highway, Ibagué has plenty of buses running east and west along this road.

**To Bogotá** Expreso Bolivariano is the major operator on this route, but several other companies service Bogotá as well (US$7.50 climatizado, US$6.50 pullman, US$5.50 corriente, five hours).

**To Cali** A bus by one or other of several companies should depart every 15 to 30 minutes (US$9.50 climatizado, US$8.50 pullman, seven hours).

## PLACES TO STAY

| | |
|---|---|
| 7 | Hotel Pacandé |
| 16 | Hotel Bremen |
| 17 | Hotel Ambeima |
| 18 | Nelson's Inn Hotel |
| 21 | Residencias Acapulco |
| 23 | Hotel Bolivariano |
| 25 | Hotel Cordillera No 2 |
| 28 | Hotel Athabasca |
| 29 | Hotel Cordillera No 1 |
| 30 | Hotel Farallones |
| 31 | Hotel Suiza |
| 32 | Hotel Lusitania |

## PLACES TO EAT

| | |
|---|---|
| 2 | Burger Pizza |
| 8 | Restaurante Marcos |
| 11 | Pollo Frito Frisby |
| 19 | Restaurante Chamaco |
| 22 | El Mesón Tolimense |
| 24 | Restaurante Vegetariano Govinda's |
| 26 | Restaurante Tienda Vegetariana |

## OTHER

| | |
|---|---|
| 1 | Aires Office |
| 3 | Avianca & Post Office |
| 4 | Banco de Colombia |
| 5 | Catedral |
| 6 | Turtolima Tourist Office |
| 9 | Telecom |
| 10 | Banco de Occidente |
| 12 | Banco de Bogotá |
| 13 | Banco del Estado |
| 14 | Banco Industrial Colombiano |
| 15 | Banco Popular |
| 20 | Iglesia del Carmen |
| 27 | Transportes La Ibaguereña |
| 33 | Plaza Chapinero |
| 34 | Iglesia de San Roque |
| 35 | Bus Terminal |

They all go via Armenia and some of them continue on to Popayán and Pasto.

**To Honda** Rápido Tolima has half-hourly departures (US$4.50 pullman, US$3.75 corriente, three hours). All these buses pass via Armero and Mariquita.

**To Ambalema** Rápido Ochoa has departures every three hours (US$2.50, 2½ hours).

**To El Silencio** Transportes La Ibaguereña has one lechero at 7.30 am, departing from the company office at Carrera 1 No 13-12 (US$2, two hours).

## GIRARDOT
• *pop 70,000* • *290 m* • *28˚C* • ☎ *(9834)*

Girardot is an undistinguished town on the east bank of the Río Magdalena, 130 km from Bogotá. The town lies in the south-western tip of Cundinamarca, but you're most likely to come here while travelling around Tolima, and therefore it has been included in this chapter.

Founded in 1852, it was once a thriving port but today the importance of the Magdalena as a waterway is insignificant. The climate is hot, and Bogotanos come here on weekends to relax and warm up. You may choose to do the same, though it's not a very attractive place to hang around.

You might like to visit the large, lively, two-storey market, between Calles 10 and 11 and Carreras 9 and 10, and walk across one of the two bridges that cross the Magdalena to see the river and the riverside part of town. Other than that, there is little to do here.

### Places to Stay
There are lots of hotels throughout the town, eagerly awaiting weekends when most tourists come. You are most likely to use them just as an overnight stop on your way to more interesting destinations, maybe Ambalema or Cueva del Cunday.

There are several hotels in the bus terminal area, of which the basic *Residencias Tamaco* is the cheapest (US$4/6 a single/double). In the town's centre, inexpensive places include the *Hotel Camellón* (☎ 25783), at Calle 16 No 9-52 (US$3.50/4.50 per person in rooms without/with own bath); the *Residencias Tex*, diagonally opposite at Calle 16 No 9-41 (the same price); and the *Nuevo Hotel Emperador* (☎ 22533), at Carrera 10 No 19-50 (US$5 per person in rooms with bath).

Far better than any of the above is the *Hotel Bocachica* (☎ 33708), at Carrera 9 No 18-39. It has good rooms with bath and TV, costing US$9 per person. For much the same you can stay in the large *Hotel Río*, at Carrera 10 No 16-37, which has preserved its atmosphere (but not its standards) of the post-war years when it was probably the poshest

THE NORTH-WEST

venue in town. The *Hotel Bachué* (☎ 34790), at Carrera 8 No 18-04, has air-con rooms, swimming pool and a restaurant, but costs US$40/50 a single/double.

*El Peñón* outside the town (US$5 by taxi from the centre) is a large recreational bungalow complex with a lake, swimming pool, restaurant, casino, disco and other facilities.

### Getting There & Away

**Bus** All buses arrive at and leave from the spacious bus terminal, 10 blocks east of the town's centre.

**To Bogotá** Buses operated by several companies run every 15 minutes or so (US$5.25 climatizado, US$4.50 pullman, US$3.75 corriente, three hours).

**To Cali** Buses coming through from Bogotá depart approximately every half-hour (US$13 climatizado, nine hours). They all go through Ibagué and Armenia.

**To Neiva** Buses go every half-hour (US$6.25 climatizado, US$5.50 pullman, US$4.50 corriente, three hours).

**To San Agustín** There are three buses daily, or you can go to Neiva, from where there are more departures.

**To Ambalema** Take a bus to Cambao (with Cooperativa de Transportes de Girardot), get off in Gramalotal (US$2.50, two hours) and take a boat across the Magdalena to Ambalema (US$0.30).

## CUEVA DEL CUNDAY

This is the nearest cave to Bogotá. It's about 10 km south-west of the town of Cunday in Tolima. The cave is long but not very high – in parts you have to walk bent double through narrow passageways. The stalactites and stalagmites are impressive. There are plenty of bats flying around, and the noise of the San Lorenzo River flowing through the cave adds to the mysterious atmosphere.

The cave has two entrances; the main one is from the lower end. After about a 20-minute walk through the cave you get to a place called El Baño. From here you can return the same way or continue for one hour to another entrance at the upper end of the cave. Wear your worst clothes and sensible shoes as the way is slippery in many parts. A

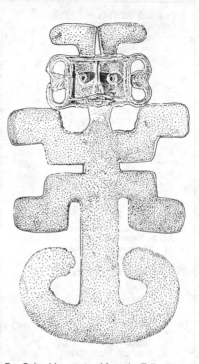

Pre-Columbian pectoral from the Tolima area

good torch is a must and you need more than one if you are in a group.

The cave has side galleries and it is possible to get lost. A guide is recommended if you want to go deeper into the cave. You can find one in the last house before the cave, a few hundred metres below. The boy living there knows the place well and is willing to show you through for a modest fee. Leave your gear in the house, as it is difficult to walk in the cave with a backpack.

### Places to Stay

The nearest accommodation is in Cunday, where there are several hospedajes. Possibly the best budget place is *Las Palmas* at the end of Calle 8 near the police station, a five-minute walk from the main plaza. It costs US$3 per person in a rustic room, but is quiet and pleasant. Otherwise you have *Las Acacias* on the main plaza, next to the church, at US$5 for a *matrimonio*, or the *Balmoral*, at Carrera 5 No 6-31, just off the square, which costs US$6 a double.

## Getting There & Away

The usual starting point for the cave is Cunday. There are several buses daily from Melgar to Cunday (US$2, 1½ hours); some of these buses come through from Bogotá or Girardot.

From Cunday, take a bus to Valencia or Tres Esquinas and get off in El Revés about five km from Cunday. If you leave early from Melgar you won't have to stop in Cunday, as most buses go through to Valencia and will drop you in El Revés.

From El Revés, walk along a dirt road branching off to the right for about three km until you get to a white house and a cattle gate on the road. Carry on for half a km more, passing three more cattle gates. Near the last one you will see a white concrete drinking trough for cattle, from where a path leads down to the Río Cunday. Cross the river and follow the path upstream, parallel to the river, until you pass a house, where the path turns up the hill. Ten minutes more and you get to the last house where you will find a guide. The cave is a 15-minute walk uphill from there but the path is almost nonexistent.

## AMBALEMA

• *pop 5500* • *240 m* • *28°C* • ☎ *(982)*
Ambalema is a charming colonial town on the bank of the Magdalena River, characterised by its unique architecture. The streets are lined with houses that have wide, overhanging tiled roofs supported on rustic, usually crooked wooden pillars. Note the decoration of the windows.

The town is unspoiled by tourism and the people are friendly. Cross over one of the two small bridges to the other section of the town to see some interesting old houses, particularly the Escuela María Auxiliadora and the Casa Inglesa. In the 18th century, the latter

was one of the most important tobacco-processing factories in the Americas.

## Places to Stay

The *Hotel Barcelona*, on the corner of Carrera 2 and Calle 8A, one block off the main plaza, is a pleasant though very simple place with shared bath facilities, and costs US$2 per person. If you don't want to be woken up at dawn by roosters, you will probably need earplugs. Also, beware of the psychotic parrot which likes to peck ankles.

Perhaps even more basic is the friendly *Hotel Magdalena* on the main square, at Calle 8A No 4-41. Doubles without/with bath in this slowly decaying colonial house cost US$3/5.

The best place to stay in town is the *Hotel Los Ríos*, at Carrera 6 No 21. Rooms in either the house or its cabañas cost US$7 per person (perhaps overpriced). There's a swimming pool in the compound which can be used free of charge by the hotel guests; nonguests have to pay a US$1 entrance fee.

## Places to Eat

One of the cheapest places is *Restaurante La Manuela*, on the corner of Calle 8 and Carrera 4, but it closes early in the afternoon. The *Hotel Barcelona* serves cheap set meals, as does the *Hotel Los Ríos* for a bit more. Other options include *Asadero de Pollo*, on the corner of Carrera 2 and Calle 8A, and a couple of simple eateries around the plaza.

## Getting There & Away

Buses and colectivos depart from the main plaza.

**To Ibagué** Rápido Ochoa has five buses daily (US$2.50, 2½ hours).
**To Bogotá** One bus a day goes to Bogotá via Mariquita, departing at 6 am (US$6.50, 5½ hours). Alternatively, take a colectivo to Cruce de Armero, then catch one of the half-hourly buses or a colectivo to Honda; from Honda there's frequent transport to Bogotá and Medellín.
Yet another possibility is via Girardot; cross the Magdalena River by boat to Gramalotal, from where there are regular buses to Girardot.

## ARMERO

Armero was a prosperous town of 25,000 inhabitants until 13 November 1985, when a swollen mud slide, caused by the eruption of the Nevado del Ruiz, buried it almost instantly with mud. Tragically, about 20,000 people lost their lives in what has been the largest disaster of its kind in the country's history. The layer of mud was so thick that only the second floors of the buildings escaped the flood. Now they stick out of the dried mud, as a bizarre, surrealistic reminder, marking what once was the heart of the town. Most of the buildings were one-storey structures which simply disappeared under the mud along with their dwellers.

One site, however, was fortunate to survive almost intact because it was on a hillside. Ironically enough, this was the town's cemetery.

The town was abandoned after the tragedy and the area turned into a vast, eerie cemetery, dotted with crosses left behind by the relatives and survivors where once there were houses. An open chapel topped with a tall white cross was built where Pope John Paul II celebrated mass during his visit to Colombia in 1986.

The town has never revived and remains a terrifying sight, though the landscape changed a lot. The climate and fertile mud have caused the ground to become overgrown with bushes and grass. Neglected and abandoned crosses still stick out through the grass but many have fallen into it. This only adds to the feeling of poignancy.

Many Mariquita-Ibagué buses pass through Armero, now called Cruce de Armero. It is just a pair of roadside soft-drink stands. If you are feeling up to strong impressions, stop here and have a look around.

## MARIQUITA

• *pop 25,000* • *495 m* • *27°C* • ☎ *(989)*

Mariquita, a town in the far north of Tolima, was founded in 1551. It was here that Gonzalo Jiménez de Quesada, the founder of Bogotá, died in 1579. Today, Mariquita is just an average town and the centre of the surrounding fruit-growing region.

There are still a handful of old houses dating from colonial times; you'll find them around the main square. Visit La Ermita, a lovely small, stone church a couple of blocks off the plaza. The house opposite the church is the former Casa de la Moneda, one of the oldest in town.

Mariquita is noted for its fruit, particularly the great variety of avocados and mangos. Sunday is market day, held in the main square.

### Places to Stay

The cheapest accommodation is in the area around the bus offices; for example, try the *Hotel El Terminal*, at Calle 7 No 5-26. It's nothing special but cheap at US$4/6 for a double without/with bath. Similar is the *Hotel Paisa*, at Calle 7 No 4-49. Marginally more expensive and better are the *Residencias Savoy*, at Carrera 4 No 7-50, and the *Hotel Imperial*, at Carrera 4 No 7-33. Probably the best in the area is the *Hotel Jari* (☎ 522392), at Calle 7 No 3-18, costing US$5/7 a single/double.

There are several better hotels in town, including the *Hotel Tolaima* (☎ 522282), on the corner of Carrera 4 and Calle 5, close to the plaza, and the *Hotel Las Acacias* (☎ 522016), on the corner of Carrera 4 and Calle 15, on the outskirts of town on the road to Ibagué.

### Getting There & Away

The bus company offices (Expreso Bolivariano, Rápido Tolima, Empresa Arauca and Velotax) are all on Calle 7 between Carreras 5 and 6.

**To Bogotá** All the listed companies operate buses to Bogotá (US$6.50 climatizado, US$5.75 pullman, four to 4½ hours); you shouldn't have to wait more than an hour for a departure.

**To Manizales** Rápido Tolima runs busetas (US$4.50, 3½ hours), while Expreso Bolivariano operates climatizados (US$6) and pullmans (US$5.25).

**To Ibagué** Rápido Tolima has half-hourly buses (US$3.25, 2½ hours).

**To Ambalema** Take the Ibagué bus, get off at Cruce de Armero (US$1, half an hour), from where colectivos depart to Ambalema (US$1.25, half an hour).

## HONDA
* *pop 40,000* • *230 m* • *28°C* • ☎ *(989)*

Set on the left bank of the Río Magdalena, Honda was the first river port in the interior of the colony. Originally an Indian settlement, it was come upon in 1539 by Gonzalo Jiménez de Quesada, Sebastián de Belalcázar and Nicolaus Federmann, the three conquerors at variance, on their way from the just-founded Bogotá back to Spain. A year later the Indians were eventually defeated by Baltazar de Maldonado and the town began to grow, taking advantage of its proximity to the capital. A century later Honda was the most important fluvial port in the interior of the colony and a busy trade centre.

The earthquake of 1805 affected 80% of the urban fabric but the importance of river transport in that period prompted a swift revival and kept the town developing for another century. Today, navigation on the Magdalena is of marginal importance but the town has turned into an important road-transport hub, as it sits on the convergence of the Bogotá, Medellín and Manizales roads.

For Bogotanos, Honda is a weekend holiday resort, where they come to warm up. An extensive array of hotels has been built over the past decades in and around the town, many of which contain swimming pools.

Honda has preserved some of its colonial architecture, though it's in deplorable shape. The authorities only recently realised the value of the town's cultural heritage and plan to restore the historic quarter. Honda is also known as a town of bridges.

The cobbled streets, old houses and bridges make Honda a pleasant stop if you are travelling this route. It's also worth strolling along the bank of the Magdalena (or hanging around on one of two bridges spanning the river) to watch the river life go by, particularly the fishermen with their atarrayas. February is the best month, as the fish migrate upriver and the fishermen are abundant. The Festival Nacional del Río y la Subienda is celebrated annually during that month.

Like many other towns in the region, Honda suffered from the eruption of the Nevado del Ruiz. You can still see the damaged hotel buildings along the bank of the Río Gualí.

### Information
**Tourist Office** The Oficina de Cultura y Turismo (☎ 514145) is in the Casa de los Conquistadores, one of the few restored colonial mansions. It's worth a visit for both good information and for the building itself. The office is open Monday to Friday from 7 am to noon and 2 to 5 pm, Saturday from 10 to 11.30 am.

### Things to See
The colonial quarter, south of the Río Gualí has been declared a national monument, though it will probably be a long time before it recovers its original splendour. It's noted for a few picturesque, narrow streets. The best known of these is Calle de las Trampas (Calle 12). Drop into the Plaza de Mercado, a large market building dating from 1917.

**Museums** Of the town's museums, the most interesting is the **Museo del Río Magdalena**, set in a lovely 17th-century house on the corner of Carrera 10 and Calle 10. It features a somewhat haphazard collection of stuffed crocodiles, old photos and minerals, but it's worth visiting to see the fine pre-Columbian ceramics, mainly funeral urns, excavated in the region. The museum is open Monday to Saturday from 8 am to noon and 2 to 6 pm, Sunday from 9 am to 4 pm.

The **Casa Cultural Alfonso López Pumarejo**, at Calle 13 No 11-65, has photos and documents related to this former president (1934-38 and 1942-45) who was born in Honda in 1886.

The **Museo de Arte Religioso**, in the 17th-century Catedral de Nuestra Señora del Rosario, is not much more than a handful of old statues of saints without captions. If the church is closed, ask to have it opened at the Despacho Parroquial next door.

**Bridges** The local sources list 20 bridges within the urban limits and a further nine in the surroundings. The most interesting is the

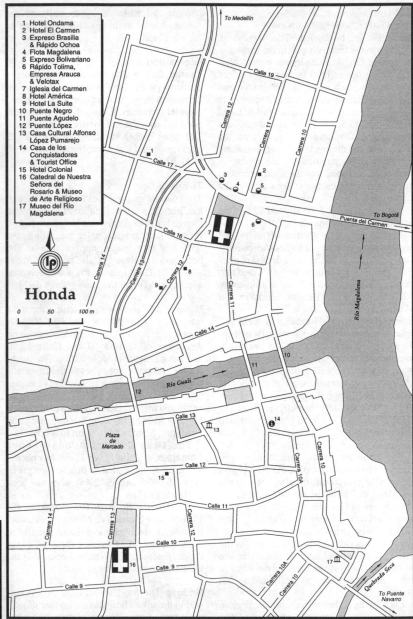

1 Hotel Ondama
2 Hotel El Carmen
3 Expreso Brasilia
  & Rápido Ochoa
4 Flota Magdalena
5 Expreso Bolivariano
6 Rápido Tolima,
  Empresa Arauca
  & Velotax
7 Iglesia del Carmen
8 Hotel América
9 Hotel La Suite
10 Puente Negro
11 Puente Agudelo
12 Puente López
13 Casa Cultural Alfonso
   López Pumarejo
14 Casa de los
   Conquistadores
   & Tourist Office
15 Hotel Colonial
16 Catedral de Nuestra
   Señora del
   Rosario & Museo
   de Arte Religioso
17 Museo del Río
   Magdalena

Honda

0    50    100 m

To Medellín

Calle 19

Carrera 12
Carrera 11
Carrera 10

Calle 17

Calle 16

To Bogotá
Puente del Carmen

Carrera 14
Carrera 13
Carrera 12
Carrera 11

Río Magdalena

Calle 14

Río Guali

Calle 13

Plaza
de
Mercado

Calle 12

Calle 11

Calle 10

Carrera 14
Carrera 13
Carrera 12
Carrera 10A
Carrera 10

Calle 9

Quebrada Seca

To Puente
Navarro

iron **Puente Navarro** built in 1898; it's the oldest bridge over the Magdalena.

## Places to Stay

There are lots of hotels in town, the result of its status as a holiday resort. If you need to be close to the bus offices, the best budget bet in the area is the *Hotel El Carmen*, at Carrera 11 No 17-34, just around the corner from the Expreso Bolivariano office. Rooms with baths are priced at US$3.50/5 for a single or matrimonio/double.

In the colonial part of the town, go to the old-style *Hotel Colonial* (☎ 513429), at Calle 12 No 12-09, ideally located on the Calle de las Trampas. Singles/doubles with bath cost US$4/7.

The small *Hotel La Suite* (☎ 514408), at Carrera 12 No 12-09, is a recently opened, friendly place offering comfortable rooms for US$7 per person.

For somewhere with a swimming pool, air-con and TV in your room, try the *Hotel Ondama* (☎ 513127), on the corner of Carrera 14 and Calle 17 (US$30/40/50 a singe/double/triple), or the slightly more expensive *Hotel América* (☎ 513222), at Carrera 12 No 15-58. Both have their own restaurants and bars.

## Getting There & Away

All the bus companies which call in at Honda (Expreso Bolivariano, Flota Magdalena, Expreso Brasilia, Velotax, Rápido Tolima, Rápido Ochoa and Empresa Arauca) have their offices packed at the foot of the Puente del Carmen (the main bridge). Colectivos also depart from here. A new terminal is under construction in the northern part of the town, on the road to Medellín, one km from the bridge.

**To Bogotá** There are plenty of buses by several companies (US$6 climatizado, US$5 pullman, US$4 corriente, 3½ to four hours). They all pass through Guaduas (see that section in the Bogotá chapter), only 33 km away; there are also colectivos to Guaduas (US$1).

**To Medellín** Buses by several companies run about every half-hour (US$11 climatizado, US$9.50 pullman, five to six hours).

**To Manizales** There are at least 30 departures per day. Expreso Bolivariano operates climatizados (US$6.50, four hours) and pullmans (US$5.75), while Empresa Arauca and Rápido Tolima run cheaper busetas (US$5).

**To Puerto Boyacá** Rápido Tolima has buses every two hours or so (US$3, two hours). This is the bus to take for Caverna del Nus.

**To Ibagué** Rápido Tolima has half-hourly buses via Mariquita and Armero (US$3.75, three hours); there are also colectivos (US$4.75, 2½ hours).

# The South-West

Like almost every region in Colombia, the south-west is widely diverse, both culturally and geographically. Here you will find beaches and snow-capped peaks, jungles and deserts, hot springs and icy streams, fertile valleys and arid wastelands, volcanoes, páramos, lakes, caves and waterfalls – virtually every kind of landscape you could wish for. Some of these natural features are protected in the region's eight national parks.

On the cultural front, the south-west boasts a collection of colonial towns (of which Popayán undoubtedly heads the league), several important religious sanctuaries (don't miss Las Lajas), a number of old haciendas (among which El Paraíso and Piedechinche are the best known) and two of the most significant archaeological sites in all of the Americas – San Agustín and Tierradentro – which are possibly the region's biggest tourist attractions.

The Indian population of the region is composed of several groups from different ethnic backgrounds. The dominant group is the Páez Indians living in the Tierradentro area, who belong to the Chibcha linguistic family and number some 40,000 people. The most traditional, however, are the Guambianos (numbering about 12,000), from the mountainous region around Silvia, northeast of Popayán.

This chapter covers the departments of Valle del Cauca, Cauca, Huila and Nariño. With a population of nearly two million, Cali is the region's dominant urban centre, six times larger than the second biggest city, Pasto.

## Valle del Cauca

The department of Valle del Cauca bears the name of the Cauca Valley, the agricultural heart of the region. The valley accounts for most of Colombia's total sugar production and it is possible to harvest the crop all year round. The valley produces many other crops, including cotton, tobacco, maize, grapes and coffee. Amidst all this rich agriculture sits Cali, the departmental capital.

The valley is flanked on its east and west sides by the mountain ranges of the Cordillera Central and Cordillera Occidental, respectively. Beyond the latter stretches the wide lowland of thick rainforest which slopes down to the mangrove swamps on the Pacific coast. Here is the port of Buenaventura, the second largest city of the department and Colombia's most important port on the Pacific.

### CALI
• *pop 1,800,000* • *1005 m* • *24°C* • ☎ *(923)*
Set in the verdant Cauca Valley, Cali is a prosperous and lively city with a fairly hot yet tolerable climate. Apart from a few fine old churches and good museums, the city has no great sights. Its appeal lies rather in its

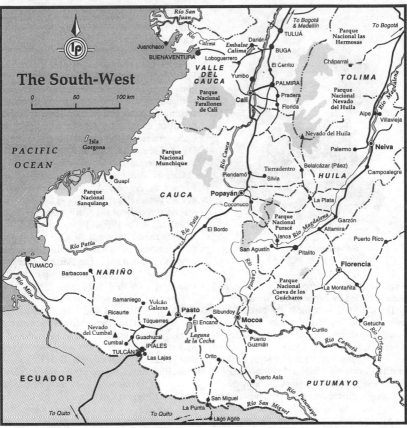

The South-West

0    50    100 km

PACIFIC
OCEAN

atmosphere and in the character of the *caleños*, as the city's inhabitants are known. This ambience is best appreciated in the evenings, when a refreshing breeze dissipates the heat of the day and the city dwellers take to the streets, open-air cafés and salsa spots.

Cali was founded in 1536 by Sebastián de Belalcázar, one of Francisco Pizarro's lieutenants, who had taken part in the conquest of the Incas. When the Inca Empire was effectively at an end after the execution of Atahualpa in August 1533, Belalcázar founded Quito (1534) on the ruins of a former Inca city. The intrigues between the

two conquerors, however, prompted Belalcázar to desert from Pizarro's army and make his way northward. It took him almost a year to get to the Cauca Valley.

At the time of the arrival of the Spaniards, the valley was inhabited by various indigenous tribes, of which the people, indigenous; Indians were the most advanced. Despite Indian attacks, a new settlement was founded and called Santiago de Cali. Belalcázar briefly explored the region (founding Popayán in the process) and then moved further northward. He was only a little too late to found yet another important city,

Sebastián de Belalcázar

industrial, agricultural and commercial centre of the south-west and the capital of the Valle del Cauca, housing half the department's population.

Cali is renowned as a centre for sports. The Pan-American Sports Complex was built here in 1971 for the international games, with a stadium, Olympic-size gymnasium, swimming pools and the like. The city is also proud of its bullring: La Plaza de Toros de Cañaveralejo is the biggest in the country (19,000 seats) and one of the most modern in the Americas.

Cali is also noted for the beauty of its women, *las caleñas*. Another source of pride in Cali is its salsa music. These hot rhythms spread throughout the Caribbean, reaching Colombia in the 1960s. Today, salsa is heard all over the country, but the Cali region and the Caribbean coast have remained the major centres of this music. The African ancestry of a sizeable part of the population is largely responsible for this.

Finally, Cali is known as the home of the Cartel de Cali and the world capital of cocaine trafficking. This supremacy, recently taken over from Medellín, doesn't make the place an oasis of peace. Even though the city looks quieter than Bogotá or Medellín, don't be deceived by its easy-going air, summery heat and beautiful women. Muggers and thieves aren't inactive here, nor are they less clever or violent than elsewhere. Be extremely careful while wandering around the streets at night. Avoid the park along Río Cali in the evening, and don't walk east of Calle 13 after dark.

Bogotá, arriving there shortly after it had been founded by Jiménez de Quesada.

The town's development was based principally on the fertile soil of the valley. The Spaniards shipped in thousands of African slaves to work on plantations of sugarcane and other crops. The African legacy is still very much in evidence today: a significant proportion of the population is black and mulatto.

Cali's political and religious importance, however, was minor. Popayán was the province's real capital and the principal centre of regional power during the whole colonial period and for a long time after.

Cali's growth was very slow and progress really came only at the beginning of the present century, first with the establishment of a large-scale sugar industry, followed by dynamic development in other sectors. A remarkable economic boom, especially since the 1940s, has helped the city to grow tenfold in the last 50 years. Between 1985 and 1993 alone the city's population increased by almost half a million.

Today Cali is Colombia's third-largest city, but it's expected to surpass Medellín soon to become the second-biggest metropolis after Bogotá. Cali is the dominant

## Orientation

The city centre is split in two by the Río Cali. To the south is the city's original heart, laid out on a grid plan and centred around the Plaza de Caycedo. This area has the most tourist attractions, including old churches and museums.

To the north of the river is the new centre, whose main axis is Avenida Sexta (Avenida 6N). This sector is essentially modern, packed with trendy shops and good restaurants, and comes alive in the evening. This is the area to come and dine after a day of sightseeing on the opposite side of the river.

## Information

**Tourist Office** The departmental tourist office, Cortuvalle (☎ 675614), is at Avenida 4N No 4N-20. It's open Monday to Friday from 8.30 am to 5 pm. There is another outlet at the airport.

If you need a good map of the city and the region, go to the Fondo Mixto de Promoción del Valle of the Cámara de Comercio (☎ 823271), Calle 8 No 3-14, Piso 4. The office is open Monday to Friday from 7 to 11.30 am and 2 to 5.30 pm.

**Money** Most of the major banks are grouped around the Plaza de Caycedo. Banco Popular appears to be the only bank which changes cash (at a good rate), but it's always packed with people, so you'll probably spend a lot of time in the queue.

The Banco Popular and the Banco Industrial Colombiano seem to be the only two banks changing travellers' cheques. The former pays better rates, but has long queues, while the latter has no queues but is totally inefficient, so the paperwork will take at least half an hour.

To withdraw cash on a Visa card, try the Banco Anglo Colombiano, Banco de Bogotá or Banco de Colombia. MasterCard is honoured in the Banco de Occidente and the Banco Industrial Colombiano.

The Tierra Mar Aire office (☎ 676767; for lost or stolen American Express travellers' cheques) is at Calle 22N No 5BN-53.

**Red de Reservas Naturales** Founded in 1991, this is an association which collects information about nature reserves operated by rural communities and nongovernment organisations. These reserves are independent from the governmental Inderena-run array of national parks and other protected areas. As of 1994, there were 53 private reserves affiliated to the association, and there are likely to be more by the time you read this. The reserves are scattered countrywide, although most of them are in the Andean region. They are usually small, sometimes very small, but often contain an interesting, diverse sample of an ecosystem. More importantly, many of them are run by genuine nature lovers, aware of the importance of ecological preservation and dedicated to their work. Some reserves have tourist facilities, allowing for longer stays, whereas others can only be visited on a day trip, unless you are prepared to camp.

The association has information about the reserves' location, features and facilities, complete with names and phone numbers of people who can provide further details. The association also publishes the *Redservando* bulletin on the reserves. Its head office (☎ 542294, 542300) is at Carrera 35A Oeste No 3-66.

You may also want to make direct contact with the operators of those reserves which have their headquarters in Cali. They include:

Fundación Farallones (☎ 568335), Carrera 24B No 2A-99, operates the Reserva Natural Hato Viejo near Cali (refer to the Parque Nacional Farallones de Cali section for details).

Fundación FES (☎ 822524, 845933), Carrera 5 No 6-05, runs the Reserva Natural La Planada in Nariño (read the Reserva Natural La Planada section for full details).

Fundación Herencia Verde (☎ 808484, 813257), Calle 4 Oeste No 3A-32, has the Reserva Natural Acaime in the department of Quindío (see the Reserva Natural Acaime section for information).

**Consulates** Cali's consulates include:

Bolivia
    Carrera 40 No 5C-102 (☎ 536386)
Brazil
    Calle 11 No 1-07, Oficina 304 (☎ 804914)
Chile
    Avenida 6N No 17AN-51, Piso 3 (☎ 687479)
Costa Rica
    Avenida Colombia No 1B-70 Oeste (☎ 806551)
Ecuador
    Carrera 3 No 11-32, Oficina 409 (☎ 801937)
El Salvador
    Avenida 4B Oeste No 3-70 (☎ 811719)
Guatemala
    Carrera 5 No 47-165 (☎ 474411)
Panama
    Calle 11 No 4-42, Oficina 316 (☎ 809590)
Peru
    Avenida 5N No 23BN-41 (☎ 672752)

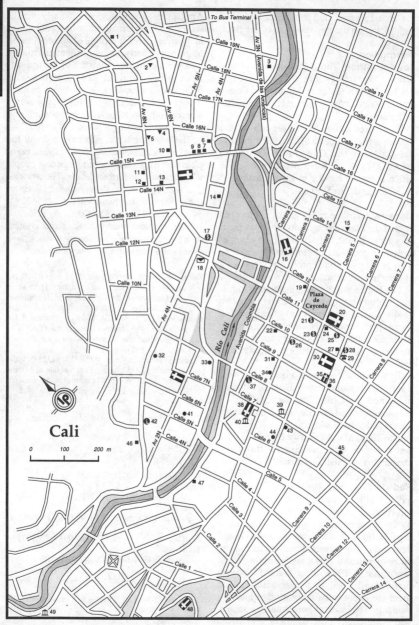

To Bus Terminal

Calle 19N

Calle 18N

Calle 17N

Calle 16N

Calle 15N

Calle 14N

Calle 13N

Calle 12N

Calle 10N

Av 8N

Av 6N

Av 5N

Av 4N

Av 3N

Avenida de las Américas

Calle 19

Calle 18

Calle 17

Calle 16

Calle 15

Calle 14

Carrera 2

Carrera 3

Carrera 4

Carrera 5

Carrera 6

Carrera 7

Río Cali

Avenida Colombia

Plaza de Caycedo

Calle 12

Calle 11

Calle 10

Calle 9

Calle 8

Calle 7

Calle 7N

Calle 6N

Calle 5N

Av 4N

Av 2N

Calle 4N

Carrera 8

Carrera 9

Carrera 10

Carrera 12

Carrera 13

Carrera 14

Calle 6

Calle 5

Calle 4

Calle 3

Calle 2

Calle 1

**Cali**

0    100    200 m

## PLACES TO STAY

1  Hostal Santor
3  Hotel La Torre de Cali
6  Residencial Chalet
7  Hotel Granada
8  Hotel California
9  Casa del Viajero
10  Hotel Don Jaime
11  Residencial JJ
12  Residencial 86
13  Hotel La Familia
14  Residencial Paseo Bolívar
19  Hotel Royal Plaza
22  Hotel María Victoria
24  Hotel Astoria
27  Hotel Plaza
31  Hotel Camino Real
46  Pensión Stein
47  Hotel Intercontinental

## PLACES TO EAT

2  Restaurante Vegetariano
    Raíces
4  Restaurante El Caballo Loco
5  Restaurante El Fuerte del
    Norte
15  Restaurante Vegetariano Hare
    Krishna

## OTHER

16  Iglesia de la Ermita
17  Banco de Occidente
18  Avianca Post Office
20  Catedral
21  Banco Anglo Colombiano
23  Banco de Bogotá
25  Banco de Colombia
26  Banco Popular
28  Banco Industrial Colombiano
29  Telecom
30  Iglesia de San Francisco
32  Sifonería Martyn's
33  Avianca Office
34  Club Bingo Social
35  Capilla de la Inmaculada
36  Torre Mudéjar
37  Fondo Mixto de Promoción del Valle
38  Iglesia de la Merced
39  Museo del Oro
40  Museo de Arte Colonial & Museo
    Arqueológico
41  Taberna Alexander
42  Cortuvalle Tourist Office
43  Teatro Municipal
44  Fundación FES
45  Teatro Experimental de Cali (TEC)
48  Iglesia de San Antonio
49  Museo de Arte Moderno La Tertulia

**Tours** There are plenty of travel agencies in Cali. They offer tours both within and outside the department (El Paraíso-Piedechinche, Popayán-Silvia, Roldanillo-Cartago-Buga, Buenaventura-Juanchaco-Ladrilleros), as well as city tours and Cali by night in a chiva. Contact Cortuvalle, which has some tours and whose staff will direct you to the appropriate agency if they don't have what you want.

### Churches

Located on the corner of Carrera 4 and Calle 7, **Iglesia de la Merced** is the city's oldest church. It was begun around 1545 on the site where the first mass was held in 1536 to commemorate the town's foundation. It's a lovely whitewashed building in the Spanish colonial style. Once inside, your attention will immediately be captured by a beautiful high altar topped by the Virgen de las Mercedes, the patron saint of the city. The church is only open for mass, Monday to Saturday at 7 am and 6 pm, and Sunday and holidays at 9 am and 6 pm.

Overlooking the parks on the Río Cali from Avenida Colombia, the Gothic-style **Iglesia de la Ermita**, constructed between 1930 and 1948, has become one of the best known landmarks of the city. The marble altar was brought from Italy. Don't miss seeing the famous 18th-century painting of El Señor de la Caña (displayed in the side altar), to whom many miracles are attributed. The church is open most of the day.

**Iglesia de San Francisco**, on the corner of Carrera 6 and Calle 10, is a neoclassical construction dating from the 18th century. The large marble-and-wood altar was made in Spain at the beginning of the present century and shipped to Colombia. It landed at Buenaventura and was then carried to Cali by mule along the ancient *camino de herradura*.

Next to the church are the Convento de San Francisco and the Capilla de la Inmaculada with the adjacent **Torre Mudéjar** (corner of Carrera 6 and Calle 9), an unusual brick bell tower and one of the best examples of Mudéjar art in Colombia. The tower was built in the 18th century and its pealing bells served as the town's timepiece for many years.

**Iglesia de San Antonio** is set on the top of a hill, the Colina de San Antonio. This fine, small colonial church was built in 1757. It shelters valuable *tallas quiteñas*, 17th-century carved-wood statues of the saints, representing the style known as the Quito School. The church's 19th-century bells, cast in a gold, copper and bronze alloy, are said to have the merriest sound in Cali; they ring for mass at 9 am and 6 pm (on Sunday at 5.30 pm only). Even if you miss the opening hours of the church it's still worth walking there for a good view of the city; it's just a 10-minute walk from the Torre Mudéjar.

### Museums

The convent adjoining the Iglesia de la Merced houses two good museums: the **Museo de Arte Colonial** (open Monday to Saturday from 9 am to noon), with mostly religious artefacts from the colonial period, and the **Museo Arqueológico** (open Monday to Saturday from 9 am to 12.45 pm and 1.45 to 6 pm), with pre-Columbian pottery of several cultures from southern Colombia. Admission to either museum is US$0.50.

The **Museo del Oro**, one block away, on the corner of Carrera 5 and Calle 7, is open Monday to Friday from 10 am to 6 pm. It has a small but well-selected and arranged collection of gold and pottery of the Calima culture.

The **Museo de Arte Moderno La Tertulia**, Avenida Colombia No 5 Oeste-105, a 15-minute walk from the city centre, presents temporary exhibitions of contemporary painting, sculpture and photography. It is open Tuesday to Saturday from 9 am to 1 pm

and 3 to 7 pm, Sunday and holidays from 3 to 7 pm. Admission is US$0.50, half-price for students.

The **Museo de Historia Natural**, at Carrera 2 No 7 Oeste-18, a five-minute walk uphill from La Tertulia, has a selection of Colombian fauna. It's open Monday to Friday from 9 am to noon and 2 to 5 pm.

The small **Museo del Mar**, in the bus terminal building, has a collection of marine species. It's open daily from 10 am to 6 pm. You can have a look if you have some time to kill before your bus departs.

### Zoológico de Cali

Founded in 1970, the zoo is on the corner of Carrera 2 and Calle 14 Oeste in the suburb of Santa Teresita, a short walk west of the Museo de Historia Natural. Its 10 hectares are home to a variety of animals, both native and imported from other continents. The zoo is open daily from 9 am to 5 pm. The admission fee is US$1.

### Hacienda Cañasgordas

This fine old hacienda is on the southern outskirts of the city beyond the Universidad del Valle. It was used as the setting for the novel *El Alférez Real* by the local writer Eustaquio Palacios. It is a lovely 18th-century country mansion filled with period furniture and colonial objects. At the time of writing, the hacienda was closed for refurbishing, but it may have reopened by the time you read this. Ask at the Cortuvalle office for news before you decide to set off.

To get there, take a Transur bus from the terminal; it goes along the main Popayán road and will drop you at the entrance to the hacienda. Alternatively, take a city bus (Ruta No 1) from the centre which goes along Calle 5. Get off after the university when the bus turns to the right off the main road. Continue walking for 10 minutes along the main road to the hacienda.

### Festivals & Events

The main city event is the Feria de Cali, which breaks out annually on 25 December and goes till the end of the year (some events

May, brings an increase in cultural activity, including music concerts, theatre performances and art exhibitions.

### Places to Stay – bottom end

Budget accommodation in Cali, as in most of the big cities, is generally poor or overpriced, or both. Avoid places called amoblados – most of them are sex hotels which rent rooms by the hour.

There is a choice of budget accommodation right in the heart of the new (northern) city centre, which is a relatively secure and pleasant area. The dark side is that the residencias are pretty poor, and some double as love hotels.

Three hotels side by side on Calle 15N are used by budget travellers despite their not-very-innocent status: the *Hotel Granada* (☎ 612477), at Calle 15N No 4N-44; the *Hotel California* (☎ 612483), at Calle 15N No 4N-52; and the *Casa del Viajero* (☎ 610906), at Calle 15N No 4N-60. All have rooms with private bath and cost US$5/7 for a single/double. The California seems to have the highest ratio of passing couples per day and, apparently, a few tenant prostitutes. Check the other two and take your pick. Just around the corner, at Avenida 4N No 15N-43, is the *Residencial Chalet* (☎ 612709). It's quieter, perhaps cleaner, and a dollar cheaper than the previous three.

If you prefer somewhere with a better reputation (though not a higher standard), there are three small hotels around the corner of Calle 14N and Avenida 8N: the *Residencial 86* (☎ 612054), Avenida 8N No 14N-01; the *Hotel La Familia* (☎ 612925), at Calle 14N No 6N-42; and the *Residencial JJ* (☎ 613134), at Avenida 8N No 14-47. The first has rooms with bath (US$5/7) and is the best of the lot. Another basic hotel, the *Residencial Paseo Bolívar* (☎ 682863), is at Avenida 3N No 13N-43. All four rent rooms by the week or the month, and may often be full.

One of the best budget places to stay in the Avenida Sexta area is the *Hostal Santor* (☎ 686482), at Avenida 8N No 20N-50, which has rooms with bath for around

Sloth

continue into the first days of the new year), with parades, masquerades, music, theatre, bullfights and lots of fun. One of the highlights is a marathon concert of salsa bands, usually well attended by renowned international groups. Given the legendary beauty of the caleñas, it's no surprise that the beauty contest also draws in hordes of spectators.

The Festival Internacional de Arte, in

US$10/12. There are also several cheaper rooms without bath, but they are of poor quality.

On the southern side of the Río Cali, in the historic centre, there's not much budget accommodation, except for the maze of seedy hospedajes east of Calle 15. However, you shouldn't walk there as this is one of the most dangerous areas of central Cali.

### Places to Stay – middle
There's quite a choice of mid-range hotels within a couple of blocks of the Plaza de Caycedo, a convenient area to stay. Most of them, however, especially the cheaper ones, are quite undistinguished.

The one which does have an *ambiente distinguido* – as its business card says – is the *Hotel María Victoria* (☎ 823242), at Calle 10 No 3-38. It's set in an old, once fine but now dilapidated house. The rooms are large but not that well kept, and cost US$11/15 a single/double.

The *Hotel Plaza* (☎ 822560), at Carrera 6 No 10-29, is one of the uninspiring modern options. It has private baths and TVs in the rooms and is reasonably priced (US$15/20). Better is the *Hotel Camino Real* (☎ 834684), at Calle 9 No 3-54, which has larger rooms and costs US$20/24.

Perhaps the best value for money in this price bracket is the *Hotel Astoria* (☎ 830140), at Calle 11 No 5-16, on the corner of the plaza. Airy, comfortable rooms with TV and private bath cost US$20/25. Ask for a room on one of the top floors, as these are less noisy and have better views.

### Places to Stay – top end
The *Hotel Royal Plaza* (☎ 839243), at Carrera 4 No 11-69, on the corner of the Plaza Caycedo, is a good and reasonably priced choice. The rooms are slightly better than those in the Astoria and cost US$26/33/39 for a single/double/triple. Here, too, the rooms on the upper floors are more attractive. There's a fine restaurant on the top floor.

If you are looking for something with a special style, there's one exceptional place, the *Pensión Stein* (☎ 614927), at Avenida 4N

No 3N-33, in a large, beautiful house. Run by a Swiss couple, the hotel offers spotlessly clean rooms with bath, and also has its own restaurant. Singles/doubles cost US$30/40, breakfast included.

If you need somewhere close to the city's pulse, on Avenida Sexta, try the *Hotel Don Jaime* (☎ 614598), at Avenida 6N No 15N-25, which has good air-con rooms for US$80/100.

More expensive (but with a swimming pool) is *La Torre de Cali* (☎ 675097), at Avenida de las Américas (Av 3N) No 18N-26. It's located in Cali's highest building, and its top-floor restaurant provides good bird's-eye views over the city. The management sometimes gives permission for nonguests to go up to a viewpoint on the 43rd floor.

Anyone with adequately lined pockets might take the plunge in the five-star *Hotel Intercontinental* (☎ 823225), at Avenida Colombia No 2-72, which is the best in Cali.

### Places to Eat
The best sector for eating is on and around Avenida 6N, where loads of restaurants and cafés are packed together; you can get nearly everything, from simple snacks, burgers and pizzas, through regional Colombian cuisine, to rich Chinese, Arab and German specialities. There are also an adequate number of cheap restaurants in the area, which serve set meals for around US$1.50.

For vegetarian food, the best budget place is the attractive *Restaurante Vegetariano Raíces*, at Calle 18N No 6N-25, but it only serves meals between 11.30 am and 2.30 pm. Not as pleasant, but open from 6 am to 8 pm, is the *Restaurante Vegetariano Hare Krishna*, at Calle 14 No 4-49.

For a satisfying dinner, try *El Caballo Loco*, at Calle 16N No 6N-31 (ask for the castellana – a roast-beef or pork roll with cheese and ham, served in béchamel sauce); *El Fuerte del Norte*, Avenida 8N No 15AN-06 (good seafood); or *Los Girasoles* (mainly fish) and *Las Dos Parrillas* (steaks), both on the corner of Avenida 6N and Calle 35N. There are plenty of other, equally good restaurants in the area.

## Entertainment

**Cinema** Cinemateca La Tertulia, next to the Museo de Arte Moderno, is the only regular art cinema in Cali. Check the programme in the local newspaper, *El País*, or at the museum.

**Theatre** Colombia's national theatre started with the foundation of the Teatro Experimental de Cali (TEC). It continues to be one of the city's most innovative theatre companies. If you understand Spanish well enough, go to the TEC theatre, at Calle 7 No 8-63, and see one of its current productions.

The Teatro Municipal, at Carrera 5 No 6-64, is the city's oldest existing theatre, completed in 1918. Today it's used for various artistic forms, including musical concerts, theatre and ballet, performed mostly by visiting groups.

**Music** Cali is known for its salsa music, so it comes as no surprise that there are many salsotecas (discos with salsa music) in the city. The most famous place is Juanchito, a popular suburb on the Río Cauca, which gained fame for its cafés blasting with salsa music, frequented mostly by blacks. This is the archetypal place to go on weekends to listen to salsa, dance and watch the locals dancing. Note that the area can be dangerous; the aguardiente flows fast and the atmosphere is hot if not boiling. It's best to find some locals to take you there. Don't take anything of value with you.

If you are not up for exploring Juanchito, there are several salsa spots around Avenida Sexta and in the old centre close to the Plaza de Caycedo. Another, better area to look for salsa is on and just off Calle 5, especially between Carreras 38 and 44. Here you'll find two good salsotecas, Taberna Latina and Taberna Nuestra Herencia, both near the corner of Calle 5 and Carrera 38. Tin Tin Deo, on the corner of Calle 5 and Carrera 22, is renowned for good salsa and old Cuban rhythms. Clásico Jazz, at Avenida de las Américas No 2N-58, features bands playing salsa and Latin jazz.

Sifonería Martyn's, at Avenida 4N No 7N-10, and Taberna Alexander, at Calle 5N No 1N-74, are two pleasant, central places for a night-time drink to the rhythms of salsa/reggae/rock and the like.

For opera buffs, there's the Video Taberna El Trovador, at Avenida Circunvalación No 4 Oeste-42, open Tuesday to Saturday from 8 pm to 2 am. It serves drinks, and has 50 operas on video and twice that number on compact disc. The programme is designed by the customers.

A night tour in a chiva is a convenient and easy way of visiting some of the night spots, if you are wary of setting off on a nocturnal adventure on your own. Chiva tours are organised on weekend nights by several operators, including the Hotel Intercontinental. Its chiva departs from the hotel on Friday and Saturday at 8 pm. The five-hour tour calls at several music spots, includes half a bottle of aguardiente and a snack, and costs US$15 per person.

**Bingo** Bingo is a feature of Cali. There are several bingo halls in the centre, one of the more popular being *Club Bingo Social*, at Carrera 4 No 9-21 (open 24 hours), where anyone may enter and people of all ages do so.

### Things to Buy

Cali has a choice of handicraft shops. Artesanías Pacandé, at Avenida 6AN No 17AN-53, has a selection of fine basketwork and other handicrafts. You can also buy crafts at either branch of the Museo de Artesanía de Colombia, at Calle 12 No 1-20 or Avenida 6N No 23N-45, and at Artesanías Quimbaya, Avenida Colombia No 2-72.

The main posh shopping area is Avenida Sexta and the adjacent streets.

### Getting There & Away

**Air** The modern, international Palmaseca Airport is 16 km north-east of the city, off the road to Palmira. Minibuses between the airport and the bus terminal run every 10 minutes until about 8 pm (US$1, half an hour).

There are plenty of flights to most main Colombian cities, operated by all major

## Salsa

The music of the Caribbean basin, commonly referred to as Afro-Caribbean music, is essentially a blend of African and Spanish musical traditions with minor borrowings from the English, French and Dutch. The African element, the legacy of hundreds of thousands of black slaves shipped in by the Spaniards from Africa, is mainly represented by an arsenal of percussion instruments, which gives this music a strong, vital beat.

Afro-Caribbean music was born when the first blacks arrived, in the 16th century, and evolved down different paths on different islands of the region. Its beginnings and early history are not well documented, and it is only possible to trace its musical development closely after the 1920s, the time when the first recordings on rolls were made.

**Cuban Roots**  Cuba came to be the most prolific source of Afro-Caribbean music, to the extent that a separate term – Afro-Cuban music – was coined. An infinity of genres, including *son, guajira, guaguancó, danzón, conga, guaracha* and, later, *mambo, bolero, rumba* and *cha-cha-cha*, were all born either in Cuba's countryside or on Havana's backstreets. Son was one of the earliest and most important rhythms and is seen as the ancestor of salsa.

Cuban music began to travel beyond Cuba's borders, mostly to the USA, in the 1920s. Many US jazz musicians, from Jelly Roll Morton to Dizzy Gillespie, incorporated Cuban rhythms into jazz. On the other hand, millions of North Americans flocked to Havana's taverns and dance halls to enjoy hot music, sexy dances and tropical sun. The rapid development of recording techniques contributed to the spread of Cuban beats.

One of the first great ambassadors of Cuban music was the seven-sister group Anacaona, which was later enriched with a further four female participants and had gained considerable fame by the mid-1930s. An all-woman orchestra – brass and percussion included – wasn't at all a common sight in those days.

Guillermo Portabales, an unsurpassed interpreter of guajira, hit Havana's saloons in the 1930s with his beautiful tunes from the countryside. A vocalist, composer and guitarist, he later fled the Cuban communist regime to Puerto Rico, where he died in a car accident in 1970.

Mambo's birth is attributed to Orestes López, who composed his early mambos towards the end of the 1930s. Pérez Prado, a pianist, and conductor of his own orchestra, made them famous a decade later, but perhaps no-one sang mambo as beautifully as Beny Moré. Mambo became a craze during the 1950s, but by that time a new rhythm, cha-cha-cha, had emerged and conquered Havana's great dance halls.

Plenty of bands flourished during the 1930s and 1940s and brought pure, rural rhythms into Havana's music houses. The Trío Matamoros and the duet Celina y Reutilio were possibly the best known small groups of those days. The great classic Cuban orchestras of the time included La Sensación, La América, La Aragón and, most famous of all, La Sonora Matancera, which has become a living legend.

La Sonora Matancera gathered together some of the finest musical figures of the day; many of them later joined Fania All Stars and laid the foundations of salsa. Of all the band's stars, Celia Cruz is the best known – her distinctive, husky voice has immortalised many Afro-Cuban classics. Born in Havana in 1928, she made her first record in 1951 in Cuba and performs throughout the Americas to this day.

**Son**  Son is the backbone of Afro-Cuban music. Although it never enjoyed the booms of popularity which befell mambo and cha-cha-cha, it has always been highly esteemed by Cubans. Keeping closely to its generations-old roots, son didn't run after the hearts of North American tourists and remained largely unaffected by passing fashions. It perhaps best embodies the very essence of traditional Afro-Cuban music. As well, it gave rhythmic and harmonic patterns to other musical genres, and set the scene for salsa.

Son employs a variety of percussion instruments, including *tumbadoras* or congas (large, one-metre-high, barrel-shaped drums), bongos (a pair of small, bucket-shaped drums joined together by a bar), *claves* (a pair of hardwood sticks struck together to produce a sound), *güiro* (a gourd of the güira fruit, notched with a row of cuts and scratched with a wooden stick) and maracas (gourd rattles). Also very characteristic of traditional son is the *tres*, a guitar-like instrument with six strings grouped in three pairs (hence its name).

Isaac Oviedo was one of the first important tres players. He began his career in the 1920s and contributed much to the accepted style of playing the instrument. He still performs today.

However, Oviedo has never gained the renown of another brilliant tres player, composer and band leader, with whom he performed in Havana in the 1930s – the legendary Arsenio Rodríguez. Born in 1911 as one of 16 children of a humble family, Rodríguez revitalised old Afro-Cuban music, filling it with new dynamics and energy. His band was among the most popular Cuban groups of the 1940s and caused a sensation in New York. His compositions became standards of the son repertoire, and he is considered the father of modern son. He died in the USA in 1972.

One of the most highly regarded Cuban bands today is Sierra Maestra. Formed in 1976, this nine-piece ensemble has quickly became an outstanding interpreter of classic sones and son-derived rhythms, including some amazing compositions by Arsenio Rodríguez.

**The Rise & Evolution of Salsa** Salsa was created in New York in the 1960s by Cubans, and some Puerto Ricans, who blended traditional rhythms from their native countries with elements of the music that dominated the grand metropolis, such as jazz and rhythm and blues, to produce a distinctive sound.

The main reason for the emergence of salsa was the break in political and economic relations between the USA and Cuba, which took place in 1960. This rupture drastically reduced contacts between the two nations, leaving US-based Cubans stranded, away from their native country. There was no longer a permanent, fresh supply of nostalgic guajiras and sones, as there had been before the revolution. As no other music could fill the vacuum, the US-based Cubans themselves, strengthened by a newly arrived stream of immigrants, set about recreating their beloved tunes. The result was a different strain, since it had to rely on accessible, local sources of talent and local instruments.

There's no precise definition of salsa. Broadly speaking, it's a fusion of musical expressions reflecting a range of Caribbean styles. Salsa is a hot dance music, whose most evident feature is its strong Afro-Cuban pulse. In contrast to its mostly rural origins, salsa is an urban product. It's performed by a band and is almost always sung. Salsa has a vibrant, vital, energetic and intense beat, which makes your hips begin to sway and moves your feet to dance.

Of all the styles which contributed to the creation of salsa, son played the most important role – it gave salsa its rhythmic and harmonic patterns. Yet salsa has gone far beyond son's musical boundaries; it has developed its own form of expression, its own instruments and arrangements, and also incorporated many other traditional and new rhythms.

While salsa borrowed son's basic instruments, including tres, congas and bongos, it also added others such as piano, flutes and violins. A typical salsa band now consists of somewhere between eight and 12 performers, including one or more vocalists. A brass section, composed of a couple of trumpets and trombones (and, occasionally, saxophones), has become the norm for a modern salsa band.

No-one knows for sure where the term 'salsa' came from. Some say it was taken from the famous son 'Échale Salsita', composed in 1928 by Ignacio Piñeiro and wonderfully interpreted by Guillermo Portabales. Others point to a band formed in the 1940s in Cuba and named Los Salseros. A popular radio music programme, put to air by a Venezuelan disc jockey and titled 'La Hora del Sabor, Salsa y Bembé', might also have been one of the sources.

What we do know is that at some point the Cuban community in New York began to use the name 'salsa' frequently to label their new music. The meaning of the word 'salsa' – sauce, or a preparation eaten with food to enhance its flavour and add piquancy – goes some way towards giving us an explanation.

The record *Hommy*, by Fania All Stars, a sort of Caribbean opera, which was released in 1972 in response to The Who's rock musical *Tommy*, became a success on the US market and contributed to the popularisation of salsa. The music gained even wider acceptance after the release of Jerry Masucci's film *Salsa* (1973), which featured a Fania All Stars concert in New York. Since then, the term has been adopted universally and entered the dictionaries.

Fania All Stars was – as its name suggests – a group of salsa stars. In fact, the band gathered together almost all the great salseros, including Johnny Pacheco, Ray Barreto, Willie Colón, Ismael Miranda, Héctor Lavoe, Cheo Feliciano, Richie Ray and Ismael Quintana. Many of these musicians had cut their teeth with the old Cuban orchestras long before salsa was born and, after a time with Fania, they went their independent ways.

The group of Richie Ray (piano) and Bobby Cruz (vocal) was one of the longest lived salsa bands. The group was formed in 1965 and performed successfully until the late 1980s. Curiously, it achieved greater fame in the Caribbean than in New York, where its career began. The melodic section of the group was based on two trumpets.

Eddie Palmieri was one of the first salsa musicians to introduce trombones when he added them to his group, La Perfecta. His music was based on *pachanga*, an old Cuban genre, but acquired a new sound through its use of the brass section. By the mid-1970s he had become one of the first of salsa's big names, and overshadowed his probably equally gifted brother, Charlie, a pianist and arranger, who meanwhile was experimenting with trumpets in his own band. The two brothers occasionally played together and their imaginative experiments with sound and instrumentation contributed greatly to the transformation of the old Caribbean rhythms into contemporary salsa.

Willie Colón, a trombonist and composer, formed a group with two trombones and employed Héctor Lavoe as a vocalist. The band performed for several years and gained remarkable popularity. After his separation from Lavoe, Colón continued creatively throughout the 1980s and became, like Eddie Palmieri before him, one of the pillars of salsa. It was he who discovered a new voice, Rubén Blades.

Blades was born, raised and educated in Panama, where he studied law and became involved in university leftist circles. Many of his lyrics expressed Latin American socio-political conflicts, topics which at first were not well received by New York audiences and made his first steps difficult. However, once he was engaged to sing with Willie Colón's orchestra in 1977, his poetic yet politically charged references broke down the public's reserve, and made Blades the most remarkable author and performer of ideologically committed salsa. Blades later split from Colón and formed his own group, Seis del Solar, with which he achieved international acclaim and won various musical prizes (among them a Grammy). In 1994 he was one of the leading candidates in Panama's presidential elections, but didn't win. Salsa was the winner.

While the experiments of some bands led to a creative new music, increasingly independent from its Cuban origins, other musicians, such as Henry Fiol, Alfredo 'Chocolate' Armenteros, Mario Muñoz 'Papaíto', Miguel Quintana and Roberto Torres, took on the task of interpreting traditional son with due respect and produced many pearls – songs which reverberate with the authentic feel and rhythm of a bygone Cuba.

Another product of all this experimenting with salsa was Latin jazz, a fusion of salsa and jazz. Actually, Latin jazz is nothing new – it has a history of more than half a century. The influence the old Cuban music and North American jazz have had on each other dates from the 1920s.

Musicians who took the Latin jazz course include Tito Puente, Mongo Santamaría and Paquito D'Rivera. More recently, the music of Irakere, an 11-piece combo from Havana led by the pianist Jesús 'Chucho' Valdés, is one of the most extraordinary examples of contemporary Latin jazz.

Latin jazz, despite the many excellent musicians who have performed it, has never been a big discographic business. Record companies looked for musical styles easier to commercialise and found the *merengue*. Merengue, which has its roots in old rhythms from the Dominican Republic, conquered New York in the 1980s. Many musicians have jumped on the merengue bandwagon; of them, Wilfrido Vargas is perhaps the best known. Like salsa, merengue has spread widely throughout the Caribbean and is also popular in Colombia. In contrast to salsa, however, merengue discography is full of low-quality, repetitive, commercial stuff with uninspiring lyrics.

In the early 1980s salsa began to make its way into Europe but, except in Spain, it hasn't got much further than scattered Latin communities. It also spread to the west coast of the USA, especially Los Angeles, but has never become as popular there as in New York. Furthermore, it has largely lost its Cuban rhythms, instrumentation and sound. Californian salsa searches for references not in son but in rock and soul, and its interpreters are mostly Mexican.

**Salsa in Colombia** The influence of Cuban music began to be felt in Colombia during the 1930s, partly thanks to the establishment of a local record industry (Colombia's first two record companies were founded in Barranquilla and Cartagena in the early 1930s) and partly as a result of concerts given by visiting groups. These musical links declined in importance during the 1950s and 1960s, firstly because of the outbreak of La Violencia in Colombia, and later because of the isolation imposed on the communist regime in Cuba.

The era of salsa in Colombia really began in February 1968 with the concerts given by the band of Richie Ray and Bobby Cruz in Barranquilla. The new sound conquered the city and began to spread throughout the Caribbean coast. Around Christmas of the same year the group arrived in Cali and was again met with massive applause. A factor which facilitated the spread of salsa in these two centres is their significant black and mulatto population. Barranquilla and Cali have since become the main bastions of salsa in Colombia, competing fiercely for supremacy. Most salsa addicts agree that Cali deserves the title of Colombia's salsa capital.

In Bogotá, salsa began to gain popularity in 1977, after the concert of Héctor Lavoe, but did not bocome trendy until the 1980s. It was at first regarded by many people as vulgar music of the lower classes. Today, however, it is fashionable with young people right across the social spectrum.

Medellín greeted the arrival of salsa with reserve, despite the fact that Colombia's largest record company, Discos Fuentes, was located there and had already released heaps of salsa records. In a city of tango and among an essentially white culture, salsa didn't at first find favourable soil and its popularity grew only slowly. Not until quite recently did salsa make a more vigorous assault on the city's airwaves.

Today, Colombia has perhaps more than 50 salsa groups and plenty of excellent musicians. The best known of these is Joe Arroyo, who began his career in the mid-1970s in Cartagena, but gained fame in Barranquilla after he formed his own group, La Verdad, in that city during the early 1980s. Arroyo's music is not a pure salsa; it has elements of *cumbia* and rhythms from the Lesser Antilles, yet it's very creative and attractive.

Grupo Niche is the best known salsa band of the Cali region. Formed in 1978 by Jairo Varela, the group has since changed its line-up and its style several times. It doesn't play typical salsa either.

The only Colombian who has successfully entered the New York salsa market is Eddie Martínez. Born in Nariño, he went to New York and joined Ray Barreto's combo. A pianist, composer and arranger, Martínez has since played with most of salsa's big names. He feels equally at home in salsa and Latin jazz. ■

national carriers. The major domestic routes include Bogotá (US$66 with Avianca, Sam and Aces, US$46 with Satena, US$42 with Intercontinental), Medellín (US$64 with Sam and Aces, US$48 with Intercontinental), Barranquilla (US$118 with Avianca and Aces, US$90 with Intercontinental) and Cartagena (US$115 with Sam and Aces, US$88 with Intercontinental).

Sam flies to San Andrés (US$142) but Intercontinental and AeroRepública will take you there more cheaply (US$109). Pasto is serviced by Avianca (US$62) and Intercontinental (US$42). Aces is the only airline which flies to Ipiales (US$62). To Leticia, you have to fly to Bogotá and take another flight from there.

Satena has a number of flights to the Pacific coast, including Bahía Solano (US$64), Quibdó (US$42), Buenaventura (US$26), Guapí (US$35) and Tumaco (US$48). Tumaco can also be reached with Intercontinental (US$47).

Aires operates flights to Ibagué (US$44), Neiva (US$75), Florencia (US$107) and Puerto Asís (US$65).

Among international flights, Avianca flies three times a week directly to Panama City (US$158), while Intercontinental has recently opened routes to Esmeraldas and Tulcán (both in Ecuador, US$63 to either). Add the 19% Colombian tax on top of international fares.

**Bus** The bus terminal is about one km northeast of the city centre; it's a 15-minute walk or less than 10 minutes by one of the frequent city buses.

**To Bogotá** Expreso Bolivariano, Flota Magdalena and Expreso Palmira have plenty of buses (US$19 climatizado, 12 hours).
**To Medellín** Empresa Arauca, Flota Magdalena and Expreso Palmira have buses (US$18 climatizado, US$15.50 pullman, nine hours).
**To Pasto & Ipiales** Several bus companies (Expreso Bolivariano, Flota Magdalena, Trans Ipiales, Cootranar and Supertaxis del Sur) operate the Cali-Pasto route (US$16 climatizado, US$14 pullman, 10 hours). You shouldn't have to wait more than an hour for the next departure. Many of these buses continue on to Ipiales (US$3 extra plus two hours), or change in Pasto.

**To Popayán** Any Pasto/Ipiales bus will drop you off in Popayán (US$5.50 climatizado, US$4.50 pullman, three hours).

**To Buenaventura** There are frequent buses with Expreso Palmira, Expreso Trejos and Flota Magdalena (US$3.50, three hours). The scenery along the road is spectacular; grab a window seat on the left-hand side of the bus.

**To Darién** Trans Calima has departures approximately every other hour (US$3, 2½ hours).

**Car Rental** Car-rental agencies operating in Cali include:

Avis
    Carrera 3 No 1-39, Piso 1 (☎ 811586)
Dollar
    Avenida 6N No 42N-30 (☎ 640515)
Hertz
    Avenida Colombia No 2-72 (☎ 822428)
Ready
    Calle 2 No 2-28 (☎ 808357)

## PARQUE NACIONAL FARALLONES DE CALI

This national park lies to the south-west of Cali and covers 150 sq km of rugged, verdant terrain. The park contains the highest part of the Cordillera Occidental, topped by the Pico Pance (4100 metres), and stretches far to the west over the western slopes of the Cordillera down to an altitude of 200 metres near the Pacific coast. Given such a wide bracket of altitudes and climatic zones, there's considerable diversity of habitats. The lowest, westernmost part of the park is covered with thick, humid rainforest, with trees growing up to 40 metres. Small communities of Cholo Indians live in this area. The eastern, upper reaches of the park, between about 2000 and 3500 metres, are equally lush, though the composition of plant species differs. This area is covered with dense Andean cloudforest, which is particularly impressive if you come here from the agricultural Cauca Valley. Above 3600 metres is the páramo which, curiously, doesn't feature frailejones but is rich in other low-growing plants, many of which flower.

These diverse strata of vegetation are reflected in a variety of animal life. Here you can find several species of monkey, the spec-

tacled bear, anteaters, rodents, bats (80 species), snakes (mostly nonvenomous), vultures and some 60 other bird species.

Access to the park is from the east, the village of **Pance** on the park's border being the major jumping-off point. One km downhill from Pance is the Centro de Educación Ambiental El Topacio, with several observation trails. It is well run and has a few small kiosks and two campsites, one of which is located on a small lake. Pance, El Topacio and the surrounding area have become the favourite weekend spot for caleños eager for recreation.

There are several paths heading uphill to the **Pico del Loro** (2670 metres). This is a single elevated cone lying outside the main range of the Farallones. A spectacular walk through dense forest up to the top takes about two hours. The Cascada de la Chorrera is no more than a 10-minute walk from El Topacio.

The hike to the top of the **Pico Pance** is a more adventurous proposition. The footpath begins in Pance and roughly follows the Río Pance, crossing it several times over small rustic bridges made of guadua. The path winds through lush cloudforest and is steep on some stretches. It's muddy in parts, especially in the rainy season. If the weather is clear (which occurs mostly in the morning), you'll get marvellous views over the Cauca Valley and beyond, as far as Nevado del Huila and the Volcán Puracé. Further up, upon reaching the crest (about a six-hour walk from Pance), you may also be lucky enough to have breathtaking views towards the west as far as the Pacific coast and Buenaventura. This, however, happens very seldom (and usually only very early in the morning) as this area is clouded almost all the time. Following the crest northward for another two hours, you'll get to the top of the Pico Pance. This part of the hike leads through the páramo, without any major changes in altitude. The walk from the pico back down to Pance village will take about six hours.

Given the total walking time, the trip will take three days (hard trekkers may do it in two days) and, consequently, you need camping gear. There are several places on the way which are good for camping, the best ones lying up in the páramo near the ridge. Alternatively, use the accommodation in the **Reserva Natural Hato Viejo**.

Hato Viejo is the private nature reserve operated by the Fundación Farallones. It was created in 1989 on the site of a former cattle ranch which had been acquired by the foundation and is being gradually reforested. It lies inside the national park, in the uppermost reaches of the Río Pance, eight km up from the village of Pance (a three-hour walk).

### When to Go
The dry season on the eastern slopes (where you are most likely to hike) is from January to March and July to August. It's far more pleasant to do walks then, although it's possible to hike during the other months. It's always wet on the western slopes and rainfall becomes heavier as you descend to the Pacific coast. The average annual rainfall reaches 6000 mm (or even surpasses it) in the far western parts of the park.

### What to Bring
If you plan on camping, you'll need your camping equipment. As even the highest peaks are below the snowline, there's no need for special equipment apart from the usual trekking gear. Since the dry season can be tricky, bring a reliable rainproof jacket. Make sure to pack insect repellent and a torch. The average temperature on the ridge is 5°C (it can drop below freezing point at night), so bring enough warm clothing and a good sleeping bag if you are going to camp up there.

### Places to Stay & Eat
There are several small (but not very cheap) hotels along the access road to the park, between La Vorágine and Pance. They tend to be packed with caleños during weekends; most of them are closed on weekdays. There are also numerous restaurants in the area, and again, they mostly operate on weekends.

You can pitch your tent on either of two campsites in El Topacio, or further up on the path to the Pico Pance.

The only accommodation and eating facilities up in the mountains are in Hato Viejo. The foundation operates the cabaña (US$12 a bed plus three meals); you can camp for free next to the cabaña and buy food only (US$6 for three meals). It also offers other facilities such as horse rental (US$6 per day) and guides. Accommodation and food have to be booked and paid for in the Cali office of Fundación Farrallones (☎ 568335), Carrera 24B No 2A-99. It will also collect the US$1.50 entrance fee to the reserve. The office is open Monday to Friday from 8 am to noon and 2 to 6 pm. It's recommended you book several days in advance. You may arrange at the office for a guide to come down to Pance and take you up to the cabaña.

### Getting There & Away
Colectivos from the Cali bus terminal depart for Pance from 7 am on, frequently at weekends, but not so often during the week (US$1.50, 45 minutes). There are also buses on weekends.

## HACIENDAS EL PARAÍSO & PIEDECHINCHE
There are a number of old haciendas in the Cauca Valley, in the environs of Cali. Most of them date from the 18th and 19th centuries and were engaged in the cultivation and processing of sugarcane. El Paraíso and Piedechinche, close to each other about 40 km north-east of Cali, are the two best known haciendas.

**El Paraíso**, also called the Casa de la Sierra, is a country mansion built in colonial style in 1815. It owes its fame to having been the setting for a tragic love story depicted by Jorge Isaacs in his tear-jerking romantic novel, *María*. The book was published in 1867 and has remained unwaveringly popular to this day.

The house has been restored and decked out with period furnishings, and looks much the same as it is described in the novel. It's open to the public as a museum, Tuesday to Sunday from 9 am to 4 pm, closed on Monday (if

Monday is a holiday, it stays open but closes on Tuesday). Entry is US$0.50. The place will mean much more to you if you have read the book, but if not, it is still a nice house surrounded by a pleasant garden.

**Piedechinche**, dating back to the second half of the 18th century, is a bigger hacienda and once had its own sugar refinery; the original *trapiche* (traditional sugarcane mill) is still in place, next to the colonial house.

The **Museo de la Caña de Azúcar** (Sugarcane Museum) was founded here in 1981 and is very well organised. There is an exhibition hall where various aspects of sugarcane production are displayed, and a large park where a collection of old trapiches from all over the country have been put on view. The house itself, with its collection of period objects, can also be visited.

The hacienda is open Tuesday to Sunday from 9.30 am to 3.30 pm, closed on Monday (open on Monday if it's a holiday, but then closed on Tuesday). Entry is US$1, US$0.50 for students. All visitors are guided in groups at no extra charge. The tour takes about 1½ hours and includes visits to both the original mansion and the museum.

### Getting There & Away
As the haciendas are near one another, it is convenient to visit both of them in one trip. However, there's no regular public transport all the way to the haciendas, so if you want to visit them on your own, the trip will involve quite a bit of walking.

Many buses run along the main Cali-Buga road; get off on the outskirts of the town of Amaime (the drivers know where to drop you) and walk or hitch the rest of the way to Piedechinche (5.5 km). El Paraíso is still further off the road. Occasionally, you can catch a chiva.

Tours from Cali are organised on weekends; contact the Cortuvalle tourist office in Cali, which has possibly the cheapest tours.

### BUGA
• *pop 95,000* • *970 m* • *24°C* • ☎ *(9222)*
Buga, 76 km north of Cali, was founded in 1555 by Giraldo Gil de Estupiñán and would

probably be just an ordinary town today had it not been for a miraculous vision. Legend has it that in 1570 Christ – the Señor de los Milagros, or Lord of Miracles – appeared before an Indian woman on the bank of the Río Guadalajara, near the town. As is usually the case, the faithful who prayed to his image began to experience miraculous cures. The wondrous powers of Buga's Christ image have gradually made this town one of the major religious sanctuaries in the country. Pilgrims gather here all year round, but mostly in September for the Fiesta del Señor de los Milagros.

### Things to See
The town has lost much of its original colonial character, but it's still worth strolling about the central streets to explore what is left. Note the palmas de cera growing in the main plaza (see the Cocora section in the North-West chapter for information about these palms). The northern side of the plaza is taken up by the massive **Palacio de Justicia**, which has been recently restored. On the opposite side stands the **Catedral de San Pedro**, also known as the Antigua Ermita del Señor de los Milagros. The cathedral dates from 1773 and has an ornate, gilded high altar. The miraculous image of Christ was kept here until 1937. The church is only open for mass, daily at 6 pm and additionally at 11.30 am on Saturday and Sunday.

One block south of the plaza, on the corner of Carrera 14 and Calle 5, is the beautiful, though unrestored, **Iglesia de San Francisco**. This small church is rarely open.

Another block south and you'll get to the monumental **Basílica del Señor de los Milagros**. The church is 80 metres long and 35 metres wide, and its twin towers are 50 metres high. It was built between 1892 and 1907 as a new home for the image of Christ, which now resides over the high altar. You can get right to the foot of the crucifix by specially constructed steps. Predictably, this is the destination of the pilgrims. The church is open all day long.

Diagonally opposite the church, at Carrera 14 No 3-35, is the religious **Museo del Milagroso**, open Tuesday to Saturday from 11 am to noon and 2 to 3 pm, and Sunday from 9 am to 5.30 pm. Entry is free.

The square in front of the church is packed with stalls selling all imaginable kinds of religious stuff. Watch out for the wax figurines of men, women and children, and separate parts of the body such as legs, arms and eyes. They are supposed to make it easier for Christ to determine what you are suffering from. You buy the relevant part (or the full corpus if the disease affects the whole of your body) and leave it at the foot of the crucifix.

## Places to Stay

There are three areas to stay in Buga. The first is near the bus offices, where there are half a dozen cheapies. One of the cheapest is the basic *Hospedaje Las Vegas*, at Calle 6 No 18-68, which offers doubles without/with bath for US$6/7, but a bit of negotiation with the manager will probably beat these prices down.

Round the corner, the *Hotel Los Balcones*, at Carrera 19 No 6-20, may be a basic alternative, though it's overpriced. One of the best in this area is the *Hotel Los Faraones* (☎ 74131), at Calle 5 No 18-64, which has singles/doubles/triples with TV and bath for US$10/14/18.

The second area is in the vicinity of the market, which occupies the entire block between Calles 7 and 8 and Carreras 12 and 13. There are plenty of shabby residencias around, with a particular concentration on Calle 9 between Carreras 11 and 13.

Finally, you can stay in the centre, near the basilica. This area is more pleasant and the hotels are better, but they are more expensive. They are also overpriced: after all, they cater for pilgrims who are not necessarily worried about saving a few pesos after they've come from hundreds of km away to ask the Señor de los Milagros to cure them.

If you want to stay near the basilica, be prepared to pay some US$5 to US$7 per person. In that price bracket are the *Hotel La Casona* (☎ 77850), at Carrera 15 No 6-33, the *Hospedaje Su Casa* (☎ 75862), at Carrera 14 No 4-40, the *Hotel Los Ángeles* (☎ 71018), at

Carrera 14 No 4-34, and the *Hotel San Carlos*, at Carrera 14 No 4-13.

Better but more expensive is the *Hotel Cristo Rey* (☎ 78311), at Carrera 14 No 5-50; again, it's probably not worth the price.

If you feel like being a pilgrim, go to the *Casa del Peregrino* (☎ 75308, 72868), Calle 4 No 14-45, where decent singles/doubles/triples/quads go for US$10/15/18/22.

## Places to Eat

There are plenty of restaurants in each of the three hotel areas. Predictably, those around the bus offices and the market are mostly basic but cheap. The restaurants around the basilica are better and, accordingly, more expensive. Most of the listed hotels have their own restaurants. You'll also find restaurants closely packed on Calle 4 between Carreras 14 and 17.

## Getting There & Away

**Bus** The bus companies have their offices clustered around the square in front of the unused railway station, on the corner of Carrera 19 and Calle 6, four blocks west of the main plaza. Services are operated by Expreso Bolivariano, Expreso Palmira, Flota Magdalena, Empresa Arauca and Expreso Trejos.

**To Bogotá** There are frequent buses operated by most of the listed companies (US$16.50 climatizado, 10½ hours).

**To Medellín** Empresa Arauca has about 10 climatizados a day (US$14, 7½ hours), while Flota Magdalena runs several cheaper pullmans (US$13).

**To Cali** Buses to Cali depart at most every half an hour (US$3, 1½ hours).

**To Buenaventura** Expreso Trejos and Expreso Palmira have regular departures throughout the day (US$4.50 climatizado, US$3 corriente, three hours). Choose a seat on the left-hand side of the bus for better views.

**To Darién** Trans Calima buses leave from Calle 9 No 12-36 approximately every two hours, from 6.30 am to 6.30 pm (US$1.50, 1½ hours).

## EMBALSE CALIMA

Embalse Calima is a reservoir formed by the construction of a dam in the upper course of the Río Calima. It's a picturesque, 11-km-long lake set in a wide valley, and has become a popular weekend and holiday spot for people from Cali. Many of them have built summer houses along the lakeside, especially on the southern shore and slopes of the valley. The northern side has also experienced considerable tourist development and the shore is now lined with several holiday centres.

At the far northern end of the reservoir lies Darién, the only town on the lake (refer to the following section for details). The dam is at the westernmost end of the lake. There's a scenic road skirting the western and northern sides of the lake, which provides splendid views and gives a good idea of the lie of the land.

Before the Spanish conquest, the Calima Valley was home to the Calima Indians, who developed an advanced culture, confirmed by numerous artefacts excavated in the area. A good number of these finds are now exhibited in the museum in Darién.

## DARIÉN

• *pop 7000* • *1485 m* • *21˚C* • ☎ *(92226)*
Darién is the southernmost town founded by paisa colonisers. It was established in 1907, and preserves some features of Antioquian architecture. Over the past decade, the town has achieved popularity as a lakeside holiday resort for caleños and is packed with visitors at weekends.

Darién doesn't lie right on the lakeside but is within easy walking distance of the shore, and is a good base for walks around the lake and for water sports. The town itself is also interesting and is worth a visit if only to see its museum.

The local Fiestas del Verano are held over four days in the middle of August. It may be difficult to find accommodation at that time.

### Information

The Secretaría de Turismo (☎ 3157), at Calle 10 No 6-33, on the main plaza, is open Monday to Friday from 8 am to noon and 2 to 6 pm, and Saturday from 8 am to noon.

There's nowhere to change money, so bring enough pesos with you.

### Things to See

The sloping main plaza and adjacent streets still boast some of the original Antioquian houses, though the general character is gradually being lost because of an increasing number of modern constructions.

The town's star attraction is the **Museo Arqueológico**, at Calle 10 No 12-50, five blocks uphill from the main plaza. The museum focuses on Calima culture, which flourished in the area before the arrival of the Spaniards. The exhibition features the pottery of the three major groups that shaped the culture: Ilama (2000 BC to 1000 AD), Yotoco (1000 BC to 1000 AD) and Sonso (900 BC to the 16th century AD). Replicas of the original dwellings have been constructed in the surrounding park. The museum is open Tuesday to Friday from 9 am to 12.30 pm and 1.30 to 6 pm, as well as weekends and holidays from 10 am to 6 pm.

### Places to Stay

The accommodation options have expanded over the past decade and there are now perhaps a dozen budget hospedajes in town.

One of the cheapest places to stay is the *Hotel del Parque*, at Carrera 7 No 10-31, on the upper side of the main plaza. It's very simple and has shared baths only, but it's set in an old house and so has a certain style. It costs US$2 per person.

The *Casa del Viajero*, at Carrera 6 No 11-10, just off the lower corner of the plaza, offers much the same for US$3.50 per bed (single or matrimonio).

For somewhere cheap with a private bath, go to the *Hotel Zulevar* (☎ 3219), at Carrera 8 No 10-13, which is good and clean and costs US$4/7/8 a single/matrimonio/double. Alternatively, try the *Hotel Darién*, at Carrera 6 No 7-40, where doubles go for around US$7, though the management may try to charge more on weekends.

One of the best in town is the *Hotel Punto Rico* (☎ 3243), at Carrera 7 No 7-35, which has rooms with double beds (for single or matrimonio) and private bath with hot water for US$10. Add US$5 if you need a colour TV in your room.

Other budget options include the *Hospedaje El Campesino*, at Carrera 7 No 9-60, the *Hotel del Lago*, at Carrera 6 No 10-44 (main square), and the *Hotel La Séptima*, at Carrera 4 No 11-25, opposite the hospital.

Outside the town, the *Hostería Los Veleros* (☎ 3232), about six km west of Darién, is a posh, new hotel, with rooms for up to four people costing around US$80.

It's possible to camp rough along the northern shore of the lake, west of Darién, but ask the landowners for permission. There is an organised campsite near the dam, about 10 km from Darién.

### Places to Eat

There are quite a few eating outlets serving snacks, pizzas, fast food and set meals – nothing very sophisticated or expensive. Among restaurants, the *Delicias Vallunas*, Carrera 8 No 9-37, has possibly the best set meals. Other options include *Restaurante La Casona*, Carrera 6 No 10-02 (lower side of the main square), *Restaurante Delicias del Calima*, Calle 10 No 9-21, and the restaurant at the *Hotel Punto Rico*.

Pizzas are served in *Maia's Pizzas*, Calle 11 No 5-37. *Panadería y Pastelería La Cigarra*, Carrera 7 No 10-43 (upper side of the plaza), has probably the best tinto in town, while *Fuerza Latina*, Calle 11 No 5-59, is one of the places where you can enjoy an evening beer to the rhythms of salsa.

### Getting There & Away

Trans Calima, on the corner of Carrera 6 and Calle 9, opposite Telecom, operates buses to Buga and Cali. Buses to Buga depart every 1½ hours until 6.30 pm (US$1.50, 1½ hours). Buses to Cali run approximately every two hours (US$3, 2½ hours).

### BUENAVENTURA

• *pop 160,000* • *7 m* • *28°C* • ☎ *(9222)*

Buenaventura is Colombia's largest port on the Pacific coast. It's the only port on this coast with the capacity to service large vessels, and the only coastal city on the Pacific which is connected to the centre of the country by paved road. Understandably, most of the city's life has traditionally revolved around the port, fishing and other maritime activities.

Buenaventura was reputedly founded on 14 June 1539 on the Isla Cascajal by Juan de Ladrilleros. There's disagreement among historians about the site, the year and the founder's name. The only fact they agree upon is that it took place on 14 June, the holy day of San Buenaventura – hence the town's name.

The discovery of gold and platinum in the region prompted the development of the port. The Spaniards shipped in large numbers of black slaves and put them to work in mines. Although the exploitation of these two precious metals is now insignificant in the region, the descendants of the slaves remain, and are a feature of the city. In modern times, Buenaventura has expanded beyond Cascajal Island on to the mainland and has been connected to it by a bridge, the Puente El Piñal.

The city has an unpleasantly hot, humid climate. The annual rainfall is about 6500 mm, and heavy rains are frequent. There's no dry season as such, although the period from January to March is not as wet as the rest of the year.

Don't expect to find great tourist attractions in Buenaventura other than its omnipresent port atmosphere. If you are looking for some local colour, you can walk along the southern shore of the island where the people live in poor wooden shacks built on stilts over the ocean. Preferably, find a local to accompany you – the area is not safe.

The city is the main hub of transportation for virtually the whole of the Colombian Pacific coast. This is the best jumping-off point for Isla Gorgona and the Chocó coast. There are also some attractions closer by, including the beaches of La Bocana, Juanchaco and Ladrilleros (see the following sections).

### Information

**Tourist Office** The Cortuvalle tourist office (☎ 24415) is in the building of the Cámara de Comercio at the foot of the Muelle

**PLACES TO STAY**

1 Hotel Estación
5 Hotel Palermo
6 Hotel La Ceiba
7 Hotel Katherine
8 Hotel Residencias El Faro
9 Hotel Cordillera
11 Cascajal Hotel
14 Hotel Miramar
15 Hotel Colombia
16 Hotel Ensenada
17 Hotel Confort
18 Hotel del Mar
19 Hotel Felipe II

**OTHER**

2 Inderena
3 Banco de Occidente
4 Bus Terminal
10 Catedral de San Buenaventura
12 Cortuvalle Tourist Office
13 Banco de Bogotá
20 Restaurante Los Balcones
21 Banco de Colombia

*Bahía de Buenaventura*

Port Area

Tourist Pier

Parque Santander

## Buenaventura

0    100    200 m

Turístico (tourist pier), on the corner of Calle 1A and Carrera 2. It is open Monday to Friday from 8 am to noon and 2 to 6 pm.

**Money** Buenaventura has perhaps a dozen banks but apparently none of them change cash or travellers' cheques. The potentially useful banks for credit-card transactions have been marked on the map, but nonetheless you'd do better to bring with you enough Colombian currency from an inland big city.

**Inderena** Inderena (☎ 23862) is at Calle 3 No 2-50. The office is open Monday to Friday from 8 am to noon and 2 to 6 pm.

### Places to Stay – bottom end

Typically for a port, Buenaventura has a number of seedy brothels, which are often recognisable by the presence of prostitutes hanging around their doorways. Don't end up staying in one of them. There's also a good supply of suspicious dives operating as sex hotels on an hourly basis, but these are more difficult to detect. However, the first question of the incredulous staff – 'For the whole night?!' – will usually give you the answer.

One of the cheapest of the more 'orthodox' places is the big *Hotel Residencias El Faro*, at Calle 6 No 4-19, which costs US$3.50/4.50/6 for a single/matrimonio/double. There are only shared baths but rooms have fans. Choose a room with a window as the others are very unattractive.

One of the cheapest places with private baths is the *Hotel Miramar* (☎ 22100), at Calle 6 No 4A-24. It has large singles/doubles (though in a decayed state) for US$4.50/8.

There's a choice of hotels offering a fairly acceptable standard of rooms with private baths for around US$7/9/10 a single/ double/triple. Choose between the *Hotel Palermo* (☎ 23096), at Calle 7A No 4-17; the *Hotel Cordillera* (☎ 22008), at Calle 6 No 3B-59; the *Hotel Ensenada* (☎ 24282), at Carrera 5 No 4-27; and the *Hotel Colombia* (☎ 23969), at Carrera 5 No 5-22.

Slightly better than the above is the *Hotel Katherine* (☎ 23853), at Calle 7 No 4-32, which costs US$8/10/12 a single/matrimonio/double in rooms with bath and TV.

### Places to Stay – middle

In this category, you usually get an air-con room with TV, but don't expect much space or style. Possibly the cheapest is the *Hotel La Ceiba* (☎ 24267), at Calle 7A No 4-08, which costs US$12/14 for a single/double. Marginally more expensive is the *Hotel Felipe II* (☎ 22820), at Carrera 3A No 2-44.

The *Hotel del Mar* (☎ 24183), on the corner of Carrera 4 and Calle 3, is a more costly alternative at US$15/20. The recently refurbished *Hotel Confort* (☎ 23722), at Carrera 5 No 4-17, is indeed comfortable but has rather small rooms which are probably not worth the price (US$17/25/33/41 a single/double/triple/quad).

### Places to Stay – top end

One of the few options in this price bracket is the well-located *Cascajal Hotel* (☎ 22806), at Carrera 2A No 1-20, which has doubles/triples for US$36/44. Undoubtedly the fanciest place in town is the *Hotel Estación* (☎ 34070), at Calle 1 No 2-08. Built in 1928, this spacious, elegant mansion is in fact the only hotel with style and atmosphere; it costs around US$62/84/100 for a single/double/triple.

### Places to Eat

Cheap restaurants are clustered around the budget hotels; many of them are on Carrera 5. Comidas go for US$2 and other dishes from US$3 upwards. These restaurants are nothing special, but their fish is usually quite good.

There is a scarce choice of better restaurants. Try the *Restaurante Los Balcones*, Calle 2 No 3-94, which is good for mariscos (seafood) but is not very cheap, with dishes from US$7 to US$10. The restaurant of the *Hotel Estación* is reputedly the best in town.

### Getting There & Away

**Air** The airport is on the mainland, about 15 km from Buenaventura. Satena is the only airline which operates flights. They go to Cali (US$26), Guapí (US$31) and Bogotá (US$55).

**Bus** The new bus terminal is on Carrera 5 between Calles 7A and 7B, a five-minute walk from the city centre. Several bus companies, including Expreso Palmira, Expreso Trejos and Flota Magdalena, have frequent buses to Cali (US$3.50, three hours) and Buga (US$3, three hours). The road skirts the gorge of the Dagua River and pierces steep slopes through five tunnels near Loboguerrero. Take a seat on the right-hand side.

**Boat** A lot of unscheduled cargo boats go north (to Nuquí, Bahía Solano and Juradó) and south (to Guapí and Tumaco) along the coast. They usually take passengers and some have cabins. Most of the boats leave from El Piñal, the bridge that joins Cascajal Island to the mainland. Enquire in the office that is in the building right near the bridge (on the mainland side).

There is no regular transport to the Isla Gorgona but boats going to the ports further south pass by the island and can drop you off there. Count on about US$15 to US$20 one way and eight to 12 hours' travelling time. See the Isla Gorgona section for further details.

There are no boats up the Río San Juan to

Istmina. You have to take a chiva to San Isidro on the Río Calima (a long and bone-shaking trip) and look for a boat there. The lower course of the Río San Juan is reputedly unsafe, so it's perhaps better to avoid this trip. Instead, you can get to Istmina and Quibdó by road (via Buga, Cartago and Tadó).

Boats to La Bocana and Juanchaco leave from the tourist pier on the corner of Calle 1A and Carrera 2 (see the respective sections for more details).

## LA BOCANA

La Bocana is a hamlet with a beach at the mouth of the Bahía de Buenaventura. Although the beach is not very attractive, it has become a popular destination among tourists in the region. There are a number of simple, family-run hotels and restaurants; most of them will charge about US$5 for a bed or US$15 for full board.

A half-hour walk west along the coast will take you to the Piangüita beach, which sees fewer tourists. You can continue for about 40 minutes to yet another beach, Piangua.

### Getting There & Away

There are passenger boats operated by Cootransmar between Buenaventura and La Bocana. They depart from the tourist pier in Buenaventura. Information and tickets can be obtained in the Cootransmar office in the Cámara de Comercio building at the foot of the pier. Count on one boat daily in either direction on weekdays and about three boats daily on weekends. A return ticket costs US$8 and the trip takes 45 minutes one way. You can go by one boat and return by the other, but make sure there will be another boat to take you back.

If money is not a problem, or if you're with a large group, you may want to *pagar expreso* (rent a boat), which costs about US$90 return for up to 10 people. These boats can also take you to Piangüita and Piangua for a little extra.

## JUANCHACO & LADRILLEROS

These two small fishing villages are set on the Pacific coast at the outlet of the Bahía de Málaga. Both have become popular weekend spots for people from Cali and the region. Juanchaco is bigger but Ladrilleros has better beaches. Like elsewhere on the Pacific coast, the beaches have dark sand, the tides are high and the sea is rough. Boats anchor in Juanchaco, and from here it's a 20-minute walk to Ladrilleros.

There are a few caves on the beach at the foot of Ladrilleros that you can get to at low tide. Cholo Indians come to the beach in Ladrilleros to sell their traditional basket-ware, which is good and cheap.

You can walk several km north along the beach to another fishing village, La Barra, where some Cholo Indians live.

### Places to Stay & Eat

Both Juanchaco and Ladrilleros live off tourists and just about every house is a hotel, a restaurant, or both. Although Ladrilleros is a more pleasant place to stay, the choice of restaurants is better in Juanchaco. The usual price of most hotels is US$5 per person or US$15 with full board (it's possible to bargain on weekdays). Food and drink are not cheap as they have to be shipped in from Buenaventura. Fish, though it comes straight from the ocean, is not cheap either.

### Getting There & Away

Cootransmar has passenger boats between Buenaventura and Juanchaco. The return ticket costs around US$15 in the *barco* (large boat) and US$18 in the *lancha* (launch). The ride can be rough if the weather is stormy. The barco trip takes 2½ hours either way (the lancha is one hour faster) and you can return on any boat, on any day.

There are theoretically three boats a day in either direction, but there may be only one or two on weekdays. Boats are supposed to leave from both towns at 10 am, noon and 4 pm. There may be more boats on puentes (extended weekends). Keep in mind that this theoretical timetable is subject to change at any time depending on the number of passengers, the captain's mood, damage to the

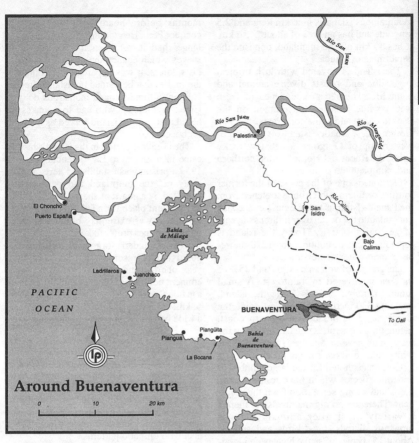

Around Buenaventura

```
0          10          20 km
```

boat, the weather and a myriad of other unpredictable developments.

## AROUND JUANCHACO

The region around Juanchaco is interesting. The coast in this area is precipitous in parts, and there are some small, lovely islets, which you will pass by when going to Juanchaco. Other attractions include the **Bahía de Málaga**, a large, picturesque bay with more than 30 islands, and the delta of the Río San Juan. The **San Juan delta**, which empties into the ocean the largest volume of water of all the rivers on the Pacific coast from Alaska to Chile, is 50 km wide and has several

mouths. The islands between the channels are covered with rainforest and mangroves. There are some tiny settlements on the coast and on the banks of the channels.

Negotiate a motorboat with the fishermen in Juanchaco (not in Buenaventura); they are eager to earn some extra money. Be prepared to pay about US$12 to US$15 an hour for a small boat that takes up to five people. The four to five-hour trip around Málaga Bay can be organised for US$50.

## ISLA GORGONA

Gorgona Island is Colombia's largest insular possession in the Pacific Ocean. This lovely, mountainous island is nine km long and 2.5 km wide and has an area of about 24 sq km. It lies 55 km off the mainland, opposite the department of Cauca.

The island is covered with lush tropical vegetation and boasts diverse animal and plant life. There's an abundance of fresh water, white beaches (uncommon on the Pacific coast) and some coral reefs. The Isla Gorgonilla, a smaller island off the southwestern tip of Gorgona, and a few rocky islets, the Rocas del Horno, on the northern end, complete the picture.

Gorgona is one of the peaks of the former fourth Cordillera, which once stretched from the Panama Isthmus to the Ecuadorian coast, but sank into the ocean over millions of years of geological activity. Today the island is separated from the continent by a 270-metre-deep underwater depression.

Gorgona is of volcanic origin and 85% of its area is covered by rainforest. A small mountain range extends along the island, reaching 330 metres at its highest point, the Cerro de la Trinidad. The eastern coast, facing the continent, is much calmer than the west, with several beaches (some of them white) and coral reefs along the shore.

Gorgona is noted for the large number of endemic species which have resulted from the island's long separation from the continent. There are no big mammals but there's a variety of smaller animals such as monkeys, lizards, bats, birds and snakes. About 15 species of snake have been identified here, including the boa. Two species of freshwater turtles and a colony of babillas (spectacled caymans) live at the Laguna Ayatuna. The waters surrounding the island are seasonally visited by dolphins, humpback whales and cachalots, and sea turtles come for their breeding period and lay eggs on the beaches.

In the remote past Gorgona was reputedly inhabited by Indians, but which Indian group it was is a matter of speculation. Suggested groups range from the Cunas of Panama to the Sindaguas from the southern part of the Colombian coast. Francisco Pizarro landed on the island in 1527 and stayed for several months before heading further south to conquer Peru. He would perhaps have stayed longer had it not been for the poisonous snakes which caused the deaths of some of his soldiers. It was apparently in honour of the snakes that he named the island after the Gorgon, a three-winged monstrous deity in Greek mythology, who had live snakes for hair. Later on, the island served as a shelter for buccaneers.

The cruellest period in the island's history came in response to La Violencia, when in 1959 a prison was established here. Tucked away off the mainland and permanently patrolled by a guard of sharks, Gorgona was an excellent place for a jail. Some witnesses say that it was extremely brutal and cruel; official sources prefer to keep silent. In 1975 Inderena included Gorgona on its list of proposed nature reserves. It took almost 10 years of effort and negotiations with the government before the island eventually became a national park in 1984. The park covers 492 sq km, comprising Gorgona, Gorgonilla and a wide belt of the surrounding ocean.

### When to Go

The island can be visited all year round. The high season is in December, January, Holy Week, June, July and all puentes. This season corresponds with the periods of Colombian holidays (and, accordingly, the island sees most national tourists in these times) rather than with climatic patterns.

The climate is hot and wet throughout the year. The mean temperature is about 27°C and the relative humidity is close to 90%. The sky is frequently overcast.

Average annual rainfall exceeds 4000 mm. There's no dry season, but there are significant monthly differences in the amount of precipitation: September and October are the wettest months, whereas the rainfall is lowest in February and March.

### What to Bring

Bring boots, a long-sleeved shirt, long trousers, rain gear, a swimsuit, hat and sun screen. If you plan on snorkelling, bring

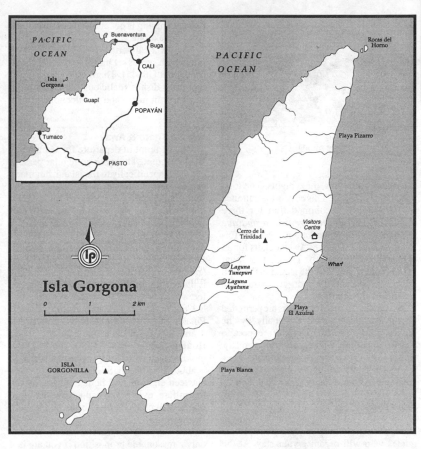

Isla Gorgona

along your gear. A torch is recommended; the use of candles is not permitted.

It's not necessary to bring food. Don't plan on cooking on the island – it's not permitted. Nor, according to the park regulations, are you allowed to bring in alcoholic beverages.

All nonbiodegradable products (bottles, cans, batteries etc) have to be taken off the island, so make sure you have some plastic bags with you.

### Permit

Before you visit Gorgona, you need a permit from Inderena. Unlike permits to many other national parks, this one is essential: you won't be allowed to visit the island without it.

The permit should be obtained from the Inderena office in Bogotá. The Buenaventura office may give you the permit in some particular cases (for example, if you are coming from Ecuador and, understandably, haven't passed through Bogotá) but it's not guaranteed. There's no Inderena office in Cali.

While applying for the permit, you also have to book and pay for accommodation on Gorgona. There's a fixed duration of stay on

Giant Anteater

the island: four days, three nights. The total to be paid is US$35. This covers the entrance fee (US$3.50), accommodation for three nights (US$30) and *embarque/desembarque* (embarkation/disembarkation – see the following Getting There & Away details for an explanation) (US$1.50). The cost is about US$3 more if you visit the island in the high seasons. Food and transport are extra – see the following details.

As a limited number of visitors are permitted on the island (restricted essentially by the limited accommodation capacity), expect to wait for some time. Waiting times differ greatly, from a week to two or even three months. They are much longer during the high season. It's advisable to book as early as possible.

### Activities

Upon arrival on the island you'll be in the hands of friendly Inderena rangers or private guides who will organise your stay. At the beginning, you will be given an introductory lecture concerning the island. Then, in the following days, you'll take part in excursions, which will introduce you to the most interesting parts of the island. All the walks are accompanied by a guide. The Inderena programme allows some time for recreational activities such as swimming, sunbathing and snorkelling.

### Places to Stay & Eat

Inderena has a spacious visitors centre for 70 guests. It has mostly four-bed rooms, each equipped with its own bath and fresh water. The electricity is provided by a small local plant. Camping is not allowed because of the risk of snakebite.

There's a cafeteria, open from 7 am to 8 pm, which serves set meals (three meals will cost about US$11). There's also a choice of à la carte dishes (delicious fish), fast food, snacks, fruit juices and nonalcoholic drinks.

### Getting There & Away

The usual point of departure for Gorgona is Buenaventura. There are no regular passenger boats specifically to the island, but many cargo boats go to the ports further to the south and pass by Gorgona en route. They don't dock at the island, but will call Inderena's launch, which will come and pick you up from on board. A similar operation is performed when you leave the island: Inderena staff will hail a passing cargo boat and deliver you on board in their launch. This is the reason for the embarque/desembarque fee.

Cargo boats depart daily from Puente El Piñal in Buenaventura, at some time between 4 and 8 pm. Check in the morning at the Bodega Lizcano (☎ 34580, 34680), the building next to the bridge. The one-way fare is about US$15 to US$20 and the trip takes between eight and 12 hours. Never pay the return fare, even if the captain swears blind that he will pick you up to bring you back to Buenaventura.

You can also contract a launch, but it's only a reasonable proposition if you are in a larger group, as it will cost some US$100.

Other possible (but seldom-used) jumping-off points for Gorgona are Guapí and Tumaco. Guapí is a seaside village in Cauca, just opposite Gorgona, 56 km away. Guapí is not connected by road with the rest of the country and can only be reached by air (flights from Cali with Satena and Aces) or sea (cargo boats from Buenaventura and occasionally from Tumaco). Once in Guapí, you have to rent a boat (expensive), which will take you to Gorgona in two hours.

Tumaco is accessible by road from Pasto and Ipiales after a long, bone-rattling trip. Irregular cargo boats (a couple per week)

Top: Iglesia de la Ermita, Cali
Bottom: Old hacienda of Cañasgordas near Cali

Stone statues of San Agustín

going to Buenaventura can put you down on Gorgona (US$15 to US$20).

## Tours

As Gorgona has become an increasingly popular tourist destination, several private operators have emerged on the market, offering all-inclusive tours to Gorgona. They have their own boats and provide a more comfortable and attractive way to visit the island than doing it on your own – at a price, of course.

One of the major agencies organising trips to Gorgona is Cruceros de Colombia, which has the luxurious *Tropic Surveyor* boat. Cruceros offers the standard four-day/three-night programme, including all excursions on the island you'd otherwise take with Inderena. The difference is that you'll sleep and eat on the boat (both accommodation and food are very good). The company provides transport from Cali (where you can be picked up from the airport) to Gorgona and back, and will arrange the Inderena permit for you. There is diving equipment on board and provision is made for up to three dives a day. The whole package costs about US$400.

Cruceros de Colombia has offices in Bogotá (☎ 257 3894), Calle 95 No 13-22; Medellín (☎ 266 6414, 266-3932), Carrera 43A No 1A Sur-69, Oficina 801; and Cali (☎ 612153, 612154), Calle 19N No 5N-34, Piso 8.

These tours don't set off until they collect 32 people (the capacity of the boat), which may take some time. Contact Cruceros de Colombia in advance for further information and schedules.

---

# Cauca & Huila

These two departments boast Colombia's most important archaeological sites, San Agustín (in Huila) and Tierradentro (in Cauca). The colourful Guambiano market in Silvia, the volcanoes and hot springs of the Parque Nacional Puracé, the caves of the Parque Nacional Cueva de los Guácharos and the white pearl of colonial architecture, Popayán, are some of the region's other highlights.

The Popayán-San Agustín-Tierradentro triangle is one of the most popular areas in Colombia among foreign travellers, and it's well worth a trip – set aside at least one week for this loop.

## POPAYÁN

• *pop 210,000* • *1740 m* • *19°C* • ☎ *(928)*

Popayán is one of the most beautiful colonial cities in Colombia. Founded in 1537 by Sebastián de Belalcázar, the town quickly became an important political, cultural and religious centre, and was an obligatory stopover on the route between Cartagena and Quito. Its mild climate attracted the wealthier Spanish families owning sugar haciendas in the hot Cali region. They came to live here, building mansions and founding schools. Several imposing churches and monasteries were built in the 17th and 18th centuries.

During the 20th century, while many other Colombian cities were caught up in the race to modernise and industrialise, Popayán somehow managed to retain its colonial character. Unfortunately, on 31 March 1983, as the much-celebrated Maundy Thursday religious procession was just about to depart, a violent earthquake shook the city, seriously damaging many of its historic buildings and most of its churches. The difficult job of restoration continued for a decade, and the result is truly admirable – little can be seen of the effects of the disaster.

Apart from its beauty, Popayán is an inviting, tranquil and clean city. It has a competent tourist office and a range of good places to stay and eat, and is not expensive by Colombian standards.

The weather is pleasant most of the year, although the best time to visit is from November to January. From June to September, the rains are more frequent and it is often cloudy.

## Information

**Tourist Office** The Caucatur tourist office (☎ 242251), at Calle 3 No 4-70, is a recommended first stop in town. The staff are

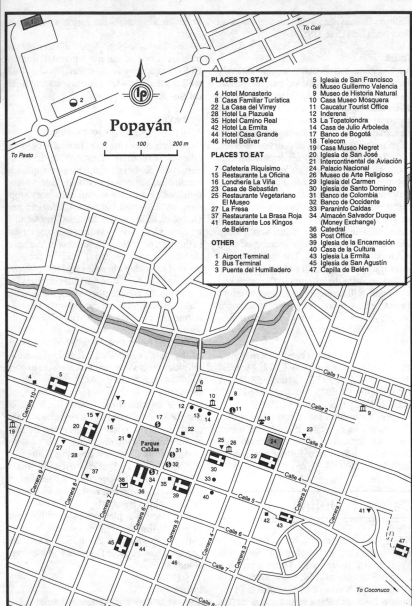

# Popayán

0    100    200 m

**PLACES TO STAY**

4   Hotel Monasterio
8   Casa Familiar Turística
22  La Casa del Virrey
28  Hotel La Plazuela
35  Hotel Camino Real
42  Hotel La Ermita
44  Hotel Casa Grande
46  Hotel Bolívar

**PLACES TO EAT**

7   Cafetería Riquísimo
15  Restaurante La Oficina
16  Lonchería La Viña
23  Casa de Sebastián
25  Restaurante Vegetariano
    El Museo
27  La Fresa
37  Restaurante La Brasa Roja
41  Restaurante Los Kingos
    de Belén

**OTHER**

1   Airport Terminal
2   Bus Terminal
3   Puente del Humilladero

5   Iglesia de San Francisco
6   Museo Guillermo Valencia
9   Museo de Historia Natural
10  Casa Museo Mosquera
11  Caucatur Tourist Office
12  Inderena
13  La Topatolondra
14  Casa de Julio Arboleda
17  Banco de Bogotá
18  Telecom
19  Casa Museo Negret
20  Iglesia de San José
21  Intercontinental de Aviación
24  Palacio Nacional
26  Museo de Arte Religioso
29  Iglesia del Carmen
30  Iglesia de Santo Domingo
31  Banco de Colombia
32  Banco de Occidente
33  Paraninfo Caldas
34  Almacén Salvador Duque
    (Money Exchange)
36  Catedral
38  Post Office
39  Iglesia de la Encarnación
40  Casa de la Cultura
43  Iglesia La Ermita
45  Iglesia de San Agustín
47  Capilla de Belén

helpful and friendly, and will provide good information about the city and the region. They will also store your luggage free of charge. The office is open Monday to Friday from 8 am to noon and 2 to 6.30 pm, and on Saturday and Sunday from 10 am to 5 pm.

**Money** No bank in Popayán will change cash or travellers' cheques, so come prepared. If you happen to run out of money, the best place to go is the Almacén Salvador Duque, a shop on the main square at Calle 5 No 6-25. The owner changes both cash and cheques and his rate is consistently among the best in town, though it's less than you would get in banks in Cali or Pasto, the two nearest cities with useful banks. Note also that San Agustín and Tierradentro, two popular tourist destinations from Popayán, don't have banks, so bring along enough pesos to last you the whole trip around the region.

Banco de Bogotá, Banco de Colombia and Banco de Occidente, all on the main square, might deal with your credit cards.

**Inderena** The Inderena office is at Calle 3 No 5-73.

### Churches

Most of the churches have been meticulously restored and are open for worship. They are only open for mass, usually early in the morning and late in the afternoon, so plan your sightseeing accordingly and , of course, remain quiet while the mass is in progress.

Don't miss the **Iglesia de Santo Domingo**, famous for its rich original decoration, particularly the side altarpieces, and the **Iglesia de San Agustín**, which has probably the most magnificent high and side altars in Popayán. **Iglesia La Ermita** is Popayán's oldest church (from 1546), worth seeing for its fine main retable, and for some fragments of old frescoes which were only discovered after the earthquake.

The **Catedral** dates from the second half of the 19th century. It was almost completely destroyed by the earthquake (as was its internal decoration) and rebuilt virtually from the ground up. It's now the most carefully tended church in town, but there's a somewhat soulless air to the place.

The **Iglesia de San Francisco**, reputedly the best of all the city churches, is still waiting for restoration. Its cracked façade gives a good idea of just how destructive the earthquake was.

### Museums

All of Popayán's renowned museums are open again, daily from 9 am to noon and 2 to 5 pm. The **Casa Museo Mosquera** contains a collection of colonial art, including some religious objects. More sacred art is to be found in the **Museo de Arte Religioso**. The **Casa Museo Negret** features abstract sculpture by the distinguished contemporary artist Edgar Negret, while the **Museo Guillermo Valencia** is dedicated to the poet who once lived here.

The **Museo de Historia Natural** is possibly the best of its kind in the country, noted for its extensive collection of insects, butterflies and, in particular, stuffed birds. Part of the top floor is taken up by an archaeological display of pre-Columbian pottery of several cultures from southern Colombia.

### Other Attractions

Churches and museums are only a part of what Popayán has to offer. The best approach is to take a leisurely walk along the central streets, which are lined with whitewashed, two-storey colonial mansions, savouring the architectural details and stepping inside the public buildings to see their fine patios.

Have a look at the Palacio Nacional, the Puente del Humilladero, the Casa de la Cultura and a curious house, different from the others, the Casa de Julio Arboleda. The Universidad del Cauca, in the old Dominican monastery, is worth entering to see the ornate Paraninfo Caldas meeting hall.

The Capilla de Belén, a chapel set on a hill just east of the city centre, offers good views over the town, but don't walk there under any circumstances: there have been repeated armed attacks on travellers on the serpentine access alley to the chapel. El Morro de Tulcán, a hill topped by an equestrian statue of the town's founder, provides even better views, but it's equally dangerous to walk there.

## Festivals & Events

Since 1558, Popayán's fame has grown on account of its Easter celebrations, especially its Maundy Thursday and Good Friday night-time processions. Thousands of believers from all over Colombia come to take part in this religious ceremony, the most elaborate in the country. The Festival of Religious Music is held concurrently. Note that hotels are full around this time, so get there earlier or book in advance.

## Places to Stay

Popayán has a good array of accommodation to suit every pocket. Many hotels are set in old colonial houses and have a style and atmosphere which is not often to be found in Colombian hotels.

**Places to Stay – bottom end** If you are really hard up, there are half a dozen residencias on Carrera 5 between Calles 7 and 8. They are basic but very cheap: about US$2.50/3.50 for a single/double. The best of the lot seems to be the *Hotel Bolívar*.

The place which has recently become the most popular among foreign backpackers is the *Casa Familiar Turística* (☎ 240019), Carrera 5 No 2-41 (no sign on the door). It has a friendly, family atmosphere, and just five rooms (you pay US$3.50 per bed). You can have a filling breakfast for US$1, and leave your gear free of charge if you go for a trip around the region. The Casa Familiar is the only budget hotel from which you can make overseas reverse-charge calls. If reverse-charge calls to your country are impossible, the manager will let you have a one-minute call to ask your party to call you back. As this book was in production, a traveller's letter announced that the Casa Familiar had moved to Carrera 8 No 3-25 (☎ 242100).

**Places to Stay – middle** The friendly *La Casa del Virrey* (☎ 240836), Calle 4 No 5-78,

just off the main plaza, is a place deserving a warm recommendation. This beautiful colonial house with a fine patio has comfortable rooms with bath attached (choose one facing the street) which cost US$9/15/20 a single/double/triple. The *Casa Grande* (☎ 240908), Carrera 6 No 7-11, has similar prices and standards but lacks the old-time atmosphere.

**Places to Stay – top end** The *Hotel La Ermita* (☎ 241936), Calle 5 No 2-77, near the church of the same name, combines old and new, with airy modern rooms and a delightful old patio. It costs US$25/35/45.

There's a choice of colonial mansions which have been turned into stylish hotels, including the *Hotel La Plazuela* (☎ 241084), Calle 5 No 8-13, and the *Hotel Camino Real* (☎ 241254), Calle 5 No 5-59. Either costs about US$30/40 for a single/double; the latter is better (ask for a room with a balcony facing the street).

*Hotel Monasterio* (☎ 242191), Calle 4, on the corner of Carrera 10, is the fanciest place in town. Check whether it has reopened after refurbishing.

## Places to Eat

Popayán has plenty of good places to eat. The cheapest set meals are served at *La Brasa Roja*, on the corner of Calle 6 and Carrera 8. The *Lonchería La Viña*, Calle 4 No 7-85, is open till late and is popular among locals for its filling set meals. *La Oficina*, Calle 4 No 8-01, just a few steps along the street from La Viña, has rich Antioquian food at reasonable prices, and also serves large set meals at lunch time. For tasty vegetarian food, go to *Restaurante Vegetariano El Museo*, Calle 4 No 4-62.

*Los Kingos de Belén*, Calle 4 No 0-55, has good regional food; try the bandeja típica and wash it down with champús. For delicious and very cheap empanadas de pipián and tamales de pipián (local specialities not to be found elsewhere), the place to go is *La Fresa*, a small cubbyhole (with no sign) at Calle 5 No 8-83. You can also have tamales and a variety of other snacks at the *Cafetería*

*Riquísimo*, at Carrera 8 No 3-61. The owner, Silvio, has plenty of information about the region.

*Casa de Sebastián*, Calle 3 No 2-54, is an atmospheric colonial pizzeria-cum-bar with a beautiful patio and friendly management. It's open from 7 pm to 1 am. An alternative place for a drink (but not for food) is *La Topatolondra*, a night bar at Calle 3 No 5-69 with good salsa music.

The restaurant of the *Hotel Camino Real* is commonly and justly acclaimed as the best in town: you won't find such mouthwatering steaks and French specialities for miles around.

### Getting There & Away
**Air** Machangara Airport is just behind the bus terminal, a 15-minute walk from the city centre, but to get there you have to walk through a reputedly unsafe area so it's recommended you take a taxi (US$1.50).

Intercontinental de Aviación has daily flights to Bogotá (US$54), where you can change for flights to other destinations throughout the country. Satena flies twice weekly to Guapí (US$34).

**Bus** All buses arrive at and leave from the bus terminal, on the main Cali-Pasto road. It's a short walk from the city centre, but it's better to go by taxi (US$1).

**To Cali** There are plenty of buses operated by several companies (US$5.50 climatizado, US$4.50 pullman, three hours).

**To Bogotá** Flota Magdalena and Expreso Bolivariano service this route; expect a bus to depart every hour or two (US$24 climatizado, 15 hours).

**To Pasto** Buses depart regularly, every 30 minutes to an hour (US$12 climatizado, US$10 pullman, six to seven hours). The scenery along the road is captivating. Night buses on this route have been waylaid and passengers robbed, so avoid night-time travel.

**To Silvia** Coomotoristas has several morning buses (US$1.50, 1½ to two hours). See the Silvia section for more information.

**To Tierradentro** Take a Sotracauca bus to Belalcázar (Páez) at 5 or 10.30 am, or 1 or 3 pm, and get off at El Cruce de San Andrés (US$6.50,

five hours). From El Cruce, walk two km to the museum.

**To San Agustín** Two buses daily (with Cootranshuila and Sotracauca) run to San Agustín along a road via Coconuco and Isnos (US$10, six to seven hours). The road is very rough, but the trip through the lush cloudforest of the Cordillera is spectacular. Note that you can walk to San Agustín; there's an attractive and popular trek via the Laguna de la Magdalena. The tourist office will give you the necessary information. See the Parque Nacional Puracé section for details.

**To Coconuco** Cooptranstimbío has a couple of buses a day (US$1.50, one hour); or take either of the San Agustín buses, which pass through Coconuco.

## SILVIA
• *pop 4500* • *2620 m* • *15°C* • ☎ *(928)*

Silvia, a picturesque small town 60 km from Popayán, is the centre of the Guambiano Indian region. The Indians don't live in Silvia itself, but in small mountain villages such as Pueblito, La Campana, Guambia and Caciques, scattered throughout the area. The whole community numbers about 12,000 Indians.

The Guambianos are considered one of the most traditional Indian groups in Colombia. They have preserved their culture surprisingly well given their proximity to, and contacts with, the 'civilised world'. They speak their own language, dress very traditionally and still use rudimentary techniques in agriculture. They are excellent weavers.

On Tuesday, which is market day, they come to Silvia to sell fruit, vegetables and handicrafts. This is the best time to visit the town – a perfect day trip from Popayán. Silvia market is possibly the most colourful Indian gathering in the country.

There are plenty of Indians in town on that day, almost all in traditional dress, the women in handwoven garments and wearing an impressive collection of beaded necklaces, busily spinning wool. They come in chivas and tend to congregate around the main plaza.

The market begins at dawn and goes until the early afternoon. You can purchase ruanas, shawls, blankets, scarves and sweaters, as well as, of course, an amazing variety of fruit and vegetables. Don't forget to bring a sweater (or buy one at the market) – it can be pretty cold if the weather is cloudy.

There's the Museo de Artesanías del Mundo in the Casa Turística, Carrera 2 No 14-39, which displays a haphazard assortment of tourist souvenirs from all over the world. It's hardly an essential port of call unless you're curious to see what they have from your country.

Freddy Vargas, the local guide (you'll find him in the Casa Turística), can arrange tours around the region in a jeep. For shorter excursions, you can rent horses next to the Centro Vacacional Silvia, a large, expensive hotel just off the main square.

### Places to Stay

Most travellers visit Silvia as a one-day trip from Popayán, but, if you feel like staying longer, there are at least half a dozen cheap residencias, including the *Hotel Cali* on the main plaza. The *Casa Turística* is a more expensive place (US$9/17 a single/double), but you'll actually stay in the museum. In the top bracket is the *Centro Vacacional Silvia*.

### Getting There & Away

Coomotoristas has buses from Popayán to Silvia at 8, 9.30 and 11 am (US$1.50, 1½ to two hours). Take the first bus, otherwise you'll miss a lot of the market action. Better still, take any of the frequent early-morning buses from Popayán to Cali, get off in Piendamó (US$0.80, 45 minutes), then take a colectivo to Silvia (US$0.80, another 45 minutes). On Tuesday there are also direct colectivos between Popayán and Silvia. The tourist office was planning to provide its own transport for the Tuesday market, so ask there about this.

You may consider coming to Silvia on Monday to stay overnight and catch the spectacular sight of the Guambianos arriving in their chivas at dawn on Tuesday, then preparing for the market. If you plan to do this, get to Piendamó before 5 pm, the time when the last colectivo departs for Silvia.

## COCONUCO

* *pop 2000* • *2460 m* • *16°C*

This village, set in the valley of the Río Cauca at the foothills of the Volcán Puracé, 25 km from Popayán, is noted for its hot sulphur springs. The best known are the Aguas Hirviendos (Boiling Waters), three km from the village, a 45-minute walk on the road or a 30-minute walk by a short cut along a path that climbs just past the Hotel de Turismo. The water is really hot but the setting is not very pleasant. The other springs, the Aguas Tibias (Warm Waters), are four km along the road towards Paletará.

The Hacienda del General Tomás Cipriano de Mosquera, the old summer house of a former president of Colombia, is about one km from the village on the road to Popayán, but you aren't allowed inside.

### Places to Stay & Eat

There are a few budget hospedajes in the village, including the hospedaje of *Marino Legarda*, a house 20 metres off the main road, three blocks up from the church. It charges US$3.50/5 for a single/double, and serves set meals.

The *Hotel de Turismo*, a big, stylised building, is about 0.5 km past the village. Rooms cost US$14/20, and it has a reasonably priced restaurant but the menu is limited.

### Getting There & Away

There are two buses to Popayán, departing at 8 am and 5 pm (US$1.50, one hour), plus a chiva at about 6 am coming through from Paletará. In addition, two buses from San Agustín pass through on their way to Popayán early in the afternoon. In the opposite direction, to San Agustín, buses pass through Coconuco in the morning (US$8, five to six hours).

## PARQUE NACIONAL PURACÉ

This national park, about 60 km east of Popayán, covers 830 sq km of one of the most spectacular parts of the Cordillera Central. Encompassing rugged terrain between altitudes of 2500 and almost 4800 metres, the park offers a wide variety of

**Parque
Nacional
Puracé**

landscapes and sights. Several volcanoes, more than 20 mountain lakes, the sources of three of the main Colombian rivers (Magdalena, Cauca and Caquetá), sulphur springs, waterfalls, lush vegetation and diverse animal life are all to be found in the park.

The principal volcanic peaks are in a mountain range known as the Sierra de los Coconucos, in the northern part of the park. The highest of them are Pan de Azúcar and Puracé, the latter being the only active volcano in the park. Its last violent eruption took place in 1889, when rocks were thrown as far as Popayán. At the beginning of the present century all the peaks were covered by permanent snow. Today only Pan de Azúcar has a snowy cap all year round; the others have only patches of snow that may disappear altogether in the dry season.

### When to Go
The dry season is from December to February, but even this period is not very reliable. The weather is precarious all year round, so take good rain gear. Generally, only the early mornings are sunny; later in the day, the volcanoes are covered by clouds.

### Things to See & Do
If you are not going to trek, then you can only visit the northern part of the park, which is accessible by the Popayán-La Plata road, serviced regularly by buses. There are several interesting places in this area, most of which are within a short walking distance of the road.

The hot sulphur springs known as the **Termales de San Juan** are set in beautiful surroundings and are a most spectacular sight. Multicoloured moss, algae and lichens grow where the hot waters meet the icy-cold mountain creeks. The springs are a 15-minute walk from the Inderena building on the Popayán-La Plata road (the entrance fee is US$0.40). Inderena also has a museum there, which features exhibits on the region, its history, geography, flora and fauna (the entrance fee is US$0.80).

Two km west of the springs, just off the

main road, is a fine 12-metre-high waterfall, the **Cascada de Bedón**.

Another waterfall, the 25-metre-high **Cascada San Nicolás**, is three km east of the springs by the main road, then a 15-minute walk south along a path. This path gets very muddy in the rainy season.

**Pilimbalá**, set at 3350 metres, two km off the main road, is the only place with lodging and eating facilities within the park (see Places to Stay & Eat), and has thermal baths. It is a starting point up to the summits of the volcanoes.

The **Volcán Puracé** (4780 metres) can be reached by a footpath from Pilimbalá after a steady four-hour climb (three hours back down). The path is clear all the way up to the top. If you're lucky, the view from the top will stretch as far as Nevado del Huila. You can easily do this trip within a day, but start early.

From the top of Puracé, you can walk on to the **Volcán Pan de Azúcar** in about three to four hours – there is no path, just head for the snowy cone of the volcano – but you won't be able to get back the same day. Camping equipment is a must.

There's more splendid trekking territory in the central and, particularly, southern regions of the park. In the southernmost part of the park, the trek from Valencia to San Agustín (or vice versa) is becoming increasingly popular. You can do it in two to three days on foot or on horseback; horses can be hired at either end. Camping gear is not necessary. Tourist offices in San Agustín and Popayán will provide the most recent information on this trek.

If you plan on trekking further afield in the park, you should be well prepared: a tent, sleeping bag, warm clothes, good shoes and food are necessary. Buy the 1:25,000 maps in the IGAC in Bogotá, and get a permit from Inderena.

### Places to Stay & Eat

The only accommodation in the park is in Pilimbalá, where three cabins and a restaurant have been built next to the thermal pools. Each cabin can sleep up to seven people and costs US$36. If there are not many guests, you may be allowed to pay US$7 for just a bed. All the cabins have baths with hot water, and open fireplaces with firewood provided. The restaurant serves breakfasts (US$2) and set lunches and dinners (US$4 each). The management is friendly and helpful. The water in the thermal pools is quite cold – only about 30°C. If you are not a guest of the hotel, you pay a US$1 entrance fee to the pools.

On weekends, the place may fill up with tourists; you can book ahead at the tourist office in Popayán.

### Getting There & Away

The northern part of the park is the easiest to reach; buses along the Popayán-La Plata road run every two hours or so, passing near Pilimbalá and the other sites of interest. Make sure you tell the driver where you want to get off.

Popayán-San Agustín buses (two daily in either direction) pass through the central part of the park. Unless you are prepared to camp, it's probably too risky to get off and count on the later bus to take you back down. The area is uninhabited; the closest village is Paletará, but it would be a long walk.

Finally, the southernmost part of the park is only accessible on foot or horseback, from either San Agustín or Valencia. There's one bus daily in either direction between Popayán and Valencia.

### SAN AGUSTÍN

• *1695 m* • *18°C* • ☎ *(988)*

This is one of the most important archaeological sites on the continent. The region was inhabited by a mysterious civilisation which left behind several hundred freestanding monumental statues carved in stone, as well as a number of tombs.

There is still little known about the people who created the statues. Some archaeologists have drawn parallels between these monuments and the statues on Easter Island in the Pacific Ocean, but most experts relate San Agustín to the pre-Columbian Mesoamerican

San Agustín Area

0     1     2 km

(Mexico, Guatemala) and Andean (Peru, Bolivia) cultures.

Most probably, the culture began to flourish about the 6th century AD and reached its apogee around the 14th century. The best statuary was made in the last phase of the civilisation's existence. The people who inhabited the region had presumably vanished before the Spaniards arrived. Perhaps, like many other civilisations of the Andean region, theirs fell victim to the Incas – this area of Colombia was the northernmost point of the Inca Empire. All this is still open to discussion. What is certain is that the statues

were not discovered until the middle of the 18th century, when a Spanish monk, Fray Juan de Santa Gertrudis, passed through San Agustín and gave a written account of the sculptures.

So far, some 500 statues have been found and excavated. A great number of them are anthropomorphic figures – some of them realistic, some very stylised, resembling masked monsters. Others are zoomorphic, depicting sacred animals such as the eagle, the jaguar and the frog. The statues vary in size, from some 20 cm up to seven metres, and in their degree of detail.

The site was no doubt a ceremonial centre where the Agustinians buried their dead, placing statues next to the tombs. Pottery and gold objects were left in more important tombs.

San Agustín is not a compact archaeological site but rather a collection of a few dozen sites scattered in groups over a wide area on both sides of the gorge formed by the upper Río Magdalena. The main town of the region is San Agustín, where you'll find most of the accommodation and restaurants. From there, you can explore the region; count on three days for leisurely visits to the most interesting places.

The most important place is the Parque Arqueológico, which boasts the largest number of statues and a museum. The second most important place in the region is the Alto de los Ídolos, another archaeological park.

You buy one entrance ticket (US$6 for foreigners), which is valid for two days for entry to both parks. A student card saves you half this price. There's no admission fee to other, outlying archaeological sites.

The weather is varied, with the driest period from December to February and the wettest from April to June. In certain periods of the year, there may be many annoying, biting insects. Carry insect repellent for excursions, and wear trousers and long-sleeved shirts at these times.

### Information

**Tourist Office** The tourist office (☎ 373019), at Calle 5 No 14-75, is very friendly and helpful, probably the best in Colombia. Staff members speak English, French and Italian. They have comprehensive information about the region, and plenty of leaflets on the whole country – stock up here, as they can be difficult to find elsewhere. They sell a good booklet (Spanish/English edition) about the San Agustín and Tierradentro cultures, which contains a description of the sights and is illustrated with maps. The tourist office offers jeep tours and horse rentals, and has a full list of routes, with prices, licensed guides etc. The staff also have a complete list of hotels in the area. The office is open daily from 8.30 am to 12.30 pm and 1.30 to 5.30 pm.

**Money** There are no banks which change money in San Agustín. The tourist office will help you to change cash dollars, but at a poor rate. Travellers' cheques are apparently impossible to change. The Caja Agraria may give peso advances to Visa card holders.

### Parque Arqueológico

The 78-hectare archaeological park is about 2.5 km west of the town of San Agustín, a pleasant half-hour's walk along a paved road. The park covers an area where several important archaeological sites have been found close to each other. There are in total about 130 statues in the park, either found *in situ* or collected from other areas, and including some of the best examples of San Agustín statuary. Even if you are on a tight schedule, don't miss the park.

At the entrance to the park is the **Museo Arqueológico**, which displays smaller statues, pottery, utensils, jewellery and other objects, along with background information about the culture. It's a useful first stop to learn something about the people who created this mysterious cult of statuary.

Just in front of the museum is the **Mesita D**, one of four burial sites identified by consecutive letters of the alphabet. The statues assembled here date from the earlier phase of the culture's development and are noted for their cruder designs and less polished appearance.

A path leads from the museum to the so-called **Bosque de las Estatuas** (Forest of the Statues), where 35 statues of different origins have been placed along a footpath that snakes through lush vegetation.

Return to the museum and go to see the three remaining mesitas. **Mesita A** has two mounds, each with a central figure accompanied by a statue of a warrior on each side. There are also a few statues standing around, remaining at the sites where they were found.

**Mesita B** is the most important mesita. It has three mounds and several freestanding figures, of which the most outstanding are a

## San Agustín - Parque Arqueológico

To Quinchana

To San Agustín

Museum

Mesita D

School

Bosque de las Estatuas

Quebrada de Lavapatas

Mesita B

Mesita A

To La Parada

Alto de Lavapatas

Fuente de Lavapatas

Mesita C

0    100    200 m

four-metre-high statue known as the Bishop, unusual for the human faces carved on both top and bottom, and a statue depicting an eagle with a serpent in its talons.

The path continues for about 500 metres to **Mesita C**, which features yet another cluster of statues. A short walk downhill will bring you to the **Fuente de Lavapatas**, an important ceremonial site, presumably used for ritual ablutions and for the worship of aquatic deities. In the rocky bed of the stream, a complex labyrinth of ducts and small, terraced pools, with representations of serpents, lizards and human figures, has been chiselled out.

From here, the path winds uphill to the **Alto de Lavapatas**, the oldest archaeological site found in San Agustín. You'll find here a few tombs guarded by statues, and you'll get a panoramic view over the surrounding countryside.

The park is open daily from 8 am to 6 pm; entry is until 5 pm but Alto de Lavapatas closes at 4 pm. The museum is open from 9 am to 5 pm, and is closed on Monday. Plan on spending at least three hours in the park.

### Alto de los Ídolos

This is another archaeological park, established on the site where a number of large stone sarcophagi and statues have been excavated. The largest statue in the San Agustín area, about seven metres high, is to be found here. The park is five km from San José de Isnos, on the other side of the Río Magdalena from the town of San Agustín. The park is open daily from 8 am to 4 pm. You can get there on foot from San Agustín by crossing the deep Magdalena Gorge, a spectacular three-hour walk. Ideally, you should not walk alone, since some travellers have been attacked and robbed on this route. You can also walk from Isnos, which is reached from San Agustín by road.

### Alto de las Piedras

This site is seven km from Isnos and contains tombs lined with stone slabs painted red, black and yellow. One of the most famous statues, known as Doble Yo, is here; look carefully as there are actually four figures carved in this statue. You'll also find an intriguing statue representing a female figure in an advanced state of pregnancy.

To get there, walk from Isnos, or take one of the irregular chivas from Isnos on Saturday and Sunday mornings, which go as far as Salto de Bordones and return in the early afternoon. An easier but more expensive way of visiting the place is a jeep tour (see Getting Around for more details).

### El Tablón, La Chaquira, La Pelota & El Purutal

These four interesting sites are relatively close to each other, so they can be seen in one trip. It is a pleasant five-hour walk from the town of San Agustín, or you can do it on horseback. La Chaquira is noted for its divinities carved into the mountain face, overlooking the gorge of the Magdalena River. In El Purutal you can see the only surviving painted statues in the region.

### Other Attractions

There are several more archaeological sites to see if you are not in a hurry, including La Parada, Quinchana, El Jabón and Naranjos (see the map for locations), and Quebradillas.

Apart from its archaeological wealth, the region is also noted for its natural beauty, and features two spectacular waterfalls, **Salto de Bordones** and **Salto de Mortiño**. **El Estrecho**, where the Río Magdalena passes through a two-metre narrows, is also worth a walk or ride. All these sights are accessible by road.

**Laguna de la Magdalena**, where the Río Magdalena has its source, is yet another popular destination. The trip can be done on foot or horseback. See the Parque Nacional Puracé section for information. San Agustín's tourist office will give you a map and up-to-date details about this trip.

### Places to Stay

The accommodation in San Agustín is good and cheap. There are a dozen residencias in town, most of which are clean and friendly and have hot water; all cost much the same – about US$2 to US$3 per person in rooms without bath, and a dollar more in rooms with private bath.

If you don't feel like walking when you arrive, there are a few residencias right near the bus offices, including the *Colonial* (☎ 373159), at Calle 3 No 11-54, and the *Central* (☎ 373027), at Calle 3 No 10-54. Both are good, if a bit noisy from the passing traffic, and cost US$3.50 per person in rooms with bath.

If you prefer a quieter area, walk five blocks west along Calle 4, where you will find several residencias, including *Mi Terruño*, at Calle 4 No 15-85, with a long balcony overlooking the garden. It has some rooms with private bath. Also, try the two others just a few steps away (they don't have signs): the *Luis Tello* (☎ 373037), at Calle 4 No 15-33, and the *Eduardo Motta* (☎ 373031), at Calle 4 No 15-71. A block away, on the corner of Calle 5 and Carrera 16, is one more budget place, the *Ñáñez* (☎ 373087).

Another option is to stay in a pleasant family house, the *Posada Campesina Silvina Patiño*, one km outside town towards El Tablón. You can also camp there.

The *Nelly*, run by a French woman, is a good new place popular with travellers. It's on the western outskirts of town.

There are two up-market hotels, the *Osoguaico* (☎ 373069) (US$18/24 a single/double) and the *Yalconia* (☎ 373013) (US$22/30). Both are outside town, on the road leading to the Parque Arqueológico.

There are two simple campsites, *Camping San Agustín* and *Camping El Ullumbe*, both near the Hotel Yalconia.

Should you need somewhere to stay in Isnos, there's the cheap *El Balcón*, on the main square.

### Places to Eat

*Brahama*, Calle 5 No 15-11, is recommended for cheap set meals, vegetarian food and fruit salads. *Los Ídolos*, Carrera 11 No 2-48, serves inexpensive, tasty meals.

*La Martina*, Carrera 12 No 3-40, known locally as Las Negras, serves good regional food. It's open only on weekends and Mondays.

Outside town, opposite the Hotel Yalconia, there is the reasonably priced *La Brasa*, good for churrasco, carne asada and the like.

### Getting There & Away

**Air** The nearest airport is in Pitalito, 35 km from San Agustín. Aires has flights from there to Neiva, on Thursday and Sunday (US$46); these flights continue on to Bogotá (US$84 from Pitalito). Flights in the opposite direction are on the same days.

**Bus** All bus offices are clustered on Calle 3 near the corner of Carrera 11. San Agustín is linked to Bogotá (via Pitalito and Neiva) by paved road. If you are heading elsewhere (Popayán, Cali or Tierradentro), expect bumpy travel over rough roads.

**To Pitalito** There are frequent jeeps between San Agustín and Pitalito (US$1, 45 minutes). As there is not much room inside, luggage is put on the roof. Keep a constant eye on your backpack, especially if you board the jeep in Pitalito. There have been many reports of travellers whose packs were loaded in Pitalito but then disappeared somewhere along the way.

**To Bogotá** There are two buses daily with Coomotor (US$16, 12 hours).

**To Popayán** Two buses run early in the morning via a rough road through Isnos (US$10, six hours if everything goes well).

**To Tierradentro** There are no direct buses to Tierradentro; you must first go to La Plata (US$7, 4½ hours, two buses daily). If you don't want to wait, go by jeep to Pitalito, from where there are more buses to La Plata. See the La Plata section for details on how to go from there to Tierradentro.

### Getting Around

The tourist attractions close to the town of San Agustín can be easily visited on foot. You can also walk to the sights tucked further away, but these will be long hikes. This is where horse and jeep trips become an attractive alternative.

The tourist office offers a number of excursions, by jeep or on horseback, to practically all places of interest. Horses are hired out for a specific route, or by the hour (US$2) or the day (US$10). One of the most popular horseback trips includes El Tablón, La Chaquira, La Pelota and El Purutal; it costs US$6 per horse, and takes five hours. The group of riders is usually accompanied by a *baquiano* (horse handler/guide), so add US$6 on to your budget for him and another US$6 for his horse. It is now also possible to rent a horse without a baquiano.

Jeeps, which take up to five people, cover sights accessible by road. The most popular jeep tour includes Alto de los Ídolos, Alto de las Piedras, Salto de Bordones and Salto de Mortiño. It takes six hours and costs about US$50 per jeep.

A five-day round trip on horseback to the Laguna de la Magdalena is offered for US$75. Don't even think about it if you're not used to horse riding – it may turn into torture. Put your bottom to the test with a couple of short excursions on horseback before making any decision on a longer trip.

### CUEVA DE LOS GUÁCHAROS

Cueva de los Guácharos was Colombia's first nature reserve to be declared a national park, in 1960. Covering an area of 90 sq km, the park is located along the western flank of the Cordillera Oriental, in the southernmost tip of Huila department. The park is noted for a chain of caves formed by the erosive activity of the Río Suaza, and for the presence of the *guácharo*, a species of bird after which the park was named.

The reserve is a long way from any human settlement. There are no roads leading to the park, and the only access is by a long and strenuous walk (see Getting There & Away). Visitors are few and far between.

Another deterrent is the weather, as it rains most of the year. December to March are the driest months (and the only suitable period in which to tackle the trip) while April to August are the wettest.

### The Guácharo

The guácharo, or oilbird *(Steatornis caripensis)*, is a nocturnal, frugivorous (fruit-eating) bird, the only one of its kind in the world. It inhabits caves in various parts of tropical America, living in total darkness and leaving the cave only at night for food, principally the fruits of some species of palms. The guácharo has a sort of radar-location system similar to that of bats, which enables it to get around in the dark. The adult bird is about 60 cm long, with a wingspan of a metre. It has reddish-brown feathers and a curved beak. The bird played an important part in the religion of some Indian tribes, including the Nazca and Inca. It is likely that some of the San Agustín stone statues represent the guácharo.

The bird was first classified by a famous German scientist, Alexander von Humboldt, who explored several countries of Central and South America. He found the birds in 1799, in a cave in north-eastern Venezuela, which has since come to be known as the Cueva del Guácharo. This cave has the largest guácharo population living in a single cave – about 15,000 birds.

In Colombia, the guácharo inhabits numerous caves in different regions of the country; the biggest colony, estimated at over 2000 birds, lives in the Cueva de los Guácharos. ∎

### Things to See & Do

The pride of the park is its namesake, the **Cueva de los Guácharos**. The oilbirds that live here are easily disturbed by the presence of visitors and the light of torches, and raise a tremendous din. You can see them pouring out of the cave mouth after dark, and returning before dawn. Many of the birds fly away for their breeding season, from February to June, but a small colony remains in the cave all year round.

The Cueva de los Guácharos has a main cavern about 20 metres high and 50 metres long (through which the river flows), but otherwise is pretty small. Its calcium formations are relatively poor. The best in this respect is the **Cueva del Indio**, which is the biggest (750 metres long) and most spectacular cave in the park, remarkable for its stalactites and stalagmites. There are a few other caves of minor interest, including the Cueva Chiquita and the Cueva del Hoyo (the latter can only be reached with the help of a rope).

The caves apart, you can walk along observation trails traced through the cloudforest to view the rich vegetation with its mosses, lichens and other epiphytes.

The rangers are friendly and will guide you through the caves. Get a permit to visit the park from Inderena; there are Inderena offices in Neiva (☎ 722580), Calle 10 No 6-61, and in Pitalito, Carrera 4 No 4-21. Remember to bring a torch, reliable rain gear and clothing adequate for temperate weather.

### Places to Stay & Eat

Inderena has a cabaña in the park, which offers simple accommodation for a maximum of 10 visitors. Camping is possible, and you can also string up your hammock if you bring one. Food is not provided, but there are cooking facilities to prepare your own provisions.

### Getting There & Away

A long walk is the only way of getting to the park. There are two possible routes; the more frequently used one begins in Palestina, a small village 23 km south of Pitalito. Cootranshuila has about 10 chivas daily (more on market days), departing regularly between 6.30 am and 5.30 pm from the corner of Carrera 3 and Calle 7 in Pitalito. They cost US$1 and take a little over an hour. There's a basic hospedaje or two in Palestina, and simple meals are available.

From Palestina, go two km along a rough road (there is also a short cut) to the bridge over the Río Guarapas. Cross the bridge and take the path climbing straight up the hill. From the bridge, it's about 25 km to the park – a hard six-hour walk along an eroded path.

The trail goes up and down over several mountain ridges, and is often muddy even in the dry season. During the rainy season it can be virtually impassable in parts. The scenery is wonderful.

The trail is unclear and confusing in some parts, so it's easy to get lost. Ask for directions whenever you encounter someone or pass a hut on the way, though they are few and far between. Get detailed information about the trail from Inderena offices beforehand. Better still, look for a guide in Palestina, who may provide mules as well.

The alternative route to the caves goes from Acevedo, a village 28 km east of Pitalito and linked to it by a rough road. From here, a sort of jeep track winds along the valley of the Río Suaza up to the hamlet of San Adolfo. You then continue by a path to the park. This route is even longer, although probably easier – as you at least know that you have to follow the river.

## LA PLATA

• *pop 13,000* • *1020 m* • *23°C* • ☎ *(988)*

La Plata is a small, uninspiring town, where you have to change buses if you're heading for Tierradentro from San Agustín or Neiva. There's no other reason to come here.

There was a serious earthquake in June 1994 on the area north of La Plata. The landslides which followed the quake caused the Río Páez to overflow its banks, and the resulting mud flow destroyed several villages and a few bridges in its path. The effects of the disaster are still very much in evidence in the region, but the roads have

already been repaired and transport has returned to normal.

### Places to Stay & Eat

There are quite a number of residencias scattered throughout the central part of the town, including some in the vicinity of the main plaza, the market and bus company offices.

One of the better budget places is the *Hotel Berlín* on the main plaza, at Calle 4 No 4-76, which costs US$4/7 a single/double and also serves meals. There are two more basic (and cheaper) options on the same side of the square.

You may also want to stay in one of the shabby hospedajes around the square from which buses depart, two blocks off the main plaza, which is convenient if you plan to catch the early-morning bus to Tierradentro. The *El Viajero*, at Carrera 2 No 5-27, just opposite the Sotracauca bus office, is very basic but cheap – US$2 per person. One block away, at Calle 5 No 2-62, is the slightly better *Brisas de Plata*, which also costs US$2 per person (US$3 in rooms with private bath).

There are several food stalls opposite the bus offices. Cheap meals are also available in the market, bounded by Carreras 3 and 4 and Calles 5 and 6.

### Getting There & Away

All the bus companies are clustered around the square on the corner of Calle 5 and Carrera 2. Jeeps also depart from here, but chivas to Belalcázar leave from the corner of Carrera 4 and Calle 6, next to the market.

**To Bogotá** Coomotor has a morning climatizado (US$15, nine hours) and an evening corriente (US$13, 10 hours).

**To Neiva** There are regular departures throughout the day with several companies (US$5, three hours).

**To Popayán** Several buses a day run along a rough road through the Parque Nacional Puracé (US$7.50, six hours).

**To San Agustín** There are two buses daily (US$7, 4½ hours). If there's no bus due to depart promptly, go to Pitalito (at least half a dozen departures a day) and change for a jeep to San Agustín. Or take any of the frequent jeeps to Garzón, change for a bus to Pitalito (which depart at least once an hour) and change again for a jeep to San Agustín.

**To Tierradentro** The only bus (operated by Sotracauca) leaves at 5 am (US$3, three hours). Get off at El Cruce de San Andrés and walk 20 minutes to the museum of Tierradentro (or 45 minutes to San Andrés de Pisimbalá). Don't count on the hotel staff to wake you up for this bus. If you arrive later at La Plata (or don't wake up for the bus) and don't want to waste the day, take a chiva to Belalcázar (they depart from the market until about 4 pm) and get off in Guadualejo. From there, you can catch the Belalcázar-Popayán bus passing through at about 11.30 am, or another (less reliable) one at around 2 pm.

## TIERRADENTRO

• *1750 m* • *18°C*

Tierradentro is an archaeological zone where a number of hypogea, or underground vaults, have been found. They are circular chambers ranging from two to seven metres in diameter, scooped out of the soft rock in the slopes and tops of hills. The dome-like ceilings of the larger vaults are supported by massive pillars. The walls, ceilings and pillars were decorated with geometric motifs painted in red and black (representing life and death, respectively) on a white background. Anthropomorphic figures were carved on the columns and walls of many chambers. The tombs vary widely in depth; some of them are just below ground level, while others are as deep as nine metres, with spiral staircases of volcanic rock leading down into them.

The underground chambers were hewn out of the rock to house the remains of tribal elders. Their ashes were kept in ceramic urns decorated with dotted patterns and, sometimes, with representations of animals. The pottery is now displayed in the museum of Tierradentro.

The burial chambers of Tierradentro are the only example of their kind in the Americas. About a hundred of them have been discovered to date. In some of the chambers the decoration has been preserved in remarkably good shape.

A number of stone statues similar to those of San Agustín have also been found in the region, probably the product of a broad cultural influence. Human figures predominate, but animal representations are not unusual.

Little is known about the people who built the tombs and the statues. The most likely hypothesis is that they were of different cultures, and the people who scooped out the tombs preceded those who carved the statues. Some researchers have placed the 'tomb' civilisation somewhere between the 7th and 9th centuries AD, while the 'statue' culture shows links with the later phase of San Agustín development, which is estimated to have taken place some 500 years later.

Today the region is inhabited by the Páez Indians, who have lived here since before the Spanish conquest, but it is doubtful whether they are the descendants of the sculptors of the statues.

### Things To See & Do

There are four sites with tombs and one with statues, as well as a museum and the village of San Andrés de Pisimbalá. Except for El Aguacate, all the sites are quite close to each other, so they can easily be visited on foot. You can also hire horses, which are rented out near the museum and, sometimes, in San Andrés. Allow yourself two to three days in the area. A torch is necessary for almost all the tombs.

**Museum** You begin your visit from the museum, where you buy a ticket (US$6) which is valid for two days at all archaeological sites and the museum itself. Apparently there's a 50% discount for students but the attendants are very reluctant to admit it, unless you insist.

The museum consists of two sections, in two separate buildings across the road from one another. The Museo Arqueológico contains pottery urns which have been found in the tombs, while the Museo Etnográfico has utensils and artefacts of the Páez Indians. Both museums are open daily from 8 am to 5 pm. There are several statues, collected from the region, distributed in the park adjacent to the museum buildings.

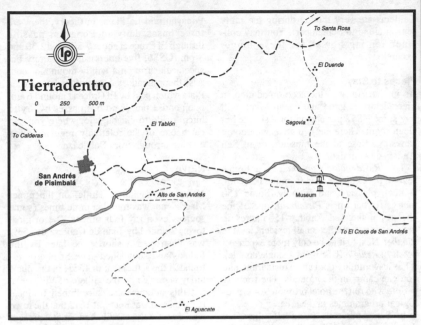

**Tierradentro**

0    250    500 m

To Calderas

San Andrés
de Pisimbalá

*El Tablón*

*Alto de San Andrés*

*El Aguacate*

To Santa Rosa

*El Duende*

*Segovía*

Museum

To El Cruce de San Andrés

**Burial Sites** A 10-minute walk up the hill from the museum will take you to **Segovia**, the most important burial site. There are 28 tombs here, some with very well preserved decoration. Seven of them are lit but not well enough to take photos unless you have a very fast film; it is officially forbidden to take photos with a flash. The other tombs are unlit, so you will need a torch. The tombs are open from 8 am to 5 pm; at other times they are kept locked.

A 15-minute walk uphill from Segovia will bring you to **El Duende**, where there are four tombs whose decoration hasn't been preserved.

More interesting is **Alto de San Andrés**, where you'll find five tombs, two of which boast their original paintings in remarkably good condition.

In the same area is **El Tablón**, where there are 10 stone statues, similar to those of San Agustín, excavated in the area and now thrown together under a roof in a fenced-in field.

**El Aguacate** is the only remote burial site, located high on a mountain ridge, a two-hour walk from the museum. There are a few dozen tombs there, but most have been destroyed by the guaqueros. Only a few vaults still bear the remains of the original decoration. It's worth taking this walk anyway, for the sweeping views it provides over the whole region.

**Churches** The tiny village of **San Andrés de Pisimbalá**, a 25-minute walk from the museum, is noteworthy for its amazing thatched church. You can see its very simple interior through the gap in the entrance doors.

There are several churches similar in style to that in San Andrés scattered through the region; the one in **Santa Rosa** (a two-hour walk) is perhaps the most beautiful. The nuns living in the house near the church have the keys. Another church in the same style is in **Calderas**, a three-hour walk from San Andrés. The footpaths to Santa Rosa and

Calderas are very muddy during the rainy season (June to September). You may consider renting horses for these longer excursions.

### Places to Stay

As in San Agustín, the accommodation in Tierradentro is good and cheap – you will pay some US$2 per person for a simple but clean room. There are two areas where you can stay: close to the museum or in San Andrés de Pisimbalá.

The *Residencias Lucerna*, in a house several paces up the road from the museum, is neat, pleasant and friendly. Some 150 metres further on is *Pisimbalá*, one of the cheapest in the area. Another 150 metres up the road is yet another small residencias, the *Ricabet*. Next to it is the only more expensive hotel, *El Refugio* (US$10/14 a single/double). It has a swimming pool and a restaurant, and you can camp on the grounds. The friendly people who run the hotel promote some ecological programmes in the area.

In San Andrés de Pisimbalá, there are three residencias: *El Viajero*, *El Cauchito* and *Los Lagos de Tierradentro*. El Cauchito has a campsite (US$1 per person). Los Lagos is the cheapest and friendliest – recommended. It's 100 metres down the road past the church; if you can't find it, ask anybody for directions to Edgar Bolaños Velasco, the owner.

### Places to Eat

In the museum area, the *Pisimbalá* (see Places to Stay) is the cheapest place to eat, serving set meals for about US$1.50. Slightly more expensive and better is the *Restaurante 86*, just across the road. Possibly the best option is the restaurant of *El Refugio*.

In San Andrés de Pisimbalá, *El Viajero* offers cheap meals, or you can eat in *La Gaitana*, next to the church.

### Getting There & Away

Only occasional buses call at San Andrés de Pisimbalá, so you'll normally have to walk to El Cruce de San Andrés (20 minutes from the museum), where you can catch the bus to Popayán and La Plata. In theory, there are three buses daily to Popayán, passing through El Cruce at about 7.30 am, 12.30 and 3 pm (US$6, five hours). It's a bumpy but spectacular trip on a windy mountain road. Also theoretically, there are three buses to La Plata which pass by El Cruce at around 6 am, noon and 3 pm. If no bus passes by, try to hitch a ride to Guadualejo, where you can catch one of the relatively regular chivas coming through from Belalcázar.

## NEIVA

• *pop 250,000* • *442 m* • *27°C* • ☎ *(988)*

Neiva, the capital of Huila, on the upper Magdalena, was founded three times (some sources even say four times). The original town, founded by Juan de Cabrera in 1539, was destroyed a short time later by the Indians and abandoned. The Spaniards refounded the settlement in 1551, in the place today occupied by the village of Villavieja, but this attempt also succumbed to local resistance. It was not until 1612 that the town was eventually established in its present location. Today it is a hot, unremarkable city, not much more than a stopover on the way to the Tatacoa Desert, San Agustín, Tierradentro or elsewhere.

### Information

**Tourist Office** The Inturhuila tourist office (☎ 712792, 712827) is on the ground floor of the Edificio de la Gobernación, on the main square. It is open Monday to Friday from 7.30 am to 1 pm and 3 to 6 pm.

**Money** Probably only the Banco Industrial Colombiano will be able to change your cash and travellers' cheques. Cash advances on Visa cards may be obtained at the Banco de Colombia and Banco de Bogotá, whereas for MasterCard they can be obtained at the Banco de Occidente and Banco Industrial Colombiano.

### Things to See

If you have some time to spend in the city, take a look at the **Templo Colonial**, the 17th-century church fronting the main plaza

(Parque Santander), one of the few structures in the city that recall Spanish times. The other church on the square, the large, neo-Gothic, brick **Catedral de la Inmaculada Concepción**, is a much more recent construction.

The **Museo Arqueológico**, right behind the tourist office, features the artefacts (mostly pottery) of the two pre-Columbian Indian groups of the region: the Santana from the north of present-day Huila and the Yalcones from the south. The museum is open Tuesday to Friday from 9 am to noon and 3 to 6.30 pm, and on Saturday from 10 am to 4 pm. The **Museo de Artes y Tradiciones Populares Rumichaca**, Calle 9 No 6-98, has regional handicrafts.

The city has two interesting monuments designed by Rodrigo Arenas Betancur. The **Monumento a la Gaitana**, on the bank of the Magdalena, is a striking composition depicting the battle between La Gaitana, a female Indian chief, and the Spanish conquerors. The **Monumento a los Potros**, on the corner of Avenida La Toma and Carrera 3, is dedicated to the local writer José Eustasio Rivera, author of the poem 'Los Potros'.

### Festival

The Festival Folklórico y Reinado Nacional del Bambuco and the Fiesta de San Juan y San Pedro (the latter celebrated throughout Huila and Tolima) take place at the end of June. The town celebrates them with music and dancing, and the Bambuco Queen is elected in a beauty and dancing contest.

### Places to Stay

There are plenty of hotels in the city centre to suit every budget. All hotels listed below have fans (or air-con where indicated) and private baths (unless otherwise specified). Note that during the June festival the prices of budget accommodation go through the roof and it's difficult to find a room except, perhaps, in the top-class hotels.

One of the best budget bets is the *Hospedaje La Posada* (☎ 711700), at Carrera 3 Bis No 7-82, only half a block from the main plaza. Neat, large singles/doubles cost

US$6/7. Just round the corner is the *Hotel Suizo* (☎ 712395), at Carrera 3 No 8-10, which is more basic, but may be an option if you want a cheap room and don't need a private bath (US$5 for a matrimonio).

*Hotel La Gaitana* (☎ 712104), Calle 7 No 3-27, in the same area, has a choice of rooms without/with bath for US$3.50/5 per person. Next door at Calle 7 No 3-25 is the *Gran Hotel* (☎ 710043), which is not exactly 'grand' but is nonetheless better than La Gaitana. It offers airy rooms with bath for US$8/11 a single/double.

On the opposite side of the main plaza is the *Hotel Nicol's* (☎ 712171), which is good value in itself (US$6/10/13 a single/double/triple), but has a billiard hall downstairs, which can be noisy till late.

If you need more comfort, try the *Hotel Tupinamba* (☎ 713990), at Carrera 3 No 9-17, which has rooms with fan (US$14/20/24) and air-con (US$18/24/28).

Going up the price scale, you have an array of hotels which provide decent standards and facilities (including a swimming pool), and offer a choice between rooms with fans and air-con. Among them, there is the *Hotel Americano* (☎ 729241), at Carrera 5 No 8-67 (US$22/28 a single/double with fan, US$27/35 with air-con); the *Hotel Neiva Plaza* (☎ 710806), at Calle 7 No 4-62 (US$26/34, US$32/44); and the *Hotel Dinastía* (☎ 711940), at Carrera 4 No 9-43 (US$27/36, US$33/46).

One of the best in the city is the *Hotel Pacandé* (☎ 711766), at Calle 10 No 4-39, which is fully air-conditioned and costs US$60/80 a single/double.

### Places to Eat

There are plenty of budget restaurants throughout the city centre, particularly in the market area. The market itself is a good place for cheap meals. The two self-service outlets on the main plaza, *Autoservicio Pare* and *Punto Verde*, are open 24 hours a day. If you feel like having chicken, go to *Kokoriko*, on the corner of Calle 10 and Carrera 5. You'll find several Chinese eateries in the vicinity of the main plaza; *Hong Sing*, Carrera 6 No 7-66, is one of the best.

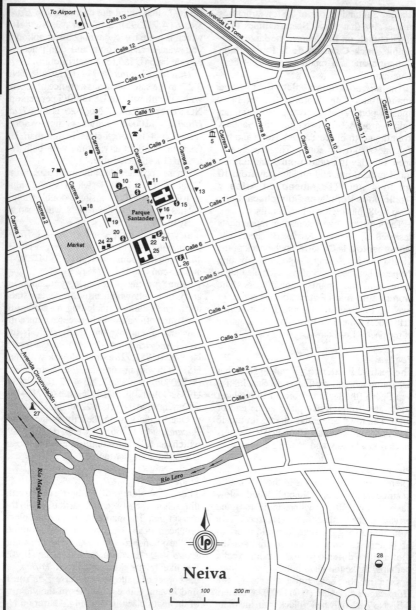

Neiva

0    100    200 m

## PLACES TO STAY

3   Hotel Pacandé
6   Hotel Dinastía
7   Hotel Tupinamba
8   Hotel Americano
11  Hotel Nicol's
18  Hotel Suizo
19  Hospedaje La Posada
22  Hotel Neiva Plaza
23  Hotel La Gaitana
24  Gran Hotel

## PLACES TO EAT

2   Kokoriko
13  Restaurante Hong Sing
16  Autoservicio Pare
17  Punto Verde

## OTHER

1   Aires Office
4   Telecom
5   Museo de Artes y Tradiciones
    Populares Rumichaca
9   Museo Arqueológico
10  Inturhuila Tourist Office
12  Banco de Colombia
14  Templo Colonial
15  Banco Industrial Colombiano
20  Banco Popular
21  Banco de Occidente
25  Catedral de la Inmaculada
    Concepción
26  Banco de Bogotá
27  Monumento a la Gaitana
28  Bus terminal

There's also a number of restaurants around the (no longer used) railway station, on the corner of Carrera 16 and Calle 7. This is also the area for night-time entertainment, with music (live and taped) blasting on weekend nights, and drawing in some of the local youth.

### Getting There & Away

**Air** La Manguita Airport is a 15-minute walk north from the centre, or take the local bus marked 'Granjas'. A taxi between the main plaza and the airport will cost about US$1.

Flights are operated by Aires (with an office at Carrera 5 No 13-09) and Satena (whose office is at the airport). Aires has half a dozen flights a day to Bogotá (US$48), three flights daily to Florencia (US$42), two flights to Puerto Asís (US$65) and one flight to Cali (US$78) via Ibagué. It also flies twice weekly (Thursday and Sunday) to Pitalito (US$46), near San Agustín.

Satena has three flights a week to Bogotá, Florencia and Puerto Leguízamo, and its fares are marginally lower than those of Aires.

**Bus** The new, purpose-built bus terminal is south-east of the city centre, beyond the Río Loro. It's a 10-minute walk or a five-minute ride by frequent city buses. Taxi (US$1) is a more comfortable option.

**To Bogotá** Coomotor and Expreso Bolivariano have frequent buses (US$10 climatizado, US$9 pullman, US$8 corriente, six hours).

**To San Agustín** There are several buses daily with La Gaitana and Coomotor (US$6.50, six hours), plus infrequent colectivos (US$7.50, 4½ hours).

**To La Plata** There are a dozen buses a day (US$4, three hours). From La Plata, you can continue on to Tierradentro or Popayán. There are also a few direct Neiva-Popayán buses (US$10.50, nine hours).

**To Florencia** Coomotor, Cootranshuila and La Gaitana have a dozen buses a day altogether (US$10 climatizado, US$7.50 corriente, six to seven hours).

## VILLAVIEJA

• *pop 3000* • *430 m* • *28°C*

Villavieja is a lazy village about 35 km north of Neiva. It was here that Neiva was founded in 1551 but destroyed by Indians and abandoned. The settlement later revived, took the name of Villavieja ('Old Town') and adopted the year of Neiva's foundation as its own.

There are two churches on the main plaza. The smaller one, the Capilla de Santa Bárbara, dating from 1748, houses the **Museo Paleontológico**, open Tuesday to Sunday from 8 am to noon and 2 to 5 pm. The collection of fossils on display comes from the Desierto de la Tatacoa, the spectacular arid wasteland to the north-east of Villavieja (see the following section).

## Places to Stay & Eat

There are two places to stay in Villavieja. The *Parador Turístico La Portada*, on the corner of Carrera 2 and Calle 7, has a capacity for 20 guests in simple but neat rooms, for US$4 per person. It has its own restaurant.

The only other place is the informal hospedaje in the house of Gerardo Calderón, at Carrera 2 No 4-41. The conditions are probably more rustic, but the owner charges only US$1.50 per person, and even less if you're with a group.

Of the few basic eateries, the *Restaurante El Desierto*, at Calle 4 No 7-32, has perhaps the best food in the village.

You have more options for accommodation and food in Aipe, just across the Magdalena (refer to the Aipe section).

## Getting There & Away

Villavieja is accessible from Neiva by a partly unpaved road, and from Aipe by boat.

There are four Cootranshuila buses a day from Neiva to Villavieja, at 6 and 10.30 am, noon and 2 pm (US$1.25, 1½ hours), which then turn round and go back to Neiva. Alternatively, take any of the frequent buses heading north to Bogotá or Ibagué, get off in Aipe and cross the Magdalena to Villavieja.

Boats across the Magdalena run on demand as soon as passengers turn up (US$0.50). The landing site in Villavieja is at the far western end of Calle 4, a five-minute walk from the main plaza.

## DESIERTO DE LA TATACOA

The Tatacoa Desert stretches over roughly 300 sq km to the north-east of Villavieja. It's not exactly a desert – the name is somewhat misleading – but rather a vast, arid, eroded land sparsely covered with shrubs, cacti, grasses and other xerophytic species.

The landscape changes significantly across the region, and is often fascinating. Perhaps the most spectacular place is the site known locally as **El Cuzco**, where you can find a maze of eroded standing rocks protruding out of the rugged terrain, which is cut by dry washes. The reddish ochre colour of the rock adds to the overall effect.

Further afield, the place called **Los Hoyos** is remarkable for its gently rolling desert dunes in a sober, pearly colour. Locals give names to several other areas, including Cardón and Los Mezones, each noted for its own distinctive features.

The climate is hot and dry. Although the average temperature is 28°C, it can easily rise to over 40°C at midday.

## Getting Around

The main gateway for Tatacoa is Villavieja, from which you can explore the desert on foot or by vehicle. There's an eroded dirt road which heads from the village into the desert, passing near El Cuzco and reaching Los Hoyos.

A guide to accompany you for a full-day hike shouldn't cost more than US$10. Nelson Martínez Olaya is the best known guide in Villavieja. Ask for him at the Restaurante El Desierto. He can go with you for a walking trip or organise a vehicle. A three to four-hour car trip, which includes visits to El Cuzco and Los Hoyos, will cost US$12 to US$15.

Make sure to take with you plenty of water and good sun protection (hat, sun screen, sunglasses). If you plan to do walks without a guide, a compass is not a bad idea.

## AIPE

• *pop 4000* • *435 m* • *28°C*

Aipe is a small town 37 km north of Neiva on the main Bogotá road. It sits on the opposite bank of the Magdalena from Villavieja. There's nothing much to do here, but you may be stuck for the night if you are coming from the north (Bogotá, Ibagué or Armenia) and arrive too late to cross the river to Villavieja.

## Places to Stay & Eat

There are three places to stay in Aipe, and all three serve meals. The unnamed hospedaje at Carrera 4 No 3-19, opposite the police station, is basic but acceptable and the cheapest at US$2/3 a single/double. The *Hospedaje Real*, at Calle 5 No 6-55, 1½ blocks from the main plaza along the Neiva road, is better but costs

US$3 per person. Much the same standard and price are to be found at the *Hotel Aipe*, at Carrera 5 No 5-27, just off the plaza.

### Getting There & Away

Frequent buses pass through Aipe's main plaza (you catch them on the corner of Calle 5 and Carrera 5) on their way north to Bogotá and Ibagué, and south to Neiva. Just wave down the bus going in your direction.

To get to Villavieja, walk eastward along Calle 5 to its end and continue for 10 minutes along the path to the river. Then take a boat (there are usually some waiting) for a trip of only a few minutes to Villavieja (US$0.50).

### PIEDRA PINTADA

Piedra Pintada is a large rock covered with petroglyphs. Despite its name ('Painted Rock'), the petroglyphs are not painted but engraved. Their meaning is unknown; nor is it known which group of Indians left behind these mysterious messages. It is unlikely that they were done by the Pijaos who dominated this region during the Spanish conquest.

The rock lies just off the main Bogotá-Neiva road, 10 km north of Aipe. There is a sign on the road.

# Nariño

Nariño is Colombia's south-westernmost department, adjoining the border with Ecuador. In remote pre-Columbian times, this land was home to two remarkable centres of culture: Tumaco on the Pacific coast and Nariño in the Andean highlands. In the mid-15th century, less than a century before the arrival of the Spanish, Nariño was conquered and incorporated into the Inca Empire. Once the Incas had been defeated by Pizarro, the Spaniards pushed northward into what is now Colombia. In effect, Nariño was conquered by the Spanish earlier than any other part of Colombia except for the Caribbean coast, which was invaded independently from the north.

Present-day Nariño comprises two very

Gold ear ornament from Nariño

different geographical regions. The western part is a vast lowland covered with thick rainforest, whereas the eastern section is mountainous and topped with several volcanic peaks. Here is the so-called Nudo de los Pastos, the area where the Andean range splits into three cordilleras, which then fan northward into Colombia. The Nudo is a zone of serious seismic activity.

Nariño's mountains are picturesque and worth exploring, even though most travellers do no more than pass through on their way to or from Ecuador. You can do some volcano hikes or relax beside the Laguna de la Cocha, one of the country's most beautiful lakes.

The cultural side of Nariño is also interesting. The department's inhabitants, known as the *pastusos*, are skilful artisans, and the local crafts are known for their originality and quality. Its history and people give Nariño a special atmosphere which reflects the cross of Colombian and Ecuadorian cultures.

### PASTO

• *pop 290,000* • *2530 m* • *13°C* • ☎ *(927)*

The capital of Nariño, Pasto is set in the fertile Atriz Valley at the foot of the Galeras Volcano. The town was founded by Lorenzo de Aldana in 1536, and is thus one of the oldest cities in Colombia. It played an active role in Colombia's history and was an important cultural and religious centre. Today it is a commercial city which has lost much of its colonial character. Yet its churches still retain some of the splendour of the past.

The city is known throughout Colombia for its *barniz de Pasto*, a kind of processed vegetable resin used on wooden bowls, plates, boxes, furniture etc to decorate them with colourful patterns. The technique is not new; in the past, the Indians used the resin (known to them as *mopa mopa*) to coat their pottery and wooden articles.

Because of Pasto's high altitude, it gets cold at night – have something warm handy.

### Information

**Tourist Office** The Oficina Departamental de Turismo de Nariño (☎ 234962) is at Calle 18 No 25-25. The office is open Monday to Friday from 8 am to noon and 2 to 6 pm.

The Instituto Geográfico Agustín Codazzi (IGAC), Calle 18A No 21A-18, sells departmental and city maps. The office is open Monday to Friday from 7.30 to 11 am and 2 to 5 pm.

**Money** Most major banks are located around the main square, the Plaza de Nariño. Only the Banco Industrial Colombiano changes cash. It also changes travellers' cheques, as does the Banco de Bogotá. Other banks marked on the map only handle credit-card transactions.

Óptica San Francisco, on the main square, changes cash till 7 pm on weekdays and is the best private moneychanger, though it pays less than the banks.

### Churches

Pasto is a city of churches; it still boasts perhaps a dozen colonial churches, most of which are large constructions with ornate interiors. The decoration, in particular the carved wood statuary, shows noticeable influences of the *escuela quiteña*, the style of art which developed in Quito during the colonial era.

The **Iglesia de Cristo Rey**, with its fine stained-glass windows, is perhaps the most beautiful. Also have a look at the richly decorated **Iglesia de San Juan Bautista**. This is the city's oldest church, dating from Pasto's early days, but was rebuilt in the mid-17th century after damage caused by earthquakes. See the city map for the location of these and other churches.

### Museums

There is a small but good **Museo del Oro** in the building of the Banco de la República, Calle 19 No 21-27, containing gold and pottery of the pre-Columbian cultures of Nariño. It's open Monday to Friday from 8 am to noon and 2 to 6 pm.

Another interesting museum, the **Casona de Taminango**, is at Calle 13 No 27-67. Installed in a meticulously restored 17th-century house, the museum displays artefacts and other antique objects from the region. It's open Monday to Friday from 9 am to noon and 2 to 6 pm, and on Saturday from 9 am to 1 pm.

The **Museo Maridíaz**, Calle 18 No 32A-39, and **Museo María Goretti**, off Avenida de las Américas, both have missionary collections and consequently resemble antique shops crammed with anything from images of the saints to cannonballs. However, you may want to visit them for their modest archaeological and fauna collections. Maridíaz doesn't have regular hours and is open when *la hermana* (the nun) happens to be around; leave an offering. María Goretti is open Monday to Friday from 8 am to noon and 2 to 6 pm.

### Festival

The city's major event is the Carnaval de Blancos y Negros, held on 5 and 6 January. Its origins go back to the time of Spanish rule, when slaves were allowed to celebrate on 5 January and the masters showed their approval by painting their faces black. On the following day, the slaves painted their faces white. The tradition is quite faithfully maintained and on these two days the city goes wild, with everybody painting or dusting one another with grease, chalk, talc, flour and any other substance even vaguely black or white in tone. It's a serious affair – wear the worst clothes you have and buy an *antifaz*, a sort of mask to protect the face, widely sold for this occasion.

### Places to Stay

There are plenty of cheapies around the bus offices but not many that can be recommended. The *Residencias Colonial*, at Carrera 21 No 19-32, is one of the few places worth trying if you need somewhere at the rock-bottom end – it costs only US$1.50 per person. It is clean and quiet, and has hot water early in the morning. It's highly improbable that you will find anything cheaper in town.

There's a good new budget hotel, the *Koala Inn* (☎ 221101), at Calle 18 No 22-37, which within a short time of its opening has become the most popular place among travellers. The friendly owner, Oscar, a long-time traveller himself, speaks English and has a good idea of what backpackers want. The hotel offers simple yet adequate rooms with bath (US$3.50 per person), a little café, free morning tinto, book exchange and information.

If the Koala Inn is full, there is the *Hotel Manhattan*, at Calle 18 No 21B-14. It is a pleasant place to stay, with old-world style and atmosphere. It has large, clean rooms, some with private bath, which cost US$3 per person.

Alternatively, go to the *Hotel Canchalá*, Calle 17 No 20A-38, which provides perhaps better comfort but lacks style. It has ample rooms with bath (US$5/7/9 a single/double/triple).

Marginally better is the *Hotel Isa* (☎ 235343), at Calle 18 No 22-23 (US$7/10/14). Rooms have bath attached, but, as in most low-budget and many mid-range hotels in Pasto, hot water is only available in the morning.

Yet another reasonably priced place is the *Hotel El Duque* (☎ 237390), at Carrera 20A No 17-17, at US$12/15/18. Rooms have TV, bath and hot water round the clock.

For something up-market, try the *Hotel Agualongo* (☎ 235216), at Carrera 25 No 17-83, possibly the best in town. It costs about US$40/50/60, with discounts available at times. Alternatively, check the *Hotel Don Saúl* (☎ 230618), at Calle 17 No 23-52, where comfortable, if small, singles/doubles cost US$32/42.

### Places to Eat

There are several cheap restaurants and cafés around the bus offices where you can get a meal for not much more than a dollar, but it obviously won't be anything special.

There are also some cheap eateries in the central sector of the city. For vegetarian food, go to *Govinda's*, Carrera 24 No 14-04. The self-service *Punto Rojo*, on the main square, is a good place to put together a reasonably priced meal. It's clean and is open 24 hours.

The *Picantería Ipiales*, Calle 19 No 23-37, has food typical of the region; try the lapingacho. The restaurant in the *Casona de Taminango* (closed on Monday) lacks atmosphere but has a choice of regional dishes at reasonable prices.

In the *Don Pancho*, Calle 18 No 26-93, you'll get a filling plate of comida criolla (such as sobrebarriga, chuleta or arroz con pollo) for less than US$3. The restaurant at the *Hotel El Paisa*, Carrera 26 No 15-37, serves good Antioquian food, including bandeja paisa. *La Cabaña*, Calle 16 No 25-20, has good churrasco and parrillada.

The *Salsa Cazuela & Ceviche*, Carrera 23 No 20-40, is the place to go for ceviche and cheap beer, with good taped salsa music.

The restaurant at the *Hotel Don Saúl*, Calle 17 No 23-52, is one of the best places to eat in the city centre, with a long menu that includes some Arab specialities.

### Things to Buy

Pasto barniz artefacts can be bought in Casa del Barniz de Pasto Mopa Mopa, on the corner of Carrera 25 and Calle 13, which has possibly the best choice and quality. Before you purchase anything here, however, check the small craft stand in the Casona de Taminango, which has limited choice but

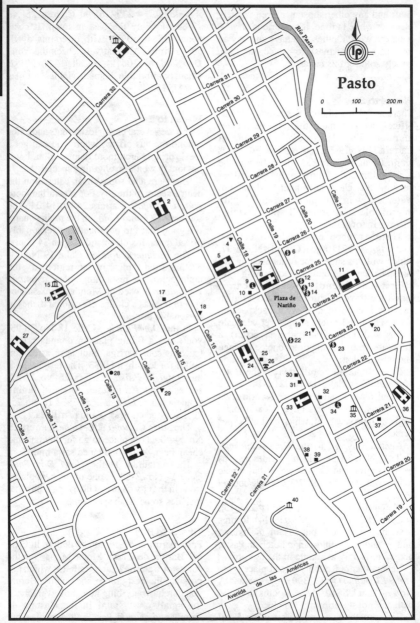

Pasto

Río Pasto

0    100    200 m

Carrera 32
Carrera 31
Carrera 30
Carrera 29
Carrera 28
Carrera 27
Carrera 26
Carrera 25
Carrera 24
Carrera 23
Carrera 22
Carrera 21
Carrera 20
Carrera 19

Calle 21
Calle 20
Calle 19
Calle 18
Calle 17
Calle 16
Calle 15
Calle 14
Calle 13
Calle 12
Calle 11
Calle 10

Plaza de
Nariño

Avenida de las Américas

## PLACES TO STAY

10 Hotel Agualongo
17 Hotel El Paisa
25 Hotel Don Saúl
30 Koala Inn
31 Hotel Isa
32 Hotel Manhattan
37 Residencias Colonial
38 Hotel Canchalá
39 Hotel El Duque

## PLACES TO EAT

4 Restaurante Don Pancho
18 Restaurante La Cabaña
19 Punto Rojo
20 Salsa Cazuela & Ceviche
21 Picantería Ipiales
29 Restaurante Vegetariano
    Govinda's

## OTHER

1 Museo Maridíaz
2 Iglesia de San Andrés
3 Plaza de Bomboná
5 Catedral
6 Banco Industrial Colombiano
7 Avianca & Post Office
8 Iglesia de San Juan
   Bautista
9 Oficina Departamental de
   Turismo de Nariño
11 Iglesia de Cristo Rey
12 Óptica San Francisco
    (Money Exchange)
13 Banco de Bogotá
14 Banco de Colombia
15 Casona de Taminango
    (Museum & Restaurant)
16 Iglesia de Lourdes
22 Banco de Occidente
23 Banco del Estado
24 Iglesia de San Agustín
26 Telecom
27 Iglesia de San Felipe
28 Casa del Barniz de Pasto Mopa
    Mopa
33 Iglesia de la Merced
34 Instituto Geográfico Agustín
    Codazzi
35 Museo del Oro
36 Iglesia del Rosario
40 Museo María Goretti

does have good crafts and is cheaper than Mopa Mopa. Also try Plaza de Bomboná, Calle 14 between Carreras 28 and 30. There are a few other handicraft shops around. Pasto is also a good place to buy leather goods (at Bomboná and the nearby shops).

### Getting There & Away

**Air** The airport is 35 km north of the city on the road to Cali. Shared taxis go there from the corner of Calle 18 and Carrera 25 (US$2.50). You can pay this fare the day before your flight in the Avianca office, on the corner of Calle 18 and Carrera 26. Doing this not only assures you of a seat but also means that the colectivo will pick you up from your hotel. If you want to save money, take any bus to Cali, which will drop you near the airport.

Avianca has two flights a day to Bogotá (US$92) via Cali (US$62). Intercontinental de Aviación has three flights daily to Bogotá (US$71), two of which stop over in Cali (US$42). Connections to other destinations are possible in either Cali or Bogotá with both carriers.

**Bus** All bus companies are clustered around the square on the corner of Calle 18 and Carrera 20.

**To Ipiales** Supertaxis del Sur and Cootranar have plenty of buses until 7 pm (US$2.75, two hours).

**To Cali & Popayán** Frequent buses go along a spectacular route to Cali (US$16 climatizado, US$14 pullman, 10 hours). These buses will put you down in Popayán (US$12 climatizado, US$10 pullman, seven hours). Trans Ipiales, Flota Magdalena, Expreso Bolivariano, Cootranar and Supertaxis del Sur all have services on this route. Do this trip during the day for the beautiful scenery and, more importantly, for safety: there have been quite a number of armed attacks on night buses and passengers have been robbed.

**To Bogotá** Expreso Bolivariano has climatizados every two hours (US$33, 22 hours); Flota Magdalena also has a few buses every day, and the fare may be a couple of dollars cheaper.

**To Tumaco** Trans Ipiales has five buses daily (US$11.50, 10 hours). Supertaxis del Sur has another five buses a day.

**To Puerto Asís** Cootransmayo and Trans Ipiales have several buses daily (US$11.50, at least 11 hours). All buses go via Mocoa. Book beforehand as the buses are often full. The Pasto-Mocoa road is rough, often muddy, narrow in parts and dangerous, with frequent landslides which block traffic. It is only 140 km long but the bumpy trip takes at least seven hours. The road snakes through the mountains up to the páramo, passing near the beautiful Laguna de la Cocha and through the verdant, picturesque Sibundoy Valley. It is one of the most scenic routes in Colombia; do it in daylight. Many locals, however, prefer to travel at night to avoid seeing the breathtaking gorges dropping several hundred metres right next to the wheels of the bus.

## VOLCÁN GALERAS

The Galeras Volcano (4276 metres) is about eight km west of Pasto as the crow flies. It has an extensive crater, more than one km in diameter. The upper slopes of the volcano are covered with páramo, below which stretches a wide belt of lush Andean cloudforest. In 1985 all this area, about 76 sq km, became a Santuario de Fauna y Flora administered by Inderena.

The rim of the volcano provides splendid vistas over the crater, the vast surrounding countryside and the city. The trail to the top passes through different climatic zones and corresponding strata of vegetation, and the walk down into the crater is an added attraction.

However, there is some bad news. The volcano's level of activity rose dangerously in mid-1989, putting Pasto and the surrounding region in a state of emergency. Since that time, it has erupted several times and is still smoking. The access road was (and may still be) closed to visitors. Check with the tourist office.

### Getting There & Away

There is a rough, 22-km-long road leading up to the top of the volcano from Pasto. This road is suitable for vehicles of all kinds, not only 4WDs, but there's no public transport along it. You can negotiate a taxi in Pasto, which shouldn't be too costly provided you are travelling with a few companions.

An alternative is to walk. Take an urban bus marked 'Anganoy' from the city centre to get to the suburb of that name, the most distant point you can reach by public transport. From there, it takes about six hours to

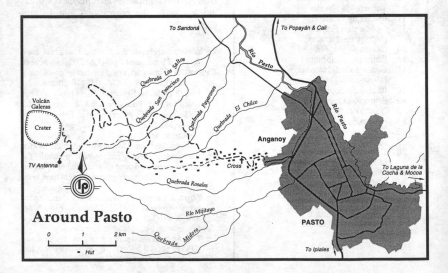

**Around Pasto**

follow the road up to the top of the volcano. It is at least two hours quicker to take short cuts which considerably shorten two long bends in the road. The first short cut branches off the road not long after you pass a large cross on the left. This area is inhabited and there are many side paths so ask for the one which finally rejoins the road. The next short cut begins about one km further on, next to a small bridge. After a long, steep ascent through a páramo you come to the road again, which will eventually lead you to the top.

The driest months are July to September, but even then the top is usually hidden in cloud in the afternoon, so start your trek early in the morning.

## LAGUNA DE LA COCHA
• *2760 m* • *13°C*

Laguna de la Cocha, also called Lago Guamués (or Guamuez), is one of the biggest and most beautiful lakes in Colombia. It is spectacularly set amidst forested mountains, about 25 km east of Pasto.

The small, eight-hectare island of **La Corota**, at the northern end of the lake, has been declared an Inderena nature reserve – the Santuario de Fauna y Flora Isla de la Corota – because of its highly diverse flora, particularly trees; some 500 species have been found here. In 1985 a small chapel, the Templete a Nuestra Señora de Lourdes, was built on the island. From the chapel, a footpath leads through the forest to a *mirador* (viewpoint) on the opposite end of the island, less than a 10-minute walk away. The Day of the Virgin is celebrated with colourful boat processions on the second Sunday in February.

La Corota apart, there are two dozen small nature reserves, collectively known as the **Reservas Naturales de la Cocha**, established by the local peasants on their fincas scattered around the lake. They will be happy to show you around, and some of them can provide modest accommodation and food for visitors. For information about the reserves, enquire at the Asociación para el Desarrollo Campesino (☎ 231022) in Pasto, Carrera 24 No 16-66, Piso 3, before you set off for the lake.

1 Hotel Quechua
2 Chalet Guamuez
3 Hotel Sindamanoy
4 Templete a Nuestra
  Señora de Lourdes

To Pasto

Pueblo
El Encano

Puerto
El Encano

To Mocoa

Santa Rosa

Isla
La Corota

El Motilón

Laguna
de la
Cocha

Laguna de la Cocha

0    1    2 km

Río Guamués

The main village on the lakeside is Puerto El Encano, two km from Pueblo El Encano on the road. There is a market on Sunday in Puerto.

The rainy season is from June to mid-September; note that this is the reverse of the climatic pattern in Pasto, only 25 km away.

### Places to Stay & Eat

There are a few pleasant places to stay near the lake. The *Hotel Quechua* is one of the cheapest – it costs US$6 per person. It is simple but clean and friendly and has hot water and a restaurant.

The *Chalet Guamuez* is a charming place, although it doesn't look that impressive from the outside. All rooms have private bath and hot water, and cost US$25/30 for singles/doubles. You can also stay in a cabaña; these take up to five people. The cosy restaurant has a fireplace and offers a reasonably priced menu. The owner, who is Swiss, has a fascinating collection of masks from the Sibundoy Valley, which is displayed on the walls.

The *Hotel Sindamanoy* is a large, Alpine-style house overlooking the lake. It has comfortable singles/doubles for about US$20/30 and a good restaurant.

In the high season, December to January, all these places tend to fill up with guests. If so, look for accommodation in El Encano (Pueblo or Puerto). Both have budget residencias and restaurants. In Pueblo El Encano, try *La Casita*, on the road, which costs US$4 per person and serves comidas. In Puerto El Encano, there's a very pleasant, family-run hotel, the *Reflejos del Lago* (US$5 per night); the friendly family can serve you hot meals (delicious trout) and has a boat.

As previously mentioned, you can also stay and eat in some of the private reserves, including the Casa del Búho, Tunguragua and Rumi Inti. Accommodation costs about US$6 per person. It is also possible to camp on the lake shore.

### Getting There & Away

All buses from Pasto heading towards Putumayo (to Sibundoy, Mocoa, Puerto Asís

etc) will drop you off near the lake (US$1, one hour). Get off at the turn-off shortly past Pueblo El Encano (the drivers know where to stop) and walk for half an hour to the lake.

You can also get to the lake from Pasto by jeep (US$1, 40 minutes), which departs from the back of the Hospital Departamental, near the corner of Calle 22 and Carrera 7. Frequent urban buses (Nos 2, 8, 11 and 15) will take you from the city centre to the hospital.

### Getting Around

Motorboats to La Corota Island depart from the Hotel Sindamanoy. The operators charge US$5 to US$8 per boat for the return trip and give you some time on the island (half an hour or so). Up to 10 passengers fit in each boat. In the off season you can bargain considerably.

A trip to the far southern end of the lake can be arranged for about US$20 to US$30 per boat; the price depends on the season, route, journey time and number of passengers. Negotiate with the people who do the La Corota route, or with the boat owners in Puerto El Encano. They can also take you to the nature reserves. Rowing boats can sometimes be hired from villagers for US$5 to US$10 for a full day.

### SIBUNDOY

• pop 4000 • 2600 m • 14°C

Sibundoy is the main settlement of the Sibundoy Valley. This village lies in the department of Putumayo, but is easier and faster to reach from Nariño; it's a two-hour bus trip from the Laguna de la Cocha.

The Sibundoy Valley is home to two Indian groups: the Inga, who live in the region of Santiago and Colón; and the Kamzá (or Kamtsá), around Sibundoy. They speak different languages (belonging to different linguistic families) and so communicate with each other in Spanish. Both communities, but particularly the Kamzá, have been known for using *yagé*, an extract of a plant noted for its clairvoyant properties. However, the legendary yagé *brujos* (witch doctors) have almost died out; only a few are left and it is difficult to find them. You may encounter some Indians claiming to be brujos and willing to offer you a yagé experience. Be careful: your constitution is probably not accustomed to such treatment and, instead of a hallucinogenic 'trip', you may end up with awful diarrhoea and vomiting.

The Indians live in huts scattered throughout the valley. Like most other indigenous communities on the continent, they have been converted to Catholicism and come to Sibundoy's church on Sunday for the morning mass, then stay in the village for the market. This is the best day to visit Sibundoy, to see the men dressed in their traditional *sayos* (the local style of poncho), and the women wrapped in *rebozos* (the women's equivalent of the sayo) and adorned with *chaquiras* (necklaces made of beads).

There are two handicraft shops on the main road (Calle 16), but the selection is not impressive. The Indian carnival and handicraft fair is held in Sibundoy just before Ash Wednesday.

### Places to Stay & Eat

The *Sibundoy* and the *Oriente* are two cheap, if basic, residencias on the main road where the buses stop. Either will cost about US$3 per person and both have restaurants. You'll find a few more places nearby, including the more pleasant *Residencias Turista*, which has rooms with bath and hot water, and costs about US$5/8 a single/double.

### Getting There & Away

Trans Ipiales and Cootransmayo have 10 buses a day to Pasto (US$3.50, three hours). There are several buses to Puerto Asís coming through from Pasto (US$8, nine hours or more), but they are often full by the time they reach Sibundoy.

### IPIALES

• *pop 60,000* • *2900 m* • *11°C* • ☎ *(92725)*
Ipiales, the last Colombian town before the Ecuadorian border, is an uninteresting, busy commercial centre driven by the contraband trade across the frontier. There is little to see, except for the big, colourful Saturday

market, where the campesinos from surrounding villages come to sell and buy goods. The Banco de la República has a small collection of pottery from the pre-Columbian Indian groups from around the region on display. You can also pop into the Catedral on the Plaza de la Independencia; in the left-hand aisle is a vivid sculptured representation of souls burning in hell. A short side trip to Las Lajas is a must (see the following section).

### Information

**Money** No bank in Ipiales changes cash or travellers' cheques. The Banco de Bogotá and Banco de Colombia may give advances on Visa card, while the Banco de Occidente will do the same on MasterCard. Plenty of moneychangers on the main square and at the border will interchange US dollars, pesos and Ecuadorian sucres.

**Immigration** All passport formalities are conducted at the border, not in Ipiales or Tulcán. On the Colombian side of the border, there's a newly constructed brick building which houses the DAS office, the Ecuadorian consulate (see next section) and the Telecom office. The DAS office is open nonstop from 6 am till 8 pm, but don't plan to cross during lunch time: the Ecuadorian immigration post, on the Ecuadorian side of the border, closes from noon to 2 pm. Make sure you get exit and entry stamps in your passport from both Colombian and Ecuadorian officials.

**Ecuadorian Consulate** The consulate on the border, in the same building as the DAS office, is open Monday to Friday from 8.30 am to noon and 2.30 to 6 pm, and it's your last chance to get a visa, if you need one. There's no Ecuadorian consulate in Ipiales or in Pasto; the nearest is in Cali.

### Places to Stay

The hotels in Ipiales tend to fill up early (particularly on Saturday), and you may have to look around a bit if you arrive late. The nights are quite chilly, so check the

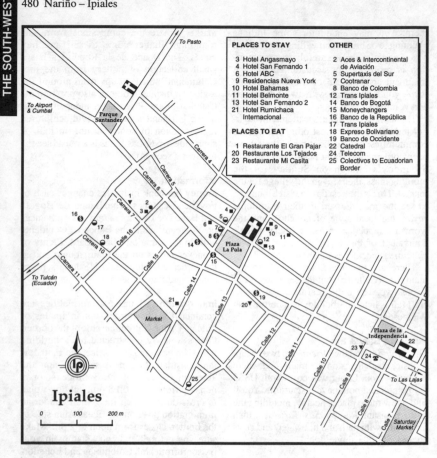

To Pasto

To Airport & Cumbal

Parque Santander

Carrera 4

Carrera 6

Carrera 5

Carrera 7

Calle 16

Carrera 10

Carrera 11

Calle 15

Calle 14

Calle 13

Calle 12

Calle 11

Calle 10

Calle 9

Calle 8

Calle 7

Plaza La Pola

Plaza de la Independencia

To Tulcán (Ecuador)

To Las Lajas

Market

Saturday Market

**Ipiales**

0      100      200 m

| PLACES TO STAY | OTHER |
|---|---|
| 3 Hotel Angasmayo | 2 Aces & Intercontinental |
| 4 Hotel San Fernando 1 | de Aviación |
| 6 Hotel ABC | 5 Supertaxis del Sur |
| 9 Residencias Nueva York | 7 Cootranar |
| 10 Hotel Bahamas | 8 Banco de Colombia |
| 11 Hotel Belmonte | 12 Trans Ipiales |
| 13 Hotel San Fernando 2 | 14 Banco de Bogotá |
| 21 Hotel Rumichaca | 15 Moneychangers |
| Internacional | 16 Banco de la República |
| | 17 Trans Ipiales |
| PLACES TO EAT | 18 Expreso Bolivariano |
| | 19 Banco de Occidente |
| 1 Restaurante El Gran Pajar | 22 Catedral |
| 20 Restaurante Los Tejados | 24 Telecom |
| 23 Restaurante Mi Casita | 25 Colectivos to Ecuadorian |
| | Border |

number of blankets before you book a room in a cheapie.

The cheapest one of an acceptable standard is the *Residencias Nueva York*, at the corner of Carrera 4 and Calle 13, which has fairly good rooms but without bath or hot water. It costs US$1.50 per person. Next door is the *Hotel Bahamas* (☎ 2884), which has hot water in shared baths and costs US$2 per head.

The *Hotel San Fernando 1* has rooms with private bath and hot water (US$3/5 for a single/double). The *Hotel San Fernando 2* has similar standards but shared baths only, for the same price.

The *Hotel Belmonte* (☎ 2771), at Carrera 4 No 12-111, is a small, friendly, family-run place, possibly the most popular with foreign backpackers. It has no private baths but does have hot water. It costs US$3 per person.

The *Hotel ABC* (☎ 2311), at Carrera 5 No 14-43, is another place offering good value for money. Singles/doubles/triples with bath and hot water cost US$3.50/6.50/8.

For something appreciably better, check the *Hotel Rumichaca Internacional* (☎ 2692), at Calle 14 No 7-114 (about US$10/15/18). The best in the region is the expensive *Hostería Mayasquer* (☎ 2643), on the road to Ecuador, a few hundred metres before the border.

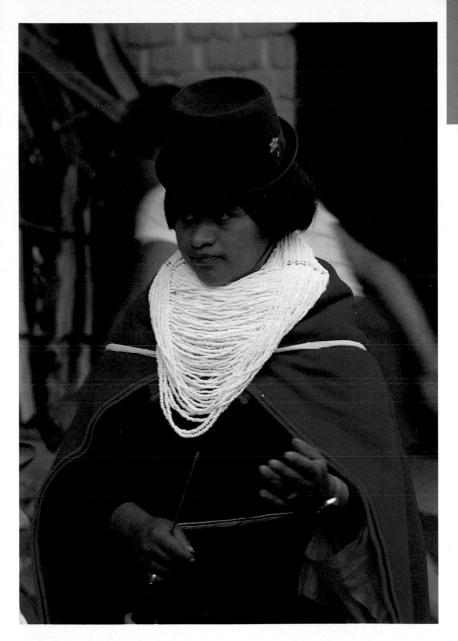

Guambiano Indian from Silvia region

Top: Market in Ipiales
Bottom: Kamzá Indians in Sibundoy

## Places to Eat

Several cheap restaurants on the main square serve set meals, and many more are scattered around the town. Better eating places include *Mi Casita*, *El Gran Pajar* and *Los Tejados*. The last two are more expensive.

## Getting There & Away

**Air** The San Luis Airport is seven km north-west of Ipiales, on the road to Guachucal. Colectivos to Aldana from the Parque Santander will drop you at the airport (US$0.50), or take a taxi (US$4).

Aces has daily flights to Cali (US$62). Intercontinental de Aviación has one flight a day to Popayán (US$38), and from there you can continue with Intercontinental to Bogotá (US$70 from Ipiales).

There are no direct flights from Ipiales to Ecuador, but you can easily get to Tulcán, and from there Tame has daily flights (often full) to Quito (US$15). The Tulcán airport is two km before the town from the border.

**Bus – within Colombia** The offices of the bus companies are scattered throughout the town. Ipiales has plenty of bus connections with Cali and the intermediate cities on the Pan-American Highway.

**To Pasto** Cootranar and Supertaxis del Sur buses leave from the main square every 15 minutes till 7 pm (US$2.75, two hours).

**To Bogotá** Expreso Bolivariano has direct climatizados every two hours from 6.30 am to 8.30 pm (US$37, 24 hours).

**To Cali** Apart from the above-listed Expreso Bolivariano climatizados, Cootranar and Trans Ipiales have pullmans which depart regularly throughout the day (US$17, 12 hours). Alternatively, go to Pasto and change; there are more buses from there.

**To Tumaco** Trans Ipiales has one bus a day (US$10, nine hours).

**Bus – to Ecuador** The border between Colombia and Ecuador is on the Rumichaca Bridge over the Carchi River, 2.5 km from Ipiales.

Frequent colectivos travel to the border, leaving (until around 6 pm) from the corner of Calle 13 and Carrera 11 (US$0.30). After

crossing the border on foot (don't forget to get exit and entry stamps in your passport), you take another colectivo (US$0.40) or a minibus (US$0.30) to Tulcán (six km). On both routes, Colombian and Ecuadorian currencies are accepted.

Both colectivos and minibuses go to the Parque Isidro Ayora, the square on the northern edge of Tulcán. The long-distance bus terminal is a long way from there, at the opposite end of Tulcán, so take a local bus or taxi. Buses to Quito depart regularly throughout the day (US$2.50, five to six hours).

In Tulcán visit the cemetery, which is just two blocks from the Parque Isidro Ayora. There is a busy market on Sunday, attended by hordes of Colombians.

## SANTUARIO DE LAS LAJAS
• *2600 m* • *14°C*

Santuario de Nuestra Señora de las Lajas is a Gothic-style church built on a bridge which spans a spectacular deep gorge of the Guáitara River, seven km south-east of Ipiales. The church was erected to commemorate the appearance of the Virgin Mary; legend has it that an image of the Virgin appeared in the mid-18th century on an enormous vertical rock about 45 metres above the river.

The first chapel was constructed in 1803, then replaced by another. Today's church, designed by an architect from Nariño, Lucindo Espinoza, was built between 1916 and 1948, and is an unusual construction. The church is set on a bridge up against the cliff in such a way that the rock with the image is preserved as its high altar. The Virgin is accompanied by Santo Domingo and San Francisco.

Pilgrims from all over Colombia and Ecuador come here all year round. Some local sources maintain that this is the most visited religious sanctuary in the Americas. Many pilgrims have left thanksgiving plaques along the alley leading to the church. Note the number of miraculous occurrences which are attributed to the Virgin.

## Places to Stay

You can stay in Las Lajas, in the convent up

the road from the church. Double rooms with bath attached, hot water and a beautiful view over the gorge cost US$3.50 per person. The place is a little hard to find – look for the basketball court in front of the primary school, just off the main road; the convent is immediately behind the school.

### Getting There & Away

Getting to Las Lajas is very easy. Frequent colectivos run from Ipiales, departing from the corner of Carrera 6 and Calle 4 (US$0.40, 15 minutes). A taxi from the main square, Plaza La Pola, to Las Lajas will cost about US$3.50. A return taxi trip for four people, including a one-hour wait in Las Lajas, shouldn't cost more than US$10. You'll get a spectacular view of the gorge and the church just before you reach Las Lajas.

## VOLCÁN CUMBAL

Cumbal is Nariño's highest volcano, reaching a height of 4764 metres. It is set in the Nudo de los Pastos, a volcanic range near the Ecuadorian border. The volcano has two peaks: the southern one is extinct and is covered with a snow cap, while the northern one is active and has several craters. The last major eruption took place in the 1920s.

The campesinos living in the hamlets near the volcano climb to both peaks: to the active one to dig out the sulphur rock, and to the snowy one to collect ice for ice creams and juices. Haven't refrigerators come to Nariño yet?, you might ask. Yes, they obviously have, but the ice from the summit of Cumbal is said to have extraordinary properties, including an almost miraculous power to cure hangovers.

There are footpaths heading up to both peaks. The usual jumping-off point for trekking to either top is the village of Cumbal, 15 km east of the volcano. Market day in Cumbal is Sunday.

If you don't plan to climb the volcano and only want to see it from a distance, the best view is from the Ipiales-Guachucal road, a few km before Guachucal.

### When to Go & What to Bring

The driest months are July to September but even then the mountain tops are often shrouded in clouds, showing themselves only early in the morning. During the rest of the year it rains a lot, the paths are muddy and you are unlikely to get panoramic views. The winds are strong higher up. Take rain gear and a windproof jacket; gloves and a warm hat can also be very useful.

### Maps

Don't waste time on a visit to IGAC in order to get maps. It does have maps of the region but there is a blank area where the volcano should be, as it was hidden by cloud (no wonder!) when the aerial photos were taken.

### The Trek

The trek to either peak is not technically difficult except in the extreme upper parts. It is possible to do it in one day but you must start very early as the climb is long and strenuous – you have about 2000 metres to ascend. If you have a tent and food, you can do it in a more leisurely fashion over two days.

From Cumbal village go west along Calle 18, which turns into a rough road that leads to Laguna del Cumbal (about eight km). Halfway there you'll find a side road branching off to the left to Ortiga village. This is the road to take. The village is just a collection of huts loosely scattered over a few km along the river. The road goes to the far western end of the village, where it terminates. There are several misleading turn-offs – use the map for orientation. You can also get to Ortiga by jeep (US$0.80), which saves about an hour's walking.

After passing the last hut you'll come to the footpath leading to the volcano. Follow it for about 1½ hours until it divides. Here you must decide which peak to climb. The left branch leads to the snowy top; it's a three-hour ascent to the snowline. The right fork climbs to the sulphur mines of the active peak and you can identify the route by the marks left by the small sledges the locals use to transport the sulphur rock down from the mines. Cloud and fog, which are common

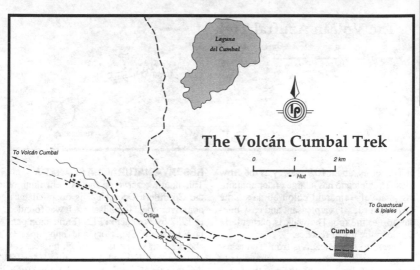

The Volcán Cumbal Trek

from about noon on, can make the trails hard to find and follow.

It takes two to three hours of hard uphill walking to get to the mines. They are no more than small caves where the people dig the sulphur rock. They make the climb every day and work all day in terrifying conditions – the heat and the sulphur fumes are unbearable – and then transport the rock down to sell it for next to nothing. You can see them working in the caves, but you're unlikely to stay inside for more than a minute. The sulphur fumes will immediately make you weep and breathing is impossible. It is hotter than the hottest desert, yet as soon as you leave the 'sauna' to catch a breath, you will be assaulted by biting, icy winds.

The surrounding scenery is breathtaking: huge white ice pillars stand beside the yellow sulphur holes, all submerged in a mysterious fog of acrid vapours. The top of the volcano is nearby, but as you go higher the vapour becomes denser and visibility more limited, not to mention the worsening smell and cold.

### Places to Stay & Eat

There are a few places to stay in the village of Cumbal, including the unnamed residencias at Carrera 8 No 20-47. It has shared baths and cold water only, and costs US$5 for a *matrimonio*. There are a couple of simple eateries in town, of which *El Rincón de Colombia*, Calle 18 No 8-48, is the best: a filling, tasty meal will cost US$1.50.

### Getting There & Away

You can get to Cumbal from Pasto, but there is only one direct bus daily, at 1.30 pm with Trans Ipiales (US$3.50, three hours). It's easier to reach Cumbal from Ipiales: jeeps depart when full (approximately every hour or so), from about 8 am till 4 pm, from the garage next door to Calle 15 No 7-23 (US$1.50, one hour). In the opposite direction, from Cumbal to Ipiales, jeeps leave from 6 am till about 3 pm from the main plaza. If you finish your trek later and want to leave the area, you'll have to walk or hitch eight km to Guachucal, where you'll find transport to Ipiales until about 6 pm.

### VOLCÁN AZUFRAL

If you are not up to climbing Cumbal, go to Azufral, another volcano in the Nudo de los Pastos, which is lower (4070 metres) and easier to get to. Azufral lies west of the town

THE SOUTH-WEST

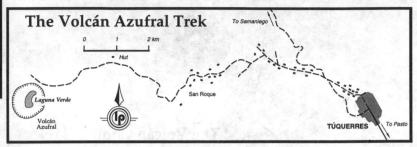

# The Volcán Azufral Trek

of Túquerres, about 10 km away as the crow flies. The volcano has a large crater containing a lovely emerald-coloured lake, the Laguna Verde. It is a pleasant and easy one-day trip to the top. The walk is particularly scenic in the upper reaches.

Access to the volcano is from Túquerres along a jeepable road. Jeeps occasionally ply this road but they only go as far as the farms near Túquerres. The walk from the town to the volcano will take you about four hours uphill and three hours back down. If you don't want to walk, try to hire a jeep in the market area in Túquerres; it will bring you near the crater (the road becomes impassable shortly before reaching the crater). The weather pattern is the same as on Cumbal. There's a good market in Túquerres on Thursday, with some great ruanas.

### Places to Stay

Túquerres has a modest choice of accommodation. *Pensión Quito*, Carrera 14 No 17-29, just off the main square, costs US$3 per person and is acceptable. Two other budget hotels, *Santa Rita* and *Londres*, are on the road to Pasto, a 10-minute walk from the plaza. Túquerres lies at 3000 metres, so the nights are cold.

### Getting There & Away

Túquerres can be easily reached from Pasto by a colectivo; they run when full (US$4, two hours). In addition, all buses from Pasto going to Tumaco pass through Túquerres (US$3, 2½ hours). There are no direct buses between Ipiales and Túquerres.

## RESERVA NATURAL LA PLANADA

This nature reserve on the western flank of the Cordillera Occidental is operated by a nongovernment organisation. It was founded in 1982 by Fundación FES (Fundación para la Educación Superior) and encompasses about 33 sq km of land stretching between altitudes of 1300 and 2100 metres. Most of the reserve's area is covered with humid cloudforest rich in plant species (many of which are endemic) and wildlife.

The reserve has a research station which focuses on ecological issues, and has facilities for visitors. There are a few paths traced through the forest which give an insight into the local flora and fauna. A trip to the Nevado del Cumbal can be done from the reserve.

The average temperature in the reserve is about 15°C and the annual rainfall is 4500 mm. Regardless of when you come, bring rain gear, good walking boots, warm clothes and a torch.

### Places to Stay & Eat

The reserve provides accommodation and food in the pleasant, purpose-built Centro de Visitantes (visitors centre). A bed plus three meals costs about US$25.

### Getting There & Away

The reserve lies roughly midway between Pasto and Tumaco, close to the road linking these two cities. From Pasto, take the Tumaco bus (there are about 10 a day) to the village of Chucunés (US$5.50, five hours). A two-hour walk from Chucunés will bring you to the Centro de Visitantes.

If you are coming from Cali, contact the

head office of Fundación FES (☎ 822524, 845933), Carrera 5 No 6-05. The staff will provide further information and book your visit. You also may be able to arrange with them for a guide to come from the reserve down to Chucunés to pick you up and accompany you to the visitors centre.

## TUMACO

• *pop 65,000* • *6 m* • *28°C* • ☎ *(927272)*

Tumaco is Colombia's second largest port on the Pacific coast, but it's far less important than Buenaventura, the largest. The town is connected to Pasto and Ipiales by a partly unpaved road. This is gradually being upgraded and surfaced, but the work is advancing at a remarkably slow pace.

Often subject to earthquakes, fires and floods, it is a poor, neglected town; only a few main streets are paved and many of the houses are ramshackle wooden constructions, some of them built on stilts over the sea. There are problems with the electricity and water supplies, and it rains most of the year. The region was once the centre of the pre-Columbian Tumaco culture, but today the population is predominantly black.

### PLACES TO STAY

| | |
|---|---|
| 3 | Residencias Porvenir |
| 8 | Hotel Villa del Mar |
| 10 | Hotel Colón |
| 12 | Hotel Ipiales |
| 13 | Hotel Don Luis |
| 14 | Hotel del Pacífico |
| 15 | Hotel La Sultana |
| 18 | Residencias M-C |
| 19 | Hotel Don Pepe |

### PLACES TO EAT

| | |
|---|---|
| 5 | Restaurante El Paisa |
| 7 | Restaurante Las Velas |
| 20 | Restaurante La Tropicana |

### OTHER

| | |
|---|---|
| 1 | Telecom |
| 2 | Police Station |
| 4 | Supertaxis del Sur |
| 6 | Trans Ipiales |
| 9 | Minibuses to El Morro Island |
| 11 | Post Office |
| 16 | Almacén Caracol (Money Exchange) |
| 17 | Market |

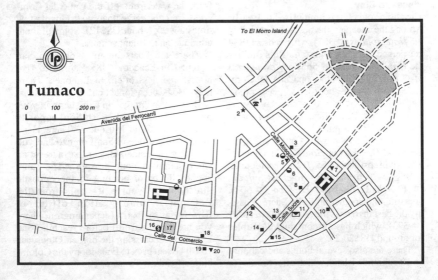

Tumaco

There's no good reason to visit Tumaco unless you feel the urge to get to the Ecuadorian coast by sea. Few travellers make this effort.

## Information

**Money** There doesn't seem to be a useful bank in Tumaco; some shops and hotels change greenbacks but give a poor rate. Try Almacén Caracol near the market or the Hotel Villa del Mar.

## Things to See & Do

The poor north-eastern suburb built on stilts over the sea is an astonishing sight. It is quite large, and has its own chapel, medical centre, shops, restaurants etc. Take some precautions when walking there. It's probably best to get to know some locals and ask them to show you around.

You can do a short trip to the natural rock arch on El Morro Island. Take a minibus from the square behind the market to El Morro and get off at the end of the line. For a beach, go to Bocagrande Island, which is admired by local tourists but is not very good.

## Places to Stay

The choice of hotels is limited, so book early. Among the cheapies, the best bet is probably the *Hotel Ipiales* (☎ 387), which costs US$4 per person in rooms with fan. If it's full, try the *Hotel Don Pepe* (☎ 565) or *Residencias M-C*, opposite each other on Calle del Comercio (both charge about US$5 per person). *Residencias Porvenir*, opposite the Supertaxis del Sur bus office, is another basic option at a similar price.

If you need a room with a private bath, try the *Hotel Don Luis* or *Hotel Colón*, either of which will cost about US$7/12 a single/double.

Slightly better are the *Hotel La Sultana* (☎ 438) and *Hotel del Pacífico* (☎ 607), opposite one another on Calle Sucre. Possibly the best in town is the *Hotel Villa del Mar* (☎ 393), which has air-con singles/doubles for around US$20/25.

There are also several hotels and cabañas on Bocagrande Island, which offer rooms for around US$5 per person (US$15 with full board).

## Places to Eat

There are several basic eateries around the bus offices; *El Paisa* has possibly the best set meals. Better restaurants include the *Claudia* in the Hotel Don Luis, *La Tropicana* on Calle del Comercio (good seafood) and *Las Velas* (arguably the best in town).

## Getting There & Away

**Air** The airport is on El Morro Island. Take a minibus from the square behind the market (US$0.40) or a taxi (US$4). Satena has three flights a week to Cali (US$48) and one to Guapí (US$34). Intercontinental also operates flights to Cali (US$33).

**Bus** There are 10 buses a day to Pasto, five with Trans Ipiales and another five with Supertaxis del Sur (US$11.50, 10 hours). To Ipiales, there's only one Trans Ipiales bus daily (US$10, nine hours).

**Boat** A few boats go daily to Bocagrande (US$4 one-way, 30 minutes); they depart from the waterfront, off the Calle del Comercio. Irregular cargo boats go to Guapí a few times a week (about US$12). Some of them continue on to Buenaventura.

There are boats on most days to San Lorenzo in Ecuador (US$8, three to five hours) and, less often, to Limones. There may also be occasional boats to Esmeraldas.

Before leaving, get an exit stamp in your passport at the police station opposite Telecom on Calle Mosquera. There is no immigration office in San Lorenzo and you need to go to Esmeraldas or Ibarra to get an entry stamp in your passport. The same applies if you're heading in the opposite direction: get your exit stamp from the Ecuadorian immigration office in Esmeraldas or Ibarra (depending on where you are coming from) before reaching San Lorenzo and crossing the border. Otherwise you'll be sent back to Ecuador by the Colombian officials in Tumaco.

# The Amazon Basin

Most people on hearing the word 'Amazon' immediately think of Brazil. While it is true that most of the Amazon basin is in Brazil, half a dozen other countries, including Bolivia, Peru, Ecuador, Colombia, Venezuela and Guyana, share part of this immense green carpet.

In Colombia, the Amazon basin takes up the entire south-east portion of the country, an area of about 400,000 sq km, more than a third of the national territory. Administratively, Amazonia (as it's known to Colombians) falls into six departments: Amazonas, Caquetá, Guainía, Guaviare, Putumayo and Vaupés.

Almost the entire region is clad in thick rainforest, crisscrossed by a labyrinth of rivers and sparsely inhabited by Indian groups and colonists. The total population is estimated at some half a million, but most people live in a narrow belt at the foot of the Andes, leaving the rest of the area almost devoid of inhabitants.

The longest rivers of the Colombian Amazon basin are the Caquetá (2200 km), part of which is not navigable, and the Putumayo (1800 km), an important waterway forming the border between Colombia and Ecuador/Peru. Both these rivers are tributaries of the Amazon. As for the Amazon itself, Colombia contains only about 130 km of its more than 6400-km course. This is a result of a treaty signed in the 1920s between Colombia, Brazil and Peru. The agreement granted Colombia a somewhat curious, narrow strip of land penetrating south between the two neighbouring countries down to the bank of the Amazon, with the town of Leticia sitting at its south-eastern tip.

Very early on, the dream of El Dorado enticed the Spaniards into the Amazon region. Soon after the discovery of the Amazon River by Francisco de Orellana (in 1542) the region became the object of various expeditions. The explorers were followed by missionaries, first the Jesuits, later the Franciscans and Capuchins, who

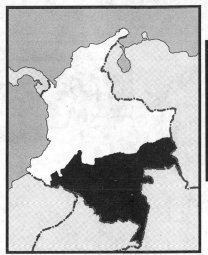

founded new settlements and brought the gospel to the Indians. At the end of the 19th century, the rubber boom marked the beginning of economic exploitation of the jungle on a large scale. It brought with it probably the cruellest period for the indigenous people. Slavery was introduced in its most inhuman form and decimated the Indian population.

By the 1930s, when the rubber fever came to an end, a new danger had emerged. In 1932 the construction of the Altamira-Florencia and Pasto-Mocoa roads opened up the Amazon region. A stream of settlers rushed in, turning into a flood from the 1950s onwards. Uncontrolled colonisation continues but, so far, has mostly affected the fringes of the Amazon basin, with very few migrants heading deeper into the jungle.

Large parts of Colombian Amazonia still remain invincible. Its central part, while inhabited by different Indian communities, is otherwise almost unexplored. The region

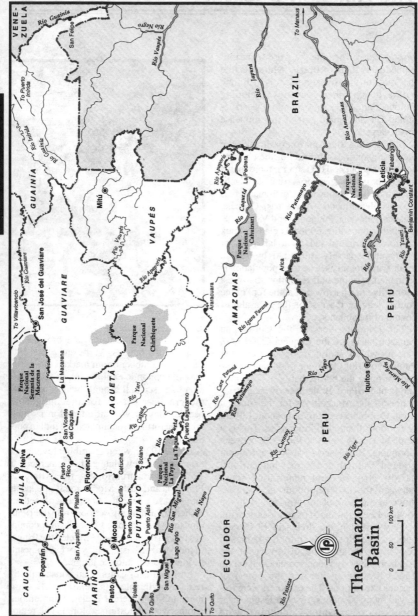

The Amazon Basin

is a linguistic mosaic of more than 50 languages (not counting dialects) belonging to some 10 linguistic families.

The largest Indian group of Colombian Amazonia are the Huitotos (also spelled Witotos), who live scattered throughout the extensive territory between the middle stretches of the Caquetá and Putumayo rivers. Today their population is estimated at roughly 10,000. See the sketch map in the Population & People section of the Facts about the Country chapter for the location of the Huitotos and some other major indigenous groups.

The climate is not uniform throughout Colombian Amazonia. In its south-eastern part (Amazonas department) it rains most heavily in January. At the same time, the opposite end of Amazonia (the northern parts of Caquetá, Guaviare and Guainía) is in the middle of the dry season. The further north one goes, the longer the dry period lasts. In July, while the north has heavy rains, the extreme south enters the *veranillo*, a short period of drier weather, though it's not a dry season by any standards.

The water levels of the rivers don't follow local climate patterns, as they depend a great deal on the rainy season in the Andes, where the rivers originate. In most rivers (excluding the Amazon) the water rises from April to June, subsides somewhat in July and August, then rises significantly from September to November, only to drop from December to March to its lowest level. On the Caquetá and Putumayo rivers, the difference between the highest and lowest water levels can exceed eight metres.

The flora and fauna, as you might expect, are fabulously varied. Studies carried out to date have revealed only a part of the real picture. According to the records, there are more than 200 species of mammals, 600 species of birds, 200 species of reptiles and 600 species of fish. The world of insects remains largely unstudied.

The possibilities for exploring the Amazon are virtually unlimited and depend only on your experience, preparation, funds, time and imagination. This said, few foreign travellers venture into the region except to make the easy, if costly, trip to Leticia. If you plan on doing any boat trips, you will need plenty of time, huge doses of patience, some of your own food and quite a lot of money. Travel in the Amazon is not cheap but it is, without doubt, a memorable adventure.

### Orientation

Road access to Colombian Amazonia is only from the west. There are three roads that pass over the Cordillera Oriental and lead down to the western periphery of the Amazon: Altamira-Florencia, Pasto-Mocoa and Pitalito-Mocoa. All these roads are very rough and dangerous. Landslides are a way of life, particularly in the second half of the rainy season from August to September. Still, all the roads are spectacular and offer marvellous scenery. The Pasto-Mocoa road is possibly in the worst shape and the most dangerous, yet it's very scenic and the trip is breathtaking. You'll certainly remember it for a long time.

Florencia, Mocoa and Puerto Asís aren't in the Amazon rainforest proper. The region along the eastern foothills of the Cordillera is a sort of savannah populated by colonists who mostly devote themselves to raising stock. Jungle vegetation and wildlife begin far beyond the settled area.

There are two principal starting points for excursions into the wilderness: from Florencia by the Orteguaza and Caquetá rivers, and from Puerto Asís by the Putumayo.

The easiest trip, but only a foretaste, is the excursion from Florencia to San Antonio de Getucha and on to some Indian settlements along the Río Orteguaza. A more· exciting route is the Florencia-La Tagua-Puerto Leguízamo-Puerto Asís (or vice versa) loop. This trip can be done in a week but it is worth taking longer. Florencia and Puerto Asís are connected by road and river transport through Curillo and Puerto Guzmán. This gives you the possibility of closing the loop.

The most fascinating part of Amazonia stretches further to the east, where various Indian tribes live in almost total isolation from 'civilisation'. The Indians generally don't live on the banks of the biggest rivers, preferring to build their settlements on the smaller and quieter tributaries. Outsiders come here only sporadically, and tourists are virtually unknown.

At the far south-eastern end of the Colombian Amazon lies Leticia, the town which has become the most popular destination for tourists (both locals and foreigners) eager to get an insight into the region.

### Information
Perhaps the best source of information on the Colombian Amazon basin is the Corporación Colombiana para la Amazonia Araracuara (COA) in Bogotá, Calle 20 No 5-44. It has specific information on flora and fauna, the Indian groups, geography, history etc. It has its own publications as well as a library, and has published an almost complete bibliographical catalogue on Colombian Amazonia, comprising over 4000 books, articles and studies, with notes on where to find them.

You will find a good synthesis of information on the Colombian Amazon basin (but only in Spanish) in *Amazonia Colombiana* by Camilo A Domínguez (Banco Popular, Bogotá, 1985). This book gives general information on the area's history, geology, climate, hydrography, inhabitants etc. It also has a comprehensive dictionary of flora and fauna with local names and descriptions. The book is almost unknown and hard to obtain in bookstores but can be bought directly from the Banco Popular bookshop in Bogotá, next door to the Museo Arqueológico.

There are no good maps of the Amazon. The IGAC in Bogotá has only general maps of individual departments. The names of villages, small rivers, rapids etc often differ from the names used locally.

### What to Bring
For any serious trip to the Amazon, a hammock is a must, as are a mosquito net, insect repellent, rain gear (though you will probably get wet anyway, either from rain or perspiration), a water container, antimalarials, water-purifying tablets, a torch and a machete.

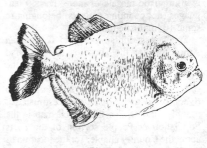

Piraña

Long sleeves are essential for protection against the bush and insects. Take proper footwear as paths are muddy and swampy. Also take your own food, as the local diet is lacking both in quantity and nutritional value. Don't forget a well-stocked medical kit (see the Health section in the Facts for the Visitor chapter for details). Take some 'alternative money', ie useful, practical items which can be easily exchanged for food or local handicrafts, or just presented as gifts. Knives and clothing are obvious examples, but use your imagination and common sense.

### Getting Around
As there are no roads in the Amazon region, transport is by either boat or plane. Travel is very expensive. Petrol is shipped in and doubles or even trebles in price. The cost of river transport is not much less than that of flying, which makes air travel a good alternative in order to skip difficult areas or simply to get out of the jungle.

**Air** Satena airline has regular flights throughout Amazonia, linking about 10 major points. Contact its office before your trip (best in Bogotá) and get a complete schedule to plan your route. Apart from Satena there are several local carriers with mostly chartered flights between the small villages of the region.

**Boat** Boat trips can take weeks, as none of the boats run on any regular schedule. Most are cargo boats, which leave when sufficient freight has been accumulated. The conditions on board are primitive – you sleep in a hammock or on deck – and food, if provided, is poor and monotonous. Water is taken straight from the river. There are plenty of mosquitoes on the smaller rivers, though rarely any out in the middle of the larger ones.

Although traffic on the main rivers is relatively frequent, the distances are enormous and the boats are usually far from fast. As soon as you get off the main routes you can wait days for a lift. You can't plan a schedule when travelling along the rivers.

### Warning

Bear in mind that some parts of the Amazon basin harbour coca plantations and guerrillas. Don't venture on your own into remote, unknown areas. Local guides are well worth considering. They can make contact with the Indian communities, and are essential as interpreters. They will usually organise transport and help you to find food and a place to sleep. Most importantly, they know the dangerous areas and will help you to avoid the 'red zones'. If you stumble upon a red zone, a guide is practically your only protection.

### FLORENCIA

• *pop 105,000* • *450 m* • *26˚C* • ☎ *(98835)*

Florencia, the capital of Caquetá, is the only important urban centre on the fringes of the Colombian Amazon. The town was founded in 1902 by Italian missionaries who named it after the famous Italian city. Today it is the base for intensive colonisation of a wide region. It is quite big, busy and lively but not very pleasant.

Since the electricity comes from Huila, passing over the Cordillera, power cuts are frequent and random. The town also has problems with its water supply. The only road which passes over the mountains to Altamira, connecting Florencia with the outer world, is poor and sometimes blocked by landslides, particularly between July and September.

The town has a good museum but other-wise there is little to do here. It is just one of the possible gateways to the Amazon. The FARC guerrillas operate in the region east of Florencia, so check the current situation carefully before you decide to set off for the wilderness. Police checkpoints on the roads are frequent and searches thorough.

### Information

**Tourist Office** The Instituto de Cultura y Turismo, Calle 15 No 10-11, is open Monday to Friday from 7 am to noon and 2 to 5 pm.

**Money** There are several banks in the city centre but none of them seems to handle foreign-exchange transactions. Bring sufficient pesos with you.

### Museum

The Museo Etnográfico del Centro Indigenista is in the Emisora Armonías del Caquetá building, next to the cathedral. The museum features a collection of crafts of the Indian groups living in the region, mainly of the Huitotos and Coreguajes. It is open Monday to Friday from 8 am to noon and 2 to 5 pm.

### Places to Stay

Accommodation is rather expensive in Florencia. There are a lot of basic residencias in the central area, particularly on Carrera 10 between Calles 16 and 17 and on Calle 16 between Carreras 10 and 11. They tend to fill up early and the minimum charge is US$4 per person. Not all have fans, which are essential here. Due to water shortages, the toilets may leave a bit to be desired.

Probably the best among the cheapies is the *Hotel Central* (☎ 2677), at Carrera 11 No 15-26, just off the main square. It costs US$4 per person in clean rooms with fans but without private bath. Alternatively, try the *Apartamentos Tumaco*, at Carrera 11 No 16-41, which costs US$6/10 for singles/doubles with bath and fan.

Other central options include the *Apartamentos Petecuy* (☎ 3244), at Carrera 11 No 15-20 (US$8/13 with private bath and fan), and the *Hotel Metropol* (☎ 3916), at

Carrera 11 No 16-52 (US$10/15). The *Hotel Apartamentos Chairá* (☎ 2635), at Calle 16 No 12-51, is appreciably better but costs US$15/20. It has its own restaurant. The *Hotel Royal Plaza* (☎ 3030), on the main square, is the best in town and it, too, has a restaurant.

### Places to Eat

Like accommodation, food tends to be expensive in Florencia. You'll find a number of restaurants within a couple of blocks of the main plaza. They serve the usual fare of set meals (around US$3 each) plus a short menu of carne asada, arroz con pollo and the like. There is a good choice of fruit in the market. The pineapples are delicious.

### Getting There & Away

**Air** The airport is on the road to La Montañita. Any bus to Puerto Rico, San Vicente, San Antonio de Getucha etc will drop you there. Otherwise take a taxi for US$5.

Aires has two flights a day to Neiva (US$42) and Bogotá (US$81); one flight daily to Ibagué (US$67), Cali (US$111) and Medellín (US$114); and one flight a week (on Tuesday) to Puerto Asís (US$34).

Satena flies three days a week to Neiva (US$37), Bogotá (US$78), Puerto Asís (US$32) and Puerto Leguízamo (US$46).

**Bus** The bus terminal is a 10-minute walk north-east of the main plaza. Coomotor has direct buses to Bogotá (US$20 climatizado, 12 hours). There are about 10 buses daily to Neiva with various companies (US$10 climatizado, US$7.50 corriente, six to seven hours).

If you are heading for San Agustín, take any Neiva or Bogotá bus, get off in Altamira and catch a bus coming through from Neiva to San Agustín. The Florencia-Altamira road, passing over the Cordillera Oriental, is rough but spectacular. Travel during the day to catch the splendid scenery.

There are buses or chivas to Curillo (10 daily) and San Antonio de Getucha (six daily) with Coomotorflorencia and Cootranscaquetá. To reach either destination costs US$5.50 and takes about 4½ hours.

### SAN ANTONIO DE GETUCHA

Usually labelled on the maps as Getucha, this is a small river port south-east of Florencia and linked to it by a 100-km road, more than half of which is unpaved and in poor shape. San Antonio de Getucha is a rather unremarkable minor settlement but it's Florencia's main gateway to the Amazon: it lies on the navigable Río Orteguaza (the river in Florencia is not navigable), which flows down to the Río Caquetá, and thus provides access to numerous small localities in Caquetá and Putumayo which would otherwise remain inaccessible.

San Antonio de Getucha is also a good base from which to visit the nearby Indian communities. The Indians, mainly Coreguajes but also Huitotospeople, indigenous; and Tamacunas, inhabit the region along the Orteguaza River, and some live in Getucha itself.

There is a Catholic mission in Mama Bwe, about 20 km down the Orteguaza River from Getucha, which operates a school for Indian kids from the area. A few tiny Indian settlements, including Agua Negra, are within a short walking distance of the mission.

Before you set off for this trip, go to the tourist office in Florencia for specific information and a letter of introduction for the mission. The sisters from the mission will then introduce you to the local Indian communities.

### Places to Stay & Eat

There are a few residencias in San Antonio de Getucha; try *Buenos Aires* or *Florida*. The sisters at the Catholic mission in Mama Bwe may offer you food and accommodation.

### Getting There & Away

**Bus** Getucha is connected to Florencia by about half a dozen buses (or chivas) per day (US$5.50, four to five hours, depending on the road conditions).

**Boat** There is regular boat transport to some of the nearby Indian settlements, including Mama Bwe and Agua Negra (US$3, one hour), but you have to hire a boat to get to the others.

Passenger boats (known locally as *deslizadores)* depart from Getucha for La Tagua, on the Río Caquetá, on Thursday and Saturday at 6.30 am (US$30, six hours). Buy the ticket in Florencia at Heladería Caleña, Carrera 12 No 16-52, and go to Getucha a day before to catch the boat. From La Tagua, the boat returns to Getucha on Monday and Friday. The Río Caquetá is navigable below La Tagua until cut by rapids several km above Araracuara. There's no scheduled transport on this stretch of the river.

A 25-km-long road links La Tagua to Puerto Leguízamo on the Río Putumayo. From there you can hunt for a cargo boat heading upstream to Puerto Asís or down to Leticia. Traffic is busy but there are no passenger boats.

Puerto Leguízamo is a gateway to the Parque Nacional La Paya, a vast, 4420-sq-km expanse of rainforest between the Caquetá and Putumayo rivers, but the park has no tourist facilities.

## CURILLO

Curillo is a tiny port on the Río Caquetá, linked to Florencia by a largely unsurfaced, poor road. It has no tourist interest, except as a stopover between Florencia and Mocoa.

### Places to Stay & Eat

There are a few budget residencias; they cost around US$3 to US$5 per person. Try *El Viajero* or *Plaza*. Two or three budget eateries will keep you going.

### Getting There & Away

**Bus** Buses or chivas to/from Florencia run fairly regularly till the early afternoon (US$5.50, 4½ to five hours).

**Boat** There are passenger boats daily at 6 am travelling upstream to Puerto Guzmán (US$10, five to six hours). From there you can continue by road to Mocoa or Pasto, or to Puerto Asís and on to Ecuador.

There is no regular transport from Curillo down the Río Caquetá. Boats occasionally

go as far as Solita (about US$7, three hours). In Solita, you must look for another boat to Tres Esquinas or Puerto Solano, where the traffic is heavier.

## PUERTO GUZMÁN

Puerto Guzmán is another tiny port on the Río Caquetá, about 100 km upstream from Curillo. Like Curillo, it serves as a transit point between Mocoa and Florencia, but otherwise there is no reason to come here.

This is a guerrilla region so expect more rigorous army checks. The army barracks in the village are 100 metres uphill from the church; stay well away from the barracks.

### Places to Stay & Eat

There are at least five basic residencias on the main street, all charging US$4 to US$5 per person; *Caquetá* is probably the best. A couple of basic eateries, including *Turista,* serve uninspiring almuerzos and comidas.

### Getting There & Away

**Bus** One Cootransmayo bus departs every day directly to Pasto (US$10.50, 11 hours). A few chivas (locals call them *escaleras)* go to Mocoa (US$3.50, three hours).

**Boat** Passenger boats depart daily at 6 am to Curillo, heading down the Río Caquetá (US$10, five to six hours).

## MOCOA
• *pop 12,000* • *595 m* • *25°C* • ☎ *(988)*

Mocoa, the capital of Putumayo, is a small, unremarkable agricultural and cattle centre. You'll pass it if you're heading from Pasto to Puerto Asís or Puerto Guzmán, but there is no point in stopping here unless you need an exit stamp in your passport from the DAS office. Note that there's no longer a DAS office in Puerto Asís.

### Places to Stay

There are a few budget hotels just off the main plaza, close to the bus offices. The *Residencias Voz del Putumayo*, round the corner from the Cootransmayo bus office, costs US$3 per person. It is basic but acceptable. The *Santa Ana* costs US$5 per person in clean rooms with baths. The *Hotel Central*, just off the main plaza, and the *Residencias Colonial*, a block further north, are both reasonable deals; either costs US$4 per person.

### Getting There & Away

There are several buses that travel daily to Pasto along a very scenic road (US$7, seven to eight hours). Read the Pasto section for more about this route. To Puerto Asís, buses cost US$4.50 and take four hours. Chivas ply the route to Puerto Guzmán two or three times a day (US$3.50, three hours).

There are two buses a day to Pitalito (US$7, six hours) along the recently opened, rough road. It's a beautiful ride when the potholes aren't bouncing you out of your seat, but, as always, beware of thieves. There are two army checks along the way.

### PUERTO ASÍS

• *pop 14,000 • 250 m • 28°C • ☎ (927)*

Founded in 1912, Puerto Asís is today the largest port on the Putumayo River, but it is nothing more than a spreading, impoverished town where everything is a problem – the water and electricity supplies, health and educational services and road connections. Puerto Asís is the place to hunt for boats down the Putumayo to explore the Amazon or to get to Brazil and Peru by river. This is also a stopping point on the unpopular backyard route to Ecuador. There is nothing else to do in town.

The surrounding region is an important coca-growing area. It is also infested by guerrillas, with the FARC and EPL operating here. Predictably, the zone is swamped by the military and anti-drug forces. There are two police checkpoints on the Mocoa-Puerto Asís road which are more thorough than most.

The area has high rainfall, with June to September being the wettest months.

### Information

**Money** There are no useful banks in Puerto Asís. Bring enough pesos from Pasto, as the rate for greenbacks given by local shops, hotels and moneychangers is poor.

If you are heading for Ecuador, you can easily change pesos for sucres (and vice versa) with moneychangers in Puerto Asís, San Miguel, La Punta and Lago Agrio.

**DAS** There's no longer a DAS office in Puerto Asís; it has moved to Mocoa. Get an exit stamp in your passport there if you're heading for Ecuador or Brazil.

### Places to Stay

There are plenty of basic hotels throughout the town. There is no big difference between them, just look around and choose one which looks less scruffy than the others. Many of them have matrimonios. The cheapest places cost US$4 per person and US$6 per matrimonio. Note that cheap hotels fill up early, so look for a bed as soon as you come.

The better hotels (in ascending order of price) include: the *Hotel Mery* (☎ 397160), at Calle 10 No 19-32; the *Hotel Continental* (☎ 397219), at Calle 12 No 17-68; the *Hotel Camba Huasi* (☎ 397087), at Carrera 22 No 10-27; and the *Hotel Chilimaco* (☎ 397218), at Calle 10 No 20-06.

### Getting There & Away

**Air** The airport is on the northern outskirts of the town, a short walk from the centre. Aires and Satena service Puerto Asís.

Satena flies three days a week to Florencia (US$32) and Bogotá (US$100). Aires has one flight daily to Bogotá (US$107), four flights a week to Cali (US$90), three flights a week to Neiva (US$69) and Puerto Leguízamo (US$49) and one flight weekly to Florencia (US$34).

Aires has recently introduced flights to Lago Agrio, in Ecuador, on Tuesday, Thursday and Saturday (US$16).

**Bus** There are several buses daily to Pasto through Mocoa, operated by Trans Ipiales and Cootransmayo (US$11.50, 12 hours). About 10 chivas a day go to San Miguel on the Ecuadorian border (US$5, five hours); the last one departs around 2 pm. From San

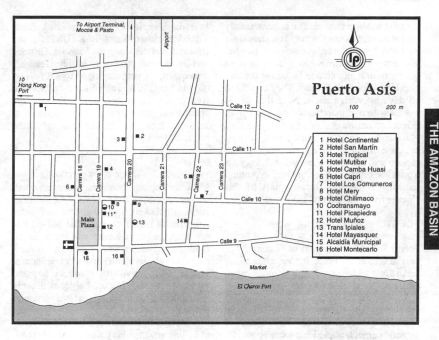

**Puerto Asís**

0    100    200 m

1 Hotel Continental
2 Hotel San Martín
3 Hotel Tropical
4 Hotel Mutibar
5 Hotel Camba Huasi
6 Hotel Capri
7 Hotel Los Comuneros
8 Hotel Mery
9 Hotel Chilimaco
10 Cootransmayo
11 Hotel Picapiedra
12 Hotel Muñoz
13 Trans Ipiales
14 Hotel Mayasquer
15 Alcaldía Municipal
16 Hotel Montecarlo

THE AMAZON BASIN

Miguel, take a boat to La Punta in Ecuador (US$4, half an hour). From La Punta, chivas regularly run to Lago Agrio (US$0.80, one hour). Get an entry stamp in your passport in the Oficina de Migración at Avenida Quito 111.

From Lago Agrio, there are regular buses to Quito, operated by a few bus companies (US$4.50, eight to 11 hours), and one Tame flight daily except Sunday (US$15).

**Boat** Puerto Asís has two ports. One, locally called Hong Kong, is 2.5 km west of town; it's here that bigger boats and army boats (generally long-distance vessels) berth. The other port, called El Charco or La Cocha, is in town near the market. It is busier, particularly on market days (Friday to Sunday), when plenty of small boats come from the nearby villages. However, the larger boats to Puerto Leguízamo and Leticia also leave from here, so you must check both ports. Contact the Oficina de Inspección Fluvial in the Alcaldía Municipal on the main square

for a list of arrivals and departures. Also visit Transportes Fluviales del Amazonas, on the corner of Carrera 20 and Calle 10, for information.

There are no passenger boats as such. They all carry cargo and those carrying gasoline don't take passengers at all. The main destination ports are Puerto Leguízamo (takes two to four days) and Leticia (takes 10 to 15 days, sometimes even longer).

If you are heading for Leticia try to find a direct boat in Puerto Asís; Puerto Leguízamo does not have a larger choice of boats and most come from Puerto Asís anyway, so why do the same work twice? The fare is up to the captain and is usually open to negotiation. In general, you must be prepared to pay US$20 to US$30 to Leguízamo and US$80 to US$150 to Leticia. This is only a rough guide; you may sometimes strike it lucky and find a bargain ride.

The price and the time taken to complete the journey differ widely from one boat to the next so shop around. The price normally covers food, but not always. You should fix everything with the captain before departure. The army boats (SENARC) leave at most once a month and charge US$6 for the fare plus US$4 for food per day. They take 12 to 15 days to reach Leticia. Note that this is more expensive than the airline ticket from Bogotá to Leticia.

If you have already found a boat, keep an eye on it as it may leave at short notice. The captain will probably allow you to hang your hammock on deck. See the Getting Around section in the introductory part of this chapter for some general information.

## PUERTO INÍRIDA
• *pop 10,000* • *85 m* • *26°C* • ☎ *(9816)*

Puerto Inírida, the capital of Guainía, was only founded in 1965. It's an uninspiring small town which serves as an administrative centre of the vast department.

South-west of Puerto Inírida, up the Río Inírida, are the Cerros de Mavecurí, three impressive rocky outcrops reminiscent of gigantic camel humps. They loom about 300 metres out of the plains, right next to the river. There are some Curripaco and Puinave Indian settlements scattered along the Río Inírida; the Puinave settlement of El Remanso is the best known.

A round trip to the Cerros can be organised in Puerto Inírida; a *voladora* (a fast speed-boat) for four to five people will cost about US$100 to US$120 and the ride takes two to three hours one way. You can climb one of the rocks, but only in the dry season. It is possible to camp on the beach at the foot of the Cerros.

### Places to Stay & Eat
There are a few hotels (including the *Hotel Safari* and *Hotel Orinoco*, either of which costs US$5 per person) and restaurants in town.

### Getting There & Away
Satena has two flights per week to/from Bogotá (US$80), both of which stop in Villavicencio. You can also get to Puerto Inírida overland: take the bus from Villavicencio to Santa Rita (US$35), and continue by boat along the Vichada, Orinoco and Inírida rivers to Puerto Inírida. Boats are infrequent, so you may need to wait a few days in Santa Rita. The voladora takes about five to six hours but it's expensive; the cheaper cargo boats can take up to three days. In Santa Rita you can stay and eat in the house of Doña Teresa.

## MITÚ
• *pop 5000* • *180 m* • *26°C* • ☎ *(9816)*

Mitú, the capital of Vaupés, is another small settlement lost deep in the Colombian Amazon, tucked away hundreds of miles from major urban centres. The village has not a single paved street, and there are no roads to anywhere. There are only 20 vehicles (brought in by air) and 135 telephones. Electricity is provided six hours a day and water is rationed. It's unlikely you'll come here unless you are taking part in a particular project.

Vaupés is noted for a remarkable diversity of Indian groups living along the main river, the Río Vaupés, and its tributaries. However, in order to get to the really remote villages, you have to travel for at least several hours by boat, and these trips will be extremely expensive because of the cost of gasoline. An additional problem is posed by the *raudales*

Anaconda

(rapids) which cut the river and may be impassable in some periods.

Indians living close to Mitú have partly adopted the 'advantages of civilisation'. This can be noticed in their dress and manners and in the appearance of their villages. They come to Mitú on Sunday, market day, to sell fish, fruit and yucca and to buy supplies.

It may be possible to visit the Indians at their village by tagging along with a voluntary medical team which goes to a different place every Saturday and talks to the villagers about tuberculosis, cholera and general hygiene, and distributes medicines and gifts provided by the local hospital.

### Places to Stay & Eat

Mitú has a good hotel run by the friendly Señor Leone – anyone will direct you there. Clean rooms with bath cost US$5 per person, and you can have tasty meals for US$3 each. The manager can organise trips along the river for you.

### Getting There & Away

Mitú is linked to Bogotá by two flights a week with Satena (US$71). Make sure to reconfirm your return flight. Keep in mind that flights may be cancelled due to lack of demand or bad weather, leaving you there for a few days more till the next one.

There's no way into or out of Mitú other than by air.

### LETICIA

• *pop 23,000* • *96 m* • *27°C* • ☎ *(9819)*

Leticia is a small town on the Amazon River, at the south-easternmost tip of Colombia, on the tripartite border with Brazil and Peru. When it was founded in 1867, under the name of San Antonio, it was part of Peru, but it was transferred to Colombia under the treaty of 1922 and its name changed to Leticia.

Leticia is the most popular place in Colombian Amazonia, principally due to its developed tourist facilities and its good flight connections with Bogotá and, through there, with the rest of the country. Leticia has become the leading tourist centre for Colombians eager to see Indian tribes and buy their handicrafts and to get a taste of the jungle. The influx has, to some degree, upset the natural balance, and today the Indians work hard on their crafts to keep up with tourist demand.

For foreign travellers, Leticia is also interesting because it is linked via the Amazon to Manaus and Iquitos and therefore offers reasonably easy travel between Brazil, Colombia and Peru.

As most products such as food, petrol, machinery and consumer goods have to be shipped or flown in from far away, Leticia is expensive for food and accommodation, and (especially) for the jungle trips offered by travel agents and independent operators. Bring enough mosquito repellent from Bogotá because you can't get good stuff in Leticia. Take high-speed film – the jungle is always dark.

Leticia is hot and humid and the only hint of respite is late in the afternoon when a gentle breeze comes from the river. The best time to visit the region is in July or August, which are the only relatively dry months.

### Orientation

Leticia lies right on the Colombian-Brazilian border. Just across the frontier sits Tabatinga, smaller and poorer than Leticia but with its own airport. Leticia and Tabatinga are virtually merging together, and there are no border checkpoints between the two. Frequent colectivos link the two settlements, or you can just walk from centre to centre in 20 minutes. Traffic of both locals and foreigners is allowed without visas, but if you plan on heading further into either country, you must get exit/entry stamps in your passport from DAS in Leticia and the Policía Federal in Tabatinga (not on the actual border).

On the island in the Amazon opposite Leticia/Tabatinga is Santa Rosa, a Peruvian village. A boat goes there from Tabatinga wharf, and the one-way fare is US$1.50.

About 20 km from Leticia/Tabatinga, on the opposite side of the Amazon, is the Brazilian town of Benjamin Constant, the main port for boats heading downstream to

Manaus. Tabatinga and Benjamin Constant are connected by one boat daily in each direction (US$2.50 one way). If you go by this route, make sure to visit the Indian Museum in Benjamin Constant, which gives a good introduction to the Indian cultures in the area (past and present).

### Information

**Tourist Office** Leticia's tourist office (☎ 27505) is at Carrera 11 No 11-35.

**Money** The Banco de Bogotá, at the corner of Carrera 10 and Calle 7, is the only bank which changes travellers' cheques for pesos (from 10.30 am to 1.30 pm). It also gives advances to Visa card holders, as does the Banco Ganadero, on Carrera 11. No bank in Leticia will exchange cash dollars.

There are plenty of casas de cambio on Calle 8, from Carrera 11 down towards the river. They change US dollars, Colombian pesos, Brazilian cruzeiros and Peruvian nuevos soles in any direction. They are open till 5 or 6 pm on weekdays and till about 2 pm on Saturday. Shop around, as the rates vary.

Many shops in the same area also change money, at rates similar to those in the casas de cambio. One which might be of interest is the Importadora Miscelánea No 1, Calle 8 No 10-90. It pays slightly better rates for your greenbacks than its neighbours, and is one of the few places that will change travellers' cheques, though at a poor rate.

There are also moneychanging facilities in Tabatinga and Benjamin Constant. They have roughly similar rates to those in Leticia, though it seems better to buy cruzeiros for pesos in Leticia than in Tabatinga. Check the exchange rates on both sides of the border if these small differences are important to your budget or if you have a lot of money to change. Don't carry pesos further into Brazil or Peru as it will be difficult to change them.

In Tabatinga there are three casas de cambio: Casa Blanca, Casa Verde and Casa Amarela, all on Avenida Internacional, 400 metres past the border, opposite the Hotel Miraflores. There are no moneychangers in the port area in Tabatinga.

If you have a Visa card and are travelling from Colombia or Peru into Brazil, the Banco do Brasil in Tabatinga will pay you a cash advance in cruzeiros.

**Immigration** The DAS office in Leticia, on Calle 9, is open Monday to Saturday from 7 am to noon and 2 to 6 pm. This is where you get your passport stamped when leaving or entering Colombia.

Brazilian entry and exit stamps must be obtained at the Policía Federal, on the main road in Tabatinga, near the hospital. The office is open daily from 8 am to noon and 2 to 6 pm. A yellow-fever vaccination certificate is required by officials if you're entering Brazil. Dress neatly for a visit to either office.

If you arrive or depart by air, you get your passport stamped at the Leticia or Tabatinga airport. If travelling to/from Iquitos (Peru) by boat, you get your entry/exit stamp in Santa Rosa.

**Consulates** The Peruvian consulate in Leticia, on Carrera 11, next to the Hotel Anaconda, is open Monday to Friday from 8.30 am to 2.30 pm. Most Western nationals don't need a visa for Peru, but if you need one, it will be issued within a couple of hours (around US$12).

The Brazilian consulate, on Calle 13, is open Monday to Friday from 8 am to 2 pm. A visa is given within a day and is valid for a stay of 90 days.

**Inderena** The Inderena office (☎ 27619), on Carrera 11, will give you information about the Parque Nacional Amacayacu, sell you an entry permit (US$1) and book accommodation there if you haven't already done it in Bogotá.

**Tours** If exploring the jungle on your own seems too daunting, several travel agencies in Leticia run tours. Tours don't usually have a fixed timetable; the agents wait until they have enough people, usually a minimum of

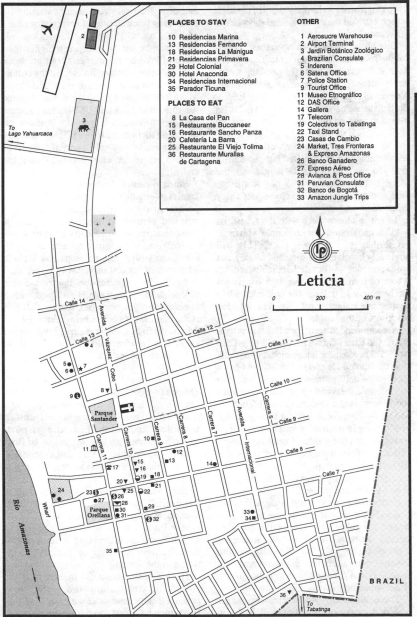

**PLACES TO STAY**

10 Residencias Marina
13 Residencias Fernando
18 Residencias La Manigua
21 Residencias Primavera
29 Hotel Colonial
30 Hotel Anaconda
34 Residencias Internacional
35 Parador Ticuna

**PLACES TO EAT**

8 La Casa del Pan
15 Restaurante Buccaneer
16 Restaurante Sancho Panza
20 Cafetería La Barra
25 Restaurante El Viejo Tolima
36 Restaurante Murallas
de Cartagena

**OTHER**

1 Aerosucre Warehouse
2 Airport Terminal
3 Jardín Botánico Zoológico
4 Brazilian Consulate
5 Inderena
6 Satena Office
7 Police Station
9 Tourist Office
11 Museo Etnográfico
12 DAS Office
14 Gallera
17 Telecom
19 Colectivos to Tabatinga
22 Taxi Stand
23 Casas de Cambio
24 Market, Tres Fronteras
& Expreso Amazonas
26 Banco Ganadero
27 Expreso Aéreo
28 Avianca & Post Office
31 Peruvian Consulate
32 Banco de Bogotá
33 Amazon Jungle Trips

**Leticia**

0     200     400 m

To
Lago Yahuarcaca

Calle 14
Calle 13
Calle 12
Calle 11
Calle 10
Calle 9
Calle 8
Calle 7

Avenida Vázquez Cobo
Carrera 11
Carrera 10
Carrera 9
Carrera 8
Carrera 7
Avenida Internacional
Carrera 5

Parque
Santander

Parque
Orellana

Wharf

Río Amazonas

BRAZIL

To
Tabatinga

five. Thus there can be daily tours in the high season but you may wait several days in the off season.

One of the best known operators is Anaconda Tours, in the Hotel Anaconda. These days it focuses on standard one-day tours, rarely offering anything more adventurous. A seven to eight-hour trip to Monkey Island, Bellavista or Puerto Nariño, with a visit to an Indian village on the way, will cost roughly US$30, lunch included.

These short excursions are well organised, comfortable and trouble-free but can hardly give you a real picture of the jungle or of the Indians. They are probably not worth the time and money unless you have just a day to spend in the region.

To get in closer touch with the forest, its wildlife and the indigenous people, you must get further off the tourist track. This will obviously involve more time and money, but the experience will be much more rewarding. A tour of some three to five days is perhaps the best way to balance the cost of the trip against the insight it will give you into the workings of the jungle.

A recommended agent for adventurous trips is Antonio Cruz Pérez of Amazon Jungle Trips (☎ 27377), Avenida Internacional No 6-25, near the border. He speaks English and has a good guide and boatman/cook who will take you into wild areas of the region in Brazil, Peru and Colombia (no visas necessary). Tours of two to 10 days (or more) can be organised. You'll sleep in the huts of locals or in camps arranged by your guides. Count on around US$35 per person per day in a group of six, all inclusive. Four people are usually the minimum for a trip unless you are prepared to pay substantially more.

Contact the agent soon after arrival in Leticia, as it may take a couple of days to collect the party and arrange the trip. He usually waits at the airport for incoming flights from Bogotá. You might also want to check other agencies, such as Amazon Explorers and Amaturs, both next door to the Hotel Anaconda.

There are many independent operators who don't have offices; they will find you and offer their services, usually starting by presenting thick albums of photos from their previous tours. The prices they quote initially may be similar to or even higher than those offered by the agencies, but are open to negotiation. Always fix clearly the conditions, places to be visited, time and price. Make it clear who's going to pay the entrance fee to Monkey Island (US$4) and to some Indian settlements. If you don't insist on including them in the tour's price, you'll pay all these extras. Pay only a part of the cost of the trip before departure and the rest at the end.

Some travellers have recommended Luis Daniel González as a good independent guide. On the other hand, there have been repeated complaints about the services of Joel Mendoza, known locally as Tattoo.

Note that it's cheaper to take one long excursion with overnight stops and include all places of interest on the way rather than to make a few separate one-day trips. Some independent operators may lure you with a lower price if you take your own food. If this is the case, remember to bring along lots of drinks. As fizzy drinks are expensive, a good solution is the water sold widely in Leticia in one-litre plastic bottles.

### Things to See & Do

There's not much to see or do in the town itself. You can visit the small **Jardín Botánico Zoológico**, near the airport, which has almost nothing in the way of flora but does have some snakes and crocodiles. It's open daily from 7 am to 6 pm; the admission fee is US$1.

The modern library of the Banco de la República, on Carrera 11, contains the **Museo Etnográfico** (open Monday to Friday from 8 am to noon and 2 to 6 pm), which features interesting artefacts and household implements of Indian groups living in the region.

Have a look around the market near the river and stroll along the waterfront, crammed with boats and with stalls selling fish which have just come from the river. On

Sunday evening there are cockfights at the local *gallera*.

Leticia has become a tourist spot not for what the town itself offers but for the surrounding region, which is populated by several indigenous tribes, among which the Ticuna and Yagua are the dominant groups. This is also a place to explore the jungle and its exuberant flora and fauna. See the Around Leticia section for information.

### Places to Stay

**Leticia** Accommodation in Leticia is not plentiful but is generally sufficient to cope with the tourist traffic. There are a dozen places to stay, offering a fairly good standard. All have private bath and fan. However, they are not that cheap.

At the bottom end, expect to pay around US$5/7 for a single/double. At this price, among the best are the *Residencias La Manigua* (☎ 27121), *Apartamentos Jolamar* (☎ 27016) and *Residencias Marina*, all of which are clean and friendly.

The *Residencias Primavera* (no sign on the door), across the street from La Manigua, is more basic and noisy for the same price, but you have a good chance of getting a room here if the other hotels are full. The *Residencias Internacional* (☎ 28066), on Avenida Internacional, near the border, is better than Primavera and it, too, usually has vacancies.

The *Residencias Fernando* (☎ 27362) is a pleasant place to stay, though it's a bit over-priced at US$8/12.

If you need somewhere with air-con and a swimming pool, go to the *Hotel Anaconda* (☎ 27119), which is the best place to stay in town. It's modern though rather styleless, and costs US$40/55. It has good views over the Amazon (particularly at sunset), if you are lucky enough to get the room on the top floor facing the river.

Alternatively, try the *Hotel Colonial*, which costs the same as the Anaconda but isn't as good, either in location or in the standard of the rooms.

Until recently you had a third up-market option, the pleasant *Parador Ticuna*

(☎ 27241), with a spacious courtyard filled with tropical plants. The hotel operated the Monkey Island Lodge on the Isla de los Micos and housed the office of the Turamazonas travel agency. The hotel was closed down after its US owner was charged with drug trafficking and ended up in a Miami jail. Check it anyway, as it may reopen under new ownership.

**Tabatinga** Tabatinga is a less attractive place than Leticia but is cheaper. Both pesos and cruzeiros are accepted in most establishments.

The cheapest place to stay is the *Hotel Halley*. It's very basic, but rooms have their own bath and cost US$4 a double. Next door is the considerably better *Hotel Pajé*, also with private bath, charging US$4/5.

If you need a room with air-con, try the *Hotel Miraflores*, 300 metres past the border from Leticia (US$7/11), or better still, the *Hotel Belo Brasil*, on the road to the wharf (US$15 a double).

### Places to Eat

**Leticia** The food is not bad in Leticia, though it is fairly expensive. The local speciality is fish; don't miss the delicious gamitana. Another fish typical of the region and worth trying is the pirarucú, which can weigh up to 300 kg. You can get either of these fish in most restaurants. Also try cupuasú juice, from a local fruit somewhat similar in taste to the guanábana. Fizzy drinks and beer are expensive.

The *Sancho Panza*, on Carrera 10, is possibly the cheapest restaurant for set almuerzos and comidas (US$1.75), though the food is not very inspiring. For marginally more, you can have tastier set meals at the *Buccaneer*, next door, or at *El Viejo Tolima*, on Calle 8, one block away. The latter looks pretty ordinary but has good fish and meat dishes and fruit juices. *Murallas de Cartagena*, next to the frontier, is also worth a mention and is open till late at night. For more up-market fare, you can eat in the restaurant of the *Hotel Anaconda*.

*Cafetería La Barra*, on Calle 8, opposite El Viejo Tolima, is a place popular with locals for a good tinto and cheap fruit juices, while *La Casa del Pan*, in the Parque Santander, is a tiny café which has fresh bread and pastries – a good place for breakfast.

**Tabatinga** Like accommodation, food is cheaper in Tabatinga than in Leticia. The restaurants to try here are the *Bella Época* (diagonally opposite the church), the *Canto da Peixada* (near the Banco do Brasil) and the *Tres Fronteras* (which has recently moved from Leticia to Tabatinga).

### Getting There & Away

**Air – within Colombia** Avianca has three direct flights per week to/from Bogotá, on Monday, Wednesday and Friday (US$112). Satena flies to/from Bogotá on Sunday, and is cheaper (US$96). Satena's flights are in light planes and call at one or two small Amazonian ports on the way. Consequently, the trip takes longer than with Avianca, but you'll see more. It may be difficult to get on these flights without advance booking. Satena also flies from Leticia to Mitú (US$55), Araracuara (US$55), La Pedrera and some other Amazonian localities. AeroRepública has recently introduced Bogotá-Leticia flights, and is cheaper still (US$88), possibly only for the promotional period.

Before you book on a commercial flight to Bogotá, check the cargo flights. Aerosucre shuttles between Leticia and Bogotá almost daily and usually takes passengers. Avesca, another cargo carrier, comes to Leticia a few times per week and is also willing to generate some extra cash by carrying passengers. The fare with either carrier is about US$75. They both use large jet planes. You must hunt for them at the airport as there is no fixed schedule. The Aerosucre *bodega* (warehouse) is just behind the passenger terminal. In Bogotá, the departure point for Aerosucre planes is the cargo building (Edificio de Carga No 1) just before the El Dorado passenger terminal (refer to the Getting There & Away section of the Bogotá chapter for further information).

**Air – to Brazil** There are no flights into Brazil from Leticia, but from Tabatinga,

Varig/Cruzeiro has three flights per week to Manaus, on Monday, Wednesday and Saturday (US$140). The airline's office is on Tabatinga's main road, 300 metres past the frontier. The airport is about two km from Tabatinga and is accessible by colectivo.

**Air – to Peru** Varig/Cruzeiro has a flight on Saturday at noon from Tabatinga to Iquitos (US$121 one way, US$156 return, minimum five days, maximum two months). Expreso Aéreo, a new and still unestablished Colombian carrier, has flights from Leticia to Iquitos on Wednesday and Sunday in light Fokker planes (US$102, 19% Colombian tax included).

**Boat** Sitting on the border between Brazil, Colombia and Peru, Leticia is an attractive transit point for travellers looking for a somewhat adventurous, backwater route between these three countries. Although boat fares have risen considerably over the past few years, they are still interesting for the adventure they provide.

**Boat – to Puerto Asís (Colombia)** Irregular cargo boats depart from Leticia to Puerto Asís, on the upper reaches of the Putumayo. The trip can take up to 20 days, and the price varies substantially, from US$100 to US$150, food included. It's better to do this route in reverse (ie downstream), as it is faster and cheaper this way. See the Puerto Asís section for further details.

**Boat – to Manaus (Brazil)** Boats down the Amazon to Manaus leave from Benjamin Constant, but they usually come up to Tabatinga to unload/load. They anchor in Porto de Tabatinga, one km south of Tabatinga's fishing wharf.

Theoretically, there are two boats per week, leaving Tabatinga on Wednesday and Saturday morning and Benjamin Constant the same evening. The trip to Manaus takes four days and costs US$85 in your own hammock, or US$250 for a double cabin. Food is included but is poor and monotonous. It's a good idea to buy some snacks as a supplement, and also bottled water, easily available in Leticia, because that on board comes from the river. At certain times of the year the nights can be fairly cold, so a sleeping bag is not a bad idea. Unless you decide to take a cabin, you must have your own hammock (or sleep on the hard deck).

You can buy a typical net-like Indian hammock made of the fibre of a species of palm known as *chambira*. They are sold in artefact shops in Leticia, and around the market near the riverfront. These hammocks are decorative, but not very comfortable if you are not used to them. It's better to buy an ordinary cloth hammock. The cheapest place to get one (for US$6 to US$8) is the Esplanada Tecidos shop, near the wharf in Tabatinga.

The boats come to Tabatinga a couple of days before their scheduled departure back down the river. You can string up your hammock or occupy the cabin as soon as you've paid the fare, thus saving on hotels. Food, however, is only served after departure. Beware of theft on board. If the boat doesn't come up to Tabatinga but only to Benjamin Constant, you must go there by passenger boat, which departs daily from Tabatinga around 5 pm (US$2.50), or pagar expreso (hire a boat) for 10 times as much.

In the opposite direction, upstream from Manaus to Benjamin Constant, the trip takes six to seven days.

**Boat – to Iquitos (Peru)** Expreso Loreto in Tabatinga, near the wharf, initiated the *rápido* (fast boat) passenger service from Tabatinga to Iquitos. The boats are supposed to depart on Tuesday and Sunday at 5 am and reach their destination 10 to 12 hours later (in reverse, the trip is about two hours shorter). The boats call at Santa Rosa's immigration post. The journey costs US$50 in either direction.

There are irregular cargo boats to Iquitos once or twice a week, departing from Santa Rosa. The journey takes three days and costs US$25 to US$30 after some negotiation. In reverse, downstream from Iquitos to Santa Rosa, it takes around 36 hours.

Note that there are no roads out of Iquitos into Peru. You have to fly or continue by river to Pucallpa (five to seven days), from where you can go overland to Lima and elsewhere.

## AROUND LETICIA

The region around Leticia is covered with thick rainforest and sprinkled with small, widely scattered Indian settlements. Although no longer virgin territory, the area still provides an insight into what the Amazon basin really is – including its principal fluvial artery, the legendary Río Amazonas.

The Amazon River changes markedly depending on the season. The river begins to rise in November and reaches its highest level from March through to May. In June, the water rapidly drops. It reaches its lowest level in July and doesn't change much until October.

The difference between low and high water can be as great as 10 metres. At the same time the river's width changes dramatically. While it is 'only' one km wide (in the area of Leticia) at the time of the lowest water, it spreads for several km and floods the neighbouring areas when it reaches its maximum level.

There are several attractions along the river (described separately further in this section), but the genuine wilderness only begins well away from the Amazon proper, on its small tributaries. The further you go, the more chance you have to observe wildlife and see Indians in relatively undamaged surroundings.

However, as all transport is by river and there are almost no regular passenger boats, it's difficult to get around cheaply on your own. All trips are monopolised by tourist agents and by locals with their own boats, and are expensive (see Jungle Tours at the end of this section).

Probably the most intriguing plant species of the region is the famous *Victoria regia* (or more correctly – since it was renamed – *Victoria amazonica*), a kind of water lily with gigantic round leaves which can carry the weight of a child. You can see small

examples of this lily in the Parque Santander in Leticia.

The main Indian groups living in the region are the Ticunas and Yaguas. Ticunas, the second most numerous community of the Colombian Amazon (after the Huitotos), occupy a vast area of Peru, Colombia and Brazil to the south of the Putumayo River. Their best known settlement in the Leticia area is Arara, but the village is on the route of almost every tour and has become something of a theatre with Indians as the actors.

More authentic is the village of Bellavista (on the Peruvian side), which also appears on itineraries of tour operators but is less frequently visited. Even though the village was hard hit by the recent cholera epidemic, it remains an interesting place to see. Some Ticuna Indians live in Atacuari, Puerto Nariño, Santa Sofía, Nazareth and on Mocagua Island.

The Ticuna men traditionally paint themselves with a black-blue dye extracted from the *huito* or *genipa*, an orange-like fruit, and dress in vegetable-fibre skirts. Only a few still do so, except for tourist shows. Their typical crafts include textiles, *cerbatanas* (blowpipes), necklaces and *yanchanas* (bark paintings).

The Yaguas are a semi-nomadic group, more traditional than the Ticunas, ethnically distinct and belonging to a different linguistic family. Most of them live in Peru; in Colombia they inhabit the Tucuchira and Atacuari rivers but not the village of Atacuari itself. Some Yaguas live in the region of Santa Sofía and on Mocagua Island.

Yagua means 'red' in Quechua. The name comes from the red paint of the *achiote* plant, used on the face to prevent the approach of evil spirits. This paint also protects from insect bites and is employed as an ornament. The Yaguas are essentially hunters and fishers, but handicrafts have recently become an important source of revenue. They make fine seed necklaces, mochilas, ritual masks, bark paintings, blowpipes and totems, the most distinctive being the sticks with carved human figures on top.

### Isla de los Micos

Monkey Island, about nine km long and only one km wide, lies some 40 km up the Amazon River from Leticia and is a popular spot on the tour routes. The island was bought in the 1950s by a US entrepreneur, who introduced several thousand yellow-footed monkeys. These used to be sent to research laboratories and zoos in the USA. When in 1974 the Colombian government prohibited their exportation, the owner removed all the monkeys he managed to catch, but the remaining specimens reproduced at a startling rate and today number over 15,000.

The comfortable Monkey Island Lodge, complete with restaurant, offered visitors to the island a variety of services, including night photo-hunting for alligators. A footpath has been traced through a wilder part of the island to allow visitors to enjoy the jungle vegetation, among it the *Victoria amazonica*.

Since the owner found himself behind bars, the lodge has been closed down, but the island can still be visited for a US$4 fee. However, it's probably not worth the trip; you'll find more interesting habitats and more diverse wildlife elsewhere – say, in the Amacayacu national park.

### Parque Nacional Amacayacu

This national park takes in 2930 sq km of jungle on the left (northern) bank of the Amazon, 75 km upstream from Leticia. The terrain is flat throughout most of the park, though its northern part has some gently undulating areas.

The park is perhaps the best place in the region to get a good image of the Amazon wilderness for a reasonable price. A few days' exploration (using the park's accommodation, food and guide services) will cost far less than any tour of equal length of time organised from Leticia.

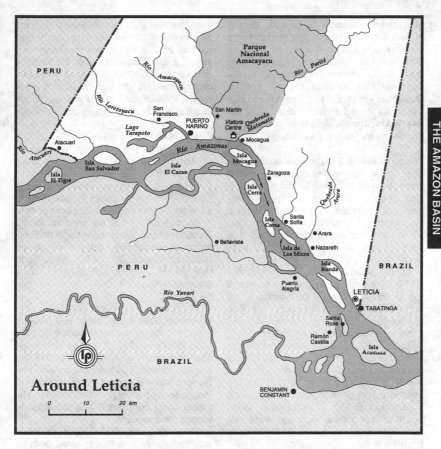

Around Leticia

0    10    20 km

A spacious visitors centre, constructed by Inderena on the bank of the Amazon at the confluence of the Quebrada Matamata, provides a good base for excursions into the park. From the centre, you can explore the park either by marked paths or by water. The rangers will explain the recommended routes and places to see, and park guides (mostly local Indians) will show you around for a modest fee.

**Things to See & Do** As might be expected, the park has abundant wildlife, featuring caymans, snakes (including the boa and ana-

conda) and various species of monkeys, not to mention a profusion of fish and birds. You probably won't be lucky enough to spot big animals, but you'll see a variety of birds, butterflies and insects. You may also wish to try fishing for piranhas.

In the high-water period (March to June), much of the land turns into swamps and lagoons, greatly reducing walking options, but motorboat excursions are organised at this time. It is also possible to rent a canoe so you can get around the nearby small rivers by yourself.

There are some Ticuna Indians living

near the boundaries of the park; the hamlet of **San Martín** is their major settlement in the area, and can be reached by water or land from the visitors centre (three to four hours' walk one way). Other popular nearby destinations include the village of **Mocagua** (just across the Quebrada Matamata from the visitors centre) and the **Isla de Mocagua** with its two small internal lagoons (a half-day trip in a canoe).

**Places to Stay & Eat** The visitors centre has large, mosquito-proofed communal rooms equipped with beds and hammocks, and is well set up with showers and toilets. Blankets are provided so you don't need a sleeping bag. A small generator allows light for around four hours each evening; you need a torch for the remaining hours of darkness.

Accommodation in a bed/hammock costs US$7/5 per person; you have to book and pay for this in advance at the Inderena office in Bogotá (preferably) or Leticia, as well as paying the US$1 entry fee to the park. Camping in the park is not permitted.

Three meals (breakfast, lunch and dinner) will run to about US$9. There are also drinks and snacks available but they are expensive. Water is collected from rainfall, so it's reputedly safe to drink untreated. You are allowed to take in your own food provided you take the rubbish with you when you leave. However, you cannot use the cooking facilities at the centre.

**Getting There & Away** Two small boat companies, Tres Fronteras and Expreso Amazonas (both of which have their offices near the waterfront in Leticia), operate scheduled fast passenger boats to Puerto Nariño, daily between 11 am and noon. They will put you down at the park visitors centre (US$8, 1½ hours). Buy your ticket the day before.

Returning from the park to Leticia may sometimes involve a day (or even two) of unexpected waiting. The boats come through from Puerto Nariño (normally passing by the visitors centre around 10 am) but can be full. If this is the case, they simply pass by without stopping. Sometimes it's possible to wave down other boats, but they are mostly slow cargo vessels. If you happen to catch a fast boat, it will probably charge you much more than the scheduled passenger boat.

### Puerto Nariño

About 90 km up the Amazon from Leticia (15 km upstream from the Amacayacu park), Puerto Nariño is the second largest town of the region. It is built on a square plan and is inhabited mainly by colonists, though there are some Ticuna Indians living here as well.

Another 10 km to the west of Puerto Nariño is a beautiful lake, the **Lago de Tarapoto** (accessible only by river), with varied flora including the famous lily. If you are in luck, you may see the pink dolphins. There are some Indian settlements scattered around the lake.

**Places to Stay & Eat** There is a pleasant hotel, the *Brisas del Amazonas*, built by a paisa family in 1983. It is fairly simple but neat and quiet, and costs US$12/18 for singles/doubles. The hotel has its own restaurant serving good food (excellent gamitana) and it's not that expensive. The management are friendly and can organise tours around the area.

There are a couple of cheaper options in accommodation and food in town, both on the riverfront.

**Getting There & Away** Puerto Nariño and the Lago de Tarapoto feature on the itineraries of the Leticia tour operators. If you want to get there on your own, Tres Fronteras and Expreso Amazonas boats will bring you from Leticia to Puerto Nariño in two hours for US$10. There's no regular transport further on to the Lago de Tarapoto; you'll have to negotiate a boat with the locals or at the Brisas del Amazonas.

# Los Llanos

Los Llanos, or, fully named, Los Llanos Orientales, are the vast plains stretching from the Cordillera Oriental east as far as the Venezuelan border. They lie in the Orinoco basin, cover over 250,000 sq km and comprise four departments: Meta, Casanare, Arauca and Vichada. They extend north-eastwards well into Venezuela, taking up as vast an area of that country as they do of Colombia.

Los Llanos (literally 'the plains') are billiard-table flat, low-lying savannahs. A result of the accumulation of sand, clay and mud deposited by rivers over millions of years, these eerie expanses lack any notable topographical features. Most of the terrain is covered with grass, with ribbons of gallery forests along the creeks and rivers, and scattered islands of woodland here and there. Rivers are numerous and, in the wet season, voluminous; the main ones are the Meta, Vichada, Guaviare and Inírida – all of which are left-bank tributaries of the Orinoco.

The climate of Los Llanos follows a definite pattern, and reaches the extremes in both the rainy and dry season. The former (referred to as *invierno*) lasts from April to November and is characterised by frequent and intense rains. In that period the rivers overflow, turning much of the land into shallow lagoons. Humboldt, who was here during this season, compared Los Llanos to 'an ocean covered with seaweed'. In December the rains stop and the rivers return to their normal courses, steadily getting thinner and thinner as the dry season (called *verano*) progresses. The sun bakes the parched soil and the winds blow dust all around.

The annual rainfall is high and ranges from 2500 mm in northern Arauca and Vichada to over 4000 mm in western Meta. June is usually the wettest month. Although Los Llanos are low-lying and the average temperature varies between 25° and 28°C, cold fronts in the rainy months can cause it to drop to only 10°C at night. In the dry

season, by contrast, daytime temperatures of over 40°C are not unusual.

In this inhospitable climate, the *llaneros* – as the local inhabitants are referred to – have mainly dedicated themselves to cattle raising. They are tough and resistant people, used to the hard life. Bolívar knew this, and enlisted them in his army to fight the Spanish and – as it turned out – they had great success. The llaneros have developed a distinctive culture, music and folklore of their own, quite different from those elsewhere in Colombia but with close affinities to the culture of Los Llanos of Venezuela.

Most of the region's population, about 800,000 in total, live at the *piedemonte* (foothills) of the Andes. The rest of Los Llanos, crossed by an array of rivers and virtually without roads, remain sparsely populated and little exploited. Although these areas have potential for food production and are rich in natural resources, difficult access hinders their development. So far, progress

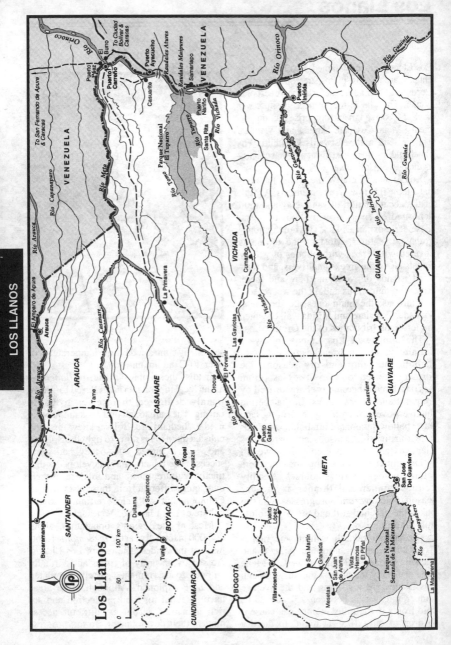

has only reached limited areas through either cattle ranching and agriculture (western Meta and Casanare) or oil (Arauca and, recently, Casanare).

The everyday life of Los Llanos is essentially ruled by the climate. The dry season is a period of activity and prosperity thanks to the possibility of transporting goods out to the markets of the highlands. The rest of the year brings hard times for the inhabitants, with storms, floods, impassable roads and links with the outer world considerably limited or completely cut.

Stock raising makes an important contribution to the country's economy, and Los Llanos have became one of the most important regions for meat production. Recently, they have also gained importance as a crop producer, supplying the Andean region, particularly Bogotá, with rice, tropical fruits and vegetables.

Until 1936, when the first road to Los Llanos was built (Bogotá-Villavicencio), the region had virtually no reliable form of transport or communication. Although the Spaniards introduced cattle to the area as early as the 16th century, it was only with the influx of colonists that the grazing industry came into being. Villavicencio, the main urban centre of Los Llanos, is today one of the most rapidly growing of Colombia's cities.

Petroleum may before long significantly change the socioeconomic picture in the region. Oil has been exploited in Arauca for more than a decade, but production suffered as a result of mismanagement and, in particular, because of the activities of the ELN guerrillas, who repeatedly blew up pipelines. New oilfields, discovered in the early 1990s in Cusiana, in south-western Casanare, are thought to contain the biggest oil reserves found anywhere in the world during the last decade. These installations began production early in 1995 and the export of Casanare oil is expected to bring the country an additional US$5 billion in annual revenue by the turn of the millennium.

Los Llanos are home to several Indian groups. There are not many of them: the official statistics put their total number at around 25,000. Over 75% of them live in Vichada, where the dominant group are the people, indigenous; (or Guajibos), who still live in *malocas* (their traditional houses) scattered between the Guaviare and Vichada rivers. In Arauca, there are some Tunebos living at the foot of the Sierra Nevada del Cocuy, whereas in Casanare, the Cuivas and Sálivas are the main groups, though they don't surpass 2000 in number.

Los Llanos are difficult to explore. If you come to Colombia in the rainy season, you probably won't get far afield. The road network is poor, unpaved and impassable for most of the year. Tourism as such doesn't exist. Facilities are scarce and, except for a handful of places, including the tourist centres in Orocué and Las Gaviotas, they are found only in the towns along the Cordillera, an area not really representative of the region. Los Llanos seldom see travellers; in fact they are Colombia's least visited region.

Yet, if you have time and an adventurous spirit, and want to experience something other than the usual tourist sights, the region is a worthy challenge. Los Llanos are noted for their abundant and diverse wildlife, particularly their impressive variety of birds. There are two beautiful national parks in the region, Serranía de la Macarena and El Tuparro (both described separately in this chapter).

Another special attraction of Los Llanos is their famous sunrises and sunsets. Lastly, much of the charm of Los Llanos lies in the everyday life of the inhabitants. To stay for a while with the locals, sharing their work, listening to their music and tasting such distinctive food as armadillo and capybara, can be an inspiring and rewarding experience.

### Getting There & Around

Los Llanos are bordered in the west by the Cordillera Oriental, where you are most likely to start your trip, by air or road.

**Air** Satena has flights to several of the main towns in Los Llanos including Arauca, Yopal and Puerto Carreño, giving you an alternative to the long bus rides. Minor carriers,

## The Wildlife of Los Llanos

Los Llanos are one of Colombia's greatest repositories of wildlife – especially birds, which live here permanently or gather seasonally to breed and feed. About 500 bird species have been recorded in the region, which accounts for nearly a third of all bird species found in Colombia. Water birds predominate, and the list includes ibis, herons, cormorants, egrets, jacanas, gallinules and darters. The *corocora*, or scarlet ibis *(Eudocimus ruber)*, noted for its bright orange-red plumage, is a spectacular sight when it comes in large colonies in the dry season.

Among the more than 50 mammal species that inhabit the region is the *chigüiro*, or capybara *(Hydrochoerus hydrochaeris)*. This is the world's largest rodent, growing up to about 60 kg. It has a guinea-pig face, bear-like coat and is equally at home on land and in the water, feeding mainly on aquatic plants. It's the most visible mammal in Los Llanos (apart from ubiquitous zebu herds) and is often seen in families of two adults and several young, or in large groups.

Other local mammals include armadillos, peccary, opossums, anteaters, tapirs, ocelots and the occasional jaguar. Two particularly interesting aquatic mammals are the *tonina*, or freshwater dolphin *(Inia geoffrensis)*, and the *manatí*, or manatee *(Trichechus manatus)*, which inhabit the larger tributaries of the Orinoco. Both are endangered species, but the numbers of the latter are dangerously low.

Also threatened with extinction is the largest American crocodile, the *caimán del Orinoco*, or the Orinoco cayman *(Crocodylus intermedius)*. This huge reptile, which once lived in large numbers and reached up to eight metres from head to tail, has been decimated by ranchers killing it for its skin. Far more numerous is the *babilla*, or the spectacled cayman *(Caiman crocodylus)*, the smallest of the family of local crocodiles, growing up to three metres in length. ■

using light aircraft, call at a number of other localities that would otherwise be virtually inaccessible.

**Bus** There are four roads leading to the western outskirts of Los Llanos. By far the most popular access route is the Bogotá-Villavicencio road that is paved but not in good condition and occasionally blocked by landslides. Another gateway to the area is the Sogamoso-Aguazul road (completed in 1962), which will take you to Yopal, the capital of Casanare. You can also get to Yopal by the road leading from the Valle de Tenza to Monterrey. Finally, there is the unsafe (because of guerrillas) Pamplona-Saravena road, opened in 1964, which continues on to Arauquita. On all these roads there are bus services.

Villavicencio, Yopal and Saravena are connected by a road which runs along the eastern foothills of the Cordillera and may eventually extend as far south as Florencia. Despite its importance and efforts to improve it, the existing road is in poor condition and in parts can be impassable during the rainy season.

The roads heading further east into Los Llanos are with a few exceptions fit for traffic only in the dry season. There are two roads from west to east across Los Llanos: Villavicencio-Santa Rita, which is theoretically passable all year round; and Villavicencio-Puerto Carreño, only from December to March. Scheduled buses ply both these roads (see the Villavicencio section for details).

A new road is being built across the north-western part of Los Llanos, and is intended to provide a good, direct route between Bogotá and Caracas. At present, all traffic between these two cities uses the long, mountainous road which goes via Bucaramanga and Cócuta. The new road is expected to shorten travel time between the capitals by at least 10 hours.

## VILLAVICENCIO

• *pop 280,000* • *470 m* • *26˚C* • ☎ *(9866)*

Villavo – as it is known to the locals – is a busy, sprawling city and the principal gateway to Los Llanos. Founded in 1840 by colonists from the highlands, it has become the main cattle and agricultural centre of the region and one of Bogotá's major suppliers of meat, rice, fruit and vegetables. The city owes its fast development to the road built in the 1930s linking it with Bogotá, and has grown into the largest urban centre in the eastern half of Colombia.

With an annual rainfall of over 4000 mm, it receives heavy downpours during the rainy season. The days are hot but the temperature drops to a pleasant level in the evening.

## Information

**Tourist Office** The Corporación Departamental de Turismo del Meta is on Carrera 36 next to the corner of Calle 35. It is open Monday to Friday from 8 am to noon and 2 to 6 pm.

**Money** Don't count too much on the possibility of changing cash or travellers' cheques in the banks. Probably the only bank to handle these operations is the Banco Industrial Colombiano. It may also give you a peso advance on your MasterCard, as may the Banco de Occidente. Banco de Colombia and Banco de Bogotá can do the same on your Visa card.

**Inderena** The Inderena office (☎ 22862) is at Carrera 30 No 36-45. Contact Inderena if you plan to visit La Macarena National Park.

**Fundación Horizonte Verde** This is one of the foundations involved in ecotourism. It plans to open a nature reserve in the region, probably on the eastern slopes of the Cordillera Oriental. At the time of writing, it was organising two-day tours (on weekends) to Caño Cristales in the Serranía de la Macarena (US$160 per person, including return air transport to La Macarena, accommodation in tents or hammocks, food and a guide). The foundation also operates the Hacienda Yamato, on the Río Meta, about 30 km beyond Puerto Gaitán, where it offers accommodation, food and boat trips. The foundation's office (☎ 30354) is at Calle 35 No 37-35. You may also contact Álvaro Ocampo (the head of the foundation) at the university (☎ 31291), where he works.

## Things to See

Villavicencio doesn't have much to show tourists. Its urban fabric is the product of rapid, chaotic development – a ragbag of uninspiring architecture, without any eye-catching features.

Just about the only place worth visiting is the **Estación de Biología Roberto Franco**, which has turtles (26 species) and crocodiles from Los Llanos. It is at Carrera 33 No 33-76, five blocks south of the main square along the road towards Puerto López. It is open Monday to Friday from 9 to 11.30 am and 1.30 to 5 pm.

If you want a bird's-eye view of the city, climb the **Cerro de Cristo Rey**, topped with a statue of Christ, just west of the city centre, but don't expect a miraculous vista – the city doesn't look any better than it does from street level.

## Places to Stay – bottom end

There are lots of budget hotels scattered throughout the central area within a few blocks of the main plaza, the Parque Los Libertadores. On the whole, their standards are rather poor. Many of the cheapest ones don't have fans, though these are not essential as the nights are not especially hot.

Among the cheapest places, check two family-run hotels just to the north of the main plaza: the *Residencias Graciela*, at Carrera 32 No 39-32, and, next door, the *Residencias Cóndor*. Both are basic but acceptable and cost US$4/7 a single/double.

The *Hotel Maipore* (☎ 23707), at Calle 31 No 37-69, is marginally more expensive and has rooms with private baths. The *Hotel*

Capybaras

LOS LLANOS

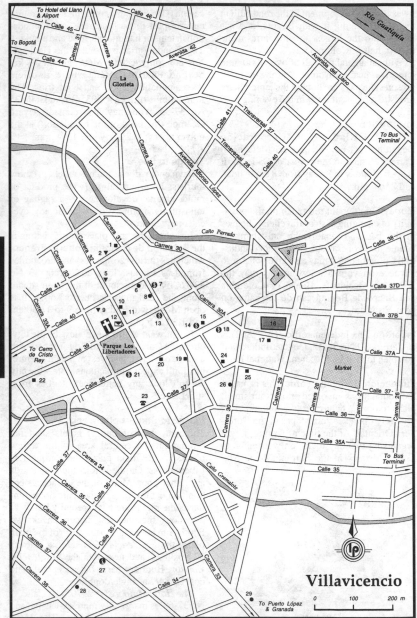

**LOS LLANOS**

**Villavicencio**

0        100        200 m

## PLACES TO STAY

1   Hotel Savoy
10  Residencias Cóndor
11  Residencias Graciela
15  Hotel Montana
17  Hotel Serranía
19  Hotel Maipore
20  Hotel Galerón
22  Hotel Medellín
24  Hotel Central
25  Hotel Tía Juana

## PLACES TO EAT

2   Restaurante Llano Son
5   La Fonda Quindiana
9   Restaurante La Baranda

## OTHER

3   Mercado San Andresito
4   Mercado Popular Villa Julia
6   Tagua Office
7   Banco Industrial Colombiano
8   Satena Office
12  Adpostal Office
13  Banco de Bogotá
14  Banco de Occidente
16  Supermercado Ley
18  Banco Popular
21  Banco de Colombia
23  Telecom
26  Inderena
27  Tourist Office
28  Fundación Horizonte Verde
29  Estación de Biología Roberto
    Franco

*Medellín* (☎ 24751), at Calle 39 No 33A-81, offers much the same.

There are several basic residencias on Carrera 33 between Calles 37 and 38, but be careful as some of them rent rooms by the hour.

Possibly the best budget place in the city centre is the *Hotel Montana* (☎ 26290), at Calle 38 No 30A-42. It has rooms with bath and fan; singles/doubles/triples cost US$7/12/16.

If you want to escape from the noisy city centre, try *Los Girasoles* (☎ 42712), a 10-hectare forested finca (ranch) on the north-western outskirts of the city, off the road to Bogotá. Accommodation costs US$7 per person (or US$15 complete with three meals). To get there, take the urban bus going from the city centre along the Bogotá road, get off by the CAI police post in the suburb of Gaitán and walk a few blocks up a side road.

### Places to Stay – middle

*Hotel Central* (☎ 25167), Carrera 30A No 37-06, has rooms with bath, fan and TV. Singles/doubles/triples cost US$12/16/22. Slightly better is the *Hotel Savoy* (☎ 22666), Calle 41 No 31-02, for US$14/22/28.

### Places to Stay – top end

There's quite a choice of centrally located hotels at the lower end of this price bracket, including the *Hotel Galerón* (☎ 26379), at Calle 38 No 31-45; the *Hotel Tía Juana* (☎ 24504), at Calle 37 No 29-57; and the *Hotel Serranía* (☎ 24190), at Calle 37A No 29-63. They are all rather styleless venues, but all offer air-conditioned rooms with bath and TV, and all cost around US$22/28/35.

The best in town is the four-star *Hotel del Llano* (☎ 41119), Carrera 30 No 49-77, about one km north of the city centre.

### Places to Eat

The central area is packed with budget restaurants serving the usual set meals plus the typical local dish, carne llanera. You can also get cheap meals (and buy a variety of fruits) at the market, between Carreras 27 and 28 and Calles 37 and 37A. Vegetarians can eat in the restaurant of the Hotel Savoy.

*La Baranda*, Calle 40 No 32-37, is popular among the locals for its good, reasonably priced food, as is *La Fonda Quindiana*, Carrera 32 No 40-36. Another place to try is *Restaurante Llano Son*, Calle 41 No 31-32.

One of the best eateries in the city (but also the most expensive) is the restaurant of the Hotel del Llano. The hotel also has a tavern with live joropo music.

### Things to Buy

If you are heading further east and still

haven't got a hammock, Villavo is the right place to buy one. San Andresito market, on Avenida Alfonso López, has several stalls which sell hammocks. Probably the most interesting variety among them are the hammocks made of *cumare*, a fibre extracted from the leaves of a species of palm. These hammocks are made by Indians and brought from Vichada, and are expensive.

Just across the road from San Andresito is the Mercado Popular Villa Julia, where you'll find more stalls selling hammocks and other crafts.

### Getting There & Away
**Air** The Vanguardia Airport is two km northeast of the town as the crow flies, but it's four km by road. The airport is accessible by busetas which leave from the corner of Calle 38 and Carrera 30 in front of the Ley supermarket. There are flights with Satena (office at Carrera 31 No 39-37) to Bogotá (US$32) and the main towns of Los Llanos and the Amazon basin, including Yopal, Arauca, Puerto Carreño and Araracuara.

Tagua, the local carrier (office at Calle 40 No 31-15), has flights to San José del Guaviare (US$40), and to several other destinations in Meta. Other small airlines have their offices at the airport and mostly operate on a charter basis. Be prepared to pay around US$150 per hour for a three-seater plane.

**Bus** Villavicencio has a new bus terminal, located on the eastern outskirts of the city, about four km from the central area. Frequent urban buses and colectivos shuttle between the terminal and the centre.

**To Bogotá** Flota La Macarena and Expreso Bolivariano have frequent buses (US$5.50 pullman, US$4.50 corriente, four hours). All these buses pass near the city centre along Calle 44 and Avenida 42, and normally stop at the roundabout known as La Glorieta to drop off passengers coming from Bogotá or pick up those going to the capital. It's a good saving on the trip to and from the bus terminal.

**To Puerto López** Flota La Macarena has buses every hour (US$2.50, 1½ hours).

**To Orocué** Flota La Macarena has buses three times a week, on Monday, Wednesday and Saturday at 3 am (US$10, eight to 10 hours).

**To San José del Guaviare** Flota La Macarena has a few buses daily (US$15, 12 hours).

**To Santa Rita** Flota La Macarena has two buses a week, on Tuesday and Friday at 2 am (US$35). The trip takes two days (about 25 hours of net bus ride) with an overnight stop in Las Gaviotas or Cumaribo; it is not very reliable in the rainy season.

**To Puerto Carreño** Flota La Macarena has a bus on Tuesday at 3 am, in the dry season only (December to February or March). The trip costs US$45 and can take up to 40 hours – two full days with an overnight stop in La Primavera.

## PARQUE NACIONAL SERRANÍA DE LA MACARENA
The Serranía de la Macarena, set in southern Meta, is a flat-topped mountain about 120 km long and 25 km wide. It's all that remains of the mountains which existed in South America prior to the Andes. It is a nearly cuboid, sandstone formation towering nearly 1000 metres above Los Llanos; its highest point, 1096 metres above sea level, is in the northern part of the plateau. The interior of the Serranía is largely unexplored, but initial studies have shown that it is one of the richest biological reserves in the world, home to numerous endemic species.

The national park, which was founded in 1948 to preserve this unique habitat, comprises the outcrop proper and the adjoining lowland area, and covers 11,313 sq km. This makes it just about the largest national park in Colombia; it's also one of the most unusual and spectacular.

The Serranía has impressive sandstone formations, deep river canyons and abundant fauna and flora, and is well worth a visit of several days. There are also Indian stone carvings beside the Río Cafre in the south of the park, and lovely cascades on the Río Guayabero. The showpiece is probably the multicoloured **Caño Cristales**, in the southern part of the park, which some consider the most beautiful nature spot in the country. It's at its best in the rainy season.

Although it is more pleasant to visit the park in the dry season, there are no obstacles to road access or trekking during the rainy months, except perhaps in the time of heavy rainfall, which is from April to June.

There's some occasional guerrilla activity in the lowlands surrounding the Serranía, so check the current situation with Inderena before you set off for the wilderness.

### Trekking

Trekking is the only way to explore the Serranía. If you plan on a one-day excursion only, go to a place called La Curía, on the Granada-Mesetas road, four km past the turn-off to San Juan de Arama. There is a small chapel on the hill just off the road, from where you can walk uphill to the Cuchillo El Tablazo. This is a beautiful walk along the top of the range, which reaches 690 metres, with spectacular views into the narrow Güejar canyon and of the Serranía proper.

You can then descend into the canyon, cross the river and walk along the base of the Serranía, but there is no route to the top of the plateau from here. The bigger rivers can be crossed using wooden 'cable cars' suspended on steel cables, which you drive with your own muscle power. To cross smaller rivers you may just have to wade, taking off shoes and trousers.

If you plan on ascending to the main plateau, you'll have to bring all your trekking and camping gear and food with you. The last chances to shop are in San Juan de Arama and Mesetas in the north, and Piñal and Vista Hermosa in the east. Buy the relevant IGAC maps in Bogotá. These are accurate and very useful. Don't let yourself be confused by the inaccurate map of the region in the Inderena guide.

There are four principal jumping-off points for the Serranía: Mesetas; the Inderena post near San Juan de Arama; Piñal; and the village of La Macarena on the Río Guayabero, which is only accessible by plane or by boat. The latter is the gateway to Caño Cristales.

From each of these points you can trek across the Serranía to another one. These are long and adventurous hikes. For example, the Piñal-La Macarena or Piñal-Mesetas treks will each take six days to complete. A guide is essential, both to help you to find the right way and for safety. Enquire at the offices of Inderena and Fundación Horizonte Verde in Villavicencio. If you come up with nothing, ask around in Mesetas, San Juan de Arama, Piñal or La Macarena, depending on where you begin. The rangers in the park may either guide you themselves or may suggest a local who could do this.

### Places to Stay & Eat

San Juan de Arama, at the northern end of the park, has two residencias; both are on the main road (running parallel to the road to Vista Hermosa) and both cost US$2 per person. They are clean and friendly and have mosquito nets but no private baths. All the buses, pick-up trucks and taxis stop at this road and you don't need to walk more than five minutes to reach all the shops, restaurants and cafeterias. There are more lodging and eating places in Mesetas.

The Inderena post near San Juan de Arama is an excellent base for trekking tours. There is a big Inderena sign on the Granada-Mesetas road, about three km past the road branching off to San Juan de Arama. From here, it is another two-km walk on a plain dirt road to the post, which is attended all year round and has simple sleeping facilities. No food is provided (don't rely on the small shop), so bring provisions with you. Other Inderena posts are in Mesetas, Piñal and La Macarena but they usually don't take in visitors.

### Getting There & Away

Flota La Macarena has buses every two hours from Bogotá to Mesetas (US$9 pullman, US$8 corriente, about eight hours); all buses pass through San Juan de Arama (US$7/6 respectively, seven hours). Alternatively, take the hourly bus from Bogotá to Granada, from where you can take a pick-up truck or taxi to San Juan de Arama (33 km).

## PUERTO CARREÑO
• *pop 4500* • *80 m* • *27°C* • ☎ *(9816)*

Set on the bank of the Río Orinoco at its confluence with the Río Meta, on the frontier with Venezuela, Puerto Carreño is the capital

**The Music of Los Llanos**

Music is an important part of local life in Los Llanos, probably more so here than in other regions of the country. The llaneros are shaped by their work, and their whole way of life and philosophy are clearly reflected in their music. The *música llanera*, which has direct flamenco roots, is known by the general term of *joropo*, and has two major forms – the *golpe* and the *pasaje* (some purists claim that true joropo consists only of golpes). The golpe is a musical form, usually sung, with variations that have developed around a definite harmonic pattern. There are over 30 different golpe rhythms, such as the *pajarillo*, the *zumba que zumba* and the *seis por derecho*. The golpes are folkloric and are often traditional compositions. By contrast, pasajes are sung with set lyrics and music, and their composers are usually known. Generally speaking, they are slower and gentler than golpes.

The música llanera is nowadays played on an *arpa llanera* (a sort of local harp), a *cuatro* (a kind of small guitar) and maracas. The harp was introduced by the Spainiards during the colonial period but it was not until the 1920s that it made its way into Venezuelan joropo, and from there, in the 1940s, into the music of the Colombian Llanos. By that time it had evolved into quite a different instrument: it's smaller and less elaborate than its European parent. The cuatro is a small guitar with four nylon strings, and it accompanies the melody played by the harp. It is also of European origin and had already changed before coming to Colombia from Venezuela. The maracas are the only instrument of the three that is American in origin.

In Casanare, the harp isn't as common as is the *bandola* (another guitar derivative), which has grown in popularity over the past decade. Obviously, there was music in Los Llanos long before these instruments were introduced, and initially *tiple*, *requinto* and guitar were used, but they have almost disappeared.

The llaneros lead hard lives and this is expressed in their music. The harp is normally associated with lyrical, soft salon music, but it is played quite differently in the songs of the llaneros; it sounds clear and sharp, at times even wild.

Listen out for this music – it is interesting and original, typical of Venezuela and Colombia, and is almost unknown beyond the borders of these two countries. It may take some time to become accustomed to joropo, but once you do, you are likely to fall in love with it. Needless to say, you'll absorb it most swiftly in Los Llanos.

If you plan on buying some records, CDs or cassettes (almost unprocurable outside Colombia and Venezuela), among the best musicians of joropo are Orlando 'Cholo' Valderrama, Dumar Aljure and Alfonso Niño (all vocalists), and several outstanding harpists, such as Mario Tineo, Carlos Rojas and Darío Robayo. ■

of the department of Vichada. It's the smallest departmental capital in the country – a village rather than a town. It spreads for two km along its main road, which links the wharf with the airport. Most activities are concentrated along this road, between the main plaza and the wharf.

Puerto Carreño has no tourist attractions except, perhaps, a feeling of being at the end of the world. There's no good reason to come here unless you use this unusual route between Colombia and Venezuela.

### Information

**Money** Several shops in Puerto Carreño will exchange pesos to bolívares (and vice versa). If you are leaving Colombia, change all pesos for bolívares on the Colombian side;

it's difficult to change in Puerto Ayacucho, and the rate is poor.

**Immigration** The DAS office is one block west of the main plaza, just off the main road, and is open daily from 8 am to noon and 2 to 6 pm. Be sure to have your passport stamped here when leaving or entering Colombia.

**Venezuelan Consulate** The Venezuelan consulate is on the main road, one block east of the plaza. It's open Monday to Thursday from 8 am to noon and 1 to 3.30 pm, but the afternoon hours are not reliable. It may or may not give you a Venezuelan visa.

**Inderena** There's no longer an Inderena office in Puerto Carreño.

## Places to Stay

There are at least half a dozen hotels in town, most of which are on or just off the main road. The cheapest are the *Hotel Samanaff*, a hundred metres from the Orinoco riverfront, and the *Hotel La Vorágine*, near the main plaza. Either costs around US$4/7 for a single/double.

The *Hotel Safari* and the *Hotel Orinoco*, next to each other, midway between the wharf and the main square, are both pleasant and cost around US$10 per double. The former has a few rooms with air-con.

## Places to Eat

Food is not cheap in Puerto Carreño but is not bad either. There's an adequate array of restaurants on the main road, gathered mainly near the plaza (eg *El Prado* and *Donde Mery)* and in the wharf area. Most restaurants open around 6 or 7 am and close before 8 pm.

## Getting There & Away

**Air** Satena has flights to and from Bogotá on Wednesday and Sunday. They cost US$74, and all stop over in Villavicencio (US$64 from Puerto Carreño).

**Bus** One bus a week departs in the dry season (mid-December to early March,

approximately) for Villavicencio, on Saturday at 3 am (US$45). It takes a full day to reach La Primavera, a village where there's an overnight stop. The bus then departs the next day at 3 am to reach Villavicencio late in the afternoon. The trip may take much longer if the bus breaks down or gets stuck in mud, which happens frequently.

**To Venezuela** There are two routes across the frontier between Puerto Carreño and Venezuela: to Puerto Páez or Puerto Ayacucho. The choice depends on where you are heading on to from there, and when you do it. In the rainy season (May to November) you have practically no choice but to go through Puerto Ayacucho.

If you plan on continuing northward (eg to Caracas) in the dry season, it's better to go to Puerto Páez, right across the Río Meta. Boats between Puerto Carreño and Puerto Páez shuttle regularly from 6 am to 6 pm. Puerto Páez is no more than a village but has a few places to stay and eat. Don't forget to get an entry stamp in your passport from DIEX (the Venezuelan counterpart of DAS).

Three or four buses a day depart from Puerto Páez for an interesting ride through the Venezuelan Llanos north to San Fernando de Apure (US$9, six hours). The first part of the road is unpaved and can usually be accomplished only during the dry season (December to April). The road is steadily being upgraded in order to make it usable all year round. Check for news when you come.

To date, travelling from Puerto Carreño to any destination in Venezuela in the rainy season has involved passing through Puerto Ayacucho. Getting to Puerto Ayacucho from Puerto Carreño is pretty straightforward. A voladora (high-powered boat) departs every morning at 6 am from Puerto Carreño's wharf for Casuarito, a small Colombian village on the bank of the Orinoco, right opposite Puerto Ayacucho. The trip costs US$6 and takes 1¼ hours. Buy your ticket the previous day. The boat from Casuarito to Puerto Carreño leaves at 4 pm.

There's a rough road linking Casuarito to Puerto Carreño, serviced irregularly by jeeps. There's also a weekly bus in the dry season, departing from Puerto Carreño on Thursday at 8.30 am (US$3.50, three hours).

From Casuarito, take the boat across the river to Puerto Ayacucho (US$1, 15 minutes). The boat shuttles between the two banks every hour or so, depending on demand.

Upon arrival at Puerto Ayacucho's wharf you are likely to be thoroughly searched at the police post, and your passport will be inspected, but no entry stamp will be put in it. For this, you must go to the DIEX office in the town, on Avenida Aguerrevere. The office is open Monday to Friday from 8 am to noon and 2 to 6 pm, though it doesn't seem to keep strictly to these hours.

Puerto Ayacucho is a rapidly sprawling town of some 60,000 people. It has a wide choice of hotels (Residencia Internacional, Avenida Aguerrevere 18, is perhaps the best budget bet, for US$5/8 a single/double) and restaurants. The town is linked with the rest of the country by a paved, all-season road, serviced by public transport. Two buses a day run to Caracas via Caicara (US$20, 16 hours), and there are a dozen buses a day to Ciudad Bolívar (US$11, 10 hours). Puerto Ayacucho has an airport, from which two flights go daily to Caracas (US$65).

## PARQUE NACIONAL EL TUPARRO

Covering 5480 sq km, El Tuparro is one of Colombia's largest national parks. It is situated on the bank of the Río Orinoco on the Venezuelan border, and comprises forests, savannahs and swamps. It lies between altitudes of 80 and 315 metres and is mostly flat.

The park boasts some beautiful sights, the most well known being the **Raudales Maipures**, the rapids on the Orinoco near the mouth of the Tuparro River. Give yourself a few days for the visit as there are several scenic sites scattered over a large area. The Inderena rangers will guide you to nearby sights. Don't forget to get a permit to visit the park from the Inderena office in Bogotá.

Accommodation facilities are being built; so far, only camping is possible. Nonetheless, the rangers will probably offer you a spare mattress or a bed, and they'll certainly allow you to sling your hammock under the roof. They may even offer food, but it would be wise to take your own provisions.

### Getting There & Away

There are basically two ways of getting to the park, from the west and from the east, and both are difficult.

The first one is by a track suitable for jeeps, which branches off from the Villavicencio-Santa Rita road at a place called Tibabisco and runs for 180 km to El Tapón at the western entrance of the park. There are several fincas along this road. From El Tapón, the track (passable in this part in the dry season only) continues for another 180 km through the park before reaching the administrative centre at the far end, on the bank of the Río Orinoco. This route is possible only if you have access to a jeep, as there is virtually no transport on the access road. If you do this trip, remember that the last petrol station is in Puerto Gaitán, about 520 km before arriving at the administrative centre of the park.

The other route is from the Orinoco, the frontier river between Colombia and Venezuela. The Orinoco is cut by rapids, the Raudales Atures to the north of the park and the Raudales Maipures just south of the park. Consequently, El Tuparro cannot be reached via the Orinoco River from the Colombian side, from either the north (Puerto Carreño) or the south (Puerto Nariño). You must go to Venezuela and cross the river back to Colombia between the two rapids. The best place to organise a boat trip to the park is the small hamlet of Agua Blanca, midway between Puerto Ayacucho and Samariapo (all on the Venezuelan side).

Technically, it's quite easy: go from Puerto Carreño to Puerto Ayacucho, where frequent pick-up trucks leave for Samariapo. They will drop you off in Agua Blanca, 25 km south of Puerto Ayacucho. From there, a hired boat will take you across the river to the administrative centre of the park for around US$10. To do this trip, however, you will need a Venezuelan visa, which will be checked upon arrival at Puerto Ayacucho.

# Glossary

For the names of food and drink, see the Food & Drink section in the Facts for the Visitor chapter. For geographical and other general terms, refer to the Language section in the Facts about the Country chapter. For medical and health terms, see the Health section in the Facts for the Visitor chapter. Note that this glossary is arranged according to the Spanish alphabet, in which 'ch', 'll' and 'ñ' are considered separate letters and follow 'c', 'l' and 'n', respectively.

**adobe** – sun-dried brick made of mud and straw, used in traditional rural constructions

**alpargatas** – sandals used by country people, originally with a *fique* sole, today made mostly of rubber from old tyres

**amoblado** – 'love hotel' which rents out rooms by the hour

**atarraya** – circular fishing net widely used on the coast and rivers

**ayudante** – driver's assistant on intercity buses

**azulejos** – ornamental hand-made tiles, mostly in blue tones (hence their name), which originated in Portugal and were brought to South America in colonial times

**balneario** – seaside, lake or river bathing place with facilities

**bambuco** – musical style of the Andean region based on a rhythm of Spanish origin

**bandola** – an instrument derived from the mandolin, used in the music of the Andean region; also an entirely different kind of instrument, more like a guitar, played in Los Llanos

**bandolero** – bandit, brigand; term increasingly used to refer to guerrillas to undermine their political aims, emphasising their criminal activities

**baquiano** – a peasant who hires out horses or mules for horseback excursions, and usually accompanies the group as a guide

**basuco** or **bazuco** – base from which cocaine is refined; smoked in cigarettes

**bomba** – petrol (gasoline) station

**bordado** – decorative needlework done on cloth, typical of the city of Cartago

**brujo** – a witch doctor, shaman

**burundanga** – a drug used by thieves to render their victim unconscious; extracted from the plant known commonly as *borrachero* or *cacao sabanero*

**buseta** – small bus; a popular means of city transport

**cabaña** – cabin, usually found on the beaches or up in the mountains

**cacique** – Indian tribal head; today, the term is applied to provincial leaders from the two traditional political parties, also called *gamonales*

**cachaco/a** – person from Bogotá, although for the *costeños* anyone not from the coast is a cachaco

**CAI** – Centro de Atención Inmediata; one of a network of police posts established in the cities in order to upgrade public security; there's an extensive and still growing array of them

**caleño/a** – person from Cali

**caminata** – trek, hike

**camino de herradura** – bridle path, partly or entirely paved with stone; these were the early tracks built under Spanish rule by Indian slave labour, often following the original Indian trails

**campero** – jeep

**campesino/a** – rural dweller, usually of modest economic means; a peasant

**caneca** – wastepaper basket or bin

**carriel** – a typical Antioquian leather bag used by men

**carro** – car

**casa de cambio** – money-exchange office

**caserío** – hamlet

**casona** – big, rambling, old house

**cédula** – ID of Colombian citizens and residents

**ceiba** – a common tree of the tropics; can reach a huge size

**celador** – security guard (usually armed) at a public building or private house; a very common job these days – there are at least 100,000 of them in Bogotá alone

**cinemateca** – cinema which focuses on screening films of a higher artistic quality

**climatizado** – air-conditioned; term used for deluxe buses

**colectivo** – a shared taxi; a popular means of public transport

**coleo** or **las coleadas** – a game of the Los Llanos region; the aim is to overthrow a bull in full flight by grabbing its tail from a galloping horse

**conuco** – a small piece of cultivated land

**corraleja** – a dangerous kind of bullfight in which spectators can take their chance with the bull; popular mainly in the Sucre department, it originated in Pamplona, Spain

**corrida** – bullfight

**corriente** – ordinary bus

**costeño/a** – inhabitant of the Caribbean coast

**criollo/a** – Creole, a person of European (especially Spanish) blood but born in the Americas

**cuadrilla** – a kind of popular theatre group or play, always using disguises, usually accompanied by music and sometimes by dance

**cuatro** – a small, four-stringed guitar, used in the music of Los Llanos

**cumare** or **chambiro** – vegetable fibre extracted from a palm and used in weaving; typical of some parts of the Amazon region

**cumbia** – one of the most popular musical rhythms (and a corresponding dance) of the Caribbean coast, Afro-Cuban in origin

**currulao** – the most popular dance of the Pacific coast, of mixed African-Spanish origin, usually accompanied by a marimba

**chalupa** – term used in some regions for a small passenger boat powered by an outboard motor

**chichamaya** – traditional dance of the Guajiro Indians

**chigüiro** – capybara, a large rodent typical of Los Llanos

**chinchorro** – a hammock woven of cotton threads or palm fibre like a fishing net; they are typical of many Indian groups, but probably the best known are the decorative cotton hammocks of the Guajiros

**chirimía** – type of street band popular on the Pacific coast and in the Andean region

**chiva** – traditional bus still widely used in the countryside; also known as *bus de escalera*

**chulo** – vulture

**danta** – tapir; large, hoofed mammal of tropical and subtropical forests; a distant relative of the horse

**DAS** – Departamento Administrativo de Seguridad; the security police, who are also responsible for immigration

**derrumbe** – landslide; the main cause of blocked roads, particularly in the rainy season

**(los) desechables** – literally, 'the disposables'; term referring to the underclass including the homeless, beggars, street urchins, prostitutes, homosexuals and the like, who are treated as human refuse and are the object of an abhorrent process of 'social cleansing' by death squads known as *los limpiadores*, or 'the cleaners'

**deslizador** – term used in some regions for a high-powered boat

**droguería** – pharmacy

**encomienda** – estate granted to Spaniards in the colonial period; the Indians living on the land were put to work on the estate or had to pay taxes to the owner

**estadero** – a roadside restaurant which often offers accommodation

**finca** – anything from a country house with a small garden to a huge country estate

**fique** – sisal obtained from the agave, widely used in handicrafts

**flota** – general term for intercity buses

**frailejón** – espeletia, a species of plant typical of the *páramo*

**furruco** – typical musical instrument consisting of a drum and a wooden stick piercing its drumhead; sound is produced by striking the drumhead by moving the stick up and down; used in popular music of some regions

**galería** – normally a shop exhibiting and selling art; also the eating section of the market

**gallera** – cockfight ring

**gamín** – street urchin; originated from the French *gamin*; the word was adopted in Colombia when the French media began reporting on the appalling conditions of street children in Bogotá

**gamonal** – provincial leader from either of the two traditional political parties

**greca** – large, cylindrical coffee-maker; the old ones, still in use in some regions, are often lavishly decorated with engraved patterns and are vaguely reminiscent of Russian samovars

**gringo/a** – actually any white foreigner, not only a Yankee; sometimes, not always, derogatory; *hacerse el gringo* – to play the fool

**guacharaca** – percussion instrument consisting of a stick-like wooden body with a row of cuts and a metal fork; used in *vallenato* music

**guácharo** – oilbird, a species of nocturnal bird living in caves

**guadua** – a species of tree of the bamboo family, common in many regions of moderate climate

**guaquero** – robber of pre-Columbian tombs

**guayabera** – men's embroidered shirt popular throughout the Caribbean region

**guerrilla** – irregular, usually politically motivated insurgent group that aims to change existing political order through armed struggle; a radical form of opposition to the established political system

**hacienda** – a country estate, often large

**hospedaje** – cheap hotel

**invierno** – literally, winter; the rainy season

**isleño/a** – inhabitant of San Andrés and Providencia islands

**IVA** – the *impuesto de valor agregado*, a value-added tax (VAT)

**jején** – a species of small, biting fly

**joropo** – music played in Los Llanos, also referred to as *música llanera*

**ladrón** – thief, if you still don't know it

**lancha** – launch, motorboat

**lechero** – literally, milk truck; popularly used of any means of transport which is slow or stops a lot, eg a flight with several stopovers

**ligre** – a cross of Bengal tiger and African lion, first bred in Pereira, Colombia

**liqui-liqui** – men's traditional costume, typical of most of the Caribbean; a white or beige suit comprising trousers and a blouse with a collar, usually accompanied by white hat and shoes

**llanero/a** – inhabitant of Los Llanos

**(Los) Llanos Orientales** – the vast plains between the Andes and the Río Orinoco, often simply called Los Llanos

**machismo** – the exaggerated masculine pride of the Latin American male

**mafioso** – a member of the mafia; big fish of the drug business

**maloca** – large, communal house of some Indian tribes; a wooden structure packed with earth and thatched with palm leaves

**manta** – long, loose dress worn by Guajiro Indian women; also a bedspread

**maracas** – gourd rattles; an indispensable rhythm instrument of the *joropo* and some other musical genres

**marimba** – musical instrument of African origin; a sort of wooden xylophone; see also Informal Glossary

**matrimonio** – a hotel room with a double bed intended for married couples

**mecha** – small triangular envelope with gunpowder, used in *tejo*

**merengue** – musical rhythm of the Dominican Republic, today widespread throughout the Caribbean

**mestizo/a** – person of mixed European-Indian ancestry

**metropolitano** – 1st-class bus

**mirador** – lookout, viewpoint

**mochila** – a bucket-shaped shoulder bag, traditionally made by Indians, today produced commercially; also a rucksack

**mola** – colourful, hand-stitched appliqué textile of the Cuna Indians; a rectangular piece of cloth made of several differently coloured, superimposed layers sewn together and then cut to form patterns; the motifs usually represent animals or geometrical designs

**mopa mopa** – also known as *barniz de Pasto*; a kind of vegetable resin used for decorating wooden handicrafts, typical of Pasto

**moriche** – a palm common in Los Llanos, used for construction, household items, handicrafts etc

**motorista** – boat driver

**múcura** – a kind of traditional pottery jar of the Muisca Indians

**muelle** – pier, wharf

**mulato/a** – mulatto, a person of mixed Spanish-African blood

**narcoguerrilla** – term coined for the guerrillas involved in drug production and trafficking to finance their activities, an increasingly common practice nowadays

**narcotraficante** – drug dealer; mafioso

**Navidad** – Christmas

**nevado** – snow-capped mountain peak

**ñapa** – a little bit extra for having bought something; don't forget to ask for it if buying in the market

**orquídea** – orchid

**paisa** – person from the department of Antioquia; *pueblo paisa* – a typical Antioquian town

**panga** – term used in Chocó for a high-powered speedboat

**papagayo** – popular term for macaw

**paradero** – bus stop; in some areas called *parada*

**páramo** – open highlands between about 3500 and 4500 metres, typical of Colombia, Venezuela and Ecuador

**parqueadero** – car park

**pasillo** – a type of music/dance played in the Andean region

**pastuso/a** – a person from Pasto, but also anyone a bit slow or stupid; the pastuso is the butt of many jokes

**piso** – storey, floor

**pito** – car horn; used indiscriminately in and outside the city, often without apparent reason; also used extensively to express happiness after winning sporting contests, elections, beauty contests or whatever

**plaza de toros** – bullfight ring

**poporo** – a vessel made from a small gourd, used by the Arhuacos and other Indian groups to carry lime; the lime is used to activate the coca from masticated coca leaves

**porro** – musical rhythm of the Caribbean coast

**propina** – tip (not a bribe)

**puente** – literally, bridge; also means a three-day-long weekend including Monday

**pullman** – 1st-class bus

**rancho** – a rural house, usually made of adobe with a thatched roof

**refugio** – a rustic shelter in a remote area, mostly in the mountains

**requinto** – a small, 12-stringed guitar used as a melodic instrument

**requisa** – police document search, sometimes a body search; very common

**residencias** – cheap hotel

**retén** – a police checkpoint on the road

**rolo/a** – person from Bogotá, with a noticeable accent marked by a very rolled 'r'

**ruana** – Colombian poncho

**salinas** – seaside saltpans or shallow lagoons used for extraction of salt

**salsa** – a type of Caribbean dance music of Cuban origin; evolved and matured in New York, from where it conquered the whole Caribbean basin and the surrounding countries

**salvoconducto** – safe-conduct pass issued by DAS

**sanjuanero** – music/dance of the Andean region, particularly Huila and Tolima

**Semana Santa** – Holy Week, the week before Easter Sunday

**sicario** – paid killer hired to eliminate adversaries; widely used by the drug cartels

**soborno** – a bribe

**son** – one of the main rhythms of Afro-Cuban music

**soroche** – altitude sickness

**taberna** – a pub/bar/tavern

**tagua** – the hard, ivory-coloured nut of a species of palm; used in handicrafts

**taita** – term for daddy; used by children in certain regions

**tejo** – a traditional game, popular mainly in the Andean region; played with a heavy metal disk, which is thrown aiming to make a *mecha* (a sort of petard) explode; players invariably drink huge amounts of beer while playing

**Telecom** – state telephone company

**teleférico** – cable car

**telenovela** – TV soap opera

**tiple** – small, 12-stringed guitar used as an accompanying instrument

**torbellino** – music/dance typical of the Andean region

**totuma** – cup-like vessel made from a hollowed-out pumpkin cut in half; used in some areas for drinking, washing etc

**trapiche** – traditional sugarcane mill

**tugurios** – shantytowns built of waste materials by the poor on invaded public or private land around big cities, particularly extensive in Bogotá and Medellín; they are found throughout South America, though under a different name in each country: for example, *favelas* in Brazil, *villas miserias* in Argentina, *cantegriles* in Uruguay, *barriadas* in Peru, *callampas* in Chile and *ranchos* or *barrios* in Venezuela

**tunjo** – a flat, gold figurine, often depicting a warrior; typical artefact of the Muisca Indians

**turmequé** – traditional name of *tejo*

**vallenato** – music of the Caribbean coast, especially Valledupar and La Guajira, today widespread all over Colombia

**vaquero** – cowboy

**verano** – literally, summer; the dry season

**(La) Violencia** – a bloody period of civil war (1948-57) between Colombia's two political parties

**vivero** – plant nursery

**voladora** – high-powered speedboat

**yagé** – a plant with hallucinogenic properties used by traditional healers of some Indian groups

**yanchana** – a fabric made from the bark of the ojé tree, sun-dried and bleached, then dyed with vegetable colours and decorated with simple drawings of animals etc; made by some Indian groups of the Amazon

**zambo/a** – person of mixed Indian-African ancestry

# Colloquialisms

Colombians pepper their language with a plethora of strange oaths and odd expressions that are collectively referred to as *colombianismos*. Some are used within certain social groups or circles, others only in certain regions. Some are common nationwide but almost unknown outside Colombia's borders. Although they are rarely to be found in the written language, they are frequently used in everyday conversation. Following are some of the more common of these terms and expressions. You probably won't find them in any conventional dictionary. Be careful if using them, as some change meaning depending on the context, and may be very offensive if used inappropriately.

**aguacate** – literally, avocado; in *gamín* language it refers to the police, whom they also call *iguanas*, *boteros*, *tallos* or *terobos*

**atracador** – mugger, robber

**bareta** – marijuana

**bareto** – a joint, a marijuana cigarette; also known as *barillo*, *coso* and, on the Caribbean coast, as *tabaco*

**bicho** – any small, annoying insect; used figuratively to refer to people

**bobada** – see *maricada*

**boleteo** – a guerrilla practice, which consists of 'taxing' local landowners in exchange for leaving them in peace; 'a bourgeois contribution to the revolution'; people who refuse to pay are often hijacked or assassinated

**bollo** – a problem

**brocha** – literally, paintbrush; used to refer to a negligent or careless person

**cabrón** – asshole, jerk; this word can give grave offence

**caco** – a thief

**cacharro** – old car looking like a pile of junk

**cagada** – a screw-up

**camellar** – to work hard

**camello** – literally, camel; a difficult task

**carajo** – hell!; *qué carajo* – what the hell; also applied to persons as a general term of insult

**cochino** – literally, pig; dirty; a dirty person

**colarse** – to enter a show, cinema etc without paying for a ticket; also to queue-jump, to jump the line

**colmo** – used in the saying *es el colmo* – that's the last straw, that's the last thing I need

**conchudo** – barefaced, shameless

**corroncho** – disrespectful term for a person from the coast or someone without manners

**culebra** – literally, snake; money debt

**cháchara** – bullshit

**chambón** – careless; a careless person

**chambonería** – a job done in a careless, superficial or irresponsible manner

**charro** – bad taste

**chasco** – a disappointing surprise

**chepa** – good luck

**chepazo** – stroke of luck

**chévere** – good, nice

**chicharra** – literally, cicada; the butt of a marijuana cigarette, or roach

**chimbo** – false; of bad quality; not as good as expected

**chino/a** – literally, Chinese; used in Bogotá to refer to a child

**chirriao** – nice, good-looking; an expression used in Bogotá

**chiviado** – false, fake

**chucu-chucu** – contemptuous term referring to tropical music

**churro** – good-looking person

**chusco** – cute

**chusma** – used disrespectfully to refer to people of low class and little education

**dar papaya** – to give someone the opportunity to take advantage of you

**despelote** – a complete mess; total chaos

**echar carreta** – to talk much about nothing; to bullshit

**embarrada** – a real mess, a big problem

**envolatado** – missed or forgotten somewhere in one of the steps of a bureaucratic process (a document); busy (a person)

**estar encarretado** – to be in love or emotionally involved with somebody; to be deeply involved in something

**estar mosca** – literally, to be a fly; to be vigilant, ready to flee from trouble

**filo** – literally, cutting edge; hunger; *tener filo* – to be hungry

**fregado** – difficult

**fresco** – take it easy

**fulano** – so-and-so; a person whose name has been forgotten or is unknown

**godo** – initially, a term of contempt for a Spaniard; later, for a member of the conservative party; today, applied to any conservative view, or person holding such a view

**gomelo** – yuppie

**guache** – Chibcha word for man, used in pejorative sense

**guayabo** – hangover; warranted after an aguardiente session

**hablar mierda** – much the same as *hablar paja* but much stronger

**hablar paja** – to speak a lot without saying anything substantial

**hacer conejo** – literally, to act the rabbit; to sneak out of a restaurant, bar etc without paying the bill

**harto** – very much

**huevón** or **güevón** – a silly prick, idiot

**indio** – literally, Indian; in Colombia it has acquired a pejorative connotation and is used to insult someone, regardless of their race; to refer respectfully to Indians, use *indígena*

**inmamable** – unbearable

**jartera** – drag; *qué jartera* – what a drag

**jarto** – fed up; *estar jarto de* – to be fed up with, to be sick of

**jíbaro** – drug dealer

**jincho** – stone drunk

**joder** – to bother

**jodido** – very difficult, hard; *está jodido* – it's stuffed (doesn't work)

**jurgo** – a great amount; *un jurgo de plata* – a fortune

**lagarto** – literally, lizard; obsequious person

**lobo** – literally, wolf; a person or thing with, or in, bad taste

**locha** – laziness; inclination for doing nothing

**machera** – same as *verraquera*

**maluco** – baddy

**mamar gallo** – to take the piss out of someone, to pull somebody's leg; in conventional Spanish, *tomar el pelo*

**mamera** – same as *jartera*

**mamerto** – pejorative term for a communist

**mamón** – boring; a boring person

**marica** – gay; usually used in a derogatory sense

**maricada** – something stupid, a waste of time; also *bobada* or *pendejada*

**marimba** – marijuana

**marimbero** – grower of marijuana; also used for a heavy marijuana smoker

**meter** – to use drugs

**mijo/a** – a familiar term used between members of a couple or between parents and children; a contraction of *mi hijo/a* - my child

**milicos** – disrespectful term for the military

**mono/a** – a person of fair complexion, but used very flexibly

**mozo/a** – pejorative term for a lover

**mula** – literally, mule; a person hired by drug traffickers to smuggle drugs overseas

**niña** – literally, a young girl; used familiarly to refer to women of any age

**ñero/a** – a person who lives by collecting recyclable materials from the streets

**olla** – literally, pot; a place which sells drugs; *estar en la olla* – to be broke, out of money

**pagar expreso** – to hire a boat or car like a taxi

**palanca** – literally, lever; a connection or person with influence to help out when the regular avenues don't work; it's very important to have them in Colombia

**papaya** – literally, papaya; opportunity

**papayazo** – opportunity; a stroke of good luck

**papeleo** – paperwork

**paquete chileno** – literally, Chilean package; a swindle; an arrangement, transaction etc which looks great but turns out very badly

**parar bolas** – to pay attention

**pea** – a drunken stupor

**pendejada** – see *maricada*

**pendejo** – a silly prick

**perica** – cocaine

**perra** – literally, bitch; also a drunken stupor

**pilas** – literally, batteries; look out! get your act together; *estar con las pilas puestas* – to be alert, to work hard

**pilo** or **piloso** – responsible, studious and hard-working

**piropo** – any macho street comment or remark referring to a woman's appearance or behaviour; its intent may range from complimentary to offensive

**pisco** – a guy, fellow (a term used mainly in Bogotá); also a turkey

**putería** – something very, very good or very, very bad; *qué putería* – how terrific!

**raponero** – thief, robber

**rumba** – fiesta; private or public party with music and drinking

**rumbeadero** – discotheque, usually with salsa music

**rumbear** – to party; a Colombian speciality

**ruso** – literally, Russian; a term used for a construction worker

**salseadero** – a disco playing salsa music

**salsoteca** – a more common term for *salseadero*

**sapo** – literally, toad; informer

**sardino/a** – literally, sardine; teenager, inexperienced

**sumercé** – originated from *Su Merced*, old-fashioned, respectful form of address; used mostly in rural areas of the Andean region

**tenaz** – intense, difficult, wild

**tierrero** – a confusing and violent situation, often in a crowded place

**tira** – plain-clothes police or police informer

**tombo** – the most common informal term for police

**traba** – the state of being stoned

**tumbar** – to rip off, to steal; *qué tumbada* – what a rip-off

**turco** – literally, Turk; refers to any migrant from the Middle East; since many have dedicated themselves to commerce, the term is today generalised to describe a tough merchant

**vacano** or **bacano** – fantastic, great; *un vacán* – a great guy

**vacuna** – literally, vaccine; term used to refer to the payments made to guerrillas by farmers to avoid being harassed

**vaina** – thing; *qué vaina* – what a problem

**verraco** – great, fantastic; a great guy

**verraquera** – something great, terrific

**zorra** – literally, vixen; horse-drawn cart

# Index

## MAPS

Amazon Basin 488
Armenia 402
   Around Armenia 406

Barichara 234
Barranquilla
   Centro 291
   El Prado 296
Bogotá 145
   Around Bogotá 184
   Central Bogotá 158-159
   Northern Bogotá 172-173
   Chapinero 168
Boyacá, Santander
   & Norte de Santander 195
Bucaramanga 238
Buenaventura 442
   Around Buenaventura 445

Cali 426
Caribbean Coast 254
   Central Caribbean Coast 289
Cartagena 300
   Around Cartagena 317
   Bocagrande 311
   Old Town 304
Cartago 399
Caverna del Nus 382
Chiquinquirá 212
Colombia 11
   Administrative Divisions 27
   Avianca Domestic Flights 131
   Geographical Regions 29
   Major Indian Groups Living
      Today 38
   National Park System 34
   Pre-Columbian Cultures 12
   North-West 348

   South-West 423

Cúcuta 246

Darién – Urabá Routes 121

Girón 240

Honda 420

Ibagué 414
Ipiales 480
Isla Gorgona 447

Jardín 378

La Guajira 259
Laguna de la Cocha 477
Leticia 499
   Around Leticia 505
Los Llanos 508

Maicao 260
Manizales 384
Medellín 356
   Around Medellín 366
   Central Medellín 362
Mompós 319

Nabusímake-Pico Colón Trek
   277
Neiva 468

Ocaña 250

Pamplona 242
Parque Nacional Chingaza 189
Parque Nacional Los Katíos 334
Parque Nacional Los Nevados
   410
Parque Nacional Puracé 455
Parque Nacional Tayrona 287

Pasto 474
   Around Pasto 476
Pereira 392
Popayán 450
Providencia 345
Puerto Asís 495

Quibdó 350

Río Claro Area 380
Riohacha 266

San Agustín Area 457
   Parque Arqueológico 459
San Andrés 338
San Andrés Town 340
San Gil, Around 232
Santa Fe de Antioquia 369
Santa Marta 282
Sierra Nevada de Santa Marta
   269
Sierra Nevada del Cocuy 222
Sincelejo 322
Socorro 229
Sogamoso 218

Tenza, Around 197
Tierradentro 465
Tumaco 485
Tunja 198
Turbo 328

Valledupar 256
Villa de Leyva 206
   Around Villa de Leyva 209
Villavicencio 514
Volcán Azufral Trek 484
Volcán Cumbal Trek 483

## TEXT

Map references are in **bold** type.

Abejorral 376
Acandí 331-333
accommodation 96-98
Acevedo 463
Acuario & Haynes Cay 339
Aipe 470-471

air travel
   airfares 130-132
   Colombian airlines 130
   glossary 112-113
   onward ticket requirements 110
   passes 132
   to/from Colombia 109-119
   within Colombia 130-132

Alcom 146
Alianza Democrática M-19
   23, 24
Almeida 197
Alta Guajira 264
altitude sickness 85
Alto de la Cueva 227
Alto de las Piedras 460

Alto de los Ídolos 459-460
Alto de San Andrés 465
Amazon Basin 487-506, **488**
Amazon River 30, 502
Ambalema 417
Andes 377
Antioquia 355-383
Aquitania 221
Aratoca 235
Arboletes 326-327
Arcabuco 211
architecture 41-42
Armenia 401-405, **402, 406**
Armero 409, 418
art, pre-Columbian 39-40
arts, visual 42-43
Atlántico 290-299

Bahía de Málaga 445
Bahía Solano 352-354
Balsa Muisca 186, 187, 188
Barichara 232-235, **234**
Barranquilla 290-297, **291, 296**
Bastidas, Rodrigo de 14, 281
beaches 95
Belalcázar, Sebastián de 15, 423
Belén de Umbría 397-398
Benjamin Constant 497, 498, 502
Betancur, Belisario 25, 28
boat travel within Colombia 139
Bocas de Ceniza 298
Bogotá 142-193, **145, 158-159, 168, 172-173, 184**
    bookshops 150
    churches 157-163
    embassies & consulates 149-150
    entertainment 176-178
    festivals & events 164-165
    getting around 181-183
    getting there & away 179-181
    history 142-143
    Jardín Botánico José Celestino Mutis 163-164
    La Candelaria 153-154
    maps 151
    museums 154-157
    places to eat 170-176
    places to stay 165-170
    Plaza de Bolívar 153
    Plaza de Toros de Santamaría 163
    shopping 178-179
    Spanish courses 152
    things to see & do 153-165
    tourist offices 144-146
    tours & guides 147-148
Bojacá 192
Bolívar 318-321, 507

Bolívar, Simón 16-17, 18, 204, 249, 281, 283, 299, 507
books 67-70
Boyacá 194-221, **195**
Bucaramanga 236-240, **238**
Buenaventura 441-444, 448, **442, 445**
Buga 438-439
bullfighting 106
Buritaca 200, see Ciudad Perdida
burundanga 94-95
bus travel 132-135,
    see also land travel
    chiva 134
    colectivo 135, 140
    local 140
business hours 64
bicycle, see cycling

Cabo de la Vela 263, 264
Calarcá 405
Caldas 383
Calderas 465
Cali 422-436, **426**
Cali Cartel, see Cartel de Cali
Cañón del Chicamocha 235-236
Cañón del Río Claro 379
Capitanejo 223
Capurganá 331-333
Caquetá 491-493
car & motorcycle travel 135-138
    car rental 136
    carnet de passage 137
    driving in Colombia 138
    your own vehicle 136-138
Caribbean Coast 253-335, **254, 289**
Carmen de Viboral 374
Carnaval de Barranquilla 293-294
carnivals, see cultural events
Cartagena 299-316, **300, 304, 311, 317**
    entertainment 314
    festivals & events 309-310
    getting around 315-316
    getting there & away 314-315
    history 299-301
    Old Town 302-308, **304**
    places to eat 312-314
    places to stay 310-312
    shopping 314
    Spanish forts 308-309
    things to see 302
    tourist offices 302
Cartago 398-400, **399**
Cartel de Cali 25-28, 424
Cartel de Medellín 25-28, 359
Cauca 449-471

Caverna del Nus 382-383, **382**
Cesar 255-258
Chinavita 196
Chiquinquirá 212-214, **212**
chiva, see bus travel
Chivor 197
Chocó 347-355
Ciénaga Grande de Santa Marta 288-290
Ciénagas de Tumaradó 335
cinema 44-45, 106
Circasia 405-407
Circuito de Oriente 371
Ciudad Perdida 270-275
climate 30-32, 61
cocaine 25-28, 36, 93, 358
cockfighting 106
Coconuco 454
Cocora 407-408
colectivo, see bus travel
Columbus, Christopher 13
Cordillera Central 29, 409, 422, 454
Cordillera Occidental 28, 422
Cordillera Oriental 28, 183, 194
Córdoba 322-327
Corporación Colombiana Para la Amazonía Araracuara 146-147
Corporación Ecofondo 147
Coveñas 324-325
crafts 40-41
credit cards 60
Cúcuta 244-249, **246**
Cueva de los Guácharos 95, 461, 462-463
Cueva del Cóndor 380-381
Cueva del Cunday 416-417
Cueva del Indio 462
Cueva del Yeso 235
cultural events 64-65
Cumbal 482
Cundinamarca 183
Curillo 493
customs 58
cycling 106, 138-139

Darién 440-441
Darién Gap 119-126, **121**
Desierto de la Tatacoa 470
'dirty war' 22, 26
disabled travellers 63
Drake, Sir Francis 299
driving, see car & motorcycle travel
drug cartels 21, 25-28, 424
    Cartel de Cali 25-28, 424
    Cartel de Medellín 25-28, 359
    Lehder, Carlos 25
    Search Block 26

Tranquilandia 25
US Drug Enforcement Agency
26
drugs 25-28, 93-94
Duitama 215-217
Duriamelna 279

economy 36-37
Ejército de Liberación Nacional,
see ELN
Ejército Popular de Liberación,
see EPL
El Aguacate 465
El Caribe, see Caribbean Coast
El Cocuy 221, 223
El Dorado, legend of 13, 14,
143, 187, 270, 487
El Duende 465
El Jabón 460
El Libertador,
see Bolívar, Simón
El Peñón 372-373
El Purutal 460
El Rancho 411
El Rodadero 285
El Ruiz 409
El Silencio 411
El Tablón 460, 465
El Valle 352-354
electricity 67
ELN 23, 24, 224
Embalse Calima 439-440
Embalse de Chivor 197
embassies 56-57
emeralds 106
entertainment 106
EPL 25
Escobar, Pablo 22, 25, 26, 359,
361, 379

Facatativá 192
FARC 25, 224, 271, 326, 491
fauna, see flora & fauna
fax services 67
Federmann, Nikolaus 15, 216
Feria de Manizales 388
Festival Latinoamericano de
Teatro 388
festivals, see cultural events
Filandia 407
fishing 95
flamingos 263, 268
flora & fauna 32-36, 221, 263,
268, 288, 290, 394, 407, 436,
462, 503, 510
Florencia 491-492
food & drink 98-105
Frente Nacional 21, 22, 23, 24, 25

Fuerzas Armadas Revolucionarias
de Colombia, see FARC
Fusagasugá 191

Gaitán, Jorge Eliécer 143
Galapa 298
Garagoa 196
García Márquez, Gabriel 44, 70,
292
Gardel, Carlos 357
geography 28-30
Girardot 415-416
Girón 240-241, **240**
Golfo de Urabá 347
government 28
Gruta de la Cascada 379-380
Gruta de la Danta 381
Guácharo 462
Guaduas 192-193
Guainía 496
Guane 235
Guatavita 185-186
Guateque 196
Guayatá 197
Guerrillas 20, 22-24, 224, 271
Güicán 221-223
Güicán-El Cocuy Trek 223-227

Hacienda El Paraíso 437-438
Hacienda Fizebad 375-376
Hacienda Piedechinche 437-438
health 56, 74-88
    altitude sickness 85
    glossary 87
    medical problems & treatments
    78-87
    predeparture preparations 74-77
    women's health 87
Heredia, Pedro de 14
heroin 25, 28, 94
hiking, see trekking
history 10-28
    20th century 19-21
    colonial period 15-19
    La Violencia 19, 22
    post-Independence period 19
    pre-Columbian period 10-13
    Spanish Conquest 13-15
hitching 139
holidays, public 64
Honda 419-421, **420**
Huila 449-471
Huitotos 492
Humboldt, Alexander von 462,
507

Ibagué 411, 412-415, **414**
Inderena 146

Infierno Verde, see Ciudad
Perdida
Ipiales 479-481, **480**
Isla de los Micos 504
Isla de Mocagua 505
Isla de Salamanca 288-289
Isla Gorgona 445-449, **447**
Islas de San Bernardo 325
Islas del Rosario 316-318
Istmina 352

Jardín 377-379, **378**
Jericó 376-377
Jiménez de Quesada, Gonzalo
15, 142, 217, 281, 418
Johnny Cay 339
Jordán 236
Juanchaco 444-445
Juntas 411

La Bocana 444
La Boquilla 316
La Candelaria 211-212
La Capilla 196
La Ceja 374-375
La Chaquira 460
La Costa, see Caribbean Coast
La Cueva 411
La Guajira 30, 36, 258, **259**
La Parada 460
La Pelota 460
La Plata 463-464
Ladrilleros 444-445
Lago de Tarapoto 505
Laguna de Chingaza 188
Laguna de Guatavita 186, 187
Laguna de Iguaque 210
Laguna de la Cocha 477-478,
**477**
Laguna de la Plaza 227
Laguna de Tota 221
Laguna del Avellanal 226
Laguna del Pañuelo 226-227
Laguna Grande de la Sierra 227
Laguna Grande de los Verdes
225-226
Laguna Naboba 279, 280
Lagunillas 227
land travel
    Darién Gap 119-126
    from Brazil & Peru 127
    from Ecuador 127
    from Panama 119-126
    from Panama along the
    Caribbean Coast 120-123
    from Panama through the Jungle
    123-126
    from Venezuela 127
    to/from Colombia 119

language 47-55
  Spanish courses 152
Lehder, Carlos 25
Leticia 497-503, **499**
Lezo, Don Blas de 299
literature 43-44, 70
Los Cocos 288
Los Estoraques 252
Los Llanos 507-518, **488, 508**
Los Naranjos 211
Los Nevados 29
Los Santos 236
Lost City, *see* Ciudad Perdida

M-19, *see* Alianza Democrática
  M-19
Magdalena 281-290
Maicao 258-262, **260**
Manaure 262-264
Manga Island 309
Manizales 383-390, **384**
maps 71-72, 150
marijuana 36, 94
Marinilla 371-372
Marmato 391
Marsella 396
Medellín 355-368, 370, **356,
  362, 366**
  entertainment 365
  festivals & events 361
  getting around 368
  getting there & away 365-368
  history 355-357
  places to eat 364
  places to stay 361
  shopping 365
  things to see 359
  tourist offices 358
media 72
Medellín Cartel, *see* Cartel de
  Medellín
Mitú 496-497
Mocagua 505
mochilas 276
Mocoa 493-494
Mompós 318-321, **319**
money 58-61
  changing money 59-60
  costs 61
  credit cards 60
  currency 58-59
  exchange rates 60-61
Monguí 220
Monkey Island, *see* Isla de los
  Micos
Montería 325-326
Morgan, Henry 336
mountaineering 95

music 41
  bolero 432
  golpe 512
  guajira 432
  latin jazz 434
  merengue 434
  música llanera 512
  opera 431
  pasaje 512
  rumba 432
  salsa 424, 431, 432-435
  son 432
  tango 355
  vallenato 255
Musichi 264

Naboba 278
Nabusímake 275-276, **277**
Naranjos 460
Nariño, Antonio 18, 207,
  471-486
National Front, *see* Frente
  Nacional
national parks 33-36
Necoclí 331
Neiva 466-469, **468**
Nemocón 185
Nevado del Huila 28
Nevado del Ruiz 28, 409, 412
Nevado del Tolima 409
newspapers 72
Norte de Santander 241-252, **195**
Núñez, Rafael 20

Ocaña 249-252, **250**
oilbirds, *see* guácharos
Ojeda, Alonso de 13
Orellana, Francisco de 487
Ortiga 482

Pachavita 196
Paipa 215
Pamplona 241-244, **242**
Pantano de Vargas 215
Parque de Chicaque 191-192
Parque Nacional Amacayacu
  504-505
Parque Nacional Chingaza
  188-190, **189**
Parque Nacional del Darién 120
Parque Nacional El Tuparro 518
Parque Nacional Ensenada de
  Utría 354-355
Parque Nacional Farallones de
  Cali 436-437
Parque Nacional Los Katíos
  120, 327, 333-335, **334**
Parque Nacional Los Nevados
  409-412, **410**

Parque Nacional Macuira 264
Parque Nacional Puracé
  454-456, **455**
Parque Nacional Serranía de la
  Macarena 515-516
Parque Nacional Tayrona
  286-288, **287**
Parque Ucumarí 398
Partido Revolucionario de los
  Trabajadores, *see* PRT
passports 57, 128
Pasto 471-476, **474, 476**
Península de la Guajira 264
people 37-39
people & cultures, indigenous
  Andean 457
  Arhuaco 271, 275, 276, 278
  Calima 10, 40
  Coreguaje 492
  Cuiva 509
  Cuna 333
  Guajiro 258
  Guambiano 422
  Huitoto 489
  Ijka 270
  Inca 423, 462, 471
  Kogi 270, 271, 273
  Mesoamerican 456
  Mestizo 18
  Muisca 183, 185-187, 192
  Mulato 18
  Nazca 462
  Páez 422, 464
  Sáliva 509
  San Agustín 10, 39, 462
  Sanká 210, 271
  Tamacuna 492
  Tayrona 10, 40, 41, 253, 270,
    273, 286
  Ticuna 503
  Tierradentro 10
  Tolima 10, 40
  Tumaco 10, 471
  Tunebo 509
  Yagua 503
  Zambo 18
Pereira 391-396, **392**
photography 72-74
Pico Cristóbal Colón 30, 268,
  277, 278, 280, **277**
Pico Simón Bolívar 30, 268, 280
Piedra Pintada 471
Playa Blanca 221
police 93
Popayán 449-453, **450**
population 37-39
postal services 65-66
Providencia 336, 343-346, **345**
PRT 24

Pueblo El Encano 478
Puente de Boyacá 204
Puente de Occidente 370-371
Puente de Pumarejo 297-298
Puerto Asís 494-496, **495**
Puerto Carreño 516-518
Puerto Colombia 298
Puerto El Encano 478
Puerto Guzmán 493
Puerto Inírida 496
Puerto Nariño 505-506
Puntalarga 216-217
Putumayo 493-496

Quebrada Yebosimeina 279
Quebradillas 460
Quibdó 349-352, **350**
Quinchana 460
Quindío 383
Qintín Lame 24

radio 72
Ráquira 211
Raudales Maipures 518
Red de Reservas Naturales 146
religion 47
Reserva Natural Acaime 408-409
Reserva Natural La Planada
    484-485
Retiro 375
Río Atrato 347
Río Caquetá 492, 493
Río Chicamocha 236
Río Claro 379-382, **380**
Río Combeima 411
Río Lagunillas 409
Río Orteguaza 492
Río San Juan 347
Riohacha 264-267, **266**
Rionegro 373-374
Riosucio 390-391
Risaralda 383
Ritacuba Blanco 30, 221
rock climbing 95
Roldanillo 401

safety 88-93, 152-153
Sal Si Puedes 147
Salamina 390
Salento 407
salinas 263
salsa 424, 431, 432-435
Salto de la Tigra 334
Salto de Tequendama 190
Salto de Tequendamita 375
Salto de Versalles 193
Salto del Tendal 334
Salto del Tilupo 334
Samper, Ernesto 22

San Agustín 456-461, **457, 459**
    Parque Arqueológico 458-459,
    **459**
San Andrés 336, 337-343, **338,**
    **340**
San Andrés de Pisimbalá 465
San Antonio de Getucha 492-493
San Gil 230-231, **232**
San Jacinto 318
San Juan Delta 445
San Martín 505
Santa Fe de Antioquia 368-370,
    **369**
Santa Marta 281-285, **282**
Santa Rosa 465
Santander 227-241, **195**
Santander, Francisco de Paula
    16, 204, 249
Santuario de Iguaque 210-211
Santuario de Las Lajas 481-482
Santuario Los Flamencos 268,
    272
Sapzurro 331-333
scuba diving 95
sea travel 127
Segovia 465
Serranía de la Macarena 30
shopping 106-108
Sibundoy 478-479
Sierra de los Coconucos 455
Sierra Nevada de Santa Marta
    30, 36, 268-280, **269**
Sierra Nevada del Cocuy 30,
    221-227, **222**
Silvia 453-454
Sincelejo 322-324, **322**
slavery 15, 487
snorkelling 95
soccer 106
Socorro 227-230, **229**
Sogamoso 217-220, **218**
Somondoco 197
Sonsón 376
South American Explorers Club
    63
Sucre 322-327
Sucre, Antonio José de 17
Suesca 186-188

Tabatinga 497-502
Taganga 285-286
Tausa 185
taxis 140-141
telephone services 66-67
Tenza 194-196, **197**
Termales de Santa Rosa 396-397
theatre 44-45
Tierradentro 464-466, **465**
Tolima 412-421

Tolú 324-325
Tópaga 220-221
tourist offices 63
tours 127-128, 139
    environmental 128
    overland 127
train travel 135
Tranquilandia 27
trekking 62-63, 95, 152
    Ciudad Perdida 274-275
    Güicán-El Cocuy 223-227
    Nabusímake-Pico Colón
        276-280, **277**
    Nevado del Cumbal 482-483,
        **483**
    Nevado del Tolima 411-412
    Parque Nacional Puracé 454-456
    Parque Nacional Serranía de la
        Macarena 515-516
    Villanueva-Los Santos 236
    Volcán Azufral 483-484, **484**
Tumaco 485-486, **485**
Tunja 197-204, **198**
Túquerres 484
Turbo 327-331, 370, **328**
TV 72

Urabá 327-335
Uribia 262
US Drug Enforcement Agency 26

Valle del Cauca 30, 422-449
Valle del Magdalena 30
Valledupar 255, 256-258, **256**
Vaupés 496-497
Vernon, Edward 299
Vichada 516
Villa de Leyva 205-209, **206, 209**
Villa del Rosario 249
Villanueva 236
Villavicencio 510-515, **514**
Villavieja 469, 470
Viñedo de Puntalarga 216
visas 56-57
Volcán Azufral 483-484, **484**
Volcán Cumbal 482-483, **483**
Volcán de Lodo El Totumo
    298-299
Volcán Galeras 476-477
Volcán Pan de Azúcar 455, 456
Volcán Puracé 455

wildlife, *see* flora & fauna
women travellers 88

Zabriskie 191
Zipaquirá 183-185
Zona Cafetera 383-412
Zoológico Santa Cruz 190-191

# PLANET TALK
*Lonely Planet's FREE quarterly newsletter*

*We love hearing from you and think you'd like to hear from us.*

*When...is the right time to see reindeer in Finland?*
*Where...can you hear the best palm-wine music in Ghana?*
*How...do you get from Asunción to Areguá by steam train?*
*What...is the best way to see India?*

For the answer to these and many other questions read PLANET TALK.

*Every issue is packed with up-to-date travel news and advice including:*

- *a letter from Lonely Planet founders Tony and Maureen Wheeler*
- *travel diary from a Lonely Planet author - find out what it's really like out on the road*
- *feature article on an important and topical travel issue*
- *a selection of recent letters from our readers*
- *the latest travel news from all over the world*
- *details on Lonely Planet's new and forthcoming releases*

*To join our mailing list contact any Lonely Planet office (address below).*

## LONELY PLANET PUBLICATIONS
**Australia:** PO Box 617, Hawthorn 3122, Victoria (tel: 03-9819 1877)
**USA:** Embarcadero West, 155 Filbert St, Suite 251, Oakland, CA 94607 (tel: 510-893 8555)
TOLL FREE: (800) 275-8555
**UK:** 10 Barley Mow Passage, Chiswick, London W4 4PH (tel: 0181-742 3161)
**France:** 71 bis rue du Cardinal Lemoine – 75005 Paris (tel: 1-46 34 00 58)

*Also available: Lonely Planet T-shirts. 100% heavyweight cotton (S, M, L, XL)*

# Guides to the Americas

### Alaska – a travel survival kit
Jim DuFresne has travelled extensively through Alaska by foot, road, rail, barge and kayak, and tells how to make the most of one of the world's great wilderness areas.

### Argentina, Uruguay & Paraguay – a travel survival kit
This guide gives independent travellers all the essential information on three of South America's lesser-known countries. Discover some of South America's most spectacular natural attractions in Argentina; friendly people and beautiful handicrafts in Paraguay; and Uruguay's wonderful beaches.

### Backpacking in Alaska
This practical guide to hiking in Alaska has everything you need to know to safely experience the Alaskan wilderness on foot. It covers the most outstanding trails from Ketchikan in the Southeast to Fairbanks near the Arctic Circle – including half-day hikes, and challenging week-long treks.

### Baja California – a travel survival kit
For centuries, Mexico's Baja peninsula – with its beautiful coastline, raucous border towns and crumbling Spanish missions – has been a land of escapes and escapades. This book describes how and where to escape in Baja.

### Bolivia – a travel survival kit
From lonely villages in the Andes to ancient ruined cities and the spectacular city of La Paz, Bolivia is a magnificent blend of everything that inspires travellers. Discover safe and intriguing travel options in this comprehensive guide.

### Brazil – a travel survival kit
From the mad passion of Carnival to the Amazon – home of the richest ecosystem on earth – Brazil is a country of mythical proportions. This guide has all the essential travel information.

### Canada – a travel survival kit
This comprehensive guidebook has all the facts on the USA's huge neighbour – the Rocky Mountains, Niagara Falls, ultramodern Toronto, remote villages in Nova Scotia, and much more.

### Central America on a shoestring
Practical information on travel in Belize, Guatemala, Costa Rica, Honduras, El Salvador, Nicaragua and Panama. A team of experienced Lonely Planet authors reveals the secrets of this culturally rich, geographically diverse and breathtakingly beautiful region.

### Chile & Easter Island – a travel survival kit
Travel in Chile is easy and safe, with possibilities as varied as the countryside. This guide also gives detailed coverage of Chile's Pacific outpost, mysterious Easter Island.

### Costa Rica – a travel survival kit
Sun-drenched beaches, steamy jungles, smoking volcanoes, rugged mountains and dazzling birds and animals – Costa Rica has it all.

### Eastern Caribbean – a travel survival kit
Powdery white sands, clear turquoise waters, lush jungle rainforest, balmy weather and a laid back pace, make the islands of the Eastern Caibbean an ideal destination for divers, hikers and sun-lovers. This guide will help you to decide which islands to visit to suit your interests and includes details on inter-island travel.

### *Ecuador & the Galápagos Islands – a travel survival kit*
Ecuador offers a wide variety of travel experiences, from the high cordilleras to the Amazon plains – and 600 miles west, the fascinating Galápagos Islands. Everything you need to know about travelling around this enchanting country.

### *Guatemala, Belize & Yucatán: La Ruta Maya – a travel survival kit*
Climb a volcano, explore the colourful highland villages or laze your time away on coral islands and Caribbean beaches. The lands of the Maya offer a fascinating journey into the past which will enhance appreciation of their dynamic contemporary cultures. An award winning guide to this exotic fregion.

### *Hawaii – a travel survival kit*
Share in the delights of this island paradise – and avoid its high prices – both on and off the beaten track. Full details on Hawaii's best-known attractions, plus plenty of uncrowded sights and activities.

### *Honolulu – a travel survival kit*
Honolulu offers an intriguing variety of attractions and experiences. Whatever your interests, this comprehensive guidebook is packed with insider tips and practical information.

### *Mexico – a travel survival kit*
A unique blend of Indian and Spanish culture, fascinating history, and hospitable people, make Mexico a travellers' paradise.

### *Peru – a travel survival kit*
The lost city of Machu Picchu, the Andean altiplano and the magnificent Amazon rainforests are just some of Peru's many attractions. All the travel facts you'll need can be found in this comprehensive guide.

### *South America on a shoestring*
This practical guide provides concise information for budget travellers and covers South America from the Darien Gap to Tierra del Fuego.

### *Trekking in the Patagonian Andes*
The first detailed guide to this region gives complete information on 28 walks, and lists a number of other possibilities extending from the Araucanía and Lake District regions of Argentina and Chile to the remote icy tip of South America in Tierra del Fuego.

### *Venezuela – a travel survival kit*
Venezuela is a curious hybrid of a Western-style civilisation and a very traditional world contained within a beautiful natural setting. From the beaches along the Caribbean coast and the snow-capped peaks of the Andes to the capital, Caracas, there is much for travellers to explore. This comprehensive guide is packed with 'first-hand' tips for travel in this fascinating destination.

### *Also available:*
**Brazilian** phrasebook, **Latin American Spanish** phrasebook and **Quechua** phrasebook.

# Lonely Planet Guidebooks

Lonely Planet guidebooks cover every accessible part of Asia as well as Australia, the Pacific, South America, Africa, the Middle East, Europe and parts of North America. There are five series: *travel survival kits*, covering a country for a range of budgets; *shoestring guides* with compact information for low-budget travel in a major region; *walking guides*; *city guides* and *phrasebooks*.

## Australia & the Pacific

Australia
Australian phrasebook
Bushwalking in Australia
Islands of Australia's Great Barrier Reef
Outback Australia
Fiji
Fijian phrasebook
Melbourne city guide
Micronesia
New Caledonia
New South Wales
New Zealand
Tramping in New Zealand
Papua New Guinea
Bushwalking in Papua New Guinea
Papua New Guinea phrasebook
Rarotonga & the Cook Islands
Samoa
Solomon Islands
Sydney city guide
Tahiti & French Polynesia
Tonga
Vanuatu
Victoria
Western Australia

## North-East Asia

Beijing city guide
China
Cantonese phrasebook
Mandarin Chinese phrasebook
Hong Kong, Macau & Canton
Japan
Japanese phrasebook
Korea
Korean phrasebook
Mongolia
North-East Asia on a shoestring
Seoul city guide
Taiwan
Tibet
Tibet phrasebook
Tokyo city guide

## South-East Asia

Bali & Lombok
Bangkok city guide
Cambodia
Indonesia
Indonesian phrasebook
Jakarta city guide
Laos
Malaysia, Singapore & Brunei
Myanmar (Burma)
Burmese phrasebook
Philippines
Pilipino phrasebook
Singapore city guide
South-East Asia on a shoestring
Thailand
Thai phrasebook
Thai Hill Tribes phrasebook
Vietnam
Vietnamese phrasebook

## Middle East

Arab Gulf States
Egypt & the Sudan
Arabic (Egyptian) phrasebook
Iran
Israel
Jordan & Syria
Middle East
Turkey
Turkish phrasebook
Trekking in Turkey
Yemen

## Indian Ocean

Madagascar & Comoros
Maldives & Islands of the East Indian Ocean
Mauritius, Réunion & Seychelles

# Mail Order

Lonely Planet guidebooks are distributed worldwide. They are also available by mail order from Lonely Planet, so if you have difficulty finding a title please write to us. US and Canadian residents should write to Embarcadero West, 155 Filbert St, Suite 251, Oakland CA 94607, USA; European residents should write to 10 Barley Mow Passage, Chiswick, London W4 4PH; and residents of other countries to PO Box 617, Hawthorn, Victoria 3122, Australia.

## Indian Subcontinent
Bangladesh
India
Hindi/Urdu phrasebook
Trekking in the Indian Himalaya
Karakoram Highway
Kashmir, Ladakh & Zanskar
Nepal
Trekking in the Nepal Himalaya
Nepali phrasebook
Pakistan
Sri Lanka
Sri Lanka phrasebook

## Africa
Africa on a shoestring
Central Africa
East Africa
Trekking in East Africa
Kenya
Swahili phrasebook
Morocco
Arabic (Moroccan) phrasebook
North Africa
South Africa, Lesotho & Swaziland
Zimbabwe, Botswana & Namibia
West Africa

## Central America & the Caribbean
Baja California
Central America on a shoestring
Costa Rica
Eastern Caribbean
Guatemala, Belize & Yucatán: La Ruta Maya
Mexico

## North America
Alaska
Backpacking in Alaska
Canada
Hawaii
Honolulu city guide
USA phrasebook

## South America
Argentina, Uruguay & Paraguay
Bolivia
Brazil
Brazilian phrasebook
Chile & Easter Island
Colombia
Ecuador & the Galápagos Islands
Latin American Spanish phrasebook
Peru
Quechua phrasebook
South America on a shoestring
Trekking in the Patagonian Andes
Venezuela

## Europe
Baltic States & Kaliningrad
Britain
Central Europe on a shoestring
Central Europe phrasebook
Czech & Slovak Republics
Dublin city guide
Eastern Europe on a shoestring
Eastern Europe phrasebook
Finland
France
Greece
Greek phrasebook
Hungary
Iceland, Greenland & the Faroe Islands
Ireland
Italy
Mediterranean Europe on a shoestring
Mediterranean Europe phrasebook
Poland
Prague city guide
Scandinavian & Baltic Europe on a shoestring
Scandinavian Europe phrasebook
Switzerland
Trekking in Spain
Trekking in Greece
USSR
Russian phrasebook
Vienna city guide
Western Europe on a shoestring
Western Europe phrasebook

## The Lonely Planet Story

Lonely Planet published its first book in 1973 in response to the numerous 'How did you do it?' questions Maureen and Tony Wheeler were asked after driving, bussing, hitching, sailing and railing their way from England to Australia.

Written at a kitchen table and hand collated, trimmed and stapled, *Across Asia on the Cheap* became an instant local bestseller, inspiring thoughts of another book.

Eighteen months in South-East Asia resulted in their second guide, *South-East Asia on a shoestring*, which they put together in a backstreet Chinese hotel in Singapore in 1975. The 'yellow bible' as it quickly became known to backpackers around the world, soon became *the* guide to the region. It has sold well over half a million copies and is now in its 8th edition, still retaining its familiar yellow cover.

Today there are over 140 Lonely Planet titles in print – books that have that same adventurous approach to travel as those early guides; books that 'assume you know how to get your luggage off the carousel' as one reviewer put it.

Although Lonely Planet initially specialised in guides to Asia, they now cover most regions of the world, including the Pacific, South America, Africa, the Middle East and Europe. The list of *walking guides* and *phrasebooks* (for 'unusual' languages such as Quechua, Swahili, Nepali and Egyptian Arabic) is also growing rapidly.

The emphasis continues to be on travel for independent travellers. Tony and Maureen still travel for several months of each year and play an active part in the writing, updating and quality control of Lonely Planet's guides.

They have been joined by over 50 authors, 110 staff – mainly editors, cartographers & designers – at our office in Melbourne, Australia, at our US office in Oakland, California and at our European office in Paris; another five at our office in London handle sales for Britain, Europe and Africa. Travellers themselves also make a valuable contribution to the guides through the feedback we receive in thousands of letters each year.

The people at Lonely Planet strongly believe that travellers can make a positive contribution to the countries they visit, both through their appreciation of the countries' culture, wildlife and natural features, and through the money they spend. In addition, the company makes a direct contribution to the countries and regions it covers. Since 1986 a percentage of the income from each book has been donated to ventures such as famine relief in Africa; aid projects in India; agricultural projects in Central America; Greenpeace's efforts to halt French nuclear testing in the Pacific; and Amnesty International.

Lonely Planet's basic travel philosophy is summed up in Tony Wheeler's comment, 'Don't worry about whether your trip will work out. Just go!'